MW01010018

THE OXFORD HANDBOOK OF

ETHICS OF WAR

THE OXFORD HANDBOOK OF

ETHICS OF WAR

Edited by

SETH LAZAR

and

HELEN FROWE

UNIVERSITY PRESS

Oxford University Press is a department of the University of Oxford. It furthers the University's objective of excellence in research, scholarship, and education by publishing worldwide. Oxford is a registered trade mark of Oxford University Press in the UK and certain other countries.

Published in the United States of America by Oxford University Press
198 Madison Avenue, New York, NY 10016, United States of America.

CIP data is on file at the Library of Congress
ISBN 978-0-19-994341-8

3 5 7 9 8 6 4 2

Printed by Sheridan Books, Inc., United States of America

Seth Lazar dedicates this book to his son, Amos, who is its coeval.

Helen Frowe dedicates this book to her lovely little niece, Katherine Frowe.

Contents

PART III RESORT

PART IV CONDUCT

Acknowledgements

This volume was the result of many years of concerted effort by a large group of people, most notably the authors, who were united in their effort to make this Handbook serve not only as an introduction, but also as a significant event in the field, advancing debates on many fronts. The editors would like to thank the authors for all their efforts and, of course, for their patience in some cases and persistence in others. Seth Lazar would also like to thank the School of Philosophy, in the Research School of Social Sciences at the Australian National University, for providing the ideal environment in which to develop this project—as well as several models of how to efficiently edit an Oxford Handbook. His work on this volume was supported by the Australian Research Council's Discovery Early Career Award, DE130100811. Helen Frowe would like to thank the Department of Philosophy at the University of Stockholm. Her work on this volume was supported by a Wallenberg Academy Fellowship from the Knut and Alice Wallenberg Foundation and the Stellenbosch Institute for Advanced Study.

Contributors

Christian Barry, Director of the Centre for Moral, Social, and Political Theory, School of Philosophy, Research School of Social Sciences, ANU College of Arts and Social Sciences, Australian National University.

Saba Bazargan, Department of Philosophy, University of California, San Diego.

Yitzhak Benbaji is a Professor of Philosophy at Tel-Aviv University, Israel.

Allen Buchanan is James B. Duke Professor of Philosophy and Professor of Law at Duke University, where he is also an Investigator at the Institute of Genome Sciences and Policy.

Lars Christie, University of Oslo.

Rory Cox, University of St Andrews, Scotland, UK.

Patrick Emerton, Faculty of Law, Monash University, Australia.

Cécile Fabre, Senior Research Fellow, All Souls College, Oxford, UK.

Helen Frowe is Professor in Practical Philosophy at Stockholm University. She is also a Wallenberg Academy Research Fellow in the Department of Philosophy and directs the Stockholm Centre for the Ethics of War and Peace.

Toby Handfield, Associate Professor, Department of Philosophy, Monash University, Australia

Adil Ahmad Haque, Professor of Law, S.I. Newhouse Center for Law and Justice, Rutgers School of Law–Newark.

Pablo Kalmanovitz is an Assistant Professor at the Universidad de Los Andes in Bogota, Colombia.

F. M. Kamm is Littauer Professor of Philosophy and Public Policy, Harvard Kennedy School, and Professor of Philosophy, Department of Philosophy, Harvard University.

Seth Lazar, Associate Professor and Head, School of Philosophy, Australian National University

Catherine Lu, Associate Professor, Department of Political Science, McGill University, Canada.

David Luban, University Professor in Law and Philosophy, Georgetown University.

David R. Mapel, Associate Professor, Department of Political Science, University of Colorado Boulder.

Jeff McMahan is Professor of Philosophy at Rutgers University.

Darrel Moellendorf, Goethe-Universität Frankfurt, Institut für Politikwissenschaft.

Jens David Ohlin is a Professor at Cornell Law School, specializing in international law, criminal law, and the laws of war.

Jonathan Parry, The Stockholm Centre for the Ethics of War and Peace, Stockholm University, Sweden.

Gregory M. Reichberg is Research Professor at the Peace Research Institute Oslo (PRIO) and Adjunct Professor in the Department of Political Science at the University of Oslo. He heads the Oslo-based Research School on Peace and Conflict (a consortium that offers doctoral courses) and is an associate editor of the *Journal of Military Ethics.*

Cheyney Ryan is Director of Human Rights Programs for the Oxford Institute for Ethics, Law, and Armed Conflict (ELAC), co-chair of the Oxford Consortium on Human Rights, and a member of Merton College at University of Oxford.

Daniel Schwartz, Department of Political Science and Department of International Relations, The Hebrew University of Jerusalem, Israel.

Henry Shue is Senior Research Fellow, Department of Politics and International Relations, Oxford University, and Fellow, Merton College. He was a founding member, and later Director, of the Institute for Philosophy and Public Policy at the University of Maryland (1976–87) and was then the first Director of the Program on Ethics and Public Life at Cornell University (1987–2002).

Daniel Statman, University of Haifa, Israel.

Anna Stilz is Associate Professor of Politics at Princeton University.

Victor Tadros, University of Warwick, UK.

Suzanne Uniacke is Director of the Centre for Applied Philosophy and Public Ethics, Charles Sturt University, Canberra.

Jeremy Waldron teaches legal and political philosophy at New York University School of Law.

THE ETHICS OF WAR

HELEN FROWE AND SETH LAZAR

1. Overview

On the global scale, war and other forms of political violence are not significant sources of human mortality. According to the World Health Organization, in 2012, global mortality rates from 'collective violence and legal intervention' were 1.7 per 100,000 (among those older than five).[1] Self-harm, by contrast, accounted for 11.4 deaths per 100,000 members of the population. Road injury accounted for 17.7 deaths per 100,000. If we care about saving people's lives, then, perhaps before thinking about war, we should direct our attention to, for example, improving water supplies to mitigate the 32 per 100,000 deaths from digestive diseases. And yet global figures do not tell the whole story. Consider Western Asia. In 2000, deaths from collective violence and legal intervention totalled 0.9 per 100,000. In 2012? 34.2. Deaths from intentional injuries rose in the same period from 10.2 to 41.5 per 100,000. It is not hard to conjecture what caused this massive increase, putting conflict and violence into the top ten causes of mortality in the region. The attack on the World Trade Center and the Pentagon, the invasion of Afghanistan, the invasion of Iraq, and the subsequent breakdown of Northern Iraq and Syria into poisonous civil war, together with other factors, account for an increase in mortality that equates to (on the assumption that the regional population is about 300 million) almost 200,000 excess deaths in 2012 relative to 2000. What's more, deaths are just part of the story. For every person killed, hundreds have been displaced by war. The UNHCR reported in 2015 that worldwide displacement hit an all-time high, with refugees making up almost 1% of the world's population.[2] War visits its victims with every other known kind of suffering as well.[3]

Still, with all that said, many more people die from easily curable diseases and malnourishment than die from war. Why, then, should we care so much about war? Perhaps, although many do not acknowledge it, we are all somewhat responsible for the many avoidable deaths caused every year by poverty and its associated ailments. But at least some of us are *surely* responsible, to at least some degree, for the deaths caused by our governments in war. And citizens of those countries that have launched and supported the wars in Western Asia over the past two decades are indirectly responsible—to at least some degree—for those additional 200,000 deaths a year. We had better be very sure, then, that we understand the rights and wrongs of our governments' and our combatants' actions; otherwise, by any reckoning, an inordinate moral burden lays on our shoulders.

In the past, many serious thinkers believed that there were fundamental differences between people, such that we need treat only those with whom we share important traits in common as moral equals. But every decent person now believes that all people are created equal. And in war we use the vast power of the state (or the inchoate power of collective action in the absence of a state) to aim at the death and destruction of our moral equals. War matters not only because of the terrible toll it takes on human lives and the environment, but because it is practically the only sphere of human conduct in which we actively aim at such terrible ends—and believe that it might be justified to do so.

Some think that war is in decline.[4] We question the validity of social scientific predictions based on a small sample size that is so clearly skewed by geopolitical factors, such as whether there is a hegemon. We also note that, if war is in decline, political violence is not.[5] And we note that even if the 'total wars' of the twentieth century are a thing of the past, we are now in an age where the effects of war can permeate ordinary life as never before. One man can bring havoc to the streets of Nice with little more than a shipping truck. Unmanned aerial vehicles can target individuals in their homes, far from any identifiable 'front line'. Mortality from war might be on the decline. But the practice of war—and the war machine—are in rude health.

With this background in mind, this Handbook offers a guide to thinking through the ethics of war. We have two aims: to introduce the reader to a broad (though not exhaustive) range of the central topics in just war theory and to make significant advances in each of those debates. Our focus has been squarely on shedding light on a perennial moral problem. But 'just war theory', taken broadly, is one of the most exciting areas in contemporary moral and political philosophy, and we also hoped to showcase this burgeoning field. Thus, the chapters in this handbook share an overarching methodology. They are all either engaged in or informed by contemporary analytical moral and political philosophy. We do address methodological disputes, but those disputes are in-house. We cover the history of just war theory, but only the Western tradition in which contemporary analytical just war theory has its roots.

Much of the most exciting work of the past twenty years has radically called into question the traditional, Western way of doing just war theory, and we are sympathetic to that scepticism. Nonetheless, we structured the volume conventionally, allowing the chapters to do the questioning, rather than the table of contents. Accordingly, the handbook has five parts. The first focuses on methodology, allowing us to explore how to think about the morality of war (within an analytical approach). The second part focuses on historical just war theory in the Western tradition to which analytical just war theory has the greatest debts.[6] The remaining parts are structured according to the conventional categories of '*jus ad bellum*', '*jus in bello*', and '*jus post bellum*'. *Jus ad bellum* governs the morality of the resort to war, *jus in bello* governs conduct in war, and *jus post bellum* governs the aftermath of war. The Latin labels have shallower roots than one might believe: they are a sometimes useful shorthand, nothing more.[7]

2. Part One: Method

In the opening chapter, Seth Lazar offers an overview of recent debates in analytical just war theory. He notes the divide between 'traditionalist' writers, seeking very broadly to vindicate the moral foundations of the laws of armed conflict, and 'revisionists' who call those foundations into question. The most prominent issues at stake have to do with the *jus in bello* and, in particular, with the principle of noncombatant immunity (also known as the principle of discrimination) and the moral equality of combatants. The former protects noncombatants (those who are not part of the armed forces of a party at war, nor directly participate in hostilities) against intentional attack in war. The latter is the moral equivalent of the legal position that the permissions and prohibitions in the laws of war apply to all combatants equally, regardless of whether their aims are just or unjust. Lazar argues that the substantive dispute between revisionists and traditionalists is in part sustained by their different approaches to thinking about the morality of war. Traditionalists tend to start by thinking about war and drawing on the resources of contemporary political philosophy. Revisionists tend to start by thinking about the ethics of harm outside of war and drawing on contemporary moral philosophy. But, Lazar argues, revisionists can (indeed must) also draw on political philosophy, and traditionalists must also attend to the insights of moral philosophy. Just war theory must not be conducted solely through hypothetical thought experiments that bear little connection to the reality of war. But we must not allow the pervasive horror of war to blind us to the underlying moral reality—that people have fundamental rights, and killing in war can be justified only if we can explain how those rights are either lost or overridden.

Helen Frowe's chapter addresses the distinction between *jus ad bellum* and *jus in bello* that structures most discussions of just war theory (and indeed this Handbook). She argues that this framework is misleading since it implies that there are two aspects of war—the war 'as a whole' and the way in which the war is conducted—and that each is subject to distinct moral constraints. But, Frowe argues, there is a single set of moral principles that determines the justness of actions that cause nonconsensual harm. If this is correct, there cannot be distinctive *ad bellum* or *in bello* principles. Frowe also denies that this distinction reflects a contrast between a limited range of goods and harms that determines the justness of specific offensives in war and a wider range of goods and harms that determines the justness of the war as a whole. She argues that when we are assessing the justness of combatants' actions, there is no principled reason to restrict the range of relevant goods and harms to those that are a direct upshot of their particular offensive. Whether an offensive is proportionate, for example, depends on all the goods and harms to which it contributes or which it prevents and not on some morally arbitrary subset of goods and harms directly caused by the agent or members of her military unit. Frowe also rejects the notion that the concept of *jus ad bellum* is valuable because it enables us to evaluate whole wars, arguing that such summative assessments of war are often misleading. We would do better, she argues, to focus on more nuanced assessments of individual actions.

In his contribution to this section, Gregory Reichberg examines the historiography of just war theory. He argues that the idea of the just war as a scholarly tradition emerged comparatively late in the early modern period, when the label 'just war' is applied retrospectively by writers attempting to identify a canon of the ethics of war, often in order to reject the idea that war might sometimes be justified. Reichberg rejects the popular view that Augustine is the first systematic writer on just war, arguing instead that it is Gratian who first compiles disparate works into a single text (his *Decretum*).

Reichberg identifies various ways in which recent debates in the ethics of war are pre-empted by historical texts. For example, Luis de Molina viewed war as an essentially legal mechanism for resolving disputes, thereby placing warring parties on an equal footing in a manner evocative of more recent defences of the moral equality of combatants, such as Michael Walzer's. Vanderpol, in contrast, rejects the legal model in favour of a moral standard, prefiguring work by critics of Walzer such as Jeff McMahan.

The final chapter in this section, by Jeremy Waldron, explores the implications of the ethics of war for the laws of war. In particular, Waldron cautions against undermining international law through philosophical discourse. While in most modern states domestic law is sufficiently robust to withstand critique and often adapt accordingly, international law is comparatively nascent and fragile. Waldron is especially concerned by the recent erosion by moral philosophers of the principle of noncombatant immunity. Revisionist just war theorists have argued that the correct approach is to discriminate not between combatants and civilians, but between those who are morally liable to harm and those who are not. Many revisionists nonetheless grant that, as a matter of law, the existing principle of discrimination is a useful convention that helps to minimize the harms of war. Waldron rejects both the thought that the principle is mere convention and the thought that such a convention is justified if, but only if, it minimizes harm.

Waldron's chapter highlights an ongoing concern for those proposing revisionist accounts of war—namely, whether the laws of war should (if they could) be altered to reflect what these philosophers take to be the morality of war. Moreover, Waldron urges revisionists to take seriously what he call the 'ethical burden' of publicly criticizing and potentially undermining laws that, he argues, represent 'elementary moral restraint' in the midst of war.

3. Part Two: History

Although contemporary analytical just war theorists rarely focus on their debt, they owe much to a Western tradition of thinking about the just war, grounded in Ancient Greece and Rome, substantially developed by the early Church fathers and later the Scholastics, and becoming most influential among the post-Westphalian theorists of public international law. This Western tradition is, of course, just one among others (and, of course, treating it as a single tradition is somewhat artificial). Nor was it hermetically sealed: Western just war theorists drew on the work of their various counterparts. But our focus in this Handbook is on contemporary analytical just war theory, and its roots are in this Western tradition.

Part Two begins with Rory Cox's survey of the early development of, and relationship between, *jus ad bellum* and *jus in bello* in the Western just war tradition up to Aquinas. Cox rejects several orthodoxies concerning the evolution of these branches of the ethics of war. In particular, he denies James Turner Johnston's claim that *jus ad bellum* was primarily developed by theologians, whereas *jus in bello* was developed by lawyers and soldiers. For example, it is popularly believed that Augustine focused exclusively on the justice of resorting to war. But, Cox argues, his demand that soldiers fight with right intention entails that they eschew cruelty, using only proportionate and necessary force. Thus, properly understood, Augustine is making both *ad bellum* and *in bello* prescriptions. Similarly, writers often thought to be solely concerned with the conduct of war also impose restrictions upon the waging of war. Adomnán's *Cáin*, for example, primarily aims at developing a form of noncombatant immunity, but also recognizes a constraint of legitimate authority on the waging of war. Cox argues that writings on *jus ad bellum* and *jus in bello* are consistently intermingled in this way, and, over time, culminate into a substantial body of morally sophisticated work on the ethics of war.

In his chapter, Daniel Schwartz tackles the late Scholastics: Francisco de Vitoria, Gabriel Vázquez, Francisco Suárez, and Luis de Molina. He begins by exploring Suárez's judicial model of offensive war—that is, war undertaken with the aim of rectifying past injustice—and contrasting Suárez's and Vitoria's accounts of the scope of a sovereign's jurisdiction. In this debate, we can see the early roots of disagreement about humanitarian intervention. For Suárez, the sovereign's jurisdiction is limited to his or her own territory, and he or she may wage war only to fend off incursions into that territory. But Vitoria posits a community of the 'whole world' that can rightfully wage war to prevent or repair wrongdoing against others—arguing that one could permissibly wage a war of intervention against the Aztecs to prevent their widespread practice of human sacrifice.

Much of Schwartz's chapter examines the late Scholastics' views on the morality of individual combatants' refusing to fight in what they believe to be an unjust war. Greg Reichberg has argued that, since Vitoria thought that combatants who wrongly believe their side's cause to be just are merely excused, he cannot be enlisted in support of the moral equality of combatants. Schwartz challenges this view, arguing that while the Scholastics did indeed distinguish between justifications and excuses, they nonetheless took excuses to be action-guiding. Combatants whose evidence wrongly suggests that their war is just have duties to fight. While this doesn't generate complete moral parity between just and unjust combatants, it moves them closer to parity than others have thought. The final part of this chapter explores the Scholastics' take on the permissibility of killing innocent people in war.

Pablo Kamanovitz's chapter explores the writings of the seventeenth- and eighteenth-century theorists Hugo Grotius, Christian Wolff, and Emer Vattel, focusing on the notion of 'regular war'. Kalmanovitz identifies three central features of regular war:

it is fought by sovereign states (or groups that aim to be such states) to settle disputes between them in the absence of any higher authority, it requires a formal declaration of war that marks the transition to the laws of war, and it concludes with a formal peace treaty. He contrasts this with the typical understanding of the just war as an entirely moral project focusing on the justice of the cause, the liability of the aggressor, and the vindication of the victim's rights. Regular war is a rejection of, in particular, the view that war can be reduced to the morality of ordinary life and interpersonal relationships. Rather, it takes the institutional features of states and the relationships between them to determine the morality of war.

Kalmanovitz elucidates how writers such as Grotius distinguish between how we judge individual actors and states and how we draw up our laws. Grotius, he argues, does not seek to justify the actions of unjust soldiers, 'but rather to justify the legal permissions that are granted to them'. Similarly, while we might criticize a given state for engaging in an unjust war or failing to assist in a just war, the *laws* of war should nevertheless be neutral about *jus ad bellum* since international law is ill-equipped to make reliable judgments about when war is warranted. These weaknesses of international law appear again in the work of Wolff and Vattel, who lament the endemic uncertainty and indeterminacy of the law. However, Kalmanovitz argues that the demand that belligerents make public declarations of war that set out their cause and that must persuade a 'global audience' of its justice have the (perhaps often unrealized) potential to serve as a check on aggression.

4. Part Three: Resort

In the first chapter of Part Three, Allen Buchanan offers a critical assessment of contemporary analytical just war theory and, in particular, its focus on objective moral principles at the expense of 'action-guiding norms'. Military and political leaders suffer from both epistemic limitations and potentially corrupting motivations, such as the desire to be re-elected. Asking them to determine the objective justification of their actions might yield worse results than insisting that they adhere to clear norms, even if the content of these norms departs from the objective moral facts. For example, rather than enjoining political leaders to wage interventionist wars only when war is proportionate—which requires them to make an assessment of proportionality that they may skew in favour of whatever verdict is most likely to lead to their re-election—we should instead insist that they follow a rule, according to which wars of intervention are permissible only to prevent genocide or mass killing. Similarly, a heuristic proscribing preventive war might be advisable even if preventive war can in principle sometimes be justified. Some justifications for war are 'practically dangerous' even if theoretically sound. Buchanan then explores the implications of this heuristic approach for our practices of praising and blaming leaders. The final part of the chapter explores the practical aims of theorizing about *jus ad bellum*, considering the ways in which such theorizing might be brought to bear on the law or communicated to practitioners and policy-makers.

David Luban's contribution also tackles the practicality of *jus ad bellum* theorizing, focusing on the predicament of an individual combatant who is ordered to fight but is unsure whether her war is unjust. Luban's main target is Jeff McMahan's proposal that we should provide moral guidance to combatants by establishing an *ad bellum* 'court' that could offer authoritative judgments about whether a war is just. Luban argues that merely compiling a panel of experts each of whose presence is uncontroversial will be a mammoth task; once compiled, the panel must then try to agree on particular cases. This, too, would be near impossible: even analytical just war theorists—a small and otherwise homogeneous group—disagree vehemently on many issues in just war theory. Any broader sample would be still more disputatious. Making an informed judgment will also require vast amounts of information that might be very dangerous or costly to obtain. And, since international bodies such as the UN Security Council already offer judgments on the use of force, combatants will need to decide which body to trust when those judgments conflict. In such cases, a *jus ad bellum* court might well increase rather than diminish a combatant's uncertainty about what to do.

However, Luban also rejects the idea that a combatant can simply ignore her conscience and be obedient to her state. Combatants are moral agents, capable of deliberation; they must obey orders to fight manifestly just wars and disobey orders to fight manifestly unjust wars. But, in the face of doubtful wars, combatants may defer to their state. He defends this third claim by invoking the moral importance of retaining civilian control of the military—a factor that he claims is largely overlooked by just war theorists but that provides compelling support for a presumption in favour of combatant obedience in cases of uncertainty.

A 'bloodless invasion' is an act of aggression that initially threatens only political or territorial rights but in which defending these rights will lead to bloodshed on both sides. International law and conventional morality suggest that national defence is permissible against such lesser aggressions, but many just war theorists argue that this conclusion lacks defensible moral foundations. In his contribution to this section, David Mapel explores the permissibility of resisting bloodless invasions, especially from the perspective of interpersonal morality. *Prima facie*, it seems that if a mugger threatens lethal force unless his victim hands over her purse, she ought to hand over the purse rather than try to kill him. Killing to defend her purse is disproportionate. But Mapel points out that these kinds of 'conditional threats' are nearly always accompanied by uncertainty. And it is not clear that the victim must take the risk that the mugger is trustworthy and will not try to kill her even if she complies. This speaks in favour of allowing force in the face of conditional threats.

However, Mapel suggests that considerations of proportionality have significantly more weight when defence risks harm to innocent people—as war invariably does—than in cases that involve only an attacker and a victim. When defence aims at protecting only lesser interests, such as political rights, it will likely be disproportionate to kill innocent people as a side effect. Perhaps we should revise the laws of war and conventional morality to reflect this more restrictive stance on national defence.

Anna Stilz's chapter explores the neglected question of when, and why, states have territorial rights and the circumstances under which these rights give rise to a just cause for war. Stilz argues that individuals' interests in 'located life plans' are nearly always sufficiently weighty to generate duties for others not to interfere with their occupancy of a given piece of land. Excepting cases in which respecting such a duty compromises another agent's capacity to live a minimally decent life and cases where occupancy was preceded by unjust expulsion, Stilz argues that occupancy generates a preinstitutional moral right to land. And, since individuals have justice-based reasons to accept the authority of a just state, a state that offers a just system acquires jurisdiction over the land that its citizens occupy. When that state is also self-determining, this provides an additional reason for other potentially just states not to interfere with its territory. However, like Mapel, Stilz is sceptical about whether territorial rights can generate a just cause for defensive war in the range of cases in which it is commonly supposed to do so. In cases where the imposed political system is not radically different from the system arising from self-determination, arguably, the harms of war—again, most notably the deaths of innocent people—would not be justified in order to defend territorial rights.

Henry Shue's contribution focuses on the *ad bellum* requirements of proportionality and last resort. Shue thinks we have a just cause for war only if going to war will avert a great evil; war is a last resort only if, of all the means for averting that evil, war is the least harmful. Proportionality may be assessed only if the last resort condition has been met. Shue argues that all the evils that would not occur but for the war being fought count when determining whether the war is proportionate, including those that the enemy will inflict if we resist their aggression. He distinguishes five types of evil relevant to *ad bellum* proportionality: (1) the evil one directly inflicts (roughly, harm to civilians caused by one's own offensives); (2) the evil that will be inflicted by others on people to whom one owes a duty of care (roughly, harm to one's own civilians caused by the enemy's offensives); (3) the evil that will be inflicted by others on people to whom one does not owe a duty of care (harms to foreign civilians caused by the enemy's offensives); (4) a 'moral contingency' of unpredictable evils that one cannot yet identify, but that inevitably occur in war; and (5) environmental damage. Shue argues that since the proportionality calculation judges the total evil of war—and does not assign blame or responsibility for those evils—it would be 'fundamentally dishonest' to exclude some of these evils because they are inflicted by the enemy. After all, if one is fighting a defensive war, *all* the evils of war are in some sense the responsibility of the aggressor. Insofar as we grant the need for *ad bellum* proportionality judgments at all, we have already accepted the relevance for our actions of the evils for which others are responsible.

Shue argues that the proportionality of resort differs from the proportionality of conduct since *in bello* proportionality considers only one of the evils just listed—civilian losses that one's own operation inflicts—and compares this to the military advantage sought. His argument here draws on existing international law. For Shue, the *in bello* rules are meant to limit the destruction caused by people who have already decided to fight, even if they should not be fighting at all. He thus supports the familiar Walzerian position that each individual offensive of a war can be *in bello* proportionate, even if the war as a whole is *ad bellum* disproportionate.

In his chapter, Cheyney Ryan carefully distinguishes between personal pacifism and political pacifism. He describes personal pacifism as an opposition to all forms of killing, including in personal self-defence. Political pacifism, in contrast, opposes war as a social practice, seeking to undermine what Ryan calls 'the war system': 'the practices of killing and destruction that characterize war *making*, and the practices of mobilizing human and material resources to those ends that characterize war *building*'. It focuses on developing institutional alternatives to war that enable the peaceful resolution and avoidance of conflicts. Political pacifism is compatible with the permissibility of killing in personal self-defence.

Ryan further contrasts political pacifism with 'just war pacifism'—the view that, although war could in theory be just, all actual wars have failed to satisfy the just war conditions (and are likely to continue to do so). Ryan suggests that as societies have become increasingly reluctant to fight wars—and as individuals have become increasingly reluctant to serve in them—it has become harder to distinguish pacifism from a general aversion to war. However, he argues that pacifism's absolute rejection of war is its defining characteristic: any practically possible war is *always* wrong, under any circumstances. He thus dismisses the challenge posed to absolutism by hypothetical wars (such as wars in which only culpable people are harmed, and only to the extent to which they are liable, in order to prevent some utter catastrophe). Whether such a war could be just is irrelevant since there is no practically possible war that could satisfy these conditions.

Yitzhak Benbaji's chapter examines the *ad bellum* requirement that wars be fought by a legitimate authority. Historically, this has been interpreted as granting only states or representatives of aspiring states the power to wage a just war. The requirement has been rejected by some revisionist writers who argue that if a war satisfies the other *ad bellum* conditions, then ordinary individuals may fight it regardless of whether they are authorized to do so by their state.

Benbaji describes what he calls a Factual Condition that summarizes the background of most wars: (1) there is a group (Actor) that fights the war, made up of decision-makers (typically a government) and enactors (typically the armed forces); (2) Actor represents a larger group in whose the name the war is fought—the Political Society; (e) the war is fought to secure a good for a third group, Beneficiaries; and (4) the war uses resources that belong to, and imposes risks on, a fourth group, Bearer. Benbaji suggests that, usually, Political Society is identical with Beneficiaries and Bearers—that is, wars are usually fought in the name of the group that it is intended to defend, using that group's resources and exposing that group to the risks of war. However, these groups can come apart—a war of humanitarian intervention might be undertaken in the name of one group, using their resources, but be intended to benefit an entirely different group. Benbaji suggests that each of these groups can confer or withhold its authorization with respect to a war. However, while the vetoing of a war by the Beneficiary or Bearer groups is evidence that the war fails the other *ad bellum* conditions, a failure to obtain Political Society authorization is not indicative of the war's being otherwise unjust. It instead shows that a decision to fight the war would be 'morally defective'.

The final chapter in the Resort section is Jonathan Parry's exploration of civil wars and revolutions. As Parry points out, only a small percentage of recent wars have been fought exclusively between states. The overwhelming majority involve substate groups. Parry suggests that thinking about these conflicts can shed light on the theoretical debates between reductive individualists, who argue that war is morally continuous with the use of force outside of war, and exceptionalists, who argue that there are some justifications for killing that obtain only in war. Parry identifies four kinds of exceptionalism: (1) *collectivist* exceptionalism, which invokes the fact that war is a group activity; (2) *authority-based* exceptionalism, which invokes the legitimacy of orders issued by institutions fighting wars; (3) *contractualist* exceptionalism, which invokes the mutually beneficial status of agreements between warring parties to accept certain norms; and (4) *pragmatic humanitarian* exceptionalism, which invokes the humanitarian importance of accepting exceptional justifications for killing in war as a means of reducing the overall suffering of war.

Parry argues that each of these forms of exceptionalism is challenged by substate conflicts. For example, contractualist exceptionalism has been developed in the context of agreements between (minimally decent) states. It is thus silent on the topic of non-state actors. The force of collectivist exceptionalism rests on the controversial idea that when sufficiently robust structures are in place, a group can count as acting together in a way that effects some change in its actions' normative status. But substate groups will often be much less robust than states, which makes it even harder to show that they have genuine collective agency of the sort that can generate the exceptional justification for killing. More generally, since these exceptions are meant to apply only to killing in war, exceptionalism seemingly requires some account of whether a conflict counts as a war—what Parry calls the Demarcation Problem. But the myriad forms of substate conflict suggest that there will be a substantial range of indeterminate cases in which exceptionalism neither prohibits nor permits killing. The second part of this chapter considers the circumstances in which substate groups might be justified in resorting to violence—specifically, whether the standard *jus ad bellum* criteria apply to insurgencies. In particular, Parry explores the role that consent plays in the permissibility of resorting to force.

5. Part Four: Conduct

In their chapter, Christian Barry and Lars Christie consider in depth the moral equality of combatants (the doctrine, recall, that combatants on all sides of any conflict have the same rights and immunities). They argue that views that categorically reject *or* support Equality are problematic, whether mounted from an individualist or collectivist position. They defend an individualist approach to the morality of war, according to which nonculpable combatants may retain their rights to life even if on the unjust side in war.

This would yield a limited defence of Equality since it would not hold for all unjust combatants, and it would entail only that many combatants on both sides of a war have the same immunities; it would not entail that they have the same permission to kill.

Saba Bazargan's chapter tackles one of the central tenets of traditional just war theory—namely, the idea that noncombatants enjoy moral immunity to intentional harm. According to international law, combatants may be intentionally attacked, but noncombatants may only be unintentionally harmed as a proportionate side effect of pursuing a legitimate military objective. The moral counterpart to this legal position is set out most famously in Walzer's *Just and Unjust Wars*, where he argues that all combatants have lost their rights not to be killed because they have allowed themselves to be made into dangerous men. Noncombatants, in contrast, do nothing to forfeit their usual rights against being harmed. As Bazargan outlines, Walzer's defence of noncombatant immunity has been substantially undermined by revisionist critics such as Jeff McMahan. McMahan argues that moral responsibility for causally contributing to an unjust threat is sufficient for liability to defensive harm, provided that harming the responsible person is necessary to avert the unjust threat for which she is responsible. This criterion will not map onto the distinction between combatants and noncombatants since many noncombatants are causally responsible for unjust threats, and combatants on the just side of a war are not typically responsible for *unjust* threats.

Bazargan argues that while the revisionist view is largely correct, it is incomplete. Specifically, he argues that the focus on liability through causation has led its proponents to overlook other grounds of liability, such as being a beneficiary of an unjust war. Bazargan claims that a certain type of war profiteers—those trading in large quantities of goods stolen from a civilian population as part of an unjust war—can be liable to be killed if they fail in duties of restitution. Such profiteers have an obligation to transfer the benefits that they obtain through wrongdoing—for example, the money that they make from trading the stolen goods—to the victims of the theft. Of course, this is fairly plausible—more controversial is the claim that profiteers may be killed if they fail to discharge this duty. But, as Bazargan argues, in war, the victim's very survival may be at stake precisely because someone has stolen her resources. In such cases, the duty to disgorge the relevant benefits is especially stringent, and a refusal to do so can render lethal force proportionate.

Adil Ahmad Haque tackles the moral status of human shields. Both active shielding (moving civilians to military targets) and passive shielding (moving military targets into proximity with civilians) are prohibited by international law. But some philosophers have recently argued that the moral reasons against using civilians as shields may be less weighty than the law suggests and that the harming of civilians who are being used by the enemy as shields may be 'discounted' compared to the harming of other civilians.

Haque begins by rejecting Cécile Fabre's arguments that civilians on an unjust side of a war can render themselves liable to be used as shields by just combatants and that innocent civilians can sometimes permissibly be forced to serve as shields for their just combatants. Fabre suggests that using civilians as shields is easier to justify than intentionally killing civilians since it is the enemy who will be killing them—from the perspective of the side using the shields, their deaths are unintentional. Haque rejects Fabre's claim that individuals have distinct rights not to be unintentionally killed and not to be intentionally killed in favour of the view that we each have a single right not to be killed. He then argues that there is 'hardly any moral difference' between using a person in a way that inflicts unintended harm upon her and using a person in a way that occasions her being unintentionally harmed by someone else.

Haque also addresses the idea that, although using shields oneself is morally impermissible, one can nevertheless disregard or discount the deaths of people who have been forced into shielding by the enemy. According to this view, unintentionally killing a civilian who is being used as an involuntary shield is easier to justify than unintentionally killing a civilian who is not a shield. A comparison with conscripts is sometimes used to support this view. Conscripts, like shields, are forced to participate in the war. And yet most people believe that conscripts lack rights not to be killed and are legitimate targets of force. So, the fact that civilians are being forced to serve as shields does not show that they cannot be legitimate targets as well. Haque invokes a difference in the sorts of contribution that shields and conscripted combatants make to the war effort to argue that conscripts, but not shields, lack rights not to be killed. He suggests that the role of shields is sufficiently close to allowing harm that they need not bear very significant costs to avoid playing that role. Thus, they do not forfeit or weaken their rights against being harmed if they shield as a result of serious duress. However, he grants that voluntary shields who intend to dissuade or prevent attacks on unjust combatants or military targets can compromise their rights not to be harmed.

Perhaps one of the most familiar aspects of moral reasoning about killing in war is the Doctrine of Double Effect (DDE). As Victor Tadros explains in his chapter, there are various competing formulations of the DDE. But each formulation includes two components: a strict constraint on intentional harming and a less stringent constraint on unintentional, side-effect harming. The DDE is commonly thought to underpin the *in bello* requirement of discrimination—that is, the requirement that force be aimed only at combatants. Civilians may be collaterally harmed as an unintentional side effect of pursuing a military objective but must never be intentionally harmed. However, despite its apparent centrality to the ethics of war, the truth of the DDE is deeply contested. Tadros offers a defence of the DDE, arguing that it is an important part of the most plausible general account of the permissibility of killing in war.

Much of the controversy surrounding the DDE focuses on the significance of intentions to permissibility. Some writers believe that we are more responsible for the outcomes that we intend compared to the outcomes we do not intend and that the more responsible we are for harms, the harder they are to justify. We might also think that (at least some) intentional harms involve using the victim in an especially objectionable way. Tadros suggests that both ideas help explain why there is a stricter restriction on intentional harming. In particular, he argues that we should not distinguish between directly intended harms and directly intended actions that result in harm, and he defends the DDE against putative counterexamples. Moreover, he argues that this version of the DDE is superior to Frances Kamm's purely causal account of broadly the same moral phenomena. Even though he grants the force of related distinctions, such as that between eliminative agency and opportunistic agency, and between opportunistic agency and manipulative agency, Tadros argues that intentions (and the DDE) still have work to do in the ethics of war.

Jeff McMahan's chapter offers a careful investigation of the notion of proportionality and the related issue of necessity. He begins by drawing attention to some features of *ad bellum* proportionality, arguing that harm to combatants, if it exceeds what they are liable to, can render war disproportionate. McMahan also offers an account of the range of goods relevant to *ad bellum* proportionality, arguing that only the prevention or correction of a moral wrong can be a just cause for war and that it can be so only when those who must be attacked to prevent the wrong are liable to be harmed and there is a lesser-evil justification for killing nonliable people as a side effect of those attacks.

Turning to *in bello* proportionality, McMahan rejects the traditional just war idea that the relevant good is its contribution to a military advantage, irrespective of whether one's war is just. Military advantage is an essentially instrumental notion, and its value is derived from the end that it serves. Unjust combatants cannot satisfy *in bello* proportionality because their actions contribute to unjust ends. McMahan grants that there might be morally bad consequences were combatants to come to accept this view, but he insists that this is irrelevant to the view's truth. He then sketches four alternatives for how international law might interpret proportionality but suggests that none is appealing. He concludes that, for now, keeping the current law may be preferable to the alternatives, but notes that changes in the guidance provided by legal institutions might also effect a change in the best way to legislate.

Suzanne Uniacke's chapter considers how reflecting upon the structure and moral character of terrorism can illuminate our understanding of the *in bello* requirement of discrimination. Uniacke defines terrorism as, paradigmatically, a violent attempt to further a political agenda by coercion—typically, by generating terror or insecurity by unpredictable attacks on illegitimate targets. These tactics are typically employed by non-state groups who attack innocent people as a means of coercing a larger group or government into behaving in a particular way. However, Uniacke recognizes that one or several of these features may be missing from actions that we nonetheless regard as terrorism—these features are indicative, rather than constitutive, of terrorism. And, although her account does not insist that terrorism is impermissible by definition, its features of coercion and violence make it presumptively wrongful.

Uniacke argues that terrorism should be judged by the moral standards that govern war, in particular the requirement not to target noncombatants. Much of the philosophical discussion of terrorism has focused on whether what appear to be instances of justified terrorism show that the requirement of discrimination is not an absolute prohibition, but rather an especially high moral hurdle. However, she also points out that the features of terrorism that most obviously speak to its wrongness—that it is coercive and harms innocent people—are not unique to terrorism, either in isolation or combination. Even the 'structural' feature of terrorism—that it objectionably makes use of people by harming them in order to coerce others—is not unique to terrorism: kidnappings for ransom, for example, harm the abductee in order to influence others.

Whether torture is a legitimate tactic of war has been the topic of significant public debate, particularly since the 2001 war in Afghanistan and the 2003 war in Iraq. Frances Kamm's chapter begins by comparing and contrasting accounts of torture, such as the UN Convention Against Torture and Other Cruel, Inhumane or Degrading Treatment or Punishment, and the United States Torture Statute, and also accounts from Henry Shue and David Sussman. These accounts vary with respect to, amongst other things, whether only someone acting in an official capacity can count as engaging in torture and whether torture must be aimed at a defenceless person (and whether being able to reveal information counts as a form of available defence).

Kamm's central interest is in the relationship between what we may do to a person while she is actively threatening someone else and what we may do to her once she has completed her threatening act—for example, once she has planted the bomb and need do nothing else in order for the bomb to kill her victim. Kamm thus considers cases in which inflicting the sort of harm that one might inflict in a standard case of torture—such as giving a person repeated electric shocks—is necessary to prevent a threatener from completing threatening actions. She calls this *torture** and argues that inflicting such harm could be permissible if it were necessary to prevent the killing of innocents. Even though certain acts of torture* and other forms of manipulation can be more disrespectful than killing a person, it is more important not to kill people than not to disrespect them. Moreover, Kamm suggests that torture* is permissible not only as a less harmful substitute for killing in cases where killing is permissible. Even when it is not permissible to kill a person while she is in the midst of threatening, torture* could be proportionate, given the lethal threat she poses to her victim. Thus, even if it is impermissible to kill people once their threatening action is complete, this does not show that it is impermissible to torture them.

The last chapter in this section is Daniel Statman's exploration of one of the most widely discussed topics in both academic and public debates on the ethics of war—namely, the moral permissibility of using unmanned aerial vehicles (UAVs, or drones) and robots as means of fighting. Statman defends the use of these forms of technology on several grounds. He argues that they are more discriminate than available alternatives and more likely to be proportionate. He also cites their capacity to reduce the risk of harm to combatants and to increase the likelihood that states will wage justified wars of humanitarian intervention. These technologies also make it easier for states to resist aggression without resorting to the much more harmful means of full-scale war. Finally, they are cheaper than conventional wars, which makes resources available for pursuing other valuable ends.

Statman suggests that arguments that try to show the wrongness of using UAVs and robots often struggle to show any significant distinction between these weapons and conventional weapons. For example, it's not clear why being killed by a remotely operated drone is more of a 'faceless' or inhumane killing than being killed by a bomb dropped from a plane 20,000 feet in the air. He also rejects Paul Kahn's argument that combatants who fight using drones, thereby avoiding risk to their own lives, cannot have a right to use lethal force against their targets. Kahn believes that a combatant's 'licence to kill' rests upon what he calls the 'reciprocal imposition of risk' between opposing combatants. Statman argues that, amongst other problems, Kahn's view renders humanitarian intervention impermissible since combatants who undertake interventions cannot claim to have antecedently been at risk in a way that would legitimize their use of force.

6. Part Five: Aftermath

The Handbook concludes with a section on endings and aftermath in the ethics of war. Darrel Moellendorf argues that the justice of ending a war—what he calls *jus ex bello*—raises distinct moral problems. We cannot determine whether a war should be ended by focusing exclusively on whether it should have been started in the first place. It's possible that a war that was unjustly begun—that failed the condition of being a last resort, for example—could be justly continued if the war itself has now made alternative resolutions impossible. Moellendorf therefore rejects David Rodin's claim that such situations constitute a dilemma in which one would act wrongly in continuing the war, but also in stopping the war.

Moellendorf also rejects the view that the costs of a war that have already been incurred should be treated as 'sunk costs' that are irrelevant to the proportionality of continuing the war. He suggests that if we disregard past killings, there may be no principled point at which a war becomes disproportionate, no matter how much destruction lies in its wake. The chapter also outlines the principles that Moellendorf takes to determine the constraints on ending war. Foremost amongst these are that the war be ended as quickly as possible insofar as this is compatible in minimizing injustice and moral costs. But Moellendorf also grants a defeasible principle that one should negotiate in good faith and that negotiating parties should not make unjust demands based on their success in the war.

Cécile Fabre focuses on the role of *jus post bellum*—justice after war—in just war theory and its relationship to *jus ad bellum* and *jus in bello*. She begins by addressing the question of whether *jus post bellum* is properly part of just war theory at all, rather than part of political philosophy more generally construed. Whereas some writers have urged the need for the development of *jus post bellum*, Fabre finds their motivations for this project wanting. However, she also resists Seth Lazar's claim that we should think of just war theory as having little to offer a full account of the ethics of peacebuilding. Lazar argues that when building peace after war, we need to look forward, whereas reliance on the tools of just war theory promotes recrimination and claims for compensation instead of prioritizing peacebuilding. Fabre defends a middle ground that grants the role of broader moral and political philosophy in developing an account of justice after war, but nonetheless insists that it makes a difference that what is aimed at is peace after war and not peace *simpliciter*.

For example, Fabre argues that a state's duties in the aftermath of war can be partly determined by whether its resorting to war was just and whether the war was justly fought. She distinguishes between substantive justice—that is, who is entitled to what—and procedural justice—that is, who should decide whether those entitlements are received. She then argues that the *ad bellum* and *in bello* justice of a belligerent's war affects which peace terms will count as substantially just and who has the standing to negotiate peace terms. Fabre argues that those who have contributed to injustice can be liable to bear costs that it would be unfair to impose on innocent people. However, this interaction between the justice of the war and *jus post bellum* must be tempered by whether and how imposing such costs undermines the prospects for peace. She also suggests that some leaders, such as Hitler, can come to lack the standing to negotiate peace terms by engaging in especially egregious wrongdoing.

Jens Ohlin's chapter offers a deontological defence of the anti-impunity norm: the principle that wrongdoing in conflict should not go unpunished. He argues that criminal trials, rather than nonpenal processes, best serve this norm. This contrasts with an instrumental justification that upholds the anti-impunity norm as the best way to prevent recidivism by belligerents and to deter others from engaging in wrongdoing. Ohlin suggests that this debate in international law mirrors the debate in domestic criminal law. However, he also points out empirical differences between international crimes and domestic crimes that, he suggests, undercut the force of the instrumentalist justification as applied to international crimes. Those who engage in genocide, he argues, are already acting irrationally in a way that makes them much less responsive to the sort of incentives and sanctions provided by a system of punishment. Instrumentalist justifications of the anti-impunity norm may be plausible in the domestic context, but less so in international law.

In the final chapter of this section, Catherine Lu explores two kinds of reconciliation. Relational reconciliation concerns how we repair alienating relationships between individuals in the aftermath of conflict. Structural reconciliation concerns how we amend or replace the alienating social and political systems and practices that mediate these individual relationships. These forms of reconciliation have international counterparts, addressing the relationships between states and the systems that govern these relationships, respectively. Of these two forms of reconciliation, Lu argues that, despite being neglected by theorists in favour of relational reconciliation, structural reconciliation is 'analytically prior and normatively fundamental' since it establishes the background conditions that bestow legitimacy on attempts to reshape relationships between agents.

Lu outlines two concerns: first, that the project of reconciliation might be misguided at the individual level, placing undue burdens on victims and setting unrealistic goals of unity and harmony; and second, that reconciliation might not be demanding enough at the structural level since it focuses on the individual actors involved at the expense of reflection on the systems that allowed wrongdoing to occur. Lu argues that when we conceive of relational and structural reconciliation as political projects, we circumvent the concern that reconciliation places excessive or inappropriate burdens on victim.

And, of course, her proposal for structural reconciliation speaks directly to the concern that systems escape critical reflection.

Notes

1. Statistics taken from http://apps.who.int/gho/data/node.home
2. http://www.unhcr.org/news/latest/2015/6/558193896/worldwide-displacement-hits-all-time-high-war-persecution-increase.html
3. For a gruelling rundown of the horrors of war, see, e.g., Hugo Slim, *Killing Civilians: Method, Madness and Morality in War* (London: Hurst, 2007).
4. Steven Pinker, *The Better Angels of Our Nature: Why Violence Has Declined* (New York: Viking, 2011).
5. Keith Krause, 'From Armed Conflict to Political Violence: Mapping and Explaining Conflict Trends', *Daedalus* 145 (4: 2016) Issue 4, Fall 2016.
6. This is, of course, one tradition among others. Readers seeking a comparative approach to the ethics of war should consider Gregory M. Reichberg and Henrik Syse, *Religion, War, and Ethics: A Sourcebook of Textual Traditions* (New York: Cambridge University Press, 2014).
7. Gregory M. Reichberg, 'Jus Ad Bellum', in *War: Essays in Political Philosophy* edited by Larry May and Emily Crookston (Cambridge: Cambridge University Press, 2008), 11–29.

PART I

METHOD

CHAPTER 1

METHOD IN THE MORALITY OF WAR

SETH LAZAR

1. Introduction

When your topic is the ethics of maiming and killing, it is hard to care about methodology, still harder to care about which theorists of maiming and killing fall into which camp. Most essays about war should be about war, not about thinking about war. This is not only a philosophical but perhaps also a moral imperative.

Yet unless we periodically step back, take an overview of the debate and engage in some self-conscious reflection about how and why we write just war theory, we are likely to find ourselves ploughing ever narrower and less productive furrows. In this chapter, I attempt such an overview. I show how disputes over first-order questions about the permissibility of particular act-types in war have been conflated with second-order disputes about how to do just war theory. We can make progress by separating the two kinds of enquiry, giving each the independent attention that it deserves.

The 'first-order' history of contemporary just war theory is easy to write. Michael Walzer's 1977 book, *Just and Unjust Wars*, defined, if not created the field.[1] It presented a philosophical vindication (with some revisions) of the central principles of the international law of armed conflict. States may go to war to defend their political sovereignty and territorial integrity. Humanitarian interventions are justified only to avert rare and extreme catastrophes. Noncombatants are immune from attack in war but may be killed as an unintended side effect if that is proportionate to the military advantage combatants thereby achieve and if the combatants take on additional risks themselves to reduce risk to noncombatants (here Walzer anticipated international law: Article 57 of the first additional protocol to the Geneva conventions, also promulgated in 1977, caught up). Combatants, regardless of the justice or injustice of their cause, face the same liabilities and constraints and enjoy the same permissions. As Article 43(2) of the first additional protocol states: 'combatants have the right to participate directly in hostilities'. And, as the preamble states, its strictures and permissions apply 'without any adverse distinction based on the nature or origin of the armed conflict or on the causes espoused by or attributed to the Parties to the conflict'.

Although these views substantially depart from much that was traditional in just war theory,[2] we can call it the orthodoxy since it dominated intellectual discussion of the ethics of war for at least two decades. Outside of philosophy—in military education, public policy and other academic disciplines—it remains the orthodoxy. Only in philosophy has it come under sustained attack. In rough chronological order, David Luban, Charles Beitz, Robert Holmes, Jeff McMahan, Richard Norman, and David Rodin repeatedly put pressure on each element of Walzer's orthodoxy.[3] We can call these philosophers and the many who followed them with similar arguments the 'revisionists'.

Revisionists are not a unified camp; they share only their rejection of Walzer's orthodoxy. The most significant divides are between those who advocate outright pacifism, those who espouse contingent pacifism (wars could be just in theory, but never will be in practice) and those who think that some actual wars can be just.[4]

The revisionists did not only disagree with Walzer about which acts of war were permissible. They disagreed about how to do just war theory. Walzer's method was to start with international law and military history and present his arguments as an interpretation of 'the war convention'. His opponents built their critiques from analyses of permissible harm outside of war. As their isolated criticisms became a groundswell, they coalesced into a distinct methodological approach. They were *reductivists* because they thought that any justified killing in war must be justified by appeal to the same properties that justify killing outside of war. And they were *individualists* because they thought that considering interpersonal interactions between individuals sufficed to explain permissible killing both in war and outside of it.[5] Walzer developed his account of the morality of war by thinking about war; the revisionists theirs by thinking, at least in the first instance, about individual self- and other-defence.[6]

As barbaric as they might appear when considered in abstraction, the laws of war, and the orthodoxy they express stand among the great moral advances made by humanity, alongside the abolition of slavery and the advance of social and political equality worldwide. They contrast with customs and practices that preceded them, according to which wars could be launched for naked political purposes and fought without restraint. Unsurprisingly, then, the orthodoxy has its defenders.[7] They are normally called 'traditionalists', though few believe that every aspect of Walzer's picture can or should be saved.

Traditionalists have often assumed that Walzer's first- and second-order positions must be defended together. To refute the revisionists' verdicts on the permissibility of killing in war, they would have to refute their reductivism, their individualism or both. Some have adopted an *exceptionalist* stance, according to which there are properties that justify (or prohibit) killing in war that do not justify killing outside of war. These properties, they argue, deflect the arguments advanced by the revisionists against the first-order orthodoxy.[8] Some also reject individualism (note that this is consistent with endorsing reductivism).[9] They argue that some of the values that justify some killing in war are irreducibly collective or that the actions of which war is composed are irreducibly collective.[10]

Although the dialectic between revisionists and reformists has been fruitful, it has become too polarized. There is a significant danger that the first- and second-order disputes will hypostasize, so that reductive individualism becomes a necessary corollary to revisionism and reformism goes hand in hand with exceptionalism, collectivism or both. This would be a mistake. Reductivism is conceptually independent from individualism, and reductive individualism does not entail revisionism. Traditionalists need not be exceptionalists or collectivists. And exceptionalists and collectivists can be revisionists.

My aim in this chapter is to substantiate the narrative just given (although, for reasons of space, I will say no more about the Walzerian orthodoxy). In each section, I will illustrate the claim that first-order disagreements have been underpinned by second-order disputes but that the connection between methodological and substantive commitments is contingent. In Section 3, I discuss the revisionist critique of Walzer and its stance on how just war theory should be done. Although there is a natural connection between one kind of reductive individualism and revisionism, the reductivist individualist church is broader than one might think, also encompassing traditionalist arguments. In Section 4, I discuss traditionalist responses to revisionism, which have for the most part presupposed exceptionalism. And yet, exceptionalists can be revisionists, too. In Section 5, I discuss collectivist approaches to the morality of war, which can support both traditionalist and revisionist conclusions.

I begin, however, with some generic observations about how killing can be justified on which (with a little strategic vagueness) most should be able to agree.

2. What Justifies Killing?

In such a disputatious field as just war theory, it might seem hard to find common ground. And yet, over the past thirty years, a basic picture has emerged of the generic kinds of justification that one can offer for killing a person. Although each philosopher will have his or her own species of each genus, most should accept something like this generic classification.

I think that almost all contemporary just war theorists agree that people have a presumptive right not to be killed. This, in the most abstract terms, grants additional moral protection to their interest in survival.[11] Killing someone who retains that right cannot be justified by the mere fact that doing so would realize a marginally greater good for someone else. Once we agree that people start out with this right, the path to justifying killing becomes quite simple: killing is permissible if and only if either the target has somehow lost the protection of his right to life or he has not lost that protection but the good achieved by killing him is sufficiently great to render killing him permissible, thus overriding his right.[12] Call these the 'loss of rights' and 'lesser evil' justifications for killing.

Satisfying the loss of rights condition is not sufficient for an act of killing to be permissible. Three further conditions must be met.[13] Killing a person must be *proportionate*: that is, the good achieved by killing him (e.g., averting an unjustified threat) must be great enough to justify imposing that much harm on him. It must be *necessary*, in the sense that there must be no other less harmful means available to that end, or, if there are such means, the reduction in harm is more than offset by a reduction in prospects of success.[14] And killing must not have *other adverse consequences* which might render it impermissible even if the other conditions are satisfied. For example, suppose that one's target is the only person who knows the cure to cancer. Satisfying the lesser evil condition *is* sufficient for killing to be permissible—but it also entails that each of these three other conditions is met.

These two genera of justification are extremely capacious. Loss of rights justifications typically include those grounded in consent, desert or liability to be harmed in self- or other-defence. But they can also include views for which one's rights depend on the persistence of favourable background conditions so that when those conditions are absent, the right no longer obtains. Or they could be underpinned by a rule consequentialist or a contractarian argument: the right fails to obtain when the rule, obedience to which realizes the best consequences overall, does not support the right or when the underlying hypothetical contract on which the right is grounded does not obtain.

Some act-consequentialists will deny that there are any rights. They think that killing (like everything else) is permissible if and only if all alternatives realize worse outcomes. Those who believe in rights think that killing is a permissible lesser evil if and only if all alternatives realize worse outcomes. So, for act-consequentialists, lesser evil justification is all there is (although, of course, they will evaluate outcomes quite differently from nonconsequentialists). The same can be said, *mutatis mutandis*, for some forms of rule-consequentialism.

3. Reductive Individualism

Reductivism claims that we can reduce the morality of war to the morality of life outside of war: reductivists think that people lose the protection of their right to life on just the same grounds in war as they do outside of war; and they think that the lesser evil justifications that apply in war are no different from those that apply outside it. This amounts to a clear stance on how to think about the morality of war: start by working out the principles that govern liability and lesser evil justifications in life outside of war, then apply those principles to war.

Presented in this schematic form, reductivism is a capacious doctrine. It is consistent, for example, with a thoroughgoing act consequentialism. In practice, however, it has been interpreted much more narrowly. With some minor disputes, many just war theorists affirm something like the following picture of the ethics of killing inside and outside of war. I will call this 'paradigmatic reductivism'. It has two key tenets.

The first concerns loss of rights justifications for killing. Paradigmatic reductivists think that although there are several ways one can lose the protection of the right to life outside of war, only one of them is relevant to the ethics of killing in war: liability to be killed in self- or other-defence. A person loses the protection of her right to life in this way when she is sufficiently responsible for an unjustified threat to another person or persons and killing her is a necessary and proportionate means to avert that threat. Those who are liable to be killed in self- or other-defence may permissibly be killed either intentionally or unintentionally provided doing so does not have excessively adverse consequences.

The second tenet concerns lesser evil justification. *Intentionally* killing those who retain their right to life can be a permissible lesser evil only if it is necessary to realize some extremely valuable goal.[15] Most think that lesser evil justifications like this are extremely rare, appropriate only in what Michael Walzer calls 'supreme emergencies', if even then.[16] *Unintentional* killing, by contrast, can be a lesser evil provided it is necessary to achieve a substantial, but nonetheless more pedestrian good.

We can extract from this the following criteria for permissible intentional and unintentional killing in war: killing in war is permissible if and only if

(a) Those whom one intentionally kills are either unavoidably killed in pursuit of an extremely valuable goal, or they are liable to be killed in self- or other-defence where killing them is necessary and proportionate to that end.
(b) Those whom one unintentionally kills are either unavoidably killed in the pursuit of a sufficiently valuable goal, or they are liable to be killed in self- or other-defence where killing them is necessary and proportionate to that end.[17]

Notice that satisfying (a) and (b) does not ensure that this account of the morality of war is reductivist. We need to add a further condition:

(c) None of the properties that render killing the liable necessary and proportionate, and killing the nonliable a permissible lesser evil, justifies killing only in war.

This view has been most explicitly articulated by David Rodin, in his *War and Self-Defence*, where he coined the term 'reductive individualism'.[18] In a response to Rodin, McMahan gave a simple and powerful statement of the view. It is worth quoting at length, to be clear that reductive individualism is no caricature but the doctrine at the heart of contemporary revisionist just war theory:

> First imagine a case in which a person uses violence in self-defense; then imagine a case in which two people engage in self-defense against a threat they jointly face. Continue to imagine further cases in which increasing numbers of people act with increasing coordination to defend both themselves and each other against a common threat, or a range of threats they face together. What you are imagining is a spectrum of cases that begins with acts of individual self-defense and, as the threats

> become more complex and extensive, the threatened individuals more numerous, and their defensive action more integrated, eventually reaches cases involving a scale of violence that is constitutive of war.[19]

In his *Killing in War*, the most influential book in the revisionist critique of Walzer, McMahan adds:

> The difference between war and other forms of conflict is a difference only of degree and thus the moral principles that govern killing in lesser forms of conflict govern killing in war as well. A state of war makes no difference other than to make the application of the relevant principles more complicated and difficult.[20]

This view has recently received robust defence by Helen Frowe and Cécile Fabre and has underpinned discussions of war by Robert Holmes, Richard Norman, David Rodin, Lionel McPherson, and Richard Arneson.[21] And all of these philosophers have used reductive individualism as the key element in their critiques of the Walzerian orthodoxy.

Walzer argued that combatants in war face the same liabilities, permissions, and constraints irrespective of whether their cause is just or unjust. Reductivists show that people using force in ordinary cases of self- and other-defence outside of war do not stand in the same symmetrical relationship. And they conclude that if combatant moral equality has no analogue in conflicts outside of war, then it must be a mistake.[22] Indeed, many revisionists go further than this: not only do they argue that just combatants retain their rights to life; they also argue that many combatants on the unjust side are not liable to be killed.[23] This is because they are not responsible for contributing to unjustified threats—either they are ineffective, so barely contribute to any threats at all, or they contribute but are not responsible for doing so because they are acting under duress or in the belief that fighting is permissible. Hence, it is impossible to fight a just war without intentionally killing many innocent people. Some think this means we should endorse pacifism.[24]

Walzer argued that all noncombatants retain their rights to life. Reductivist revisionists show that the principles grounding liability to be killed outside of war, when applied to war, would allow some—perhaps many—noncombatants to be liable to be killed.[25] This is because liability does not require that one *pose* an unjustified threat, only responsibility for *contributing* to it. Noncombatants contribute to the unjustified threats of their state by paying their taxes, voting, providing services to the military, boosting public support for the war, and so on. If these contributions are enough to render them liable to be killed, then the principle of noncombatant immunity must be false. If we insist that loss of one's right to life requires a greater degree of responsibility or a more significant causal contribution, then we are returned to the problem that many unjust combatants will not be liable to be killed either.

Walzer contended that states could (indeed, sometimes must) defend themselves against attacks on their political sovereignty and territorial integrity. Some reductivist revisionists have argued that we cannot make sense of this permission in terms of individual rights of self- and other-defence.[26] And in some of the first responses to Walzer, reductivists argued that the constraint on humanitarian interventions is unsustainable. Individual self- and other-defence are justified to protect individual rights to life and security, so, when those rights are threatened there is a *prima facie* case for intervention irrespective of whether the threat is a rare calamity of the kind Walzer envisages as being a prerequisite for justified intervention.[27]

For these philosophers, the path from methodology to substantive commitments is clear. They start by thinking about liability and lesser evil justification outside of war, they then endorse something close to paradigmatic reductivism, and they derive from it their revisionist critique of Walzer's just war theory. This leaves open the possibility of a methodologically equivalent stance that has different substantive conclusions: if we can show paradigmatic reductivism to be false, or at least underinclusive, then we might be able to vindicate broadly Walzerian conclusions on reductive individualist grounds.

In my own work, I have argued for a more expansive role for lesser evil justification in the morality of killing by showing that there are many ways in which some rights-violating killings are morally worse than others, along similar lines to the distinction already drawn between intended and merely foreseen killing.[28] Most importantly, noncombatants—but not combatants—are defenceless against attack, and, in killing noncombatants, one takes a greater risk of killing an innocent person than when killing combatants, which aggravates the former right-violation and mitigates the latter.

Attending to these factors helps to mitigate one of the most controversial implications of revisionism: the 'responsibility dilemma', according to which, whatever degree of responsibility for contributing to an unjustified threat one thinks is necessary for liability to be killed, one faces problems. If only a very slight degree of responsibility is sufficient for liability, then too many noncombatants on the unjust side will be liable; if a higher degree of responsibility is necessary, then too many unjust combatants will *not* be liable. On my view, liability to be killed presupposes a high degree of responsibility for contributing to an unjustified threat, so many unjust combatants, as well as almost all unjust noncombatants, are not liable to be killed in war. However, killing nonliable soldiers is, in various respects, less *pro tanto* wrongful than killing nonliable civilians. So it can be permissible to kill nonliable unjust combatants and avoid a counterintuitive endorsement of pacifism while it remains impermissible to kill nonliable noncombatants on the unjust side.

This does not get us all the way to Walzer's doctrine of noncombatant immunity and his account of the permissibility of going to war in national defence. But it is an essential first step, one that is wholly consistent with reductive individualism if not with its paradigmatic form. Crucially, it presupposes the same methodology: it identifies principles relevant to the ethics of killing outside of war, then shows how they apply in war. In a similar vein, David Rodin has argued that principles of self-defence, properly understood, would not license the wholesale onslaught on noncombatant immunity threatened by paradigmatic reductivism because the causal remoteness of noncombatants' contribution protects their immunity.[29]

Using the same methodology, Uwe Steinhoff has argued that the ethics of force outside of war *does* license something close to Walzer's moral equality of combatants, permitting combatants fighting on the unjust side in war to use lethal force against just combatants.[30] This is because even unjust combatants are entitled to use lethal force to defend those of their compatriot noncombatants who are at risk of being killed unintentionally by the enemy. With a similar aim in mind, I have also argued that citizens' associative duties to protect one another, grounded in the value of their relationship *qua* co-citizens, as well as in their deeper relationships, can render some killing in war a justified lesser evil even if carried out in the service of the unjust side.[31]

In a more radical departure from the mainstream reductive individualist positions, but also with a view to vindicating the moral equality of combatants, Thomas Hurka has argued that soldiers on either side of most conflicts consent to be exposed to the risks of war. In doing so, they waive their rights to life, thus vindicating something like the moral equality of combatants.[32] This is a loss of rights justification for killing, which has nothing to do with self- or other-defence.

Emerton and Handfield argue that there are distinct principles governing self-defence in circumstances of 'affray'.[33] When conflict erupts around one, and it is not clear who is in the right, we plausibly have moral privileges to use lethal force that cannot be justified under the standard principles of self- or other-defence. They develop this argument in an institutionalist way, but we could venture a simpler version: suppose you find yourself in a chaotic brawl where nobody really knows what is going on, but everyone knows that if they don't defend themselves, they'll be seriously harmed. It's plausible that, provided you know you're no more at fault for the riot than is anyone else (which is consistent with everyone being at fault), you're licensed to use lethal force to defend yourself. After all, why should it be morally preferable to let someone else unjustly kill you rather than unjustly kill him first? This argument might give further limited support for something close to moral equality between some combatants in war and would also help underpin noncombatant immunity since noncombatants are not parties to the affray that might plausibly extend combatants' permissions.

4. Exceptionalism

Reductivists start with the principles governing interpersonal violence and aggregate up into an account of the morality of war. Exceptionalists start by thinking about war itself. In particular, they identify properties of warfare that are not present in conflicts short of war, which might play some normative role and in particular help vindicate some of the pretheoretical intuitions about the morality of war that are so hard to ground in reductivist reasons alone. Given this ambition, it is unsurprising that exceptionalists tend to be traditionalists, defending aspects of the Walzerian orthodoxy against the revisionist critique. But we can quickly see that an exceptionalist revisionism is also possible, as I will show at the end of this section.

First, though: if we start not with self-defence, but with war itself, then what do we find? What, in particular, do exceptionalists mean by war? It is important not to caricature their view. There is nothing magical about the fact that we call a certain conflict a war, as though crossing some bright line between war and other conflicts transforms the array of salient principles. Exceptionalists need endorse only two relatively conservative theses. First, there are some properties of war that do not widely obtain in conflicts outside of war, especially not in the cases of individual self- and other-defence that reductivists use as their model. Second, these properties can determine whether a loss of rights or a lesser evil justification for killing obtains. I will not attempt an exhaustive list of these properties, but these are the ones that are most commonly invoked:

(i) Wars are *large-scale* conflicts. The interests of many people are at stake. And wars have an inherent tendency to increase in scale.
(ii) There is widespread and egregious *noncompliance* with any principles that could plausibly govern killing outside of war.
(iii) Among the interests at stake, some are *political*. For example, they have to do with preserving political sovereignty and territorial integrity.
(iv) At least one party to the conflict is a *state*.
(v) The conflict is governed by *institutions*, in particular the laws of war.
(vi) The conflict takes place against the backdrop of, and usually disrupts, the *international state system*.

This second-order stance—when thinking about the morality of war, think first *about war*—has underpinned much of the reaction to the revisionist critique of Walzer. Walzer himself dismisses McMahan's views as a 'precise account of what individual responsibility in war would be like if war were a peacetime activity'.[34] A number of other philosophers have argued that the properties just listed undermine the revisionist position. Because these properties are heterogeneous, the exceptionalist camp is less unified than their revisionist counterparts, but the following seem to be the most promising approaches.

Henry Shue and Jeremy Waldron focus most on (i) and (ii)—scale and widespread noncompliance.[35] They argue that war is hell in two senses: the scale of suffering that it involves and the moral depravity that it inevitably entails. Shue in particular argues that it is absurd to direct moral prescriptions at those who are inevitably set on disregarding those prescriptions. This basic point could be developed in many different ways—one could argue that the presence and preservation of our rights to life depends on there being a minimal degree of willingness to comply with the dictates of morality (this would be a loss of rights justification for killing). That is, rights are *practice-dependent*, just as many think that principles of distributive justice are dependent on favourable material conditions obtaining. When conditions are less favourable, it is every man for himself.

Or, one could argue that morality in general is rule consequentialist: the right principles are those which will in fact have the best consequences in the long run (with respect to whatever makes consequences best). Outside of war, the principles governing the use of force that have the best long-run consequences are the very restrictive ones with which we are all familiar. If we carry those over to war, we get disastrous results because of the scale of the violence and the widespread predictable noncompliance. So the best principles for war are something close to Walzer's orthodoxy (this would fit with a lesser evil justification).

Appealing to the political nature of the interests at stake in war (iii), I have argued that to vindicate a plausible account of national defence, the goods that render killing in such wars proportionate and necessary must include political goods, such as the preservation of political sovereignty and territorial integrity, for the sake of which it is permissible to kill only in war (revolutions and civil wars are governed by the same principles as wars of national defence).[36] Reductivists sometimes concede this point: they argue that defensive wars are rendered proportionate in part by the aggregated political interests of large populations of people.[37] They think this remains consistent with reductivism, but although it is certainly consistent with *evaluative individualism* (which we will come to in the next section), those political interests do not justify killing outside of war, so this is an exceptionalist justification for killing. It is only in virtue of the scale of the conflict—which scale obtains only in wars—that killing for these ends is permissible.

Perhaps reductivists and exceptionalists can reasonably disagree on this point. Still, to invoke these political interests in the proportionality calculation, a belligerent needs to be appropriately authorized to do so by the polity at large because the value of these political goods reflects the degree to which people actually care about them, and their nature is such that they must be subject to the direction of the polity whose political interests are at stake.[38] The good in question is, broadly, *political independence*: the capacity of a group of people to decide their own collective fate. If we go to war to defend the political independence of a people who do not want us to go to war, then we are contravening the very interest that we claim to be defending. So, the good for which we are fighting and the process by which we are licensed to fight for it are both unique to conflicts over political sovereignty and territorial integrity: that is, to wars.

The fact, (iv), that wars often involve states on at least one side is crucial to another key traditionalist argument, one grounded in the authority of particular democratic states.[39] David Estlund has argued that citizens of democratic states can be under an obligation to defer to their state's judgment on matters such as the justice of war except in cases when the injustice is obvious. This lends a qualified support to the moral equality of combatants: unjust combatants have some reason to obey the orders of their state to fight even unjust wars.[40] In a similar vein, Cheyney Ryan has argued that a democratic state's military must be subordinate to its government, which gives its combatants reasons to fight unjust wars as well as just ones.[41] One might respond that these authority-based reasons help justify some acts of killing outside of war.[42] No obvious examples spring to mind, however, and while we might be able to conjure up hypotheticals, I suspect that these would depend for their intuitive support on how closely they approximate the conditions under which killing is permissible in war.

Properties (v) and (vi)—the institutions that structure warfare and the international state system—are at the heart of Yitzhak Benbaji's accounts of just conduct and resort to war, respectively. Benbaji argues that the institutions governing war constitute the basis of a hypothetical contract among states and their armies, according to which soldiers know, when they choose to fight, that they are participating in a system in which they are legitimate targets for the enemy regardless of which side is in the right.[43] In signing up to fight on these terms, they reciprocally waive the obligation on the part of enemy combatants to verify whether their cause is just, thus allowing them to obey orders to fight without having to examine them on every occasion. This, in turn, is necessary for them to be able to provide both actual security and deterrence against future threats.

Adil Haque argues for the authority of international law in a different way by contending that it enables just combatants to do better by their moral reasons than they would if they attended to them directly, as well as allowing unjust combatants to do less wrong than they otherwise would.[44]

Benbaji separately defends the restrictive, Walzerian account of resort to war, arguing that a more permissive stance on interventionist wars would be abused to the detriment of all, whereas a relaxed stance on defensive wars provides a deterrent to unwarranted aggression.[45] Benbaji's paper brings to the table a recognition of the strategic realities of warfare that is almost wholly absent from the rest of the philosophical debate (barring loose allusions to the importance of deterrence).

In more recent work, Ian Fishback and, separately, Allen Buchanan have argued that the reductivist project is based on a fundamental mistake: the assumption that the ethics of killing outside of war is governed by natural rights, which must therefore also be relevant to the ethics of killing in war.[46] On their view, typical hypothetical cases invoked by reductivists presuppose the institutional context of an ordered domestic society. We therefore cannot extend those intuitions to the quite different institutional context of warfare. Perhaps there are natural rights appropriate to a pre-institutional state of nature, but all rights are ultimately dependent on the institutions structuring our interactions, so since warfare is structured by different institutions from those that obtain outside of war, we can learn little about the ethics of killing in war from thinking about the ethics of killing outside of war.

Now, it is possible to argue for each of the properties on which these exceptionalists draw that they could justify killing in some conflicts that we would not typically call wars, in which case the label 'exceptionalist' might be undeserved. I confess that my imagination rather fails here: I cannot think of cases outside of war in which, for example, the arguments from democratic authority or the vindication of political interests can justify killing (bear in mind that I assume revolutions and other insurgencies count as wars). But rather than try to dream up suitable scenarios, it is better to take a more detached approach to the methodological positions at stake. Ultimately, what matters is not whether one is a reductivist or an exceptionalist. What matters is when one thinks war and acts of war are permissible.

The reductivist and exceptionalist labels are useful because they identify two different methodologies. One understands the morality of war by thinking first about the use of force outside of war. The other starts by thinking about war. Perhaps the latter approach would ultimately entail that there are some situations outside of war when killing is justified, on the same grounds as one might otherwise imagine would apply only in war (maybe some assassinations? Some revolutions too small in scale to plausibly be called wars?). Perhaps, ultimately, there is really no such thing as 'war', just a number of overlapping properties, none of which is unique to war. So be it.

Still, this would simply mean that these so-called exceptionalist just war theorists have merely identified a plethora of properties relevant to the justification of killing outside of war that have been overlooked by the paradigmatic reductivists. And the central methodological difference between them would still stand: reductivists start with self-defence and work up to war; exceptionalists start with war directly.

McMahan has discussed many of the exceptionalist positions that I have just canvassed. But he presupposes that the task is to vindicate or refute Walzer's doctrine of the moral equality of combatants.[47] I think the debate should move on. That doctrine is false. It is not true that all combatants, regardless of what they are fighting for, face the same liabilities, constraints, and permissions.

What *might* be true, and what we can just as easily understand the exceptionalists as arguing for, is that combatants who fight for the unjust side in a war enjoy more extensive permissions and face weaker constraints than do individuals fighting for unjustified aims outside of war, whereas combatants fighting for the just side might enjoy less extensive permissions and face stricter constraints than individuals fighting for justified aims outside of war. In plain terms, the revisionist critique of the moral equality of combatants aimed to show that there is no morally relevant difference between an unjust combatant and an unjustified attacker outside of war and between a just combatant and a justified defender outside of war. The exceptionalists have, to my mind, refuted *this* claim, but they have not vindicated the moral equality of combatants.

And it is worth recognizing that although exceptionalists have, for the most part, developed their views to vindicate some element in Walzer's orthodoxy, we can equally develop exceptionalist arguments that challenge the orthodoxy from all possible angles. For example, one could motivate a revisionist rejection of the moral equality of combatants by combining a Walzerian view about the distinctive collective liability of members of armed forces with a McMahan-style view that 'justification defeats liability', so all members of the armed forces of the unjust side are liable and all those of the just side (if there is one) are not.[48]

Or one could challenge the orthodox principle of noncombatant immunity by arguing that, since wars are hell (in virtue of their scale and the widespread noncompliance with morality), we ought simply to minimize the number killed without regard to combatant or noncombatant status. This is the 'realist' doctrine that Michael Walzer saw as his primary competitor but is today largely discredited. Or one could argue for what Cheyney Ryan calls *political pacifism* on the same grounds, as well as because of the distinctively political character of war and the institutions that fight and sustain wars.[49] On this approach, even if fighting wars could sometimes be in principle permissible, sustaining the institutions that we use to make war has too many adverse consequences to be defensible, all things considered.

These are just some possibilities; it seems likely that as more *political* philosophers start thinking about just war theory, many more versions of exceptionalism will be developed. It is important that, as those new theories are developed, we keep an open mind on what their first-order implications will be. The fact that exceptionalists have thus far mostly been traditionalists should not lead us to prejudge where these new theories will lead us.

5. Collectivism

Since David Rodin first introduced the term 'reductivism' to the just war debate, it has always been paired with *individualism*. But, for the most part, what that individualism entails has been left open. Revisionists mining this seam emphasize that they are showing how justified wars must be composed of justified acts of individual self- and other-defence. But there is no serious discussion of just which kinds of individualism philosophers mean to invoke.

I think we can distinguish between three relevant kinds: *evaluative*, *descriptive* and *metaphysical*. Evaluative individualism is the doctrine that only the well-being of individuals matters morally; groups and collectives either lack well-being entirely, or their well-being is morally unimportant. Descriptive individualism is the doctrine that wars, and other complex human interactions, are wholly reducible to the individual actions of which they are composed. This means that, to justify war, we would have to break it down into these composite actions by individuals and ask whether they are justified (I return to this point later). The third kind of individualism entails the first two but is not entailed by them. Metaphysical individualism is the doctrine that only individuals are agents. Groups, collectives, states, are not agents. They do not exist; therefore, it is unsurprising that they cannot act and that they do not have morally significant interests.

Although I think war is a useful test case for theories of metaphysical and evaluative individualism, I do not think just war theory as such has any special insight into these fraught questions. What's more, I think they *are* extraordinarily fraught—that merely pumping pretheoretical intuitions about cases is an inadequate substitute for serious study of the rich philosophical debates that they involve. In other words, if a just war theorist professes commitment to evaluative or metaphysical individualism or to their collectivist counterparts without engaging with or drawing on these debates, then their profession is little more than a statement of allegiance.

Descriptive individualism is another story, however. I think that just war theorists do have something distinctive to offer discussion of this position. Indeed, I think that a sensible understanding of just war theory gives us reason to reject descriptive individualism. The central problem is that it prevents us from sensibly asking whether a war as a whole is justified (it also prevents us asking whether it is proportionate or necessary). And yet we both do and need to be able to evaluate wars as a whole.

If wars are to be understood just as composites of individual actions, then there is no meaningful question of the form: 'was the war justified?'[50] We can ask only whether the individual actions that compose the war were justified. We could then say that a war was justified just in case all the actions of which it was composed were justified, but this raises two problems. First, it is far too demanding. Surely, a war can be justified even if it includes some unjustified actions. To deny this is to make justified wars practically impossible. Second, it is quite unclear how to identify the actions of which a war was composed! For instance, we obviously would not want deaths inflicted by the enemy to count in the evaluation of whether our side's war was justified in the same way as deaths that we ourselves inflict. But to make that distinction we need to distinguish between the two sides. It is not clear how to do this without some account of how those on our side are acting together. One could say that only those actions that contribute to the goal of our side winning the war count. But then this would disqualify lots of both justified and unjustified individual actions from the tally that should not be excluded.[51] Justified individual actions that saved the life of combatants whose survival in no way contributes to the victory of their side would be excluded, as would unjustified actions aimed at wrongful goals.

McMahan suggests that we might ask: 'whether the war is such that it is better that it be fought than not'.[52] But, obviously, for almost all wars it's better that they not be fought! We need to know which individual actions count as part of a *side's* war—who counts as acting together such that, for those people, it's better that *their* war be fought. This is such a basic part of just war theory that it is usually built into the very language we use—we individuate wars according to the sides that fight them (World War II, for example, consists of a war fought by the British, a war fought by the Germans, and so on).[53] Of course, we could simply abandon these usages and deny that talking about a 'side's war' being just makes any sense, concentrating instead only on evaluating actions by individuals.[54] But this seems to omit an important and familiar aspect of the morality of war. At the very least, it stands in need of justification.

One could consider the decision of the military leaders who declare the war and ask whether *that decision* was justified. But that doesn't seem as if it will track the right kind of judgment. Suppose that the president knows that if he does not launch an aggressive war, there will be a coup and the generals will launch a much more destructive war. Then he might do the right thing by declaring war; yet, clearly, we should not judge the war as justified for that reason.

Partly in virtue of the fact that there is a morally significant sense in which the members of a community act together to fight a war—and a question of whether *their* war was just—descriptive collectivism has further important normative implications. In particular, I think those who stand in the kinds of institutional relationships to one another that can facilitate joint action of this kind have special obligations to coordinate to ensure that the overall impact of what they do together satisfies what I call a *collective necessity constraint*.[55] Consider this example:

> *Multiple Threats*: Alf, Barney, and Charlotte each face unjustified threats from, respectively, Dave, Edison, and Ferdy. Acting alone, Alf, Barney, and Charlotte can each avert the threat to his life only by killing Dave, Edison, and Ferdy, respectively.

> Acting together, however, they could avert all threats by subduing their attackers, inflicting serious, but nonfatal harms.

Most accounts of the morality of self- and other-defence contend that the infliction of harm that is unnecessary to achieve one's objective is impermissible. For each of Alf, Barney, and Charlotte, if they act on their own, killing their attacker is necessary. Only if they act together can they nonlethally avert the threats they face. But acting together is not an option that is available to any one of them considered individually. So, the individual necessity constraint suggests that it is permissible for each to kill his assailant, and yet this is intuitively deeply implausible. If they are able to coordinate, they ought to do so. The necessity standard that applies to their actions is set by what they can do together, not what they can do on their own.

But what if Alf wants to coordinate with Barney and Charlotte but does not believe that they will work together with him? In circumstances like this, the character of the collective of which they are part is especially relevant to their obligations to coordinate with one another. If the three are a random aggregate of people thrown together by circumstance, then the costs that they are required to bear in order to coordinate will be relatively low. After all, if Barney and Charlotte refused, Alf might miss his opportunity to save himself from the threat posed by Dave. But if the three of them have roles in an institutional structure, the purpose of which is precisely to enable them to coordinate their actions, then their obligations to do so are correspondingly more exacting. They must be prepared to bear a greater risk of being killed by their respective assailants in the course of securing the cooperation of their fellow victims.

And again, it is important to remember that rejecting descriptive individualism neither necessitates rejecting reductivism, nor endorsing reformism. For example, Saba Bazargan has argued against the moral equality of combatants by arguing that unjust combatants who are not sufficiently responsible, as individuals, to be liable to be killed are liable in virtue of their complicitous participation in the wrongful wars fought by their comrades-in-arms. Bazargan's view is reductivist—he thinks complicitous liability to be killed obtains outside of war, too. It is collectivist—he grounds liability to be killed in collective action. And it is revisionist—he argues against the moral equality of combatants.

6. Conclusion

There are two main ways to think about the ethics of war. The first is to start by thinking about war. The second is to think about the ethics of killing outside of war, then apply those principles to the case of war. In recent just war theory, the first approach has most commonly been associated with Michael Walzer and his contemporary defenders; the second with Jeff McMahan and Walzer's other revisionist critics. This conflation, however, is mere accident. Perhaps the richest terrain to be ploughed is in the combinations that have been relatively neglected—reductivist vindications of international law; exceptionalist critiques. Although reductivism has most commonly been paired with individualism, the understanding of descriptive, evaluative, and metaphysical individualism and collectivism in just war theory is still in its infancy. There is fertile ground there, too.

It is worth noting, in conclusion, an *a priori* argument in favour of exceptionalism. The reductivist says: to understand the ethics of killing in war, we need to think about permissible killing outside of war. The exceptionalist says: that might be useful, but we need also to think about what is distinctive about war. If one were considering the debate *de novo*, the exceptionalist starting point would be more compelling simply because, outside of war, cases of permissible killing are extraordinarily rare, whereas most agree that they are quite common in war.

The reductivist, by contrast, asks us to place more stock in our intuitions about hypothetical cases outside of war, which track the experiences of thankfully few people, than in our intuitions about realistic cases within war, of which plenty of people—including some philosophers—have direct experience. The approach is similar to defending principles of distributive justice by asking how to distribute cowrie shells if we were to land on a desert island.[56] We are much more familiar with the concrete, situated problems of a modern political society than we are with how castaways should share shells, and even that outlandish hypothetical is closer to most people's lived experience than is the permissible use of lethal force outside of war.

Notes

1. Michael Walzer, *Just and Unjust Wars: A Moral Argument with Historical Illustrations* (New York: Basic Books, 1977).
2. As Greg Reichberg and Pablo Kalmanovitz show in their chapters for this volume, Walzer's approach owes its origins to the 'regular war' tradition. *Just war* theorists, such as Vitoria and Suárez, have more in common with Walzer's critics.
3. David Luban, 'Just War and Human Rights', *Philosophy and Public Affairs*, 9 (2: 1980), 160–181; Charles R. Beitz, 'Nonintervention and Communal Integrity', *Philosophy and Public Affairs*, 9 (1980), 385–391; Robert Holmes, *On War and Morality* (Princeton: Princeton University Press, 1989); Jeff McMahan, 'Innocence, Self-Defense and Killing in War', *Journal of Political Philosophy*, 2 (3: 1994), 193–221; Richard Norman, *Ethics, Killing and War* (Cambridge: Cambridge University Press, 1995); David Rodin, *War and Self-Defense* (Oxford: Clarendon Press, 2002); Jeff McMahan, 'The Ethics of Killing in War', *Ethics*, 114 (1: 2004), 693–732. Luban, however, is definitely now in the traditionalist camp.
4. Holmes and Norman are outright pacifists; Larry May has used revisionist arguments to defend contingent pacifism; David Rodin often appears to be a contingent pacifist; Uwe Steinhoff has defended a similar view. All the other revisionists think that some actual wars can be justified, although most leave open the possibility that contingent pacifism is true. See Larry May, 'Contingent Pacifism and the Moral Risks of Participating in War', *Public Affairs Quarterly*, 25 (2: 2011), 95–111; David Rodin, 'The Myth of National

Self-Defence', in *The Morality of Defensive War*, edited by Seth Lazar and Cécile Fabre (Oxford: Oxford University Press, 2014), 69–89; Uwe Steinhoff, *On the Ethics of War and Terrorism* (Oxford: Oxford University Press, 2007).

5. The terminology is owed to David Rodin, although my usage is more general than his, which relates to his specific typology for theories of justified killing. See Rodin, *War and Self-Defense*.
6. Most recent books on the ethics of war, by revisionists and traditionalists, have this structure: the first chapter or part of the book determines what the correct principles are for permissible killing in self- and other-defence; the rest applies those principles to war. See, for example, ibid.; Cécile Fabre, *Cosmopolitan War* (Oxford: Oxford University Press, 2012); Helen Frowe, *Defensive Killing* (Oxford: Oxford University Press, 2014); Seth Lazar, *Sparing Civilians* (Oxford: Oxford University Press, 2015).
7. Including: Noam J. Zohar, 'Collective War & Individualistic Ethics: Against the Conscription of "Self-Defense"', *Political Theory*, 21 (4: 1993), 606–622; Yitzhak Benbaji, 'A Defense of the Traditional War Convention', *Ethics*, 118 (3: 2008), 464–495; Henry Shue, 'Do We Need a Morality of War?', in *Just and Unjust Warriors: The Moral and Legal Status of Soldiers*, edited by David Rodin and Henry Shue (Oxford: Oxford University Press, 2008), 87–111; Michael Walzer, 'Response to McMahan's Paper', *Philosophia*, 34/1 (2006), 43–45; Adam Roberts, 'The Principle of Equal Application of the Laws of War', in *Just and Unjust Warriors: The Moral and Legal Status of Soldiers* edited by David Rodin and Henry Shue (Oxford: Oxford University Press, 2008), 226–254; Larry May, *War Crimes and Just War* (Cambridge: Cambridge University Press, 2007); Christopher Kutz, 'Fearful Symmetry', in *Just and Unjust Warriors: The Moral and Legal Status of Soldiers*, edited by David Rodin and Henry Shue (Oxford: Oxford University Press, 2008), 69–86; David Estlund, 'On Following Orders in an Unjust War', *Journal of Political Philosophy*, 15 (2: 2007), 213–234; Cheyney Ryan, 'Democratic Duty and the Moral Dilemmas of Soldiers', *Ethics*, 122 (1: 2011), 10–42; Patrick Emerton and Toby Handfield, 'Order and Affray: Defensive Privileges in Warfare', *Philosophy & Public Affairs*, 37 (4: 2009), 382–414; Uwe Steinhoff, 'Jeff McMahan on the Moral Inequality of Combatants', *Journal of Political Philosophy*, 16 (2: 2008), 220–226. Much of my own work also falls into the traditionalist camp, especially Seth Lazar, 'Responsibility, Risk, and Killing in Self-Defense', *Ethics*, 119 (4: 2009), 699–728; Seth Lazar, 'The Responsibility Dilemma for *Killing in War*: A Review Essay', *Philosophy & Public Affairs*, 38 (2: 2010), 180–213; Seth Lazar, 'Morality & Law of War', in *Companion to Philosophy of Law*, edited by Andrei Marmor (New York: Routledge, 2012), 364–379; Seth Lazar, 'Necessity in Self-Defense and War', *Philosophy & Public Affairs*, 40 (1: 2012), 3–44; Seth Lazar, 'Necessity and Non-Combatant Immunity', *Review of International Studies*, 40 (1: 2014), 53–76; Seth Lazar, 'Associative Duties and the Ethics of Killing in War', *Journal of Practical Ethics*, 1 (1: 2013), 3–48; Seth Lazar, 'National Defence, Self-Defence, and the Problem of Political Aggression', in *The Morality of Defensive War*, edited by Seth Lazar and Cécile Fabre (Oxford: Oxford University Press, 2014), 11–39; Lazar, *Sparing Civilians*.
8. With the possible exception of May and Steinhoff, and my arguments in the two papers criticizing McMahan, and *Sparing Civilians*, I think this move is present in all the work cited in the previous footnote.
9. In particular, Zohar, 'Collective War'; Christopher Kutz, 'The Difference Uniforms Make: Collective Violence in Criminal Law and War', *Philosophy & Public Affairs*, 33 (2: 2005), 148–180; Michael Walzer, 'Response to Jeff McMahan', *Philosophia*, 34 (1: 2006), 19–21; Lazar, 'Necessity in Self-Defense and War'; Lazar, 'National Defence, Self-Defence,

and the Problem of Political Aggression'; Margaret Moore, 'Collective Self-Determination, Institutions of Justice, and Wars of National Defence', in *The Morality of Defensive War* edited by Cécile Fabre and Seth Lazar (Oxford: Oxford University Press, 2014), 185–202.

10. See, for example, Lazar, 'Necessity in Self-Defense and War'; Saba Bazargan, 'Complicitous Liability in War', *Philosophical Studies*, 165 (1: 2013), 177–195.
11. Those who disagree can be represented within this schema as construing all justified killing as falling under the lesser evil heading.
12. Some philosophers think that there can be hybrid justifications—the protection afforded by the target's right to life has been somewhat reduced plus the good achieved is somewhat less than would be needed to override an unreduced right.
13. Some would think that these conditions determine whether the target has lost the protection of his right to life. Some think they are additional conditions that must be satisfied. Some think that some fall in one category, some in the other. They can reinterpret what I say in accordance with their conceptual framework.
14. I discuss the necessity constraint in much greater depth in Lazar, 'Necessity in Self-Defense and War'.
15. In recent years, revisionist and traditionalist just war theorists have revised this position, recognizing that not all intentional killings of those who retain their rights to life are equally seriously wrongful. See, for example, Helen Frowe, 'Threats, Bystanders and Obstructors', *Proceedings of the Aristotelian Society*, 108 (1: 2008), 365–372; Jeff McMahan, 'Who Is Morally Liable to Be Killed in War?', *Analysis*, 71 (3: 2011), 544–559; Lazar, *Sparing Civilians*.
16. Michael Walzer, *Just and Unjust Wars: A Moral Argument with Historical Illustrations* (New York: Basic Books, 2006). Jeff McMahan describes the kind of unusual case in which he thinks lesser evil justifications would apply in Jeff McMahan, 'Just Cause for War', *Ethics & International Affairs*, 19 (3: 2005), 1–21: 16. Cécile Fabre takes a similarly restrictive view of lesser evil justification, see Fabre, *Cosmopolitan War*.
17. If they are killed unintentionally, then can we say that killing them was necessary? Some people think that killing Ant was necessary to save Bee entails that killing Ant is a means to saving Bee. I disagree. A harm is necessary to achieving some end if there is no way to achieve that end that does not involve at least that much harm. This is consistent with the harm being an intended means, but also consistent with it being an unintended side effect.
18. Rodin, *War and Self-Defense*.
19. Jeff McMahan, 'War as Self-Defense', *Ethics & International Affairs*, 18 (1: 2004), 75–80: 75. McMahan continues: 'But if war, at least in some instances, lies on a continuum with individual self- and other-defense, and if acts of individual self- and other-defense can sometimes be morally justified, then war can in principle be morally justified as well. It follows that the only coherent forms of pacifism are those that reject the permissibility of individual self- or other-defense—for example, those based on an absolute prohibition of violence or killing.'

    Cheyney Ryan's contribution to this volume, in particular his discussion of political pacifism, refutes McMahan's last sentence.
20. Jeff McMahan, *Killing in War* (Oxford: Oxford University Press, 2009), 156.
21. Norman, *Ethics, Killing and War*; Holmes, *On War and Morality*; McMahan, 'Innocence'; Rodin, *War and Self-Defense*; Lionel McPherson, 'Innocence and Responsibility in War', *Canadian Journal of Philosophy*, 34 (4: 2004), 485–506; Cécile Fabre, 'Guns, Food, and Liability to Attack in War', *Ethics*, 120 (1: 2009), 36–63; Frowe, *Defensive Killing*; Richard J.

Arneson, 'Just Warfare Theory and Noncombatant Immunity', *Cornell International Law Journal*, 39 (2006), 663–688. I think that Fabre conceives of her project as being reductive individualist, but that in fact in her book she (quite rightly, in my view) strays from reductivism. See Seth Lazar, 'Review of Cécile Fabre, Cosmopolitan War', *Ethics*, 124 (2: 2014), 406–412; Fabre, *Cosmopolitan War*.

22. McMahan, 'Innocence'; Norman, *Ethics, Killing and War*; Rodin, *War and Self-Defense*; Mcpherson, 'Innocence and Responsibility in War'; David Rodin and Henry Shue (eds.), *Just and Unjust Warriors: The Moral and Legal Status of Soldiers* (Oxford: Oxford University Press, 2008).
23. Lazar, 'Responsibility Dilemma'.
24. Holmes, *On War and Morality*; Norman, *Ethics, Killing and War*; Rodin, *War and Self-Defense*; May, 'Contingent Pacifism and the Moral Risks of Participating in War'.
25. McMahan, 'Innocence'; Norman, *Ethics, Killing and War*; McMahan, 'Killing in War'; Fabre, 'Guns, Food'; Frowe, *Defensive Killing*.
26. Beitz, 'Nonintervention and Communal Integrity'; Norman, *Ethics, Killing and War*; Rodin, *War and Self-Defense*; Lazar, 'National Defence, Self-Defence, and the Problem of Political Aggression'; Rodin, 'The Myth of National Self-Defence'.
27. Luban, 'Just War and Human Rights'.
28. Lazar, *Sparing Civilians*.
29. David Rodin, 'The Moral Inequality of Soldiers: Why Jus in Bello Asymmetry Is Half Right', in *Just and Unjust Warriors: The Moral and Legal Status of Soldiers*, edited by David Rodin and Henry Shue (Oxford: Oxford University Press, 2008), 44–68. For a (decisive, in my view) response to Rodin, see Frowe, *Defensive Killing*.
30. Steinhoff, 'Jeff McMahan on the Moral Inequality of Combatants'.
31. Lazar, 'Associative Duties and the Ethics of Killing in War'.
32. Thomas Hurka, 'Proportionality in the Morality of War', *Philosophy & Public Affairs*, 33 (1: 2005), 34–66.
33. Emerton and Handfield, 'Order and Affray'.
34. Walzer, 'Response to McMahan's Paper', 43.
35. Shue, 'Morality of War'; Janina Dill and Henry Shue, 'Limiting the Killing in War: Military Necessity and the St. Petersburg Assumption', *Ethics & International Affairs*, 26 (3: 2012), 311–333; Jeremy Waldron, *Torture, Terror, and Trade-Offs: Philosophy for the White House* (Oxford: Oxford University Press, 2010). See also Roberts, 'Equal Application'.
36. Lazar, 'National Defence, Self-Defence, and the Problem of Political Aggression'. See also Jonathan Parry's contribution to this volume.
37. See especially Frowe, *Defensive Killing*.
38. For more on this point, see Seth Lazar, 'Authorisation and the Morality of War', *Australasian Journal of Philosophy*, 94 (2: 2016).
39. Estlund, 'On Following Orders in an Unjust War'. For a critique of Estlund, although with a similar overall approach, see Massimo Renzo, 'Democratic Authority and the Duty to Fight Unjust Wars', *Analysis*, 73 (4: 2013), 668–676.
40. Advocates of this kind of view might reject my dichotomy of loss of rights versus lesser evil justification, arguing that some reasons exclude others from consideration. I don't think much turns on this difference: if the authority-based reason is going to exclude, for example, a just combatant's right to life from constraining an unjust combatant, then it is going to have to be extremely weighty. The structure of justification is much the same as for lesser evil justification.

41. Ryan, 'Democratic Duty and the Moral Dilemmas of Soldiers'.
42. Jonathan Parry thinks this. See Jonathan Parry, 'Authority and Harm', unpublished ms. (2014).
43. Benbaji, 'A Defense of the Traditional War Convention'; Yitzhak Benbaji, 'The Moral Power of Soldiers to Undertake the Duty of Obedience', *Ethics*, 122 (1: 2011), 43–73.
44. Adil Ahmad Haque, *Law and Morality at War* (Oxford: Oxford University Press, forthcoming).
45. Yitzhak Benbaji, 'Distributive Justice, Human Rights, and Territorial Integrity: A Contractarian Account of the Crime of Aggression', in *The Morality of Defensive War*, edited by Seth Lazar and Cécile Fabre (Oxford: Oxford University Press, 2014), 159–184.
46. Allen Buchanan, 'The Flawed Methodology of Contemporary Just War Theory', *Unpublished MS.*, Ian Fishback, 'Necessity and Institutions in Self-Defense and War', *The Ethics of Self-Defense*, edited by Christian Coons and Michael Weber (Oxford: Oxford University Press, 2016), 274–291.
47. McMahan, *Killing in War*, chap. 2.
48. McMahan discusses such a view in ibid. Saba Bazargan defends something similar in Bazargan, 'Complicitous Liability in War'. Bazargan's view is probably best described as reductivist collectivist.
49. See his contribution to this volume.
50. McMahan acknowledges this at McMahan, 'Just Cause', 20.
51. Thanks to Jonathan Parry for discussion here.
52. McMahan, 'Just Cause', 20.
53. McMahan is always very clear about this.
54. James Pattison, 'When Is It Right to Fight? Just War Theory and the Individual-Centric Approach', *Ethical Theory and Moral Practice*, 16 (1: 2013), 35–54.
55. I draw here on Lazar, 'Necessity in Self-Defense and War'.
56. R. Dworkin, 'What Is Equality? Part 2: Equality of Resources', *Philosophy and Public Affairs*, 10 (4: 1981), 283–345.

CHAPTER 2

THE JUST WAR FRAMEWORK

HELEN FROWE

1. *Jus ad Bellum* and *Jus in Bello*

The last decade or so has witnessed a surge of interest in the ethics of war amongst philosophers. Prior to this revival, both philosophical and public debates on the ethics of war adhered to a fairly broad consensus on two central points. First, that war is to be understood as a relation between collectives—most obviously states—rather than as a relationship between individuals. Second, that making judgments about war involves judging whether the war satisfies two sets of established criteria: the principles of *jus ad bellum* and the principles of *jus in bello*. *Jus ad bellum* is commonly interpreted as determining the justice of resorting to war, although, as I'll argue here and has been observed elsewhere, this is misleading, since on any plausible view these principles also apply across the duration of a war. *Jus in bello* is commonly understood as determining the justice of combatants' conduct during war. As Michael Walzer puts it in his influential *Just and Unjust Wars*, 'The moral reality of war is divided into two parts. War is always judged twice, first with reference to the reasons states have for fighting, second with reference to the means they adopt.'[1] This framework has lately been extended to include *jus ex bello* (the justice of ending war) and the development of *jus post bellum* (justice after war).[2]

More recent work on the ethics of war has challenged the claim that war is a relationship between states. For example, one prominent school of thought known as *reductive individualism* holds that war is to be understood in terms of the rights and duties of individuals and can be judged by the rules governing harming between individuals outside of war.[3] This approach has revisionary implications for many substantive issues in the ethics of war. For example, it undermines the idea that noncombatants are not legitimate targets in war. In ordinary life, people making indirect contributions to unjust harms can forfeit their rights against being intentionally harmed. Reductive individualism thus implies that noncombatants can forfeit their rights against being intentionally harmed by contributing to unjust wars.[4] It also challenges the widespread belief that combatants fighting in unjust wars can be the moral equals of those fighting in a just war. When we think about conflicts between individuals, we draw a sharp moral asymmetry between those engaged in unjust aggression and those engaged in justified defence against that aggression. If this asymmetry obtains in war, we must reject the thesis of moral equality between combatants.[5] This entails a rejection of one aspect of the bifurcation of war: if just cause matters for the status of combatants, it cannot be true that *ad bellum* and *in bello* judgments are, as Walzer claims, 'logically independent' of each other.[6]

But, surprisingly, Walzer's model of the structure of just war theory, with the *ad bellum–in bello* distinction at its core, has survived these revisionist critiques largely intact.[7] While few now endorse the view that issues of *jus in bello* can be settled independently of *jus ad bellum*, just war theorists still routinely distinguish between the principles that determine the justness of resorting to war and the principles that determine the justness of combatants' conduct during the war. Questions about just cause, for example, are described as *ad bellum* questions, even though the justness of a cause clearly matters *in bello*. Even those who reject traditional, collectivist approaches to war develop their work around this familiar framework. For example, in *Cosmopolitan War*, Cécile Fabre cites the way in which just war theory is 'standardly divided' into principles governing resort to war and principles governing conduct within war, adopting this distinction for the structure of her book.[8] Jeff McMahan distinguishes between, for example, *ad bellum* proportionality and *in bello* proportionality.[9] David Rodin suggests that the *ad bellum–in bello* distinction articulates 'moral reasons appropriate to distinctive forms of moral problem generated by different aspects of conflict'.[10] Books on the ethics of war—such as this one—are typically structured around the *ad bellum–in bello* distinction, reinforcing the idea that these categories raise distinct moral problems or address different questions. And, of course, international law sharply distinguishes between the laws governing recourse to war and the laws governing conduct in war: as Carsten Stahn puts it, *jus ad bellum* and *jus in bello* are as regarded as 'distinct normative universes'.[11]

Given the prevalence of the *ad bellum–in bello* distinction and its apparently ingrained place in our just war thinking, one could be forgiven for assuming that it must have an ancient lineage in the just war tradition. But, as Robert Kolb puts it, while 'the august solemnity of Latin confers . . . the misleading appearance of being centuries old', the structural use of the distinction that Walzer describes is a comparatively recent phenomenon.[12] Oliver O'Donovan describes the 'modern (not traditional) distinction between just resort to war (*ius ad bellum*) and just conduct in war (*ius in bello*)' as a 'secondary casuistic distinction, not a load-bearing one'.[13] Nicholas Rengger argues that whilst the distinction is a useful heuristic, '[t]he problem is that the modern revival of the [just war] tradition has elevated it to an architectonic'.[14] This doesn't mean, of course, that early just war scholars were not writing about the justness of resorting to war or about the just conduct of war. But it does mean that we should be cautious about suggesting, as McMahan does, that just war theory 'has traditionally been divided into two sets of principles'.[15] Given what McMahan says immediately afterwards—that classical theorists such as Francisco de Vitoria took the justness of actions within war to rest on the justness of resorting to war—it seems neither helpful nor accurate to regard the *ad bellum–in bello* distinction as a historical *division* between two sets of principles if that division is meant to reflect mutual independence. (Indeed, it's a bit hard to make sense of the idea of dividing sets of principles at all.[16] The view McMahan has in mind is more accurately described as the claim that war itself is divided into resort and conduct and that some moral principles can be sensibly applied to only one, but not both, of these aspects of war.)

The view that I will defend here—that the categories of *jus ad bellum* and *jus in bello* are not useful—perhaps looks less heretical against this historical background. In Section 2, I suggest that there are no distinctive *ad bellum* or *in bello* principles. Any principle that matters for the justness of declaring war matters for the justness of a specific offensive in war.

We might grant that this claim but argue that these principles are sensitive to different goods and harms depending on whether we are talking about *jus ad bellum* or *jus in bello*. When we make *ad bellum* proportionality judgments, for example, we take into account all the (predicted) harms and benefits of the war. But when we make *in bello* proportionality judgments, we take into account only a comparatively small range of goods and harms pertaining to a specific offensive. In Section 3, I argue that this view is mistaken: the justness of *in bello* actions is not limited in this way. The justness of an action depends on all its interactions with other actions, and this is no less true for the justness of individual offensives than for the justness of the decision to declare war. Given this, there's no principled demarcation of relevant effects and harms that is reflected by the *ad bellum–in bello* distinction.

Seth Lazar has suggested that anyone who endorses some kind of collectivism in ethics will need some analogue of the *ad bellum/in bello* distinction. I agree that if one endorses collectivism, one will need to do some demarcating of relevant actions (e.g., if one believes that an individual can be 'on the hook' for the wrongful actions of other members of her collective, one will be picking out a subset of actions for which she can be thus responsible). I'm not a collectivist, although I don't defend anti-collectivism here. However, it's not clear to me why we would call this an analogue of the *ad bellum–in bello* distinction: the relevant collectives and subset of actions aren't going to map onto that distinction. So I think collectivists can share the reasons I give here for scepticism about this pervasive bifurcation of war.

Section 4 addresses the thought that *jus ad bellum* gives us valuable summative assessments of war. I suggest that summative assessments of war—understood as a single verdict on the war as a whole—are not useful and that it is a mistake to focus our moral evaluations in this way. In any war, some individual actions will be just and some will be unjust. Even wars that we typically describe as just—such as the Allies' war against Nazi Germany—contain many instances of wrongdoing, ranging from mildly disproportionate or overly risky offensives to appalling atrocities. Given this, it is unsurprising that people often baulk at sweeping evaluations that purport to give us an overall assessment of a war (commonly expressed as the thought that 'there's no such thing as a just war'). One response to this kind of scepticism is to embrace pacifism, concluding that war is always impermissible. But those who think that war can be permissible typically respond by disaggregating the actions of the war. We grant that, of course, some of the offensives were wrong, and some atrocities were committed, and that these actions were unjust. But the decision to resort to war can still be justified in light of the importance of securing the just cause despite foreseeing the concomitant wrongdoing. I suggest that if we're interested in the morality of a war, we should be primarily interested in these more nuanced, individualized evaluations, rather than summative assessments of wars.

2. The Principles Governing Nonconsensual Harming

In this section, I argue that there is no difference in content between *jus ad bellum* and *jus in bello*. There is, rather, a single set of principles that governs both the justness of resorting to war and the justness of particular acts within war. This is a formal claim that holds irrespective of the substantive content of this set of principles: it holds simply that whichever principles determine the justness of harming as part of a specific offensive within war also determine the justness of declaring or continuing war. Contrary to Rodin's suggestion, there are no distinctive moral reasons that matter only, for example, *in bello* and not *ad bellum*.

I think this formal claim is a natural upshot of various arguments that have been put forward in support of reductive individualism as well as of the more general view, reductivism (which might or might not be individualist). Defences of reductivism in just war theory typically focus on the relationship between harming in war and harming in self-defence. But the more general reductivist claim is simply that there is a single set of principles governing all actions that cause nonconsensual harm, whether those actions are part of self-defence, policing, measures short of war, or war. If this is correct, there cannot be different principles that govern the resort to war compared to the conduct of war, and so reductivists should find the view defended here appealing. However, the claim that actions that cause nonconsensual harm are always judged by the same principles is also open to those who take a nonreductivist or 'exceptionalist' approach to war (although exceptionalists will think that some of the justifications for harming generated by these principles are satisfied only in war).

I'll defend the formal claim by considering the principles traditionally identified as governing *jus ad bellum* and *jus in bello*. I'll argue that each of these principles either matters both *ad bellum* and *in bello* or is subsumed under one of the other principles. Thus, there are no distinctive *ad bellum* or *in bello* principles. However, the focus on these particular principles is primarily illustrative. It's compatible with the formal claim that a completely different set of substantive principles govern the inflicting of nonconsensual harm.

On traditional accounts of *jus ad bellum*, a war is just if and only if it has a just cause, is a last resort for securing that just cause, is proportionate to that just cause, is waged in order to secure that just cause, is waged by a legitimate authority, fought for the right intention, and has a reasonable prospect of success. The standard account of the content of *jus in bello* is a requirement to discriminate between legitimate and illegitimate targets and to cause only harm that is necessary for securing and proportionate to a military advantage.

It is uncontroversial, then, that the constraints of necessity and proportionality apply to the resort to and continuation of war and to specific offensives within war. And, I think it is now fairly widely accepted that the criterion of just cause plays a central role in our judgments about specific actions and offensives in war.[17] As Jeff McMahan and Thomas Hurka have argued, having a just cause is a prerequisite of any individual offensive's satisfying proportionality. Proportionality weighs morally relevant harms against morally relevant goods. If one lacks a relevant moral good to secure—if one's aim is simply to contribute to the unjust expansion of territory, for example—there's nothing to outweigh the harms that one causes.[18] A similar argument applies with respect to necessity. The fact that force is the least harmful means of achieving an end can form part of a justification for using force only when the end is morally good. The fact that I need to kill you to steal your wallet does not provide some partial justification for killing you. When the end is morally wrong, there's no role for necessity to play.[19]

Notice that this does not mean that the only just cause for using force is the just cause that initially gave rise to war. As McMahan has pointed out, there could be other just causes for using force, such as defending noncombatants whose country lacks a just cause from unjust attacks by combatants whose country is fighting for a just cause.[20] A combatant might have a just cause for some of her actions and lack a just cause for others.

I'm somewhat sceptical about the importance of right intention, where this is understood as requiring that a war be fought for the reasons that in fact justify it and not as a pretext for furthering some other national interest, even if the war would in fact secure the just cause via (otherwise) legitimate means.[21] Similarly, I'm not sure how much intentions matter for the permissibility of individual actions. But whilst this debate will affect the substantive content of the set of principles governing harming, it poses no threat to the formal claim I'm defending here since it's hard to see how intentions could matter for the justness of declaring or continuing of a war but not for the justness of specific offensives that make up the war. If one's intentions partly determine the permissibility of one's actions, this will be equally true for combatants engaged in fighting and politicians engaged in declaring war. That is, if there is a right intention constraint on the use of force, it will equally constrain the declaring, continuing, and fighting of war.[22]

I'm also sceptical, as are many other just war theorists, that the traditional notion of legitimate authority plays any role in determining the justness of war.[23] The idea that only heads of state are eligible to declare war, or that only their wars can be just, is shown to be implausible by civil wars and just revolutions. The more recent appeals to consent or authorization as a way of capturing what seems morally relevant about authority strike me as attractive,[24] but I also think that these considerations will come under the remit of the proportionality constraint. Roughly, whether, for example, the intended beneficiaries of a war consent to being exposed to the (risk of the) harms of war affects the goods that can be included in the proportionality calculation.[25] But again, if one thinks legitimate authority important for the justness of resorting to war, one should extend this to *jus in bello*: it will also matter whether a combatant is killing on behalf of a state or other relevant group.

Finally, I'm also unsure whether the requirement that wars should have a reasonable prospect of success is best conceived of as an independent constraint on the use of force or as part of the proportionality constraint. But, whichever model we prefer, it will matter for the declaring, continuing, and fighting of war—all must have a reasonable prospect of achieving their ends if they are to justify the inflicting of collateral harm. Even if a combatant may kill twenty civilians as a side effect of securing a given military advantage, it does not follow that she may kill twenty civilians as a side effect of an offensive that has only a very low chance of securing the military advantage.

The foregoing supports the view that those principles typically identified as governing *jus ad bellum* also apply *in bello*. But to secure the conclusion that there are no distinctive *ad bellum* or *in bello* principles, we also need to show either that we can omit the requirement of discrimination from our principles governing the use of force or that discrimination also matters for the resort to and continuation of war. This requirement enjoins combatants to distinguish between legitimate and illegitimate targets—traditionally interpreted as the distinction between military personnel, equipment, and installations, on the one hand, and civilians and civilian infrastructure on the other. More recently, some writers have urged that discrimination should be interpreted as a requirement to discriminate between people who are liable to be harmed and people who are not so liable.[26]

There are two ways in which the requirement of discrimination might be employed (whatever the relevant criterion for discrimination turns out to be). The first is as an absolute prohibition on intentionally harming the members of the relevant group (e.g., on intentionally harming civilians or intentionally harming nonliable people). The second is as a claim that intentionally harming the members of the relevant group is harder to justify than harming other people. Whichever model we choose, though, it will matter for the justness of declaring war as well as the justness of specific offensives. If one predicts that the war will be fought in a way that involves intentionally harming members of the relevant group, this will either make it impermissible to declare war (on the absolutist model) or harder to satisfy proportionality (on the higher justificatory threshold model).

3. Relevant Goods and Harms

Say we grant that whatever moral principles determine the justness of conduct within war also determine the justness of resorting to war or of continuing a war. Nevertheless, we might insist that there are still important differences between our *ad bellum* and *in bello* judgments. Specifically, we might think that, even once just cause is satisfied, the range of goods and harms relevant to *in bello* judgments is much narrower than the range of goods and harms relevant to *ad bellum* judgments. I'll address this objection in the context of our judgments concerning proportionality and necessity.

3.1. Proportionality

Henry Shue argues that there are two proportionality principles:

> a macro-level test concerning the resort to war, as well as a micro-level test concerning the conduct of war . . . thought each to apply independently. One must ask prior to going to war, would the evil to be prevented by military action in this case be worth engaging in a war overall, and ask throughout any war engaged in, would this particular military engagement make a sufficiently great contribution to potential victory to be worth the death and destruction likely to result?
>
> (Shue, 2005, p. 748)

David Rodin similarly suggests that, with respect to *jus in bello*, 'proportionality requires balancing the harm of a particular action in the course of a war against the requirements of military necessity. It prohibits military actions which are "excessive in relation to the concrete and direct military advantage anticipated"'. But, in contrast, 'proportionality in the context of the *jus ad bellum* . . . requires a fundamentally different kind of balancing—between the harms brought about by the pursuit of a defensive war and the nature of the threat to which the war is a response'.[27] The language of the 'harm of a particular action' and the 'direct military advantage' reflects the narrow range of outcomes that is typically thought relevant to combatants' conduct in war compared to the broad array of goods and harms that determine *ad bellum* proportionality.

According to the view I will defend here, it's true that the justness of declaring and continuing war is grounded in a very wide range of goods and harms. But, I will argue, all these goods and harms are also relevant to the justness of specific offensives. Nothing that is relevant to the justness of a political leader's decision to continue a war is irrelevant to the justness of a combatant's decision to continue fighting in that war, and vice versa. There's thus no difference between what I'll call the sensitivity of moral principles that varies depending on whether we are talking about an '*ad bellum*' action or an '*in bello*' action.

Here's a simple case that demonstrates why the relevant goods and harms for proportionality are not limited to those that one directly causes.

> *Prediction*: A runaway trolley is heading to where it will break innocent Engineer's leg. Engineer can divert the trolley down a sidetrack to where it will break Workman' finger. But Engineer knows that if she diverts the trolley, Workman will then divert it

again down a second side-track, killing innocent Pedestrian in order to spare himself the cost of a broken finger.

If Engineer's proportionality calculation were sensitive only to the goods and harms that she herself causes, it would not be disproportionate for her to divert the trolley. She would be permitted to break Workman's finger as a side effect of defending her leg, and she does not directly cause the death of Pedestrian since that death depends on Workman's intervening agency. But the fact that Workman will predictably kill an innocent person to avoid the broken finger renders Engineer's defence disproportionate. She may not divert the trolley away from her leg if she knows that Workman will then lethally divert the trolley towards Pedestrian. The range of harms that are relevant to the permissibility of her defence extend beyond those that she will directly cause.

This doesn't mean, of course, that actions that give rise to wrongdoing are always impermissible. The interactions between our actions are more complex than that. For example, one can sometimes be justified in acting even if one foresees that others will then engage in wrongdoing as a consequence, as in *Prediction Two*:

> *Prediction Two*: A runaway trolley is heading to where it will kill fifty people. Bystander can divert the trolley down a sidetrack to where it will break Workman's legs. But Bystander knows that if she diverts the trolley, Workman will then divert it again down a second side-track, killing an innocent person in order to spare himself the cost of broken legs.

In this case, Bystander is justified in diverting the trolley despite knowing that, if she does so, Workman will then engage in the wrongful killing of an innocent person. It would have been proportionate for Bystander to directly divert the trolley to where it would kill one innocent person as a side effect of saving the fifty, and so her prediction that Workman will wrongly inflict this harm does not make Bystander's action disproportionate. But Workman's actions are still relevant to the proportionality of her Bystander's actions: if she knows that Workman will divert the trolley to where it kills a hundred people, she may not divert it away from the fifty.

There can also be cases in the permissibility of our actions that can depend upon wrongdoing, such as *Murderous Prediction*:

> *Murderous Prediction*: A runaway trolley is heading to where it will kill Walker. Passer-By can divert the trolley away from Walker down a side-track. Jogger is on the side track, and will be killed if the trolley hits her. However, Murderer is just about to shoot Jogger in the head, so she will already be dead when the trolley hits her.

It would be disproportionate for Passer-By to divert the trolley if she would thereby kill Jogger. But when she sees that Murderer will unavoidably kill Jogger anyway, diverting the trolley becomes proportionate and permissible in virtue Murderer's wrongdoing.

These are just some of the myriad ways in which our actions can interact and that will affect their permissibility. Notice that none of these claims depends on any underlying commitment to collective responsibility or notions of acting together. There's no sense in which Bystander and Workman are acting together, or Passer-By and Murderer are acting together. And yet what Workman does can determine the proportionality of Bystander's actions, just as what Murderer does can determine the proportionality of Passer-By's saving Walker.

How our actions interact with other actions is equally important in war: whether a specific offensive is justified is not, as Rodin suggests, determined only by the goods and harms that it directly produces. Consider *Torture*:

> *Torture*: Captain A is leading Unit A on a mission to break into the enemy's military base. Captain B is going to provide Captain A with essential information for getting through the base's security. Once inside, Captain A's unit will kill a proportionate number of combatants to secure the base. There is no less harmful way to secure the base, which is important for winning a just war. However, the information that will be provided by Captain B will be extracted by Unit B from a captured enemy combatant by torturing his children in front of him.

Assume that torturing the children is so harmful as to make Unit B's actions disproportionate. Considered independently of Unit B's actions, nothing that Unit A does is impermissible. They will use proportionate force to secure an advantage that is necessary for winning their just war. But the harms that Unit B will inflict are surely relevant to whether Unit A acts permissibly. If refusing to carry out their offensive might prevent the torture of the children, for example, it's plausible that Unit A should refuse to capture the base, even though the harm of torture is not a direct result of their offensive. It is false, then, that the range of goods and harms relevant to *in bello* judgments is limited to those directly caused one's own actions or by the actions of a very small subset of individuals tied to a specific offensive. It also matters how one's actions causally influence, or depend upon, the actions of others.

Moreover, there's no reason to think that the range of relevant goods and harms is limited to those brought about by one's own unit, or platoon, or regiment. Those are not morally significant demarcations. Even if one is more likely to causally influence the actions of one's own unit, this is a merely contingent fact, not indicative of some genuine moral boundary. Any goods and harms—whether they are inflicted by one's own side or even by the opposing side—can affect the permissibility of one's own actions. Once we recognize this, it looks like the range of goods and harms that determines the justness of any individual combatant's decisions could in principle be as extensive as the range of goods and harms that determines the justness of a political leader's *ad bellum* decisions.

We might object that it is surely implausible that a combatant's actions could be rendered impermissible by the actions of some other individual or individuals who are perhaps thousands of miles away. But closer reflection suggests otherwise. We can see this most clearly with respect to just cause: if a political leader is offered reasonable peace terms that she declines, continuing to fight may be unjust because war is no longer the least harmful means of securing the just cause. But fighting can also be rendered disproportionate by the excessive destruction of troops elsewhere. If a combatant's evidence is that the war will continue to be fought in a disproportionate way, this, too, could make it impermissible for her to continue to fight. The fact that those troops are not physically close to her or part of her own unit does not make their excesses irrelevant to the justness of her participation in the war.

Note that this claim is not vulnerable, on either a fact-relative or an evidence-relative account of justification, to the objection that no combatant could possibly know such an extensive range of facts as a political leader.[28] On the fact-relative account, the justness of action depends on objective truths. It does not matter whether the combatant (or the political leader) knows these truths. If her action is fact-relative unjustified, she will act wrongly in performing it. What she believes or has evidence of might furnish her with an excuse, but it won't provide her with a justification for acting.

On an evidence-relative account, the justness of an action depends on whether that action is the right thing to do in light of the agent's available evidence. It is possible that, if she has different evidence available to her, an ordinary combatant's continuing to fight might be justified even if her leader's continuing the war is unjustified (and vice versa). But that doesn't undermine the claim that there is no limited range of goods and harms that determines the permissibility of specific offensives compared to the wide range of goods and harms that determines permissibility of declaring or continuing war. Both should act according to their evidence—which, for a combatant, includes her evidence about the goods and harms arising from other people's actions even if they are causally or physically remote from her own. All that matters for the view being defended here is that there is no evidence that might be significant for the justness of a leader's actions but irrelevant to the justness of a combatant's actions.

It looks implausible, then, to hold that the *ad bellum–in bello* distinction does useful work by directing our attention to distinct sets of goods and harms that determine the answers to different sorts of questions we can ask about war. The justness of specific offensives is not sensitive to only a narrow range of goods and harms that are a direct upshot of that offensive. Anything that might be relevant to the justness of declaring or continuing a war is relevant to our evaluation of specific offensives not only because combatants' just cause for using force will typically be the cause justified the leader's decision to declare war, but also because the justness of the means by which that cause is pursued depends on how those means interact with other actions.

3.2. War-Dependent Goods

We might think that the sensitivity of *ad bellum* proportionality differs from the sensitivity of *in bello* proportionality in the following way. *Ad bellum* proportionality weighs the harm we expect to cause in war against the harm we hope to prevent by waging war. But this cannot exhaust what is weighed *in bello*. Consider the following case:

> *Rescue*: Ten members of Unit A, whose country is fighting a just war, are captured by a group of enemy combatants, who will kill them at dawn. Unit B have a plan to rescue them. In doing so, they will collaterally kill one civilian.

It looks like Unit B's proportionality calculation should weigh the good of rescuing the ten combatants against the harm of killing of the civilian. But the good of saving the captured combatants cannot be a factor in our *ad bellum* proportionality calculation—not because rescuing people can't be a just cause for resort to force, but because (in this case) the existence of the good of the rescue is conditional on whether we resort to force. One cannot count in one's decision about whether to go to war the good of rescuing a person from a harm that he will face only if one decides to go to war. These are, in a sense, goods that don't yet exist since their existence turns on the decision to fight. Thus, it looks like there will be goods that matter *in bello* that do not count *ad bellum*.[29] (This is compatible with thinking that the harms of cases like *Rescue* count *ad bellum*. We can predict that our combatants will be captured and that rescuing them will cause harm, and we should include these harms in our assessments of whether to go to war.)

I think that this objection plays upon the fairly pervasive, but mistaken, idea that the principle of *jus ad bellum* apply to a one-off judgment made prior to resort to war. Some people explicitly endorse this idea. Brian Orend writes that '*jus ad bellum* . . . concerns the justice of resorting to war in the first place'.[30] Megan Braun and Daniel Brunstetter claim that 'in war, principles such as just cause and last resort need only be satisfied at the outset of a conflict'.[31] Others slip into this terminology when speaking rather more loosely: Fabre recently suggested that *jus ad bellum, jus in bello*, and *jus ex bello* are 'a convenient way to demarcate various phases in the initiation, conduct and termination of a war', even though she also claims that the categories lack 'deep conceptual or normative significance'.[32]

But we can see that this understanding of *jus ad bellum* is mistaken by thinking about ways in which a war might satisfy the conditions for the just use of force at its outset but cease to satisfy one or more of those conditions as the war progresses. For example, it might become apparent some months into a war that it cannot be won without a disproportionate loss of life. Or, a less harmful alternative to war might suddenly present itself. Most obviously, a group may not continue to fight after it has secured its just cause (unless some other just cause arises, such as ensuring stability in the defeated state or defending civilians against revenge attacks). We can ask of a war at any time whether it is just, and our answer might vary between different stages of the same war.[33]

How does this bear on the objection concerning the role of war-dependent goods in proportionality? Well, we can grant that when a leader is thinking about declaring war, she cannot factor in savings that don't yet need enacting and that will need enacting only because of the war. If *jus ad bellum* judgments were restricted to the declaration of war, it would seem that there are indeed some *in bello* goods that don't count *ad bellum*. But once the war is being fought and the combatants need saving, the good of saving them becomes relevant to whether the leader may continue to use force—that is, to the *ad bellum* question of whether she may continue the war. Preventing unjust imprisonment and killings are legitimate aims of force. Thus, rescuing combatants who have been captured in the course of their legitimate defence is a good of the war that can be factored into her proportionality calculation about whether the war should continue to be fought. We can see this clearly if we imagine that peace terms are offered that are satisfactory in every respect except that the enemy proposes to execute all of its prisoners of war. These people would not have been endangered were it not for the war. But the good of saving them certainly matters for our assessment of whether continuing to fight the war is proportionate. The fact that these goods aren't included in the *ad bellum* proportionality calculation prior to war is irrelevant—they can't be included in any *in bello* calculations prior to war either since there is no *in bello* at that point. Cases such as *Rescue* suggest that there are some goods that might matter when we're considering the continuation of war that don't count when we're considering the resort to war. But that doesn't support a difference in sensitivity between *jus ad bellum* proportionality and *jus in bello* proportionality. All that matters for the purposes of my argument is that, at any time at which there is an *in bello* proportionality calculation that is sensitive to these kinds of goods, *ad bellum* proportionality will be similarly sensitive to them.

3.3. Necessity

On the standard view, *ad bellum* necessity governs the whole war, such that war is justified only if it is the least harmful means available of securing the just cause. For example, a political leader who is wondering whether to continue with a war should compare the costs and harms of war with, for example, those of diplomacy or surrender. *In bello* necessity, in contrast, governs specific offensives, such that an offensive is justified only if it is the least harmful means available of securing some specific end that will contribute to winning the war. A combatant who is deciding whether to carry out a particular offensive has no option of ending the war or accepting peace terms. Thus it seems that her *in bello* deliberations about necessity are very different from the *ad bellum* deliberations of a political leader.

But the idea that necessity is indexed to a particular agent and her available options is a familiar one.[34] Consider *Attack*:

> *Attack*: Attacker is trying to simultaneously kill Amy and Beth. Amy has a shotgun that she can use to defend herself by killing Attacker. Beth has a taser with which she can nonlethally disable Attacker, but she refuses to use it.

Beth acts impermissibly in refusing to use the taser. But her refusal means that the least harmful means of defence available to Amy is killing Attacker with the shotgun. Amy's action of killing Attacker therefore satisfies the necessity condition.

Similarly, from the perspective of a political leader, it might be that an unnecessarily violent (but still proportionate) war is the least harmful means of securing a just cause available to her. She may predict that her troops will cause more harm than is necessary and that a less bloodthirsty army would secure the just cause less harmfully. And yet, since those are the only troops she has and their fighting will still be proportionate, it could still be permissible for her to order the war. But the observation that what is necessary depends on the set of actions available to an agent doesn't show the distinction between *jus ad bellum* and *jus in bello* to be a useful one. It merely shows that it's still true in war that necessity is indexed to an agent's options. At any point in the chain of command, combatants will have different option sets available to them: some will direct entire campaigns, whilst others will lead particular missions or participate in specific offensives. Nothing helpful follows from singling out the perspective of the political leader and calling this *ad bellum* necessity, as if this is somehow tells us that the war overall is the least harmful means of achieving the just cause. In the case described, the war as it will be fought is *not* the least harmful means—many of the offensives will be gratuitously violent. It can be important, of course, that we recognize that it was still the least harmful means available to the political leader. But privileging her option set as determining the overall necessity of the war seems to me wrongheaded. As I'll suggest next, our moral judgments of war should primarily involve a more nuanced assessment of individual actions rather than summative assessments of the perspective of a political leader.

4. Summative Assessments of War

Surely, we might insist, there is value in asking whether, for example, the Kosovo intervention was just or ought to have been fought—that, as Seth Lazar claims, 'we both do and need to be able to evaluate wars as a whole.'[35] Lazar argues that if we focus on the justification of individual actions, we can no longer engage in this valuable practice. Rather, we can ask only about the justification of individual actions that make up the war and then offer the thought that a war is justified only if each of those individual actions is justified. He argues that this sets the bar for justification too high, making 'justified wars practically impossible'.[36]

I think we should be cautious about how valuable summative assessments of wars really are. By 'summative assessments', I mean assessments that purport to aggregate all the actions of the war to produce a single verdict of 'just' or 'unjust'—as Lazar puts it, to 'evaluate the war as a whole'. O'Donovan suggests that such assessments are not, in fact, the purpose of just war theory:

> [I]t is very often supposed that just war theory undertakes to *validate or invalidate particular wars*. That would be an impossible undertaking. History knows of no just war, as it knows of no just peoples. Major historical events cannot be justified or criticised in one mouthful; they are concatenations and agglomerations of many separate actions and many varied results. One may justify or criticise acts of statesmen, acts of generals, acts of common soldiers or of civilians . . . but wars as such, like most

> large-scale historical phenomena, present only a great question mark, a continual invitation to reflect further on which decisions were, and which were not, justified.[37]

A more nuanced approach of this sort, one that does not try to aggregate all the component actions and harms of a war into a single verdict, strikes me as a much more useful way to evaluate wars.

For example, imagine that we want to know whether a given war was proportionate. One way to assess this is to simply take the total harm inflicted—lives lost, injuries inflicted, cities destroyed—and ask if this total harm was warranted by (trying to) avert the threat that was the cause for war. If it was, we might think that we don't need to know anything more to know whether the war was proportionate—that we don't need to know how many specific offensives were proportionate and how many were not.

But this strikes me as morally misleading: it's unclear why we should be interested in that kind of overall judgment. Imagine a war in which some very important targets were captured or destroyed with very little collateral harm, even though their capture or destruction would have warranted significant collateral harm, and many comparatively minor targets were captured or destroyed with vastly disproportionate force. It might be that the total amount of harm inflicted in this war was proportionate to the just cause. But pronouncing the war *ad bellum* proportionate simply fails to capture the fact that many of the composite actions of the war were disproportionate. And if we're concerned with the morality of a war, then the more nuanced, individualized approach strikes me as much more interesting. In the example just given, the overall proportionality of the war would not undercut our duties to compensate those harmed in disproportionate offensives or to punish those involved in carrying out those offensives. Nor would the fact that a combatant fought in this war tell us whether she acted permissibly. Asking whether the war as a whole was proportionate seems akin to asking whether Bystander and Workman's actions in the *Prediction* cases are, taken together, proportionate.

This doesn't mean that we cannot answer questions about whether, for example, war should be declared. It can be true that a politician ought to pursue a war that could be fought less harmfully if fighting it less harmfully is not an option for her, and that it is better that she declare war than not, and so on. But even if we determine that the action of declaring war is justified, this should not be viewed as a verdict that the actions of the ensuing war are justified. It's merely an assessment of the leader's action, given the options available to her. We can similarly assess whether Bystander in *Prediction* is justified in diverting the trolley without taking our answer to provide an overall assessment of whether Bystander and Workman's actions taken together are justified.

In some sense, Lazar is correct that this approach entails that a war can be properly described as justified only if each composite action is justified. But this is not an objection since this approach holds that the overall description of a war as justified is not terribly interesting. What we should be interested in is whether a political leader was justified in declaring or continuing a war, and she can be so justified even foreseeing that others might engage in wrongdoing as a result, as in *Prediction*.[38] Indeed, one can be justified in acting even if the success of one's action depends upon wrongdoing, as in *Murderous Prediction*. The upshot of focusing on individual actions is not that we set the bar for justified resort to war impossibly high. It's rather a recognition that, just as it's unhelpful to ask in the *Prediction* cases whether the agents' actions 'taken together' or 'as a whole' were justified, it's unhelpful to ask whether all the actions of a war, taken together, were justified. There can be no meaningful single verdict on those actions taken together.

5. Conclusion

I have suggested that there is no difference in content between the principles of *jus ad bellum* and the principles of *jus in bello*. Rather, a single set of principles governs the declaring, continuing, and fighting of war. I have also argued that we should reject the idea that judgments about the justness of particular offensives in war are limited to the evaluation of goods and harms directly caused by that offensive. The justness of any action depends on how it interacts with other actions, which can include actions performed by other units, even if they are physically or temporally remote, or by members of allied or opposing forces. Once we widen the scope of relevant effects in this way, the idea that the *ad bellum–in bello* distinction helpfully demarcates the range of relevant evaluanda for moral principles looks false.

I also rejected the idea that the category of *jus ad bellum* enables us to make valuable summative assessments of war, understood as a single verdict on the justness of the war as a whole. There is no helpful evaluation to be made about whether the set of individual actions that compose a side of a conflict are, taken together, 'overall' just or justified. This is compatible with saying that a political leader was justified in declaring or continuing a war. But it denies that we should take the perspective of the political leader—whether a war was necessary from her perspective, for example—and take this to determine whether the war 'taken as a whole' was necessary. A war that was necessary from the leader's perspective could include many gratuitously harmful offensives. If we know this, it is misleading to nevertheless declare the war just with respect to necessity. Our moral evaluations of war should be more nuanced, focusing on the justification of individual actions rather than on attempts to pronounce on the war as a whole.

Acknowledgements

Thanks to Daniel Statman for helpful suggestions, and to Seth Lazar, Victor Tadros, Jonathan Parry, and Cécile Fabre for helpful written comments. Thanks also to Tom Dougherty, Massimo Renzo and J. P. Smit for helpful discussions.

Notes

1. Michael Walzer, *Just and Unjust Wars: A Moral Argument with Historical Illustrations* (New York: Basic Book, 1977).
2. See, e.g., Darrel Moellendorf, 'Two Doctrines of Jus Ex Bello', *Ethics* 125 (3: April 2015), 653–673. David Rodin prefers the term *jus termination* to *jus ex bello*. See, e.g., Rodin, 'The War Trap: Dilemmas of Jus Terminatio', *Ethics* 125 (3: April 2015), 674–695.
3. See, for example, Jeff McMahan, *Killing in War* (Oxford: Oxford University Press, 2009); Cécile Fabre, *Cosmopolitan War* (Oxford: Oxford University Press, 2011); Helen Frowe, *Defensive Killing* (Oxford: Oxford University Press, 2014); Victor Tadros, 'Orwell's Battle with Brittain: Vicarious Liability for Unjust Aggression', *Philosophy and Public Affairs* 42 (1: 2014), 42–77. Of course, there are other theoretical approaches to war—see Seth Lazar's contribution to this volume for an excellent taxonomy.
4. See, e.g., Frowe, *Defensive Killing*; Kai Draper, *War and Individual Rights* (New York: Oxford University Press, 2015).
5. E.g. McMahan, *Killing in War*.
6. Walzer, *Just and Unjust Wars*, 21.
7. In 'War's Endings, and the Structure of Just War Theory', Seth Lazar argues that we should replace the *ad bellum–in bello* distinction with what he claims is a more useful a distinction between Command Ethics and Combatant Ethics. I think that proposal is vulnerable to the same objections that I'll level here against the *ad bellum–in bello* distinction.
8. Fabre, *Cosmopolitan War*, 4.
9. McMahan, *Killing in War*, 19.
10. David Rodin, 'The War Trap: Dilemmas of *jus terminatio*', *Ethics* 125 (3: April 2015), 674–695, at 676.
11. Carsten Stahn, '"Jus ad bellum", "jus in bello" . . . "jus post bellum"? Rethinking the Conception of the Law of Armed Force', *The European Journal of International Law* 17 (5: 2007), 921–943, at 925.
12. Robert Kolb, 'Origins of the Twin Terms *Jus Ad Bellum and Jus in Bello*', *International Review of the Red Cross* 37 (Special Issue 320: 1997), 553–562. Thanks to Greg Reichberg and Rory Cox for helpful discussion of this.
13. Oliver O'Donovan, *The Just War Revisited* (Cambridge: Cambridge University Press, 2003), 15.
14. Nicholas Rengger, '*Jus in bello*', in *War: Essays in Political Philosophy*, edited by Larry May and Emily Crookstone (Cambridge: Cambridge University Press, 2008), 32.
15. McMahan, 'War', in *The Oxford Handbook of Political Philosophy*, edited by David Estlund (New York: Oxford University Press, 2012). 298.
16. Thanks to Victor Tadros for pointing this out.
17. See, e.g., Estlund, 'On Following Orders in an Unjust War', *Journal of Political Philosophy* 15 (2: 2007), 213–234; Lazar, this volume.
18. Thomas Hurka, 'Proportionality in the Morality of War', *Philosophy and Public Affairs* 33 (1: 2005), 34–66, at 37; and Jeff McMahan, 'Just Cause for War', *Ethics and International Affairs* 19 (3: 2005),1–21, at 5.
19. Seth Lazar suggests that gratuitously harming someone is worse than harming a person because it's necessary to achieve an unjust end (see *Sparing Civilians*, chapter 3) I disagree: I

don't think that an unjust harm becomes less bad if it also contributes to achieving some further unjust end.

20. McMahan, 'Just Cause for War', 2. See also Saba Bazargan, 'Aiding and Abetting Unjust Wars', *Journal of Moral Philosophy* 8 (2011), 513–529; Uwe Steinhoff, 'Debate: Jeff McMahan on the Moral Equality of Combatants', *Journal of Political Philosophy* 16 (2: 2008), 220–228; and James Pattison, 'When Is It Right to Fight? Just War Theory and the Individual-Centric Approach', *Ethical Theory and Moral Practice* 16 (1: 2013), 35–54, at 40.
21. See Frowe, 'Judging Armed Humanitarian Intervention', in *The Ethics of Armed Humanitarian Intervention* edited by Don E. Scheid (Cambridge: Cambridge University Press, 2011). For the view that intentions do matter, see Tadros, ' *Journal of Practical Ethics*, and his contribution to this volume.
22. Rengger argues that, e.g., Augustine also took there to be a right intention constraint on ordinary combatants that 'cut across the "dividing line" of *jus ad bellum* and *jus in bello* that is in fact absent in Augustine . . .'.
23. See, e.g., Cécile Fabre, 'Cosmopolitanism, Just War Theory and Legitimate Authority'.
24. See, e.g., Jonathan Parry, this volume; Seth Lazar, 'Authorisation and the Morality of War', *Australasian Journal of Moral Philosophy* 94 (2: 2016), 211–226.
25. See Jonathan Parry, this volume.
26. McMahan, *Killing in War*; Frowe, *Defensive Killing*.
27. David Rodin, *War and Self-Defense* (New York: Oxford, 2002), 114.
28. Fact-relative, evidence-relative, and belief-relative permissibility are distinguished by Derek Parfit in *On What Matters: Volume One* (Oxford: Oxford University Press, 2011), 143. But see also Frank Jackson, 'Decision-Theoretic Consequentialism and the Nearest and Dearest Objection', *Ethics* 101 (3: 1991), 461–482.
29. See, e.g., Seth Lazar, 'War', *The Stanford Encyclopedia of Philosophy* (Summer 2016 Edition), edited by Edward N. Zalta, http://plato.stanford.edu/archives/sum2016/entries/war/, §4.5.
30. Ibid.
31. Braun and Brunstetter Megan Braun and Daniel Brunstetter, 'Rethinking the Criterion for Assessing CIA-Targeted Killings: Drones, Proportionality and Jus ad Vim', *Journal of Military Ethics* 12, (4: 2013), 304–324, 317.
32. Fabre, 'War Exit', p. 632. In an exchange between myself and Fabre on Pea Soup, she concedes that it may be a mistake to talk of the categories as useful. See http://peasoup.typepad.com/peasoup/2015/05/ethics-discussions-at-pea-soup-cecile-fabres-war-exit-with-critical-precis-by-helen-frowe.html
33. See, e.g., McMahan, 'Just Cause for War', 2; Frowe, *The Ethics of War and Peace: An Introduction*, 2nd edn. (New Abington: Routledge, 2015), 54, 57; Cécile Fabre, 'Guns, Food and Liability to Attack in War', *Ethics* 120 (1: 2009), 36–63, at 49 and 57; Seth Lazar, 'War's Ending and the Structure of Just War Theory' (forthcoming); Darrel Moelloendorf's work on *jus ex bello* and David Rodin's work on *jus terminatio*, e.g., 'War Termination and the Liability of Soldiers for the Crime of Aggression', in *Jus Post Bellum: Towards a Law of Transition from Conflict to Peace*, edited by Carsten Stahn and Jann Kleffner (T. M. C. Asser, 2008).
34. See, e.g., Lazar, 'Necessity in War and Self-Defence', *Philosophy and Public Affairs*, 40, 1 (2012), pp. 3–44.
35. Lazar, this volume.
36. Ibid.

37. Oliver O'Donovan, *The Just War Revisited*, 13.
38. For discussion of what I have elsewhere called *mediated harms* that are triggered (but not enabled) by one's otherwise permissible behavior, see Frowe, *Defensive Killing*, chapter 5, and Rodin, 'The Myth of National Defense', in *The Morality of Defensive War*, edited by Cécile Fabre and Seth Lazar (Oxford: Oxford University Press, 2014).

CHAPTER 3

HISTORIOGRAPHY OF JUST WAR THEORY

GREGORY M. REICHBERG

THE aim of this chapter is not so much to survey the history of ethical thinking about war[1] as it is to examine what approaches have been adopted by those retelling this history. Prima facie, historical reflection on the ethics of war would seem to be a second-order initiative that is parasitic upon the primary task of disentangling the substantive moral issues to which war gives rise. Nonetheless, just war theorising assumed this systematic form only after it had evolved for several centuries. Largely prompted by Aquinas's succinct formulation of just war principles in his '*Quaestio de bello*', the idea that the morality of war could be discussed on its own terms as a distinct field of inquiry at the time represented a novel development.

At its inception, reflection on just war was inherently historical. Thucydides (ca. 460–395 BC), arguably the first normative theorist of war,[2] examined the relevant issues through the prism of history, in his case by reconstructing the history of the Peloponnesian War. His approach was largely descriptive; he contrasts alternative viewpoints on the rights and wrongs of war but does not overtly reach conclusions about the truth or falsity of these views. This task he left to the discernment of his readers. Plato seems to have picked up the cue because he, for the first time in Western thought, assessed in a theoretical vein (by implicit reference to the Peloponnesian War[3]) the substantive issues that can be raised concerning human engagement in armed conflict.

Not, however, until the canon lawyer Gratian compiled his *Decretum* in the twelfth century do we find a sustained attempt (in bk. 2, Causa 23) at detailing normative conclusions about war. Here, too, the approach is historical, yet in a very different sense from what may be found in Thucydides. Little is said about past battles and wars, apart from some stock examples drawn mainly from the Old Testament. Causa 23 begins with an idealized case—a hypothetical armed seizure of property from heretical bishops—but then proceeds to reproduce copious citations from earlier authors. Cataloguing their statements about the rights and wrongs of war served as Gratian's vehicle for normative reflection. And, despite the speculative cast of his writing, Aquinas followed very much the same procedure as Gratian. Conclusions on, for instance, whether any war could be just or whether lying might be deemed permissible in war were dialectically linked with an exposition of the views that had been advanced by his predecessors. Grotius adopted a similar methodology in his *De jure belli ac pacis*. The state of affairs that we now take for granted was thus inverted: historical reflection of the ethics of war came first; only afterwards could there be reasoned judgment about the issues in their own right.

The classical theorists of just war[4] understood that our reasoning about the rights and wrongs of war would be only as good as the premises that form our point of departure. On their view, theoretical reflection would be strengthened through the examination of positions articulated by earlier thinkers. Thereby set in motion was a comparative hermeneutic in which earlier positions were reviewed, not so much out of historical interest, but rather for the didactic purpose of grounding sound reasoning about issues of contemporary import.

For these authors, a historical approach was considered beneficial for several reasons: it widened the range of available premises and thereby directed the theorist's attention to issues that might otherwise go unnoticed, it facilitated critical self-reflection by bringing into greater relief the theorist's own cherished assumptions, it showed how a single premise could be drawn towards very different and even opposing conclusions, and it explained the appeal of errors that were operative in contemporary practice, thereby enabling their persuasive refutation. This, in sum, was the idea behind the 'disputed question' methodology that Aquinas and later scholastics exploited to such great effect within their treatment of war and related issues.[5]

Dialectical engagement with earlier viewpoints was essential to the classical theorists, but none of them sought to write narrative histories of just war thought. In fact, it was not until the late nineteenth century that such histories were first written. In this formative period, the main interest of these historians was to situate just war reflection in relation to public international law, a branch of jurisprudence that had emerged only the century before. Given its relative novelty, there was much concern to show how it was solidly anchored in the work of respected past thinkers. The resulting just war histories consequently had an apologetic cast that emphasized the continuity between the earlier period of normative reflection on war and the newly codified rules of the international community. Later, this continuity would be questioned. In this there lies an important lesson for readers today. Few (if any) histories of just war have been written as purely descriptive exercises. Most have a decidedly normative thrust, articulated by the authors themselves with varying degrees of transparency. Explaining the normative options that have oriented historical methodology in this field is the principal task of this chapter.

It goes without saying that historical accounts of just war theorising, while concentrated on the 'classical' authors of the Middle Ages and early modernity, are in no wise restricted to this period. The emergence of public international law, the French Revolution and the rise of the nation-state, new kinds of weapons, and the establishment of institutional arrangements for regulating resort to war (for instance the League of Nations and the UN Charter) have, *inter alia*, left an imprint on the historical retelling of just war theory.

The historiographical account that I develop herein begins (Section 1) with a comment on how the underlying concept of 'war' has remained far from constant from one period to another. Acknowledging the various shifts in meaning—and the attendant danger of equivocation—is a prerequisite for broad historical reflection in this domain. Later, in Section 2, I consider how the idea of a 'just war tradition' first emerged. Usually described by contrast to 'pacifism', on the one hand, and 'political realism', on the other, nowadays we take for granted that 'just war' represents a set of philosophical postulates that are shared by a recognizable group of authors. But this was not exactly how the formative ('classical') authors viewed their own activity; taken as the name of a distinctive school or approach, the label 'just war' was affixed by later historians who were intent on establishing a just war 'canon'. Why modern histories of just war theory were first written and their criteria for inclusion in the canon is taken up in Section 3. Implicit in every canon are normative presuppositions about the ideal shape of a tradition and a retelling of its history in terms of inclusion and exclusion, rise and decline. Just war is no exception; hence, in Section 4, I examine several accounts that have an explicitly normative cast. Finally, to exhibit the salience of just war historiography for contemporary theorising, this chapter concludes (Section 5) with a reflection on the antecedents to our present debate on the moral equality of combatants.

1. 'War': Contrasting Usages

Historical analysis of normative conceptions of war over a broad time span must grapple with the fact that the very term—*war*—that underlies this investigation has not remained constant from one author or historical setting to another. The lack of a unitary concept of war, even among authors who employ the same word, has not infrequently resulted in equivocation and thus confusion about the main issues at stake.[6]

In the medieval period, writers such as Aquinas typically spoke of 'war' from an action-centred perspective such that the noun *bellum* (war) functioned as an equivalent for the infinitive *bellare* (to wage war). 'War' thus signified the act of a belligerent using force against his opponent. In any particular armed conflict, there would accordingly be two wars: a just war waged by one side and the unjust war waged by the other. A single conflict could also encompass two unjust wars if neither of the respective belligerents was possessed of a just cause. In early modernity, a shift occurred. From the action-centred meaning of the previous period, 'war' came to designate a state in which two (or more) parties have the express will to contend against each other by force.[7] Such a state could exist even if no hostilities had yet taken place, as for instance, during the so-called Phoney War (1940–41) between Britain/France and Germany. Conceptualized as a 'state', war was a 'distinctly marked out period of time in which a special legal regime [the 'state of war'] was substituted for the ordinary one [the 'state of peace'] that generally prevailed'.[8] For Aquinas and his scholastic successors, by contrast, there was 'no state of war but only *acts* of war—either wrongful acts by the unjust side or lawful ones by the just party'.[9] They understood that the overall condition of war is indeed an evil, in the sense that it is both an affliction (*malum poenae*) and, more acutely still, the manifestation of wrongful choice (*malum culpae*)—since in every war at least one of the parties must be in the wrong. But this negative judgment on war qua condition was nonetheless compatible with asserting that some wars are just, in the sense that one party to the conflict may be justified in using force against the other.

If one is unaware of this shift in meaning confusion can easily result. The contemporary Roman Catholic teaching on war can provide a useful illustration. The Church magisterium most often employs the term 'war' in the modern sense, as the state or condition of mutual conflict. By the same token, statements abound to the effect that this condition is sinful and an affront to reason because it presupposes at a minimum that one of the two (or more) contending parties is gravely at fault. On a superficial reading, the two different usages—scholastic and modern—can easily become entangled. Thus, on reading the very negative appraisal of the state of war in contemporary writings of Church authorities, one could easily be misled into thinking that their intent was to repudiate the very idea of just war.

Other terminological shifts have occurred as well. The classical just war theorists typically employed *bellum* to designate any resort to force, at a small or large scale, whether by organized armies, opponents of established order, or even single individuals defending themselves.[10] In the lexicon of Grotius, these were differentiated, respectively, as 'formal', 'mixed', and 'private' war.[11] By contrast, from the nineteenth century forward, 'war' has typically been reserved only for the first of these categories, and even then only for the largest of conflicts, with smaller-scale military engagements receiving the euphemistic name 'measures short of war'.[12] Moreover, in some lexicons, 'war' has assumed an entirely pejorative meaning, so that any *justifiable* employment of violent means will be designated under the labels[13] 'enforcement measures', 'armed force', 'defensive action', and so forth.[14]

Along similar lines, the Catholic magisterial teaching on war, as it emerged in the early twentieth century, was framed as a reaction against the doctrine of *raison d'état*, which had reached its apogee in European state practice during the nineteenth century, a practice that received doctrinal articulation in the legal positivism of the day. On this conception, 'war was, above all else, an exercise of will on the part of the state—i.e., a determination made by a state, reached entirely on the basis of its own interest, that a certain foreign-policy goal will be more effectively pursued by force of arms than by alternative means such as negotiation or the exercise of the unheroic virtue of patience'.[15] The pursuit of policy by other means (to repeat the famous turn of phrase from Clausewitz), war was taken to be a recognized institution, codified in international law, to which states could appeal in order to adjudicate their disagreements. This procedure, in which two states mutually agreed (hence the idea of a 'war contract') to settle their quarrel 'by rolling the dice of Mars'[16] was fundamentally at odds with the classical doctrine of just war as it had been taught in the Church.[17] Yet, even while rejecting this view, Church writers nonetheless adopted positivist semantics when speaking of 'war'. As a consequence, the modern popes may frequently be found condemning resort to war.[18]

Thus understood after the fashion of *raison d'état*, the pontiffs had necessarily to declare war a sin; it was per se *malum* such that the expression 'just war' would be an oxymoron. Yet, in uttering this condemnation of war, the popes did not intend to target the *jus ad bellum* as it had earlier been conceptualized by the scholastics, and which continues to be taught in the Church. It was rather 'war' in the positivist sense of the term that was the target of exclusion.

Finally, the related terms 'aggression' and 'defence' have undergone transformation as well. Whereas scholastics distinguished just from unjust *bellum aggressivum* (equivalently called *bellum offensivum*), for moderns, 'aggression' has an unqualifiedly negative connotation,[19] with the result that modes of armed action the former would have placed under the heading of just offensive war have in modernity gravitated into a bloated category of 'defence'.[20]

2. Identifying a Just War 'Tradition'

The difficulty in assessing doctrinal shifts in just war theory over a broad span of time points to an even deeper challenge that is in a sense presupposed: namely, in what measure it is possible to identify over multiple authors across a span of time sufficient continuity so as to speak of a 'just war tradition'. Any attempt at defining such a tradition will necessarily be obliged to designate insiders and outsiders.

The idea that there exists a line of thinkers, joined by a set of shared premises on the justifiable uses of armed force such that together they constitute a 'just war tradition', appears to have emerged only in early modernity, when opponents grouped these authors into a single category the better to criticize them. It was in this vein that Kant in *Perpetual Peace* (1795) famously spoke of Grotius, Pufendorf, and Vattel as 'sorry comforters', whose normative teaching on war had little effect on the actual behaviour of warring states. Francis Bacon had earlier placed (in a letter written ca. 1620) in a single category the idealistic opponents of preventive war (most likely he had in mind Vitoria and other followers of Aquinas), whom he called 'schoolmen, otherwise revered men, yet fitter to guide penknives than swords [who assume] that every offensive war must be "ultio", a revenge, that presupposeth a precedent assault or injury'.[21] Although Kant and Bacon did not name their alternative approaches to the ethics of war, today, these go under the headings of 'perpetual peace' and 'realism', respectively. Other competitors to 'just war' that standardly receive mention in the historical literature are 'pacifism' and 'holy war' (also termed 'crusading').[22]

Significantly, however, the long line of authors, from Cicero to Augustine, Gratian, Aquinas, Cajetan,[23] Vitoria, Molina, to Suárez, who are standardly classed as members of a 'just war tradition' rarely if ever designated themselves in this manner. What we do find, however, is a running discussion, visible in the form of citations, wherein a continuous pattern of textual references (from the Bible, Church fathers, canon lawyers, etc.), leading ideas (just cause, legitimate authority, or right intention), principles (of double-effect, proportionality, or combatant/noncombatant discrimination), and negations (of, e.g., pacifism) may be discerned.

Although all of the above authors utilized the label 'just war' (originally coined by Aristotle[24]), Grotius was arguably the first to have consciously thought of himself as a theorist within the specialized domain of moral-legal reflection that might go under this name. Recognising that his predecessors had covered portions of this field, he nevertheless took credit for being the first to treat 'this subject-matter as a whole'.[25] Referring to the sort of realist sentiment earlier expressed by Bacon, he made it clear that his goal would be to refute those who viewed the theory of just war 'with contempt as having no reality outside of an empty name'.[26] Yet, unlike Descartes, who several years later would seek to construct a new science of 'first philosophy' from scratch, Grotius was at pains to demonstrate that his juridical science of war and peace was not a construct born of his own mind, but rather a discipline that emanated from a set of pregiven norms (*jus naturae*—natural right) that had already been acknowledged by a broad array of Greek, Roman, and Christian thinkers. That he was but a member of a long-standing tradition of reflection on these matters (hence the care he took in citing *inter alia* his scholastic predecessors) testified in his eyes to the emanation of these norms ('a common law among nations, which applies both to wars [*ad bella*] and in wars [*in bellis*]'[27]) from a source outside of human contrivance. Indeed, the centrality assigned to *lex naturalis*, a moral instruction that ultimately derives from God but that does not inherently depend on special religious revelation, was a common thread that bound together all the classical just-war theorists.[28]

The central postulates of just war theory are ordinarily traced to St. Augustine. It has been argued, however—convincingly in my opinion[29]—that his diverse writings on this topic are far from constituting a theory; namely, an express attempt at thematising the issue of just war on its own terms. Instead, his comments on just war had an ad hoc character. The references to war that may be found in his diverse writings usually play a supporting role for arguments that bear on quite different matters; for instance, to explain how an unconditional obedience is owed to God's commands, he proceeded by analogy with a better known case—namely, the chain of command in military affairs.[30]

The paternity of just war theory is more credibly traced to the canon lawyer Gratian, who, around 1140 in Bologna, assembled (in Causa 23 of his *Decretum*, bk. II) disparate texts on war and violence—from Augustine and other theologians, the Bible, Church councils, and the popes—under selected headings (named 'canons') that highlighted concepts that later historians would view as integral to the just war 'tradition'.[31] This he did by lifting these texts out of their original context and placing them in juxtaposition to other texts either by the same author or from other authors who were thought to be making a similar point. Thus, in the passage from Augustine about duty of obedience, the original structure of the argument has practically disappeared in Gratian's citation; no longer is there any mention of divine injunctions: instead, the supporting point about obedience to military superiors is alone retained.[32]

The *Decretum* quickly become the standard reference work for medieval lawyers and theologians on all manner of normative issues. For these authors, the texts that were collected in Causa 23 took on the status of a canon on matters relating to participation in war and violence. By sifting through opposing positions[33] on a variety of issues relating to war (on, e.g., whether it was permissible for Christians to serve as soldiers, or whether the authorization of a prince was necessary for the waging of a just war, or whether war could justifiably be waged against heretics) and by citing well-known authorities in support of the conclusions reached, Gratian laid out the boundaries of legitimate discourse (within the Latin-speaking Church) on this subject for centuries to come. His work had a twofold audience. On the one hand, it served as a basic manual in canon law,[34] so that subsequent efforts at defining the legal status of acts relating to war—on the scope of pre-emptive defence, the permissibility of ambushes, the obligation to defend the weak and powerless from aggression, and similar questions—would proceed by reference to this seminal work, either in the form of glosses on selected passages or through later papal legislation (decretals). On the other hand, it also provided theologians such as Thomas Aquinas with the basic materials from which they could reflect more systematically on the moral aspects of armed force. Instead of sitting down to read, say, Augustine, in the original texts, Aquinas and those like him would advert to Gratian's compilation, so that, in effect, they found the materials already organized along certain key lines. In either case, the reflection was inherently practical in the sense that it was meant to inform the conscience of individuals who, in one way or another, had contact with war. Hence, Aquinas situated his analysis of just war within a concrete treatment of the moral virtues,[35] and his Dominican predecessor Raymond of Peñafort elaborated a just war casuistry (writing on this topic in his *Summa de casibus poenitentiae*, ca. 1225) that was specially geared to the needs of the confessional. By their power to absolve penitents from their sins, confessors exercised a role akin to judges and were expected to apply the law within a special jurisdiction: the inner domain of conscience.[36]

A close linkage of decision-making and concrete action would remain constant throughout the classical period of just war reflection. Even at its late, most systematic stage, as in Grotius's *De jure belli ac pacis*, this linkage was retained by the copious selection of historical cases drawn mainly from Greek and Roman antiquity (which in Grotius's eyes reflected a superior level of civilization). For Grotius, these cases served a twofold function. On the one hand, they showed actual agents engaged in concrete choices, thereby aiding in the classification and evaluation of current cases; on the other hand, these cases were conveyed along with determinate moral or legal judgments (which the historians often placed into the mouth of their protagonists). The first provided manifestations of *jus naturae* (an imprint of divine rationality in the created world) that could enable the jurist to deduce appropriate conclusions about current cases. The second was equivalent to the modern *opinio juris* (decision of law), which, by a concordance of decisions from one jurisdiction to another could reveal something essential about the positive norms of *jus gentium*. These two sources of judgment were considered mutually reinforcing.[37] Neither in Grotius nor in his predecessors[38] do we find a purely deductive approach to the normative issues of war (with an imaginative modelling of cases replacing historical reflection), as has become prevalent today in philosophers of the analytic school.[39]

3. The Emergence of Just War Historiography

In the preceding section, we saw how out of Gratian's *Decretum* a tradition was born, not so much in name as in practice. The explicit conceptualization of this practice as a distinctive tradition emerged not from the thinkers themselves, but from historians who, invoking the seventeenth-century School of Natural Law and the Law of Nations (associated with Grotius, Pufendorf, et al.), began in the late nineteenth century to delineate a subsidiary current that was itself devoted to matters of just war.

Among the first manifestations of the new trend was the publication in 1882 of a book by Ernest Nys (a jurist who was a member of the Permanent Court of Arbitration in The Hague and a professor at the University of Brussels) on the precursors of Grotius and their respective views on just war.[40] Nys tells us in the introduction that his main purpose in writing this book was to trace out the beginnings of public international law, which he viewed as a technical elaboration on the precepts of *jus gentium* (law of nations). Identifying the origin of this discipline ('the last to emerge of the legal sciences'[41]) with the need to establish order in medieval Christendom after the fall of the Roman Empire, he held that, in the period before Grotius, the theorists of *jus gentium* were concerned almost exclusively with articulating norms of war. Once limitations on the resort to war (as well as the conduct of war) were recognized, a space could open up for the advancement of positive norms of peace. In writing this history, Nys hoped that it would reinforce the growing influence of international law. Nearly all historians of just war, from the time of Nys up until the post World War II period, advanced with the same normative thrust; namely, that international law (and its affiliated institutions such as the League of Nations) would be strengthened if its roots in the just war teaching of the medieval and early modern theorists were better understood. Only much later would legal historians question the alleged continuity of classical just war theory with the League of Nations and related international law initiatives that were implemented between the two World Wars.[42]

Writing in the wake of Nys, other continental authors sought to trace out the history of just war doctrine as it emerged in the Middle Ages. First, there appeared a translation into French of Gratian's Causa 23, which was presented, tellingly, as a treatise in public international law.[43] It was followed a decade later by a book, also written by a professor of law, Hippolyte Pissard, that demarcated holy war as a subset within the broader legal/canonical tradition of just war.[44] A milestone was passed in 1911–12, when another French historian, Alfred Vanderpol, an engineer by training and a fervent member of the Catholic internationalist movement, wrote two books[45] that sought to show how a set of thinkers—including not only Gratian, Aquinas, Vitoria, but also Bonet, Pisan, and Gentili—represented a veritable school, organized around the core idea that resort to war should be governed by a set of limitative rules. To his credit, Vanderpol did not present this school as monolithic, for, as we shall see shortly, he detected several distinct strands within the broader stream.

The idea that historical study of the just war tradition could reinforce the development of international conventions to regulate war was central to the ambitious project, initiated by James Brown Scott in 1906, to republish the classic writings on war and peace that were believed to have given birth to international law. Comprising more than twenty works (each reproduced in the original language with English translation) by the time of its completion in 1950, *The Classics of International Law*, as the series was called, did much to solidify belief in the existence of a just war canon that could enable its readers to 'trace the history of international law to its sources'.[46] The unity of this canon was presented by Brown as a given, but, like most other canons, it was in fact a reconstruction. The principal flaw in the eyes of its later critics was the canon's teleological foundation: the cohesion of the tradition was attributable to the service it would render only in the future vis-à-vis the formation of public international law. Beyond highlighting this anachronism,[47] later scholars would also emphasize how some central postulations of the classical just war literature (roughly from Aquinas to Grotius) were in fact inconsistent with the basic framework of international law as it emerged in the eighteenth and nineteenth centuries.[48] Even the alleged unity of just war writings in the classical period would be called into question, as, for instance, when Peter Haggenmacher (and before him Carl Schmitt) maintained that authors such as Bartolus, Legnano, Ayala, and Gentili, usually categorized under the heading of 'just war', actually represented a competing tradition, 'regular war', which in turn was the main progenitor of international law (more about this later).

4. Accounts of Decline and Progress

Of the early works on the history of just war reflection, Vanderpol's was by far the most influential. His *La doctrine scholastique du droit de guerre* (scholastic teaching on the law of war) sought to demonstrate how, in the Catholic Church, from Ambrose and Augustine in late antiquity, through the high Middle Ages until the seventeenth century, there arose a doctrinal consensus on the justifiability and limits of the resort to armed force. While acknowledging that this doctrine was born and nurtured within the Church, Vanderpol emphasized that it nevertheless did not bear on matters inherently religious but pertained rather to the sphere of natural right, and, as a consequence, it could subsequently lay the foundations for a nondenominational ('secular' as we would now say) international law. Not content merely to unite disparate authors under a loose family resemblance, Vanderpol sought to identify the key premise that, on his view, constituted the core of just war doctrine and by reference to which any purported instantiation of this doctrine could be judged. Citing Aquinas's famous definition of just cause in his '*Quaestio de bello*'—'those who are attacked should be attacked because they merit it on account of some fault'[49]—Vanderpol defined just war as 'an act of vindicative justice, namely the punishment of foreign malefactors'.[50]

On Vanderpol's understanding, war could be justifiably undertaken only when it was posited as a reaction to a grave, culpable offence. Modelled on the procedures of criminal justice, this standard of just cause was extremely stringent. Instances of wrong-doing wherein the culpability (*mens rea*) of the unjust side could not be demonstrated would accordingly not warrant an armed response. In formulating this requirement, Vanderpol sought to discredit a more permissive view that he associated especially with Molina. The Spanish Jesuit was singled out for special criticism as having argued that the commission of (material) injustice, apart from any inner culpability (formal injustice), was sufficient to warrant a response of just war. Vanderpol thus maintained that the Jesuit scholastic had opened the door to the idea, later to be taken up in nineteenth-century international law, that states were entitled to resort to war as a legitimate means of resolving their grievances. Just war, on Molina's logic as understood by Vanderpol, was akin to a civil lawsuit undertaken by parties who were juridically equal. By abandoning the paradigm of criminal law, the moral barrier to war was thereby lowered to the point whereby it could be viewed as a normal procedure for resolving conflicts in the international sphere.[51] Here it can be noted that a similar logic is operative in the recent work of Jeff McMahan. His claim that soldiers who fight on behalf of an unjust cause bear liability for this wrongdoing and may unilaterally be attacked is (like the argument of Vanderpol before him) motivated by the project of reducing resort to war. On McMahan's view,[52] the initiation of unjust war can best be prevented if rank-and-file combatants are made to understand that they bear personal liability for their participation in such wars. This awareness will lead them to exercise selective conscientious objection when necessary. Should this become a majority option, it will impede the wrongful initiatives of their political leaders, who depend on a compliant military to advance their programs of aggression. For this reason, McMahan argues against Walzer's idea that combatants confront each other on the battlefield as moral equals whose obligation of obedience to their superiors removes from their purview any substantive engagement on the underlying just cause of the wars in which they are called to fight (see Section 5).

Returning to Vanderpol, we note how, in his eyes, an additional factor further aggravated the trend towards a more permissive understanding of just war: namely, the introduction of a 'probabilist' calculus into the assessment of just cause. Levelling this charge against Suárez, Molina, and their followers, Vanderpol maintained that they had moved away from grounding just cause on the certitude of a grave fault committed by the adversary, replacing this epistemic requirement with a mere judgment of probability that the evidence was weighted in favour of the claims put forward by one's own side.[53] Once this was conceded, it would be a short step to recognising that each party to a conflict would readily construe the probable reasons in favour of itself, thereby leading to a situation wherein each side would simultaneously have a right to declare war against the other. Whereas the classical doctrine as articulated by Vitoria had allowed solely for an *appearance* of simultaneous justice (premised on the invincible ignorance of one party to the conflict), by the acceptance of probabilism, the central condition of just cause would be adulterated so that, *substantively*, each side would have an equal right to fight. The core of the just war doctrine would thereby be jettisoned, in effect replaced by the modern conception, according to which war, when declared by two sovereigns, was a legitimate way to adjudicate disputes that could not be settled by other means (the 'war contract'[54]).

The two prongs of Vanderpol's critique were vigorously countered by Robert Regout, a Dutch jurist whose comprehensive account of the historical development of just war theory, *La doctrine de la guerre juste de Saint Augustin à nos jours* ('The doctrine of just war from St. Augustine to the present'), appeared in 1934.[55] An ardent proponent of a system of international law rooted in classical just war theory who would later die at the Dachau concentration camp (after airing legal views critical of the German occupation of his country),[56] Regout's main claim was that war could be resorted to only when it might serve as an instrument of justice. The justice in question he did not construe quite so narrowly as had Vanderpol, who, as we have seen, maintained that only a culpable offence (formal injustice) might be countered by means of war. This could leave grave wrongs unanswered if they were committed out of invincible ignorance, for example. The harm done to the recipient of this wrong would thereby be left to stand, an outcome hardly incompatible with justice,[57] namely, the 'free exercise of [legitimate] rights'.[58] Inversely, by characterising just war as a form of punishment, Vanderpol had unwittingly construed the legitimate objectives of war too broadly. For, on his formulation, not only defence and restitution, but also punishment of wrongdoing could be included under the category of just cause.[59] Against this overly broad construal of just cause, and by reference to Vitoria and Molina, Regout maintained that offensive war ideally should be waged only to repair (overturn) a wrong.[60] This is what he termed a 'war of recuperation'.[61] Punishment he argued (by reference to Vitoria), should never be the proximate aim of war; when deserved, punishment should be secured solely *post bellum*, by the prosecution of the guilty. To put the same point otherwise: just war can be a means to apprehend the guilty such that they are brought to justice afterwards, but war itself should never be imposed as a form of punishment.[62]

As to Vanderpol's accusation of probabilism, Regout countered that it resulted from a misreading of Suárez and Molina. The two Spanish Jesuits had indeed conceded that disputes could arise wherein one or both parties found it very difficult to render firm determinations of just cause. They accordingly devised a subtle casuistry to guide decision-making about such 'doubtful cases'. On this account, heads of state have an obligation to submit their grievances to arbitration or be willing to attend conferences where their competing claims could be dispassionately discussed. Contested land should never be unilaterally seized, and, if both parties are in doubt about the rights of possession, a presumption would vest in favour of the current owner. Molina and Suárez likewise held that whereas a weighing of probabilities might be altogether apposite in an initial phase of deliberation, to embark on war without having first achieved a reasoned certitude about the matter at hand would be unjustifiable. Unduly conflating the initial process of deliberation with the subsequent decision, Vanderpol had wrongly attributed to the two Jesuits the belief that war could justly be declared on merely probable grounds.[63]

Vanderpol's further contention that this probabilism had paved the way for the view, prominent among lawyers in the nineteenth and early twentieth centuries, that war could be accepted as an ordinary means of resolving intractable disagreements between states, resulted, on Regout's estimation, from another undue conflation, in this instance between the casuistry of hard cases (i.e., the method promoted by Suárez and Molina) and the idea of a 'war contract'. [64] Regout pointed out that Suárez (and by extension Molina) had hesitated to condemn the latter practice solely with respect to the obligation of restitution. Since the parties had voluntarily entered into this arrangement, commutative justice could not require that the goods thus gained by victory in war should be returned. This concession aside, Suárez took care to state how the war contract was wholly incompatible with the virtue expected of those who wage just war.[65] Although the war contract would subsequently find some acceptance among nineteenth-century lawyers, only by considerable distortion could its paternity be traced to Suárez and his kin in just war theory.[66]

Closer to our own time, the thesis that the just war tradition has gone into decline due to a betrayal of its core principles has been revived by James Turner Johnson, a historian who works in the field of religious studies.[67] On several occasions,[68] he has argued that contemporary versions of just war—particularly as articulated within the Christian churches (especially Catholic)—are 'radically at odds with the classical idea of just war'.[69] The difference between the classical and contemporary versions he has summed up with his widely cited contrast between two incompatible starting points for moral reflection on war: 'the presumption against injustice' (the classical theory), on the one hand, and 'the presumption against war' (the contemporary theory), on the other. For Johnson, the discrepancy between these two forms of just war theory is to the discredit of the contemporary version. Describing it as an 'intellectual deterioration . . . in influential quarters' which has 'altered the ground on which the theory itself has stood for more than a thousand years',[70] he maintains that the 'presumption against war' view underestimates the weight of injustice in human affairs, thus hindering the ability of moral leaders to counter it effectively. Moreover, he faults this approach for unduly limiting the legitimate scope of the *jus ad bellum* to self-defence, thereby 'trammel[ing] action and initiative in foreign policy'.[71] Harking back to the classical doctrine because it provides a more robust understanding of just war (allowing, *inter alia* for humanitarian interventions), Johnson, referring to the same authors as Vanderpol (Augustine, Aquinas, and, to some extent, Vitoria) nonetheless reaches a diametrically opposed conclusion: namely, that the classical doctrine is better than the contemporary version (as taught, e.g., by the popes) precisely because it is less restrictive. Moral empowerment to confront injustice is more central to the just war ethos than its attendant teaching on *jus in bello* restraint.

Significantly, Johnson is far from alone in his assessment that contemporary Christian teaching (especially by the Catholic magisterium) represents a departure from the 'classic canons of just-war thinking'.[72] An almost identical appraisal may be found in a 1962 monograph[73] by René Coste, who argues that, for Pope Pius XII (the pivotal figure in the articulation of contemporary Catholic just war doctrine), offensive war, in the juridical and moral sense of the term, must be entirely excluded. This represents, Coste affirms, 'a key divergence with the traditional doctrine'.[74] Unlike Johnson, however, Coste views this doctrinal shift as a positive development, one in keeping with the progress of humanity (as reflected notably in international law) towards a less sanguine view of the nobility of war. Similar views have been echoed by other historians of just war thinking.[75]

From the preceding it should be manifest that historical interpretations of just war are often teleologically driven. Doctrinal positions are not merely classified into their variants according to an order of origination and family resemblance, but, moreover, they are assessed by reference to some normative ideal. Some historians are more overt than others in disclosing their normative preferences, but, in any case, readers must be alert to these preferences and how they structure the historical narratives of just war theory.[76]

5. Conclusion

The salience of just war historiography to contemporary theorising about war and ethics can be illustrated by the contemporary debate on the moral equality of combatants.[77] The idea that *in bello* rules of armed conflict can be defined without reference to the *ad bellum* status of belligerents (the 'independence thesis'), such that the same rules apply to all soldiers, irrespective of the justice of the cause for which they fight (the 'symmetry thesis'),[78] was advanced by Michael Walzer as a central presupposition of traditional just war theory. Indeed, Walzer maintained that the 'medieval' distinction between *jus ad bellum* and *jus in bello* presupposes 'two sorts of judgments' that 'are logically independent'. 'War is always judged twice', he famously states at the outset of *Just and Unjust Wars*, 'first with reference to the reasons states have for fighting, secondly with reference to the means they adopt'.[79]

Against this just war 'orthodoxy', Jeff McMahan has elaborated over the last few years a 'revisionist' theory that assesses the *in bello* conduct of soldiers by reference to the *ad bellum* justice of their cause.[80] Soldiers possessed of a just cause may direct force against their adversaries in proportion to the degree of liability that the latter bear for the unjust cause that, de facto, they represent on the battlefield. Within this normative framework, soldiers do not confront each other on the battlefield as moral equals, for only those possessed of the just cause have a right to bring lethal force upon their peers, whereas those prosecuting the unjust cause have no such entitlement; on purely moral grounds, they should simply lay down their arms. McMahan's theory has received sustained criticism from various quarters,[81] mainly on grounds that it would undermine the *in bello* rules that have enjoyed wide acceptance under international law since the late nineteenth century. The excesses of, say, the Allied powers during World War II (obliteration bombing of urban centres) or the United States during its so-called War on Terror (with its unwillingness to recognize the fighters on the opposing side as 'lawful combatants') would seem to bear out the worry that rejection of the symmetry thesis (motivated by strong belief in a unilaterally applicable just cause) would foster a neglect of long-standing international norms in the conduct of war.

How would just war historiography contribute to this debate? First of all, it would contest Walzer's claim that his postulation of combatant equality represents an embrace of traditional just war teaching. From Aquinas to Grotius, the common assumption of leading authors in the tradition was that the right to kill, which is conferred on soldiers in war, is a prerogative of the just side only. Soldiers on the unjust side enjoy no such right even if, under some circumstances, they may be excused on grounds of ignorance or their adherence to the requirements of obedience for killing without just title. *Jus in bello* was viewed largely through the prism of the *jus ad bellum*; thus, the default position operative in the tradition was that unjust combatants are unilaterally liable to attack.[82]

What Walzer had identified as the 'traditional' theory was indeed a doctrine that had emerged in the Middle Ages; he erred nonetheless in associating it with thinkers of the just war cast. The idea that in public war combatants oppose each other as moral equals ('just enemies') is traceable to a competing line of thinkers—proponents of 'regular war'[83]—who, from the legist Raphaël Fulgosius in the late fourteenth century, to Balthazar Ayala in the sixteenth century, culminating with Christian von Wolff and Emer de Vattel in the eighteenth century, came to view the *jus in bello* as entirely separable from the *jus ad bellum*. The characteristic mark of this tradition was not a simple distinction of the two domains: when he embarked on a discussion of 'how much is permitted in a just war' Vitoria, like Suárez and other mainstream just war theorists, had implicitly recognized that the norms governing conduct in war were of a somewhat different nature than those that ought to guide the original resort to force. Yet the two sets of norms were not treated in isolation, since it was understood that the rules of *in bello* restraint were formulated for the belligerent who was possessed of the just cause; from the moral point of view, his unjust counterpart was expected, not to show restraint, but rather not to be fighting at all.

In other words, to generate combatant equality, over and above the distinction between *jus ad bellum* and *jus in bello*, an additional thesis was needed. For Fulgosius, this consisted in the insight that, whenever war breaks out between sovereign peoples or kings—over whom, by definition, there is no common judge—just cause will be indeterminable. Fulgosius does not entirely forgo the vocabulary of just war—it can have meaning within the sphere of private conscience or in the mind of God—but when sovereign powers engage in war, their very juridical status precludes reference to a just cause. By virtue of a structural condition—namely, the fact of mutual sovereignty—every belligerent has as much right to fight as any other, and, under such circumstances, victory alone will serve as the final arbiter of their underlying disputes. From the unilateral 'just war' of the scholastics we thus move to the bilateral 'public war' of the legists, and, under this condition of reciprocal *jus belli*, there extends to the rank-and-file soldiers the right to kill each other on the battlefield—a moral equality of combatants.

Originally, this was not a teaching about the reciprocal duties of restraint that should be observed in the conduct of hostilities. Rather it was about reciprocal rights, chiefly the right to kill, but also the mutually recognized right for victors to keep whatever booty they had seized and related matters. This, in other words, was about wartime liberties for which legal immunity would be granted to regular combatants (in contrast to robbers and other unrecognized fighters); very little in this connection was said about mutually binding wartime restrictions that would later be acknowledged in the Hague and Geneva conventions.[84]

A summary of these wartime liberties was spelled out by Grotius in his *De jure belli ac pacis*,[85] wherein he discusses what may be deemed permissible in a formally declared public war (i.e., a war between sovereigns). Referring to some unnamed jurists (most likely an allusion to Fulgosius and his fellow legists), as well as to the practice of the ancient Romans,[86] Grotius notes that, owing to a tacit agreement among nations (i.e., a permanent implied understanding that holds by virtue of the *jus gentium*), the parties to a public war may with impunity carry out deeds that normally would be considered impermissible under natural law. Grotius justifies this suspension of just cause by an appeal to the principle of the lesser evil. Neutral powers would inevitably get drawn into a conflict (by, e.g., being pressured to make determinations about which side had violated the laws of war or which side should be deemed the possessor of a particular territory at the close of the fighting) unless it was mutually recognized at the outset that certain legal effects would accompany the formally declared state of war. The purpose of this new bilateral regime was to narrow the circle of war with respect to the *jus ad bellum*; namely, to prevent a conflict from encompassing states that had no special stake in the matter under dispute.[87] It was, in other words, to promote *ad bellum* restraint that these *in bello* liberties were allowed (*qua* lesser evil) despite their inconsistency with the demands of 'internal justice'.[88] McMahan is similarly motivated to widen the scope of *in bello* permissions (at least with regard to the targeting of enemy combatants) in order secure an *ad bellum* gain (narrow the resort to war).

In contrast to these reciprocal liberties, the idea of *in bello* restrictions first arose among the scholastic theologians—Aquinas had prohibited lying and other forms of treachery in war, just as later Vitoria and Suárez (*inter alia*) had cautioned against direct attacks on noncombatants—but these thinkers nonetheless viewed such restrictions within the classical lens of a unilateral *jus belli*. Bilateral restrictions, on the other hand, were first proposed by Wolff and Vattel,[89] who nonetheless conceptualized this advance by establishing a theoretical system in which *jus ad bellum* and *jus in bello* were separated into two autonomous spheres. As in Fulgosius, the first pertained to the private domain of moral conscience and the second to the public domain of law. This separation allowed for what would otherwise have been a contradictory postulation of unilateral *ad bellum* norms, on the one hand, and bilateral *in bello* norms, on the other. Deriving as it did from contrasting streams of medieval thought (just war of the scholastics and regular war of the legists), the unified system that had been proposed by Wolff and Vattel (and later adopted within international law) was inherently unstable.[90]

Against this background, it should have come as no surprise that when Michael Walzer sought to revive just war theory in the mid-twentieth century, the internal tensions of the earlier systematization would still be present. Indeed, with Walzer's attempt at establishing a more robust *jus ad bellum* against the backdrop of World War II, these tensions would be considerably enhanced. But since few philosophers working systematically on just war theory paid much attention to the historiography of their discipline,[91] it would take quite some time before the tenuous co-existence of these two prongs in Walzer's synthesis would be openly acknowledged. The ensuing debate on combatant equality has mirrored the historical dialectic described earlier: reshuffled in multiple ways, the cards have nonetheless stayed the same.[92] Whitehead's quip that Western philosophy 'consists of a series of footnotes to Plato' holds equally true of the ethics of war, with the caveat that Thucydides more rightly deserves the credit as its first progenitor.

Notes

1. For a survey of the history of philosophical reflection on war, see Endre Begby, Gregory M. Reichberg, and Henrik Syse, 'The Ethics of War. Part I: Historical Trends', *Philosophy Compass* 7:5 (2012), 316–327. Many of the primary sources referred to in this chapter may be found in Gregory M. Reichberg, Henrik Syse, and Endre Begby, *The Ethics of War: Classic and Contemporary Readings* (Oxford: Blackwell Publishing, 2006), cited henceforth as *Ethics of War*.
2. Thucydides' *Peloponnesian War* was written around 400 BC. It predated by about a century the first normative accounts of warfare to emerge in China, by Mencius (ca. 372–289) and Xun Zi (ca. 312–230). The first work of this genre to appear in India, Kautilya's *Arthaśāstra*, is traced by some scholars to the fourth century BC. For background (and primary sources) on the emergence of ethical reflection on war in different civilizations, East and West, see Gregory M. Reichberg and Henrik Syse, eds. *Religion, War, and Ethics: A Sourcebook of Textual Sources* (Cambridge: Cambridge University Press, 2014).
3. For a review and analysis of the relevant passages, see Henrik Syse, 'The Platonic Roots of Just War Doctrine: A Reading of Plato's *Republic*', *Diametros* 23 (March 2010), 104–123.
4. In this chapter, 'classical theorists' (or 'classical period in just war theorising') is shorthand for medieval and early modern thinkers. The lineage begins with Gratian and his canon law commentators in the twelfth and thirteenth centuries. Under the impetus of Alexander of Hales (ca. 1185–1245) and Saint Thomas Aquinas (ca. 1225–1274), just war subsequently became a regular topic of investigation for scholastic philosopher-theologians (henceforth referred to as 'scholastics'), especially in the sixteenth and seventeenth centuries, with Francisco de Vitoria (ca. 1492–1546), Luis de Molina (1535–1600), and Francisco Suárez (1548–1617). The 'classical' period culminated with Hugo Grotius (1583–1645).
5. On the medieval 'disputed question' method of discourse, see Marie-Dominique Chenu, *Toward Understanding Saint Thomas* (Chicago: Henry Regnery, 1964), 85–98.
6. This section draws on material in my paper 'Discontinuity in Catholic Just War? From Aquinas to the Contemporary Magisterium', *Nova & Vetera* (English Edition) 10:4 (2012), 1073–1097.
7. Grotius, *De jure belli ac pacis*, I.I.II; *Ethics of War*, 393. For the transition from the scholastic understanding of war as an action to the modern idea of war as a condition (*status*), see

Delphine Thivet, 'Thomas Hobbes: A Philosopher of War or Peace', *British Journal for the History of Philosophy* 16:4 (2008), 701–721.

8. Stephen C. Neff, *War and the Law of Nations* (Cambridge: Cambridge University Press, 2005), 58.
9. Ibid.
10. Thus, on the one hand, we find Aquinas designating *bellum* as 'one multitude [i.e., a polity] contending against another' (*Summa theologiae* [henceforth ST] II–II, q. 42, a. 1), but, on the other, he recognises that it can also signify the act whereby an individual defends himself (or others) from attack (ST II–II, q. 123, a. 5, ad 2). In the latter sense, he refers to a criminal's forcible resistance to a sentence of capital punishment as an 'unjust war' (ST II–II, q. 69, a. 4).
11. Grotius, *De jure belli ac pacis*, I.I.III.1 (*Ethics of War*, 394–395).
12. On the these military engagements 'short of war', see Neff, *War and the Law of Nations*, 215–249.
13. In this connection C. A. J. Coady (*Morality and Political Violence* [Cambridge: Cambridge University Press, 2008], 4) explains how '[t]alk of "force" makes it sound as if we are proposing to move things by using superior physical strength (as we might lift protesters out of the way without seriously harming them), when what is usually on the agenda is killing, maiming, and destroying'.
14. The linguistic move away from an approving usage of 'war' is manifest, for instance, in the UN Charter (1945). Its preamble condemns the 'scourge of war', and, after noting that 'armed force shall not be used, save in the common interest', it cites 'individual or collective self-defense if an armed attack occurs' (Article 51) and 'international enforcement measures' (Article 45) including 'action by air, sea, or land forces . . . to maintain or restore international peace and security' (Article 42) as permissible applications of military might. The phraseology of 'just war' is studiously avoided, although the actions thus allowed are of the sort that scholastic theorists would have placed under this label.
15. Neff, *War and the Law of Nations*, 163.
16. Ibid.
17. See Francisco Suárez, *Selections from Three Works* (Oxford: Clarendon Press, 1944), 851.
18. See, e.g., Pope Paul VI's 1965 speech to the General Assembly of the UN '*Never Again War!*' (reproduced in Reichberg and Syse, eds., *Religion, War, and Ethics*, 126–127).
19. For instance, the UN Charter places 'acts of aggression' alongside 'threats to the peace' and 'breaches of the peace' (Article 39, all mentioned in the singular) as the sort of inherently wrongful actions that could occasion a justifiable armed reaction.
20. See Neff, *War and the Law of Nations*, 326–334ff.
21. Francis Bacon, *The Letters and the Life*, VII, edited by James Spedding (London, 1874), 477.
22. For two prominent attempts at typologising the different approaches to the ethics of war, see Roland H. Bainton, *Christian Attitudes Toward War and Peace* (Nashville: Abingdon Press, 1960), and James Turner Johnson, *The Quest for Peace* (Princeton, NJ: Princeton University Press, 1987).
23. 'Cajetan' was the scholastic nickname for Thomas de Vio, an Italian cardinal whose short theological discussions of war (written in the period 1517–24) exerted an important influence on later scholastics and even on Grotius (see *Ethics of War*, 140–141).
24. *Politics*, bk. 1, chap. 8 (1256b25).
25. *De jure belli ac pacis* (published 1624), Prolegomena, 36, in *Ethics of War*, 392.
26. Idem, 3: 387.

27. Idem, 28: 390.
28. For these thinkers, natural right (*jus naturae*) is a manifestation of divine ordering in the created world (with respect to human agents especially), whereas *lex naturalis* is its corresponding expression in the mind.
29. Haggenmacher, *Grotius et la doctrine de la guerre juste* (Paris: Presses Universitaires de France, 1983), 11–35.
30. Augustine, *Contra Faustum manichaeum*, XXII, 74.
31. For a representative sampling of texts on war from Gratian's *Decretum*, see *Ethics of War*, 109–124.
32. On the procedure utilised by Gratian, see *Ethics of War*, 106–108.
33. The work was aptly titled *Concordia discordantium canonum* (the concordance of discordant canons), although it is better known today as the *Decretum Gratiani*.
34. Alongside this Church law there also existed a civil law. Organized as *leges* (laws) rather than *canones* (canons), it was based on several collections of legal texts (*inter alia* the *Institutes, Digest,* and *Codex*) that had been compiled by the emperor Justinian around 530 AD. The study of this *Corpus juris civilis* (as the ensemble came to be known) was not of merely historical significance to the medieval civil lawyers ('Romanists' or 'Legists') because the Holy Roman Empire was thought to be a Christian continuation of ancient Rome, and Roman law was consequently deemed to be still in force. For this reason, it was understood that a careful work of interpretation was required to bring Roman law into conformity with contemporary conditions. This civil law included provisions on the waging of war that would be discussed by Legists such as Bartolus of Saxoferrato (ca. 1313–57) or Raphaël Fulgosius (1367–1427); see *Ethics of War*, 203–209 and 227–229).
35. His famous discussion of just war (ST II–II, q. 40, a. 1, apropos the theological virtue of charity) was extended into his subsequent treatment of two specific moral virtues: military prudence (ST II–II, q. 50, a. 4) and courage (ST II–II, q. 123, a. 5).
36. See *Ethics of War*, 131–134, on Raymond's casuistry of just war.
37. On Grotius's use of historical examples, see Peter Haggenmacher, 'La pratique chez les fondateurs du droit international', in *La pratique et le droit international*, edited by Societé française pour le droit international (Paris: Pedone, 2004), 49–78, at 70–71.
38. With the possible exception of Suárez, whose approach to just war, in line with his *Metaphysical Disputations*, stands out by its abstract and speculative style (*Disputation on War* 8.8–10, in *Selections from Three Works*, 862–865).
39. All the authors of the classical period were dependent on Aristotle's *Nicomachean Ethics*, which treated moral matters as part and parcel of a distinctly practical science.
40. Ernest Nys, *Le droit de la guerre et les precurseurs de Grotius* (Brussels: Librairie Européenne, 1882).
41. Idem, 6.
42. See Peter Haggenmacher, 'La place de Francisco de Vitoria parmi les fondateurs du droit international', in *Actualité de la pensée juridique de Francisco de Vitoria*, edited by A. Truyol Serra, et al. (Brussels: Bruylant, 1988), 27–80.
43. César-Auguste Horoy, *Droit international et droit des gens public d'après le* Decretum *de Gratien* (Paris: Chevalier-Maresq, 1887).
44. Hippolyte Pissard, *La guerre sainte* (Paris: Alphonse Picard et Fils, 1912).
45. *Le droit de guerre d'après les théologiens et les canonistes du moyen-âge* (Paris: Tralin, 1911) and *La guerre devant le christianisme* (Paris: Tralin, 1912). These two books were combined

to form the book (published posthumously) for which he is best known today, *La doctrine scholastique du droit de guerre* (Paris: Pédone, 1919).

46. Letter (dated 2 November 1906) of James Brown Scott 'to R. S. Woodward, President of the Carnegie Institution of Washington, relative to a project for the republication of the classics of international law', reproduced as appendix C in Hugo Grotius, *Commentary on the Law of Prize and Booty*, vol. 1 (Oxford: Clarendon Press, 1950), 288–393, at 389.
47. Haggenmacher points out that the distortions produced by reading texts in view of subsequent developments, thereby projecting onto these texts later crystallizations of their multiple latencies, is a danger that particularly besets Grotius and other thinkers who are claimed by posterity as 'fathers' of international law (*Grotius et la doctrine de la guerre juste*, 588, 605–612).
48. See Peter Pavel Remec, *The Position of the Individual in International Law according to Grotius and Vattel* (The Hague: Nijoff, 1960), and Haggenmacher, *Grotius et la doctrine de la guerre juste*, 615–629.
49. ST, II–II, q. 40, a. 1 (in *Ethics of War*, 177).
50. *La doctrine scholastique du droit de guerre*, 1.
51. Idem, 250–275.
52. For a summary, see his *Killing in War* (Oxford: Oxford University Press, 2009), 6–7.
53. Idem, section 5, ch. 2, 'Le probabilism et les controversies de la fin du XVIème siècle', 254–259.
54. On the 'war contract' as it was critically discussed by Suárez and other Spanish scholastics, see Haggenmacher, *Grotius et la doctrine de la guerre juste*, 292–295.
55. Paris: Éditions A. Pedone.
56. See Henri de Waele, 'Commemorating Robert Regout (1896–1942). A Chapter from the History of Public International Law Revised', *Journal of the History of International Law* 7 (2005), 81–92. After his death, Regout, a Jesuit, was succeeded in his chair of public international law at the University of Nijmegen by a Franciscan, Leo J. C. Beaufort, who earlier had written a work on the classical just war roots of humanitarian intervention: *La guerre come instrument de secours ou de punition* (The Hague: Martinius Nijhoff, 1933).
57. See Regout, *La doctrine de la guerre juste*, 296–297 where he sums up this assessment.
58. Idem, 269.
59. Regout, idem, 157–168, 266–273.
60. Regout explains (idem, 309–310) how the distinction between offensive and defensive war is itself (when used technically) morally neutral: it refers solely to the factual question of which party to a conflict has opened the hostilities. Concrete cases of offensive and defensive war could be deemed just or unjust depending on the circumstances.
61. Regout employs the terms 'redressement', 'vindication', and 'restitution' interchangeably, usually by contrast to 'punition' and 'défense' (in the narrow sense of repelling attack); see idem, 291–297.
62. See idem, 168–169, where Regout notes how Vitoria never uses the term 'punitive war' (*bellum vindicativum*), preferring instead to speak of war 'for the sake of vindication' (*bellum ad vindicandum*), with the understanding that this punishment can rightly be exercised only *post bellum* (or after capture in the course of a war).
63. For Regout's summary of this critique, see idem, 283–290.
64. Idem, 249.
65. See Note 17.
66. See Haggenmacher, *Grotius et la doctrine de la guerre juste*, 595–597.

67. Unlike the authors mentioned earlier (Vanderpol, Regout, and, today, Haggenmacher) who have studied just war from the perspective of legal history, James Turner Johnson has followed the approach opened up by Church historian Roland H. Bainton, whose widely read *Christian Attitudes Toward War and Peace* (Nashville: Abingdon Press, 1960) viewed just war through the lens of religious (especially Christian) history.
68. James Turner Johnson, 'The Broken Tradition', *National Interest* (Fall 1996), 27–36, at 33; 'Toward Reconstructing the *Jus ad Bellum*', *Monist* 57 (1973), 461–488.
69. 'The Broken Tradition', 33.
70. Idem, 27.
71. To cite the words of Johnson's doctoral mentor Paul Ramsey (*The Just War* [New York: Schribner, 1968], xv).
72. Ibid.
73. René Coste, *Le problème du droit de guerre dans la pensée de Pie XII* (Paris: Aubier, 1962).
74. Idem, 288.
75. See, for instance, Luigi Sturzo, *The International Community and the Right of War* (London: George Allen & Unwin, 1929), and Joseph Joblin, *L'Église et la guerre* (Paris: Desclée de Brouwer, 1988).
76. See the essays assembled in the special issue (vol. 8.3, 2009) of the *Journal of Military Ethics* on the conceptualization of just war in the thought of James Turner Johnson.
77. For an overview of this debate, see Christian Barry and Lars Christie, 'The Moral Equality of Combatants', this volume.
78. On this terminology, see David Rodin and Henry Shue, 'Introduction', in *Just and Unjust Warriors: The Moral and Legal Status of Soldiers*, edited by David Rodin and Henry Shue (Oxford: Oxford University Press, 2008), 1–18.
79. Michael Walzer, *Just and Unjust Wars*, 2nd ed. (New York: Basic Books, 1992), 21. Walzer's view that the *ad bellum* inequality of belligerents (unilateral application of just cause) is fully compatible with the *in bello* equality of combatants (bilateral application of the laws of armed conflict) was earlier proposed by the legal scholar Henri Meyrowitz, *Le principe de l'égalité des belligérents devant the droit de la guerre* (Paris: Pedone, 1970).
80. 'The Morality of War and the Law of War', in *Just and Unjust Warriors*, 19–43, and *Killing in War.*
81. See Syse, idem.
82. See Gregory M. Reichberg, 'The Moral Equality of Combatants', ch. 10 of *Thomas Aquinas on War and Peace* (New York: Cambridge University Press, 2017), 223–256.
83. The expression *regular war* ('guerre réglée') emerged in the eighteenth century from Vattel's concept of 'war in due form' (*la guerre en forme*) in his *Droit des Gens* (1758), book 3, ch. 12 (*Ethics of War*, 514–516); it signified a war that was conducted according to mutually accepted rules; hence, those who fight in such a war are termed 'regular soldiers', and, collectively, they constitute a 'regular army'.
84. The following two paragraphs draw on material in my paper 'Just War and Regular War: Competing Paradigms', in *Just and Unjust Warriors*, edited by D. Rodin and H. Shue, 193–213.
85. Bk. III, ch. III–IX (*Ethics of War*, 423–429).
86. Although Grotius does not say so explicitly, this practice was also widely accepted in his own day. To ignore it, in favour of the theological teaching of Aquinas and his successors, would imperil the credibility of his system in the eyes of his contemporaries. Grotius's account of formally declared public war (and the special bilateral effects that follow from

it) represents his attempt to assimilate a viewpoint that, on the whole, cuts against his main line of argumentation in the *De jure belli ac pacis*. On this, see Haggenmacher, 'La pratique chez les fondateurs du droit international', 49–78, especially 73–74.

87. Bk. III, ch. IV, section IV, 'why such effects have been introduced' (*Ethics of War*, 426).
88. After summarising the wartime liberties that could be allowed from the point of view of 'external justice', Grotius details subsequently the moral restrictions ('moderation') that should be observed by the just belligerent from the point of view of 'internal justice' (bk. III, ch. XI–XII; *Ethics of War*, 430–434).
89. For the relevant passages, see the chapters devoted to Wolff and Vattel in the *Ethics of War*, 469–474, 504–517, respectively.
90. See the conclusion to Haggenmacher, 'Just War and Regular War in Sixteenth Century Spanish Doctrine', *International Revue of the Red Cross* 290 (1992): 434–445.
91. By comparison with philosophers, lawyers writing on war have generally been more attuned to the historical dimensions of their discipline (see, e.g., Ian Brownlie's 'Historical Exposition of the Legal Regulation of the Use of Force by States', in his *International Law and the Use of Force by States* [Oxford: Clarendon Press, 1963], 1–18). In connection with the issue presently under discussion, Yoram Dinstein astutely notes that 'Historically, the notion of equality between belligerents has formed the underpinning of *jus in bello*. It was unchallenged as long as States were at liberty to go to war against each other. . . . The principle of equality was not easily reconcilable with the just war doctrine' (*War, Aggression and Self-Defense*, 3rd ed. [Cambridge: Cambridge University Press, 2001 (originally published 1988)], 140.
92. See McMahan's acknowledgement of this state of affairs in his *Killing in War*, 238, note 26.

CHAPTER 4

DEEP MORALITY AND THE LAWS OF WAR

JEREMY WALDRON

1. The Ethics of Moral Criticism

In this chapter, I consider the way we evaluate the laws and customs of armed conflict and the responsibilities we take on when we criticize existing laws and customs and propose or entertain possible changes to them.

By 'we', I mean 'we philosophers', particularly moral philosophers. We bring our understanding of moral values, principles, and distinctions to a set of established legal or customary rules, and we use that understanding to evaluate the rules as they exist, assessing them in terms of how well they serve the values that they purport to -serve or how well they serve the values that ought to lie behind rules of this kind. This is something we do routinely with laws and customs of all sorts in normative ethics. We do it with laws on narcotics and laws prohibiting various kinds of discrimination; we do it with the constitutional rules that establish the basic structure of our polity; we do it with laws that confer rights and responsibilities on banks and corporations; and we do it with the elementary rules of criminal law. To be sure, evaluating laws is not the whole of normative ethics. We also evaluate practices like eating animals and practices like failing to contribute money to those who are desperately poor, even when these practices are not embodied in positive law. But evaluating positive law is a very important part of the mission of normative moral philosophy, and there is no reason to suppose that it should not be applied also to the laws of war, to international humanitarian law, and to national law also, to the extent that the laws and customs of armed conflict have been incorporated therein.

Most philosophers understand that this practice of evaluating positive law has an ethics of its own, although the sense of ethical responsibility has diminished somewhat in recent years. It used to be said both by utilitarians and deontologists that, although one had a right to engage in critical evaluation of the laws, this right was always conjoined with a duty to obey. 'Argue as much as you will and about what you will; only obey!' said Immanuel Kant in his 1784 essay *What Is Enlightenment?*[1] And, in the same era, the utilitarian Jeremy Bentham said almost exactly the same: 'what is the motto of a good citizen? To obey punctually; to censure freely'.[2] In the twentieth century, philosophers were less willing to accept the view that a law that was open to moral criticism should nevertheless be obeyed punctually. Some thought this an affront to moral autonomy[3]; few paid heed to David Hume's suggestion, two centuries earlier, that there was something pathological about philosophers' obsession with the very rare cases where disobedience or resistance might be justified[4]; and almost nobody worried about the ancient concern in the *Crito* that philosophically motivated disobedience might in some circumstances do serious damage to the whole legal enterprise.[5]

The concerns of Hume and Socrates are not just about the impact of the philosopher's disobedience or the example he sets by his actions; they are concerns about the impact of his teaching. Laws depend on opinion even more than on force. Inculcation of the opinion that a given body of law, governing a certain area of life and action, is morally disreputable as it stands might do damage to the whole enterprise of legal regulation in that area because although philosophical activity can undermine a law in the opinion of its subjects, it is in its nature not capable of establishing any other, better law in its place.

These concerns may not be particularly important so far as the ordinary positive law of a society is concerned. Laws governing ordinary social life and business and personal interactions are usually strong and resilient, and, in modern circumstances, they can survive a considerable amount of noncompliance and disrepute. They are much stronger now than Athenian laws were in the time of Socrates. But international law is another matter, and there is, I think, a particular problem with what we call the laws and customs of armed conflict—that is, the laws that attempt to govern the horrors of organized fighting among the armed forces of our societies. These laws are not robust, they are not particularly resilient, they are difficult to enforce, and they depend largely on the voluntary self-application of problematic and contestable norms to the conduct of groups of men who find themselves in circumstances of mortal danger. It is the thesis of this chapter that we should take special care in bringing the resources of moral philosophy to bear on the evaluation of such laws.

2. Laws-of-War Revisionism

I focus my concerns on some suggestions made recently by an eminent moral philosopher about the deep moral justification (or lack of justification) of one of the most important laws governing armed conflict—the law of distinction. As it stands, the law of distinction requires those engaged in war to distinguish among targets: they may fire upon combatants (people in uniform or people openly carrying weapons), but they may not fire upon civilians.[6] It is not always complied with: there was an egregious violation by the United States in the deliberate use of weapons of mass destruction against Japanese civilians in 1945. But it continues to be regarded as a more-or-less viable rule, and most countries have incorporated it into their own military law and military doctrine.

However, some philosophers are on record as saying that this is a bad rule, one that lacks any justification for the distinctions it draws because it exposes to deadly attack many people who are morally innocent (like conscripts fighting in a just war against an aggressor) and immunizes against attack many people who are guilty (like civilian politicians who instigated unjust aggression and voters who supported it). Jeff McMahan is one of our most thoughtful philosophical writers about the laws of war, and he thinks that there are serious moral problems with the existing principle of distinction. In his article 'The Ethics of Killing in War', McMahan argues that there is no moral justification for any blanket prohibition on intentionally attacking civilians.[7] He thinks one could make a moral case for saying that certain civilians are properly liable to intentional attack—for example, civilians who share responsibility for an unjust war. This is because he believes that, in the eyes of critical morality, 'it is moral responsibility for an unjust threat that is the principal basis of liability to [be the target] of defensive (or preservative) force':

> The requirement of distinction should then hold that combatants must discriminate between those who are morally responsible for an unjust threat, or for a grievance that provides a just cause [for war], and those who are not. It should state that while it is permissible to attack the former, it is not permissible intentionally to attack the latter.[8]

It follows, on McMahan's approach, that soldiers who are not themselves engaged in an unjust war—soldiers who are resisting unjust aggression, for example—are not legitimate targets, whereas civilians who *are* responsible for unjust aggression may be legitimate targets of deadly force.

Notice that McMahan is not criticizing the idea of a principle of distinction. His argument does not challenge the principle 'in its most generic formulation, which is simply that combatants must discriminate between legitimate and illegitimate targets'.[9] Instead, he thinks that we need to complicate the categories we use when we apply the generic distinction by introducing a distinction between guilty and innocent civilians (and also guilty and innocent combatants) on the basis of moral responsibility for war. And he thinks this should lead us to adjust our sense of morally appropriate and morally inappropriate behaviour for soldiers. This, he says, is what morality requires.[10]

3. Law and Deep Morality

But McMahan is also cognizant of the ethical considerations that govern the philosophical activity of engaging in these moral arguments. Although he believes the case he has made provides a basis 'for the reevaluation of the rules we have inherited',[11] he acknowledges that it might be 'dangerous to tamper with rules that already command a high degree of allegiance'.[12] Perhaps any rules are better than none in this fraught area of human conflict. As I said before, destructive philosophical criticism—even justified criticism—cannot itself build up new rules in place of those it discredits. McMahan acknowledges that it may be that 'the stakes are too high to allow for much experimentation with alternatives'.[13] So he contemplates whether the critic might have a duty to pull his philosophical punches, even to the point of suppressing 'the genuine deeper principles' that morality generates.[14] But McMahan is hesitant about this: 'Must the morality of war be self-effacing in this way? I confess that I do not know what to say about this'.[15]

What McMahan *is* sure about is that a moral account of who ought to be targeted in war is not the same as a critique of the positive law that exists to cover these matters:

> [T]he account I have developed of the deep morality of war is not an account of the laws of war. The formulation of the laws of war is a wholly different task, one that I have not attempted and that has to be carried out with a view to the consequences of the adoption and enforcement of the laws or conventions. It is, indeed, entirely clear that the laws of war must diverge significantly from the deep morality of war as I have presented it.[16]

He seems to believe that it is a good idea for the laws of war to continue to prohibit and punish intentional attacks on civilians (even guilty ones). Considered abstractly as normative propositions, the legal rules may be open to moral criticism. But they do not only answer to the moral philosopher's criteria. As they stand, the conventional rules 'may be well suited to the regulation of the conduct of war in conditions in which there are few institutional constraints'.[17] And McMahan goes on to suggest that it is 'possible that the rules of *jus in bello* coincide rather closely with the laws that would be optimal for regulating conduct in battle. These rules have evolved over many centuries and have been refined, tested, and adapted to the experience of war as the nature of war has itself evolved'.[18] Deep moral critique, it seems, is not everything. 'Ideally' we should wish for laws that are as close as possible to what morality requires, but, in the real world, we must expect some divergence.[19]

All of this attests to the seriousness with which McMahan regards the laws and customs of armed conflict even as he undertakes a deep moral critique of one of their leading principles. I shall not say very much more in this chapter about the details of his critique, but I will try to explore the reasons that should lead—and I think mostly do lead—McMahan and other moral philosophers to take the positive law of the matter very seriously.

4. Conventional Rules?

Why exactly must deep morality and positive law be separated—in this arena—in this way? One answer McMahan gives has to do with the conventional character of the latter.

Criticizing a convention on moral grounds seems a little beside the point: for example, the point of the convention about driving on the right (or the left) is not to be morally right but simply to coordinate behaviour. And if the convention fails because of fatuous moral critique, the costs are considerable. Conventions exist for a reason. '[T]he laws of war', says McMahan, 'are conventions established to mitigate the savagery of war'.[20] That is in itself a moral aim, but not one that entitles us to unsettle the content of the convention itself:

> It is in everyone's interests that such conventions be recognized and obeyed.... Given that general adherence to certain conventions is better for everyone, all have a moral reason to recognize and abide by these conventions. For it is rational for each side in a conflict to adhere to them only if the other side does. Thus if one side breaches the understanding that the conventions will be followed, it may cease to be rational or morally required for the other side to persist in its adherence to them. A valuable device for limiting the violence will thereby be lost, and that will be worse for all.[21]

This claim, that the rule protecting civilians is best understood as a valuable convention, is quite common in the literature. One of its well-known proponents is George Mavrodes.[22] Noncombatant immunity, says Mavrodes, is best thought of in relation to 'a convention which substitutes for warfare a certain form of limited combat'.[23] We could substitute single combat for warfare, but it is unlikely that convention will be viable. So we substitute limited fighting among designated participants—large numbers of participants, but not as large as the number that would be involved in total warfare between all the members of rival communities. Mavrodes observes that the convention we have may actually be inferior to some other viable and morally less disreputable convention. But he denies that this means we have now have a duty to follow the improved convention that we can imagine. '[T]he results of [our] acting in conformity with a preferable convention which is not widely observed may be much worse than the results of acting in conformity with a less desirable convention which *is* widely observed'.[24] It would be like deciding, for our part, to drive on the left in the United States, on the ground that driving on the left was somehow better than driving on the right, when most others were not convinced of this.

Still, neither thinker believes that the importance of following existing and observed conventions renders moral critique redundant. If a case could in fact be made for single combat as an alternative, then Mavrodes reckons we would have a 'moral obligation to promote its adoption'.[25] And McMahan's view is that, to the extent that we have any sort of choice at all, we should seek to establish conventions for warfare that are 'best suited to get combatants on both sides to conform their action as closely as possible to the constraints imposed by the deep morality of war'.[26]

Actually I do not think the rule protecting civilians *can* be understood as a convention in the classic sense.[27] In the case of the rule about driving on the right, we know that obeying the rule makes sense for a given party only if most or all others are obeying it, and the situation in which most or all others are obeying it is better for all concerned than is a situation in which there is no rule. But this does not seem to be the case with the rule protecting civilians. When two groups, *A* and *B*, are locked in armed conflict, it is easy to imagine that any one of them, *A*, would most prefer that *B* observe the rule protecting civilians while *A* does not. After all, following the rule is costly. What could be better from *A*'s selfish point of view than that *B* bear the costs of refraining from attacking *A*'s civilians while *A* wages war in an indiscriminate manner? In a classic game of coordination, it makes no sense to violate the regularity that one expects others to conform to. But in the situation of war, it often does.

More importantly, it can also make moral sense for one side, say *B*, to continue following the rule that protects civilians even when *A* does not. This is because the rationale of the rule is partly altruistic rather than purely self-interested. One follows the rule out of concern for civilians on the other side, as well as for civilians on one's own side. The rationale usually given for the rule—mitigating the horrors of warfare—recognizes this. *B*'s refraining from targeting civilians obviously mitigates the horrors of warfare to a certain extent even if *A* does target them.[28] So, I think McMahan is making a mistake when he writes that it is rational for each side in a conflict to adhere to the rules of war only if the other side does: 'if one side breaches the understanding that the conventions will be followed, it may cease to be rational or morally required for the other side to persist in its adherence to them'.[29]

For these reasons, I do not think the rule about civilians can usefully be regarded as a convention in the classic sense. It lacks the crucial element of interdependence of interests. Some might say that the relevant interdependence of interests is established through the tit-for-tat retaliation that is typically associated with violations of the norms we are discussing. If *A* violates the rule, *A* might expect retaliation from *B*. Or *A* might expect that *B* will not long persevere in its observance of the rule once it becomes clear that *A* is not following it. And the prospect of this retaliation may lead *A* back to conformity. But these prospects do not convert the relevant norm into a convention; rather, these prospects might be associated with any norm of whatever character. They do not show that the laws of war are in themselves conventions like rules of language or rules of the road.

5. Technicality and Administrability

Still, the analysis put forward by Mavrodes and McMahan points us to a couple of things that *are* important. First, it warns us away from essaying too severe a moral assessment of the content of the rule. This warning is appropriate, trivially, in the case of pure conventions: who cares whether driving on the left has some scintilla of moral superiority over driving on the right? But it may also be appropriate for other reasons in situations that are not purely conventional.

When we are talking about positive laws, we need to take account of considerations of legal technicality that may make a norm look arbitrary by the standards of moral philosophers. There are several points to consider here.

First, the relevant norms have to be administered among people who almost certainly disagree about justice and guilt in relation to the armed conflict in question. From a practical point of view, it may be impossible to administer norms using words like 'just' and 'guilty' in their traditional moral senses or to impose tests about whose application there is likely to be irresolvable disagreement. McMahan acknowledges this:

> Perhaps most obviously, the fact that most combatants believe that their cause is just means that the laws of war must be neutral between just combatants and unjust combatants, as the traditional theory insists that the requirements of *jus in bello* are.[30]

Laws *in bello* have to use simple categories like the distinction between members of the organized military and civilians even though these categories are almost certainly both over- and underinclusive by moral standards. But the moral standards by which we judge them to be so—or by which McMahan judges them to be so—could not possibly be administered practicably in these circumstances of dissensus.

A second feature of legal technicality has to do with the reasonableness of the burdens that the laws and customs of armed conflict lay upon combatants. The laws of war (especially *ius in bello*) have to be administered not only in circumstances of moral disagreement, but in circumstances of panic, anger, and great danger. The moral burdens they impose have to be shouldered by those whose lives may be imminently at risk as a result of compliance. With regard to some of the laws of war, we just accept this: we say, for example, that prisoners are not to be executed even if this is the only way for their captors to avoid defeat and death. But too much of this, and the laws of war become utopian and impossible to enforce—especially to the extent that they rely on self-administration by the forces concerned. What is true of danger is also true of anger. We impose certain absolute prohibitions that have to stand up against and curb the worst excesses of the anger that combat involves: for example, in no circumstances may a military unit proceed on the basis that no quarter is to be offered to its opponents. So, sometimes the laws of war defy anger, just as in some respects they defy fear. But, again, a delicate balance must be struck; for the most part, the laws of war must work around the emotions like fear and anger that the circumstances of warfare impose rather than assuming they do not exist (just because morally they should not exist). Moreover, we must not assume that this is a balance that can be arrived at in the philosopher's armchair. Practicable rules have to emerge from the experience of war itself. As McMahan himself says about the existing laws of war (whose deep morality he deprecates): '[t]hese rules have evolved over many centuries and have been refined, tested, and adapted to the experience of war as the nature of war has itself evolved'.[31]

Third, laws designed to govern conduct in the fog of war cannot take account of every detail that a deep moral theory will take account of. Most laws *in bello* are self-administered by individual soldiers and their unit commanders. A deep or refined moral principle might require of our combatants a delicate inquiry into the guilt and moral status of every person or unit fired upon. But that would be utterly unworkable. Even if it is crude by moral standards, some criterion (such as the wearing of uniforms) has to be used instead. No doubt these criteria are conventional in character. They place what may seem to a philosopher undue emphasis on trivialities like uniforms or insignia and the open (visible) carrying of weapons, and they denounce, again with what must seem like uncalled-for vehemence, the perfidious use of flags and signage of various sorts. But these conventional criteria are indispensable for the administration of any norm like the rule protecting civilians in the circumstances where they have to prevail.[32]

For all these reasons, we should be wary of any 'deep' moral assessment that condemns the laws governing armed conflict on the basis of their apparent arbitrariness. My reservations about 'deep' moral critique here are rather like the conventionalist's criticism. But the apparent arbitrariness is not a function of conventionality; instead, it results from the technical demands of administrability in this area.

6. Deadly Serious Rules

I said there were two respects in which the convention analysis might be helpful to us in understanding the limits of deep moral critique even though it is not strictly applicable. The first—the apparent arbitrariness of the rules—we have just discussed. The second has to do with the distinction between the moral quality of the content of the rules and the moral importance of the telos of the rules, by which I mean the point of having rules at all in this area.

Although the conventionalist account is mistaken, what McMahan says about the point of these rules is important. The laws of armed conflict, he says, are 'established to mitigate the savagery of war'.[33] This provides an important answer to an imaginable silly question. In response either to the conventionalist account or to the account I gave in Section 5, someone may ask 'what is the big deal about killing civilians if the rule prohibiting it is just a technical device? Is the infringement of this rule a matter of any greater significance than a breach of local convention? If so, why do we judge these actions so vehemently, using terms of moral condemnation normally reserved for violations of the most serious moral absolutes?'

As it stands, the question is corrupt and irresponsible. But there is a serious issue to be faced: if we accept that the rule about civilians has important conventional elements as well as technical elements that distinguish it from familiar moral norms, how should we think about the seriousness of violating it?

We can see the shape of an answer even for a classic convention like the rule of the road. Nothing seems more trivial than the choice of driving on the left or driving on the right. But if we do not coordinate on one or the other, then the result will be chaos and paralysis at best and very likely carnage on the roads. The conventional rule aims to avoid this. But that underlying goal will not be served at all unless we choose—and stick with—a convention. The point, then, is that the justification for having a convention generates a reason for observing it. Now, in some instances, violating a convention has only trivial consequences. This is true of most linguistic conventions: misuse of the apostrophe is an example. In other cases, violating an apparently trivial rule will result in mayhem. In these cases, the convention may be arbitrary, but it is still a *deadly serious* convention.[34]

Much the same is true of technical rules. If the content of the rule about civilians is largely a technicality, it is nevertheless a *deadly serious technicality*. It is deadly serious in its responsiveness to an important underlying reason; namely, the mitigation of the savageries of war and deadly serious in the consequences of any violation. Even though the rule is administered in a technical way, looking at superficial things like uniforms to make the distinctions it prescribes, still, these features of its administration have to do with the practicalities of avoiding these consequences. Fewer bad consequences will be avoided if we try to use rules that *look* serious by the standards of deep moral critique. Unless the rules look arbitrary and technical, it will be hard to administer them in a way that avoids the terrible consequences that they aim to avoid. Maybe nothing is easily administered in this domain. But rules that look respectable in themselves by the standards of deep moral critique will not have a prayer of avoiding the terrible consequences—which is the point of having rules in this domain in the first place.

I have stuck so far with McMahan's characterization of the telos: 'to mitigate the savagery of war'. However, this is not just a consequentialist matter. The laws of war may be technical, but they have to do their work not just against a background of danger, destruction, and death, but against a background of *murder*. What I mean by this is that the norm we are considering—the rule protecting civilians—does not prohibit things that, apart from its operation, would be perfectly permissible. It is not like a set of parking regulations, introducing technical prohibition into an area where there was no prohibition before. On the contrary, the rule that prohibits attacks on civilians prohibits something that—apart from the laws of war—would already be a grave moral offence. This is because the default position, apart from any technicality, is that intentionally killing or attacking *any* human being is prohibited. The laws of armed conflict provide an exception to that; they establish a Hohfeldian privilege in relation to what is otherwise strenuously forbidden. And the rule protecting civilians is to be understood as a limitation on the scope of that privilege. Absent the laws and customs of armed conflict, almost all killing in war would be wrong.[35] The default position is emphatically *not* that you are allowed to kill anyone you like and that the rule about civilians has encroached upon *that*. The situation instead is that the laws of war have drawn an artificial line withdrawing the prohibition on killing from a certain class of killings (namely, killings of combatants). And the rule about civilians reflects the point that this withdrawal of the prohibition on killing from a certain class of killings is a partial, not a wholesale, withdrawal. So, killing a civilian is prohibited, not on account of the operation of a technical rule protecting civilians, but on account of the limit that this rule represents so far as the artificial privilege of killing combatants is concerned.

Is my account of the background too simple? Well, it is already pretty complicated. But we should also acknowledge that the moral rules prohibiting killing in general provide for various qualifications. The most notable is the exception for self-defence. But the rule protecting civilians also has a self-defence qualification built into it: a civilian aiming a rifle may be killed. That apart, killing a civilian is simply prohibited. Sometimes

I get the impression that McMahan believes that culpable responsibility for unjust war constitutes a justification for what would otherwise be murder. But I know of no plausible account of homicide that, apart from this context, yields anything like an entitlement to kill people who support unjust aggression. Crimes against peace do not now carry the death penalty, and nothing morally convincing can be built on the premise that they do.

Other consequences also follow from this understanding of the rule protecting civilians as a residuum of the rule against murder. Some of them are philosophically quite interesting. If a given rule seems like a convention or a technicality, it is tempting to think that it must be supported by consequentialist considerations—namely, the good consequences of setting up this artificial arrangement. And it is tempting to think such a rule must also be vulnerable to consequentialist considerations when the advantages of violating or abandoning it seem greatly to outweigh the good consequences of supporting it. Someone (call him Harry Truman) may say that if the point of the rule protecting civilians is to mitigate the horrors of warfare, then maybe, in an extreme situation, that same rule may be undermined by that teleology: for example, maybe the horrors of war can be mitigated more decisively by the use of terror weapons on large cities to bring a long and savage war to a speedy end. My point, though, is that this sort of calculation rests on a misleading account of the rule's underlying normative force. The basic normative force of the rule is deontological: 'Thou shalt not kill'. The wrongness of killing civilians is established independently of the goal of mitigating the horrors of warfare: killing civilians is murder.[36] Admittedly, the Truman calculation may work for those who give a consequentialist account even of the wrongness of murder; in which case, their principles will be vulnerable all the way down to consequentialist calculations. Or, it may work for those whose deontological account of murder does not have the force to withstand certain consequentialist considerations: I have in mind various forms of 'threshold deontology'.[37] Apart from such conceptions, the rule protecting civilians will not be vulnerable to Truman-style calculations. If one wants to work around it, one has to work around it as (the residuum of) a norm deontologically prohibiting murder, not as a merely technical arrangement.

This, then, is the account we should give of the importance of (what appears to be) a technical rule protecting noncombatant civilians. It looks arbitrary; it looks like something that is just a technical device. In fact, it is a rule that stands in for the general prohibition on murder in an area where murder is in danger of becoming commonplace. The rule does not only seek to mitigate the savagery of warfare, although it does do that. It also represents elementary moral restraint in the midst of the murderous horrors of war.

7. The Vulnerability of Law

In Sections 1–3, I considered the ethical issues that are raised when a philosopher offers a moral critique of rules of positive law. How dangerous is it to write and publish such a critique?

There are two things to consider: (1) there is the direct harm involved in any violations that result from the critique, and there is also (2) the prospect of damage to the rule itself and to the prospect of rule-based governance in this area. So far as (1) is concerned, we have to consider the likelihood that the critique will lead to violations of the rule times the seriousness of the harm involved in these violations. In some cases, this product may be negligible. The rule itself may not be particularly important. Or, even if it is a deadly serious rule, it may be that violations of it lead to good consequences, not bad consequences: that may be the gist of the critique. Of course, if McMahan's critique of the traditional principle of distinction is accepted, then it may be that fewer innocent people (including innocent combatants) will be killed and fewer guilty noncombatants will escape their just deserts. Or perhaps there are simply no consequences. Those whose conduct is supposed to be governed by the rule may be uninterested in moral criticism, and they will just comply (or not comply) with the rule no matter what the philosophers say about its moral quality.

But we cannot be sure that this so, and, in particular, we cannot be sure that there will be no consequences under heading (2). In the case of some conventional rules, moral critique is unlikely to have an impact. People follow (or don't follow) the rules of the road or the grammatical rule about the use of the apostrophe without any thought at all about the moral quality of the rule. It does not follow that violations are harmless. Some are, and some are not. But with some technical rules, like the one we have been considering, an element of moral consciousness may be an indispensable part of the rule's presence for those whose conduct it purports to govern. As we have seen, McMahan considers this possibility:

> Suppose . . . that . . . if combatants are to be sufficiently motivated to obey certain rules in the conduct of war, they will have to believe that those rules really do constitute the deep morality of war. If it is imperative to get them to respect certain conventions, must we present the conventions as the deep morality of war and suppress the genuine deeper principles? Must the morality of war be self-effacing in this way? I confess that I do not know what to say about this.[38]

This toys with the idea of a legal rule being sustained by a sort of noble lie. It worries that if the troops become aware of the serious moral reservations that the philosophers (and perhaps their general officers) have about the rule, they may be less inclined to follow it. Following it is already very demanding: they have to refrain from firing on civilians even when that would make them safer in a situation of terrible danger. They may not be disposed to incur this risk unless they are sure that the rule represents what morality really requires, perhaps unless they internalize it as such. At the same time, they may not think of themselves as competent to figure out the rule's moral status; they may be inclined to defer implicitly in this regard to others who are supposed to have some moral expertise. Knowing that those others doubt the moral force of the rule may therefore undermine their willingness to follow it, particularly when following it is very demanding.

Are all legal rules vulnerable in this way—or all legal rules that present themselves as morally justified? This may once have been true: I think Socrates contemplated the possibility that the laws of Athens were fragile in this way in considering the impact of his possible disobedience.[39] But it is no longer generally true: in many areas of life, positive law is so robust and funded so well with the resources of the state and its means of coercion that we need not consider the impact of our actions on it. Law flourishes when it takes on a life of its own and becomes a sort of social reality that, in large part, can be understood separately from the moral judgments that people bring to it. It flourishes when it becomes routine, internalized in the lives of individuals as habit and training or in the life of a society through institutionalization. Law never works well without relying on self-application as its basic mode of administration.[40] But it flourishes when that self-application becomes routinized and when systems of enforcement are routinized alongside it. Mostly, then, when we criticize the law, we don't have to worry about whether the law in question and the rule of law will survive.

However, the laws of war—and in particular the principle of distinction—may be one area where the fragility of the legal enterprise does still have to be taken into account. For one thing, these norms rely for their viability mostly on *unsupervised* self-application, on the part of individual soldiers and unit commanders. There are sporadic post facto prosecutions for war crimes, and these may become more common with the institution of the International Criminal Court. But, for the immediate application of the rules protecting civilians, we rely on the discipline and military doctrines of the world's armed forces. So anything that distracts from a sustained willingness to observe the rule voluntarily is a danger to the rule itself. We need to worry about a possible collapse in the rules so far as ordinary soldiers are concerned, and we also need to worry about a possible collapse or transformation in whatever there is in the way of inculcation and enforcement of these laws, not to mention the politically motivated impatience of civilian leaders with rules that seem 'quaint and obsolete' in comparison with the urgency of their security concerns.[41]

I have already made the obvious point that the laws we are considering have to operate in a most unpropitious environment. They operate in circumstances of great danger and anger, circumstances in which restraints on behaviour are already largely withdrawn. In those circumstances, we know these laws are observed imperfectly at best and sometimes not at all. Much modern warfare involves anti-terrorist operations, and the laws of armed conflict have to secure compliance in an environment in which one side, as matter of military doctrine, repudiates the laws of war—that's what terrorism involves—while still claiming the benefit of the other side's compliance. The temptation on the part of otherwise law-abiding forces to respond in kind is evident.

Any rule or any convention can withstand a certain amount of violation and still survive. But the distance from 'a certain number of violations' to the tipping point may be quite small; the amount of noncompliance it can stand and still survive may be quite limited. In the case of the laws of war, I believe they are quite close to this threshold most of the time. The principle of distinction is already honoured often in the breach and sometimes defied by whole units (indeed, by whole military organizations). The knock-on effects of perceived violations, especially if these seem like acts of policy, are likely to be extensive. Because of what is at stake for any group in armed conflict, because of the problem of the costs of compliance, because of the temptations of positional advantage and the fear of being taken advantage of, any sense that others are securing an advantage in armed conflict by violating these norms is likely to lead to other groups' violating them as well. We should remember that, despite the large numbers of people actually engaged in combat, the numbers of individual armed organizations with military doctrines is quite small (numbered in the hundreds, not the millions). In these circumstances, visible violations as a matter of policy by powerful entities or even a greater tolerance for violations as a matter of military discipline may bring us quickly and closely to the tipping point at which the rule simply collapses. No doubt some of these violations are just a product of panic, anger, or cynicism, and we can't blame the moral philosophers for that. But a widespread belief, published abroad by the philosophers, that there is nothing much morally to be said for the existing rules can certainly contribute to a collapse.

Maybe collapse of the existing rule would be no bad thing if a better rule could be put in its place. The revisionist critique aims to prevent certain killings that it regards as morally wrongful, but which are permitted by the existing laws that the critique endangers. But that may not be enough to outweigh the bad effects of the critique. A sense that existing rules are morally disreputable or 'merely' technical can undermine the force of any laws in this area. That is what is distinct about the laws of war. The establishment of new positive law in an environment fraught with stress and peril is barely possible through legislation; governance by rules probably has to emerge first as custom before being positivized as formal law. Our experience of that is that it can take decades or centuries. The most likely impact of moral criticism then—if it has any impact at all—is that it will weaken existing law, precarious already for the reasons I have stated, without putting anything better or anything at all in its place.

8. The Ethics of Moral Criticism, Again

It may seem a bit much to saddle the philosopher Jeff McMahan and his fellow revisionists with all this. McMahan is not urging anyone to open fire on guilty civilians. He is just engaging in a familiar moral inquiry, and all he has done is reserve the right to reach his own judgments on the matter of distinction in warfare—nonplussed by existence of contrary legal norms. Not only that, but McMahan and the other revisionists can be read as exploring the implications of other norms to which we are also committed—norms about human rights, about the moral equality between the members of different societies, about the importance of responsibility, about the overriding importance of justice, and the distinction between guilt and innocence. It is not their fault if these premises do not yield as conclusions the norms that we are comfortable with.

Still, I go back to the starting point of this essay. Someone who takes it upon him- or herself to offer public criticism of existing legal norms—even when that criticism is justified—does take on a certain ethical burden. A moral criticism of an existing legal rule can have an effect on it even when the critic does not urge disobedience. Legal rules are sometimes insecure; sometimes they rest on little more than opinion. And reservation of the right of deep moral criticism can make a difference to the climate of opinion in which the legal norm wilts or flourishes.

A lot will depend, of course, on what other supports there are for the norm in the culture or what other pressures it is under. It is perhaps ironic that the sort of moral challenge that McMahan's critique represents does tend to be mounted at precisely the times when the rule being evaluated is at its most insecure. It is when the country is challenged by terrorist attack and when the norms of war are under pressure from the anti-terrorist side as well that the philosophers think the opportunity is right to hold conferences and publish proceedings on the deep morality of war. In the ethical tradition of indirect utilitarianism, it was said that the best time to reconsider the status of an established rule was in a quiet hour, when we could reason in an undistracted way.[42] I think we have lost sight of that in modern normative philosophy; we reckon now that the best time to reconsider established rules is when they are brought sharply into focus by the pressure of events. That's what makes our philosophizing 'relevant'. Maybe so; but then we cannot complain if the same pressure and focus of events also brings into play a certain duty of care on the part of the moral critic.

Notes

1. Immanuel Kant, 'An Answer to the Question: What Is Enlightenment?' in Kant's, *Practical Philosophy*, edited by Mary Gregor (Cambridge University Press, 1996), 22 (8:41).
2. Jeremy Bentham, *A Fragment on Government* (Cambridge University Press, 1988), 10.
3. See, e.g., Robert P. Wolff, *In Defense of Anarchism*, revised edition (Berkeley: University of California Press, 1998), 12–19.
4. David Hume, 'Of Passive Obedience,' in Hume's *Essays: Moral, Political and Literary*, edited by Eugene F. Miller (Indianapolis: Liberty Classics, 1985), 490–491.
5. Plato, *The Crito*, in *The Last Days of Socrates* (New York: Penguin Books, 1993), 86 (50b).
6. The basic legal principles are set out in Articles 48 and 51 of the First Protocol to the Geneva Conventions. These read as follows:

   Article 48. In order to ensure respect for and protection of the civilian population and civilian objects, the Parties to the conflict shall at all times distinguish between the civilian population and combatants and between civilian objects and military objectives and accordingly shall direct their operations only against military objectives.

   Article 51. 1. The civilian population and individual civilians shall enjoy general protection against dangers arising from military operations. To give effect to this protection, the following rules . . . shall be observed in all circumstances. 2. The civilian population as such, as well as individual civilians, shall not be the object of attack. Acts or threats of violence the primary purpose of which is to spread terror among the civilian population are prohibited. 3. Civilians shall enjoy the protection afforded by this Section, unless and for such time as they take a direct part in hostilities.

7. Jeff McMahan, 'The Ethics of Killing in War', *Ethics* 114 (2004), 693. See also the discussion in Jeff McMahan, *Killing in War* (Oxford University Press, 2009).
8. McMahan, 'The Ethics of Killing in War', 722–723.
9. Ibid., 718.
10. Other authors who shard McMahan's revisionist approach include David Rodin, *War and Self-Defence* (Oxford: Oxford University Press, 2002); Tony Coady, *Morality and Political Violence* (Cambridge: Cambridge University Press, 2008), and Cécile Fabre, *Cosmopolitan War* (Oxford: Oxford University Press, 2012), esp. 71–81. For simplicity of exposition, I shall refer only to McMahan's version.
11. McMahan, 'The Ethics of Killing in War', 731.
12. Idem.
13. Idem.
14. Ibid., 732.
15. Idem.
16. Ibid., 730.
17. Ibid., 731.
18. Idem.
19. See ibid., 733.
20. Ibid., 730.
21. Idem.
22. George Mavrodes, 'Conventions and the Morality of War', *Philosophy and Public Affairs*, 4 (1975), 117.
23. Ibid., 127.
24. Idem.
25. Idem.
26. McMahan, 'The Ethics of Killing in War', 731.
27. I mean the classic sense of what is known as a *Lewis convention*: see David Lewis, *Convention: A Philosophical Study* (New York: Wiley, 2002).
28. I do not mean to suggest that Lewis conventions cannot operate in a context of altruism. There may be cases of altruistic coordination, where it makes no sense for me to play my part in a given altruistic scheme unless others are also playing theirs. But the rule about not targeting civilians is not like that. See the fine account of coordination for the common good in John Finnis, *Natural Law and Natural Rights* (Oxford: Oxford University Press, 1980), 231–232.
29. McMahan, 'The Ethics of Killing in War', 730.
30. Idem, 730.
31. Idem, 731.
32. Notice that the use of conventional criteria, like insignia, does not make the rules themselves conventions in the classic sense: they may rely on conventions, but they are not themselves conventions.
33. McMahan, 'The Ethics of Killing in War', 730.
34. Equally, we have to say that a convention can be dangerous in its observance as well as in its violation.
35. Much of what we call 'collateral damage' would be murder, too, because the category of murder is not confined to intentional killings. In ordinary criminal law, blowing up a building to kill one person you intend to kill with the predictable effect that other persons you do not intend to kill die as a result clearly constitutes the murder of the latter group. Most legal systems punish as murder reckless killings of this kind. The laws of war modify

that by permitting the intended killing (if it is of an enemy combatant) and sometimes by permitting the unintended killing if it is necessary for and proportionate to the securing of a legitimate military objective. However, if those conditions fail, then the reckless killing remains murderous or (at best) a serious form of culpable homicide such as manslaughter.

36. Of course, it is possible that someone may have a utilitarian account, in which case their principles are vulnerable all the way down to consequentialist calculations.
37. The term 'threshold deontology' seems to have been introduced by Michael Moore in 'Torture and the Balance of Evils', *Israel Law Review* 23 (1989), 327.
38. Idem, 732.
39. See note 5. See also Richard Kraut, *Socrates and the State* (Princeton, NJ: Princeton University Press, 1984), 130–131.
40. For the idea of self-application, see Henry M. Hart and Albert Sacks, *The Legal Process: Basic Problems in the Making and Application of Law*, ed. William N. Eskridge and Philip P. Frickey (Westbury, NY: Foundation Press, 1994), 120–121.
41. This was language used by White House counsel Alberto Gonzales to describe the provisions of the Geneva Conventions a few months after the terrorist attacks of September 11, 2001.
42. See, e.g., R. M. Hare, *Moral Thinking: Its Levels, Methods and Point* (Oxford: Oxford University Press, 1982), 52.

PART II

HISTORY

CHAPTER 5

THE ETHICS OF WAR UP TO THOMAS AQUINAS

RORY COX

FROM at least the first millennium BC, ideas about the justice of war, as well as customary norms regulating combat, began to be developed by Western societies. From the agonistic struggles of Greek city states, to Rome's imperial wars of conquest, and on to the Christianized warfare of medieval Europe, war has been subjected to varying degrees of ethical analysis as well as being influenced by social pragmatism. The most important intellectual and legal product of these combined developments was (and is) the concept of the 'just war', positing that violence can be justified as a means to secure peace, justice, and order. Although separated by centuries, similarities in Western ethical treatments of war exist because (1) there exists a surprisingly stable intellectual genealogy from ancient Greece up to the present day, and (2) most Western societies have sought to achieve broadly comparable objectives, utilizing violence to realize political, economic, or religious ends while at the same time wishing to regulate or restrict the use of violence (in a manner beneficial to themselves) by applying social, moral, or legal norms to the initiation and conduct of war. As a result, the concept of the 'just war' has enjoyed widespread acceptance and shown remarkable longevity.

The West was not unique in its reflections on the ethical status of war and violent action. In the Sumerian *Epic of Gilgamesh* (early second millennium BC), the two heroes debate whether or not to kill their defeated enemy Humbaba. The fearsome Humbaba begs Gilgamesh for his life, but Enkidu eventually persuades Gilgamesh to slay their prisoner—an act looked upon unfavourably by the gods.[1] Rules concerning proper conduct in war can be detected in the great Indian poem, the *Māhabhārata*, parts of which date back beyond 400 BC.[2] During the Warring States period (481–221 BC), the concept of *yi bing* was developed in China, which justified war as the highest form of judicial punishment, to be utilized by rulers alone. As such, the Chinese concept of *yi bing* focused on what the West would term *jus ad bellum* (justice to wage war), but had little to say about *jus in bello* (justice in war) norms. Much of the Chinese tradition was adopted in Japan, where war—even against foreign peoples—continued to be understood as an extension of domestic law enforcement throughout the medieval period.[3] In the Islamic world, ideas corresponding to *jus ad bellum* and *jus in bello* were developed by theologians and jurists from the ninth century onwards, contributing to a complex and dynamic doctrine of *jihad*.[4]

Although not wishing to ignore these (and other) alternative traditions, they must be laid aside. The development of just war theories in the Western tradition, from the classical period up to the completion of Thomas Aquinas's *Summa Theologiae* (1265–74), is the principal focus of this chapter. I use the plural *theories* here deliberately because the term 'just war theory' misleadingly suggests a single coherent and monolithic doctrine. Just war theories, sharing certain criteria for legitimating the use of violence under legal, moral, and/or religious considerations, often developed parallel to one another but could also diverge in numerous ways. James Turner Johnson has argued that a properly recognisable just war theory did not exist prior to 1500. Johnson particularly stresses the separation of the *jus ad bellum* and the *jus in bello* traditions, the former being largely the concern of academic theologians and canonists, with the latter belonging to the secular concerns of soldiers and chivalric law.[5] This distinction has enjoyed general acceptance but, as has been recently highlighted, this modern distinction between *jus ad bellum* and *jus in bello* has been emphasized to the point of creating an artificially impermeable divide within pre-modern just war doctrine.[6] Although much of Johnson's argument is persuasive, I believe it underestimates the implicit demands for proper conduct contained within theological and canonistic writings on war. It also underestimates the importance of proper authority and just cause contained in literature and legal writings ostensibly focused on the conduct of war, as well as the role played by clerics in establishing notions of combatant status and noncombatant immunity. It is the aim of this chapter, therefore, to revise the notion of a pre-modern just war doctrine bisected by the *jus ad bellum/jus in bello* distinction and, in doing so, to provide an analysis of the key developments of the period. For the sake of economy, I shall simply use the term 'just war doctrine' in order to refer to the variety of classical and medieval writings that may be loosely gathered under the banner of thought on justifiable war.

The period up to Aquinas also witnessed the emergence of two other important doctrines regarding war. The first is pacifism, another heterogeneous doctrine, which was present in various forms within the early Church and later re-emerged among some heterodox Christian sects from the twelfth century onwards. The second doctrine is holy war, which developed alongside the crusading movement from the end of the eleventh century and can be understood as a corollary of Christianized just war doctrine. Pacifism—essentially a rejection of the ethics of war—and holy war—an extension of just war doctrine—will not be discussed at length.

A chapter covering nearly two thousand years of ethical reflection on war cannot hope to be exhaustive, but it can indicate the richness of thought in the period up to the publication of Aquinas's *Summa Theologiae*. Many histories of just war theory, in their hurried journey towards the sixteenth century, have too often been guilty of using Aquinas as a convenient stepping-stone between Augustine and Vitoria. Not only does this ignore several centuries of thought on war, it also gives a false impression of

Aquinas's place within the history of just war doctrine. Aquinas's contribution to the development of just war doctrine was undoubtedly significant, but it was not his originality of thought, but rather the clarity of his systematized presentation of pre-existing arguments for which we owe him a debt.

1. The Greco-Roman Tradition

Informal socially mandated and enforced rules of war were developing in Europe as early as archaic Greece (800–480 BC), and, by the late fifth century BC, there appears to have been a set of established customs within intra-Hellenic warfare that included conditions such as formal declarations of war, periods of truce for sacred holidays, ransoming of prisoners, and, to some degree, the immunity of noncombatants.[7] On the other hand, Thucydides' famous account of the Melian Dialogue during the Peloponnesian War (431–404 BC), during which the Athenians inform the Melians that, 'the standard of justice depends on the equality of power to compel and that in fact the strong do what they have the power to do and the weak accept what they have to accept', has been taken as a classic example of political realism.[8]

The works of Plato in the early to mid-fourth century BC offer the first clear engagement with war as an ethical problem. In the *Republic*, Socrates (the voice of Plato) identifies the desire for luxurious living, which necessitates the acquisition of resources from neighbouring communities, as the origin of war. Socrates goes on to make an important distinction between wars fought amongst Greeks and wars fought between Greeks and barbarians (non-Hellenes):

> [W]hen Greeks fight with barbarians and barbarians with Greeks, we'll assert they are at war and are enemies by nature, and this hatred must be called war; while when Greeks do any such thing to Greeks, we'll say that they are by nature friends, but in this case Greece is sick and factious, and this kind of hatred must be called faction.[9]

This created two distinct categories of conflict: the first is war 'proper', which is natural; the second is faction, which is unnatural. It is for the latter category of conflict that Plato introduced ideas of proper conduct—including what we would now identify as proportionality and noncombatant immunity—because Greeks, as natural friends and kin, must have a view to future reconciliation:

> Therefore, as Greeks, they won't ravage Greece or burn houses, nor will they agree that in any city all are their enemies—men, women, and children—but that there are always a few enemies who are to blame for the differences. And, on all these grounds, they won't be willing to ravage lands or tear down houses, since the many are friendly.
>
> I [Glaucon] . . . agree that our citizens must behave this way toward their opponents; and toward the barbarians they must behave as the Greeks do now toward one another [i.e., without restraint].[10]

Plato clearly created an ethical distinction between war proper, which is natural and unlimited, and war as 'faction', which is unnatural and in which destructive actions should be restrained. Aristotle followed Plato in stating that intra-Hellenic warfare was a disease, whereas the wars fought against barbarians were natural and therefore legitimate and virtuous. Aristotle's emphasis on the importance of community and the common good led him to support the use of force by autonomous political communities to defend themselves, especially against barbarians. The teleological purpose of the political community was the attainment of the life of virtue, or 'good life', for its citizens. Therefore, in order to safeguard the perfecting process of civic development that would lead to the good life, governments were obliged to possess military strength in order to defend the community against internal and external threats.[11] War was not, however, an end in itself. Rather, Aristotle declared that 'we wage war in order to have peace'.[12] This influential maxim, deriving from Plato (*Laws*, 628e, 803d), was passed down to medieval theorists via Cicero (*De Officiis*, bk. 1, §35), Augustine (Letter 189 to Boniface), and Gratian (*Decretum*, Causa 23, q. 1 canon [c.] 3).[13] Nor should war be used to threaten the good of other communities without cause. Military practice 'is not to bring into subjection those not deserving of such treatment, but to enable men to save themselves from becoming subject to others'. On the other hand, liberty was not a universal right and belonged only to Greeks. Aristotle believed that slavery was the natural state of barbarian races and therefore considered wars that resulted in the conquest of 'those who deserve to be the slaves' as morally legitimate. He also appears to have condoned wars for imperial expansion, as long as they were undertaken for the good of the governed rather than for the good of the ruler.[14]

It is clear that neither Plato nor Aristotle applied an egalitarian concept of justice to war; quite the opposite, their ethical analysis of war was deeply partisan, based principally on the disparity between Greek and non-Greek. Indeed, the classical Greek consideration of war highlights a major obstacle for just war doctrine *in toto*. Differing conceptions of justice produce divergent interpretations of what constitutes a justified war; but war is, by its nature, often a clash between societies with idiosyncratic interpretations of justice, each favouring its own interpretation and its own cause. As a result, the formulation of any universal and egalitarian definition of justice in war is hugely problematic. Nevertheless, it was Greek philosophy, particularly the Stoic school from the third century BC, that provided a concept of natural law—as a universally applicable set of rules derived from reason—that was fundamental to later interpretations of justifiable warfare, beginning with Rome.

Cicero's *On Duties* (*De Officiis*, 44 BC) is probably the most cogent exposition of the Roman concept of just war; it is certainly the most cited. Cicero's treatment of war in *On Duties*, and in his earlier *On the Commonwealth* (*De Re Publica*, 54/53 BC), centred on two key criteria: just cause and proper authority.[15] These criteria remain fundamental to just war doctrine up to the present day.

Cicero stressed that justice and warfare must be closely related.[16] The end of every just war was a restoration of peace in the Platonic-Aristotelian sense, but in the Roman legal sense, it was also the restoration of justice, essentially a restoration of the *status quo ante bellum*.[17] This process began with the religious tradition of fetial law (*jus fetiale*), which demanded that for a just war to be formally declared, the guilty party should have thirty-three days to redress the wrong done or make a restitution of goods. If no redress was forthcoming after this time had elapsed, then war was declared with the approval of the gods.[18] The right to declare war was restricted to the public authority in possession of *imperium* (sovereignty/authority), but the importance of possessing authority also extended to those who fought in wars. Cicero stated that 'it is not lawful for one who is not a soldier to fight with the enemy'.[19]

Perhaps the most important aspect of Cicero's ethical analysis of war was his clear understanding that there must exist a just cause in order for a just war to be declared and subsequently waged. The condition of just cause was based on three assumptions: first, the right to defend oneself and repel force with force (*vim vi repellere*); second, a material right to recover lost property (*rebus repetitis*); and third, a punitive right to avenge injuries and punish wrongdoers (*iniuriae ulciscuntur*). These three assumptions derived from ideas about natural law and customary law (*jus gentium* 'law of nations'), with Cicero positing an intimate relationship between what is natural and what is just. A fundamental precept of natural law was the instinct for self-preservation and, as an extension of this, the right of self-defence. To defend oneself—as a natural inclination—was a just act, as was defending one's associates.[20] If one also takes the Aristotelian idea that man is naturally a political animal, then it was only a short step to justify the defence of the state on similar natural principles of self-defence.

Nevertheless, violence was only to be utilized if provoked by injustice: 'Wars, then, ought to be undertaken for this purpose, that we may live in peace, without injustice; and once victory has been secured, those who were not cruel or savage in warfare should be spared'.[21] The natural defence of material goods was slightly more problematic since, according to a strict interpretation of the law of nature, all goods should be held in common. Custom, however, had clearly legitimated private property holding, and thus the *jus gentium* provided a convenient vehicle to justify private ownership. Cicero also appears to have made room for the expansion of imperial power for the sake of glory as a just cause to wage war. Whereas wars for empire might seem to contradict the principle that 'war is for the sake of peace', Cicero argued that increased Roman *imperium* would produce greater security, and, consequently, such wars could be understood as defensive in that they defended Rome against rivals and guaranteed peace.[22]

Regarding proper military conduct, certain *jus in bello* restraints were included in Cicero's understanding of just war. Cicero recommended that states should conduct themselves honourably at all times (thereby maintaining virtue), emphasizing that faith should be kept with the enemy, that the use of poison or treachery should be rejected, and that justice should be maintained 'even towards the lowliest'.[23] Enemies who had refrained from cruelty should be spared, even those who refused to surrender immediately:

> And while you must have concern for those whom you have conquered by force, you must also take in those who have laid down their arms and seek refuge in the faith of generals, although a battering ram may have crashed against their wall.[24]

Virtue demanded that men acted reasonably and with moderation, and this extended to 'inflicting such punishment as fairness and humanity allow'.[25] Punishment, therefore, should be governed by reason not by cruelty. Cicero also explained that when Rome was engaged in 'fighting for empire and seeking glory through warfare', such wars should be waged less bitterly than defensive wars against mortal enemies because, in this latter type of warfare, 'the question was not who would rule, but who would exist'.[26] Ultimately, Cicero relied on an ethic of honour to limit the conduct of war, one based on the assumption that all just wars were for the sake of justice and peace. He recommended that soldiers should be moved by the principles of *humanitas* and *honestum*, and although they were not legally enforceable rules of engagement, it cannot be denied that they were concerned with *jus in bello* principles.

2. The Early Church

The historicity of an uncompromisingly pacifist early Church was challenged by Adolf Harnack as long ago as 1904, and a revisionist approach has gained further support since the 1970s. It has been argued that although principles of nonviolence were apparent in the early centuries of Christianity, this did not necessarily entail a universal rejection of violence nor a rejection of military service.[27] Early Christian discussion on the topic of war appears to have focussed not on the ethics of war per se, but on the problem of whether or not Christians could participate in Roman military service. Modern attempts to reconstruct an early Christian ethic of war are further problematized by the fact that the Roman army's requirements for oath-taking and idol worship, rather than a common Christian doctrine of pacifism, may have provided the principal stumbling blocks for Christian military service. What seems likely is that early Christian attitudes to military service and violence were dependent on geography and time, with different communities throughout the empire adopting and developing their own approach.[28] Moreover, early Christian writings on war, including the works of Augustine of Hippo, are not in the form of extended or dedicated analyses. Many of the remarks concerning war and military service are incidental and couched within ethical discussions of virtue, justice, and the wider role of Christians within Roman society. Therefore, to say that the early Church developed a specific 'doctrine' on war would be to endow an artificial sense of coherence and maturity on what was still an inchoate, constantly evolving collection of thoughts about violence.

The potentially conflicting attitude of early Christians is apparent in the writings of two Christian apologists, Tertullian (*c.* 160–*c.* 220) and Origen (*c.* 184–*c.* 253). Both of these writers expressed a deeply felt distaste for violence, but arguably both accepted war as an inevitable and potentially legitimate activity. Tertullian objected to military service as idolatrous and decried the killing and destruction concomitant with war,[29] but he could not deny the legitimate power of the state to wage war because, according to Romans 13, the emperor came to power by the will of God.[30] Similarly, Origen argued that Christians should not be polluted by the shedding of blood but went on to explain that Christians could pray to God, 'striving for those who fight in a righteous cause and for the emperor who reigns righteously'.[31] Certain wars were justifiable because the safety and expansion of Christianity ultimately depended on the *Pax Romana*, which was itself dependent on the use of force.[32] Therefore, although elements of early Christian thought can justifiably be described as pacifist, their pacifism was probably what Martin Ceadel has described as 'exemptionist', in so far as the stipulations for nonviolence applied to Christians as a spiritual elite but did not necessarily apply beyond the sect.[33]

By the fourth century, Christian writers were moving closer to an identifiable ethics of just war. Ambrose of Milan (d. 397), combining Ciceronian thought with Christian theology, played an influential role in producing a more detailed Christian interpretation of morally acceptable warfare.[34] Ambrose agreed with Cicero that wars to defend the *patria* were lawful, as were those that defended associates against attacks from barbarians or brigands.[35] Courage, as discussed by Ambrose, 'consists not in doing people an injury but in protecting them'. This moral obligation to defend third parties even extended into the private sphere: 'the person who fails to deflect an injury from his neighbour, when he is in a position to do so, is as much at fault as the one who inflicts it'.[36] In such a case, the right of the innocent not to suffer harm outweighed the right of the guilty not to have harm done to them. The moral duty to protect the innocent led Ambrose to condone defensive violence as an act of Christian charity (*caritas*) because justice is 'born for others rather than itself'.[37] Logically, this justified the use of force by the public authority in order to protect its subjects.

Ambrose's concern was not only with just cause and proper authority. Like Cicero, he stressed that even warring parties must maintain justice: promises made to the enemy should be honoured, no unfair advantage should be seized on the battlefield, and the defeated should be shown mercy.[38] These sentiments have a 'chivalric' tone to them that would not appear out of place in the writings of Honoré Bouvet or Christine de Pizan. Where Ambrose differed significantly from the classical tradition was his understanding of private self-defence. In the Greco-Roman tradition, the justification for waging war stemmed in large part from the natural law principle that everything possessed a right to self-preservation, from the individual to the political community. The Christian justification of war, however, did not follow this logic. Despite the legal and moral justifications that Ambrose extended to those defending their associates or the *patria*, he did not extend the same legitimacy to individual Christians faced with violence against their own person or property.[39] Doing violence to another in order to save oneself displayed an egotistical love rather than a brotherly love, and the Christian should prefer the spiritual good of salvation over corporeal health.[40] This prioritization of spiritual health applied especially to the clergy, whom Ambrose prohibited from using arms. This polarity in Ambrose's thought hinders any simplistic categorization of Ambrose as either a defender of classical just war doctrine or a pacifist. Nevertheless, he made an important step in Christian thought by drawing a distinction between specific uses of violence that were morally justified—even laudatory—and others that were not. This would be of crucial importance to the emergence of a state-centred Christian ethic of war under Augustine.

Although few modern commentators would still call Augustine's contribution to the ethics of war 'revolutionary',[41] all would agree that Augustine's contribution was fundamental to the long-term evolution of just war doctrine.[42] Augustine's approach to thinking about war was based on his concept of the imperfection of temporal government and on his view that war—a phenomenon of an essentially sinful world—was inevitable.[43] True peace, according to Augustine, would only be found in the heavenly city. Yet the prevalence of wars approved by God in the Old Testament indicated that war could indeed be used as a tool of justice. War was a product of, but also a remedy for, sin. Moreover, in order to create a stable environment for the Church to fulfil its spiritual mission of guiding souls towards true heavenly peace, it was necessary that earthly peace and justice should be defended by force.

Augustine was not the first Christian writer to justify war, nor did he create a systematic theory of just war. Nonetheless, through emphasizing the classical conditions of just cause and proper authority, as well as, crucially, the more Christian concern of charitable disposition (correct intention), Augustine provided later writers with a framework within which the legitimacy of specific wars could be assessed.

Following the classical tradition, Augustine insisted that war was not an end in itself, but a means for obtaining peace, which was a state of tranquillity founded upon justice. Wars should not be fought by choice, but according to necessity: 'Peace ought to be what you want, war only what necessity demands'.[44] Every just war, then, must have as its cause the restoration of justice:

> Those wars are customarily called just which have for their end the revenging of injuries, when it is necessary by war to constrain a city or a nation which has not wished to punish an evil action committed by its citizens or to restore that which has been taken unjustly.[45]

As can be seen, the justice served by war consisted of both a restorative element (the restitution of goods stolen or damaged), but also, more importantly, a punitive element, independent from the concept of redress for damage caused by the enemy. Augustine expanded the concept of just cause to include violations of the moral order as well as the civil, for by predicating the justice of the state on divine justice (in accordance with Pauline reasoning in Romans 13), any violation of the state's justice potentially became a violation of divine justice, thereby deserving of punishment. This increased the scope of war's punitive function and prepared the ground for later formulations of holy war against heathens and heretics. Indeed, much of Augustine's thought on war can only be properly understood in the context of his opposition to the Donatist heresy, and his belief that heretics should be forcibly returned to the orthodox faith.[46]

Accepting Old Testament precedent, Augustine declared that any war waged on divine command was just without doubt.[47] Following convention, Augustine restricted the prosecution of war to the public authority, although his lack of specificity in defining what constituted public authority would cause much disagreement among medieval theorists. Augustine believed that states that lacked justice merely committed robbery on a grand scale, but he maintained that a Christian sovereign offered the only real hope of enforcing temporal justice and peace and, by extension, also possessed the authority to wage war. The just sovereign, and those officials acting under his authority, could wage war for the sake of justice and the common good, free from motivations such as hatred or the 'lust to dominate' (*libido dominandi*).[48] As representatives of the public authority, soldiers and magistrates who killed were merely instruments of the state's justice. Like the judge or executioner, the military official committed no sin when killing by order of the sovereign authority; indeed, if a soldier disobeyed an order to kill, he was guilty of treason. In a letter to the Roman military commander Boniface, Augustine made quite clear that soldiering was a duty that could be practiced free of sin, and only those who 'took the sword' (Matt. 26:52) without authority, as opposed to 'using the sword' with authority, were guilty of breaching Christ's command to do no violence.[49]

The possibility of waging war free from sin was entirely dependent on whether the soldier could adhere to the last of Augustine's three conditions: correct intention. The New Testament injunction to preserve charity and love (*caritas*) had led Ambrose to deny the right of the private Christian to use violence in self-defence. How, then, was the soldier able to use violence without violating *caritas*? The key was Augustine's emphasis on the inward disposition of the just warrior. War itself was a morally neutral action—it was the motivations of those who waged it that determined its intrinsic justice or injustice. Lust for dominion, hatred, cruelty: these were the dispositions that made war unjust. The soldier motivated by piety, duty to the common good, and love for justice could wage war against sinners without himself committing sin. By resisting sinners, the just warrior not only defended the innocent, he also limited the capacity of the unjust to add to their sin. Therefore, the use of violence became an act of charity:

> If the earthly commonwealth observes Christian precepts in this way, then even wars will be waged in a spirit of benevolence; their aim will be to serve the defeated more easily by securing a peaceful society that is pious and just. For if defeat deprives the beaten side of the freedom to act wickedly, it benefits them.[50]

Seen in this light, war could be understood as a virtuous activity in which courage, duty, self-sacrifice, and honour could all be found. This was very much a continuation of traditional Roman attitudes to wars in defence of the *patria*; the change was that the *patria* had now coalesced with the *ecclesia*.

Augustine has been accused of giving little thought to *jus in bello* norms, allowing the just belligerent to wage wars that showed no discrimination regarding innocent or guilty, combatant or noncombatant. It is true that Augustine considered war as an arena of absolute moral truth—one side just, the other side unjust—although he did recognize that some morally good soldiers might fight for an unjust sovereign and, consequently, deserve mercy in defeat.[51] However, the accusation that Augustine disregarded *jus in bello* norms ignores the role he believed that correct intention should play in determining the actions of the just warrior. Soldiers fighting with correct intention would fulfil their duty and kill the enemy if necessary, but they would also exercise proportionality and mercy: 'The desire to do harm, the cruelty of vengeance, an unpeacable and implacable spirit, the fever of rebellion, the lust to dominate, and similar things: these are rightly condemned in war'.[52] Whereas Augustine made no guarantees that innocents would not perish in war, he certainly considered cruelty in war as a display of condemnable *malitia* (wickedness) rather than legitimate *militia* (military service).[53] It was deeply ingrained within Augustine's entire concept of justifiable warfare that soldiers would fight according to moral norms. To do otherwise was to contradict the very notion of a just belligerent engaged in a just war. Therefore, to argue that Augustine's thought on war ignores *jus in bello* principles is to miss the point of his vision of a Christian soldier 'fighting peacefully' at the command of the public authority and in defence of justice. Furthermore, Augustine was primarily interested in spiritual salvation, and he saw corporeal death as a lesser evil than spiritual damnation. Like Ambrose, he too denied the right of self-defence to private Christians: 'As to killing others in order to defend one's own life, I do not approve of this, unless one happen to be a soldier or public functionary'.[54] Augustine's acceptance that innocents will die on both sides during war is comprehensible from an eschatological perspective, but it does not follow that he believed soldiers were free to act without restraint or that all moral norms ceased to apply during war.

3. The Middle Ages

A century and a half after Augustine, the Visigothic bishop, Isidore of Seville (*c.* 560–636) briefly discussed just and unjust wars in his encyclopaedic *Etymologies*:

> A just war is that which is waged in accordance with a formal declaration and is waged for the sake of recovering property seized or of driving off the enemy. An unjust war is one that is begun out of rage, and not for a lawful reason.[55]

Isidore borrowed substantially from Cicero, emphasizing the requirements of just cause and proper authority, as well as giving a nod to the Augustinian concept of correct intention by acknowledging that rage is an unjust cause for war. He also adopted a negative stance regarding dishonourable conduct during war, judging that 'a victory acquired by guile is wicked'.[56]

Although the growth of Latin monasticism encouraged a literature extolling the benefits of peace,[57] it is usually accepted that little progress was made regarding the ethics of war until the Peace of God (*pax Dei*) movement emerged in southern France in the late tenth century.[58] Beginning with the council of Le Puy in 975, and viewed as a starting point for the medieval *jus in bello* tradition, it is argued that the peace councils initiated a debate on the status of noncombatants during war. A secondary development was the Truce of God (*treuga Dei*), which sought to limit the days on which wars could be fought. But the Peace movement was also very much an attempt to define who had the authority to wage war in order to restrict the increasing prevalence of private war-making. Prelates and magnates joined forces to restrict the right to make war, with the dual threats of excommunication and physical force utilized to compel obedience. Thus, along with its *jus in bello* concerns for distinguishing between combatants and noncombatants, the Peace movement also possessed a strong interest in *jus ad bellum* principles. Arguably, the immediate effect of the Peace of God was not the enhanced protection of noncombatants but the identification of who could legitimately resort to violence and for what purposes.[59]

Yet the Peace of God was not the first example of a concerted effort to define and protect noncombatants. As early as 697, the abbot of Iona, Adomnán, attempted to introduce into Ireland and Britain a 'Law of the Innocents', later known as the *Cáin Adomnáin*, which primarily sought to protect women from the violence of war. Under the stipulations of the *Cáin*, women were to be entirely separated from warfare and other forms of violence: they were not to be used as soldiers, they were not to suffer capital punishment (even if guilty of homicide), they were not to be subjected to magical curses or libellous accusations, and they were protected from rape and sexual assault.[60] Those who violated the *Cáin* were 'condemned to a double punishment' of mutilation prior to execution, followed by the relations of the perpetrator being forced to pay a monetary fine. The law even accounts for likely scenarios of corporate responsibility for violations committed during war:

> If it is a host that has offended, every fifth man up to three hundred is condemned to this punishment: if they are few they are divided into three groups. The first group of them, decided by casting lots, shall be put to death and a hand and foot cut off. The second group shall pay fourteen full *ancillae*. The third group is cast out on pilgrimage across the sea under the rule of a hard discipline, because it is a great sin when someone kills the mother and sister of the mother of Christ.[61]

Also protected under the *Cáin* were clergy, children, and church property, with gradations of punishment according to the severity of the injury inflicted upon these groups.[62]

The *Cáin* is certainly an unusual document, but arguably it can be considered part of a continuous tradition of ethical thought about war developed since the classical period. The assumption that the failure to protect associates is as serious as committing a crime oneself—'And it is the same payment for someone who does the injury and for one who looks on and does not protect the victim with all his might'[63]—is certainly reminiscent of Ciceronian and Ambrosian thought. Alternatively, this might merely have been a pragmatic response to law enforcement in a period in which the public authority, itself lacking the resources to enforce the law, relied on the active cooperation of the community. Even if this was the case, it need not preclude a classical influence, particularly via the medium of Ambrose.

Although the *Cáin Adomnáin* may appear to be focused on *jus in bello* concerns, there remains a strong sense that war is an activity engaged in and regulated by those with public authority. Adomnán clearly directed his law at kings, taking sureties and bonds to guarantee compliance. The law was enacted and 'imposed on the men of Ireland and Britain . . . [by] a proclamation of the nobles, the clerics and the laity', and attached to the law is a guarantor list of ninety-one named kings, prelates, and nobles.[64] The *Cáin* was effectively a contract to uphold the protected status of women, clergy, and children as noncombatants. Adomnán was no pacifist, however, and it has been shown that while he clearly sought to alleviate the sufferings of noncombatants, he accepted that legitimate authorities (kings and lords) could wage just war against unjust enemies.[65]

The ethical treatment of war gained pace after the Benedictine monk Gratian published his *Concordia Discordantium Canonum* ('Concordance of Discordant Canons'), or *Decretum*, around the year 1140.[66] In this collection, Gratian discussed the issue of war at length in Causa 23. Gratian was not the first canonist to write about war, but such was the rapid dissemination and popularity of Gratian's *Decretum* that Causa 23 became the springboard for almost every learned discussion of just war that came after it. Moreover, due to the pervasive influence of canon law on public and private life throughout Latin Christendom, the *Decretum* played the major role in disseminating Augustinian ideas of just war to a wide intellectual audience.[67]

The context for the discussion of war in Causa 23 is an ecclesiastical one: Gratian posed the question of whether it was lawful for the pope to have authorized Catholic bishops to use force to defend the faithful against heretics. Proceeding with a dialectical form of argument typical of medieval scholastic method, Gratian provided canons from scripture and the Church Fathers both prohibiting and condoning violence, before concluding that military service is not inherently sinful. For this, he relied on the Augustinian view that the maintenance of an inwardly charitable disposition could justify violent external actions.[68] Gratian showed that good men wage wars of pacification (*bella pacata*) to restrain the wicked and protect the good.[69] To clarify what made a war just, he cited the definitions of Isidore and Augustine and offered his own synthesis: 'A just war is that which is waged from an edict, and in which injuries are avenged'.[70] This definition blended both the Isidorian emphasis on authority and self-defence with the Augustinian emphasis on punitive action. Gratian outlined three principal causes of war: to repel an invasion, to recover property, and to avenge prior injuries. But what constituted an injury? By which law—natural, divine, civil, customary—was an injury to be judged? What were the limits of vengeance?[71] This lack of specificity preserved a broad application for the just war as a means of redress for all manner of grievances.

Apart from the right of self-defence and immediate defence of the *patria* and the Church, which Gratian considered licit,[72] the *Decretum* clearly echoes the traditional emphasis on authority. A just war could only be waged under the authority of God or a legitimate earthly *imperium*, and it must be waged from an authoritative edict (*ex edicto*).[73] The *ex edicto* formulation provided no precision, however, regarding what or who constituted a proper authority. In the early fifth century, Augustine had naturally presumed that *imperium* was bestowed by God on the Roman emperor and his representatives, but, in the Middle Ages, with so many competing claims to jurisdiction—emperors, popes, kings, princes, bishops, barons—the fragmentation of *imperium* created a multitude of individuals claiming authority to declare war.

Fundamentally, Gratian did not consider just wars declared by the Church as qualitatively different from those declared by the appropriate secular authorities. The right of the Church to wage war was simply an extension of divine authority to wage war, as evinced by examples in the Old Testament. By making this connection between the just war and divine authority as mediated through the Church, Gratian endowed ecclesiastical authority with the authority to wage war against any of enemy of its choosing. Foremost among such enemies were heretics and heathens.[74] It was secular authorities, however, who were charged with executing this authority.[75] Although the prohibition on clerics to bear arms remained, clergy could exhort others to fight for a just cause. Prelates could not directly command the shedding of blood, but Gratian accepted that those bishops with regalian functions had a duty to gather forces and participate in a just war.[76] Gratian did seem aware of the contradiction that a bishop could arm a man and send him to war but could not order him to shed blood, yet by making a distinction between the *possession* and the *exercise* of a right, a bishop could issue commands that might result in bloodshed so long as such commands did not directly or explicitly order bloodshed.[77]

Gratian rejected the Truce of God principle that wars should not be waged on holy days, providing a canon stating that, if necessary, war could be fought even during Lent.[78] He also made no mention of a canon of the recent Second Lateran Council (1139), which prohibited bows and crossbows in wars between Christians.[79] Nevertheless, Gratian did repeat the *jus in bello* precepts that faith must be kept with the enemy, that mercy should be shown to the vanquished and to prisoners, and that cruelty and other destructive vices should be condemned.[80] Gratian also recognized the principle of noncombatant immunity by accepting that pilgrims, clerics, monks, women, and the unarmed poor should be immune from violence.[81]

Gratian's treatment of war left many questions unresolved. From circa 1148, commentators on the *Decretum*—later known as 'decretists'—sought to clarify a number of issues, particularly what constituted just cause and proper authority. From the 1190s, a new school of commentators, 'decretalists', named after their commentaries on papal decretals (letters with legislative authority), continued the debate.[82] The natural inclination of the canonists, who were also deeply influenced by the study of Roman law that had flourished from the tenth century, was to restrict the authority to wage war to the pope, emperor, and prelates. Consequently, both decretists and decretalists have typically been associated with the *jus ad bellum* 'tradition'. However, this neglects the importance that they, too, placed on correct intention as a defining criterion for just wars and its role in regulating conduct through the prohibition of cruelty. It also neglects to give due attention to the canonists' insistence that fighting was the province of laymen, behind which is a clear belief that a combatant/noncombatant distinction did exist.

It was not until circa 1160 that the first explicit reference to 'the prince' (*princeps*) as the proper authority to wage war was given by the anonymous *Summa Parisiensis*.[83] Even then, the term *princeps* left plenty of room for interpretation, with numerous secular and ecclesiastical lords laying claim to the title despite Pope Innocent IV asserting that the right to declare war was limited to authorities who recognized no superior.[84] Private self-defence and defence of associates remained legitimate, although, strictly speaking, it was not defined as war (*bellum*) in the full legal sense. Such defence must be immediate (*incontinenti*) and proportional (*moderamen inculpatae tutelae*: lit. 'the moderation of blameless defence') to the violence suffered by the victim. This *jus in bello* principle that proportionality should regulate military conduct (including private self-defence) usually implied that the damage inflicted on the enemy should not exceed that which had been suffered by the victim. Indeed, the defender could be liable for any excessive damages because recourse to defensive violence was justified from a desire for justice and thus precluded actions motivated by malice or avarice.

Canonistic analysis of war became increasingly sophisticated during the late twelfth century and into the thirteenth century. Stephen of Tournai (d. 1203) displayed an impressively nuanced view of subjective justice when he raised the possibility that war could be just on both sides or, indeed, unjust on both sides.[85] Yet this did not enjoy general favour with canonists or theologians, and the understanding that one side held a monopoly of justice in a just war was dominant until at least the sixteenth century. Around 1210, Laurentius Hispanus provided five criteria by which the justice of a war could be assessed, which were later adopted by the canonist Raymond of Peñafort (d. 1275). Raymond explained that war must be just regarding: (1) *persona*—the persons engaged in it (the war must be fought by laymen, not clerics); (2) *res*—its object (recovery of property or defence of *patria*); (3) *causa*—its cause (a necessary cause, with no other means but recourse to arms); (4) *animus*—its state of mind (desire for justice, not hatred, revenge, or greed); and (5) *auctoritas*—proper authority (the Roman Church or a sovereign prince).[86] If *any* of these conditions were lacking, then the war would be deemed unjust. Assessing the justice of individual wars on the basis of this ethical framework may appear to be no more than an abstract intellectual exercise, but such frameworks also served pragmatic purposes. In just wars, spoils were classified as lawful restitution for damages; in unjust wars, princes and soldiers had no legal claim to spoils or territory captured during war and were liable to pay damages. For an era in which warfare was a profit-driven enterprise, the legal status of spoils was relevant to rulers and soldiers alike. Of course, it is true that in the majority of cases 'might made right'; nevertheless, many war leaders felt obliged to at least pay lip-service to the legal language of just war doctrine, even if largely ignoring its content.

By the mid-thirteenth century, the decretalist Henry of Segusio ('Hostiensis' d. 1271) had identified seven types of just and unjust wars. Just wars included the 'Roman war', waged by the faithful against infidels; the 'judicial war', waged by the faithful on the authority of a judge; and the 'war of necessity', waged by the faithful to defend themselves and their neighbours. Although generally emphasizing the importance of proper authority, Hostiensis was willing to admit that every legal system permitted the Roman maxim *vim vi repellere* for the laity. But he stressed that all force must be used 'within the limits of blameless defence' and that it must be immediate (*incontinenti*), in that it must be exercised out of necessity rather than vindictive vengeance. In this regard, the 'Roman war' stood apart as a form of unlimited warfare, reserved primarily for holy wars against infidels, although military action against rebels could also be referred to as 'Roman war' or by the more common term *guerre mortelle*. We can see here a parallel with the distinction made by Plato between the unlimited warfare waged by Greeks against barbarians and the limited warfare ('faction') of intra-Hellenic conflict. On the other hand, the very fact that the 'Roman war' was cited as an extreme form of war, waged without limits, is proof that medieval lawyers and theologians alike understood other types of just warfare to be limited. Moreover, it was very rare that the full implications of unlimited war were actually applied in practice, it being neither practicable nor profitable to do so.

Hostiensis insisted that even in wars waged for a just cause and under proper authority, the presence of soldiers who fought with a vengeful spirit or who sought to do more than recover lost goods or defend the *patria* would render a war unjust. The necessary characteristics of the soldier were a desire for justice, rejection of wilful destruction or avarice, and the possession of compassion.[87] Although the decretalists may not have provided specific prescriptions for the proper conduct of war,[88] this does not mean that questions of proper conduct and the importance of charitable disposition in regulating conduct were absent from canonistic thought.

Taken as a whole, what emerges from the writings of the canonists is a hierarchy of violent actions, each with its own proper authority and scope, ranging from immediate private self-defence to state-organized war for the restitution of justice or to counter external threats. By endowing the Church with the authority to judge on matters of justice, and thus with the ability to declare war, it was only a small step to a justification of holy war as a defensive action against threats to the faith. There was also an explicitly territorial aspect to the justification of holy war. Not only did Latin Christendom see itself as the rightful heir to Rome, but the Holy Land (particularly Jerusalem) and Iberia were regarded as Christian territories that had been illicitly conquered by heathens. Crusaders were thus waging defensive war in order to re-establish Christendom's rightful possession of the 'patrimony of Christ' and to provide protection for persecuted Christian communities. Furthermore, because these wars were waged on ecclesiastical authority they were, by definition, just. As James Brundage has argued, the Crusades were a specific type of Christian holy war, characterized especially by the exclusive authority of the pope to proclaim crusades and to grant plenary indulgences, and they occupied the principal place in the hierarchy of legitimate violence created by medieval canon lawyers.[89]

Medieval theologians largely followed the conclusions of the canonists regarding the requirements for a just war. Being primarily concerned with questions of spiritual salvation rather than ecclesiastical jurisdiction, theologians naturally emphasized that rulers and soldiers engaged in warfare should do so out of a love for justice, and Augustine's writings on this subject remained a key influence. Many theologians pointed to John the Baptist's advice that soldiers should be satisfied with their pay (Luke 3:14), arguing that John had tacitly approved of military service because he had not told the soldiers to leave the army. Moreover, with the Crusades in full swing by the twelfth century, it is unsurprising that most theologians championed war in defence of the faith.

The English Franciscan, Alexander of Hales (*c.* 1185–1245), gave an unusually detailed analysis of the problem of war and provided criteria for just war similar to that of the canonists: 'In order to determine if a war is just or unjust you must mark the authority (*auctoritas*), the state of mind (*affectus*), the intention (*intentio*), the condition (*conditio*), the desert (*meritum*), and the cause (*causa*)'.[90]

The stress placed by theologians on the personal responsibility of belligerents not to engage in unjust wars inevitably clashed with feudal customs of vassalic duty. The twelfth-century Parisian theologian, Peter the Chanter (d. 1197), held that knights had a duty to their lords to fight even in an unjust war; in contrast, Peter's contemporary, Robert of Courson (d. 1219), insisted that knights must never knowingly fight for an unjust cause. Thomas Chobham (d. 1233/6) chose a somewhat unsatisfactory middle path, stating that knights could follow their lord in an unjust conflict but must refrain from shedding blood and causing destruction. At least one theologian remained deeply sceptical of the motivations of the soldiery, and, in this scepticism, he would be joined by many more in the fourteenth and fifteenth centuries. Hugh of St Cher (d. 1263) stated that the majority of soldiers fought out of a desire for earthly glory, cupidity, and hatred: such soldiers were spiritually condemned unless they performed penance.[91] Therefore, although theologians certainly upheld the possibility and desirability of just wars, they were also attuned to the spiritual dangers faced by those who fought in war.

Like other thirteenth-century theologians, Thomas Aquinas emphasized the importance of charity in war. In his massive *Summa Theologiae*, he tackled the problem of war directly in a section dealing with vices against charity (IIaIIae, q. 34–43). The question on war (q. 40)—sometimes simply referred to as Aquinas's *De bello*—as well as the questions on Discord (q. 37), Schism (q. 39), Sedition (q. 42), and Homicide (IIaIIae q. 64), were later to become highly influential on the development of just war doctrine as a result of the adoption of Thomistic thought by a number of leading Spanish theologians and jurists of the fifteenth and sixteenth centuries: Thomas de Vio 'Cajetan' (1468–1534), Francisco de Vitoria (*c.* 1492–1546), and Francisco Suárez (1548–1617). Throughout the dialectical *Summa Theologiae*, Aquinas utilized a range of authorities (mainly scriptural, patristic, and classical texts) to posit a number of theses and antitheses for each point of inquiry. Aquinas then attempted to reconcile these conflicting authorities in his own synthetic *responsiones*.

In his question on war, Aquinas pursued four points of inquiry. The first was simply 'Are some wars permissible?'[92] In response to the initial objection that 'it would seem that it is always a sin to wage war',[93] Aquinas repeated the familiar criteria for just wars:

> Three things are required for any war to be just. The first is the authority of the sovereign on whose command war is waged. . . . Secondly, a just cause is required, namely that those who are attacked are attacked because they deserve it on account of some wrong they have done. . . . Thirdly, the right intention of those waging war is required, that is, they must intend to promote the good and to avoid evil.[94]

The *jus ad bellum* stress on authority and cause is evident, but Aquinas's direct quotation of Augustine's stipulation that warriors must not thirst for revenge, nor desire to hurt people, nor practice any other sort of cruelty, clearly indicates that Aquinas did not conceptually divorce *jus in bello* limitations from his *jus ad bellum*-focussed discussion of war.[95] Aquinas's main concern was to show that just wars were a legitimate means to obtain peace. True peace must be infused with justice, which must itself be infused with charity, and thus this type of peace was distinguished from the superficial 'peace' maintained by the cruelty of a tyrant, for example. Likewise, true justice must be informed by the Christian faith; however, influenced by the natural law teaching of Aristotle and Cicero, Aquinas accepted that even pagans could exercise natural justice within a civic community.[96]

There has been considerable scholarly debate regarding whether a presumption against violence or a presumption against injustice underpinned Aquinas's treatment of war. Although convincing cases can be made for both interpretations, Aquinas's acceptance that just wars can serve both defensive and offensive functions, as well as his acceptance that waging just war can be meritorious, would seem to indicate that Aquinas's principal concern was that injustice should not be tolerated rather than that war should be avoided.[97] Nevertheless, Augustine had forged strong links connecting charity, justice, and war—links that Aquinas and his predecessors followed closely. The effect of this was that justified violence should always be informed by and infused with love. This dictated that violence would only used—indeed, must only be used—as a last resort and in a manner consistent with the charitable intentions of the just prince and the just combatant. Extreme violence was still legitimate within a just war if it was necessary, but *unnecessary* violence or cruelty must be absent. Thus, we cannot think of the just war as being explicitly limited in terms of military conduct, but rather implicitly limited in terms of how the just combatant would be likely to act.

Within Aquinas's justification of violence is an important realization that any moral act might have more than one effect—both good and bad. In the pursuit of justice, the good intention of a moral act could justify negative consequences, such as the killing of an assailant or the deaths of innocents during war. Neither Aquinas nor any of his predecessors used the term 'double effect', but his justification of killing in self-defence, for example, essentially relied on this concept.[98]

Concerning the other major points of inquiry, Aquinas asked: May clerics engage in warfare? May belligerents use subterfuge? May war be waged on feast days? In his response to these questions Aquinas adopted wholly traditional views. Clerics should not engage in war because it was inappropriate to their sacramental and spiritual calling, although they could exhort others to wage just war. Regarding the *jus in bello* concerns of the use of subterfuge and the waging of war on feast days, Aquinas followed the interpretation of Gratian and other canonists by stating that subterfuge was acceptable but that lying to the enemy was not permitted and that just wars could 'be waged on feast days to protect the common weal of the faithful, provided that it is necessary'.[99]

Although much more could said about Aquinas's analysis of war, it remains true that his major contribution to the development of just war doctrine (which was not really felt until the fifteenth century) was his efficient systematization of the key themes and problems that had hitherto been almost exclusively the province of canonists and their laborious method of commentary. Moreover, his stress on the role of justice and natural law was to become increasingly central to the development of just war thought from the sixteenth century onwards. For these contributions alone, Aquinas deserves a prominent place in the history of just war doctrine, but it must also be recognized that the conceptual foundations of his ethics of war did not constitute a great leap forward, but were entirely typical of their time.

4. Conclusion

It is clear, then, that from the classical period through to the early Church and on to the central Middle Ages, there existed a rich tradition of ethical debate on war. This could take the form of jurisprudential analysis, theological speculation, or practical endeavours to regulate war. When Aquinas came to summarize and distil these varied discussions and customs, he did not reinvigorate forgotten knowledge or create anything particularly original: he did not need to. Equally, debate on war was not divided absolutely into independent 'traditions' of *jus ad bellum* and *jus in bello*. Concerns regarding the conduct of war, guided principally by the stress laid on the correct intention of combatants, figured consistently in canonistic and theological analyses. Vice versa, practical attempts to regulate conduct, primarily the protection of noncombatants, were inextricably entwined with a desire to limit the waging of war to magnates and prelates in possession of authority. This intermingling of *jus ad bellum* and *jus in bello* concerns produced a sophisticated and complex body of ethical thought about war and paved the way for future analysis and refinement.

Notes

1. *The Epic of Gilgamesh*, translated by M. Gallery Kovaks (Stanford: Stanford University Press, 1989), tablet V, 44–47.
2. N. Allen, 'Just War in the *Māhabhārata*', in *The Ethics of War: Shared Problems in Different Traditions*, edited by R. Sorabji and D. Rodin (Aldershot, UK: Ashgate, 2006), 138–149.
3. M. E. Lewis, 'The just war in early China', in *The Ethics of War in Asian Civilizations: A Comparative Perspective*, edited by T. Brekke (Abingdon, UK: Routledge, 2006), 185–200; K. Friday, 'Might Makes Right: Just War and Just Warfare in Early Medieval Japan', in *Ethics of War in Asian Civilizations*, edited by Brekke, 159–184.
4. J. Kelsay, 'Islamic Tradition and the Justice of War', in *The Ethics of War in Asian Civilizations*, 81–110.
5. J. T. Johnson, *Ideology, Reason, and the Limitation of War: Religious and Secular Concepts 1200–1740* (Princeton, NJ: Princeton University Press, 1975); *Just War Tradition and the Restraint of War: A Moral and Historical Inquiry* (Princeton, NJ: Princeton University Press, 1981).

6. O. O'Donovan, *The Just War Revisited* (Cambridge: Cambridge University Press, 2003), 14–15; N. Rengger, 'The *Jus in bello* in Historical and Philosophical Perspective', in *War: Essays in Political Philosophy*, edited by L. May (Cambridge: Cambridge University Press, 2008), 30–48, at 33–35.
7. *Warfare in Ancient Greece: A Sourcebook*, edited by M. M. Sage (London/New York: Routledge, 1996), 127–134; M. Goodman and A. Holladay, 'Religious Scruples in Ancient Warfare', *The Classical Quarterly* 36:1 (1986), 151–171; J. Ober, 'Classical Greek Times', in *The Laws of War: Constraints on Warfare in the Western World*, edited by M. Howard, G. J. Andreopoulos, and M. R. Shulman (New Haven, CT: Yale University Press, 1994), 12–26, at 12–13.
8. Thucydides, *The Peloponnesian War*, translated by R. Warner (Harmondsworth, UK: Penguin, 1954), bk. 5. ch. 89. It remains a matter of debate whether Thucydides himself condoned this 'realist' attitude.
9. Plato, *The Republic of Plato*, translated by A. Bloom (New York: Basic Books, 1968), bk. 5, 470c, 150.
10. Plato, *Republic*, bk. 5, 471a–b, 151.
11. Aristotle, *The Politics*, edited by S. Everson (Cambridge: Cambridge University Press, 1998), bk. 1, 1252a.1–6; bk. 2, 1267a.20–23; bk. 3, 1280b.39; bk. 5, 1308a.25–30; bk. 7, 1328b.
12. Aristotle, *Nicomachean Ethics*, translated by M. Ostwald (Upper Saddle River, NJ: Prentice Hall, 1999), bk. 10, 1177b.5–6, 289; see also Aristotle, *Politics*, bk. 7, 1333a.34–35.
13. See also J. Barnes, 'The Just War', in *The Cambridge History of Later Medieval Philosophy: From the Rediscovery of Aristotle to the Disintegration of Scholasticism 1100–1600*, edited by N. Kretzmann, A. Kenny, and J. Pinborg (Cambridge: Cambridge University Press, 1982), 771–784, at 780.
14. Aristotle, *Politics*, bk. 7, 1333b.37–1334a.10, 178.
15. Plato had earlier stated that war and peace must be controlled by the public authority, not private individuals. Violations of this law were punishable by death: Plato, *The Laws*, translated by T. J. Saunders (Harmondsworth, UK: Penguin, 1975), bk. 12, 942, 955.
16. Cicero, *On Duties*, edited by M. T. Griffin and E. M. Atkins (Cambridge: Cambridge University Press, 1991), bk. 1, §34.
17. F. H. Russell, *The Just War in the Middle Ages* (Cambridge: Cambridge University Press, 1975), 18–19.
18. Cicero, *Duties*, bk. 1, §36. See also A. Watson, *International Law in Archaic Rome: War and Religion* (Baltimore, MD: Johns Hopkins University Press, 1993), 27–28, 62–63.
19. Cicero, *Duties*, bk.1, §37, 16.
20. Idem, bk. 1, §11 and §13.
21. Idem, bk.1, §35, pp. 14–15; see also bk. 1, §§20, 23, 80; bk. 3, §§22–23; Cicero, *De Re Publica*, translated by C. Walker Keyes (London: William Heinemann, 1927), bk. 3, §23.34.
22. Cicero, *Duties*, bk. 1, §§34–38; bk. 2, §§26–29; bk. 3, §§46–49, 86–88.
23. Idem, bk. 1, §§35, 39–41; bk. 3, §99.
24. Idem, bk. 1, §35, 15.
25. Idem, bk. 2, §18.
26. Idem, bk. 1, §38.
27. A. Harnack, *Militia Christi: The Christian Religion and the Military in the First Three Centuries*, translated by D. McInnes Gracie (Philadelphia, PA: Fortress Press, 1981) [originally published as *Militia Christi: die christliche Religion und der Soldatenstand in den ersten drei Jahrhunderten* (Tübingen, 1904)]; J. Helgeland, 'Christians and the Roman

Army A.D. 173–337', *Church History* 43:2 (1974), 149–200; J. Helgeland, R. J. Daly, and J. Patout Burns, *Christians and the Military: The Early Experience* (London: SCM Press, 1987); J. T. Johnson, *The Quest for Peace: Three Moral Traditions in Western Cultural History* (Princeton, NJ: Princeton University Press, 1987), 5–65; J. H. Yoder, 'War as a Moral Problem in the Early Church: The Historian's Hermeneutical Assumptions', in *The Pacifist Impulse in Historical Perspective*, edited by H. L. Dyck (Toronto: University of Toronto Press, 1996), 90–110; A. Kreider, 'Military Service in the Church Orders', *Journal of Religious Ethics* 31:3 (2003), 415–442.

28. For example, Tertullian, *De Idolatria*, ch. 19 and *De Corona Militis*, ch. 11, printed in *The Early Fathers on War and Military Service*, edited and translated by L. J. Swift (Wilmington, DE: Michael Glazier, 1983), 41–42, 43–44; S. Gero, 'Miles Gloriosus: The Christian and Military Service according to Tertullian', *Church History* 39:3 (1970): 285–298, at 294–298. See also *The Ethics of War: Classic and Contemporary Readings*, edited by G. M. Reichberg, H. Syse, and E. Begby (Oxford: Blackwell, 2006), which provides an extremely useful selection of material in translation, inclusive of the early Church and the Middle Ages.
29. Tertullian, *De Patientia*, ch. 3 and ch. 7, in *Patrologia Latina*, edited by J. P. Migne (Paris, 1844–55) [henceforth *PL*], 1:1254 and 1:1262; Tertullian, *Adversus Marcionem*, bk. 3, ch. 14, in *PL*, 2:340; Tertullian, *Apologeticus Adversus Gentes pro Christianis*, ch. 25, in *PL*, 1:431; *De Corona*, ch. 12, in *PL*, 2:94–95.
30. Helgeland, 'Christians and the Roman Army', 150–152; Helgeland et al., *Christians and the Military*, 21.
31. Origen, *Contra Celsum*, translated by H. Chadwick (Cambridge: Cambridge University Press, 1953), bk. 8, ch. 73, p. 509. For examples of Origen's 'pacifism': idem, bk. 3, ch. 8; bk. 5, ch. 33; bk. 7, ch. 26.
32. Origen, *Contra Celsum*, bk. 2, ch. 30; J. F. Childress, 'Moral Discourse About War in the Early Church', *Journal of Religious Ethics* 12:1 (1984), 2–18, at 10.
33. M. Ceadel, 'Ten Distinctions for Peace Historians', in *The Pacifist Impulse in Historical Perspective*, edited by H. L. Dyck (Toronto: University of Toronto Press, 1996), 17–35, at 29–30.
34. See also L. J. Swift, 'St. Ambrose on Violence and War', *Transactions and Proceedings of the American Philological Association* 101 (1970), 533–543.
35. Ambrose *De Officiis*, edited and translated by I. J. Davidson, 2 vols. (Oxford: Oxford University Press, 2002) [all references are to vol. 1], bk. 1, ch. 28, §129.
36. Ambrose *Officiis*, bk. 1, ch. 36, §§178–179. Cf. Cicero, *Duties*, bk. 1, §7.
37. Ambrose, *Officiis*, bk. 1, ch. 28, §136.
38. Ambrose, *Officiis*, bk. 1, ch. 29, §§139–140; bk. 2, ch. 7, §33; bk. 3, ch. 14, §§86–88; ch. 15, §91.
39. Swift, 'St. Ambrose', 537.
40. Ambrose, *Officiis*, bk.1, ch. 28, §131; bk. 3, ch. 4, §27.
41. P. Monceaux, 'Augustine', in *L'Église et le Droit de Guerre*, edited by P. Batiffol et al. (Paris: Bloud and Gay, 1920), 40–77, at 76.
42. The scholarship on Augustine is vast, but for informative treatments of Augustine's thought on war: R. A. Markus, 'Saint Augustine's Views on the 'Just War', in *The Church and War*, edited by W. J. Sheils, Studies in Church History 20 (Oxford: Blackwell, 1983), 1–13; J. Langan, 'The Elements of St. Augustine's Just War Theory', *Journal of Religious Ethics* 12:1 (1984), 19–38; P. Ramsey, 'The Just War According to St. Augustine', in *Just War Theory*, edited by J. B. Elshtain (Oxford: Blackwell, 1992), 8–22; H. Syse, 'Augustine and Just War: Between Virtue and Duties', in *Ethics, Nationalism, and Just War: Medieval*

and Contemporary Perspectives, edited by H. Syse and G. M. Reichberg (Washington, DC: Catholic University of America Press, 2007), 36–50.

43. Augustine, *The City of God*, translated by M. Dodds (1950; repr., New York: Modern Library, 1993), bk. 17, ch. 13, 595; bk. 22, ch. 22, 846.
44. Letter 189 to Boniface, in *Augustine: Political Writings*, edited by E. M. Atkins and R. J. Dodaro (Cambridge: Cambridge University Press, 2001) [henceforth Augustine, *Writings*], 217.
45. Augustine, *Quaestiones in Heptateuchum* (*PL*, 34:545–824), bk. 6, ch. 10, translation cited Johnson, *Ideology*, 36.
46. For a collection of Augustine's anti-Donatist works in translation, see *A Select Library of the Nicene and Post-Nicene Fathers of the Christian Church*, edited by P. Schaff, 1st ser. (1886–90; repr., Grand Rapids MI: Eerdmans, 1994–96), 4: 369–651. For Augustine's views on religious coercion: R. A. Markus, *Saeculum: History and Society in the Thought of St Augustine* (London: Cambridge University Press, 1970).
47. Augustine, *Quaestiones in Heptateuchum*, bk. 6, ch. 10.
48. Augustine, *City of God*, bk. 4, ch. 1; bk. 3, ch. 3. See also Russell, *Just War*, 18n7.
49. Augustine: Letter 189 to Boniface, in Augustine, *Writings*, 216; *City of God*, bk. 1, ch. 21 and ch. 27; Letter 47 to Publicola, in *Nicene and Post-Nicene Fathers*, 1: 292–294 (also cited in *Decretum*, C. 23, q. 5 c. 8); *Contra Faustum Manichaeum*, bk. 22, ch. 70, in *Nicene and Post-Nicene Fathers*, 4: 299.
50. Augustine, Letter 138 to Marcellinus, in Augustine, *Writings*, 38 (see also *Nicene and Post-Nicene Fathers*, 1: 485); cf. *City of God*, bk. 19, ch. 16.
51. Augustine, *Contra Faustum*, bk. 22, ch. 75, in *Nicene and Post-Nicene Fathers*, 4: 301.
52. Idem, 4: 300–301.
53. Augustine, *City of God*, bk. 1, chaps. 4–5; bk. 5, ch. 23; Letter 138 to Marcellinus; Letter 189 to Boniface; Letter 229 to Darius. In 427 AD Augustine chastised the Roman military commander Boniface for allowing his troops to plunder: Letter 220 to Boniface, in *Nicene and Post-Nicene Fathers*, 1: 573–576.
54. Augustine, Letter 47 to Publicola, in *Nicene and Post-Nicene Fathers*, 1: 293 (also cited *Decretum*, C. 23, q. 5 c. 8).
55. Isidore of Seville, *The Etymologies of Isidore of Seville*, translated by S. A. Barney et al. (Cambridge: Cambridge University Press, 2006), bk. 18, ch. 1, §2. Cf. Cicero, *De Re Publica*, bk. 3, ch. 23, §35.
56. Isidore, *Etymologies*, bk. 18, ch. 2, §1.
57. T. Renna, 'The Idea of Peace in the West, 500–1150', *Journal of Medieval History* 6:2 (1980), 143–167.
58. See collection of articles in T. Head and R. Landes, eds., *The Peace of God: Social Violence and Religious Response in France around the Year 1000* (Ithaca, NY: Cornell University Press, 1992).
59. Johnson, *Quest for Peace*, 81.
60. *Adomnán's 'Law of the Innocents': Cáin Adomnáin: A Seventh-Century Law for the Protection of Non-combatants*, translated by G. Márkus (Glasgow: Blackfriars Books, 1997), §§33–34, 41–42, 45–46, 50–52. My thanks to Dr Alex Woolf for bringing this source to my attention.
61. Idem, §33, 18.
62. Idem, §§35–36, 40, 44.
63. Idem, §35, 18–19.

64. Idem, §28, 14.
65. J. E. Fraser, 'Adomnán and the Morality of War', in *Adomnán of Iona: Theologian, Law Maker, Peace Maker*, edited by J. Wooding et al. (Dublin: Four Courts Press, 2010), 95–111.
66. The standard modern edition is *Corpus Iuris Canonici*, edited by A. Friedberg, 2 vols. (Leipzig: Tauchnitz, 1879–81), 1: *Decretum Magistri Gratiani*.
67. The most accessible introduction to medieval canon law remains J. A. Brundage, *Medieval Canon Law* (New York: Longman, 1995).
68. *Decretum*, C. 23, q. 1 c. 1; dictum ante canonum [d.a.c.] 1; dictum post canonum [d.p.c.] 1. For extracts in translation, see *Ethics of War*, edited by Reichberg et al., 109–124.
69. Idem, C. 23, q. 1 cc. 3, 4, 6.
70. Idem, C. 23, q. 2 cc. 1–2; d.p.c. 2.
71. The term *ulciscuntur*, e.g., could mean repulsion, vengeance, and punishment. See Russell, *Just War*, 66–67.
72. *Decretum*, C. 23, q. 3 c. 5; q. 1 c. 7; q. 4 c. 48; q. 8 c. 15.
73. Idem, C. 23, q. 1 c. 4; q. 2 c. 2.
74. *Decretum*, C. 23, q. 8 cc. 7–8, 10, 17–18; C. 24, q. 3 c. 26.
75. Idem, C. 23, q. 8 d.p.c. 18.
76. Gratian discusses the question of clerical participation in war at length in *Decretum*, C. 23, q. 8, especially d.p.c. 6, cc. 18–20, d.p.c. 18, d.p.c. 20, d.p.c. 28. On the gradual acceptance of the permissibility of clerical self-defence in canon law, see L. G. Duggan, *Armsbearing and the Clergy in the History and Canon Law of Western Christianity* (Woodbridge: Boydell, 2013).
77. See Russell, *Just War*, 82.
78. *Decretum*, C. 23, q. 8 c. 15; *Ethics of War*, edited by Reichberg et al., 124.
79. *Concilium Lateranenses II*, Canon 29, in *Conciliorum Oecumenicorum Decreta*, edited by J. Alberigo et al. (Bologna: Istituto per le scienze religiose, 1973), 203.
80. *Decretum*, C. 23, q. 1 cc. 3–4.
81. Idem, C. 24, q. 3 cc. 22–25.
82. The major decretal collections are printed in the second volume of *Corpus Iuris Canonici*, edited by Freiberg.
83. Russell, *Just War*, 88.
84. Innocent IV, *In Quinque Libros Decretalium* (Turin: Nicolai Beuilaquae, 1581), bk. 2, f. 96r, col. B. For extracts in translation, see *Ethics of War*, 150–155.
85. Russell, *Just War*, 89–92.
86. Raymond of Peñafort, *Summa de poenitentia*, bk. 2, §§17–19, printed in *Ethics of War*, 134–147.
87. *Henrici de Segusio Cardinalis Hostiensis Summa Aurea . . . adiectis Annotationibus* (Lyons, 1597), bk. 1, f. 69v, col. B; bk. 5, f. 297v, col. A. For extracts in translation, see *Ethics of War*, 161–168.
88. Russell, *Just War*, 161.
89. J. A. Brundage, 'Holy War and the Medieval Lawyers', in *The Holy War*, edited by T. P. Murphy (Columbus: Ohio State University Press, 1976), 99–140; J. A. Brundage, 'The Hierarchy of Violence in Twelfth- and Thirteenth-Century Canonists', *International History Review* 17:4 (1995), 670–692.
90. Alexander of Hales, *Summa theologica*, bk. 3, §466, cited in Barnes, 'Just War', 773.
91. J. W. Baldwin, *Masters, Princes, and Merchants: The Social Views of Peter the Chanter and His Circle*, 2 vols. (Princeton, NJ: Princeton University Press, 1970), 1: 210–213; Russell, *Just War*, 217.

92. Thomas Aquinas, *Summa Theologiae: Latin Text and English Translation, Introduction, Notes, Appendices and Glossaries*, edited by T. Gilby et al., 61 vols. (London/New York: Blackfriars, 1964–81) [henceforth Aquinas, *ST*], 35: IIaIIae, q. 40, 80–81.
93. Aquinas, *ST*, 35: IIaIIae, q. 40, *art*. 1, *ad*. 1, 80–81.
94. Idem, q. 40, *art*. 1, *responsio*, 80–83.
95. Ibid., q. 40, *art*. 1, *responsio*, 82–83.
96. For Aquinas's treatment of justice, see *ST*, 37: IIaIIae, q. 57–62, especially q. 58 'De justitia'.
97. Aquinas, *ST*, 35: IIaIIae, q. 40, *art*. 1 and 2. For recent contributions to the 'presumption' debate, see J. F. Childress, *Moral Responsibility in Conflicts: Essays on Nonviolence, War, and Conscience* (Baton Rouge: Louisiana State University Press, 1982); D. Cole, 'Thomas Aquinas on Virtuous Warfare', *Journal of Religious Ethics* 27:1 (1999): 57–80; R. B. Miller, 'Aquinas and the Presumption Against Killing and War', *Journal of Religion* 82:2 (2002), 173–204; G. M. Reichberg, 'Is There a "Presumption Against War" in Aquinas's Ethics?', in *Ethics, Nationalism, and Just War*, edited by Syse and Reichberg, 72–98.
98. Aquinas, *ST*, 38: IIaIIae, q. 64, *art*. 7, *responsio*. See also J. Mangan, 'An Historical Analysis of the Principle of Double Effect', *Theological Studies* 10 (1949): 41–61; J. M. Boyle, Jr., 'Toward Understanding the Principle of Double Effect', *Ethics* 90:4 (1980), 527–538; D. Lefkowitz, 'Collateral Damage', in *War: Essays*, ed. May, 145–164.
99. Aquinas, *ST*, 35: IIaIIae, q. 40, *art*. 3 and 4 (quotation at *art*. 4, *responsio*, 92–93).

CHAPTER 6

LATE SCHOLASTIC JUST WAR THEORY

DANIEL SCHWARTZ

1. Introduction

ALTHOUGH medieval discussions of the ethics of war did not start with Aquinas, it was his short treatment in the *Summa Theologiae* II–II q. 40 that furnished the clearest enunciation of the basic principles of just war theory up to his time and provided the basic template for much later discussion.[1] But Aquinas's discussion of war was too concise to be a complete theory.[2] Rather it set the basis of a research program that would systematically explore the ramifications of Aquinas's views and the questions prompted directly or elliptically by him as well as those left unaddressed. This project, executed without superseding Aquinas's main insights, was undertaken by many scholastic and late scholastic theologians. Among the most prominent late scholastics (also called 'neoscholastics', 'baroque scholastics', and 'early modern scholastics' and in the just war context 'classical theorists') who wrote about war were Francisco de Vitoria (1483–1546),[3] Luis de Molina (1535–1600),[4] Gabriel Vázquez (1549–1604),[5] and Francisco Suárez (1548–1617).[6]

This late scholastic revival was possibly the most fecund and philosophically interesting phase in the just war tradition's development. It arose out of the military and political context faced by the late scholastics, foremost the Spanish and Portuguese conquest of parts of America; Spain's conquest of the Philippine Islands and its Eighty Years' War against Dutch rebels; the Portuguese commercial and political expansion in Africa, India, and China: the wars between European maritime powers and the Ottoman Empire; and the wars and disputes between the Portuguese and Castilian crowns.

Another factor contributing to this revival was the replacement of Peter Lombard's *Sentences* by Aquinas's *Summa Theologiae* as the chosen text for teaching theology at university, a change that some attribute to the commentary on Aquinas's *Summa* by Thomas de Vio, 'Cajetan' (written 1507–22, published 1540–41).[7] This change meant that most theology lecturers at some point had to engage with Aquinas's treatment of war.

In this chapter, I address some of the major questions discussed by the late scholastics. Section 2 considers the *ius ad bellum*. After discussing the judicial model of war favored by the late scholastics, I devote separate subsections to each of the three *ius ad bellum* requirements: just cause, legitimate authority, and rightful intention. My main focus here is the question of moral doubt among subject combatants. I argue that admitting the possibility of wars being just on both sides was not in fact Vitoria's original contribution to the just war tradition. Instead, he set the ground for serious reflection on a subject's refusal to fight in his country's morally doubtful wars. I relate this debate to the contemporary theme of 'the moral equality of combatants'. Section 3 considers the *ius in bello*. In its first part, after proposing an explanation of the provenance of the term 'innocent' in the textual traditions behind just war theory, I move to the question of who can enjoy the immunities provided by this status. I then discuss the permissibility of intentionally killing innocents who obstruct the achievement of the just cause. The second part of this section considers the permissibility of side-effect killing of innocents in war and the morally permitted defensive means available to potential side-effect victims.

2. Ius ad Bellum

2.1. The Judicial Model of War

Augustine's characterization of the purpose of just war, which features centrally in Aquinas's treatment as in all others, is to 'avenge injuries if some nation or state against whom one is waging a war has neglected to punish a wrong committed by its citizens, or to return something that was wrongfully taken'.[8] Augustine adds that, in such a war, the leader of the armies or the people themselves are not to be seen as the authors of war but as ministers of justice. Indeed, in the scholastic tradition, it was typical to assimilate the condition of the ruler or commonwealth waging a just offensive war to that of a judge. Justifying *defensive* wars were much easier and did not require relying on a judicial model: these wars were deemed simply cases of collective or vicarious self-defence.

In offensive war, force is used to redress an injustice that has already happened. As Suárez notes, it is not always easy to tell whether a war is offensive or defensive since it is not easy to tell when an act of injustice ends. In his view, injustice remains *in fieri* (in the making) while the wrongdoer has not yet deprived the victim entirely of his possessions, or, even when he has been successful in dispossessing the victim, but the latter is still engaged in attempts to restore the possessions to himself.

A paradoxical implication of the judicial model of just war is that the ruler features both as a judge of criminal proceedings[9] and at the same time as a party to the criminal case. This pressed the question: how can a person deliver justice when assuming at the same time the role of plaintiff and judge? Suárez notes some important differences between the case of just war and its judicial parallel. For one, he claims that rulers are less inclined than private persons to act on emotion and the thirst of vengeance.

Moreover, they are regularly assisted by the more temperate opinion of their expert advisors.[10] Recognizing that this may not be enough to surmount the problem, Suárez candidly says that, once we accept that someone must have the power to punish in the international arena, there simply aren't any better candidates for it than the sovereigns.[11] Foreigners come to fall within the punitive jurisdiction of a commonwealth by reason of the commission of wrongful harm against that commonwealth. The unjust party has only itself to blame for the judge's partiality because, by refusing to give satisfaction, it exposed itself to sentencing from a biased judge.[12]

Vitoria advanced a more expansive conception of just war than that of Suárez. He thought the prince or commonwealth could punish foreigners for harmful wrong perpetrated not only against them but also against a third, unallied, party. In order for the commonwealth's punitive jurisdiction to reach distant strangers, Vitoria had to furnish an alternative to Suárez's account of the way that the punitive jurisdiction of the commonwealth propagates beyond its borders. The solution was to posit the existence of a community endowed with punitive competence that encompasses both subjects of the realm and non-subjects. This is the community of the 'whole world'. Its authority can sometimes be embodied in the political ruler because 'everything needed to assure the governing and conservation of the world' is a matter of natural law.[13] Just as the commonwealth has punitive powers against its members, so 'the whole world' has these powers against 'any harmful and evil men'. This opened the way towards the modern idea of humanitarian intervention—the use of force by a political community to defend foreigners from foreigners in the name of humankind.

Suárez vehemently disagreed: '[T]he assertion made by some writers, that sovereign kings have the power of avenging/vindicating injuries done in any part of the world (*potestate, ad vindicandam iniurias totius orbius*), is entirely false and throws into confusion all the orderly distinctions of jurisdiction . . . '.[14]

Vitoria's view on the authority to punish foreigners for their sins against foreigners was developed as he reflected on the possible grounds of the Spanish war against American natives. These reflections were partly delivered as university lectures at Salamanca in 1539. His was a key contribution to a debate that engaged theologians, jurists, and humanists in Spain and that reached its peak in the famous confrontation between Juan Ginés de Sepúlveda and Bartolomé de las Casas in Valladolid in 1550–51. Vitoria considered seven plausible 'titles' to or grounds for war against the natives. The most compelling of these was 'the tyranny of the Lords of the barbarians or of the inhuman laws that damage the innocent, like the sacrifice of innocent human beings, or the killing of innocent persons in order to eat their flesh'.[15] This ground for the justice of the conquest pressed itself on the participants in the debate given the practice of large-scale, systematically orchestrated and executed human sacrifice and anthropophagy among the Aztecs and others, as well as by acquaintance with their political institutions. According to expert estimates, every year about 250,000 persons were killed and eaten in Central Mexico in the period preceding the arrival of the Conquistadores.[16] These were for the most part captives of wars undertaken with the deliberate purpose of capturing people alive (even the weapons used were devised to wound but not kill). Vitoria affirmed the moral imperative that one ought to defend the life of an innocent person if one can do so at reasonable price, even if the innocent is a stranger dwelling abroad. Therefore, he reluctantly recognized that, provided many conditions were met, a war against the Aztecs and other American polities to put an end to these heinous crimes could in principle be justified. Virtually all of the late scholastics who discussed the justice of the conquest agreed.[17] Vitoria argued that defending persons from blatant and serious injustice was different from the general aim of enforcing natural law as such (the violation of which may not always involve wronging others), an aim which on its own could not justify the resort to extrajurisdictional force.[18]

2.2. Just Cause

The fundamental *ius ad bellum* condition is the possession of a just cause (*causa iusta*). In line with the judicial model of just war, 'cause' here is best understood as an action by someone that gives at least presumptive reason for judicial action: 'that those who are fought against (*impugnatur*), are so fought because they deserve it on account of some fault (*culpa*)'.[19] In this section, I concentrate on the late scholastics' main interest when it comes to the just cause of war. This was determining the limits of the duty to inquire about the justice of the war as it applies to the various war participants and determining how the outcome of this inquiry affects the moral justification for the actions of these participants.

Some think that the views of Vitoria and his followers on these issues paved the way for the modern idea that combatants on both sides have the same licenses, rights, and immunities ('the moral equality of combatants') and, relatedly, that the *ius in bello* operates independently from the *ius ad bellum* ('the independence thesis'). I argue that Vitoria's main contribution lies elsewhere; namely, in making other theorists conscious of the need to think more thoroughly about the moral gravity of the subject's refusal to fight his commonwealth's doubtful wars.

The standard repertory of just war causes included the refusal to restore land or property unjustly seized, the violation of the Law of Peoples (*ius gentium*) without reasonable cause, serious damage to the prince's reputation or honor or that of the subjects,[20] the supply by a prince or republic of military aid to one's unjust enemy, the unjust protection of criminals by a prince or republic aimed at preventing their just punishment, the violation of international treaties,[21] and coming to the aid of an ally fighting a just war.

According to Molina, these wrongs could furnish a just cause for war even when no moral fault was involved. One can permissibly fight against a state that has seized alien possessions even if it inculpably believes—contrary to fact, but based on available evidence—that the possessions in dispute belong to it (in the technical scholastic language: it is in the grip of 'invincible ignorance'). However, if the attack by the state in the grip of invincible ignorance does not involve occupying alien territory or seizing alien possessions, the victim state should not react by unleashing offensive war.[22] A biblical example is the war between the People of Israel and the peoples living in the

Promised Land, who, invincibly unaware of God's promise, inculpably fought against the Israelites.[23]

Who among participants in war must inquire about the justice of the war? A distinction was made between four main classes of people. There were the rulers or leaders, the political or military hierarchies, subjects, and, finally, mercenaries (some on permanent contracts, some hired specifically for the war action at hand).

For Vitoria, Molina, and Suárez, rulers must exhaust every means to achieve certainty about the justice of their cause. They cannot be content with their own unexamined opinion. They should seek the opinion of independent moral experts and also duly consider the arguments of their opponents.[24]

According to Vitoria and Molina, political or military hierarchies whose opinions are likely to be given weight by the ruler also have a moral duty to examine the justice of the cause and convey their findings to the ruler.[25] Should they fail to do so, they will bear part of the blame for any ensuing unjust killings. Suárez, however, believed that they must convey their view only if called upon to do so. For him, the obligation to inquire into the justice of the war is one of charity not of justice.[26]

Vitoria held that subjects (including subject combatants), however, are released from these hefty epistemic duties, not so much because they are incapable of conducting this examination but because they are unlikely to be heard by the ruler.[27] Suárez bases their exception from independent inquiry on their duty of obedience.[28] Molina, after Gabriel Biel, added other reasons for this exemption: for example, that most subjects are incapable of assessing the justice of the war and that to oblige each of them resort to the advice of moral experts is overdemanding (*durum*).[29] However, according to Molina, should the subjects hear rumors or otherwise have indications about the injustice of the war, they must examine the question and individually approach experts; otherwise, they will not be able to excuse themselves by appealing to their ignorance.

Mercenaries presented an interesting case. Cajetan made a distinction between mercenaries on long-term contracts who, for him, are in the same position as subjects, and opportunistic freelancers. Because the participation of the latter in the war is fully voluntary, they should have a high degree of certainty about the justice of the war for them to be able to permissibly fight. If in doubt, the morally safer course is to abstain from fighting rather than risk being part of a criminal operation.[30] Unlike Cajetan, Suárez denied that the distinction between permanent (or long-term) and freelance mercenaries makes a difference to their moral epistemic duties. One of the six arguments that he offers is that 'if permanent mercenaries could, previously to a war, bind themselves to fight even in doubtful cases by giving their consciences into the keeping of the prince's conscience, why could not those mercenaries who enlist at the outbreak of war? For, from a moral standpoint, the same principle is involved in the performance of an action and in binding oneself to perform it'.[31]

After meeting their differential duties of inquiry, both those who decide on war and those who are called to fight may nevertheless find themselves in doubt about whether they in fact possess a just cause of war. These hard cases presented a challenge to Vitoria and the other moral theologians. The reason was that, as agreed by all, one has a moral duty to stick to one's moral judgment. If the fighter or the ruler finds himself in the grip of doubt and he nevertheless proceeds to fight, he would be contravening his—inconclusive—moral judgment. Different solutions were proposed for rulers and for fighters.

When in doubt, the ruler must diligently and impartially reconsider his purported just cause with the help of experts and listen to the arguments of the other party. If this examination does not dispel the doubt, the rule of possession comes to his aid. According to this long-standing legal and moral rule, when there is a dispute about who owns a realm, the presumption is in favor of the side that has actual possession (*in dubio melior est conditio possidentis*).[32]

But what should be done when none of the litigants has actual possession? According to Suárez, the disputed realm should be divided between the parties in proportion to the force of their respective claims, or arbitration should be sought.[33] But what if there is no agreement as to the composition of the tribunal of arbitration or the arbitrators fail to reach a deal? It would seem that, according to the account of Vitoria and Navarrus, doubtful parties are then left free to wage war on each other. This would be a war that is just on both sides.

The scope for wars that are just on both sides was expanded further with the gradual consolidation and acceptance of the doctrine of 'probabilism', which required even less moral certainty to justly engage in war. Probabilism was dominant among Catholic moral theologians during the first part of the seventeenth century. In its standard formulation given by the Dominican Bartolomé de Medina (1527/8–80) in 1577, it held that 'When an opinion is probable it may be followed even when the contrary opinion is more probable'.[34] When there are at least two conflicting opinions about the presence of a just cause of war that satisfy a certain threshold of probability, it is permitted to follow the less probable one. Probabilism made it possible to contemplate a new type of case, one in which both sides can justly fight while agreeing on all relevant facts. Neither side need deny that the other has, in principle, an actionable cause for war. Each party can say, 'We have probable just cause and so do you' not in the subjective sense ('*if* we were in their shoes we would think ourselves just') but in the objective one.

Gabriel Vázquez charged that Vitoria and Navarrus permitted two doubtful sides lacking possession of the disputed good to let war decide the issue. Yet he objected that such war could not be just. Just war is *execution* of a judicial sentence, not a way of finding out what the judicial sentence should be. 'All controversy between opinions regarding some right is to be decided by judgment, not by power and arms; it is a barbaric custom to consider the right to rule as better pertaining to the stronger party'.[35]

His solution was to drastically revise the prevalent theory of sovereignty, according to which to be a sovereign meant not to stand before the judgment of any other human being. It followed from this view that sovereigns were like judges with overlapping jurisdictions. The way to eliminate contradicting judicial sentences about the same cases is to eliminate the overlap by assigning to each sovereign a territorially bounded jurisdiction. When matters fall outside that jurisdiction, the sovereign is no longer in a position of judge but in a position of subject relative to the sovereign in that realm.[36]

The case of subject combatants presented its own difficulties. Suppose that the subject's lack of knowledge leaves him in a state of doubt. Adrian of Florisz or of Utrecht, later Pope Adrian VI, controversially held in a public disputation in Leuven in 1491 that subjects may not obey their superior when in doubt, for in doing so they expose themselves to the moral danger of acting against their own conscience.[37]

Against Adrian, Vitoria argued that a subject combatant could fight in good faith even when he remains in doubt about the justice of the war. The mistake he imputes to Adrian is to think that 'if I am in doubt about whether the cause of war is just, I must therefore doubt whether I may lawfully fight in that war'.[38] Doubts about the justice of the war need not transform into doubts about the permissibility of one's participation in the war. In putting forward this view, Vitoria surely had in mind a distinction between 'speculative' and 'practical' doubts that is explicitly relied upon in Molina's and Suárez's later treatments of war, as well as in discussions of restitution by Navarrus, Soto, and Medina roughly at the time of Vitoria's own analysis of war.[39] Speculative doubts are doubts about whether there is a just cause. Practical doubts are doubts about whether it is permissible *for me* to fight in this war. This view, that these two sorts of doubt need not entail each other can be found in a *responsa* by Cajetan from 1521.[40] According to the late scholastics, only practical doubt makes it impossible to fight in good faith.[41]

In effect, Vitoria and his followers contemplated the possibility that combatants on both sides may fight not only when they mistakenly but blamelessly believe their war to be just but also when they are not entirely certain that this is the case. This is why some see in Vitoria the inflexion point between the medieval just war theory paradigm and the regular war paradigm.[42] The latter paradigm affirms the view dubbed 'the moral equality of combatants', according to which combatants have the same licenses, rights, and immunities regardless of whether they fight for the just or unjust side. This view, in turn, is grounded in the thesis, also part of the regular war paradigm, that *ius in bello* is independent from the *ius ad bellum* (dubbed the 'independence thesis').

Graham Parsons has even argued that Vitoria actually endorses the moral equality of combatants.[43] Gregory Reichberg has rejected this claim on the grounds that, for Vitoria, good-faith unjust combatants are merely excused but not justified and therefore do not acquire a right to fight.[44] Without disputing the conclusion, one may wonder how much weight the excuse/justification distinction bore for Vitoria and the late scholastics. This is not because the late scholastics could not see a conceptual difference between excuses and justifications but because they believed that erring conscience not only excuses but also binds. One has a duty to act in conformity with the dictates of one's moral reasoning even when these dictates are objectively wrong. So, invincible ignorance excuses us insofar as it makes our acts less intentional and so removes some or all of the blame.[45] At the same time, we have a moral obligation to act according to the results of our moral reasoning, even when its conclusions result from false or restricted information. Note, however, that even if good-faith combatants have a duty to fight in an unjust war, their duty does not furnish them with an objective right to fight. Therefore, it remains the case that subject combatants on opposite sides of the trenches are not moral equals.

Even if the moral equality of combatants should not be attributed to Vitoria and the late scholastics, perhaps, as Alex Bellamy has argued, 'Vitoria's discussion of invincible ignorance and simultaneous ostensible justice unwittingly paved the way for later realists and legalists to argue that as objective knowledge of just causes was impossible, it should be assumed that war waged by sovereigns was just, placing normative emphasis on its conduct'.[46]

In response, Vitoria was not the first scholastic to advance these views.[47] It was defended by the Scottish theologian John Mair (Major) in a work published some thirty years before Vitoria wrote of *Relectio de iure belli*. Vitoria knew Mair personally from his studies in Paris. Some have argued that he even was among his disciples.[48] Mair gave the analogy, later popularized by Vitoria, that as a court executioner must obey the order of the judge and carry out the sentence even if in doubt about the guilt of the executed, so must the subject soldier carry out the ruler's command.[49]
Strikingly, Mair writes:

> It could be argued that it follows from my view that the same war can be in one respect just and in another unjust, since as regards the superior it is unjust but as regards the inferior it is just. This is problematic (*inconveniens*) because for those for whom the war is just, or is considered to be so, there is no obligation to restitute the things taken, otherwise however they must be restituted, and the same can be claimed by the opposite side. In response: I concede this, for it could happen that two opposing armies suffer from probable ignorance, sometimes affecting the superiors and inferiors and sometimes affecting only the subjects and, so Lucan seems to say in the first book of his *Civil War* [(*Pharsalia*), bk. 1-126-7] about the war between Caesar and Pompey: 'Which had the fairer right for warfare we may not know: each has high authority to support him'.[50]

Thus, Vitoria's discussion is not original in allowing the possibility of a dislocation between the *ius in bello* and the *ius ad bellum*. Rather, its originality resides in its engagement with Adrian's stand on the incompatibility of good faith with moral doubt in war.[51] We do not find an engagement with Adrian on doubt and good faith either in just war treatments before Vitoria or in Vitoria's early work. For example, there is almost nothing on this in his 1535 lectures on restitution and acquisitive prescription (a topic in which, as I show below, good faith is crucial), despite profuse referencing of other views of Adrian taken from the *Quodlibeticae*.[52] Only four years later, Vitoria engages Adrian's view on doubt in the context of just war at roughly the same time others begin to engage these same views in various other contexts in which the agent's moral and legal benefits depend on his being in a condition of good faith.

One of these other contexts was acquisitive prescription (discussed in Juan de Medina's often reprinted *De restitutione*).[53] If you are in possession of real estate for a statutory period, you may then acquire ownership rights over it. The good faith of the possessor, at least at the time of possession, is crucial in order to acquire these rights. Suppose the possessor paid a person posing as the legitimate owner. In order to grant ownership to the possessor after the statutory period, the judge will want to make sure that she thought she was purchasing it from its legitimate owner. Adrian argued—and Soto agreed[54]—that good faith is lost when the possessor finds himself in doubt about the provenance of the estate. Medina rejected this.

The debate on prescription is instructive because it shows that good faith is not only about being excused but also about acquiring rights. In war, good faith generates rights as well. It gives combatants a moral right not to restitute some of what they seized while unjustly fighting (albeit not a right to fight!).[55]

Adrian argued that, when acting under uncertainty, we should always follow the safer course (*tutior*).[56] Soto explained that this tutiorist principle operates lexically. We first weigh the gravity of the two sins that we risk committing. We should do the act that, if it should turn out to constitute a sin, will be the lesser sin of the two. We should do that act even if the alternative act presents less risk to turn out to be sinful. If the two sins we risk committing are equally grave, we should run the lower risk.[57] So what matters in the case of war is whether the sin we risk committing by disobeying the ruler's call to arms in a just war is worse than the sin of fighting in an unjust war.

Adrian seems to fail to acknowledge that failure to fight can also involve a moral risk. In his discussion of war, it is only fighting for you prince in possibly unjust war that is taken to present a moral danger: that of killing the innocent.[58] Vitoria by contrast notices that refraining from fighting for your prince can also be morally dangerous. Since no option is without danger, these two moral risks must be compared. In the *Relection* the sins are characterized as, 'assisting the enemies of the commonwealth by disobeying' which morally worse 'than fighting these enemies while in doubt' (*pugnare contra hostes cum dubio*).[59] When read in conjunction with what Vitoria had to say on this in his 1534 *Lectures* commenting on Aquinas on war, it is clear that Vitoria does not mean that the problem is the fighthing *while in doubt* (which is merely an adjuctive) but rather fighting against innocent enemies.[60]

Suárez, developing a thought that can be found in a 1540 lecture by Soto, drew a different comparison. He argued that what is at stake if we fail to fight is not just a violation of a duty of obedience but one of justice because, by failing to fight, subjects are rendering their princes (and commonwealths) unable to defend their rights. It is worse to leave your innocent compatriots defenceless than to cause the deaths of innocent foreigners.[61]

This is not an entirely implausible view. Even if we bear less responsibility for allowing the death of innocents than for causing it, allowing the death of your innocent compatriots may, all things considered, be worse than killing foreign innocents. This is so if you have an agent-relative duty to put ahead the interests of those specially related to you. This duty may offset the difference between doing and allowing harm. Suppose that your son and a stranger are fighting over car keys, and you do not know to whom the car belongs. It may be morally worse to refrain from acting in a way that will reduce the likelihood that your son will be a victim of theft (if he turns out to be the legitimate owner) than to act in a way that increases the likelihood that a stranger will be a victim of theft (if he is the legitimate owner). As a parent, you may even have a *duty* to aid your son in these circumstances. This argument does not rest on duties of obedience. Even if you are not summoned to fight by your ruler, you might have a moral duty qua citizen to privilege the doubtful claims of your compatriots over the doubtful claims of foreigners when these claims are in conflict, provided it is clear that one of the parties will act and the other will resist. Whether this is so depends on whether compatriots have duties to one another similar to those a father has to his son. This is not to affirm the moral equality of combatants, however, since the circumstances in which the combatant's duties towards his community defeat his duties towards foreign innocents apply only to those combatants who cannot reach a verdict on the justice of the war. Moreover, even when two combatants on opposite sides fight because of the force of agent-relative considerations in situations of doubt, they are not moral equals since one of them is objectively just and so has a right to fight, and the other does not.

At this stage of late scholastic discussion, it seemed that since the moral gravity of disobedience could not justify fighting in doubt, one had to invoke the moral gravity of failing your agent-relative duties to justify this. The need for this solution was a direct result of Vitoria's decision to engage Adrian's use of tutiorist reasoning on the matter of doubt and good faith in his treatise on war.

2.3. Legitimate Authority

For Aquinas, just war requires 'the authority of the prince by whose command the war is to be waged'.[62] Private persons cannot initiate war because they can seek redress and satisfaction from the wrongdoers through their superiors. Nor is it their business to summon the subjects. That is the job of the sovereign who is in charge of the common good and, in particular, of administering justice. This prohibition on private war was later understood to apply only to offensive war.[63] As a matter of natural law, every innocent person retains his or her right to self-defence, particularly when his or her life is under imminent threat.[64] However, as Cajetan says, private persons cannot avenge injuries against nor take back property from either their fellow citizens or foreigners.[65]

The requirement of legitimate authority, though merely formal in appearance, raised a number of interesting puzzles. One puzzle was: who qualifies as sovereign for the purposes of the requirement? Scholastics thought that the commonwealth transferred the power to rule to the appointed authorities.[66] But, in the Middle Ages, before the emergence of the centralized nation-state, secular political power was diffused. The Emperor of the Holy Roman Empire (in many respects a merely honorary title), kings, barons, counts, and marquees all had different and ill-defined competences.[67] It was necessary to clarify who exactly among these many authorities had the power to avenge and punish wrongs.

The standard view was that, with some exceptions (specified below), any subordinate authority, such as a marquee or baron, who initiated offensive war would be wrongfully usurping the right of the sovereign.[68] Vitoria, following Cajetan and Molina, relaxed this requirement by saying that human law and the law of nations confer to the king or commonwealth the right to allocate the power to declare war to subordinates and that such customary rights are valid.[69] Suárez restricts exceptions based on customary law only to external war, not to domestic war (so the governor of a province cannot declare war against another province).[70]

What is the commonwealth to do if it has a just cause for offensive war but the legitimate authority to declare war fails to do so? Vitoria argues that in cases of necessity a community or group need not wait for the superior to declare war. For example, if one city attacks another in the same kingdom and the king 'fails, through negligence or timidity, to avenge the damage done' then the city can not only defend itself but can also initiate war against the attacker, seize its territory, and inflict deterrent punishment.[71] This permission extends not just to defensive but also to offensive wars because sometimes one cannot effectively deter the enemy from future attack unless one goes beyond strict defence. Suárez agrees as regards interstate war but not as regards intrastate war, for, he says, 'a punishment inflicted by one's private authority is intrinsically evil' and is likely to lead to civil wars.[72] Therefore, the license of a portion of the republic to resort to war in case of necessity extends only to defensive war.[73] He adds that sometimes the tacit consent of the superior can be presumed, particularly when the war is waged against foreigners who are 'on other grounds overt enemies of the sovereign'.[74]

Is compensation due to the enemy if the condition of legitimate authority is violated but the other just war conditions obtain? According to Suárez, whose view coincides with those of Vitoria, Domingo Báñez (1528–1604), and Molina, such wars constitute an affront to justice because they involve a violation of jurisdiction and so raise just claims of restitution for all damages caused to those fought against.[75] To use an analogy, if without a judge's authorization you use force to recover items stolen from you, you do not have to return these to the thief, but you do have to compensate him for any damages or injuries caused in the attempt. Not everyone agreed, however. Francisco de Oviedo (1602–51), for one, argued that restitution to the enemy is due only if the harm inflicted in the attempted recovery is excessive or if third parties have been harmed.[76]

Enrique de Villalobos (†1637) extends the legitimate authority requirement to *ius in bello*. The requirement is violated, for example, when soldiers act beyond orders, for instance, by sacking a city for more days than allowed by the military commander.[77] Báñez, however, says that if soldiers acting on their own initiative seize back property taken by pirates, no restitution is due to the pirates themselves; the only victim of injustice would be the soldiers' own superior.[78]

2.4. Right Intention

Right intention is perhaps the just war condition that most troubled Aquinas's commentators. Aquinas himself goes little beyond citing two passages that he attributes to Augustine: 'True religion looks upon as peaceful those wars that are waged not for motives of aggrandisement, or cruelty, but with the object of securing peace, of punishing evil-doers, and of uplifting the good'.[79] And, as examples of wicked intentions: 'The passion for inflicting harm, the cruel thirst for vengeance, an unpacific and relentless spirit, the fever of revolt, the lust for power, and such like things, all these are rightly condemned in war.'[80]

The two quotations attributed to Augustine (the first of which is misattributed) point in quite different directions. The first quotation focuses on the goals fuelling the war effort, whereas the second looks into the emotions of the fighters. But is this condition a requirement of justice? Cajetan thinks that while you sin mortally when you fight out of hatred or other perverse passions, you are not bound to restitute anything to the enemy for the harm so caused, if the other conditions of just war obtain.[81] He and the rest of the tradition agree with Navarrus: 'The hangman who kills with bad intentions is not obliged to return the clothes and other belongings that he gained by executing the justly sentenced, neither is the soldier obliged to restore the horse, belongings and weapons he gained by killing [with bad intentions] an enemy soldier against whom he rightly fought.'[82] Báñez says, however, that if the prince acting out of hatred initiates an otherwise just war that results in greater harm to *his* realm, then he is under duty to restitute to the commonwealth, just as a prince should do the same if he decides to (deservedly) punish a criminal, but does so out of private animosity, knowing that the administration of the punishment will cause great harm to society.[83]

Molina creatively interprets the condition of rightful intention as a prohibition on what we may call 'moral entrapment'. We should not use our rights to provoke our neighbours to sin so as to furnish us with a just cause for war in order to vent preexisting perverse emotions such as hatred or political ambitions that in themselves do not provide just causes of war. The rights that we have should be exercised conscientiously and not as pretexts for whatever designs we have in mind. Molina, however, sets out some exceptions, cases in which provoking just wars via this sort of entrapment may be permissible.[84]

3. *Ius in Bello*

3.1. Intentionally Killing Innocents in War

As seen, the just war was conceived first and foremost as an exercise of justice. The innocent is a person who has done you no wrongful harm. It was unanimously agreed that those known to be innocents do not constitute legitimate war targets. They cannot be intentionally killed.

Note that, contrary to the etymology, the term 'innocent' is used not only to designate the person who does not endanger us (the non-*nocente*) but also to designate the person who is free of sin. Indeed, the English 'innocent' and its cognates in other vernacular languages[85] are the terms that have been chosen to translate Exodus 23:7 as 'the innocent and righteous slay thou not'. The Hebrew word translated as 'innocent' is נקי (*nakih*), which means 'clean' (as in 'clean of sin'). The Latin Vulgate has '*insontem*' (guiltless), and the Greek Septuagint has ἀθῷον (*athoon*), meaning both harmless and undeserving of punishment. Perhaps slippage from *insontem* to *innocentem* both in scholastic Latin and in the vernacular was caused by the phonetic closeness between the words. The twofold meaning of innocent as free of sin and as not harmful has been preserved in ordinary language.

Vitoria argues that just as within the commonwealth you cannot punish the innocent for the crimes of the evil, you cannot kill the innocents in the enemy population for the crimes of the wicked among them.[86] Suárez agrees: 'no one may be deprived of his life save by reason of his own guilt'.[87] Moreover, says Vitoria, if killing the innocent were permissible, it would open the way to wars that are just on both sides (here not on account of ignorance or doubt), since, plainly, the innocent are permitted to defend themselves.[88]

As Vitoria and Molina agree, innocents cannot be intentionally killed even to prevent them from future engagement in unjust war. It is forbidden in war to kill infants even when they can be assumed to eventually join their parents in their unjust war. The reason is not so much uncertainty about how these children will in fact turn out but the principle that one cannot punish for the sin that one fears will be committed but has not yet been committed (*neque fas est punire pro peccato, quod patrandum timetur, neque adhuc est commissum*).[89] Moreover, says Vitoria, there are many other ways of preventing the future sin than killing these children.[90]

The late scholastics noted that often it is difficult or impossible for combatants to tell the innocent from the culpable. Hence, they must proceed by relying on presumptions. Children, women, travelers or visitors in the enemy's territory, clergy and monks are presumed innocent.[91] Molina points out that sometimes there is evidence against a whole group of adults. He gives the example of a siege in which women can be presumed to be actively helping the unjust male defenders. Therefore, regardless of whether they can be killed or not, they should not be placed in the same category as children.[92]

All male adults capable of bearing arms among the enemy population are presumed to be non-innocents, unless it is patent that they are innocent; for example, if they are invincibly ignorant or mentally deficient. Pedro de Lorca (1561–1612) believed that the presumption of non-innocence extends to those who provide help or advice, which would include public officials who cannot bear arms.[93] Vitoria (quoted by Molina) adds that if the war is against Catholics, the presumption of innocence extends also to rural folk and peaceful civilians (*gente togata et pacifica*)—even if they can bear arms.[94]

Suárez believed that just combatants may rely on presumptive judgments about guilt and innocence based on coarse statistical generalization (age and sex) only during combat, when it is impossible or very costly to make individualized judgments. After combat is over, the examination of persons' innocence must be conducted case per case. Note that punishment, including capital punishment, may be administered after combat, both for wrongs committed by the enemy before the war (those related to the just cause) and wrongs committed in the course of war.[95] Suárez says 'if all the penalties just enumerated [the postwar indemnification for harm] seem insufficient in view of the gravity of the wrong, then, after the war has entirely ended, certain guilty enemies (*hostes nocentes*) among the enemy may also with justice, be put to death; and although the slaying of a great number [among the guilty] is not permissible unless there is a most urgent cause to kill them, nevertheless even such slaughter may sometimes be allowed, in order to terrify the rest'.[96]

There is one important exception to the prohibition to killing innocents directly and intentionally. According to Molina, one can kill an enemy combatant even if one is aware of his moral innocence (he could be nonculpable because of excusable ignorance or because he is following his sovereign's orders) and even if the ongoing war effort is not defensive but offensive. This intentional killing of the innocent is done in self-defence and 'for the common good and to recover the things that are ours, *against their resistance*'.[97] What makes the innocent enemy combatants liable to attack is their being an obstacle to the accomplishment of the just goals of the war. 'Because even as private persons, when unable to defend themselves or their possessions otherwise, can licitly kill even if the killed is an innocent whom they are resisting, so anyone in a just war can licitly kill the innocents that fight on the other side, when it is necessary to accomplish the goal'.[98] He adds, however, that the nonculpability of these enemy combatants does confer on them some special rights: if in combat you can spare some or all of them, you should try to do so.

Molina's point is that the guilty among the enemy *deserve* prima facie to be killed (although whether they should be killed, all things considered, depends on different factors including whether the war is over or ongoing). They are guilty because they are in some way responsible for the wrongful harm on account of which one can justly fight. The innocent among the enemy do not deserve to be killed but are liable to be killed during the ongoing war when they stand in the way of our just purpose (defending the country, recuperating stolen possessions, or avenging wrongs).

It follows that, while the war unfolds, just combatants may intentionally and directly kill (a) all those who can be presumed guilty of having given the occasion for war, including those who at the moment of their killing take no part in combat, and (b) those persons who while known not to be guilty of having given occasion for war, by fighting for the unjust side present an obstacle to their just goals.

3.2. Side-Effect Killing

The innocent on the side of the unjust enemy divide into those who take part in combat (and can sometimes be intentionally killed) and those who do not. Sometimes, however, the latter class of innocents can be killed as side-effects. This is the Doctrine of Double Effect (DDE).[99] Although the DDE is often attributed to Aquinas, he did not appeal to it either in his discussion of war or when considering whether the innocent can be killed.

Rather, it is in his analysis of private self-defence from an attacker that this doctrine is proposed.[100] There, he argues that two effects may follow from the act of the defender: the conservation of his life and the death of the attacker. This second effect may be beyond the agent's intention. Moral acts should be specified according to what is intended, not according to what is beyond the agent's intention (*praeter intentionem*). Therefore, when the defender repels the attack, resulting in the attacker's death (which, we assume, is not a means of his saving his life), it is only the action of saving his life by repelling the attack that should be imputed to the defender. This action, pursuant to some other conditions, is licit. Whether the attacker in question is culpable or not, he does not say, but this is not crucial since, according to Aquinas, even if he is culpable he can be killed intentionally only by public officials, not by private individuals.[101]

Not all the neoscholastics agreed that it impermissible for a private person to kill as a means. Sometimes the two effects—repelling the attack and causing death—are so close that it would be disingenuous to treat them as separate. Domingo de Soto (1494–1560), for example, argued that one may kill a person when 'searching with the sword the attacker's throat' when it is the only means of saving oneself.[102] In these cases, Soto argues, one cannot say that death was beyond the intention of the defender.

In matters of war, the late scholastics agreed that one kill can innocents when their death is foreseen but not intended, not *intenta* but *per accidens*. This happens, for example, when the weapons available do not allow for discrimination, as when using artillery fire against a walled city or setting fire to buildings that may crash on innocents or spread to their houses.[103] Or, in Molina's example, when we try to sink an enemy vessel in which we know the rowers are prisoners of war.[104] If we ban these sorts of attacks, says Vitoria, it would be impossible to wage war against the culpable.

The permission to harm and kill innocents nonintentionally is subject to considerations of proportionality. If there is only a small military advantage to taking a walled city populated by a small garrison and a great number of innocents, the indiscriminate bombardment necessary for achieving this end would be disallowed.[105] Moreover, if the military advantage thus gained is considerable, but it can be equally accomplished through a different target that does not contain innocents, then it would be morally impermissible to go for the target that contains them.[106]

Suárez bases the permission to incidentally kill the innocent on the difference between voluntarily inflicting death and merely allowing it, when you make use of your rights in time of necessity.[107] The situation is similar to that of a mother who, to save her life, uses a medicine that she knows will result in the death of the unborn child. This leads to the objection, made in the controversies about abortive medicines, that 'if help cannot be given to one person without injuring another, it is better to help neither person', a principle that holds at least from the moment the fetus has a soul.[108] Suárez replies that the objection applies when the medicine is not absolutely needed to save the mother's life but only as an aid to her better health. However, if the mother's life it at risk, this is the only medicine that can save her, and the intention is solely to save her life, the abortive medicine can be administered.[109]

Suárez argues that the attacker is not a cause per se of the death but only a cause *per accidens*. In moral terms, the attacker was exercising his right to kill the non-innocent, which he is not bound to avoid in order to prevent harm to his neighbour at great cost to himself. Although one may not perform a morally bad action (*mala moralia*) so that good may come, what we have here is a nonmoral evil (*mala poenae*) that is permitted to occur rather than one that is purposefully caused (*efficiantur*).[110]

The same principle applies to seemingly suicidal missions in war. A soldier who helps demolish a wall knowing that he will be crushed by the falling stones does not kill himself but merely allows his own death. This again must be understood relative to the good produced. So, absent other considerations, Samson's killing the Philistines along with himself by pulling down the pillars was impermissible given that punishment is not a great enough good to outweigh his own life.[111]

An interesting objection is that making side-effect killing permissible makes it possible for there to be a war that is just on both sides since potential side-effect victims could be morally permitted to fight against their just attackers. After all, they are innocents, they have done no wrong.[112] Notably, the question of the rights of potential side-effect victims has animated a lively debate among contemporary just war theorists.[113]

Suárez argued that potential side-effect victims may legitimately resort to defensive action, for example by trying to prevent the burning of the city or the destruction of the citadel. They may not, however, engage in offensive fighting against the just combatants since they suffer no *wrongful* harm from them. They can, however, offensively fight against those who gave the just cause.[114] So, an innocent civilian who is likely to be killed as side-effect in a just attack targeting a terrorist in the vicinity has the right to kill the terrorist. She can do this to save her life by making pointless the attack on the terrorist that would have killed her, even if the terrorist has done nothing to *her* directly. The terrorist is to blame for the harm the innocent will potentially suffer at the hand of just combatants. This harm can be treated as wrongful harm inflicted by the terrorist himself.

The late scholastics produced interesting discussions on additional just war issues that I have not surveyed here. These include, for example, the extent to which war prisoners can cooperate with their captors, the justice of peace settlements, and how booty ought to be divided among combatants. Their treatments of the central just war questions covered here, however, makes abundantly manifest the diversity of views within late scholastic thought and the high level of philosophical sophistication of these moral theologians, which continues to make them an inspiring model to contemporary just war theorists.

Acknowledgements

I would like to thank Greg Reichberg and Pablo Kalmanovitz for their helpful and insightful comments on a draft of this chapter and to Rory Cox for useful advice. Thanks are also due to the editors of this volume, Helen Frowe and Seth Lazar. Seth commented on various drafts and pushed me to deepen my analysis. Asher Salah kindly helped me with some of the Latin translations, as Elizabeth Miles did editing the final text.

Notes

1. On medieval and late scholastic just war theory, see Frederick H. Russell, *The Just War in the Middle Ages* (Cambridge: Cambridge University Press, 1975); Peter Haggenmacher, *Grotius et la doctrine de la guerre juste* (Paris: PUF, 1983), 23–47; Jonathan Barnes, 'The

Just War' in *The Cambridge History of Later Medieval Philosophy* edited by Norman Kretzmann, Anthony Kenny, and Kan Pinborg (New York: Cambridge University Press, 1982); Robert Hubert Willem Regout, *La doctrine de la guerre juste, de Saint Augustin a nous jours* (Paris: Pedone, 1935); Alfred Vanderpol, *La doctrine scholastique du droit de guerre* (Paris: A. Pedone, 1919); James Turner Johnson, *Just War Tradition and the Restraint of War: A Moral and Historical Inquiry* (Princeton: Princeton University Press, 1981); Stephen C. Neff, *War and the Law of Nations: A General History* (Cambridge: Cambridge University Press, 2005). Gregory M. Reichberg, Henrik Syse, and Endre Begby, eds., *The Ethics of War* (Blackwell, Oxford, 2006) contains many of the key texts as well as a very useful introduction to some of the authors and general historical background. Conventions: c.=chapter (except in Aquinas's *Summa Theologiae* where it means *corpus*); concl.=conclusion; contro.=controversy; d.=disputation; diff.=difficulty; dub.=doubt; f/fol.= folio; lib.=book; membr.=part; punct.=point; q.=question; num.=paragraph; resp.=reply; sect.=section; tract.=treatise.

2. On Aquinas on war, see Gregory Reichberg, 'Thomas Aquinas Between Just War and Pacifism', *Journal of Religious Ethics*, 28(2010), 219–241; 'Legitimate Authority: Aquinas's First Requirement of a Just War', *Thomist*, 76(2012), 337–69; 'Aquinas on Defensive Killing: A Case of Double-Effect?', *Thomist*, 69(2005), 341–370; 'Is There a "Presumption Against War" in Aquinas's Ethics?', *Thomist*, 66(2002), 337–367 and his forthcoming *Thomas Aquinas on War and Peace* (Cambridge University Press). Also Gerhard Beestermöller, 'Thomas Aquinas and Humanitarian Intervention' in *From Just War to Modern Peace Ethics*, edited by Heinz-Gerhard Justenhoven and William A Barbieri, Jr. (The Hague: De Gruyter, 2012), 71–98.
3. On Vitoria on war, see James Brown Scott, *The Spanish Origins of International Law, Francisco Vitoria and His Law of Nations* (New York: Oxford University Press, 1934); Venancio Diego Carro, *La 'communitas orbis' y las rutas del derecho internacional según Francisco de Vitoria* (Palencia: Merino, 1962); Richard Shelly Hartigan, 'Francesco de Vitoria and Civilian Immunity', *Political Theory* 1(1973), 79–91; James Muldoon, 'Vitoria and Humanitarian Intervention', *Journal of Military Ethics* 5(2006), 128–143; and Daniel Schwartz, 'The Principle of the Defence of the Innocent and the Conquest of America: "Save Those Dragged Towards Death"', *Journal of the History of International Law*, 9(2007), 263–291.
4. On Molina, see *Luis de Molina y el Derecho de la Guerra*, edited and translated by Manuel Fraga Iribarne (Madrid: Consejo Superior de Investigaciones Científicas, 1947); João Manuel A. A. Fernandez, 'Luis de Molina: On War', in *A Companion to Luis de Molina*, edited by Matthias Kaufmann and Alexander Aichele (Leiden and Boston: Brill, 2014), 227–256; Frank Bartholomew Costello, *The Political Philosophy of Luis de Molina, S. J. (1535–1600)* (Rome: Institutum Historicum Societatis Iesu, 1974); Amândio Augusto Coxito, 'O direito de guerra em Luis de Molina', *Revista Filosofica de Coimbra*, 18(2000), 261–287; Diego Alonso Lasheras, *Luis de Molina's De Iustitia et Iure* (Leiden: Brill, 2011).
5. On Vázquez, see José Antonio García Vilar, 'Teoría de la guerra y arbitraje internacional en Gabriel Vázquez', in *Pensamiento Jurídico y Sociedad Internacional: Estudios en honor del profesor D. Antonio Truyol Serra*, 2 vols. (Madrid: Centro de Estudios Constitucionales, 1986), 461–482; Daniel Schwartz, 'Probabilism, Just War, and Sovereignty in the Work of Gabriel Vázquez', *History of Political Thought*, 34(2013), 177–194.
6. Gregory Reichberg, 'Suárez on Just War', in *Interpreting Suárez: Critical Essays*, edited by Daniel Schwartz (Cambridge: Cambridge University Press, 2012), 185–204; Markus

Kremer, 'Morality and Just War According to Francisco Suárez' in *From Just War to Modern Peace Ethics*, edited by Heinz-Gerhard Justenhoven and William A Barbieri, Jr. (The Hague: de Gruyter, 2012), 155–174. On Suárez on war, see James Bernard Murphy, 'Suárez, Aquinas, and the Just War: Self Defense or Punishment?' in *From Just War to Modern Peace Ethics*, edited by Heinz-Gerhard Justenhoven and William A Barbieri, Jr. (The Hague: de Gruyter, 2012), 175–196. Also Luciano Pereña Vicente, *Teoría de la guerra en Francisco Suárez* (Madrid: CSIC, 1954) which covers also many other late scholastic authors and places their just war theory in the context of Spanish imperial policy.

7. Thomas de Vio, Cajetan, *Sancti Thomae Aquinatis Doctoris Angelici Opera Omnia iussum pensaque Leonis XIII, cum commentariis Thomae de Vio Caietani Ordinis Praedicatorum* (Rome: Typographia Polyglotta, 1895). Hereafter, *In II–II* followed by article in Aquinas's *ST* and page number in the translation by Peter Haggenmacher and Robert Andrew in Reichberg, Syse, and Begby, 247.
8. '[I]usta autem bella ea definiri solent quae ulciscuntur iniurias, si qua gens vel civitas quae bello petenda est vel vindicare neglexerit [. . .] In quo bello ductor exercitus vel ipse populus non tam auctor belli, quam minister judicandum est'. St Augustine, *Quaestiones in Heptateuchum 6.10 in Corpus Christianorum Series Latina* (Turnhout: Brepols, 1958) vol. 33, 318–319.
9. Luis de Molina, *De iustitia et iure tomi sex* (Antwerp: Ioannem Keerbergium, 1615) d.100.5 at 271 (hereafter noted as *II*).
10. Francisco Suárez, *De legibus ac Deo legislatore, d. 13 c. VI sect. 1 at 828 in Selections from Three Works of Francisco Suárez, S.J.*, James Brown Scott ed. Gwladys L. Williams, Ammi Brown, and John Waldron trans. (Oxford: Clarendon Press, 1944) with fascimil of the Coimbra 1612 edition published by Diogo Gomes Loureiro, hereafter noted as *DB* (*De bello*).
11. Suárez, *DB*, IV.7 at 819.
12. Also Cajetan, *In ST II-II* q. 40 a. 1 at 248.
13. Vitoria, *De iure belli*, 'On the Law of War'in Anthony Pagden and Jeremy Lawrence eds. *Political Writings* (Cambridge: Cambridge University Press, 1991), §19 at 305. Hereafer noted as *IB*.
14. Suárez, *DB*, IV.3 at 817. Third-party interventions are permissible by invitation only.
15. '[P]ropter tyrannidem vel ipsorum dominorum apud barbaros, vel etiam propter leges tyrannicas in iniuriam innocentium, puta quia sacrificant homines innocentes vel alias occidunt indemnatos ad vescendum carnibus eorum', *Relectio de Indis, I. 3.14. From Vorlesungen II*, edited by Ulrich Horst, Heinz-Gerhard Justenhoven, Joachim Stüben (Stuttgart, Berlin, Köln: Kohlhammer, 1997).
16. For various estimates, see Michael Harner, 'The Ecological Basis for Aztec Sacrifice', *American Ethnologist*, 4(1977), 117–135. The figure given is from an unpublished manuscript authored by Woodrow Borah, quoted by Harner with Borah's permission (119).
17. Francisco de Vitoria, *de Indis, I.3.14; In Summa Theologiae II–II, q. 40 a. 1 §6, in Comentarios a la Secunda Secundae de Santo Tomás* (Salamanca: Biblioteca de Teólogos Españoles, 1932); Vitoria, *de Indis* II, 8 (this is the fragment *De usu ciborum sive de temperantia* annexed in the Stuttgart critical edition of *de Indis* as a 'part two'). The matter was treated also by Alonso de Veracruz, Melchor Cano, Juan de la Peña, Juan de Guevara, Bartolomé de Medina, Domingo Báñez, Francisco de Toledo, Diego de Covarrubias, Domingo de Soto, Luis de Molina, and Francisco Suárez. For the references, see Daniel Schwartz, 'The Principle of the Defence of the Innocent', 263–291.

18. Vitoria, *Relectio de Indiis*, II.7. On this see Schwartz, 'The Principle of the Defence of the Innocent', 282–283.
19. Aquinas, *Summa Theologiae, II-II* q. 40 a. 1c.
20. Suárez, *DB*, IV.3 at 817.
21. Molina, *II*, d. 104.6, at 330–331.
22. Molina, *II*, d. 102.3 at 292.
23. Ibid.
24. Vitoria, *IB*, §20, 21 at 306–307, Molina, *II*, d. 103.1 at 302, Suárez, *DB*, VI.1 at 828.
25. Vitoria, *IB*, §24 at 308, Molina, *II*, 113.2 at 404–405.
26. Suárez, *DB*, VI.7 at 831.
27. Vitoria, *IB*, §25 at 308.
28. Suárez, *DB*, VI.8 at 832.
29. Molina, *II*, d. 113.3 at 406, Gabriel Biel, *Commentarius in quartum librum sententiarum* (Brescia: Thomas Bozolam, 1574) d. 15 q. 4 concl. 4 at 319.
30. Thomas de Vio, Cardinal Cajetan, *Summula caietani* (Lyon: A. de Harsy, 1581), translated by Peter Haggenmacher and Robert Andrew in Reichberg, Syse and Begby, 247. Also in Biel, *In IV Sent.* d. 15 q. 4 concl. 4 at 318–319.
31. Suárez, *DB*, VI.11 at 834–835. All the translations from this work follow Brown Scott's edition.
32. On this, see Rudolf Schussler, 'On the Anatomy of Probabilism' in *Moral Philosophy on the Threshold of Modernity* edited by Jill Kraye and Risto Saarinen (Dordrecht: Springer, 2005), 98–100 and his 'Moral Self-Ownership and Ius Possessionis in Late Scholastics' in *Transformations in Medieval and Early-Modern Rights Discourse* edited by Virpi Mäkinen and Petter Korkman (Dordrecht: Springer, 2006), 160–164.
33. Suárez, *DB*, VI. 4–5 at 830. See Juan Cruz Cruz, 'El caso del juez árbitro en caso de guerra, según los Maestros de Siglo de Oro', at http://leynatural.es.
34. Bartolomé de Medina, *Expositio in Prima Secundae Angelici Doctoris D. Thomae Aquinatis* (Salamanca: Mateo Gasti, 1582) q. 19 a. 6, at 309a. See Thomas Deman, 'Probabilisme' in *Dictionnaire de Théologie Catholique, XIII*, edited by A. Vacant, E. Mangenot and E. Amann (Paris: Letouzey et Ané, 1936), i, cols. 417–619; Ilkka Kantola, *Probability and Moral Uncertainty in Late Medieval and Early Modern Times* (Helsinki: Luther-Agricola, 1994); and Daniel Schwartz, 'Probabilism Reconsidered: Deference to Experts, Types of Uncertainty, and Medicines', *Journal of the History of Ideas*, 75(2014).
35. Gabriel Vázquez, *Commentariorum ac disputationum in primam secundae S. Thomae, tomus primus* (Alcalá de Henares: Widow of Juan Gracián, 1614) d. 64. c. 3 n. 13 at 407–408.
36. See Daniel Schwartz, 'Probabilism, Just War, and Sovereignty in the Work of Gabriel Vázquez', *History of Political Thought*, 34(2013), 177–194.
37. Pope Adrian VI, *Quodlibeticae XII* (Paris: Claudius Chevallon, 1527) q. 2 ad 1 punct. 2 at f37v-38. Also in *In IV Sent*, fol. xli B (Paris; Jodoco Badii, 1516).
38. Vitoria, *IB*, § 31 at 312.
39. For instance in Navarrus's *De poenitentia* (Coimbra: Juan Barreiro, 1542) d. 7 n. 86 at 364 (discussion starts at 340); Soto's *Relectio de legendi et delegendi* (lectures from 1540–1541) membr. 2 q. 2 at 455–457; Juan de Medina, *Codex de restitutione et contractibus* (Alcalá: Juan de Brocar, 1546) fols. 58–62.
40. Thomas de Vio, Cajetan, *Opuscula Omnia* (Antwerp: Ioannem Keerbergium, 1612). tom. 1, tract. 31 resp. XIII, 96–97.
41. Molina, *II*, d. 113.5 at 408–410; Suárez, *DB*, VI.9 at 828.

42. For example, Neff, *Just War and International Order*, 75–76. Regout rejects similar claims by Vanderpol in his *La doctrine de la guerre juste*, 182–185.
43. Graham Parsons, 'Public War and the Moral Equality of Combatants', *Journal of Military Ethics*, 11(2012), 304, and his response to Reichberg, 'What Is the Classical Theory of Just Cause? A Response to Reichberg, *Journal of Military Ethics*, 12(2013), 366.
44. Gregory Reichberg, 'The Moral Equality of Combatants—A Doctrine in Classical Just War Theory? A Response to Graham Parsons', *Journal of Military Ethics*, 12(2013), 184–185. The attribution of the moral equality thesis to Vitoria is also rejected by Peter Haggenmacher, 'Just War and Regular War in Sixteenth-Century Spanish Doctrine', *International Review of the Red Cross* 290(1992), 442. A general defense of Vitoria is found in Regout, *La doctrine*, 182–185. A similar debate took place concerning Luis de Molina who was charged by Alfred Vanderpol (*La doctrine*, 254–275) of being the main late scholastic responsible for purportedly breaking with Thomistic tradition and for allowing something akin to the moral equality of combatants. A sustained defence of Molina can be found in Manuel Fraga Iribarne, *Luis de Molina y el derecho de la guerra*, 199–127.
45. On subjective justification and permissibility, see Jeff McMahan, 'On the Moral Equality of Combatants', *Journal of Political Philosophy*, 14(2006), 389–390.
46. Alex J. Bellamy, *Just Wars: From Cicero to Iraq* (Cambridge: Polity, 2006), 55. In his reading of Vitoria, Reichberg makes the point that Vitoria usually applies the argument of simultaneous ostensible justice to the case of subordinates rather than sovereigns. 'Just ad Bellum', in *War: Essays in Political Philosophy*, edited by Larry May (Cambridge: Cambridge University Press, 2008), 20.
47. I am not the first to notice this. See, for instance, Haggemacher, *Grotius . . .* (208–209). Among humanist jurists, this view was more common, notably present in the works of Andreas Alciatus and Raphaël Fulgosius.
48. A view reported but not shared by Ricardo García Villoslada, *La universidad de París durante los estudios de Francisco de Vitoria* (Rome: Gregorian University, 1939), 95–96, 163–165.
49. John Mair, *In quartum sententiarum* (Paris: Jodoco Badio, 1519 *c.* 1509) d. 15, f120v.
50. 'Contra tertiam conclusionem cum parte quartae arguitur sic: ex illis duabus conclusionibus sequit quod aliquid bellum est in parte iustum et in parte iniustum: cum *ex parte* superioris sit iniustum et *ex parte* inferiorum iustum. Consequens est inconveniens quia quibus bellum est iustum vel tale putatum, non tenentur restituere ablatum et idem potest esse *ex parte* opposita. Respondet concedendo illatum: potest esse *ex parte* duorum exercituum oppositorum probabilis ignorantia: interdum quo ad superiores et inferiores, interdum quod ad subditos tamen. Ut Lucanus de bello inter Caesarem et Pompeium dicere videtur primo Pharsaliae "Quis iustus induat arma Scire nefas: magno se iudice quisque tuetur"', Mair, f120v. See Haggenmacher, *Grotius et la doctrine de la guerre juste*, 208–209.
51. His *Quodlibeticae* were published in 1515, seven years before his election as Pope and six after the first edition of Mair's *Sentences*.
52. In Francisco de Vitoria, *De justitia*, vol. 1, edited by Vicente Beltrán de Heredia (Madrid: Asociación Francisco de Vitoria, 1934), 102–105, 176.
53. See endnote 39.
54. Domingo de Soto, *De la justicia y el derecho* (Madrid: Instituto de Estudios Políticos, 1967) lib 4 q. 5 a. 4, at 326. Spanish trans. by Marcelino Gonzáles Ordóñez, with fascimilar of the 1557 *De iustitia et iure*.

55. Soto, *De iustitia et iure,* lib IV, q. 7 a. 2 at 369, Vitoria, *IB*, §33 at 314; Domingo Báñez, *Commentaria in Secunda Secundae* (Venice: Bernardum Iuntam, 1586) in q. 40 a. 1 dub. 7 concl. 4. at 1368.
56. On the roots of tutiorism, see Ilkka Kantola, *Probability and Moral Uncertainty* (82–84) and Thomas Deman, 'Probabilisme', cols. 424–425.
57. Domingo Soto, *De ratione tegendi et detegendum secretum in Relecciones y Opúsculos,* vol. II-1, translated by Antonio Osuna Fernández-Lago (Salamanca: San Esteban, 2000), membr. 3, q. 2 concl. 2 at 457.
58. Suárez (*DB*, VI.9 at 828) says that, for Adrian, the moral danger involved in fighting in case of doubt is 'the peril of unjust slaughtering and plundering'. Adrian, however only mentions the risk of killing the innocent. *Quodl.* q. 2. f38v.
59. Vitoria, *IB* § 32 at 32.
60. Vitoria, *Comentarios a la Secunda Secundae de Santo Tomás de Caritate et Prudentia (qq. 23-56),* Vicente Beltrán de Heredia ed. (Salamanca: Biblioteca de Teólogos Españoles, 1932) q. 40 a. 1 at 282–283.
61. 'Even though there is the danger that innocents will be killed (if the war is unjust) this danger is not more weighty than the alternative. For citizens have a duty towards their own republic and not towards a foreign one. But the prince cannot defend and care appropriately for the republic if each time he goes to war he must explain to each citizen the reasons for doing so'. Soto, *De ratione tegendi et detegendum secretum*, membr. 3, q. 2 concl. 4 at 467 (a lecture delivered in 1540–41). Domingo Báñez, *Commentaria in Secundam Secundae* (Venice: Bernardum Iuntam, 1586) q. 61 a. 1 at 1364: 'there are two dangers: to harm your prince or to harm a foreign prince, but soldiers have greater duty to impede harm to their prince, than to a foreign prince, thus they can fight'.
62. Aquinas, *ST II-II* q. 40 a. 1 c.
63. Suárez, *DB*, II. 1 at 805.
64. Vitoria, *IB*, §5 at 300.
65. Cajetan, *In ST II-II* q. 40 a. 1 at 242, Vitoria, *IB*, §5 at 300.
66. Molina, *II*, d. 100. 2 at 269, Suárez, *DB*, II.1 at 806.
67. Cajetan, *In ST II-II* q. 40 a. 1 at 242.
68. Molina, *II*, d. 100. 8 at 274.
69. Molina, *II*, d. 100.9 at 270, Vitoria, *IB*,§9 at 302.
70. Suárez, *DB*, II.2 at 806–807.
71. Vitoria, *IB*, §9 at 302.
72. Suárez, *DB*, II.2 at 807.
73. Suárez, *DB*, II.2 at 807.
74. Suárez, *DB*, II.3 at 807. Also Fernando de Castro Palao, *Operis Moralis de virtutibus & vitiis contrariis, pars prima* (Lyon: Ioannem Baptista Devenet, 1656) tract 6. d. 5 punct. 2 at 462.
75. Suárez, *DB*, II 6 at 809.
76. Francisco de Oviedo, *Tractatus Theologici, Scholastici & Morales De virtutibus fide, spe et charitate* (Lyon: Philippi Borde, Laurentii Arnauld and Claudii Rigaud, 1651), contro. 12, punct. 2. num. 20 at 423.
77. Enrique Villalobos, *Suma de la Teología Moral y Canónica, segunda parte* (Salamanca: Diego de Cussio, 1629) tract. 5, diff. 3, num. 1 at 40.
78. Domingo Báñez, *Commentaria in Secunda Secundae* (Venice: Bernardum Iuntam, 1586) in a. 40 a. 1, 1357.

79. *Decretum Gratiani* (Rome: Populi Romani, 1582) c. 23, q. 1, c. 6, at 1708; misattributed by Aquinas to Augustine.
80. St Augustine, *Contra Faustum Manichaeum*, xxii, 7–10 CSEL, XXV (Leipzig: G. Freytag, Vienna: Tempsky, 1891), at 672. All the translations from Aquinas' *ST* come from *The 'Summa Theologica' of St. Thomas Aquinas literally translated by Fathers of the English Dominican Province* (Westminster, Maryland: Christian Classics, 1980 c. 1911).
81. Cajetan, *Summula* at 177–178.
82. Martin Azpilcueta (Navarrus), *Resolutorio de casos de usura* (Salamanca: Portonaris, 1556), 118.
83. Domingo Bañez, *Commentaria in Secunda Secundae* (Venice: Bernardum Iuntam, 1586) in q. 40 a. 1 at 1372–1373.
84. Molina, *II*, 117.3 at 354.
85. Medieval Spanish bibles translated directly from the Hebrew do not make this mistake and provide 'libre' (free, free from sin) rather than 'inocente'. Américo Castro, Agustín Millares Carlo and Angel José Battistessa. *Biblia medieval romanceada según los manuscritos escurialenses I-j-3, I-j-8 y I-j-6*)Buenos Aires: J. Peuser, 1927), 101.
86. Vitoria, *IB*, §35 at 314–315, Molina, *II*, d. 119.2 at 475–476.
87. Suárez, *DB*, VII.15 at 846.
88. Vitoria *IB*, §35 at 314–315.
89. Vitoria *IB*, §38 at 316, Molina, *II*, d. 119.4 at 476.
90. Vitoria *IB*, §38 at 316.
91. Vitoria, *IB*, §35 at 315.
92. Molina, *II*, d. 119.3 at 476.
93. Pedro Lorca, *Commentaria et disputationes in secunda secundae divi Thomae* (Madrid, Luis Sanchez, 1614) membr. 3. num. 30 at 988.
94. In the edition of *Relectiones Theologicae* (Lyon: Jacob Boyer, 1557) n. 36 at 407.
95. Suárez, *DB*, VII.16 at 847.
96. Suárez, DB VII.7 at 840–841, Molina, *II*, d. 117.2 at 442.
97. Molina, *II*, d.122.2 at 498.
98. Molina, *II*, d.122.2 at 498.
99. See T. A. Cavanaugh, *Double-Effect Reasoning* (Oxford: Oxford University Press, 2006).
100. Aquinas, *ST II-II* q. 64 a. 7c. For a different interpretation of this article, see Reichberg, 'Aquinas on Defensive Killing: A Case of Double-Effect?', *Thomist*, 69(2005), 341–370, where it is argued that 'Aquinas did not in fact appeal to a version of PDE [Principle of Double Effect] in formulating his theory of justifiable defensive killing' (342).
101. Aquinas, *ST II-II* q. 64 a. 3c.
102. Soto, *De iustitia et iure*, lib. 5 q. 1 a. 8 at 402.
103. Vitoria, *IB*, §37 at 315.
104. Molina, *II*, d. 119.7 at 478–480.
105. Vitoria, *IB*, §37 at 315.
106. Vitoria, *IB*, §37 at 316.
107. Suárez, *DB*, VII.17 at 848.
108. Suárez, *DB*, VII.18 at 849.
109. Suárez, *DB*, II.19 at 850.
110. Suárez, *DB*, II.19 at 849.
111. Suárez, *DB*, VII.19 at 850.

112. Ibid.
113. See Jeff McMahan, 'The Basis of Moral Liability to Defensive Killing', *Philosophical Issues*, 15(2005), 286–405, esp. 388; and Uwe Steinhoff, 'Debate: Jeff McMahan on the Moral Inequality of Combatants', *Journal of Political Philosophy* 16(2008), 220–226.
114. Suárez, *DB*, VII.19 at 850.

CHAPTER 7

EARLY MODERN SOURCES OF THE REGULAR WAR TRADITION*

PABLO KALMANOVITZ

TODAY, the term 'irregular war' is more commonly used than 'regular war', even though conceptually and historically the former derives from the latter. The now largely neglected theory of regular war emerged from the just war tradition, but its articulation by political and legal theorists since early modernity is in important ways inconsistent with, and indeed an alternative to, medieval, early modern, and contemporary accounts of just war. Like the concept of just war, that of regular war belongs to an ethical tradition within which it has been articulated, contested, and transformed. But, unlike the just war tradition, the regular war tradition has been concerned first and foremost with institutional—conventional, formal, and ultimately juridical—means of regulating and moderating the use of armed force. In this sense, the concept of regular war may be said to belong to an *ethical* tradition of international law.[1] This chapter will look at the early stages of this tradition, starting with the transitional work of Hugo Grotius in the early seventeenth century and concluding with Emer de Vattel's Enlightenment classic *The Law of Nations* (1758), which provides a well-developed doctrine of regular warfare. Although my main focus will be on the history of ideas, I will also suggest that the historical concept of regular war illuminates the nature and ethical foundations of international humanitarian law today.

In Vattel's classic account, regular wars must satisfy three principles. First, they must be fought by *sovereign states* or at least by groups that aspire to some form of political

* Earlier versions of this chapter were presented at the 2011 meeting of the Association of Political Theory and at the Political Theory Workshop at Yale University. For helpful discussion and comments, I would like to thank specially Tom Donahue, Bryan Garsten, Casiano Hacker-Cordon, Mark Rigstad, and Daniel Viehoff.

autonomy.[2] Second, they must begin with a formal *declaration of war* that creates a legal 'state of war' in which a special regime of *war regulations* applies. Among the foremost principles governing these regulations is that the harm and destruction caused by war must be limited; in particular, the use of force must be restricted to legitimate targets, foremost among which are regular soldiers who, as such, must wear distinctive uniforms and observe the war regulations. Finally, regular wars conclude with a *peace agreement* that stipulates the conditions under which former enemies agree to end their state of war and sets the terms of future interaction between them.

These features of regular warfare contrast markedly with standard just war theorizing. From a just war perspective, a declaration of war is altogether irrelevant for establishing the justice of a war—wars are just if fought in response to an act or eminent threat of aggression, not if duly declared. Moreover, in principle, aggressors should not enjoy any of the privileges of *jus in bello*, and whoever is morally responsible for an act of aggression or for sustaining a wrongful state of affairs should be liable to attack and possibly punishment, regardless of her conventional status as combatant or noncombatant. Finally, just wars should conclude not with a peace agreement but rather with the vindication of the violated right and possibly with the establishment of conditions that will decrease the likelihood of future violations of right.[3]

The reasons for these contrasts are profound, as this chapter will show, but a fundamental methodological divergence may be stated at the outset. Theorists of regular war emphasize the fact that wars necessarily involve political associations—typically sovereign states—that pursue clashing collective interests in weakly institutionalized contexts. Consequently, the moral evaluation of war cannot be reduced to interpersonal morality or law but must be mediated by specifically institutional considerations. The background institutional structure of regular war theory is international society (i.e., a society of *de jure* equal sovereign states governed by a system of law that, in lacking centralized adjudication and enforcement, is essentially different from domestic legal systems). Due to the absence of centralized legal adjudication and enforcement in international society, insecurity and genuine disagreements among belligerents regarding the justifiability of their use of force are structural and endemic. It is a most valuable methodological feature of regular war theorizing that structural insecurity and endemic disagreements are seen as morally significant features of international society that must be reflected in any pertinent normative theorizing about war.

The regular war tradition breaks apart from its just war counterpart in two fundamental respects. The doctrine of regular *jus ad bellum* contains the possibility of a war being equally legitimate on both sides—this is the paradigmatic case of regular war—as a consequence of which the norms of regular *jus in bello* apply equally to all belligerents. The principle of belligerent equality *in bello* is a corollary of equal legitimacy *ad bellum*. The first three sections of the chapter will discuss some important elements in the complex theoretical evolution behind the principle that in war both sides are fully equals. Section 1 focuses on Grotius's brief but path-breaking epistemic and prudential arguments, and Section 2 focuses on Wolff and Vattel's argument from international legal indeterminacy and insecurity. Section 3 suggests that war declarations may be seen as embodying a demand from public reason, and that, consequently, regular war theory does not collapse into a crude form of reason of state, as some commentators have essentially suggested. Regular war theory can be construed as an alternative to just war theory in the *via media* between crude realism and pacifism. Section 4 turns to the logic and justification of the regular doctrine of *jus in bello*, and Section 5 concludes.[4]

1. Grotius and the Early Modern Origins of the Regular War Tradition

Arguably the concept of regular war can be traced back to late medieval jurisprudence and before. Relevant sources and developments can be found in the Roman *ius gentium* and in the late medieval and early modern juristic treatises of Fulgosius, Ayala, and Gentili, all of which posited bilateral rights of belligerence and emphasized the formal and procedural aspects of warfare.[5] However, a more recognizably modern and systematic doctrinal articulation, taking full account of the emergence of state sovereignty, had to wait until Wolff and Vattel in the eighteenth century.

Although Hugo Grotius was arguably a just war theorist at heart—closer in orientation to Spanish neo-scholasticism than to the emerging realities of the Westphalian system—some of his ideas are explicitly at the basis of Wolff and Vattel's work and could well be credited as laying down the foundations for later accounts of regular war. Grotius's decisive contribution to the regular war tradition is to have recognized and spelled out some reasons that could justify the validity of international laws that are in conflict with basic precepts of morality or natural law. This recognition runs against a fundamental principle of Thomistic natural law, according to which positive laws, in particular international conventions, are invalid if they conflict with natural law. Even though in *The Rights of War and Peace* Grotius ostensibly endorsed this principle, he recognized the legality of regular wars—or 'solemn wars' (*bellum solenne*), as he called them—even though they violated basic principles of natural law.[6] Because Grotius's key distinction between solemn and just wars has often been missed or misinterpreted in contemporary commentaries,[7] it is worth discussing its theoretical significance in some detail.

Grotius's discussion of solemn war begins with a distinction between two concepts of permission. An act is morally permissible, he said, if it is 'right from every point of view', and it is legally permissible if the law does not penalize it.[8] An act may thus be morally impermissible and nonetheless carry no legal liabilities or consequences. But if we think, with Grotius, that in general moral proscriptions should (morally) be reflected in the law, then a law that treats wrongdoers as if they acted permissibly grants an 'impunity' that requires justification. For Grotius these impunities amounted to more than the sheer fact that certain wrongs would go unpunished in international society—which is, I think, how Hedley Bull reads Grotius here.[9] He made clear that impunities had additional 'external' effects that could appear before the domestic courts of 'foreign peoples' and had to be 'defended as lawful', in particular regarding rights over property and territory acquired by the unjust side in a war.[10] Grotius made clear that giving equal *in bello* and *post bellum* rights and permissions to regular belligerents did not amount to a *moral* validation of unjust warfare.[11] He was consequently troubled by the mismatch that his doctrine of solemn wars created between strictly legal or 'external' rights and natural or 'internal' rights—very much like contemporary just war theorists have been troubled by the tensions between the 'deep morality' and the legality of war.[12]

The purpose of the ethical theory of regular war is not to justify the actions of unjust soldiers, but rather to justify the legal permissions that may be granted to them. More precisely, the theory seeks to justify a system of regulations that is certain to have the regrettable feature of permitting and sanctioning some wrongful acts. Instances of the law tolerating moral wrongs are not rare in domestic contexts. The enactment of a statute of limitations is an obvious example: even if irrefutable evidence of wrongdoing becomes available, if it is found beyond the duly set period, legal action is precluded. This is no doubt regrettable, but, in the interest of promoting the sound operation of a legal system, it is nonetheless valuable to have statutes of limitations. Grotius saw that international law would have to depart more than domestic legal systems from the norms and principles of interpersonal natural law. But, as in domestic law, this departure could be justified only if it contributed to the advancement of important values. The core values that regular war theory seeks to uphold, as we will see, are limitation in the use of force and, more fundamentally, the preservation of order in international society.

It may be indicative of Grotius's deeper inclination that his concise defence of the bilateral permission to use force in solemn wars is presented as a justification for an existing international consensus, not as his own view. 'The reason why [the bilateral permission to use force] met with the approval of nations', Grotius wrote, 'was this':

> To undertake to decide the justice of a war between two peoples had been dangerous for other peoples, who were on this account involved in a foreign war . . .. Furthermore, even in a lawful war [*bello justo*], from external indications it can hardly be adequately known what is the just limit of self-defense, of recovering what is one's own, or of inflicting punishments; in consequence, it has seemed altogether preferable to leave decisions in regard to such matters to the scruples of the belligerents rather than to have recourse to the judgment of others.[13]

Two strands of argument may be distinguished in this short but far-reaching passage, one epistemic, another prudential. The undertaking to which the passage refers—to establish the just proportion and proper limits of self-defence and corrective justice—is, of course, essential to the determination of *jus ad bellum* in the just war tradition. Wars fought on the basis of a mistaken belief about the disputed right are unjust even if the mistake is excusable. If the evidence available to third parties is insufficient to accurately establish where justice lies in an armed dispute, then their morally best response is to abstain from judgment—otherwise they would be in serious danger of causing wrong by mistakenly supporting the unjust party.

To be clear, Grotius is not saying that states should *always* be agnostic about the justice of armed conflicts. On the contrary, elsewhere in *The Rights of War and Peace* he advocated for third-party interventions on behalf of the just side.[14] What the passage does suggest, however, is that the law of nations itself may have to be agnostic about matters of *jus ad bellum* because international society does not fulfil the conditions necessary for the accurate or fair adjudication of armed conflicts. When it comes to adjudication, each state should have the power to decide autonomously on foreign wars and, indeed, should decide whether or not to make a judgment in the first place. The law of nations, on the other hand, cannot produce conclusive judgments and as such must remain agnostic and permissive.

Regarding the prudential strand of the argument, Grotius did not elaborate much on why giving the right to use force only to the just side would drag third parties into war, but presumably the reason is that if the law of nations gave the right to use force exclusively to the just side, all *in bello* and *post bellum* rights would have to be conditional on that right. This would mean that the unjust side would have to be made criminally liable for wrongful killings, and materially liable for property destruction and takings during war. Third-party states would have to enforce these liabilities. Enforcement need not take the extreme form of a duty to punish all unjust fighters, but third parties should at least refrain from aiding unjust belligerents and should in fact help the just side in any way they safely could (this is Grotius's doctrine of 'qualified neutrality'[15]). Most importantly, pursuant of the obligations derived from *jus ad bellum*, material exchanges with unjust belligerents involving their territorial and property acquisitions would have to be declared null and void. In sum, if the justice of a war is disputed, that dispute would spill over to third parties in virtue of their obligations of qualified neutrality and would also infect property transactions and territorial rights, thus potentially escalating to further armed conflict and more suffering and death.

This Grotian twofold argument makes two path-breaking moves for the regular war tradition: first, it acknowledges the pervasiveness of uncertainty in matters of *jus ad bellum*, and, second, it switches from the predominantly deontological normativism of late medieval and early modern just war theory to a novel form of rule-consquentialism.[16] However, Grotius did not integrate systematically these elements into a cohesive legal theory. In particular, he did not solve the question of how the positive law of nations and the natural law could fit together within a single system of law,[17] nor did he show how solemn and just wars could coexist within a single system of law. Following Grotius's lead, however, the next generation of regular war theorists reconceived the law of nations in a way that allowed for the systematic incorporation of Grotius's argument. Arguably, the most important contribution is Wolff's concept of the 'voluntary law of nations', which contains, as Vattel would put it, 'the natural principles of the law of nations'.[18]

2. Wolff, Vattel, and the Symmetry of Regular *Jus ad Bellum*

Of the four types of international legal norms identified by Wolff and Vattel—natural, voluntary, customary, and treaty law—the voluntary law is by far the most relevant for my present purposes.[19] Contrary to what the term suggests, the voluntary law of nations is not based on the actual consent of states but rather on their hypothetical consent, derived from principles constitutive of international society, to which it is assumed they have an interest in belonging. The voluntary law is obtained through a transcendental deduction of sorts because it constitutes the normative core without which a legally regulated society of sovereign states could not possibly exist.[20] And because it is valuable to have a system of law regulating international affairs, the norms and principles of the voluntary law of nations have moral value—they are in this sense both positive and moral law.

In contrast to Grotius, who, as we have seen, was ambiguous on this crucial matter, Wolff and Vattel explicitly held that, when it comes to the regulation of state interactions, the voluntary law of nations, not the natural law of nations or customary or treaty law, should (morally) rule supreme. As Vattel puts it, the law of nature, 'whose object it is to promote the welfare of human society, and to protect the liberties of all nations, which requires that the affairs of sovereigns should be brought to an issue, and their quarrels determined and carried to a speedy conclusion, that law, I say, recommends the observance of the voluntary law of nations'.[21] In contrast to Grotius, for whom the conventions regulating solemn wars were purely customary, for Wolff and Vattel the defining forms of regular war ultimately derived from the voluntary law, specifically from the moral imperatives of international order and moderation of violence.

The defining feature of Vattelian international society is the absence of supranational authorities empowered to adjudicate disputes. But although states are not assumed to have an interest in instituting a global court for the adjudication of *jus ad bellum*, they are assumed to be motivated by long-term interests in achieving cooperative, mutually advantageous terms of interaction and in limiting the destructive effects of conflict. International society is thus governed by two fundamental principles. First, states have the paramount duty of protecting the safety of their members and promoting their well-being and 'perfection'. They must normally be left to decide autonomously on what policies would best advance this self-regarding duties.[22] Second, states have enforceable duties vis-à-vis other states that limit their autonomous pursuit of security and well-being. 'In virtue of the natural liberty of nations', wrote Vattel, 'each one is free to judge in her own conscience how she ought to act, and has a right to make her own judgment the sole guide of her conduct with respect to her duties *in everything that is not determined by the perfect rights of another*'.[23]

Among the most important 'perfect' or enforceable rights are immunity to territorial invasion and, most broadly, security. Perfect rights could be enforced through reprisals—narrow and selective violations of the delinquent state's rights—or, in the extreme, by war.[24] The defining aim of the Enlightenment doctrines of regular war is to govern the enforcement of perfect rights in international society.

This may sound very much like just war theory. The novelty of Wolff and Vattel's construction becomes apparent once we consider the interaction between the two governing principles of international society. Whereas perfect rights are the hardest possible constraints on the exercise of state sovereignty, they necessarily have fuzzy boundaries and overlapping areas. Uncertainty regarding the very definition of sovereign rights led Vattel to postulate two different grounds for going to war.[25] The first is familiar from just war theory and arguably historically rare: war in response to actions that *manifestly*—clearly and indisputably—violate the perfect rights of another state. The second and novel basis is disputes arising from 'uncertain, obscure, and disputable' rights; that is, disputes over the inherently ill-defined boundaries of perfect rights.[26] In such cases, said Vattel, 'it is equally possible that either of the parties may have right on his side'. [27]It could be said more strongly, although Vattel did not quite say it, that in such cases *both sides may be justified* in using force because if the interests underlying contested rights seriously compromise the security and subsistence of the involved states, they may all permissibly wage war. Thus, the bilateral permission to wage regular war reflects the imprecise definition of sovereign rights and the pervasive insecurity characteristic of international society.

It is important to note that this argument from legal indeterminacy runs deeper than Grotius's epistemic argument. On a superficial reading, it may appear as if the argument was purely jurisdictional: because states are equal members of international society, no state may pretend to be judge of another, and because there is no authoritative organ with the competence to judge matters of *jus ad bellum*, international law must remian agnostic (this argument does appear in Wolff and Vattel,[28] but it is by no means the whole story). A purely jurisdictional argument would have no contemporary purchase and is, in fact, inconsistent with the second constitutive principle of Vattelian international society—states do have the right to judge whether their own perfect rights have been violated, which necessarily involves judging other states' actions.

Wolff and Vattel's deeper Hobbesian point is that there is prevailing and objective uncertainty about the very definition of state rights in international society because there is no supranational authority in charge of determining precisely the contours of legal rights. This is not a jurisdictional but a legal epistemic argument. As Wolff put it, 'the rights of belligerents are so involved with their underlying causes that they cannot be untangled by any one, even if an arbiter should especially be appointed, much less without judge or arbiter'.[29] Although an arbiter would be unable to *untangle* the rights, a judge, if one existed, could make an authoritative determination that *settles* the matter. So, if Grotius's point was that it is often difficult to access sufficient evidence to reach reliable judgments on the justice of disputes, Wolff and Vattel's point here is that, in the absence of binding international adjudication, there may be no truth of the matter underlying disputes over rights—or the truth of the matter may only be that both sides can make an equally plausible case for the legitimacy of their claim.

One might object that, instead of inferring from the lack of binding international adjudication that international law should be agnostic about *jus ad bellum*, binding adjudication should be instituted, either as compulsory arbitration, or as a 'minimalist global state', or as a purely epistemic court of *jus ad bellum*.[30] Full discussion of the merits of these proposals is beyond my present scope, but I do want to note that Wolff and Vattel contemplated the scenario of compulsory adjudication and rejected it. In keeping with some basic tenets of the just war tradition, both called the parties to a conflict to submit their disputes to conciliation.[31] However, both made clear that when the rights in dispute involve interests of an *existential importance*—'a right without which [a nation] could not hope to support her national existence'[32]—this requirement could not be sustained. The reason is again eminently Hobbesian. In cases of existential conflict, a state cannot be asked to trust its potential enemy to abide by the results of conciliation, not when the stakes are so high and not if the actual circumstances of international society give no assurance that the other side will comply.[33] Moreover, in existential conflicts, states cannot risk a ruling that would wrongly neglect their vital interests, which is to say they must trust not only the other side's compliance but also the equity of the conciliation mechanism. As long as international adjudication is not trustworthy and backed by reassuringly compelling power, there can be no binding obligation to defer to adjudication by a third party.

Do Wolff and Vattel's arguments from indeterminacy and insecurity have contemporary relevance? I have argued elsewhere that the structural conditions that make cases of bilateral justice possible have not been superseded in contemporary international society—security dilemmas can still generate conditions of bilaterally justified pre-emptive action.[34] As to legal definition, even though there is near consensus among contemporary just war theorists and international lawyers that unilateral military force can be justified only in self-defense against acts of aggression,[35] there is currently no legally binding definition of acts of aggression. The most accepted definition is the General Assembly Definition of Aggression (Resolution 3314 of 14 December 1974), which states that, 'aggression is the use of armed force by a State against the sovereignty or political independence of another State, or in any other manner inconsistent with the Charter of the United Nations [UN]', and indicates as clear instances attacking or invading the state's territory, blockading ports or coasts, and attacking its armed forces. These instances amount to violations of clear 'incidents' of sovereign rights—territorial integrity, access to the open sea, immunity of armed forces during peacetime—but they are only indicative, not an exhaustive catalogue of *casus belli*.[36]

It could be said that some progress towards binding codification took place at the 2010 International Criminal Court Review Conference in Kampala, which adapted the 1974 definition in its codification of the crime of aggression. If ratified by state parties, this codification will become binding after 2017. However, the Court would have jurisdiction only in pursuit of Security Council referrals and over state parties that do not exempt themselves from jurisdiction. The outcome remains to be seen, but the caution displayed by state parties in Kampala and the limited terms of their proposal illustrate clearly the historical endurance of Vattelian international society.

3. War Declarations as Demands of Public Reason

The virtual exclusion of *jus ad bellum* from international law by regular war theorists has been interpreted as either a form of moral scepticism or as a collapse of regular war doctrine into crude political realism and *raison d'état*.[37] Although inaccurate, these challenges do reflect the uneasy balance characteristic of regular war approaches, which must attempt to accommodate pragmatically the realities of international politics in post-Westphalian Europe—particularly the growing assertiveness of consolidating sovereignty states—while also seeking to efficaciously regulate armed force. In a sense, regular war theory aspires to be a form of 'realistic utopia'[38] in its attempt to find a viable middle path between realism and idealism. More precisely, regular war doctrine must, like other areas of international law, avoid the pitfalls of offering either a crude apology of the *status quo* or purely utopian and impracticable ideals.[39]

The claim that international law must be agnostic about *jus ad bellum* should nonetheless give us pause. It would seem to amount in practice to an unconditional privilege in states to use violence. Vattel was well aware of the danger. A general legal permission to use force will be abused by a nation that '*pretends* that it would be dangerous for her to attempt pacific measures' when facing an alleged threat or that only 'gives a color of justice to her precipitation in having recourse to arms'.[40] Cynicism and hypocrisy could easily substitute for genuine justification when it came to recourse to force.

The very possibility of hypocrisy indicates that the regular war tradition has contemplated resources to constrain the sovereign privilege to wage war. The most important resource is the obligation to issue public declarations of war, which in Grotius, Wolff, and Vattel have two defining features. First, typically, only a sovereign ruler can declare war, and, second and most important for present purposes, war declarations must contain the reasons why war is waged.[41] Narrowly understood, war declarations have the structure of an ultimatum. The declaring state presents its terms and asks the other side to respond satisfactorily or else face war. But, more broadly, war declarations are addressed not only to the enemy but also to the declaring state's citizens, to foreign sovereigns and diplomats, and, ultimately, to international society at large. This global audience is called to examine the plausibility of the reasons given, to assess the true intentions of the war-declaring state, and to react accordingly.

Two responses to a war declaration are possible. It may be seen as a plausible claim based on a state's 'perfect rights', in which case the war will be deemed legitimate; if plausible reasons are also given by the other side, the war will be seen as valid on both sides, which is the paradigmatic case of regular war. But a war declaration could also be widely seen as an implausible pronouncement, really a mere 'pretext' that barely disguises the fact that the war is motivated by greed, imperial expansion, or on the basis of motives that subvert the principles of sovereign equality and international society.[42] In such case, as also when a state simply refuses to give any reasons at all, the war is not valid and must elicit 'public indignation and the concurrence of every civilized people' in mobilising against the delinquent state. Collective mobilization would be most urgent when a systematic policy of undermining international society was signalled.[43] Such 'mischievous nations', wrote Vattel, are the true 'enemies of the human race'; indeed, the true and only aggressors according to regular war doctrine. Force should be mobilized collectively to stop the aggressor and preserve order in international society.[44]

Thus, both just war theory and regular war theory contemplate the existence of aggression, but there is a crucial difference. Whereas every just war has an aggressor, in regular wars, aggression is expected to be the exception rather than the norm, if collective security and the balance of power function appropriately. In regular *jus ad bellum* the standards of judgment are more forbearing and flexible than those of just war because they incorporate the indeterminacy of international rights, the inherent contestability of the right to security, and a relative toleration for isolated breaches. Regular war theory substitutes a more practicable principle of intersubjective validity for earlier ideals of objective, and necessarily unilateral, justice. Of course, just as just war doctrine creates incentives to frame one's enemy as a criminal deprived of belligerent rights, regular wars create an incentive to frame one's enemy as a 'mischievous nation' whose war would compromise the international order as a whole. However, in the context of regular wars, there are 'mischievous nation' only when a significant number of states say so. This requirement creates a multilateral check on purely strategic and spurious claims. International history furnishes attempts to use Vattel's theory in precisely this way,[45] but, unlike earlier just war theory, Enlightenment regular war excludes in principle unilateral pronouncements on the aggressive status of an enemy.

We have, then, that war declarations are embedded in a political discursive practice with forebearing but real standards of appropriateness. As such, they embody the substantive core of a regular doctrine of *jus ad bellum*. The practice of public justification requires that declaring belligerents show persuasively their recognition and respect for the governing principles of international society. And while, historically, the practice of issuing formal war declarations has long been superseded[46]—in fact it was duly followed only rarely[47]—there is currently in international law a norm of accountability that requires states to justify publicly their use of force at least *ex post*. In a weak sense of publicness, the regular war requirement of issuing war declarations may be seen as a demand of public reason. War declarations must provide public reasons why war has been waged.[48]

Can the requirement of publicly declaring war be *effective* in checking the policies of sovereign rulers? Several conditions would have to be met. It must be the case that, as Vattel put it, 'the least scrupulous sovereign would wish to be thought just, equitable, and a lover of peace: he is sensible that a contrary reputation might be detrimental to him'.[49] If not genuine virtue, then at least an interest in reputation and the 'civilizing force of hypocrisy' must be persuasive enough.[50] On the other hand, states should generally assess war declarations in good faith so that 'mere pretexts' are unmasked and generate effective denunciation and, if necessary, counterforce. These may well be the most demanding assumptions of regular war theory and clear proof of its idealism. When reacting to war declarations, states may be motivated not by a genuine concern for the integrity of international society, but by alliances of mutual interests with delinquent states or by a myopic interests in maximising their own power. Regular war theory assumes that there is a universal interest in supporting the practice of reason giving for waging war and that states will be enlightened enough to take war declarations seriously and be motivated to pool their forces and coordinate action accordingly. Arguably the development of international organizations, particularly the collective security arrangements of the UN, has made collective deliberation and action more attainable today than in Vattel's time, but we are certainly far from realising the collective security ideals associated by Wolff and Vattel to regular war.

4. *Jus in Bello* in Regular Wars

Grotius's view of 'solemn wars' as a product of customary and treaty law generates an extremely permissive doctrine of regular *jus in bello*. Grotius wrote, most troublingly, that in solemn wars not only those who bear arms were liable to attack, but also 'all persons who are in enemy territory', including children and women, prisoners of war, soldiers who surrendered unconditionally, and even foreigners living in enemy territory.[51] As proof for such sweeping permissions, Grotius cited ancient Greek, Roman, and Biblical texts, in effect interpreting regular *jus in bello* as their lowest common denominator, which was very low indeed.[52] Among the few *in bello* restrictions he recognized was the prohibition of using poison as a weapon, agreement on which, he explained, 'arose from a consideration of the common advantage, in order that the dangers of war, which had begun to be frequent, might not be too widely extended'.[53] It is impossible to square this rationale with the wide range of permissible targets he posited, but the pursuit of common advantage is indeed at the heart of regular *jus in bello*, as it was articulated, more systematically and restrictively, by Vattel.[54]

Vattel stated categorically that only 'regular forces' should be in charge of waging war and that noncombatants were immune to attack, in particular women, children, religious personnel, and also 'men of letters'.[55] In addition to citing 'enlightened' European practice, Vattel explained that the immunity of noncombatants was justified and motivated by 'common advantage'. For instance, by sparing the 'unarmed inhabitants' of the territory under its control, an occupying army general 'procures an easy subsistence for his army, and avoids many evils and dangers'.[56] Here, Vattel assumed the viability of an agreement between combatants and noncombatants, so that while the former respected the lives and livelihoods of the latter, the latter obeyed and payed contributions on a sustainable footing. In the case of prisoners of war, enemy soldiers could be taken as prisoners, but they had to be treated well, kept alive, and freed once the war had ended. Killing them when they had surrendered would be cowardly and dishonourable, but it would also expose one's own troops to similar treatment.[57]

Vattel applied analogous reasoning to the banning of certain tactics and means of violence. Poisoned weapons should be banned, Vattel said, because, 'if you poison your weapons, the enemy will follow your example; and thus, without gaining any advantage on your side for the decision of the contest, you have only added to the cruelty and calamities of war'.[58] Similarly perfidy (e.g., sending assassins under the guise of ambassadorships) should be proscribed, indeed severely punished, because it eroded the minimum trust among nations without which agreeing on a peace treaty, and future peaceful coexistence, would be impossible.[59]

This series of arguments illustrates Vattel's turn to a legitimate-interest-based form of consequentialism, which he embraced more resolutely than both Grotius and Wolff.[60] Vattel used consequentialism both to *justify* the norms of regular *jus in bello* and to make a case for their *efficacy*, thus addressing a familiar Hobbesian worry.

On the justificatory side, the norms of regular *jus in bello*, in particular the immunities of conventionally defined noncombatants, the protections of prisoners of war, and the restrictions on weaponry, were expected to limit violence and thus to reduce aggregate suffering and killing in war. In this sense, regular *jus in bello* has a humanitarian orientation, which contrasts with late medieval and early modern accounts of just war in which justice and rightful enforcement were emphasized more. In these earlier accounts, the basis for liability to attack was responsibility for the war-triggering injury or for sustaining a wrongful state of affairs, which could applie to both combatants and noncombatants. Those responsible for an unjust war, including captured soldiers and noncombatants, could be punished and even executed. As far as the law of nature was concerned, moreover, anything that was necessary to vindicate the injury suffered was thought to be in principle permissible. In Suárez's words, 'if the end is permissible, the necessary means to that end are also permissible; and hence it follows that in the whole course, or duration, of the war hardly anything done against the enemy involves injustice, except the slaying of the innocent'.[61]

Vattel rejected this view and pursued instead the more recognizibly modern insight that, in the interest of limiting war violence, strict adherence to natural rights and to responsibility-based liability criteria would have to be given up. A more adequate normative logic for regulating warfare is a form of rule-consequentialism that is ultimately grounded on the principle of lesser evil. Indeed, if the righteous discourses of natural law and moral guilt were used as guides for action in war contexts, disputes would tend to escalate and ultimately become 'more bloody, more calamitous in [their] effects, and also more difficult to terminate'.[62] Avoiding this likely outcome is a definining aspiration of the project of regulating warfare through law, for example through mutually agreed conventional limits on the means and methods of warfare.[63]

The moral force of the conventions regulating warfare stems both from their limiting orientation and from their prospects of governing force efficaciously. Vattel's argument for *efficacy* starts by assuming that all states have an interest in minimising their own losses and their own troops' and citizens' suffering. It then relies on the strategic logic of repeated interaction to make a case for their sustaining a self-enforcing equilibrium. The argument can be reconstructed using simple game theoretical language because the decision to comply with the laws of war has the structure of an iterated prisoner's dilemma game.

To see this, note that the laws of war impose a number of restrictions on the use of force, particularly on permissible targets and weapons. Generally speaking, having access to a larger set of violent means and tactics confers advantage and should, for that reason, be the top preference of belligerents. However, proscribing certain strategies and means would also be in the belligerents' interest, as long as their enemies reciprocate.[64] For instance, a norm mandating humane treatment of prisoners of war would be to all belligerents' advantage, at least insofar as each may have its own combatants captured by an enemy. But if a belligerent could enjoy the norm's protections while putting its own prisoners to forced labour or killing them to avoid the costs of care, it would gain an advantage over its enemy. In this and other areas of the laws of war, it is in everyone's best interest to stipulate certain limits on warfare, but defection confers advantage. The logic of a prisoner's dilemma dictates that, if this were the whole story, then rational belligerents would defect and the laws of war would unravel. But if belligerents should expect to face each other repeatedly, either in a single war or in future wars, the laws of war are best represented as an *iterated* prisoner's dilemma game. In such games, when the future is not too heavily discounted and effective reciprocity mechanisms are available, cooperation can emerge, with reciprocity or tit-for-tat being an equilibrium strateg.[65]

In Vattel's rendering of the doctrine of regular war, reprisals function precisely as such reciprocating mechanism. Of prisoners of war, for instance, he wrote that, 'if the hostile general has, without any just reason, caused some prisoners to be hanged, we hang an equal number of his people, and of the same rank—notifying to him that we will continue thus to retaliate, for obliging him to observe the laws of war'.[66] He also posited denial of quarter as a general reciprocating measure following breaches of the laws of war.[67] The disciplining force of these selective disciplinary measures could be effective within one single war, but also across wars, assuming that states could learn moderation from past experience [68] The upshot is that violations of the laws of war in the present will come at a later cost. The shadow of future interactions comes into play if belligerents can foresee and act on the expectation of future encounters and reprisals. These will then have a moderating effect and, ideally, lead to generalized norm compliance with actual reprisals becoming unnecessary.[69]

This conception of *jus in bello* may be contrasted with just war alternatives. In early modern just war theory, and in contemporary 'revisionist' accounts, permissions on the use of force apply exclusively to the just side. The unjust side has no right to use force; indeed, its use of force would only add to its record of injustice.[70] The only source of *in bello* limitations is the injury that justifies the war. In early accounts, armed force, like *post bellum* punishment and the exaction of reparations, had to be proportional to the injury received, which means that attacking the innocent or beyond the limits of rightful vindication would be wrong.[71]

Vattel correctly argued that this asymmetrical doctrine of *jus in bello* is inherently unstable. The practical result of framing conflicts in this way would be each side taking itself to be the only one justified in fighting and thus claiming the right to punish and execute every morally responsible enemy. The net outcome would be the unravelling of all limitations on the use of force. 'Each party asserting that they have justice on their own side', Vattel wrote, 'will arrogate to themselves all the rights of war, and maintain that their enemy has none, that his hostilities are so many acts of robbery, so many infractions of the law of nations, in the punishment of which all states should unite'.[72] Instead of the reciprocal recognition of limited belligerent rights, this just war conception of *jus in bello* fosters reciprocal blame and explosive vindictive dynamics.

Some contemporary theorists have followed Vattel in acknowledging the threat to the integrity of the laws of war of righteous emphases of *jus ad bellum*. In Hedley Bull's sober language, 'if one side in an armed conflict regards itself as specially privileged by the laws of war, then reciprocal observance of these laws, which is a basic condition of their efficacy, is undermined'.[73] Not only will legal efficacy be in jeopardy if the 'unequal application proposition' is put into practice,[74] but the overall effect of an asymmetrical *jus in bello* may be to inflame righteous passions and to escalate the use of violence.[75]

In addition to this prudential rejoinder, regular war theory can offer a principled defence of the symmetrical application of *jus in bello*. As we saw in Sections 2 and 3, Grotius's epistemic argument, together with Wolff's and Vattel's arguments from legal indeterminacy and structural insecurity, provide grounds for a *presumption* of bilateral permissions to wage war. Of course, within a bilateral regime of *jus ad bellum* there is no reason to postulate an asymmetrical doctrine of *jus in bello*. Just war theorists reject the symmetrical application of the laws of war only because they take unilateral justice—or the "aggressor-defender paradigm"[76]—to be the only possible case of just war. Regular war theorists defended the symmetrical application of *jus in bello* by arguing that often in war both sides have some plausible reason to fight. As noted earlier, this presumption of bilateral *ad bellum* justice by no means amounts to denying the existence of clear cases of unilateral justice. Vattel recognized the existence of such clear cases (e.g., that of 'mischievous nations' that sought to undermine the very foundations of international society) and in fact argued that, in the deployment of collective security to contain them, the laws of *jus in bello* could be breached or suspended.[77] However, these cases were presumed to be rare in a well-functioning international society, and whether or not they would merit breaches to the laws of war is not something that the law itself needs to contemplate, but is rather a matter of exceptional judgment.

5. Conclusion

The regular war tradition, with its institutional focus and its emphasis on the contrast between the national and international juridical orders, leads to a distinct doctrine of *jus ad bellum*. Instead of the 'aggressor-defender paradigm' of just war theory, which assumes that in just wars only one side can be justified, it proposes that *jus ad bellum* be treated as largely a matter of political morality, not to be modelled after criminal trials in domestic law. This should not be understood to amount to an abdication of moral judgment or a blanket permission to wage war. There are moral standards of regular *jus ad bellum*, but they are fluid and attuned to the deep substantive disagreements and empirical, legal, and moral uncertainties that characterize disputes behind armed conflicts. Cases of bilaterally justified regular wars are not a rare possibility, and they must be assessed not by courts of law but through public reason and political judgment. This determination may require statesmen not lawyers, but the difference between crude *realpolitik* and public justification cannot be missed.

Against this theoretical background, the doctrine of regular *jus in bello* is characterized by conventional limitations. The value of these conventions lies in their capacity to moderate the use of force and thus to mitigate the killing and suffering caused by war. For the conventions to be most effective, substantive claims of justice must be relativized and de-emphasized, for the more righteously claims are pressed, the stronger the inclination to bypass conventional limits and to degrade the enemy. In the deep tension between the value of justice and international rights, on the one hand, and the values of limitation of violence and international stability, on the other, regular war theory unequivocally sides with the latter. This choice could perhaps be questioned as reactionary,[78] but it is based partly on valid doubts about the accuracy of righteous claims made within weakly institutionalized contexts, partly on a commitment to the valuable enterprise of limiting killing and suffering in war.

Notes

1. Benedict Kingsbury, 'People and Boundaries: An "Internationalized Public Law" Approach', in *States, Nations, and Borders: The Ethics of Making Boundaries*, edited by Allen E. Buchanan and Margaret Moore (Cambridge: Cambridge University Press, 2003), 298–302.
2. In a famous passage of *On the Social Contract*, Rousseau gives a classic summary of this basic orientation: 'War is then not a relationship between one man and another, but a relationship between one State and another, in which individuals are enemies only by accident, not as men, nor even as citizens, but as soldiers; not as members of the fatherland, but as its defenders. Finally, any State can only have other States, and not men, as enemies, inasmuch as it is impossible to fix a true relation between things of different natures' (*Social Contract*, I.iv). Although in many ways Rousseau could be described as a regular war theorist, his scepticism towards the law of nations would make him a very particular one. This chapter will focus on two of his contemporaries, the Swiss jurist and diplomat Emer de Vattel (1714–1767) and the German polymath Christian Wolff (1679–1754), whose accounts of regular war were based on a firm belief in, and comprehensive theory of, international law and society. For a suggestive discussion of Rousseau's complex ideas on war, see Karma Nabulsi. *Traditions of War Occupation, Resistance, and the Law* (Oxford: Oxford University Press, 1999), 176–240.
3. Contemporary 'revisionist' acccounts of just war remarkably share some of these claims with late medieval and early modern accounts (as Jeff McMahan has acknowledged in *Killing in War* (Oxford: Clarendon Press, 2009), 238. For contemporary leading statements along these lines, see Jeff McMahan 'Just Cause for War'. *Ethics & International Affairs* 19:3 (2005), 20; Cécile Fabre, *Cosmopolitan War* (Oxford: Oxford University Press, 2012), 71–74; and David Rodin, *War and Self-Defense* (Oxford: Clarendon Press, 2004). Compare Vitoria in Anthony Pagden and Jeremy Lawrance, *Francisco de Vitoria: Political*

Writings (Cambridge: Cambridge University Press, 1991), 303, 313; Francisco Suárez and Gwladys L. Williams, *Selections from Three Works of Francisco Suárez. 2 vols, Classics of International Law* (Oxford/London: Clarendon Press/H. Milford, 1944), 828–830; and Hugo Grotius and Francis W. Kelsey, *De jure belli ac pacis libri tres. Classics of International Law* (Oxford: Clarendon Press, 1925), 565–566. For a helpful overview of late medieval and early modern just war theory, see Stephen C. Neff, *War and the Law of Nations: A General History* (Cambridge: Cambridge University Press, 2005), 54–68; and for a penetrating discussion of Vitoria's often misunderstood views on 'ostensible bilateral justice', see Peter Haggenmacher, *Grotius et la doctrine de la guerre juste, Publications de l'Institut universitaire de hautes études internationales, Genève* (Paris: Presses universitaires de France, 1983), 209–212.

4. I will not discuss in this chapter the regular war doctrine of *jus post bellum*. For discussion, see Randall Lessafer, 'A schoolmaster abolishing homework? Vattel on peacemaking and peace treaties', in *Vattel's International Law in a XXIst Century Perspective*, edited by Vincent Chetail and Peter Haggenmacher (Boston: Martinus Nijhoff Publishers, 2011); Sharon Korman, *The Right of Conquest: The Forcible Acquisition of Territory in International Law and Practice* (Oxford: Clarendon Press, 1996); and Pablo Kalmanovitz, *Justice in Post-War Reconstruction: Theories from Vitoria to Vattel*, PhD Dissertation (Department of Political Science, Columbia University, New York).
5. On these pre-modern sources, see P. Haggenmacher, *Grotius et la doctrine de la guerre juste*, 203–206; Peter Haggenmach, 'Just war and regular war in sixteenth century Spanish doctrine', *International Review of the Red Cross* 290 (1992), 434–445; and Gregory Reichberg 'Just War and Regular War: Competing Paradigms', in *Just and Unjust Warriors: The Moral and Legal Status of Soldiers*, edited by David Rodin and Henry Shue (Oxford: Oxford University Press, 2008), 200–202.
6. Grotius wrote that, 'human laws indisputably have it in their province to go further than nature in regard to many points, but never to go contrary to nature' (II.iii.6, 208). Early in *The Rights of War and Peace* he makes clar that 'law in our use of the term here means nothing else than what is just, and that, too, rather in a negative than in an affirmative sense, that being lawful which is not unjust' (I.i.3, p. 34; see also I.i.10, 38–39; II.ii.5, 192). For commentary on the significance of the tension between natural law and solemn wars in Grotius, see Benedict Kingsbury 'Grotius, Law and Moral Skepticism: Theory and Practice in the Thought of Hedley Bull', in *Classical Theories in International Relations*, edited by Ian Clark (New York: Palgrave, 1999); Tanaka Tadashi 'Grotius's Concept of Law', in *A Normative Approach to War: Peace, War, and Justice in Hugo Grotius*, edited by Yasuaki Onuma (Oxford: Clarendon Press, 1993), 39–43, and 'Temperamenta (Moderation)', 295); Peter Haggenmacher, 'On Assessing the Grotian Heritage', in *International Law and the Grotian Heritage*, edited by T.M.C. Asser Institute (The Hague: T.M.C. Asser Institute, 1985); and K. Nabulsi, *Traditions of War Occupation, Resistance, and the Law*, 128–176. For an alternative interpretation, which tends to underplay the tensions within Grotius's thought, see S. Neff, *War and the Law of Nations*, 96–102). Unless otherwise noted, all citations to *The Rights of War and Peace* are from the Carnegie Endowment edition (Grotius and Kelsey, 1925).
7. See, for example, Alex J. Bellamy, *Just Wars: From Cicero to Iraq* (Cambridge: Polity, 2006), 71–74; James Turner Johnson, *Ideology, Reason, and the Limitation of War: Religious and Secular Concepts, 1200–1740* (Princeton, NJ: Princeton University Press, 1975), 223–231.
8. H. Grotius, *The Rights of War and Peace*, III.iv.2, 641.

9. Hedley Bull, 'The Grotian Conception of International Society', in *Diplomatic Investigations: Essays in the Theory of International Politics*, edited by Herbert Butterfield and Martin Wight (Cambridge: Harvard University Press, 1966), 58.
10. H. Grotius, *The Rights of War and Peace*, III.vii.7, 695; III.x.1.1, 716.
11. Idem., III.x.1, 716.
12. Jeff McMahan, 'The Morality of War and the Law of War', David Rodin, 'The Moral Inequality of Soldiers: Why Jus in Bello Asymmetry Is Half-Right', and Henry Shue, 'Do We Need a "Morality of War"?', all in *Just and Unjust Warriors: The Moral and Legal Status of Soldiers*, edited by David Rodin and Henry Shue (Oxford: Oxford University Press, 2008). See also Seth Lazar, 'The Morality and the Law of War', in Andrei Marmor (ed.), *The Routledge Companion to Philosophy of Law* (London: Routledge, Taylor & Francis), 364–380.
13. H. Grotius, III.iv.4, 644; for the corresponding argument for civil wars, see I.iii.9.2, 111.
14. H. Grotius, II.xxv.1–8, 578–584.
15. Idem., see III.xviii.3.1.
16. For commentary emphasising the significance and novelty of Grotius's consequentialism, see Friedrich Meinecke, *Machiavellism: The Doctrine of Raison d'etat and Its Place in Modern History* (Boulder, CO: Westview Press, 1984, 208–210); Richard Tuck, 'The "Modern" Theory of Natural Law', in *The Languages of Political Theory in Early-Modern Europe*, edited by Anthony Pagden (Cambridge: Cambridge University Press, 1987), 105.
17. Hersh Lauterpacht, 'The Grotian Tradition in International Law', *British Yearbook of International Law* 23 (1946).
18. All citations to Vattel's *The Law of Nations* are to the Liberty Fund edition (Indianapolis: Liberty Fund, 2008), and all citations to Wolff's *Ius Gentium* are to the Carnegie Endowment edition (Christian Wolff and Joseph Drake. *Jus gentium methodo scientifica pertractatum*, edited by James Brown Scott, *Classics of International Law* (New York: Oxford University Press, 1995). See Vattel, III.192, 592 and Wolff, §617.
19. For valuable discussions of the theoretical significance of the voluntary law of nations, see Andrew Hurrell, 'Vattel: Pluralism and Its Limits', in *Classical Theories of International Relations*, edited by Ian Clark and Iver B. Neumann (Basingstoke/New York: Macmillan/St Martin's Press, 1996); Emmanuelle Jouannet, *Emer de Vattel el L'Émergence Doctrinale du Droit International Classique* (Paris: Editions A. Pedone, 1998), 141–164; Amanda Perreau-Saussine, 'Lauterpacht and Vattel on the Sources of International Law: The Place of Private Law Analogies and General Principles', in *Vattel's International Law in a XXIst Century Perspective*, edited by Peter Haggenmacher and Vincent Chetail (Leiden: Martinus Nijhoff Publishers, 2011); and Peter Pavel Remec, *The Position of the Individual in International Law According to Grotius and Vattel* (The Hague: M. Nijhoff, 1960), 144–157.
20. A. Hurrell, 'Vattel: Pluralism and Its Limits', 237; A. Perreau-Saussine, 'Lauterpacht and Vattel on the Sources of International Law', 173.
21. E. Vattel, III.189, 590; Wolff, Preface, 6–7.
22. For Vattel, a clear instance in which coercive interference in domestic affairs is permissible is civil wars, in which, 'by violating the fundamental laws, [the ruler] gives his subjects a legal right to resist him'. For Vattel, civil wars 'break' or 'suspend' 'the bonds of political society' and thus, from the perspective of international society, the two sides come to appear as regular belligerents in an international conflict (II.55–56, 290–291; also Prelim. §§16, 23; 74, 77.
23. E. Vattel, II.335, 456, emphasis added; see also C. Wolff, §§252–257.

24. E. Vattel, II.354, 466–467.
25. Idem., II.323, 448.
26. Idem., III.38, 489.
27. E. Vattel, III.68, 508; C. Wolff, §888.
28. E. Vattel, III.188, 589; C. Wolff, §888, 454.
29. C. Wolff, §892, 457.
30. J. McMahan, *Killing in War*,, 104–110, and 'The Prevention of Unjust Wars', in *Reading Walzer*, edited by Yitzhak Benbaji and Naomi Sussmann (London: Routledge, 2013); D. Rodin, *War and Self-Defense*, 179–188).
31. C. Wolff, §574; E. Vattel, II.326–330.
32. E. Vattel, II.332, 454.
33. E. Vattel, II.335, 456; C. Wolff, §§573–574.
34. Pablo Kalmanovitz, 'Aggression and the symmetrical application of International Humanitarian Law', *International Theory* 7:1 (2015), 1–32.
35. J. McMahan, 'Just Cause for War'; 2005; D. Rodin, *War and Self-Defense*, 103–110; Michael Walzer, *Just and Unjust Wars: A Moral Argument with Historical Illustrations* (New York: Basic Books, 1977), 50–53.
36. For legal commentary, see Yoram Dinstein, *War, Aggression and Self-Defence*, 4th ed. (Cambridge: Cambridge University Press, 2005), 125–131.
37. For an overview of these critiques, see A. Hurrell, 'Vattel: Pluralism and Its Limits', 249–250.
38. John Rawls, *The Law of Peoples* (Cambridge, MA: Harvard University Press, 1999), 11–23.
39. Martti Koskenniemi, *From Apology to Utopia: The Structure of International Legal Argument* (Cambridge: Cambridge University Press, 2005), 112–120.
40. E. Vattel, II.335, 456, emphasis added.
41. Grotius was ambivalent regarding the material content of war declarations. He wrote that it was important that declarations state reasons, 'in order that the whole human race as it were might judge the justness of [the war]' (II.xxvi.4, 593), but elsewhere he said, more formally, that the purpose of war declarations was not to publicise reasons but merely to give war the seal of sovereignty, so that 'the fact might be established with certainty that war was being waged not by private initiative but by the will of each of the two peoples or of their heads' (III.iii.9, 638). See also H. Grotius, I.iii.4–5, III.iii.1, 97–101, 630; E. Vattel, III.51–68, 500–508; C. Wolff, §§705–721, 364–373.
42. C. Wolff, §625, 318.
43. E. Vattel, III.62, 505.
44. E. Vattel, II.53, 289; III.34, 487; for commentary see Walter Rech, *Enemies of Mankind: Vattel's Theory of Collective Security* (Leiden: Martinus Nijhoff Publishers, 2013), 138–158.
45. Isaac Nakhimoksky, 'Carl Schmitt's Vattel and the "Law of Nations" Between Enlightenment and Revolution,' *Grotiana* 31 (2010), 141–164.
46. Tanisha M. Fazal, 'Why States No Longer Declare War'. *Security Studies* 21 (2012).
47. John Frederick Maurice, *Hostilities without Declaration of War* (London: Authority, 1883).
48. For a contemporary defence, see Eric Grynaviski, 'The Bloodstained Spear: Public Reason and Declarations of War', *International Theory* 5:2 (2013).
49. E. Vattel, III.64, 506.
50. Jon Elster, *Alchemies of the Mind: Rationality and the Emotions* (Cambridge: Cambridge University Press, 1999).

51. H. Grotius, III.iv.6–12, 646–650.
52. P. P. Remec, *The Position of the Individual in International Law*, 114.
53. H. Grotius, III.iv.15, 652.
54. For Wolff, in contrast to Vattel, the regular doctrine of *jus in bello* was simply the just war doctrine applied bilaterally. '[T]he voluntary law of nations', he wrote, 'allows nothing except that which is allowable by the law of nature to a just belligerent' (§890, 455). For Wolff, positive conventions do not have a special role, not even the conventional distinction between regular combatants and noncombatants. In line with Scholastic just war, Wolff claimed that, as long as someone is liable to attack in virtue of an alleged injury, the actual means used would be irrelevant (§§877–880, 450–451.) By contrast Vattel, who in most other ways was heavily indebted to Wolff, emphasized the importance of 'civilized ways' and conventions and, in so doing, gave a more distinctly modern and humanitarian account of *jus in bello*, as we shall see.
55. E. Vattel, III.145–147, 549–551.
56. Idem., III.147, 550.
57. Idem., III.150, 553.
58. Idem., III.156, 563.
59. Idem., III.155, 557–562.
60. See E. Jouannet, *Emer de Vattel el L'Émergence Doctrinale du Droit International Classique*, 147–151.
61. 'On War' VII.6, F. Suárez and G. L. Williams, *Selections from Three Works of Francisco Suárez*, 840; see also Vitoria 'On the Laws of War', in *Francisco de Vitoria*, 304–306; and Grotius, III.i.2, 599–600.
62. E. Vattel, III.188, 589–590.
63. For a concise contemporary moral justification of this approach, see George Mavrodes, 'Conventions and the Morality of War', *Philosophy and Public Affairs* 4:2 (1975); see also Jeremy Waldron, 'Civilians, Terrorism, and Deadly Serious Conventions', *NYU School of Law, Public Law Research Paper* 9:9 (2009); Robert D. Sloane, 'The Cost of Conflation: Preserving the Dualism of Jus ad Bellum and Jus in Bello in the Contemporary Law of War', *Yale Journal of International Law* 34 (2009), 47–112.
64. For further detail, see James D. Morrow, 'The Laws of War, Common Conjectures, and Legal Systems in International Politics', *Journal of Legal Studies* 31:S1 (2002); and Kenneth Oye, 'Explaining Cooperation Under Anarchy: Hypotheses and Strategies', in *Cooperation Under Anarchy*, edited by Kenneth A. Oye (Princeton, NJ: Princeton University Press, 1986.
65. Robert M. Axelrod, *The Evolution of Cooperation* (New York: Basic Books, 1984).
66. E. Vattel, III.142, 545.
67. Idem., III.141, 544–545.
68. For historical instances of this slow learning process, see Geoffrey F. A. Best, *War and Law Since 1945* (Oxford: Clarendon Press, 1994), 34–48; Wilhelm Georg Grewe, *The Epochs of International Law* (Berlin: Walter de Gruyter, 2000), 535–542; and S. C. Neff, *War and the Law of Nations*, 102–130.
69. The extent to which the logic of reciprocity is necessary or able to sustain the regime of international humanitarian law today raises hugely complex questions that are beyond this chapter's scope. I should nonetheless note that reprisals are now virtually proscribed in international law, but it is far from clear that states are willing to renounce to them (see Adam Roberts, 'The Equal Application of the Laws of War: A Principle Under Pressure',

International Review of the Red Cross 90:872 [2008], 942–945). Mark Osiel has argued that contemporary warfare has superseded the logic of reciprocity, and so the nature of legal compliance with the laws of war must be thoroughly reconceived (*The End of Reciprocity: Terror, Torture, and the Law of War* [Cambridge: Cambridge University Press, 2009]).

70. Tony Coady, 'The Status of Combatants', in *Just and Unjust Warriors: The Moral and Legal Status of Soldiers*, edited by David Rodin and Henry Shue (Oxford: Oxford University Press, 2008); J. McMahan, *Killing in War*, 14; D. Rodin, 'The Moral Inequality of Soldiers'.
71. P. Haggenmacher, *Grotius et la doctrine de la guerre juste*, 600–603; G. Reichberg, 'Just War and Regular War', 199–200.
72. E. Vattel, III.188, 589–590.
73. H. Bull, 'The Grotian Conception of International Society', 71; also M. Walzer, *Just and Unjust Wars*, 41.
74. A. Roberts, 'The Equal Application of the Laws of War'; R. D. Sloane, 'The Cost of Conflation'.
75. See further Christopher Kutz, 'Fearful Symmetry', in *Just and Unjust Warriors: The Moral and Legal Status of Soldiers*, edited by David Rodin and Henry Shue (Oxford: Oxford University Press, 2008); Hersh Lauterpacht, 'Rules of Warfare in an Unlawful War', in *Law and Politics in the World Community: Essays on Hans Kelsen's Pure Theory and Related Problems in International Law*, edited by George A. Lipsky (Berkeley: University of California Press, 1953); Carl Schmitt, *The Nomos of the Earth in the International Law of the Jus Publicum Europaeum* (New York: Telos Press, 2003), 152–171; and cf. J. McMahan, 'The Morality of War and the Law of War', 27–33.
76. Henry Shue and David Rodin, *Preemption: Military Action and Moral Justification* (Oxford: Oxford University Press, 2007), 15.
77. E. Vattel, II.56, 291.
78. For example, K. Nabulsi, *Traditions of War Occupation, Resistance, and the Law*, 142.

PART III

RESORT

CHAPTER 8

A RICHER *JUS AD BELLUM*

ALLEN BUCHANAN

1. Narrow Versus Wide *Jus ad Bellum*

The aim of most contemporary just war theorists appears to be simple: to provide an account of the necessary and sufficient conditions for war acts to be morally right—that is, to articulate *objective moral justifications* for war acts. In the case of the *jus ad bellum* part of just war theory, the goal is to determine objective justifications for acts of going to war. If one defines 'just war theory' as an account of which war acts are right, then it is trivially true that articulating objective moral justifications of war acts is the aim of just war theory: indeed, by definition, its only aim. Correspondingly, the sole aim of *jus ad bellum* would be to articulate objective moral justifications for acts of going to war.

There is nothing wrong, per se, with opting for such a definition of *jus ad bellum* (or the corresponding definition of just war theory). Yet it is important to understand that the aim referenced in this definition is very limited, given the much greater potential scope of moral theorizing about recourse to war. Even if it is true that identifying sound objective justifications for going to war is the first task of *jus ad bellum*, it is not the only important task. The following list indicates a much more expansive conception of the domain of *jus ad bellum* theorizing.[1]

1. Provide objective justifications for recourse to war (identifying criteria for justified acts of going to war).
2. Determine which directly action-guiding rules leaders, combatants, and others faced with the decision whether to go to war or to support or oppose war morally ought to employ.[2] It cannot be assumed that they should treat the elements of objective justifications as directly action-guiding. In some cases it might be the case that they ought instead to use directly action-guiding norms whose content diverges from the elements of objective justifications. 'Directly action-guiding norms' here covers, but is not limited to, heuristics. Heuristics can produce better decisions when they serve as short-cuts or reliable rules of thumb in situations

(a) where there is insufficient time for more complex decision-processes, (b) where the information required for an ideal decision-making process is not available or too complex to process adequately, or (c) where the decision-makers are subject to incentives that tend to distort their decisions (and where heuristics can function like self-binding strategies to reduce the risk of distortion).[3]

3. Provide guidance for the moral evaluation of the institutional processes within which leaders make decisions about going to war.[4]
4. Provide criteria for morally evaluating domestic or international laws regarding recourse to war (this is distinct from 3, because the actual institutional processes through which decisions to go to war are made may or may not be effectively constrained by a commitment to law).[5]
5. Provide guidance for how to achieve a division of labour between directly action-guiding rules to be employed by leaders, on the one hand, and institutional processes, on the other, that is most conducive to morally sound recourse to war.
6. Provide criteria for morally evaluating the decisions of leaders regarding recourse to war. (Note that all of the preceding tasks, 1–5, are relevant to this one.)
7. Provide an account of the virtues of leaders, so far as their decision-making regarding recourse to war is concerned. (According to moral theories that give a prominent role to virtues, this will be a central element of task 6; for other types of theories, it will be negligible or less important.)
8. Provide criteria for morally evaluating social practices regarding what counts as legitimate public justifications for recourse to war by leaders. Given the prominence of war in human life and the seriousness of its consequences, it is both unsurprising and appropriate that societies develop practices that include norms that identify some justifications for going to war as legitimate and others as illegitimate. For example, in eighteenth-century in Europe, it was widely agreed that going to war to maintain or restore 'the balance of power' was legitimate, but this is no longer the case. These practices and the corresponding norms can and should be evaluated from a moral standpoint. This item overlaps with but is distinct from item 4 because such social practices may rely more or less heavily on legal norms.
9. Provide criteria for morally evaluating leaders' public acts of justifying recourse to war. On some accounts, this evaluation will depend crucially on whether these public acts of justification count as legitimate according to the relevant social practice regarding public justifications for going to war.

Item 1 might be regarded as a purely theoretical aim. Item 2 is a practical aim, at least if it is assumed that there is some chance that the guidance provided may actually be followed. It is perfectly legitimate, of course, for a just war theorist to concentrate only on the theoretical aspects of *jus ad bellum* and leave the task of contributing to the achievement of practical aims to others. The point is simply that comprehensive moral theorizing about war should include theorizing about how best to achieve practical aims. Such theorizing will, of course, rely on empirical assumptions, but it will also be a normative enterprise and one to which moral philosophers should be able to contribute.

Moral philosophers may not be the most effective agents among all those who might contribute to the improvement of behaviour regarding recourse to war, but they are best equipped to explore the possibility that systematic moral reasoning can play some role in that worthy endeavour. So there is good reason for some moral philosophers who think systematically about war to devote their energies to the practical aims.[6]

In Section 1, I set out in detail the full set of topics that a comprehensive *jus ad bellum* should address and explain important connections among them. In Section 2, I explore neglected relationships among moral principles, institutions, and law and also argue that *jus ad bellum* theory should take seriously the idea that the relationship between the morality and the law of recourse to war is not purely instrumental but also partly constitutive—that the law, when it is appropriately institutionalized, can alter the moral landscape in significant ways. In Section 3, I examine the practical roles that an enriched *jus ad bellum* could play.

2. Elements of an Enriched *Jus ad Bellum*

2.1. Objective Versus Directly Action-Guiding Norms

This first task, the sole theoretical aim of the *jus ad bellum* part of just war theory narrowly construed, seems wholly uncontroversial. But the phrase 'criteria for justified acts of going to war' is ambiguous between (1) objective justifications and (2) directly action-guiding norms for leaders or other agents.[7] Suppose it is understood in the first way. Here is an example of an objective justification:

It is (morally) justifiable for a state to go to war in self-defence if and only if:

1. the target of the war of self-defence has perpetrated a wrongful (unjustified) attack,
2. war is a last resort (roughly, all reasonable alternatives have been exhausted),
3. the act of going to war satisfies the *proportionality requirement* (roughly, the good to be achieved by waging the war justifies the harms it will bring), and
4. the act of going to war satisfies *discrimination requirement* (roughly, reasonable care is taken to minimize harm to those not morally liable to be harmed).

I am not assuming that these are the correct elements of an objective justification for going to war in self-defence. (In fact, I believe the case has been made by myself and Robert O. Keohane that point 1 is too strong because it rules out cases of justified preventive war, situations in which the target of military action poses a dire threat of wrongful harm but one that will only be realized at some temporally distant point.)[8] I make no effort in this chapter to contribute to theorizing about objective justifications, nor will I have much to say about the fourth task, the moral evaluation of laws regarding war.

My aim, rather, is to call attention to areas of just war theorizing that have been relatively neglected: items 2–3 and 5 through 9. The sample objective justification just outlined is only intended to help ground the distinction I wish to emphasize between objective justifications and directly action-guiding norms and to lay the groundwork for showing how much of the terrain of a comprehensive *jus ad bellum* remains unexplored after the task of identifying objective justifications has been successfully completed.

2.2. Directly Action-Guiding Norms

The best way for leaders to ensure that their actions conform to the requirements of sound objective justifications for recourse to war may *not* be for them to attempt to determine whether an act of war-making they are contemplating satisfies the conditions set out in the relevant objective justification. State leaders are not ideal decision-makers who can be trusted to apply the conditions for objective justification directly. They are fallible agents labouring under all of the limitations common to human beings, including normal cognitive biases and weakness of the will. They are also subject to special incentives as a result of the institutional roles they occupy and the values that led them to come to occupy those roles—incentives that can impair their decision-making. For example, given that her country has recently suffered a humiliating defeat, and in the context of a rival political leader's allegation that she is soft on national security, a leader may rightly conclude that her grip on power requires taking a hard-line position in a current international crisis, and this in turn may bias her judgment towards recourse to war. Alternatively, a leader may understandably conclude that the political consequences for her of not taking preventive action in the event of a terrorist act or surprise military attack that could have been prevented are far more serious than the error of taking preventive action that turns out to have been unnecessary. In sum, particular institutional roles, including that of commander-in-chief, can create powerful incentives that are often not well-aligned with the requirements of objective justification.

Furthermore, even though leaders have access to information not available to ordinary people, they may nonetheless suffer serious epistemic liabilities. Their advisors may exaggerate their own expertise in order to maintain or augment their own power or may succumb to the temptation to slant the information in a direction they anticipate will please the leader, given what they know or believe they know about his preferences. And of course, advisors and leaders deliberating together are vulnerable to various other errors stemming from so-called group think. In particular, if sufficient care is not taken to distinguish expertise from loyalty, important corrective information may be excluded from the decision-making process, and the phenomenon of polarization may occur: in a group of like-minded individuals, shared views or preferences may become intensified in the absence of evidence to support making such a shift. Even when none of these distorting influences is at work, limitations on information may make attempts to apply objective justification criteria highly fallible.

The main point here should be familiar from discussions of the distinction between direct and indirect consequentialism, but it applies to both consequentialist and deontological varieties of just war theory. Because of epistemic and/or motivational limitations, an agent may do better by not attempting to apply the criteria for right action but instead relying on norms whose content is quite different.

Consider another example. Judgments of proportionality can be extremely difficult to make, even if one assumes away uncertainty as to how the principle of proportionality itself is to be understood. (A chief source of disagreement concerns which harms and benefits count and how they are to be weighted.) Beyond uncertainty as to how the principle itself is to be understood, the chief difficulty is that proportionality judgments are very epistemically demanding. Predictions about the effects of various military operations must be made but usually on the bases of inadequate evidence. One source of difficulty in making predictions is that the effects of a military intervention—in particular, how much death and destruction it will entail, as well as the distribution of harm—will depend on how the enemy reacts, how civilians in the area of operation react, and how one's own troops will behave, all of which may be difficult to predict.

Suppose that, either due to limitations of information or due to the risk that her judgment will be distorted by incentives that attach to her role in the situation at hand or other biases, a state leader is likely to err if she tries to determine whether the act of war she is contemplating satisfies the proportionality requirement in the case of a war of humanitarian intervention. In particular, she may fail to give sufficient weight to the harmful effects of the intervention on noncombatants and give undue consideration to preventing harm to her own armed forces because she is politically accountable for the latter but not the former.

Under these conditions, it may well be that the leader will be more likely to make the right decision if, instead of trying to assess proportionality, she follows a heuristic that makes no reference to proportionality: 'engage in humanitarian military intervention only in cases where the humanitarian crisis is extremely grave—a genocide or mass killing of comparable scale'. In fact, most accounts of the 'justification' (note the ambiguity) for humanitarian war include a high threshold of violence condition. The problem is that they seldom make it clear whether it is intended as a heuristic or an element of an objective justification.

Contemporary just war theorists have not ignored the epistemic obstacles to correct application of objective justification criteria.[9] Their focus, however, has been rather narrow: for the most part, theorists have discussed the epistemic issues in the context of a dispute over the moral symmetry thesis, the assertion, advanced by Michael Walzer but also reflected in international humanitarian law of war, that the rules of *jus in bello* should not discriminate between just and unjust combatants (those who fight in a just cause and those who do not).[10] Some have concluded that, in many cases, ordinary soldiers cannot be faulted for being unable to make accurate judgments as to whether the war in which they are called on to fight is just.

Some of the most prominent contemporary theorists, including most notably Jeff McMahan, have developed a theory of moral liability to be subjected to armed force according to which it is morally impermissible for unjust combatants to kill just combatants, even if in doing so they adhere strictly to *jus in bello* principles in their war-making activity.[11] In order to render this claim consistent with the conviction that, in many cases, combatants cannot be expected to know whether the cause for which they fight is just, McMahan and others have emphasized the distinction between the morality of war and the law of war.[12] Their view is that even though, as a matter of the 'deep' morality of war, Walzer's moral symmetry of combatants must be abandoned, the law regarding war should maintain symmetry. The clear assumption here is that the 'deep' morality of war should be concerned only with objective justifications and the judgments of moral culpability that follow from applying their criteria to the behaviour of agents but that the law properly has other concerns, including satisfying the conditions for just punishment.

This particular focus on epistemic obstacles is unduly narrow in two respects. First, it attends only to the implications of one sort of epistemic obstacle to morally sound acts or practices (whether legal or less formal) of holding combatants responsible for their war acts: the difficulty for ordinary soldiers of determining whether their side's war-making is just or not. It does not address the special epistemic obstacles leaders face nor does it consider how epistemic obstacles can interact with the peculiar incentives under which leaders labour to distort decision-making. Second, it does not consider other morally defensible responses to the epistemic problem it does address. More precisely, it does not acknowledge the possibility that, in some cases, the use of heuristics might mitigate the risks of acting when the information needed to apply objective justification criteria is not available.

For example, in some cases—depending on the history of one's country's recourse to war—a reasonable heuristic for soldiers or potential soldiers might be 'proceed on the assumption that any given recourse to war by the leaders of one's country is unjust, unless there is very strong evidence that it is just'. Such a heuristic might be eminently reasonable for a citizen of a country whose leaders have repeatedly shown themselves to be untrustworthy when it comes to their public justifications for going to war. In extreme cases, an individual might be morally culpable for not following it.

Clarity in theorizing *jus ad bellum* requires not only distinguishing between objective justifications and directly action-guiding principles and acknowledging that the latter are an important subject for moral reasoning. It also requires a recognition of the fact that because heuristics serve to mitigate epistemic and/or motivational defects of decision-makers and because different decision-makers have different defects, it is a mistake to assume that there is only one correct set of heuristics. In order to make the case for a particular heuristic, one must first of all provide an accurate characterization of the decision-making agent and her situation.

To illustrate this point, consider Michael Walzer's assertion that leaders contemplating the use of armed force to intervene in a conflict in another state ought to proceed on the assumption that there is a 'fit' between the political structure and the society there, unless the government is engaging in extreme violence, such as genocide.[13] Walzer could be interpreted here as proposing a heuristic designed to cope with the risk of error that a leader contemplating intervention would incur if he attempted to make more fine-grained judgments about the relationship between the government and the people and, in particular, whether the government in some sense represents or expresses the values and will of the people. But Walzer does not consider the possibility that the information needed to make such judgments may vary across agents and that different agents may be subject to a greater or lesser degree to incentives that affect their willingness or ability to utilize relevant information effectively. It is likely that different heuristics would be appropriate depending on whether a decision to go to war were being made by Dick Cheney, on the one hand, or Abraham Lincoln, on the other.

Which heuristics (if any) are appropriate will depend on the characteristics of the agent and of the situation in which the decision will be made because the function of heuristics is to mitigate the cognitive and motivational deficiencies of the agent who will apply them, and these will vary across agents and decision contexts. If, for example, a heuristic is an epistemic proxy, that is, one designed to cope with an informational deficit, it will matter whether all agents suffer this deficit or only some.

2.3. Institutional Processes for Recourse to War Decisions

An argument to justify a heuristic is, in an important sense, more complex and requires more empirical premises than a moral intuition-based argument to establish an element of an objective justification: one must first establish that there is a significant risk involved in the effort to use the objective justification as a direct guide to action. As I have just noted, this will require not only a description of the relevant epistemic and motivational features of the decision-maker but also a characterization of how features of the choice situation, when combined with these features of the agent, create the risk of bad decisions.

In the case of leaders, it will not be enough to include in the characterization the normal cognitive biases and errors to which people in general are liable. In addition, it will be necessary to note the special incentives that attach to the role of leader and these, of course, will vary depending on how the role of leader is understood in a particular society and on contingent features of the role in its particular institutional setting. After providing this complex, highly contextual characterization of the agent, one must then show that the proposed heuristic significantly reduces that risk while producing an adequate degree of congruence between what the objective justification, if perfectly applied, would recommend and what the heuristic tells one to do.

The theoretical domain of *jus ad bellum* is even more complicated than that, however. Once one takes seriously the potential effects of institutions on decision-making, it becomes clear that the only alternatives are not (1) decision-makers directly applying the elements of sound objective justifications, on the one hand, or (2) employing heuristics, on the other. Relying on heuristics is only one way of coping with the epistemic and motivational limitations of decision-makers. Institutional procedures, including requirements of transparency, consultation with relevant experts, and accountability, can also mitigate the distorting effects of both epistemic and motivational limitations. For example, as Keohane and I have argued, institutions capable of imposing costs on decision-makers who exaggerate the risk of potential, temporally distant harms can counteract incentives for making morally unjustifiable decisions.[14]

2.4. A Morally Sound Division of Labour Between Directly Action-Guiding Principles and Institutional Processes

I have argued that focusing exclusively on identifying objective justifications does not address a major moral problem regarding war: bad recourse to war decisions may be due not to ignorance of sound objective justifications but rather to the epistemic and motivational liabilities of decision-makers. I have also argued that heuristics are one solution to this problem, but not the only one and, in some cases, not the optimal one: there is also the institutional alternative. The distorting effects of decision-makers' epistemic and motivational limitations can be reduced either by encouraging them to follow heuristics whose contents are more constraining than the requirements of sound objective justifications (as with the heuristics 'engage in humanitarian intervention only when killing has reached the level of genocide' or 'engage only in pre-emptive war, never preventive war') or by embedding directly action-guiding rules that are more permissive than such heuristics within an institutional context that supplies the needed constraints. Alternatively, the best alternative might be some combination of heuristics and institutional constraints.

So, one important question for a comprehensive theory of *jus ad bellum* is this: what is the optimal division of labour between direct appeals to elements of objective justifications, the use of heuristics or other directly action-guiding principles, and reliance on institutional mechanisms for improving the decision-making of fallible agents and, in particular, of leaders, given their pivotal role? The right answer will be grounded in the facts about institutional capacities, but it will require moral reasoning as well, since some institutional arrangements will be permissible, others will be impermissible, and, among those that are permissible, some may be morally better than others.

2.5. Recourse to War Justification as a Social Practice

It can be morally preferable or even morally obligatory for a society to avoid a practice of justification in which direct appeals to certain objective justifications by leaders are regarded as legitimate. Not only justifications considered as abstract objects, but also justifications as public acts are subject to moral assessment and so is the public's response to such public acts.

In circumstances in which direct appeals to a particular kind of objective justification are highly likely to result in a leader making an erroneous judgment about whether to go to war, it is wrong for her to do so, at least if there is a sound heuristic and she either is aware of it or should be. Some types of justifications for going to war are *practically dangerous*: under the circumstances in which leaders typically find themselves when considering recourse to war, relying on them to determine how to act is very likely to produce a decision that is seriously morally defective. The public can also be morally blameworthy—either as individuals or even collectively if they ratify the leader's decision through some formal act of group decision-making—for accepting a particular practically dangerous justification as legitimate. A social practice regarding public justifications for recourse to war in which practically dangerous justifications are routinely regarded as legitimate is morally defective.

Robert O. Keohane and I have argued that, under current conditions, even the best type of preventive war justification is practically dangerous.[15] We first argue that there is a sound objective justification for preventive war (under certain highly constrained circumstances) and then make the case that the preventive war justification is practically dangerous due to the typical epistemic and motivational situation of those leaders who would be prone to rely on it. Because the harm to be averted is temporally distant, the prediction that it is likely to occur may be highly speculative, and this may provide the leader with opportunities to misrepresent or misinterpret ambiguous information in ways that serve his purposes—purposes the pursuit of which may undermine the integrity of the decision-making process.

In the light of these risks, the view that defensive war is justified only against an imminent attack looks more plausible—not as an element of a superior objective justification but as a valuable heuristic. Even if there are cases in which preventive war is justified, leaders may do better by following a heuristic that forbids preventive war and only allows pre-emptive war. In the absence of institutional processes aptly designed to reduce the special risks of deciding to go to war for preventive purposes, the most responsible course might be to rely on such a heuristic.

Whether or not leaders can be relied on to follow the heuristic 'avoid preventive war' may depend on whether they believe that the public to which they are responsible regards prevention as a legitimate justification for going to war. If the preventive war justification is very dangerous and if aptly designed institutional safeguards to guide and constrain its application are not presently available, then the best course may be to develop and sustain a social practice of regarding public justifications of war that rely on it as illegitimate.

Such a practice could be either more or less formal. A formal version would utilize a constitutional prohibition against leaders publicly justifying their decision to go to war by appealing to the preventive war justification (just as the post-World War II constitutions of both Germany and Japan included provisions against any form of war other than self-defence). A less formal version would be a widely accepted social norm serving the same purpose. The key point is that, in addition to assessing moral justifications understood as abstract objects, both particular public acts of justification and public justificatory practices are suitable subjects for the *jus ad bellum* theorist.

2.6. Morally Evaluating Leaders Who Decide to Go to War

Once we recognize that the moral quality of recourse to war decisions can be affected both by the characteristics of the specific institutional processes within which such decisions are made and by social practices regarding what counts as a legitimate public justification for going to war, it becomes clear that it is a mistake to think that a moral assessment of the actions of leaders or of ordinary citizens is simply a scaled-up version of the moral assessment of acts of violence performed by nonsituated, bare individuals.[16] For example, whether a citizen is morally blameworthy for participating in her country's recourse to war (or for supporting or at least not opposing it) may depend on the moral qualities of the institutional process and broader social practice of justification within which her country's leader made the decision to go to war. If the institutional process and the practice of justification are sound, and known to be so, then it will be reasonable for the individual citizen to be more confident that recourse to war is justified, and, other things being equal, she will be less blameworthy if that turns out not to be the case.

Similarly, if a leader operates within a highly defective institutional process for decision-making that is supported by a social practice of treating practically dangerous types of recourse to war justifications as legitimate, her blameworthiness for a bad decision may be less than it would be in other circumstances.

Contemporary just war theory has had surprisingly little to say about the morality of leadership regarding war. A leader might launch a war for which there is an objective justification and yet be morally blameworthy for doing so. This would be the case if she should have followed a heuristic that would have prohibited her from doing the (objectively) right thing. The leader would also be morally blameworthy even if she did the right thing if she failed to follow institutional procedures that would have prevented her, in this particular case, from doing the right thing or if she acted contrary to the norms of the most morally defensible practice regarding public justifications for going to war. Furthermore, an agent can be morally blameworthy for the decision-making process she actually engaged in if it was shaped by bad motives or bad intentions or involved culpable reliance on defective or incomplete information, even if it resulted in her doing the right thing. For these reasons, sound moral evaluations of the actions of leaders in deciding to go to war may require investigations into the roles of heuristics and of reliance on institutional processes that have received relatively little attention in *jus ad bellum* theory.

Consider again the fact that a leader's public justification for going to war may have little to do with his actual decision-making process. One could argue, in fact, that this is precisely what happened in the case of the Iraq War that began in 2003. Suppose that preventive war is sometimes justified in the sense that there is an objective justification for going to war to avert the threat of a temporally distant harm. That is quite compatible with the Bush administration having acted wrongly. Suppose, as appears likely, that the Bush administration invoked the plausibility of such a justification to rationalize to itself and to justify to the public the results of a deeply flawed decision-making process, one that was distorted by a willingness to overinterpret quite limited and conflicting information in the pursuit of geopolitical ends that had nothing to do with Saddam Hussein's capacity to inflict harm on the United States. If recourse to war resulted from such a flawed decision-making process, then it is correct to say that, in going to war, Bush acted wrongly, even if there is a sound objective justification for preventive war and even though Bush publicly justified the war as preventive. And he would have still acted wrongly even if, by some happy coincidence, all of the necessary and sufficient conditions specified in the objective justification had in fact obtained in the case of Iraq at the time.

This is not to say that one is blameworthy for performing a right act whenever there is any defect whatsoever in the reasoning that led to the act if one's motives or intentions are in any way less than pure. The point, rather, is that some motivations and intentions and some errors of reasoning can be so seriously defective as to render an agent blameworthy for acting even though the act he performs is a right act.

So far, I have discussed the neglected topic of the morality of leadership in recourse to war from the standpoint of directly action-guiding principles and institutional processes and by reference to the idea of social practices regarding what counts as legitimate public justifications for going to war. But a comprehensive *jus ad bellum* would also consider the possibility that virtues are relevant to the ethics of leadership. There are two quite different ways in which an account of the virtues of leaders might figure in a comprehensive *jus ad bellum* theory. First, one might take what may be called an *extreme virtue ethics* approach. According to this view, a sound account of the virtues of war-making decision-makers provides the full content of *jus ad bellum*: just wars are those that virtuous decision-makers engage in or approve, and unjust wars are those they eschew. On this view, to try to articulate objective justifications in the form of a list of right-making conditions is either impossible or superfluous, and the same holds for heuristics to be applied directly by decision-makers.

This approach is properly labelled 'extreme' because it denies any significant role either to objective justifications or to heuristics and relies solely on an account of the decision-making virtues, understood as stable dispositions (to judge, to experience various moral sentiments, and to act). Right acts of war-making are then defined as those that an agent with those virtues would engage in or approve of. Because I am convinced by the familiar criticism that such an extreme virtue ethics view fails to show how one can identify the virtuous person without recourse to moral principles that can be stated independently of reference to the virtues, I will focus on the second way in which virtue ethics might function in *jus ad bellum* theorizing.

The more modest and plausible proposal is that a comprehensive theory of *jus ad bellum* will include an account of the virtues of leaders who decide on recourse to war but without denying the importance of objective justifications, directly action-guiding principles, or institutional processes. For example, it could be argued that leaders must possess certain virtues if they are to be counted on to follow appropriate heuristics (and to know when to disregard them) and to conform to appropriate institutional requirements designed to improve their decision-making (and to know when to disregard them). To the extent that (1) there are exceptional circumstances in which disregard of generally appropriate heuristics or other directly action-guiding principles or institutional procedures is either morally permissible or morally obligatory and (2) ascertaining them is a matter of judgment and cannot be achieved by following rules, the virtues of leaders, if they include the capacity for such judgments, may be crucial. At the very least, it might turn out to be the case that, unless decision-makers are free of certain vices, even the most commendable heuristics and institutional safeguards will prove ineffective.

Finally, which virtues leaders need may depend on how effective the institutional constraints on war-making decisions are. If institutional constraints are highly effective, less robust virtues will be required for acceptable leadership, and, if leaders typically are not robustly virtuous, then greater institutional constraint will be needed. What this means is that the virtues of leaders and the institutional dimension must be theorized in a way that recognizes their interdependence.

3. Moral Principles, Institutions, and Laws

I have argued that a richer *jus ad bellum* will attend to the fact that the quality of the institutional processes within which substantive norms regarding recourse to war are invoked can affect the soundness of decisions that are made. I have not yet said anything about how the discussion thus far bears on the relationship between law and morality. To fill this gap, I first explore the relationship between the morality of law and existing institutions.

3.1. How Institutions Can Make a Moral Difference

There are two fundamentally different conceptions of the role of institutions in a comprehensive theory of *jus ad bellum*. On the first, purely instrumental conception, institutions are simply mechanisms for implementing moral norms that are justified independently of institutional considerations. On the second, constitutive conception, the validity of some moral norms depends on the institutional context in which they will be applied. I suspect that the purely instrumental conception of institutions is prevalent in contemporary just war theory generally and not just in its *jus ad bellum* part and that the partly constitutive conception has not been adequately appreciated.

Of course, in many cases, institutions are purely instrumental, and their usefulness as instruments is the sole source of their value. But, in some cases, the relationship between moral norms and institutions is more intimate.

In discussing heuristics, I have already shown that which norms a leader should follow in deciding to go to war may depend on the institutional context within which she decides. Both heuristics and institutional processes can serve to mitigate biasing factors that would otherwise distort the agent's decision. But heuristics that would be justified in the absence of institutional resources for mitigating bias may be redundant or even counterproductive if the institutions within which decisions are made are well-designed. Conversely, institutional constraints may be an unnecessary cost if heuristics do an adequate job of mitigating biasing factors. So the relationship between heuristics and institutions can be constitutive, not merely instrumental.

The same is true for norms that are elements of objective justifications rather than heuristics. Consider the case of moral norms of individual self-defence. Contrast two different situations in which an individual might act in self-defence. In the first, the individual must rely solely on her own resources to defend herself against an unjust attack by a spouse or partner. In the second, the social context provides impressive resources for protection against unjust attacks: the police are trustworthy and can be relied on to respond very quickly, and one can count on one's fellow citizens intervening on one's behalf; in addition, there are easily accessible shelters that provide sanctuary for those fleeing unjust attacks. In the first context, there may be valid moral norms regarding self-defence that are more permissive—for example, it may be justifiable, under certain circumstances, for an individual to use preventive force, not merely to try to thwart an occurring or imminent attack. In the second context, where others can be relied on, preventive force may be unjustifiable.

An analogous point applies in the case of collective self-defence, a major topic of the theory of *jus ad bellum*. Which forcible acts of self-defence a country is morally permitted to undertake may depend on whether there is an effective supranational security system. If this is the case, then a comprehensive *jus ad bellum* must take institutions seriously.

3.2. The Moral Evaluation of Legal Institutions for Constraining War

Law as an institution is both instrumental and partly constitutive in its relationship to morality. Some contemporary theorists have advanced moral assessments of some aspects of international law's treatment of group armed conflict, especially with respect to the offences that fall within the writ of the International Criminal Court. But much more work remains to be done. A comprehensive theory of *jus ad bellum* would include a moral evaluation not only of legal doctrine, but also of the institutions through which international law pertaining to recourse to war is created, interpreted, and implemented. Morally impeccable legal norms may lack legitimacy if the institutions through which they are created and applied lack legitimacy.

4. Practical Aims

In the current just war literature, there is surprisingly little discussion of whether *jus ad bellum* theory has practical aims and, if so, what precisely they are—and how achievement of the theoretical aim of providing objective justifications would contribute to them. First consider the practical aim of aiding the development of a more morally defensible international law regarding recourse to war. Even if it is true that just war thinking has in fact influenced international law in the past, it would be unjustified to assume that new advances in theory will produce further changes in the absence of an account of the causal pathways by which theoretical work can find its way into law. Providing such an account would require social science expertise that philosophers lack. If it turned out that there are serious obstacles to the theory of *jus ad bellum* influencing the international law of war, then recourse to the theory of institutional design and to work in social epistemology might be needed to propose feasible remedies, along with moral reasoning to determine whether what is feasible is also morally permissible.

4.1. How Can Contemporary Jus ad Bellum Theory Influence the Law of Recourse to War?

One way to begin this formidable task would be to undertake a critical examination of recent or current cases in which there is systematic deliberation by public bodies (whether civilian or military) or judges concerning the adequacy of the current international law of war to see whether there are adequate opportunities for 'uptake' of the results of philosophical theorizing. For example, a number of groups are working on the question of whether changes in the law of war are needed to accommodate the peculiar problems raised by the use of weaponized drones. Eventually, these deliberations might result in proposals for new treaties or amendments of existing treaties regarding permissible weapons of war. If that transpired, it would be interesting to know if moral theorizing played any role.

If it turned out that those agents who can actually influence the interpretation or development of international law regarding recourse to war are not benefiting from theoretical work, then steps might be proposed for correcting this deficiency. One option would be to try to introduce a new institutional epistemic practice: a formal recognition that *jus ad bellum* theorists constitute an important 'epistemic community' whose expertise should be utilized in evaluating the existing law of war. Something analogous has already occurred in a different domain of practical ethics: the institutionalization of high-level (in the United States, presidential) commissions on bioethics, which operate on the understanding that the interdisciplinary membership of such groups should include a prominent role for moral philosophers. This epistemic institutional innovation is now employed in a number of countries. Bioethics commissions have several purposes, including providing systematic moral thinking as an input into the process of developing new law.

The point is that it is one thing to say that *jus ad bellum* theory provides potentially valuable insights for shaping what law has to say about recourse to war but quite another to ensure that these insights are understood, much less utilized by those who are in a position to influence the character of the law. Similarly, from the fact that a comprehensive *jus ad bellum* theory provides guidance for leaders, combatants, or ordinary citizens regarding their decisions whether to make war or to support or oppose it, nothing whatsoever can be inferred about whether anyone's behaviour will actually be influenced by it. In both cases, providing valuable guidance—or, more properly, guidance that would (only) improve matters *if* it were heeded—is in itself a practical benefit only in a very anaemic sense.

4.2. From Theory to Practice

Some prominent contemporary just war theorists are to be commended for taking this problem seriously. Some have taken on the important but difficult role of public intellectual by publishing in nonspecialist outlets their thoughtful responses to actual armed conflicts—from the NATO intervention in Kosovo in 1999, to the US-led invasion of Iraq in 2003, to the 2014 Israeli incursion into Gaza. Some have also provided formal instruction in various military academies to those who will actually fight wars. In addition, several universities have standing academic units or long-term grant-funded centres that bring together just war theorists, military personnel, and government officials, and just war theorists seem to be playing an increasingly important role in their activities. Nevertheless, I think it is fair to say that both the practical aims of *jus ad bellum* and the alternatives for realizing them in a morally sound and effective way have been undertheorized. As long as the focus is on *jus ad bellum* theory narrowly construed—as a quest for objective justifications for recourse-to-war acts—the task of theorizing practical aims is likely to be neglected, in part because the gap between knowledge of which acts are right and the achievement of right behaviour, as I have argued, is so wide.

In contrast, the more comprehensive conception of *jus ad bellum* that I am recommending would provide more resources for addressing the most important practical concerns. For example, by exploring the possibility of a fruitful division of labour between heuristics and institutional processes for decision-making regarding recourse to war, a more comprehensive theory of *jus ad bellum* can inform strategies for increasing the probability that leaders will actually make decisions that conform to the requirements of sound justifications rather than merely appeal to them as cover for wrongful acts.

5. Conclusion

There are two different ways to conceive of a richer *jus ad bellum*: in a purely *theoretically* comprehensive way, that is, as an attempt to illuminate all of the morally significant aspects of recourse to war, but with no pretensions to practical efficacy; or in a way that also takes seriously the idea that theory can be a valuable resource for helping to achieve morally better behaviour regarding recourse to war. So far, contemporary *jus ad bellum* theory has not succeeded in either task, and, in that sense, it is doubly impoverished. By focusing chiefly on determining the elements of objective justifications for recourse to war, it has neglected other important aspects of the morality of recourse to war, including the moral evaluation of the actual decision-making of leaders, of the institutional processes through which decisions to go to war are made, of leaders' public justifications for going to war, and of social practices regarding what counts as legitimate public justifications. Furthermore, the role of both directly action-guiding principles and institutional processes in correcting for distortions of decision-making needs to be systematically explored. Just as important, more must be done to develop an account of the virtues of war leaders and of the partly constitutive relationship between moral principles and institutions.

From the standpoint of reasonable practical aims, contemporary *jus ad bellum* theory also comes up short to the extent that it tends to ignore the question of practical aims entirely or proceeds as if determining the elements of objective justifications for recourse to war will have good practical effects. The *jus ad bellum* part of the ethics of group armed conflict is theoretically more complex, of potentially greater practical value, and certainly more difficult than many contemporary theorists have assumed. A richer *jus ad bellum* would use a cogent account of objective justifications for recourse to war as a solid foundation from which to address a much more comprehensive set of subjects for systematic moral thinking.

Acknowledgements

I am indebted to Cécile Fabre, Jeff Holzgrefe, Robert O. Keohane, Jeff McMahan, Kit Wellman, Chad Van Schoelandt, Bas Van der Vossen, and the editors of this volume for their helpful comments on earlier drafts of this essay.

Notes

1. Most of what I say in this chapter about *jus ad bellum* will have obvious analogs for *jus in bello*.
2. For discussion of the importance of just war theory developing applied moral principles alongside its objective justifications, see Seth Lazar, 'Morality & Law of War', in *Companion to Philosophy of Law*, edited by Andrei Marmor (New York: Routledge, 2012), 364–379.

3. In ideal circumstances, even the most basic moral principles may be action-guiding, but my focus here is on principles that are intended to be action-guiding in nonideal circumstances, in which attempting to guide action by direct appeal to basic principles would be counterproductive.
4. This could, in principle, include institutions that identify authorities on war-making, on the assumption that soldiers and civilians should defer to them in deciding how to act. For examples of those just war theorists who do not consider the possibility that different norms may be appropriate depending on the institutional context in which war-making decisions are made, see all of the essays except the ones by Allen Buchanan in the following anthologies: *Ethics and Foreign Intervention*, edited by Deen K. Chatterjee and Don E. Scheid (Cambridge: Cambridge University Press, 2003) and *Humanitarian Intervention: Ethical, Legal and Political Dilemmas*, edited by Robert O. Keohane and J. L. Holzgrefe (Cambridge: Cambridge University Press, 2003). The best explanation of these authors not considering the moral difference that alternative institutions can make may be that they either implicitly assume a purely instrumental view of the relationship between principles and institutions; that is, they assume that institutions are important only as mechanisms for realizing principles whose grounding does not take institutional capacities into account, or they assume that the institutional status quo is very unlikely to change. None of these authors defends either of these assumptions. Only a small minority of contemporary just war theorists place institutional considerations at the heart of their inquiries. For perhaps the most developed examples of institutional approaches, see Allen Buchanan and Robert O. Keohane, 'Justifying Preventive War: A Cosmopolitan Institutional Proposal', *Ethics and International Affairs* 18:1 (2004), 1–22; and Allen Buchanan, 'Institutionalizing the Just War', *Philosophy and Public Affairs* 34:1 (2006), 2–38.
5. Along with 1, in contemporary just war theory, this topic has received the most discussion on this list. See especially Lazar, 'Morality & Law of War'; Jeff McMahan, 'The Morality of War and the Law of War', in *Just and Unjust Warriors: The Moral and Legal Status of Soldiers*, edited by David Rodin and Henry Shue (Oxford: Oxford University Press, 2008), 19–43; Jeff McMahan, 'Laws of War', in *The Philosophy of International Law*, edited by Samantha Besson and John Tasioulas (New York: Oxford University Press, 2010), 493–510; David Rodin, 'Morality and Law in War', in *The Changing Character of War*, edited by Sibylle Scheipers and Hew Strachan (Oxford: Oxford University Press, 2011), 446–463; Henry Shue, 'Do We Need a Morality of War?', in *Just and Unjust Warriors: The Moral and Legal Status of Soldiers*, edited by David Rodin and Henry Shue (Oxford: Oxford University Press, 2008), 87–111; Henry Shue, 'Laws of War', in *The Philosophy of International Law*, edited by Samantha Besson (New York: Oxford University Press, 2010), 511–530.
6. For examples of some such reflection in philosophical outlets, see Jeff McMahan, 'The Prevention of Unjust Wars', in *Reading Walzer*, edited by Yitzhak Benbaji and Naomi Sussman (New York: Routledge, 2014), 233–256; Henry Shue, 'Targeting Civilian Infrastructure with Smart Bombs: The New Permissiveness', *Philosophy and Public Policy Quarterly* 30:3 (2010), 2–8. Michael Walzer, David Luban, Jeff McMahan, David Rodin and others have also long sought to influence public opinion through popular outlets such as *Dissent, The New Republic, The Boston Review, The Guardian,* and *The New York Times.*
7. Of course, just war theory can and should also provide guidance for soldiers. For simplicity's sake, I will only discuss guidance for leaders, but what I say will also apply, with suitable adjustments, to guidance for soldiers.

8. Allen Buchanan and Robert O. Keohane, 'Justifying Preventive War: A Cosmopolitan Proposal', note 3 *supra*.
9. See, for example, Cécile Fabre, *Cosmopolitan War* (Oxford: Oxford University Press, 2012), 77; Seth Lazar, 'The Responsibility Dilemma for *Killing in War*', *Philosophy and Public Affairs* 38:2 (2010), 180–213, at 193; Jeff McMahan, *Killing in War* (Oxford: Oxford University Press, 2009), 119.
10. Michael Walzer, *Just and Unjust Wars* (New York: Basic Books, 1977), 36.
11. Jeff McMahan, 'On the Moral Equality of Combatants', *Journal of Political Philosophy* 14:4 (2006), 377–393. For an in-depth treatment of the issue of the moral symmetry of combatants, see *Just and Unjust Warriors: The Moral and Legal Status of Soldiers*, edited by David Rodin and Henry Shue (Oxford: Oxford University Press, 2011).
12. McMahan, 'The Morality of War'. See also Cécile Fabre, 'Guns, Food, and Liability to Attack in War', *Ethics* 120:1 (2009), 36–63, at 39.
13. Walzer, 90, n. 7.
14. Buchanan and Keohane, *supra* note 3.
15. Ibid.
16. Contra Jeff McMahan, 'War as Self-Defense', *Ethics & International Affairs* 18:1 (2004), 75–80, at 75.

CHAPTER 9

KNOWING WHEN NOT TO FIGHT

DAVID LUBAN

On the eve of battle, Shakespeare's *Henry V*, disguised as a common soldier, talks with his men:

> *King*: Methinks I could not die anywhere so contented as in the King's company, his cause being just and his quarrel honorable.
> *Michael Williams*: That's more than we know.
> *John Bates*: Ay, or more than we should seek after; for we know enough if we know we are the King's subjects. If his cause be wrong, our obedience to the King wipes the crime of it out of us.[1]

Henry thinks his soldiers' clear consciences depend on the justice of his cause. If so, Bates and Williams should refuse to follow him into battle if his cause is unjust. Bates disagrees and tethers his clean conscience solely to his duty of obedience.

Theirs is a debate about selective conscientious objection by soldiers.[2] Bates argues against it; Henry implicitly, and probably without meaning to, licenses it. But the dialogue raises an epistemic issue as well. Williams insists that the justice of Henry's cause is more than a common soldier knows. That sounds right, especially when we read the comically arcane legalisms and dubious histories Henry's advisors produce in Act 1 to convince him of his rightful title to French territory. What can Henry's soldiers be expected to know of the Salic law of succession or the genealogy of eighth-century French kings?

Bates adds a moral twist to Williams's epistemic doubts. Not only is the just cause 'more than we know', it is 'more than we should seek after'. Williams's position and Bates's are importantly different. Williams is describing the epistemic plight of the common soldier. Bates offers prescription, not description. Not only are common soldiers not in a position to know whether their cause is just, they should not try to put themselves in a better position. Bates's reason: 'we know enough if we know we are the King's subjects'.

I am grateful to the editors of this volume for their comments and suggestions on earlier drafts of this chapter.

Apparently deference to the King's political authority is supposed to imply deference to his epistemic authority as well.

Bates actually makes two distinct claims. One is that obedience to the king 'wipes the crime out of us'. Even if the soldiers knew the king's cause was unjust, they should still fight because the king's authority provides an exclusionary reason to obey. Call this the *absolute deference claim*. The other is that soldiers should not independently investigate the *jus ad bellum*—for that is the natural reading of 'more than we should seek after'. Call this the *no-inquiry claim*. In what follows, I explore these claims, first that of Williams and then the more problematic claims of Bates. To preview the conclusions: Williams is right; Bates's absolute deference claim is not. But I will defend a weaker version of Bates's prescription: not absolute deference to the King's authority, but strong presumptive deference that can be overridden only in cases where the war is manifestly unjust. This is a version of the no-inquiry claim: a *manifestly* unjust cause is one that wears injustice on its face so that no inquiry is required.

This position about the obligations of common soldiers—not to fight in manifestly unjust wars, but not to delve into the justice of wars whose injustice is not manifest—is far from novel. It is the unanimous view of the early modern just war theorists Cajetan, Suárez, and Vitoria. But my argument for the no-inquiry claim will differ from theirs. I focus on the moral importance of civilian control of the military—a value I believe contemporary just war theorists wrongly neglect, just as I fear they underrate the inherent epistemic problems soldiers confront in judging *jus ad bellum*.

1. Williams's Epistemic Claim

Michael Williams's claim is that ordinary soldiers are in no epistemic position to judge whether the king's cause is just. Like his philosopher namesake 600 years later, Williams is no radical sceptic.[3] Nothing in principle makes knowledge of just cause inaccessible to the common soldier. The problem lies in contingent and context-specific challenges arising from the fog of war, including the political fog of going to war.[4] Philosophers perhaps underestimate the epistemic difficulty of judgments about just cause. Even when the purported just cause is self-defence, it isn't always self-evident who attacked whom. Lyndon Johnson used the make-believe second Gulf of Tonkin incident to get Congress to authorize the Vietnam War; the truth took years to emerge. Even World War II, the standard example of a war of clear-cut right and wrong, began with a false flag operation, 'Operation Himmler', in which German troops in Polish uniforms 'attacked' German border towns, shooting (to miss) at the locals. They vandalized buildings, broadcast Polish nationalist slogans from a radio station they seized, and left behind the murdered bodies of political prisoners dressed in Polish army uniforms, which were displayed to journalists as proof of a Polish incursion into German territory. The next day, Hitler announced his invasion of Poland. 'This night for the first time Polish regular soldiers fired on our territory. Since 5.45 A.M. we have been returning the fire, and from now on bombs will be met by bombs'.[5] The world's worst war of aggression was off and running under the colours of self-defence.

Shakespeare well understood that politicians launch wars for deceptive reasons and ulterior motives. He depicts King Henry as an honest and honourable sovereign, but Henry's advisors are clerical schemers. The play opens with them plotting war to distract Parliament from a bill to confiscate church property. That sheds a harsher light on the legalistic argle-bargle they serve up to the King about his territorial rights in France.[6] To be sure, political mendacity and the difficulty for outsiders to know what happened on the ground are contingent obstacles to right judgment of just cause, not in-principle challenges. But they belong to the background description of the world in which just war theory has a point, so even ideal theory must not abstract from them. They are so wired into the world that we should regard them as (in the terminology of Valentini and Lazar), *parametric*.[7]

Philosophers sometimes write as though just war theory is an ideal theory of justification that should develop its principles without taking frictional forces into account. Such a theory will provide criteria for moral scorekeeping undertaken by an ideal observer. On this view of the nature of just war theory, the fact that common soldiers are epistemically poorly positioned to use a principle is said to provide an excuse for their objectively wrongful actions (maybe); indeed, it may provide a blanket excuse for all agents similarly situated—which might be nearly everyone. But an excuse is not a justification, and we have no reason to backpedal from the search for justificatory principles of *jus ad bellum* even if soldiers cannot apply them in real-world deliberation.[8]

This line of argument, in my opinion, places more weight on the distinction between justifications and excuses than it can bear. I agree with Judith Lichtenberg that

> appeals to excuses make sense where it is reasonable to expect most people to act in a certain way, but where unusual conditions sometimes prevail or where a particular individual falls short of the general requirements. . . . But if the conditions that relieve people of responsibility are pervasive, if practically everyone falls short, thinking in terms of excuses makes little sense.[9]

The language game of excuses is played against a background of typical conditions, where excusing conditions are exceptional. For the common soldier deciding whether to follow the King into battle, the fog of war and of politics are not exceptional conditions. Neither are bounded rationality, time constraints on decision-making, and limited access to information. These epistemic limitations parametrically define common soldiers' situation and constrain them to moral principles usable within the scope of those limitations.[10]

2. The *Jus ad Bellum* Court Proposal

Jeff McMahan, among the most prominent recent defenders of selective conscientious objection by soldiers, recognizes the epistemic difficulty facing ordinary soldiers judging *jus ad bellum* and offers an institutional solution: an international court (or commission or tribunal) that will provide impartial and authoritative findings on whether armed conflicts satisfy the *jus ad bellum* criteria.[11] Its purpose is to provide guidance to the war fighters—guidance that can assist their moral deliberations about whether to fight or to take the momentous step of becoming selective conscientious objectors to unjust war.[12] This would alleviate Williams's epistemic doubts.

The prominence and relevance of McMahan's proposal make it worth considering in detail. For reasons I now explain, the *jus ad bellum* court proposal is unworkable. These reasons concern its legitimacy, its fact-finding capacity, and its problematic relationship with existing international institutions and international law.[13]

2.1. Legitimacy

1. *Who sits on the jus ad bellum court, and who selects its members?* McMahan favours an unofficial court for the excellent reason that an official court would become captive of the states that establish it.[14] Then the question arises how an unofficial, non-state-sanctioned court could win the credibility and heft to do what McMahan wants it to do: provide at least some authoritative basis for a fantastically weighty moral decision by soldiers—a basis that soldiers can feel comfortable relying on if they refuse to deploy.

The *jus ad bellum* court cannot afford to be perceived as a politicized organization. Recognizing this, McMahan proposes

> international lawyers, scholars of international law, including representatives of various national organizations, such as the American Society of International Law, and veteran prosecutors, defenders, and judges from the criminal tribunals for Rwanda and Yugoslavia. This list could also include just war theorists, moral philosophers, political theorists, retired military officials, particularly former Judge Advocate Generals and their counterparts in other countries, and perhaps even some serving military personnel with training in law or ethics who might be seconded to the congress in an advisory capacity.[15]

The *jus ad bellum* court would include judges from every region of the world—a crucial structural feature adopted by all international tribunals.[16]

The problem is that the higher the stakes in any international body's decisions—and the *jus ad bellum* court has very high stakes, namely the decision by soldiers to disobey their own governments—the greater the political pressures brought to bear on it and the harder it is to maintain impartiality, either in appointing court members or in their decisions. This problem appears at two levels: not only in selecting the panelists, but also in selecting the selectors.

Suppose, for example, that the Russian Academy of Sciences proposes a candidate for an open slot on the *jus ad bellum* court, and Amnesty International proposes a candidate, and the African Commission on Human and Peoples' Rights, the Australian Philosophical Association, and the Organization of American States each propose candidates. Suppose, realistically, that all the candidates have impeccable credentials, but also have strongly opposed points of view that their critics think are ideological. Amnesty lodges strong objections against the Russian Academy's candidate, a nationalist professor and Putin crony; the Arab League objects to Amnesty's candidate, a secular feminist; and the Chinese government finds unacceptable the human rights expert who holds a chair at Oxford and defends the universality of human rights. Nobody outside the United States and the United Kingdom likes the American legal expert who argues that nothing the United States does can possibly violate customary international law because if the United States does it, its prohibition can't be custom.

Unfortunately, the soldiers who are the court's intended audience will discover in their first minutes on the Internet that reputable bodies have denounced some nominees as ideologues and complained that others were excluded for ideological reasons. Rather than alleviating their doubts, the *jus ad bellum* court will replicate them. In soldiers' minds, it will lack legitimacy, and that is because so many interested parties contest its legitimacy.

The difficulty is compounded in the case of hot-button issues, like Israel's wars. Fifty-three African countries have formally pledged 'to eliminate zionism', and anti-zionism is presumably a constant across the left–right spectrum throughout these countries, as it is in the Arab world.[17] How likely is it going to be that African representatives on a *jus ad bellum* court will agree that any of Israel's wars is ever just? But how credible would a panel be that excluded African voices? The difficulties, it seems to me, are intractable.

2. *Philosophical disagreement all the way down*. The problem is not only a matter of cultural, regional, and political diversity and conflict. Suppose we stipulate a single culture and subculture: Anglophone academic just war theorists. Is there any likelihood that a *jus ad bellum* court is going to agree on criteria of just war after they invite McMahan, Gabriella Blum, Cécile Fabre, Adil Haque, James Turner Johnson, Asa Kasher, George Lucas, David Rodin, Michael Walzer, and the editors of this volume to develop the criteria? The fact is that today significant philosophical dissensus exists on criteria of just cause.
3. *Competition with existing international organizations*. The *jus ad bellum* court is supposed to be a trustworthy epistemic resource for troubled soldiers facing the issue of conscientious disobedience. However, there are already two official world bodies authorized to make determinations of aggression: the UN Security Council (UNSC) and the International Criminal Court (ICC).[18] Suppose neither of them is willing to declare that a conflict includes acts of aggression. In fact, suppose the Security Council—determined to head off or even undermine the *jus ad bellum* court—declares there has been no aggression. How is a soldier supposed to conclude that the *jus ad bellum* court got it right while the Security Council and the ICC

are wrong? Unless the *jus ad bellum* court can somehow displace the UNSC and ICC from the epistemic field, it will have a hard time establishing its own credibility.

All the points so far are challenges to the likelihood of establishing a *jus ad bellum* court that has legitimacy yet is also able to reach consensus on controversial conclusions in the face of intense politicking around its membership and selection process. But suppose these challenges can be overcome. Daunting problems still remain.

2.2. Fact Investigation

4. *The difficulty of fact investigation. Jus ad bellum* judgments are fact-intensive. Who sank the boat? How intense is the violence? Did troops cross the border? Who fired first? Although McMahan by no means ignores the difficulty of a *jus ad bellum* court making factual findings, he underestimates those difficulties.[19] Fact-finding in conflict zones is dangerous, expensive, frustrating, and unreliable. The international criminal tribunals have a very hard time conducting fact investigations because so many people on the ground have an interest in concealing facts, including by silencing witnesses.[20] Not only witnesses and their families are threatened: investigator protection is an issue as well.

I mention these unhappy realities about international criminal investigations because it seems clear that if it is hard to gather evidence *post bellum*, it will be even harder in a hot war zone. How will the *jus ad bellum* court get investigators in while the bullets are flying to figure out who started it and whose fault it was? For that matter, why would the warring parties let them in? Perhaps the *jus ad bellum* court will rely on local investigators. They, too, will have difficulty gaining access to conflict zones, and there is no reason to suppose they will get to see anything the belligerents don't want them to see.

A related problem is:

5. *Intense disputation of facts, backed by claims of secret intelligence.* Suppose the *jus ad bellum* court must judge whether the United States has a preventive-war justification for attacking a Middle Eastern adversary. The United States claims it has secret intelligence showing that the adversary has developed A-bombs and long-range missiles. It declines to reveal the intelligence on the grounds of protecting sources and methods. How would a *jus ad bellum* court evaluate those US claims for factual accuracy? Would it develop its own intelligence assets? Would it disclose their identities? McMahan responds that

> few of us accept that our lack of access to classified information always, or even usually, renders us incapable of justifiably believing that a war in progress is just or unjust. . . . In general, however, the important question is not whether an ad bellum

> court would be infallible, but whether its judgments could be reasonably believed to be more reliable than those of any state or individual. And clearly, they could be. . . . The court might still lack information possessed by a state that refuses to divulge it, but in most cases the lack of such information would be compensated for by the absence of self-interest that inevitably contaminates the empirical and evaluative claims made by states[21]

These arguments are unconvincing. No doubt contaminating self-interest is a fatal epistemic disqualifier for many state assertions, but lack of information is an equally fatal epistemic disqualifier—and honesty does not make up for ignorance.

Furthermore, the important question is not whether a *jus ad bellum* court would be infallible (of course it won't be) or even whether its judgments are more reliable than those of any state or individual. The important question is whether the *jus ad bellum* court's judgments are reliable enough to ground a soldier's refusal to fight. That is partly the comparative question McMahan poses: is the *jus ad bellum* court more reliable than me? But it is also the noncomparative question 'how reliable is the *jus ad bellum* court?', because if soldiers think the court is only slightly better positioned than they are, there is no reason for them to take the court's deliverances seriously. If the court cannot challenge secret intelligence, why would soldiers believe the court?

6. *Making judgments in real time.* The *jus ad bellum* court is useless unless it can reach verdicts in real time.[22] Given the speed with which armed conflicts unfold, that is scarcely possible. International fact-finders cannot act in days or weeks. Even if a war lasts for a long time, its justice *ad bellum* may require continual reassessment, so the problem of making real-time judgments in impossibly short intervals never goes away.

2.3. Meshing *Jus ad Bellum* Judgments with Law

7. *Moral or legal judgments?* Would the *jus ad bellum* court make moral judgments, legal judgments, or both? I take it that McMahan wants the former: philosophers and others are to develop moral criteria of *jus ad bellum* based on the best moral theory and not necessarily consistent with international law.[23] But how should those judgments sit in relation to legal judgments? For better or worse, the *jus ad bellum* court would not operate in a normative vacuum, and just as it would have to compete for legitimacy with the Security Council and the ICC, philosophical criteria of just war would have to compete with existing international law for normative authority.[24]

I am thinking especially of Article 51 of the UN Charter, which declares that every state has an 'inherent right of self-defence'. As we know, the 'inherent right of self-defence' has proved more than a little controversial, not only among those philosophers who reject it, but also among lawyers and diplomats trying to interpret it. The International Court of Justice (ICJ) has, controversially, denied that states have an inherent right to defend themselves against terrorist attacks by non-state actors.[25] The United States, also controversially, expands the inherent right of self-defence to include preventive war, as well as drone strikes against terrorist groups in the territory of states unwilling or unable to control them.

Of course, one might think these controversies are exactly why we need a *jus ad bellum* court to settle the dispute and enunciate the normatively best criteria of self-defence. Unfortunately, the court would face a lose–lose dilemma: plunge into the morass of legal arguments or ignore them. The former course would set it in competition with official tribunals (like the ICJ and ICC) and would risk submerging morality to legalisms. But if the *jus ad bellum* court ignores the law, why should soldiers accept its normative criteria when their state is claiming 'inherent right of self-defence', which sounds pretty compelling?

Legal judgments become even more acute if the *jus ad bellum* criteria are broadened beyond the Charter requirement of self-defence to include territorial grievances, such as King Henry's quarrel with France.[26] So many conflicts arise from territorial disputes (think Kashmir, Crimea, Ethiopia-Eritrea, Turkey-Cyprus, Azerbaijan-Armenia, the South China Sea) that it seems impossible for a *jus ad bellum* court to declare justice *ad bellum* without addressing the territorial claims. And those are at least in part legal claims, often quite fact-intensive, of the kind the ICJ spends years adjudicating.

8. *Normative disagreement, the resolution of which depends on unknown, possibly unknowable, facts.* If a *jus ad bellum* finding includes judgments about proportionality and reasonable likelihood of success, the court would have to evaluate the probable consequences of a war. But those depend on the military decisions and war plans of the belligerents, which they are certainly not going to disclose (honestly) to a *jus ad bellum* court, particularly an unofficial one that states don't sanction.

Of course, an authoritative *jus ad bellum* court finding that there is no just cause could stop there; lack of just cause by itself makes a war unjust. So the *jus ad bellum* court could limit its mandate to evaluating just cause and dodge the problem of predicting the unpredictable. But if, as some theorists plausibly argue, the justice of a cause turns on proportionality and necessity, even the just cause decision will be impossible for the court to tender.

For all these reasons, a *jus ad bellum* court will not be able to do the epistemic work that soldiers confronting the question of conscientious objection urgently need. That means they will have to deliberate on their own.

Once in a blue moon, the question of *jus ad bellum* will not be hard. A war of naked aggression, unperfumed by propaganda, would present an easy case. Appian reports that when Julius Caesar was debating with his captains about crossing the Rubicon, he said, 'If I don't cross this river, I'm in trouble; if I do, everyone in the world is in trouble. Let's go!'[27] Here, at any rate, Caesar's captains could recognize a manifestly wrongful war in the making.

But easy cases are rare; even Hitler cloaked his aggression in the language of self-defence. A more plausible case would be the situation of a soldier deployed in an ongoing war, whose government justifies the fighting by claims about facts on the ground that the soldier knows are fabrications. If the government justifies its cause with palpable lies, known to be lies by soldiers who can see the truth for themselves, and no other just cause exists, then the injustice is manifest to the soldiers. As I argue later, in that case, the soldier should not continue to fight the war.

Yet even those cases are rare. Consider an example. Notoriously, in the wake of the 1994 Rwandan genocide, France militarily intervened on the wrong side, providing safe passage for *génocidaire* forces escaping to eastern Congo. Some French soldiers explained that their government told them the Hutus were the victims and the Tutsis the perpetrators of the genocide—the opposite of the truth. With few journalists on the ground and French media riddled with disinformation, they had no way to know. Being there on the ground was no help. All the soldiers could see was desperate Hutus fleeing from the victorious RPF.

We might object that matters have changed decisively since 1994. Today, scores of videos would be posted on the Internet. The genocidal broadcasts of Radio Television Milles Collines would be available for all to hear, courageous activists would live-blog the atrocities, and it would not take diligent investigation to discredit the lies the French government told its soldiers.

Yet, even now, the case would not be easy. YouTube would also show videos of the RPF's military advances into Rwanda, posted by the Hutu Power government as proof of Tutsi aggression. Sceptics and deniers would claim that the atrocity videos actually depicted Tutsis killing Hutus, not the other way around, or that the videos actually came from Burundi; the blogosphere would be filled with spin. Uncertainty would continue, and—with no reliable *jus ad bellum* court other than an institution that might seem no more credible or legitimate than the blogosphere—soldiers would remain in doubt, with the role morality of deference to command decisions as the default.

Some might say that so few wars have been just that, on purely statistical grounds, soldiers in a situation of uncertainty should always presume the war is unjust.[28] If you believe that, you should certainly not join the military. But presumably soldiers who take moral issues seriously enough to consider conscientious disobedience don't believe their country fights mostly unjust wars; otherwise, why did they enlist? Soldiers may be mistaken; but to take their dilemma seriously, we must assume they think the wars their country has fought are mostly just. To persuade them otherwise will multiply their epistemic problems rather than solving them.

In short, we have every reason to believe that Williams's epistemic claim about the disability of ordinary soldiers in judging *jus ad bellum* in the fog of war and politics remains as true today as in Shakespeare's time. Regrettably, a *jus ad bellum* court would not remedy the problem.

3. Bates's Absolute Deference Claim

What about Bates's claim that all this is beside the point because 'obedience to the King wipes the crime of it out of us'? I labelled this the 'absolute deference' claim, because if there is no moral wrong in obedience, there is nothing to balance the scales against the soldier's duty to obey. Indeed, if the King's authority suffices to wipe out the crime, there is no point even thinking about *jus ad bellum*. In Tennyson's words, 'Theirs not to make reply/ Theirs not to reason why/ Theirs but to do or die'. This is, perhaps, the most familiar and traditional view of military obedience.

But Tennyson is wrong on two counts. First, because soldiers are reasoning beings and moral agents, it is *always* theirs to reason why. No one, no matter how humble her military rank, is any less a moral agent than the most exalted princes and generals in the realm. No ignorance is invincible if soldiers have closed their eyes to injustice. This is the fundamental and valid insight behind selective conscientious objection on the part of soldiers: their own moral agency never goes away. If their participation in a war is a crime, obedience to the King cannot wipe it away. It might if obedience meant the transfer of all agency to the King, so that Bates and Williams had become nothing but instruments. But men and women are not mere instruments, and political obligation does not transfer citizens' agency to the sovereign.

Some may object that this line of argument badly misses the point. Nearly all professional soldiers would reject the accusation that by obeying orders without question they have made themselves mere instruments without conscience. Professional military organizations pride themselves on their conscience, their unswerving moral compass, and the willingness of soldiers to sacrifice life or limb for their country is an unmistakable token of moral devotion—arguably, the most unmistakable token anyone can offer. Oliver Wendell Holmes's famous Memorial Day address on 'the soldier's faith' eloquently articulates this point of view:

> I do not know what is true. I do not know the meaning of the universe. But in the midst of doubt, in the collapse of creeds, there is one thing I do not doubt, that no man who lives in the same world with most of us can doubt, and that is that the faith is true and adorable which leads a soldier to throw away his life in obedience to a blindly accepted duty, in a cause which he little understands, in a plan of campaign of which he has little notion, under tactics of which he does not see the use.[29]

Holmes gets it: Tennyson's lines are an homage to the Light Brigade's courage and devotion, not a paean to institutionalized amorality. Something along these lines is indeed 'the soldier's faith'. I can't help but think that it resonates with many of us—even if, as Holmes surely intended, the resonance is mixed with repulsion.

But I am not convinced. 'Theirs but to do or die' sentimentally obscures the fact that the doing involves not just dying but killing, and failing to notice this is Tennyson's second and fatal error. My life may be my own to sacrifice; yours is not. Moshe Halbertal nicely explains the fallacy involved in thinking otherwise: from the fact that the soldier is willing to die for the cause, she wrongly infers that the cause has objective value weightier than a human life—in which case she has moral license to kill for the cause.[30] The fallacy lies in reasoning from the strength of commitment, measured by what the soldier is willing to sacrifice in its name, to objective value. Without this fallacy, Tennyson's sentiments are a lot less appealing. 'Theirs not to reason why/ Theirs but to kill on command' is not poet laureate material—and not just because it doesn't rhyme. (No rhyme, but also no reason.)

Now Holmes was not one to confuse strength of commitment for objective value. He was a thoroughgoing sceptic about objective values. Famously, his outlook was formed by his own Civil War experiences, when he recognized that his equals in intelligence and moral seriousness on the Southern side were driven by commitments as deep as his own abolitionism.[31] Holmes doubted any decision procedure could settle the issue—that's why the war was fought.[32] In our time, Jeremy Waldron has argued that objective values are beside the point, not because there are none but because we have no reliable method for settling disagreements about them.[33] In Holmes's eyes, this leaves commitments you are willing to sacrifice your life for as bedrock, and he did not shrink from the prospect of killing for one's commitments, however ungrounded they are in anything else.

Holmes can be faulted for cranky metaphysics, but this is not the place for that discussion.[34] Fortunately, we don't need to fish in such deep waters. For, even on its own terms, Holmes's argument undermines, not supports, the absolute deference claim. If a soldier recognizes the manifest injustice of her cause—as judged by her own moral commitments—then she must decline to fight regardless of the personal sacrifice her disobedience entails. Otherwise, by Holmes's own argument, the commitment not to kill unjustly is not a wholehearted one regardless of the soldier's protestations to the contrary.

4. Manifest Injustice and the No-Inquiry Claim

Where does that leave us? I've argued that soldiers never surrender their power of moral decision—Bates's absolute deference claim fails—but that the decision might be epistemically impossible for an ordinary soldier in the fog of politics and war. Williams's epistemic claim is right. Faced with uncertainty and faint prospect of relieving it, what should the soldier of conscience do?

We can take a clue from the law of *jus in bello*. Under international law, soldiers are required to disobey manifestly illegal orders, and this legal principle straightforwardly has its moral counterpart: you must disobey manifestly immoral orders, such as orders to shoot prisoners or noncombatant civilians, to torture captives, to condone rape, or to cover up war crimes. Conversely, military discipline requires soldiers to obey lawful orders, and international law permits obedience.

In doubtful cases, those that do not 'fly the black flag of illegality', soldiers get the defence of superior orders unless they know the order is unlawful, and they disobey at their own risk, meaning that if the order was lawful, their mistaken belief that the order was unlawful will not protect them from whatever punishment their military code imposes. Thus, the *in bello* law of armed conflict incorporates a tripartite scheme of obligation and permission depending on whether an order is lawful, manifestly unlawful, or unlawful but not manifestly so. Lawful orders may be obeyed, and manifestly illegal orders must be disobeyed. Orders unlawful but not clearly so, and not known to be so, may also be obeyed (and the soldier disobeys at her own peril).[35] The parallel tripartite scheme couched in moral terms would distinguish legitimate orders, orders of unclear moral propriety, and manifestly immoral orders.

The tripartite scheme undoubtedly puts a heavy thumb on the scale in the direction of obedience: in doubtful cases, it strongly favours erring on the side of obedience—because then the soldier gets the superior orders defence—over erring on the side of disobedience. Nevertheless, the scheme incontrovertibly recognizes soldiers as moral and legal agents who are expected to evaluate the rights and wrongs of their actions. In other words, the tripartite scheme recognizes the inevitability of conscience even in a military role morality that assigns central importance to obedience and deference.

Suppose we adopt a parallel tripartite scheme for *ad bellum* judgments. A soldier ought to fight in just wars; to say otherwise is to embrace pacifism, and pacifists have no business becoming soldiers.[36] But soldiers should refuse to fight in manifestly unjust wars.

What about doubtful cases? One approach would require soldiers in doubt to err on the side of nonviolence by refusing to fight unless the war is manifestly just. The reasoning is simple: if there is even a possibility that you might kill someone in an unjust cause, don't put yourself in that position. But such reasoning is faulty because it assumes that the moral risk lies exclusively in the decision to use violence. In a just war of self-defence or a humanitarian intervention, that is not so because the soldier who errs on the side of nonviolence risks exposing those she is sworn to defend to mortal danger. Innocent lives are at stake in either direction.[37]

Under the tripartite scheme, soldiers should refuse to fight only when the war is *manifestly* unjust; in doubtful cases, the soldier may defer to her nation's political leadership and her superiors in the chain of command. That is the view articulated by several early modern just war theorists, and I think it is largely right. Consider Suárez's 1621 *De bello*: although kings and their advisors are required to make 'diligent examinations' of the justice of war, 'common soldiers, as subjects of princes, are in no wise bound to make diligent investigation, but rather may go to war when summoned to do so, provided it is not clear to them that the war is unjust'.[38] Note that common soldiers are required to judge whether the war is *clearly* (*constat*) unjust—thus, Suárez is no military amoralist, and he recognizes the inevitability of conscience. But soldiers have no obligation to delve when the war does not wear injustice on its face. Identical views, in nearly identical words, can be found a century earlier in treatises by Cajetan and his great contemporary Vitoria.[39] For all three, then, common soldiers must refuse to fight in an unjust war but only if the war is clearly, manifestly, patently unjust (I take it that their words are synonymous). Soldiers lie under no affirmative duty to investigate unclear cases.[40] And, given a baseline expectation of obedience, if they need not investigate, they should deploy.

5. Deference and Civilian Control of the Military

Why believe this? For Cajetan, Suárez, and Vitoria, the reason soldiers should obey unless their prince's cause is manifestly unjust derives from broader accounts of political authority, of debatable relevance in modern democracies. I offer a different answer: the crucial importance of maintaining civilian control over the military, which imposes a strong rather than a weak role obligation.

To see this, let's examine two central concepts of military role morality: obedience to orders and civilian control of the military. As a first approximation, we may think of obedience as the requirement of subordinates in the military hierarchy to obey orders of their military superiors. Civilian control refers to the requirement on all the military to obey orders from the civilian government.[41]

Obedience to orders is part of military discipline. It is only one part: the larger project of discipline is to train the soldier to know what to do even without orders. In combat, such discipline is a life-or-death matter.[42] So there is a prudential point to discipline. But there is a moral point as well. Highly disciplined soldiers know when they must *disobey* orders because they are illegal—which already shows that discipline is far from the same thing as absolute deference.

More broadly, military discipline is the most important antidote to war crimes. The disciplined soldier does not fire wildly out of panic. Discipline restrains soldiers from taking vengeance on prisoners and from raping and looting when their basest desires tell them to rape and loot. Disciplined obedience can lay genuine claim to being a role morality—a set of role expectations that fulfils a compelling moral purpose.[43]

Disciplined obedience has to do with *in bello* decision-making. What about the *ad bellum* decision of whether to fight at all, our focus here? That decision is equivalent to the question whether to follow the orders to deploy given by the civilian political leadership. Here, the key argument for the role morality I have called 'the tripartite scheme' is the crucial importance of maintaining civilian control of the military.

My impression is that theorists of just war have neglected the moral importance of civilian control—it is rarely discussed in the philosophical literature on just war.[44] Possibly this is because most theorists live in democratic, civilian-led countries where military coups and violence against civilians by garrisoned soldiers pose no serious threat. We lucky residents of advanced democracies take civilian control for granted.

Doing so is a mistake of monumental proportions. It's like dismissing the need for polio vaccination on the ground that polio no longer poses a threat. If polio no longer poses a threat, that is because of vaccination. If military coups no longer pose a threat, it is because of institutions of civilian control and ceaseless efforts to make it part of military culture. As a brief review of history reminds us, stable civilian control is a hard-won and recent achievement of civilization.

The oldest and most universal of all political problems involving militaries is how to domesticate a society's warriors—violent, proud men, mostly young, with a yen for action.[45] The world's oldest work of literature centres on the problem that King Gilgamesh is at once 'violent, splendid, a wild bull of a man, unvanquished leader, hero in the front lines, beloved by his soldiers . . . ', but also 'arrogant, his head raised high, trampling its citizens like a wild bull'.[46] The central theme of the epic is the domestication of Gilgamesh. In the Hebrew Bible, Samuel warns of similar problems if the Hebrews insist on appointing a king to lead them in wars.[47] Plato discussed the problem in the *Republic*, when he asks how the Guardians can be fierce toward their enemies yet gentle toward their friends. All these are literary texts, but obviously they are based on real and bitter experiences that their audiences could readily recognize.

In the European Middle Ages, feudal retainers, roaming mercenaries, and garrisoned armies were a chronic source of murder, rape, and looting. As Blackstone warned with this history in mind, 'In a land of liberty it is extremely dangerous to make a distinct order of the profession of arms. . . . The laws therefore and constitution of these kingdoms know no such state as that of a perpetual standing soldier, bred up to no other profession than that of war'.[48]

Coupled with the violence of soldiers comes the other chronic problem I mentioned: military coups. The Roman law that Caesar breached by crossing the Rubicon with his army forbade generals from bringing armed troops into the city; the Romans rightly foresaw mortal danger to the Republic. After empire replaced the republic, no fewer than a dozen emperors were deposed through military coups, and those who weren't survived by currying favour with the army. The English civil war saw five military coups and an unsuccessful mutiny within fifteen years. In founding-era constitutional debates over whether the American republic should have a standing army, the framers repeatedly warned of the dangers of 'a Caesar or a Cromwell' deposing the government or embroiling it in military adventures. They remembered that, during the Revolution, the Continental Army twice came close to mutiny.[49]

There are two additional reasons for emphasizing the stringency of civilian control of the military within the role morality of military officers. Civilian control has the paradoxical property of vesting ultimate command authority in military amateurs. Of course, responsible civilian leaders listen carefully to military advice. But nothing obligates the political leaders to heed it, and contemporary history contains notable examples of civilian leaders making awful decisions contrary to military advice. Military leaders are bound to find this structure of authority galling. This is a tension hard-wired into the very structure of civilian control.

A second tension lies in an uncomfortable fact that neither military officers nor civilians in democracies like to speak of openly: many military officers look down on their civilian society and despise its civilian leaders. The officers have sworn to put themselves in harm's way for their country and subjected themselves to a gruelling discipline; by comparison, their civilian counterparts seem like decadent, morally shallow hedonists. In some countries, where the officer corps is almost a de facto hereditary caste, the result has been military coups and military dictatorships. But even in democracies where military coups are unthinkable, part of the reason they are unthinkable is a discipline of civilian control of monastic stringency. Officers whose secret instincts tell them they are morally a cut above their civilian counterparts—including their civilian leaders—and who sometimes see the civilian leaders making gallingly bad security decisions must repress those instincts ruthlessly.

The solution to the problem of soldier violence is strict military discipline. And the solution to the problem of coups lies in placing the military firmly under civilian control, both in the formal chain of command and—more importantly—in the culture and training of military officers. Such a military culture must be built around deference to the chain of command, including above all deference to the political decisions of the civilian government. As Mark Osiel observes, we want colonels to stop and think, but 'we do not want the generals to start thinking about whether they could do a better job of running the country'.[50] That's the dilemma the tripartite scheme aims to address. It does so by insisting that soldiers take heed whether the war they are asked to fight is manifestly unjust, but obey the order to deploy when the fog of politics and war means that nothing is manifest. Bates's no-inquiry claim is wrong if it denies that manifest injustice matters, but right that the duty of inquiry stops there.

This is not a return to the unquestioned obedience celebrated by Tennyson and Holmes—a wholly exclusionary obligation that forecloses conscience and deliberation. But, between the unrestricted requirement of due diligence on the part of soldiers and more limited version of the tripartite scheme, the political arguments grounded in civilian control of the military strongly favour the latter.

Notes

1. Henry V, act 4, sc. 1.
2. This is a different issue from selective conscientious objection by civilians. The soldier has made a commitment that the civilian has not. Even the conscript has not refused to enter the ranks of the military, and, in states where the penalty for conscientious objection is not dire, this is a genuine choice. Because of this commitment, a soldier's decision to refuse orders to deploy is harder than the civilian's decision to refuse to join the military.

   Throughout, I use the word 'soldiers' to refer generically to members of the active military forces of the contesting parties—recognizing that that includes sailors, fliers, and in some cases cyberwarriors and purveyors of other exotic technologies. I am generally speaking of 'tip of the spear' war fighters; that is, those whose job directly includes committing acts of violence. Many of the same conclusions will apply to those in support roles, although the arguments must then be filtered through whatever moral principles apply to indirect participation in acts of violence.

For a thoroughgoing debate about the morality of selective conscientious objection, readers should consult the 2002 symposium issue on the subject in the *Israel Law Review*.

3. Michael Williams, *Unnatural Doubts: Epistemological Realism and the Basis of Skepticism* (Princeton University Press, 1995); *The Problems of Knowledge: A Critical Introduction to Epistemology* (Oxford University Press, 2001).
4. On the need for particularized rather than blanket challenges to knowledge claims, see Williams, *The Problems of Knowledge*, 150–151.
5. Address by Adolf Hitler, September 1, 1939, at http://www.fcit.usf.edu/HOLOCAUST/resource/document/HITLER1.htm (accessed May 8, 2015). On Operation Himmler, see Martin Allen, *Himmler's Secret War: The Covert Peace Negotiations of Heinrich Himmler* (Carroll & Graf, 2005), 51; M. R. D. Foot, 'Conditions Making for Success and Failure of Denial and Deception: Democratic Regimes', in *Strategic Denial and Deception: The Twenty-First Century Challenge*, edited by Roy Godson and James J. Wirtz (Transaction Books, 2002), 100. On the Tonkin Gulf incidents, see Pat Paterson, 'The Truth About Tonkin', *Naval History Magazine* 22 (2008), at http://www.usni.org/magazines/navalhistory/2008-02/truth-about-tonkin (accessed May 8, 2015).
6. I gratefully borrow the phrase from the late US Supreme Court Justice Antonin Scalia. *United States v. Windsor*, 570 U.S. (2013), 133 S. Ct. 2675, 2709 (2013) (Scalia J. dissenting).
7. Seth Lazar and Laura Valentini, 'Proxy Battles in the Ethics of War' (2014) manuscript, 11.
8. Jeff McMahan articulates this view in 'The Ethics of Killing in War', *Ethics* 114 (2004), 701.
9. Judith Lichtenberg, *Distant Strangers: Ethics, Psychology, and Global Poverty* (Cambridge University Press, 2014), 116–117. Lichtenberg criticizes McMahan on similar grounds in 'How to Judge Soldiers Whose Cause Is Unjust', in *Just and Unjust Warriors: The Moral and Legal Status of Soldiers*, edited by David Rodin and Henry Shue (Oxford University Press, 2008), 122–124.
10. For further reflections on the idea of usable moral principles, see Gabriella Blum and David Luban, 'Unsatisfying Wars: Degrees of Risk and the *Jus ex Bello*', *Ethics* 125 (2015), 770–771.
11. Jeff McMahan, 'The Prevention of Unjust Wars', in *Reading Walzer*, edited by Yitzhak Benbaji and Naomi Sussmann (Routledge, 2014), 229–255; the proposal for the *jus ad bellum* court is on pp. 241–252. McMahan defends selective conscientious objection in 'The Moral Responsibility of Volunteer Soldiers', *Boston Review*, November 6, 2013, http://www.bostonreview.net/forum/jeff-mcmahan-moral-responsibility-volunteer-soldiers.
12. McMahan, 'The Prevention of Unjust Wars', 240–241.
13. I note at the outset of this discussion that McMahan acknowledges most of these problems, which he believes can be solved. For the reasons that follow, I remain unpersuaded.
14. McMahan, 'The Prevention of Unjust Wars', 246–247.
15. Idem, 246.
16. McMahan agrees: idem, 247–248.
17. The undertaking appears in the preamble to the African (Banjul) Charter on Human and Peoples' Rights—the fundamental African human rights treaty.
18. Article 39 of the UN Charter; Article 5(1)(d) of the Rome Statute of the ICC.
19. McMahan, 'The Prevention of Unjust Wars', 250–251.
20. In 2014, the Prosecutor of the ICC announced that she was suspending the case against Kenya's president because of lack of evidence resulting from non-cooperation of the Kenyan government and the decisions of intimidated witnesses to withdraw their testimony reportedly in the face of threats to themselves and their families. 'Statement of the

Prosecutor of the International Criminal Court, Fatou Bensouda, on the withdrawal of charges against Mr. Uhuru Muigai Kenyatta', December 5, 2014, http://www.icc-cpi.int/en_menus/icc/press%20and%20media/press%20releases/Pages/otp-statement-05-12-2014-2.aspx. See also 'Statement of the Prosecutor of the International Criminal Court, Fatou Bensouda, on the status of the Government of Kenya's cooperation with the Prosecution's investigations in the Kenyatta case', December 12, 2014, http://www.icc-cpi.int/en_menus/icc/press%20and%20media/press%20releases/Pages/otp-stat-04-12-2014.aspx.

21. McMahan, 'The Prevention of Unjust Wars', 250.
22. Idem, 249.
23. On the other hand, his proposed composition of the *jus ad bellum* court, quoted earlier at note 15, is heavily weighted toward lawyers.
24. I say this as someone who has defended a revisionist conception of just cause and criticized the UN Charter's Article 2(4)–Article 51 regime. Luban, 'Just War and Human Rights', *Philosophy & Public Affairs* 9 (1980), 160–181.
25. ICJ, *Legal Consequences of the Construction of a Wall in Occupied Palestinian Territory*, Advisory Opinion of 9 July 2004, §§138–139.
26. As McMahan proposes in 'Just Cause for War', *Ethics & International Affairs* 19 (3: December 2005), 11–13. There, he argues that just cause consists of any severe enough wrongdoing, including seizure of territory, that would make the perpetrator state liable to force in response. If an aggressor seizes territory and the aggrieved state loses its war of self-defence, it has just cause to launch a war of recovery.
27. Raymond Geuss, *Public Goods, Private Goods* (Princeton University Press, 2001), 45. This is Geuss's free translation of a report from Appian, *Civil War* 2 §35; for Appian's Greek original and its literal translation, see 125 n. 18.
28. I am grateful to Victor Tadros for this suggestion.
29. Oliver Wendell Holmes, Jr., 'The Soldier's Faith', in *The Occasional Speeches of Justice Oliver Wendell Holmes*, edited by Mark De Wolfe Howe (Harvard University Press, 1962), 73.
30. Moshe Halbertal, *On Sacrifice* (Princeton University Press, 2012), 69–70.
31. Holmes, Memorial Day speech, in *The Occasional Speeches of Justice Oliver Wendell Holmes*, 4.
32. 'Deep-seated preferences can not be argued about . . . and therefore, when differences are sufficiently far reaching, we try to kill the other man rather than let him have his way'. Holmes, 'Natural Law', in *Collected Legal Papers* (Peter Smith, 1920), 181. Holmes had a penchant for blunt, sanguinary rhetoric.
33. Jeremy Waldron, 'The Irrelevance of Moral Objectivity', in *Natural Law Theory: Contemporary Essays*, edited by Robert P. George (Oxford University Press, 1994), 158–187.
34. I offer a discussion in Luban, 'Justice Holmes and the Metaphysics of Judicial Restraint', *Duke Law Journal* 44 (1995), 463–488.
35. Article 33 of the Rome Statute of the International Criminal Court (ICC) sets out a prototype of this liability scheme. Superior orders do not relieve a person of criminal responsibility 'unless: (a) The person was under a legal obligation to obey orders of the Government or the superior in question; (b) The person did not know that the order was unlawful; and (c) The order was not manifestly unlawful'.
36. This sentence may be objectionable to those who believe that pacifism is objectively and universally correct as a moral position—in which case, I suppose, nobody ought to become a soldier. Obviously, I am treating pacifism as an optional commitment.
37. A point noted in David Enoch, 'A Defence of Moral Deference', *Journal of Philosophy* 61 (2014), 230. For useful discussion of the decision theory of killing, see Seth Lazar, 'In

Dubious Battle: Uncertainty and the Ethics of Killing' (manuscript). I do not explore the decision theory here. All decision-theoretic methods require assigning probabilities to outcomes. But, in my view, the Williams predicament means that soldiers will often be unable to assign even subjective probabilities in a way they regard as anything more than picking numbers out of a hat. The probabilities fall into the category of 'unknown unknowns'. Moreover, when one of the questions soldiers must answer, and about which they are uncertain, is 'what is the best theory of just cause?', I believe that assigning probabilities to the competitor theories and running the numbers is a mistake. 'What are the odds that utilitarianism is the best moral theory?' strikes me as a misguided question, although I recognize that some philosophers disagree.

38. Francisco Suárez, *De bello*, part of the larger work *De triplici virtute theologica*, is excerpted in Gregory M. Reichberg, Henrik Syse, and Endre Begby, *The Ethics of War: Classic and Contemporary Readings* (Blackwell, 2006), Disputation XIII, section VI: What Certitude as to the Just Cause of War Is Required in order that War May Be Just?, at 357–359. Generals and princes called to consult with the king must also 'inquire diligently'—but not if they are not consulted. Suárez reasons that, in the former case, launching the war will be partly their responsibility, but, in the latter, 'their part in the affair becomes simply that of private soldiers'. I think the war is *always* partly the participants' responsibility—that is what it means to recognize their moral agency—and so if the generals in their nonconsultative role are closer to soldiers, it will be for the reasons I advance in this chapter: a role morality of deference grounded in the importance of civilian control of the military.

39. Thomas Cajetan, *Summula* (1524), in Reichberg et al. *The Ethics of War*, 246. Francisco Vitoria, *On the Law of War*, in Reichberg et al., 318–319.

40. Vitoria concedes that 'there may nevertheless be arguments and proofs of the injustice of war so powerful, that even citizens and subjects of the lower class may not use ignorance as an excuse for serving as soldiers'. Idem. As I read him, though, Vitoria is here spelling out what he means by a 'patently unjust' war; he is not imposing an affirmative obligation on soldiers to investigate the arguments and proofs. Vitoria makes clear that what he means to be ruling out is ignorance that is 'willful and wicked, deliberately fostered out of hostility', not negligent failure to investigate. Idem.

41. Some countries, like the United States, place the civilian leader formally at the top of the military chain of command, so that orders from the president as commander-in-chief *are* military orders. In other countries, for example Israel, the top of the chain of command is a military officer (the chief of staff), so that civilian control is formally distinct from obedience to military orders. Either way, the important point is the subordination of military decisions to those of civilians.

42. For a vivid explanation, see John Keegan, *The Face of Battle* (Penguin, 1983), 20.

43. What I mean by 'disciplined obedience' is obedience to orders as part of a broader military discipline that also teaches soldiers to disobey wrongful orders. It is constrained obedience. I develop a theory of role morality in Luban, *Lawyers and Justice: An Ethical Study* (Princeton University Press, 1988), 129–137.

44. There are exceptions. See, e.g., Dan Zupan, 'A Presumption of the Moral Equality of Combatants: A Citizen-Soldier's Perspective', in *Just and Unjust Warriors: The Moral and Legal Status of Soldiers*, edited David Rodin and Henry Shue (Oxford University Press, 2008), 224–225; Cheyney C. Ryan, 'Moral Equality, Victimhood, and the Sovereignty-Symmetry Problem', in Idem, 131–152; Cheyney Ryan, 'Democratic Duty and the Moral

Dilemmas of Soldiers', *Ethics* 122 (1: 2011), 10–42; David Estlund, 'On Following Orders in an Unjust War', *Journal of Political Philosophy* 15(2), 213–234.

45. I draw in the material that follows from my own discussion in Luban, 'On the Commander-in-Chief Power', *Southern California Law Review* 81 (2008), 467–569.
46. Stephen Mitchell, *Gilgamesh: A New English Version* (Free Press, 2004), 69, 71.
47. 1 Samuel 8:10–18.
48. William Blackstone, *Commentaries on the Laws of England*, vol. 1, 408.
49. See, e.g., Hamilton's warning in *The Federalist* No. 21, edited by Clinton Rossiter (New American Library, 1961), 140, or the equivalent by one of Hamilton's Anti-Federalist adversaries, the pseudonymous 'Brutus': Brutus, X, N.Y. J., January 24, 1788, available at http://www.constitution.org/afp/brutus10.htm.
50. Mark Osiel, *Obeying Orders: Atrocity, Military Discipline, and the Law of War* (Transaction Books, 2001), 87.

CHAPTER 10

NATIONAL DEFENCE AND POLITICAL INDEPENDENCE

DAVID R. MAPEL

It is commonly believed that states are morally justified in using necessary and proportionate military force against an armed attack or imminent threat of attack on their sovereignty or territorial integrity. It is also commonly believed that a people or nation is justified in fighting to acquire or regain a state of its own, at least under some circumstances. Are these beliefs defensible? If so, on what grounds?

Some sceptics argue that only certain kinds of defensive war can be morally justified (see Chapter 9). They distinguish between wars against 'major' and 'lesser' (or 'purely political') aggression.[1] Wars of major aggression aim at harming 'vital' interests or violating fundamental rights. Commonly accepted principles of interpersonal morality license the use of lethal force to resist such profoundly unjust harms. In contrast, wars of lesser aggression target 'nonvital' interests or violate lesser rights. Lesser aggressors pursue goals such as ideological change, the acquisition of territory, or resource extraction; major aggressors pursue enslavement, ethnic cleansing, or genocide.

The sceptic's central claim is that, if the ethics of killing in war is justified under the same principles that justify killing outside of war, then it is proportionate to use lethal defensive force only against threats that we could permissibly kill to avert outside of war. Threats to vital interests are defined as those that it would be proportionate to avert with lethal force outside of war; threats to lesser interests are those to which lethal force would be a disproportionate response outside of war. If the ethics of war is just an application of the ethics of interpersonal morality, then it is impermissible to use lethal defensive force to avert a war of lesser aggression.

Significantly, the sceptic holds this view even when a lesser aggressor makes a conditional threat to the victims' vital interests—that if they do not accede to the aggressor's war aims, the aggressor will use lethal force to achieve them. These lesser aggressors are like a mugger who threatens to kill a victim if he does not hand over his wallet. Proportionality requires that defensive force be commensurate with the loss that the victim will suffer if he complies with the aggressor's demand. In this case, the sceptic argues, the victim should hand over his wallet rather than kill the mugger. Extending this reasoning to the ethics of war, a victim state should accede to the aggressor's demands rather than fight to protect a lesser interest, such as a disputed territory, especially when a defensive war would involve intentionally or collaterally harming the vital interests of many innocent persons. The sceptical view—permitting defensive war against major aggression but not against lesser aggression backed up by a conditional lethal threat—is thus located somewhere between traditional just war theory, which (it is claimed) permits virtually all wars against lesser aggression, and pacifism, which permits no wars at all.

This sceptical challenge is related to a deeper methodological debate between 'reductivists' and 'exceptionalists'. Reductivists maintain that the morality of war should be based on principles of interpersonal morality. Exceptionalists deny that we can offer a plausible account of the morality of war on reductivist grounds alone, offering a *reductio* of reductivism. Starting with an endorsement of the commonly held assumption that most, if not all, wars of national defence against purely political aggression are morally justified, the exceptionalist then outlines the standard principles and conditions under which interpersonal morality permits defensive killing and argues that most, if not all, wars against lesser aggression are not justifiable on these terms.[2] The exceptionalist concludes that the reductivist view should be rejected as too restrictive.

Some reductivists may simply reject the exceptionalist's initial assumption: they may accept that most defensive wars against lesser aggression are unjustifiable, but they refuse to relinquish their commitment to grounding the morality of war on the principles of interpersonal morality. Pacifists agree that wars against lesser aggression are not justified, for example, yet this hardly motivates them to give up interpersonal morality as the basis of their views. Instead, they insist that the sceptic's rejection of defensive war doesn't go far enough. Some versions of just war theory also are so morally demanding that, in practice, they rule out almost all wars, thus resulting in a contingent kind of pacifism: warfare is, in principle, justified, but once contingent facts are considered almost all wars are, in fact, impermissible. The conclusion that one draws from the sceptic's *reductio* therefore depends on one's prior views about the permissibility of such wars, as well as on the strength of one's conviction that the principles of interpersonal morality are the sole basis for the morality of war. In general, though, the just war tradition takes a more permissive view of wars against lesser aggression. International law also is extremely permissive, allowing almost all such wars. Chapter 9 deals with these methodological issues more extensively, and Chapter 10 discusses a variety of just war views.

This chapter focuses on the substantive question of whether the most important kind of war against lesser aggression—in defence of political self-determination, by itself or along with basic political rights—can be justified by standard principles of interpersonal morality. If defensive war can't be justified even in this central case, this suggests that an important revision of conventional views of national defence is required: either we will have to look beyond the principles of interpersonal morality for the justification of defensive wars, or else we must concede that many wars against lesser aggression are unjustifiable.

Section 1 considers whether the reductivist position must absolutely or usually prohibit the use of lethal defensive force against lesser aggression when it is backed up by a conditional threat to kill. It suggests that reductivism may justify lethal defence more often than the sceptical challenge suggests. Section 2 discusses how the role of the proportionality requirement is to be understood. Even after making several controversial assumptions in favour of national defence, this discussion reveals that it is not so easy, after all, to justify wars against lesser aggression on the basis of interpersonal principles of morality, especially if we take seriously the likelihood of collateral harm to noncombatants. Section 3 focuses on whether protecting the 'nonvital' political interests of the citizens of a victim state might, in the aggregate, sometimes be important enough to make proportionate the harming of the 'vital' interests of a significantly smaller number of innocent enemy noncombatants. It distinguishes four kinds of wars to secure political self-determination and explores the case for each. Section 4 then considers a number of exceptionalist moral arguments for a legal right of national defence and the likely consequence were states to adopt a general duty not to resist lesser aggression.

1. Conditional Threats

To understand what interpersonal morality allows with respect to the use of lethal defensive force against lesser aggression, we must first understand more clearly the role and significance of conditional threats to kill. According to Seth Lazar, it is important to distinguish between two different kinds of conditional threats.[3] In a 'coercive' conditional lethal threat, the aggressor 'directly threatens the victim'.[4] The aggressor tells the victim that he will respond to *anything* short of the victim's full compliance with a lethal assault. In a 'defensive' conditional threat, the aggressor makes it clear he will *defend himself* against any attempts by the victim to resist his demands.[5] This is like a mugger who says, 'Don't make me hurt you, just give me your wallet. I'll fight if you attack me'.

If an aggressor issues a defensive conditional lethal threat, does interpersonal morality require you either to give up your wallet or use only the force proportionate to its loss, waiting until the risks escalate before you use lethal defensive force? Consider similar reasoning by a state facing a lesser aggressor issuing such a threat. The victim state knows that if it uses nonlethal force, say, by shooting rubber bullets, it not only forgoes the advantage of pre-emptive force, but is likely to trigger the forceful response that the aggressor has threatened. Isn't it then morally permissible to respond lethally to an imminent threat of lesser aggression if that threat is backed up by a conditional defensive threat to use deadly force?

Such reasoning, if sound, would help to explain why wars of national defence against lesser aggression are often justified. Yet Lazar argues that the foregoing reasoning is circular. A mugger who issues a defensive conditional lethal threat has the intent at T_0, only to steal the victim's wallet.[6] This mugger's subsequent action is neither predetermined nor necessary; he can always change his mind. Now, suppose you immediately respond to his demand at T_0 with lethal force at T_1. This would be disproportionate to your risk of losing your wallet. And now that you have resisted the mugger's demand in such an extreme way, he has reason to use lethal force against you in self-defence. Whereas he didn't initially intend to use lethal force, now he does. If the mugger will not use violence at T_2 *unless* you defensively attack him at T_1, then, as Lazar rightly claims, it is circular for you to use a prediction about the mugger's response at T_2, which, after all, you have provoked, to justify your otherwise (assumed to be) disproportionate response at T_1. Proportionality is determined by the actual, rather than imagined, threat.

The case of a coercive conditional lethal threat is different, however. Although the mugger may not intend to kill you immediately (after all, you may hand over your wallet and he may be satisfied with his loot), *from the very beginning*, he may truly intend to use lethal force should you fail to accede to his demands. Although he does not intend to kill you now, he does now intend to kill you if you fail to comply.[7] Not only may he kill you simply because you refuse to hand over your wallet, he also may kill you even if you *do* hand it over. In the absence of any evidence to the contrary, prudence cautions you to assume that the mugger is not bluffing when he says 'Your money or your life'. To assume otherwise, in your epistemically limited position, could be a fatal mistake. After all, the mugger did not say, 'If you resist, I will use less than lethal force to subdue you, unless you try to kill me, in which case I will kill you'. Instead, he simply issues his coercive conditional lethal threat.

An act of aggression backed up by a seemingly sincere coercive conditional threat to use lethal force therefore has a different and worse moral character than a nonlethal act of aggression without such a threat but with the same primary aim. Snatching your wallet and running away (or even simply demanding your wallet) is a less serious wrong than threatening to kill you if you do not hand over your wallet. The coercive mugger has gone beyond forming a conditional intention to making a demand and a threat, to being ready to shoot if you do not comply. Similarly, when an aggressor nation-state with a purely political objective issues a coercive conditional lethal threat to back it up, that state usually has developed a plan of attack and deployed its weapons and troops. We must assume that these troops will reliably carry out their mission.[8]

Lazar claims that a defensive model of conditional threats 'is most apt for the problem of purely political aggression'. One reason is that purely political aggressor states sometimes invade without warning and only then issue defensive conditional lethal threats. In other cases, an aggressor army follows rules of engagement permitting the use of lethal force only when necessary to stop those who resist with lethal force—the rules governing British soldiers in Iraq, for example. No doubt, most acts of lesser aggression are accompanied by some kind of conditional lethal threat, otherwise victim states would have little reason not to fight back.

The controversial empirical question is how often victim states face coercive rather than defensive conditional threats or how often they are in an epistemic position to trust that a supposedly defensive conditional threat doesn't disguise something worse. Unlike a coercive conditional aggressor, an aggressor making a defensive conditional threat promises not to defend his ill-gotten gains by killing unless threatened with death, which amounts to an implicit promise to respond with restraint to lesser forms of resistance. Victims may sometimes reasonably doubt that such promises will be kept. Cécile Fabre asserts, for example, that if a victim state were to target only unmanned military equipment, it would be 'utterly unimaginable that armies as we know them would not retaliate with lethal force'[9] rather than responding more incrementally.[10] For this reason, it is worth considering in more detail why, as a matter of interpersonal morality, a coercive conditional threat sometimes justifies lethal force as an initially proportionate defensive response.

One reason is that judgments of proportionality involve comparing defensive *harms* with offensive *wrongs*.[11] A coercive conditional lethal threat not only promises a grave harm in the future should the victim not comply; it *is* a grave wrong in the present. 'Your money or your life' is deeply coercive and unjust, no matter how much or little money is at stake. In fact, even a defensive conditional threat is a serious wrong because it, too, is aimed at compelling the victim not to resist. The wrong involved in a conditional threat is grave enough that it should be assigned substantial weight in determining what counts as a proportionate *initial* act of harmful self-defence. One may use considerable defensive force in response to such a grave wrong.[12] However, no innocent bystanders are harmed in the mugger cases, whereas national defence involves intentionally or collaterally killing nonculpable combatants. As discussed in Section 2, this makes a lethal defensive response harder to justify.

This brings us to the relative value of the lesser interest at stake; indeed, we must combine the wrongness of the conditional threat to kill the victim with the relative value of the victim's lesser interest (plus the factor of risk, discussed later) in order to decide what is an initially proportionate response. These factors may not be simply additive, but also may interact in a more complicated way to determine what counts as proportionate.[13] Consider a case in which Alfred intends to break Betty's arm for the fun of it and threatens to kill her if she resists.[14] Clearly, Betty needn't passively submit. It may even be proportionate for her to kill Alfred, if his threat is convincing and he seems capable of carrying it out. This judgment depends partly on Alfred's culpability but also reflects the fact that a broken arm is much worse than a stolen wallet. The point is that combining the wrongness of a conditional threat with a serious harm to some kinds of lesser interests increases the possibility that an initial use of lethal force is proportionate.[15]

We now come to the third relevant factor: how likely is it that an aggressor making a conditional threat to kill is trustworthy? How would one know? Doesn't the fact that he is willing to make such a threat usually make it reasonable to entertain some doubts? Matters change if an aggressor who is not initially threatening a vital interest is not trustworthy or if one has no way of knowing—which from the victim's point of view amounts to the same thing.[16] In this case, the victim could be in one of three situations. First, she may be facing an aggressor who has been lying all along about his intention not to violate her fundamental rights. Second, although initially sincere, the aggressor may change his mind—emboldened, perhaps, by his victim's surrender—and become a major aggressor.[17] Third, the original threat may be compounded by a demand to surrender any future means of self-defence. It is usually foolish to comply with such a demand because, as

Locke remarks, 'let his pretense be what he will, I have no reason to suppose that he, who would take away my liberty, would not when he had me in his Power, take away every thing else'.[18]

The point is that a victim dealing with a trustworthy aggressor faces virtually no threat to her life as long as she does what he wants, whereas a victim dealing with an untrustworthy aggressor faces some undeterminable threat to her life no matter what she does. That the victim's life is to some degree at stake means that a significant possibility of major aggression magnifies what can count as a proportionate defensive response to a lesser aggression. The problems of risk and uncertainty mean that the victim must make predictions about the future in trying to calculate the gravity of the threat she presently faces. An apparently lesser aggressor can actually be (or become) a major aggressor.

But what counts as a 'significant' risk, and how does one determine it? Are you a good shot with your own weapon, so that it wouldn't be too risky to try to disable the mugger, or are you likely to miss? Is the aggressor known to abide by his promises to his victims, or does he have a reputation for occasionally going on to kill? Analogous questions can be asked of states. Given the grave wrongfulness of a conditional threat, the great value of some so-called lesser interests, and the reasonable belief that the victim faces some 'significant' risk of worse harm to come, the use of quite a bit of initial defensive force, perhaps even lethal force, sometimes may be proportionate.

Who knows how many invasions would have been bloodless and how many occupations relatively benign had they gone unopposed or been met initially with a limited response? Although one might be inclined to think relatively few, it seems reasonable to believe that in some (perhaps many) cases, a decision to surrender to a defensive conditional lethal threat might have averted bloodshed. Lazar notes that the United States and the United Kingdom have recently engaged in acts of aggression that it is reasonable to believe would not have been particularly bloody or oppressive had they not been resisted.[19] The trouble is, of course, that such counterfactual judgments are necessarily speculative. Lazar concedes that the possibility of a significant risk of major aggression limits the practical scope of the sceptical argument, but he insists that the counterintuitive implications of merely theoretical cases are important for assessing reductivism's plausibility.[20]

Yet it is important to keep in mind that the just war tradition has always held that appeasement or surrender to a coercive or defensive conditional lethal threat may be morally required, not only when that threat is made in the service of a just cause, but also sometimes even when it is not. The question, then, is whether the principles of interpersonal morality, when applied to interstate conduct, would too often require surrender to unjust lesser aggression. Recall that the 'lesser' interest threatened may be of great importance to the victim and that the purpose of even a 'defensive' conditional lethal threat is wrongly to force the victim not to fight back. In addition, a victim sometimes may reasonably mistrust an aggressor's promise that giving in to a defensive conditional lethal threat or mounting only a proportionate response really will prevent bloodshed. Together, these considerations suggest that a reductivist might be able to justify wars of national defence against lesser aggression more often than the sceptical challenge supposes, without engaging in circular reasoning. Just how wide this range of permissible defensive wars might be depends on the answers to further questions about proportionality and the value of political self-determination.

2. Proportionality

This section examines the proportionality requirement and makes a number of favourable, albeit controversial, assumptions in order to build a robust case for national defence. Even with these assumptions in place, it will become apparent that the sceptical challenge is not as easy to meet as the previous section may have suggested.

How should a government weigh harm to its own citizens in trying to decide whether a defensive war would be proportionate? If citizens (or their representatives) have freely chosen to expose themselves to the harms involved in fighting, then a government should largely discount those harms when making this judgment. This includes harm to both volunteer combatants and to draftees, who may accept conscription as the only feasible way of raising an army in short order. Obviously, some citizens do not consent to their government's decision to fight, whereas others, such as children, must have the matter decided for them. Unanimous, completely free, and fully informed consent is never possible in political society. Instead, general acceptance by citizens of the risks of war is the first condition that must be satisfied in judging that a defensive war would be proportionate.[21] Given most citizens' deep hostility to foreign invasion, it will usually not be hard to demonstrate.

The next question is how a government should weigh the defensive harm it will inflict on unjust enemy combatants. This is more controversial, reflecting deep disagreement about the basis of individual moral liability to such harm even in domestic society. A person is liable to defensive harm if he lacks a right against such harm (e.g., if he has forfeited his right by posing an imminent unjust harm to others). We do not wrong such a person by harming him. Øverland argues that we should expect most combatants to know that an unjust, purely political aim cannot justify a conditional threat to kill.[22] Most soldiers become liable to defensive harm when participating in a war with this kind of aim; he offers the example of Nazi soldiers who should have known that establishing political control over Norway could not justify killing Norwegian soldiers.[23]

This case is too easy, however. A more difficult, and perhaps more representative, case is again the 2003 invasion of Iraq. Assume this was a war of lesser aggression aimed primarily at eliminating suspected weapons of mass destruction (WMD; that did not exist). It was not major aggression aimed at raping, expelling, or killing significant numbers of Iraqi citizens. Were Coalition soldiers liable to defensive harm because they took part in this purely political aggression? Jeff McMahan argues that we should regard most combatants as morally responsible agents who have chosen to engage in or contribute to a type of activity that foreseeably risks wrongfully harming the innocent. Having taken this risk, soldiers become liable to defensive harm if deployed to fight an unjust war.

McMahan further argues that most soldiers should be considered negligent for failing to investigate the justice of their cause, although they are partially excused by a variety of mitigating factors.[24] On this account, the Iraqi government was entitled to target (most) Coalition soldiers and to discount their deaths in trying to determine whether a defensive war would be proportionate.

Yet if we set the bar for moral liability to defensive harm this low, it seems that many enemy *non*combatants also should be considered legitimate targets, given their moral and material support for (or failure to resist) their country's unjust war.[25] In principle, Iraqi soldiers would have been justified in targeting many Coalition noncombatants. Reductivists have tried to deal with this counterintuitive implication in a variety of ways. Some argue that an individual's degree of causal contribution to an unjust war is also relevant to his liability and that most noncombatants don't make causal contributions that are proximate or significant enough to make them legitimate targets.[26] Some reductivists maintain that there is not a sufficient 'unity of intention' with combatants to make noncombatants liable to intentional killing;[27] others, that individuals are not liable to unnecessary defensive harm and that harming noncombatants is seldom, if ever, necessary to military victory;[28] still others, that many noncombatants *are* liable to defensive harm, but that we shouldn't confuse liability with the overall permissibility of such harm. It is usually difficult to target morally liable noncombatants without also impermissibly killing a disproportionate number of nonliable combatants.[29]

In contrast, exceptionalists such as Lazar and Henry Shue argue that principles of individual liability are too fine-grained to ground the morality of warfare. Lazar in particular argues that we should justify the principle of discrimination on several new grounds; for example, that it is important to respect the way in which political collectives choose to distribute harm among their citizens by nominating their combatants as targets.[30] For the sake of argument, however, I will assume that the reductivist can provide sufficient justification for limiting intentional harm to noncombatants (although this is a matter of lively debate).[31] On this basis, I also assume that war against lesser aggression should and usually can be largely fought in a discriminating manner. This brings us to the central issue: can the widespread collateral killing of innocent enemy noncombatants ever be considered proportionate?

In terms of interpersonal morality, it would seem not. It would not be proportionate to defend one's property against a thief by throwing a grenade that also foreseeably killed an innocent bystander, for example. Unfortunately, war virtually always involves the collateral killing of many enemy noncombatants who are completely innocent. This makes it difficult to believe that most wars of national defence against lesser aggression can satisfy a more general proportionality requirement. But perhaps preserving the nonvital interests of many innocent victims of lesser aggression sometimes can outweigh foreseen harm to the vital interests of fewer innocent noncombatants on the aggressor's side. This involves shifting to a wider kind of proportionality calculation involving overall comparisons of a more varied set of benefits and harms.

There are many difficulties in making such broad, aggregative judgments. The main practical problem is that predictions about the harms that will occur if a war is fought (or not) frequently turn out to be terribly mistaken. There are serious conceptual problems as well. Philosophers disagree, for example, about whether we should count only goods that are part of an 'independent' just cause (e.g., protecting political independence) or whether we may also include various 'contributory' goods, such as deterrence.[32] A deeper problem is that we must compare heterogeneous benefits and harms, including the preservation or loss of life, limb, sovereignty, territory, political self-determination, political rights, wealth, property, cultural and historical artefacts, and so on. As Lazar points out, aggregation also seems to have the counterintuitive implication that states with relatively larger populations have a stronger justification for national defence than smaller states.[33] This implication might be avoided by a more complicated consequentialism that justifies the rules of an international legal system in terms of their long-range outcomes, as discussed in Section 4.

Given such problems, some just war theorists reject any consequentialist or pluralist conception of proportionality as nonsensical. They instead offer a 'procedural' interpretation of proportionality, one based on a certain notion of fairness and appealing to the prudence of the virtuous statesman as a basis of judgment.[34] In contrast, most just war theorists argue that intelligible and relatively uncontroversial substantive judgments are possible in at least some cases (e.g., it would have been disproportionate to risk nuclear war in order to roll back Soviet aggression in Czechoslovakia). Yet, in light of the great difficulties involved in making large-scale aggregative judgments, Michael Walzer argues, 'it is our abhorrence of aggression that is authoritative, while the maxims of [last resort] and proportionality play only marginal and uncertain roles'.[35] This echoes the argument in Section 1 that the grave wrongfulness of an unjust conditional lethal threat should play a very large role in determining what counts as an initially proportionate defensive response to lesser aggression.

Even so, Walzer seems mistaken that the burden of proof lies with the sceptic because we must keep in mind that almost all wars involve the deliberate, if 'unintentional' killing or maiming of many innocent persons, not to mention myriad other wrongful harms. The prospect of such widespread collateral harm should push us towards a contingent form of pacifism with respect to purely political aggression, at least from a reductivist point of view. It is one thing to purchase political freedom by killing enemy combatants and noncombatants who are liable to defensive harm; it is quite another to purchase it by the foreseeable killing of thousands, possibly even millions, of innocent persons. A pacifist may be ready to give her life for her country by nonviolently resisting lesser aggression, but this is compatible with holding that the worst kind of lesser aggression is not bad enough to justify the foreseen killing of even a single innocent person in war. Most people reject this view as too extreme, signalling their conviction that the prevention of serious lesser harms to a sufficiently large number of citizens can be proportionate to the foreseen killing of a smaller number of innocent enemy noncombatants. Still, the lesser interests at stake must be very significant and the number of people affected over time must be very large before the collateral killing of many innocent persons can be regarded as truly the lesser evil. The next section considers what sort of political interests might have this kind of significance.

3. Political Rights and Political Independence

So far, I have suggested the possibility of a reductivist justification of at least some wars against lesser aggression. But how many such wars actually could be justified on reductivist grounds? There is an enormous range of lesser interests that might be involved, ranging from the protection of a few miles of uninhabited territory (see Chapter 10) to the defence of millions of people against tyranny. To narrow the discussion, this section focuses on the importance of the rule of law and the basic political rights of individuals and on the central issue of the rights of citizens to political self-determination. I will consider four types of war against purely political aggression, but keep in mind that there is much greater variation in the character of aggressor and victim states than this simple framework suggests.

The strongest justification for a war of national defence involves a tyrannical aggressor threatening a liberal democratic state. Suppose the aggressor aims to replace the rule of law with the arbitrary commands of a ruling clique while also severely curtailing freedoms of speech, association, and movement. Once the defending state's army has been disbanded, it will be very difficult to reverse these developments, and tyranny may persist over many generations. Some citizens are also likely to continue resisting after official surrender, even if their actions cannot be justified because they provoke wider repression. Thus, a certain amount of violence will almost certainly attend any supposedly bloodless invasion and continue thereafter, although not enough (let us suppose) to transform the case into one of major aggression. Clearly, the terms 'lesser' and 'purely political' fail to convey just how significant the consequences of surrender might be.

In addition to the destruction of the rule of law and basic political rights, let us suppose that many individuals in the conquered community lose their collective authorship of particular political institutions and their sense of communal self-esteem and solidarity. Insofar as such qualities make a contribution to individual well-being, their protection can be part of a reductivist justification of war. There also may be ways in which solidarity is a collective good valuable for a group as a whole.[36] Even if we focus only the losses for individuals, they are obviously important and should be added to the list of imposed hardships. Dictatorship is likely to harm virtually all the members of a conquered, liberal democratic state in many different, deep, and lasting ways. If these harms could be prevented by a defensive war involving the collateral killing of a relatively small number of innocent enemy civilians, then it may be justified as a lesser evil. How frequently this would be the case depends on how one compares a wide range of heterogeneous goods and evils over an indefinite period of time.

At the opposite end of the spectrum is a case offered by David Rodin, in which a just and legitimate state threatens to invade another just and legitimate state in order to make it even more just.[37] Suppose Canada threatens a military invasion of the United States in order to impose parliamentary government and a single-payer health care system. From a reductivist perspective, it would not be worth inflicting a large number of collateral deaths in order to repulse such a benign form of liberal imperialism. However, this case is highly unrealistic: it completely fails to describe the harms usually at stake in cases of lesser aggression. If our hypothetical Canadians were so concerned with justice, they hardly would threaten to invade in the first place, much less back up their aggression with a conditional threat to kill.

Consider two more debatable, intermediate types of lesser aggression. An authoritarian government wishes neither to impose an oppressive tyranny nor institute a set of just reforms, but rather to expand its authority, territory, and resources by ruling another country directly or through a puppet government. Suppose that citizens of the victim state greatly value political self-determination, which explains why they are willing to fight and why any attempt to impose radical ideological and institutional reforms from outside is likely to fail. The value that they place on self-determination also provides one explanation (in addition to the possibility of major oppression) for why they are likely to engage in a national liberation movement against a colonial ruler or to secede in order to acquire a state of their own. Yet, in this third type of case, neither the aggressor nor the victim state or group respects the rule of law or protects important political rights. From a liberal reductivist perspective, such illiberal states or movements must possess weaker defensive privileges because the form of association they are defending is less valuable *for* their members, although it may not seem less valuable *to* them.

Given that this last conclusion is frequently rejected, let's focus on a fourth type of aggression in order to consider more carefully what is lost in the suppression or destruction of a common political life. A domestically just aggressor state threatens a domestically unjust victim state with the aim of providing relief and redress to the latter's citizens. Suppose also that the aggressor—the 'reform interventionist'—intends to withdraw once its aims have been achieved. In this example, the victim state does not engage in major rights violations against its own people, but it is oppressive in other ways (e.g., it denies important political and civil rights to women). From a reductivist perspective, could the victim state justify the collateral killing of a significant number of innocent persons as a proportionate defensive response to reform intervention? By the same token, could a people justify violent secession or rebellion against a colonial power that does not engage in major rights violations, such as murder or enslavement, but that does deny them important political rights, as well as political self-determination?

The argument *for* national defence in these kinds of cases goes roughly as follows. Domestic politics is always messy and unpredictable and, in authoritarian societies, sometimes brutal as well. Nonetheless, local political life is necessary in order to give abstract human rights concrete meaning. Given that the members of an authoritarian polity greatly value their common political activity, and given that there are serious problems involved in comparing different interpretations of and tradeoffs between different human rights in different social contexts, we must recognize that there is no universal checklist of rights that we can use to justify the claim that some political societies should enjoy greater defensive privileges than others.[38] What is being protected in a war against such reform intervention is a relatively unitary, authoritative, and local interpretation of justice through particular institutions that are valued and to some extent actively participated in by the victim state's citizens. Although political philosophers dispute the precise meanings and values attached to such terms as 'public freedom', 'communal autonomy', and 'collective authorship',[39] champions of these ideas can be interpreted quite broadly as arguing that political self-determination is valuable not merely for the outcomes it produces but also for the kind of activity that it is.[40] Political self-determination is a 'participatory good' that can be realized only by individuals acting together.[41]

The liberal response, to which I am generally sympathetic, is that we should neither romanticize politics nor contextualize basic individual political rights in a way that renders repression a normal or acceptable feature of collective self-determination. It is also implausible that nonliberal polities typically provide a range of possibilities for individual well-being equal to that provided by polities governed by the rule of law and providing basic political rights. From a liberal reductivist perspective, it does not seem that in most cases protecting the participatory good of politics could be important enough to make it proportionate to kill a significant number of innocent persons as a side effect of a defensive war against lesser aggression. By the same token, wars of national liberation or secession are not likely to be a proportionate way of securing the participatory good of politics, especially if there is any chance of strengthening local autonomy arrangements instead. Indeed, national liberation and secessionist wars aimed solely at collective self-determination (rather than at the protection of vital interests) seem likely to involve disproportionate violence even when a peaceful devolution of domestic power is not in the cards. In short, liberal democratic polities generally have stronger defensive privileges than do authoritarian ones.

At this point, it is crucial to remember that invading paternalistic governments and colonial administrations usually have engaged in *major* aggression against subject populations; it is this that has generally motivated and justified wars of national defence and liberation, not merely a desire for political recognition. To be denied such recognition is a demeaning and damaging experience, yet it is difficult to believe that such harms by themselves justify the collateral killing of significant numbers of innocent individuals, at least if we stick to a reductivist point of view. We also must remember that wars of 'liberation', such as the 2003 invasion of Iraq, have often proved complete fiascos, although doubtless some nation-building projects would have turned out better in the unlikely event of encountering no military resistance. These recent misadventures strongly bolster pragmatic suspicions of any political theory that would generally forbid military resistance to such purported efforts at reform.

In principle, only some defensive wars against lesser aggression can be morally justified from a reductivist perspective, and perhaps not many at all. Even making assumptions that favour national defence, the crux of the matter is that such wars are often likely to involve disproportionate collateral killing. For those who find this restrictive conclusion about defensive war acceptable, the reductivist approach remains plausible. For those who believe that most wars of national defence against lesser aggression are morally justified, an exceptionalist approach may seem to be required after all. The next section considers one such.

4. International Law

Allen Buchanan argues that, rather than focussing on principles governing individual actions, we should shift to a kind of 'institutional reasoning' that justifies practices as a whole in terms of whether they contribute to moral progress in international governance (defined by the promotion of a list of human rights more extensive than those mentioned earlier).[42] Following Buchanan, Margaret Moore argues that precautionary principles of institutional design make the right of national defence a good institutional rule. To preclude defensive war because of the killing involved 'would have the incentive of rewarding aggression, and this would be a far worse state of affairs', whereas, in particular, 'if we do not permit defence against purely political aggression, then *all peoples are vulnerable*'.[43]

No doubt a right of national defence would be a good institutional rule within a morally progressive system of international law. Among other defects, however, international law recognizes the sovereign rights of states that abuse the human rights of their own citizens. Moreover, international law may have perverse effects on general deterrence. An effective deterrent system involves an impartial agent with a monopoly on legitimate force applying sanctions reliably and consistently. This is the main function of a legitimate state, which is one reason that general deterrence is not part of the proportionality calculation with respect to individual self-defence within such a state. In contrast, deterrence in international society is based largely on self-help (including defensive alliances). Rodin argues that, perversely, this may encourage adversaries to try to obtain a decisive military advantage, to engage in major rather than lesser aggression, or to pick a different, weaker victim, thus generally encouraging violence rather than deterring it.[44] Although these contentions remain speculative, Rodin suggests that, at the least, 'the role of general deterrence in moral reasoning should be negligible'.[45]

Which institutional rules do states have some moral reason to observe? One important standard of a proposed ethical, political, or legal principle is an universalisability test: what would the result be if states were universally to adopt a duty *not* to resist lesser aggression? How such a rule might function cannot be determined with any certainty in isolation from an entire system of rules. Nevertheless, Moore plausibly argues that adopting such a rule would build relations of domination into the structure of international law.[46] Such a duty would be deeply objectionable on this basis alone. Although Moore presents this as a lesser evil argument, it ultimately seems deontological in character. As it is applied to institutional design rather than individual action, it can be understood as an exceptionalist argument as well. Leaving such deontological considerations aside, the most likely consequence of adopting such a rule would be a significant increase in acts of lesser aggression. It is hard to imagine how such a duty of nonresistance could ever be adopted within a rule-consequentialist framework. Because this is again an argument about acceptable institutional design, it, too, can be understood as exceptionalist.

Setting these counterfactual thought experiments aside, the Kantian argument that both individuals and states have a duty to 'enter into' civil society also merits scrutiny. Without the rule of law, there can only be continually contested interpretations of what justice requires, as well as the more or less arbitrary use of force. Kant's conclusion that we have an absolute duty to obey the law is counterintuitive, however.[47] Instead, this duty can conflict with other moral rights and duties, especially if our legal system is a very imperfect one. Domestically illegitimate states have a right of national defence grounded in the moral value of current international law, but this right can hardly have the stringency that Kant's argument suggests.

To illustrate, consider two different views of NATO's intervention in Kosovo. Buchanan has argued that it was right to give current legal rights of sovereignty and national defence little or no moral weight in this case: NATO's intervention was not morally wrong.[48] A more Kantian view is that current international law does have some moral force despite its flaws. NATO's unauthorized intervention wronged other states, even though failing to rescue the Kosovars would have been morally worse, all things considered. More generally, the legal right of a domestically unjust state to defend itself against aggression sometimes may be overridden for the sake of stopping serious injustice within that state, but such extra-legal overriding necessarily involves some wronging of the other members of the society of states.[49] In contrast, there is no reason to override a domestically just state's international legal right of national defence. In this case, domestic and international justifications reinforce the case for resisting lesser aggression by military force. Those who believe that military resistance to lesser aggression is normally justified may have this kind of case primarily in mind.

Yet how much independent moral weight does an international legal right of national defence possess? If the sole justification that a victim state can offer for waging a war of national defence is that it is fighting to vindicate the rule of law among nations, this hardly warrants the destruction likely to ensue. Nevertheless, a threat of lesser aggression may involve a conditional coercive threat to kill innocent civilians, as well as some risk that the new rulers will turn out to be much worse than advertized, so that even domestically unjust states may have these justifications for national defence available. Of course, it is much harder to argue that the subjects of such a state have consented to the risk of suffering that their government's decisions involve. Even so, they may prefer war to the prospect of being ruled by a foreign power.

5. Conclusion

The justification of national defence raises complex questions about conditional threats, the proportionality requirement, the values protected by various forms of political association, and the proper theoretical approach to reasoning about the morality of war. Section 1 examined lethal defensive and coercive conditional threats and suggested that a lethal defensive response may be proportionate in a broader range of cases than the sceptical challenge suggests. Section 2, which focused on proportionality, reached a less favourable conclusion about defensive force. On the one hand, the preservation of the lesser political interests of a greater number of citizens of a victim state might outweigh harm to the vital interests of a smaller number of nonliable citizens of an aggressor state. On the other hand, war invariably involves inflicting grave collateral harm on many innocent persons. Section 3 considered four types of interstate aggression. The best case for defensive war involved a liberal democracy resisting a tyrannical aggressor; other cases offered much less justification, from a reductionist perspective, for the collateral killing and maiming of innocent noncombatants.

It seems that although some wars against lesser aggression can be justified on reductivist grounds, this is likely to be fewer than has been commonly thought. This is a more permissive view of defensive war than the sceptic alleges reductivism must take, but far less permissive than admitted by common-sense morality and international law. Thus, significant ground has been ceded to the sceptic. Arguably, this limited victory should be regarded as salutary, given how often wars against lesser aggression have been thoughtlessly romanticized and celebrated.

Should we also conclude that reductivism must be abandoned as too restrictive? As observed earlier, the answer depends on our prior substantive views about the permissibility of such wars and the strength of our conviction that the principles of interpersonal morality are the proper basis for an ethics of war. If one is convinced that many wars against lesser aggression are morally justified, then one has reason for abandoning reductivism as the sole approach to justifying war. As noted in Section 4, there are a number of exceptionalist moral arguments in favour of a legal right of national defence. In some cases, these justifications reinforce the reductivist case for resisting lesser aggression by military force.

This suggests two more general points. First, even if one ultimately rejects the reductivist's view that interpersonal morality is the sole basis for the justification of war, the moral status of the person is such a deep part of moral thinking that it can hardly be eliminated altogether from a satisfactory ethics of war. But, second, this raises the problem of how to integrate reductivist and exceptionalist approaches. We need a foundational moral theory to ground this project. To illustrate, consider rule-utilitarianism. The principle of utility yields one set of rules for permissible killing as a matter of interpersonal morality and another set of rules as a matter of institutional morality, precisely because the consequences in the former case are limited and in the latter more extensive. Rule-utilitarian institutional principles can be understood as exceptionalist in character because, as Lazar argues, they govern 'killing in war, not in ordinary life'.[50] Some forms of rule-utilitarianism focus on individual well-being, however,[51] and it is possible to envision a more radically exceptionalist view holding that states have an impersonal value apart from their value to and for individuals. Although this kind of exceptionalist view might justify a more stringent right of national defence, it would be more difficult to combine with the basic concerns of interpersonal morality.

Solving the problem of combining reductivist and exceptionalist principles in an ethics of war is a formidable task, but the first step is to try in a more explicit and systematic way to develop interpersonal and institutional principles from the same ground. Rule-utilitarianism is merely an example, for there are moderate deontological or pluralist accounts of individual *and* institutional morality as well. A Kantian account of one set of principles for individuals and another for states as moral persons is a possibility. Another is a contractualist account of principles of interpersonal morality, such T. M. Scanlon's, combined with a contractualist account of principles for domestic and international institutions, such as those offered by Rawls or by Yitzhak Benbaji.[52]

These approaches are unified by the same underlying kind of moral theory and thus hold some promise of integrating individual and institutional principles in a coherent way. Of course, this is to take the discussion in a direction that promises to become very complex. Yet it is not clear that debate about the justification of national defence or the controversy over methodological issues can be taken much further in abstraction from more definite commitments to a particular underlying moral theory. In any event, this is one avenue for exploring how a consistent set of principles for individuals and for institutions might be developed. We need to think more carefully about this problem, even if we agree that interpersonal principles should not be regarded as wholly determinative of the morality of war.

Acknowledgements

Special thanks to Jacqueline Colby and Seth Lazar for extensive comments. Thanks also to Helen Frowe, Heather Roff, Paige Digeser, Jason Robles, and David Hendrickson.

Notes

1. For one influential version of the sceptical challenge, see David Rodin, 'The Myth of National Defense', in *The Morality of Defensive War*, edited by Cécile Fabre and Seth Lazar (Oxford: Oxford University Press, 2013), 69–89. For Rodin's distinction between 'vital' and 'nonvital' interests, see 80–81, 110–142.
2. Seth Lazar presents a clear outline and a *reductio* of 'standard' reductivist views, which he associates with nonconsequentialist principles of interpersonal morality. He also criticises 'nonstandard' views, such as rule-consequentialism: see 'National Defence, Self-Defence, and the Problem of Lesser Aggression', in *The Morality of Defensive War*, 17–39.
3. Idem, 26.
4. Idem, 27.
5. Idem, 26.
6. Lazar makes this kind of assumption in an analogous case, discussed idem, 27.

7. For an extended argument that a conditional threat involves a present intention to kill, see John Finnis, Joseph Boyle, and Germain Grisez, *Nuclear Deterrence, Morality and Realism* (Oxford: Oxford University Press, 1987), 81–86.
8. See Gerhard Øverland, 'Conditional Threats', *Journal of Political Philosophy* 7 (2010), 336, 342–343.
9. Cécile Fabre, 'Cosmopolitanism and Wars of Self-Defence', in *The Morality of Defensive War*, 110.
10. As Lazar observes, however, the victim sometimes may not be in a position to respond incrementally: 'National Defence', 31.
11. See Suzanne Uniacke, 'Proportionality and Self-Defense', *Law and Philosophy* 30:3 (2011), 253–272.
12. Fabre, 'Cosmopolitanism', 111, seems to take the extreme view that a conditional lethal threat is sufficient to justify defensive killing.
13. See Shelly Kagan, 'The Additive Fallacy', *Ethics* 99 (1988), 5–31. Thomas Hurka points out that a conditional threat and a threat to a lesser interest may interact by describing this as a 'single' violation: 'Proportionality in the Morality of War', *Philosophy & Public Affairs* 33:1 (2005), 54–55.
14. This adapts Lazar's case in which *A* threatens to kill *B* if she resists his aim of insulting her: 'National Defence', 27.
15. If Betty were able to use nonlethal defence first without significantly increasing her risk at a later stage of the conflict with Alfred, then she would be required to do so, for nonlethal force may turn out to be all that is necessary to make Alfred back down. For connections between necessity and proportionality, see Seth Lazar, 'Necessity in Self-Defense and War', *Philosophy & Public Affairs* 40:1 (2012), 3–44.
16. If justification is 'evidence-relative', then some cases of mistaken self-defence will be justified; if it is 'fact-relative', some will be merely excused. The relative merits of these kinds of justification are too complicated to assess here. For an evidence-relative approach, see Helen Frowe, 'A Practical Account of Self-Defence', *Law and Philosophy* 29:3 (2009), 245–270.
17. Jeff McMahan identifies the first two situations and notes that 'if there is a serious risk that what appears to be lesser aggression is really major aggression in disguise, this is sufficient to make it reasonable for victims to threat the action as a presumptive instance of major aggression': 'What Rights May Be Defended by War?', in *The Morality of Defensive War*, 153.
18. John Locke, *Two Treatises of Government* (Cambridge: Cambridge University Press, 2005), 279–280.
19. Lazar, 'National Defence', 23–24.
20. Idem, 23.
21. This partly addresses Rodin's argument that the special duties of government officials to care for their fellow citizens support not provoking a bloody invasion by resisting lesser aggression: 'The Myth', 83–84. For a critical response, see Helen Frowe, *Defensive Killing: An Essay on War and Self-Defence* (Oxford: Oxford University Press, forthcoming), 208–210. Also see Helen Frowe, 'Can Reductive Individualists Allow Defence against Conditional Force?', in *Oxford Studies in Political Philosophy*, Vol. 1, edited by David Sobel, Peter Vallentyne, and Steven Wall (Oxford: Oxford University Press, 2015), 173–193.
22. Øverland does not distinguish between defensive and conditional threats; presumably he means both.
23. Øverland, 'Conditional Threats', 341.

24. Jeff McMahan, *Killing in War* (Oxford: Oxford University Press, 2009), 182–188.
25. See Seth Lazar, 'The Responsibility Dilemma for *Killing in War*: A Review Essay', *Philosophy & Public Affairs* 38:2 (2010), 189–213.
26. For causal proximity, see David Rodin, 'The Moral Inequality of Soldiers: Why in Bello Asymmetry Is Half Right', in *Just and Unjust Warriors: The Legal and Moral Status of Soldiers*, edited by David Rodin and Henry Shue (Oxford: Oxford University Press, 2008), 52; for causal significance or 'thresholds', see Cécile Fabre, 'Guns, Food and Liability to Defensive Killing in War', *Ethics* 120 (2009), 61.
27. David Rodin, 'Morality and Law in War', in *The Changing Character of War*, edited by Hew Strachan and Sibylle Scheipers (Oxford: Oxford University Press, 2011), 446–465, at 449.
28. McMahan, *Killing in War*, 226.
29. Frowe, *Defensive Killing*, 243–280, criticises several attempts to explain why noncombatants are not liable to defensive harm. Also see Helen Frowe, 'Non-Combatant Liability in War', in *How We Fight: Ethics in War*, edited by Helen Frowe and Gerald Lang (Oxford: Oxford University Press), 172–188.
30. See Seth Lazar, 'Complicity, Collectives, and Killing in War', under review.
31. See Jeff McMahan's response to his critics in 'Who Is Morally Liable to be Harmed?', *Analysis Review* 71:3 (2010), 544–559.
32. Thomas Hurka, "Liability and Just Cause, *Ethics and International Affairs* 21:2 (2007), 199–218.
33. Lazar, 'National Defence', 33.
34. Finnis et al., *Nuclear Deterrence*, 263–267.
35. Michael Walzer, 'Preface', *Just and Unjust Wars*, 2nd ed. (New York: Basic Books, 1992), xvi–xvii.
36. Although Lazar, 'National Defence', 35–38, notes some difficulties with the idea that a state could have an 'impersonal' value not reducible to its contributions to individual well-being.
37. David Rodin, *War and Self-Defense* (Oxford: Oxford University Press, 2002), 148.
38. For this kind of communitarian claim, see Michael Walzer, *Spheres of Justice* (New York: Basic Books, 1984); also see Patrick Emerton and Toby Handfield, 'Understanding the Political Privilege', in *The Morality of Defensive War*, 72–73.
39. For the classical republican view of 'public freedom', see Richard Dagger, *Civic Virtues: Rights, Citizenship, and Liberal Republicanism* (Oxford: Oxford University Press, 1997); for 'communal autonomy', see Michael Walzer, *Just and Unjust Wars* (New York: Basic Books, 1972), 86–91; for 'collective authorship' see Anna Stilz, 'Territorial Rights and National Defence', in *The Morality of Defensive War*, 218–224.
40. For a clear statement of this view, see Christopher Kutz, 'Democracy, Defence and the Threat of Intervention', in *The Morality of Defensive War*, 231.
41. Peter Jones, 'Group Rights and Group Oppression', *Journal of Political Philosophy* 7:4 (1999), 353–377; see also Michael Sandel, *Liberalism and the Limits of Justice* (Cambridge: Cambridge University Press, 1982), 183.
42. Allen Buchanan, *Justice, Legitimacy and Self-Determination: Moral Foundations for International Law* (Oxford: Oxford University Press, 2003); see 18–29 for institutional reasoning.
43. Margaret Moore, 'Collective Self-Determination, Institutions of Justice, and Wars of National Defense', in *The Morality of Defensive War*, 198.
44. Rodin, 'Myth', 86–87.

45. Idem, 139.
46. Moore, 'Collective Self-Determination', 195–198.
47. See Heather M. Roff, *Global Justice, Kant and the Responsibility to Protect* (London: Routledge, 2013), 16–31.
48. Buchanan, *Justice, Legitimacy*, 462.
49. See David R. Mapel, 'The Right of National Defense', *International Studies Perspectives* 8 (2007), 1–15.
50. Lazar, 'National Defence', 34–35.
51. More precisely, some utilitarian accounts are focussed on individual well-being, others on 'states of affairs'. See Will Kymlicka, *Contemporary Political Philosophy: An Introduction* (Oxford: Oxford University Press, 1990), 31–35.
52. See T. M. Scanlon, *What We Owe to Each Other* (Cambridge, MA: Harvard University Press, 1998); John Rawls, *The Law of Peoples* (Cambridge, MA: Harvard University Press, 1999); Yitzhak Benbaji, 'A Defense of the Traditional War Convention', *Ethics* 118:3 (2008), 464–495; Yitzhak Benbaji, 'Distributive Justice, Human Rights, and Territorial Integrity: A Contractarian Account of the Crime of Aggression', in *The Morality of Defensive War*, 159–184.

CHAPTER 11

HUMANITARIAN INTERVENTION AND THE MODERN STATE SYSTEM

PATRICK EMERTON AND TOBY HANDFIELD

1. Introduction

Humanitarian intervention is conventionally defined as the use of military force against a state with the principal aim of ending wrongdoing that is occurring within the state and is being perpetrated either by or with the compliance of the government of the state. The use of force in this way is importantly different from the traditional justification for the use of military force, which is defence of a state against external aggression. The central ethical question with respect to humanitarian intervention is: is it morally permissible?

If we start from the premise that violence in defence of others is sometimes morally permissible, it is very plausible that humanitarian intervention will sometimes be morally permissible. Much analysis of humanitarian intervention frames the moral question in more or less this fashion, bringing to bear various considerations that would tell for or against the use of defensive violence in a range of cases.

Although this analogy has obvious heuristic value, when examined closely, it is far from obvious that it can be reliably invoked to understand the full complexity of humanitarian intervention. In order to demonstrate this, consider first how we might go about elaborating a theory of individual defensive violence. We might begin with two postulates.

1. Normally, individuals possess rights not to be harmed by other individuals.
2. If Aggressor is culpably involved in a threat to harm Victim, and it is necessary for preventing harm to Victim to use violence against Aggressor, then Aggressor forfeits some of those normal rights not to be harmed by other individuals.

A corollary of the forfeiture described in 2 is that potential defenders of Victim are no longer under a duty not to harm Aggressor. That is, they obtain *privileges* to use violence against Aggressor. A further postulate, however, will be needed to establish the extent of the rights forfeited in such circumstances and hence the extent of the privileges to use defensive violence. May we cut off Aggressor's leg to save Victim from a moderately forceful punch? Probably not. May we kick Aggressor in the shins to avert the same harm? Probably yes.

Nor do these postulates resolve exactly *who* possesses these defensive privileges. One, very permissive, possibility is that all individuals acquire the same privileges. Another possibility is that Victim acquires more extensive privileges to engage in defensive violence than do bystanders who have less at stake in the threat situation. We need not resolve this matter for present purposes, and we simply note that a more adequate version of 2 would need to make this explicit.

With this minimal sketch of what an adequate theory of individual defensive violence would be like, we can suggest an analogous schema for humanitarian intervention.

Hypothesis 1 (H1) Normally, states possess rights not to be subject to military interference by other states.

Hypothesis 2 (H2) If a Perpetrator state is culpably involved in a threat to harm its Residents and it is necessary, for the prevention of harm to them, to use military force against the Perpetrator state, then that state forfeits some of its normal rights not to be subject to military interference by other states.

It is evident that the new schema is not analogous to the individualistic schema in a number of crucial ways. First, in the individual case, Aggressor and Victim are distinct entities of the same type: individuals. And, in standard cases, Aggressor and Victim stand in no relationship of partial constitution. In the case of humanitarian intervention, however, the Perpetrator state is arguably constituted, at least in part, by its Residents. This relationship may give rise to novel phenomena that were absent in the individual case. (We talk of *residents* rather than *citizens* because, in at least some cases where humanitarian intervention looks prima facie permissible, part of the harm that is being inflicted may take the form of denials of citizenship or of the benefits of citizenship; for instance, if certain residents are being enslaved or otherwise subjected to vicious discrimination.[1])

Second (generalizing from the first point), in the case of individual violence, the only moral agents we needed to mention in the schema were individuals. No moral standing was imputed to collectives. In our schema for humanitarian intervention, however, we have had to make reference to states, to residents, and (indirectly) to military forces. Arguably, the particular entities we chose to mention in our schema are not compulsory. Perhaps a better schema would refer to less structured collectives, such as generic groups. Or perhaps we should use Rawls's notion of a people rather than a state.[2] But whatever the nature of the agents we finally settle on, it is highly implausible that a satisfactory account could be given by mentioning individuals alone.

Third, in the individualistic schema, it is the very same agent, Aggressor, who is both culpable for the threat to Victim and is the legitimate target of defensive violence. In the case of humanitarian intervention, however, the typical target of military force used against Perpetrator will be soldiers serving in the military of that state. And it will frequently be the case that these soldiers were not involved in nor complicit in the wrongs which have given rise to the intervention. The wrongs might have been perpetrated by secret police, death squads, intelligence agencies, or simply by different branches of the military from those who are likely to be involved in defensive action against any intervention. There may be some exceptions to this. For instance, we can imagine a case of a humanitarian intervention to prevent a massacre being perpetrated by a group of soldiers, where it is precisely those soldiers who are the targets of the intervention, but these sorts of cases are unlikely to be typical. From the point of view of the intervening military, a war of humanitarian intervention will tend to resemble an aggressive war, the aim of which is to neutralize the armed forces of the enemy state so as to exercise power over its government. (In some cases, atrocities will be perpetrated by non-state actors, but this raises no special problems: either the state within which the atrocities are taking place permits intervention, in which case the scenario is closer to policing than warfare; or, the state does not permit intervention, in which case it is protecting the atrocities and hence itself becomes the target of intervention.)

Fourth, if bystanders help to defend Victim against Aggressor, they do so voluntarily, at least in the typical case. They are able to assess the gravity of Aggressor's threat and to act on their own assessments of the risks incurred by intervening. If a state intervenes against Perpetrator, however, it does so by means of distinct individuals, the intervening soldiers, who typically will have no choice in the matter, and are coercively exposed to the risk of being killed or seriously injured in warfare.

Given these significant disanalogies, one way to defend H1 and H2 may be to embrace anti-individualism in methodological and normative assumptions. Perhaps the most prominent recent example of such an approach to just war theory is provided by Michael Walzer, who explicitly invokes a value of community that is in some important way not reducible to the value of its individual members.[3] Many theorists, however, persist in attempting to understand humanitarian intervention via an individualistic analysis; we are among them. In this chapter, we cannot give anything like an adequate defence of this methodological orientation, and we simply note it as an assumption.

The typical way of pursuing an individualistic understanding of the ethics of humanitarian intervention is to undertake more detailed analyses of individualistic defensive violence, especially with respect to the permissibility of the use of violence against those *complicit* in the perpetration of wrongful harm; to analyze a range of military structures to establish the degree of complicity between soldiers and other agents of the governments they serve and, on this basis, to develop a theory of the permissibility of humanitarian intervention.[4] But we think that this approach faces serious difficulties as a justification of humanitarian intervention. Furthermore, we think that the cosmopolitan tendencies of its practitioners have tended to obscure further objections to the permissibility of intervention that are consequent on the disanalogies described earlier.

This essay will (1) bring out these objections, (2) go on to explain the aforementioned difficulties, and (3) then develop a more institutionally grounded account of the appropriate norms to govern humanitarian intervention.

2. Humanitarian Intervention and the Value of Sovereignty

The contemporary problem of humanitarian intervention is intimately connected to the modern international state system, which is grounded in the existence of (at least notionally) sovereign states. These states enjoy overwhelming legal and often factual authority in respect of their populations. They also enjoy legal immunity from outside incursion because the Charter of the United Nations forbids one state to use or threaten force against another except in self-defence.[5] This immunity is typically backed up by strong national military forces. This situation permits extremely powerful agents (states) to inflict gross harm on a large number of people (their residents). Although there are other very powerful agents (other states) with seeming capacity to stop such harm (namely, their own national military forces), the nature of the system creates a serious practical impediment to doing that because this power is territorially concentrated outside of the oppressing state.

The current international legal situation also gives rise to another problem about humanitarian intervention, namely, that it is typically unlawful: as noted earlier, the international use of force is generally unlawful, although an exception applies to intervention mandated by a resolution by the UN Security Council as necessary for international peace and security.[6] Because unilateral interventions are internationally unlawful and are carried out only selectively (typically, when in the national interest of intervening parties[7]), doubt as to the proper intentions of the intervening party is ubiquitous.[8] In this chapter, however, we will set aside these worries about illegality and focus primarily on the underlying moral issues.[9]

Many theorists of humanitarian intervention focus on sovereignty as a problem for morality because of its capacity to serve both as a license for wrongdoing and a shield against justified intervention. Less attention has been paid to the *value* of sovereignty. We concur with typical liberal thinkers that sovereignty does not possess intrinsic value, but, because of the intimate relation between a sovereign state and the interests of its citizens, there is a strong prima facie case against any incursion against sovereignty.[10]

Sovereignty is most obviously valuable because a state that has some immunity from outside interference will often be better placed to serve the interests of its resident population. A sovereign state can make plans for the allocation and exploitation of resources, can raise revenue by taxation and similar measures, and can regulate and coordinate economic behaviour to maximize well-being. All these activities can, in felicitous cases, promote the flourishing of the state's population. A war-torn state is at an enormous disadvantage in pursuing these ends and thus is much less well-placed to serve the interests of its population.

The less obvious value of sovereignty, however, is its protection of communal forms of life that play a crucial role in constituting, not just in satisfying, the interests of individual members of the population. To see how this is so, consider some of the interests that are promoted or protected in international human rights law—health (including public health), education, and certain types of labour conditions—and their (partial) constitution by certain features of social and economic organization. While it seems true that all humans have an interest in health,[11] once we consider more detailed and particular interests that issue from this general interest, certain aspects of them seem to depend on local circumstances. For instance, in a society with no mechanized industry, the interest in the existence of a robust occupational health and safety regime may be low;[12] in a society with no specialized medical professionals, there may be no distinct interest in the provision of medical services in the event of sickness[13]; and in a society in which there is no separation of domestic and other productive activities, although there would, of course, be interests in the healthy development of children, there may be less—even no—interest in making this a distinctive object of policy and social action.[14] Education is similar in this respect. In a society in which all business is transacted orally, for instance, and in which the material technology for making and preserving written records does not exist, the interest in literacy may be minimal,[15] whereas the interest in, say, learning techniques of memorization may be very great. Likewise for labour conditions: free choice of occupation,[16] for example, and the formation of trade unions[17] are far more significant matters for workers in liberal market economies than for workers in subsistence economies with little or no differentiation among productive roles.[18]

A sceptic may object that there is no genuine constitution of interests occurring in these examples. Rather, there is an invariant interest in flourishing, or in well-being, or some other suitably vague and abstract notion, and the varying material circumstances of modern economies are what give rise to contingent, particular, derivative interests in educational opportunities, access to medical care, labour protections, and the like. There are three considerations in favour of preferring to take the more concrete interests as basic, despite thereby admitting that these interests will not be held universally across all human societies. First, it is always possible to posit some suitably catch-all interests that are thought to underlie any number of international agreements or human rights documents. This threatens to trivialize the claim that the legal institutions in question serve vital interests. By allowing that the interests in question are relatively transparent in our human rights institutions, we are committing to claims that are much more readily challenged. We take this to be a beneficial counterpoint to the tendency of some theoretical discussions of human rights to produce bland motherhood statements. A second methodological benefit is that our proposal yields a simpler explanation of what is occurring when human rights claims are employed. Someone who complains that an injustice is occurring because a human right has been violated is saying something that can be simply and straightforwardly interpreted, on our view, in terms of the violation of interests.

This is a simpler interpretive hypothesis than couching human rights claims as merely instrumental and is therefore prima facie preferable. Finally, this tighter degree of fit between the interests we describe and the practices of international legal and political institutions promises to make the theory of human rights more relevant to empirical inquiry. It increases our confidence that we are theorizing actual international relations rather than a nonexistent liberal utopia.

We have talked in the previous paragraph of *societies*, but in the contemporary international environment, societies that are not located within states do not have any secure or stable existence. The facts of pre-twentieth century colonialism are testament to this. It is state sovereignty that permits societies to endure and develop in accordance with their own social and economic practices. These practices give rise both to certain of those residents' interests and to the means to satisfy those interests. The state serves as a 'shield' of these practices against disruptive external forces. The state thereby contributes both to the constitution of these interests and to their satisfaction.

That is not to say that all societies are perfect or that any is. Some practices thwart rather than satisfy interests, and many societies contain multiple cultures with different, perhaps conflicting, practices that can lead to discrimination and oppression. Arguably, once the state emerges as an institutional structure somewhat autonomous from the society within it, the risk of such things happening increases.[19] Nor is it to say that societies—and the interests that they help to constitute—should never change. Social change is endemic to human life. But periods of rapid transformation can be bad for the satisfaction of interests. This can be because interests endure but the means of securing them are lost due to social change, or because new interests arise but without the means of securing them arising also. An example of the first possibility is the enclosure of rural land happening faster than the creation of urban jobs and infrastructure, as in early industrial England or the contemporary developing world, meaning that people have an interest in material well-being but inadequate capacity to satisfy it. An example of the second is factory labour becoming widespread, but legal regimes ensuring occupational health and safety not having yet been developed.

The history of rapid social transformation therefore suggests that it should be regarded with due caution. Sovereignty plays a key role in this respect because it establishes a boundary between a society and exogenous forces that may engender rapid transformation. Even quite 'bad' states, such as the Soviet Union, can still ensure the satisfaction of interests, in part because of their exercise of these sorts of monopoly powers. Intervention, on the other hand, even when undertaken with humanitarian ends, is apt to bring about rapid and dramatic transformations in the most chaotic way (as seen, e.g., in Afghanistan since 2001 and Iraq since 2003), and this particular consequence almost always will count as a defeasible reason against it.[20]

Moreover, because sovereignty does not merely enable societies to meet individual interests but also plays a partially constitutive role in forming those interests, the value of sovereignty is not readily reducible to or comparable with other goods. This observation supports the following claims about the ethics of humanitarian intervention.

1. Humanitarian interventions that succeed in stopping egregious evils sometimes result in a state of affairs incommensurate in value with the original state of affairs.
2. Because of 1, there is reason to be relatively reluctant to undertake humanitarian intervention, even when one can be confident that egregious evils will thereby be stopped.
3. Also because of 1, there is reason to be relatively reluctant to 'undo' the effects of a humanitarian intervention, even if the intervention did not bring about a strictly better state of affairs.

To elaborate: sometimes, even a 'successful' humanitarian intervention does not bring about an outcome that is, all things considered, better than the preceding situation, but instead brings about a state of affairs that is incommensurate with that preceding it. This occurs for at least two reasons: first, humanitarian intervention is likely to involve a number of very great evils, such as unjust deaths both of combatants and noncombatants. Although a successful intervention is presumably one that has averted egregious evils—and that is naturally a very great good—the way in which we value human life does not lend itself to readily trading off unjust deaths as an appropriate price for the success of the intervention. Consequently, we can expect a degree of imprecision or vagueness in the sorts of evaluative claims that can be sustained. Although there might be some interventions that lead to strictly better or strictly worse outcomes, there will be an uncomfortably large area that is extremely difficult to classify in this fashion. For these cases, it is helpful to use the term 'incommensurate' to describe the absence of any ordinary evaluative relation.[21]

A second reason for incommensurability is the account of interests that we developed earlier. If a successful humanitarian intervention changes the socioeconomic circumstances in such a radical fashion that the individual interests of citizens are themselves very different after the intervention, then it is doubtful that there is any common currency in which the pre- and post-intervention scenarios can be meaningfully compared.

This incommensurability tells against humanitarian intervention for two reasons. First, it makes it hard to be confident that a proposed intervention will actually make things better, all things considered. Second, even if it is suggested that intervention will not make things worse, when incommensurable values are in play, there are reasons not to change the situation unless we are confident that the change will lead to a strictly better outcome. This is because the maxim, 'Don't make things worse', applied to incommensurate options, can lead to a series of choices for which the endpoint is unequivocally worse than the starting point.

To see this, consider the following simplified picture of two alternatives, which we treat as an incommensurable pair:

(I) Afghanistan pre-intervention: massive oppression of women and other human rights abuses; limited warfare.

(II) Afghanistan today: legal emancipation of women with limited practical realization, particularly in areas outside the government's control; widespread and ongoing warfare.

Now consider two alternative histories of Afghanistan. In the first history, Afghanistan never departs from alternative (I). The second history, however, is more complex. The *original situation* is alternative (I). Then another state intervenes, bringing about alternative (II) as a *new situation*. Finally, the intervening state reneges on its original intervention and brings about a state of affairs as similar as possible to the original situation, which we call the *reverted situation*. However, in bringing about the reverted situation, the intervening state inevitably incurs, and inflicts upon others, a huge array of transaction costs.

This sequence of decisions ends in an outcome that is, ex hypothesi, worse than if the intervening agent had done nothing. But note that the sequence of decisions is supported by a principle that permits choosing an option which is no worse.[22] We take this result to support our relatively conservative attitude towards humanitarian intervention.

This account of the value of sovereignty and its implications for humanitarian intervention confirms that determining the permissibility of humanitarian intervention is not merely a large-scale question about the use of force in defence of others. The role of states in international life makes a real difference. Moreover, this difference does not result from a romantic elevation of national life to some exalted status that justifies individual suffering.[23] It is, rather, the recognition—within a framework of individualism about value—that the intimate relation between sovereignty and the socioeconomic circumstances in which people live and flourish makes our choice to intervene even more weighty than a 'mere' decision whether to risk some lives in order to save others.

3. The Moral Calculus of Justifying Violence Against Soldiers

A further difficulty for humanitarian intervention, noted earlier, is that intervention typically requires attacking the soldiers of a state in order to prevent *other* agents from perpetrating egregious harms on residents. The nexus between the soldiers and the perpetrators is the state. Affirming the normative significance of that nexus in some fashion seems to be a necessary condition of the soldiers being legitimate targets.

Many arguments in favour of the permissibility of humanitarian intervention argue for such a nexus via responsibility or support, such that the soldiers defending the state against intervention thereby become complicit in the state's wrongdoing.[24] However, as a criterion for liability, this has troubling implications. We take it as a datum that civilian noncombatants in the target state are not legitimate targets of violence by intervening forces, even if they enthusiastically support the evils being carried out by the regime.[25]

Given this, any criterion of complicity cannot be grounded in mere psychological factors of support.

It might seem that the soldiers of the perpetrating state become liable to attack because they have a distinct causal connection to wrongdoing within the context of the intervention, namely, defending its perpetrators against the intervention that would stop it. But this ignores the disanalogies to the individual case noted in the introduction. Military intervention, even in a humanitarian cause, means attacking, neutralizing, and at least temporarily replacing the government of a state. The targets of that military force are therefore not readily comparable to the accomplices of an assailant who shield him from third-party defenders. In many cases, we can expect that their principal motivation will be one of national defence.[26] Hence they will not be culpable, or at least not obviously so, and hence will not have forfeited their right to life.[27] A principle of strict liability to be killed in these circumstances seems too permissive, at least when invoked to enable the defence of others.

An adequate principle of liability to attack must therefore address the value of sovereignty and the way in which it may or may not support the permissibility of violence in pursuit of national defence. We suggest the following:

> A soldier who commits acts of violence in defence of a state whose sovereignty is impugned by serious wrongdoing is committing impermissible acts of violence and hence is liable to defensive violence from the intervening soldiers.[28]

The role in this principle of 'impugned sovereignty' is consistent with our observation that the permissibility of humanitarian intervention cannot be explained without reference to the moral standing of collectives.

A principle of this sort will also give rise to an additional permission to attack the defending soldiers, namely, anticipatory self-defence on the part of the intervening soldiers. These soldiers know that, were they to attempt to peacefully enter the state and take control of its buildings, imprison its leaders, and so on (which they are entitled to do, the state's sovereignty being impugned), they would be subjected to impermissible violence by the defending soldiers. Hence, they enjoy some degree of privilege to *initiate* defensive violence against those defending soldiers.[29]

Given our account of the value of sovereignty, it seems to follow that the threshold for the impugning of sovereignty, and hence the permissibility of intervention, is quite high. Recall that, in humanitarian intervention, what is at stake is not solely the prevention of egregious harms but also the continuing existence of the institutions of the defending state. As we saw in the previous section, those institutions are essential to both the constitution and the satisfaction of the interests of those resident within it. History shows the consequences of the undoing of a state, and of the resulting social disruption, can be devastating for thousands and even millions of people.

The fact that humanitarian intervention targets not just perpetrators of atrocities but the institutions of the perpetrator state gives rise to a further reason against its permissibility. At least in many foreseeable cases, humanitarian intervention will have disproportionate consequences. Consider: the result of successful intervention is likely to be a radical reconstruction of the defeated state. This is shown by a number of historical examples: to the extent that the American Civil War had some characteristics of humanitarian intervention, it led to the (at least partial) reconstruction of the South; the wars in nineteenth- and early twentieth-century Europe that led to the secession of various Balkan states from the Turkish Empire had some characteristics of humanitarian intervention, and they dramatically changed both the territory and the geopolitical situation of Turkey; in the twentieth century, there is the secession of Bangladesh from Pakistan and the transformation of Cambodia into a Vietnamese client state; in our own century, we have experienced the radical reconstructions of Iraq and (if it can be classified as an intervention to defend the human rights of women and of minorities) of Afghanistan. Hence, so long as the state retains control over its military, it has little reason to order them to stop fighting. History further suggests that persuading the military to defect from the state that it is defending will also require infliction of a severe degree of harm (e.g., the German military defected only in the dying days of the European theatre of World War II). Hence, even if the targeted soldiers are themselves legitimate targets of defensive violence, extreme escalation of violence by both sides is highly likely and readily foreseeable, such that even very great wrongdoing on the part of the defending state may not warrant the killing that will result.

We do not offer any formula to resolve this balancing of interests, but we note that it pushes us towards a lesser evil account of humanitarian intervention, in which to launch the intervention is to knowingly set out on a path that, even if it begins with morally permissible violence, may ultimately have wrongdoing at its end and which, in bringing an end to the state's wrongdoing, may well disrupt the social and political structures upon which both the constitution and the satisfaction of the interests of many people are dependent. This dilemma is confronted not only by the political leaders of the intervening state, but also by its military leaders and by individual intervening soldiers.

A distinct question regarding the intervening soldiers is: how is it they are obliged to take part in military intervention at all, thereby risking their own lives?[30] An ordinary story of duties of national/collective self-defence is not available.[31] Buchanan appeals to a natural duty of justice 'to contribute to the inclusion of all persons in just arrangements' provided that 'this can be done with little cost to ourselves'.[32] On its own, this does not seem strong enough, however: the cost to an individual soldier facing the threat of death at the hands of defending soldiers is not a small one, and an argument that the soldier agreed to shoulder a concentrated burden of what is communally a small cost for the society of the intervening state seems to presuppose what is at issue, namely, that military structures can impose duties on soldiers that go beyond the requirements of national self-defence. McMahan discusses the situation of soldiers called upon to fight a war of humanitarian intervention but does not consider how it is that they become particularly obliged to confront the risks of such fighting.[33] (McMahan, indeed, ends his chapter with a paean to the merits of disobedience by soldiers.)

Contemporary US practice in relation to both humanitarian intervention and (ostensible) defensive warfare suggests one way of resolving the problem about the duties of the intervening soldiers: namely, ultra-mechanized warfare (e.g., high-altitude bombing during the Kosovo intervention; the use of drones in Afghanistan, Pakistan, and the Arabian Peninsula). Furthermore, at least where used against technologically less capable states, this mode of warfare does not risk the escalation of defensive violence beyond permissible levels, and, when used directly against the perpetrators of wrongdoing (which is perhaps more viable in the case of drones than of high-altitude bombing), it can be justified simply on the basis of the defence of others. But it does not lessen the consequences of undermining sovereignty. Indeed, it has the potential to exacerbate those consequences, both by making interventions likely where before they were not and because its viability as a distinctive mode of warfare turns upon a dramatic imbalance of technological and military power within the international state system.

4. Internationalizing Intervention

We have identified three difficulties regarding humanitarian intervention: the probability that a successful intervention will not lead to an unequivocally better state of affairs, given the interdependence of the value of sovereignty and individual well-being; the likely wrongdoing involved in the killing of defending soldiers that will almost certainly be part of any effective and successful humanitarian intervention; and the imposition of the risk of violence and death upon the intervening soldiers. Despite all this, in the face of atrocities such as those witnessed in Rwanda in 1994, it remains extremely hard to accept that intervention would have been unjustified. Is there an approach to humanitarian intervention that can better resolve this tension? Although it would be overoptimistic to think that these issues can be completely resolved, we do think that alternative institutional arrangements may be able to lessen the severity with which they arise. We suggest that the most promising avenues of reform will involve an institutional structure that changes the connections between interests and states, and between states and the rights and duties of soldiers.[34]

Our core suggestion is very natural and has been advanced on a number of occasions in the past: the moral problems associated with humanitarian intervention would be much less pressing if there were a properly constituted international military force empowered to carry out interventions if and when necessary. Most defences of this idea are largely prudential: such a force would be more likely to respond with the rapidity required for effective intervention and could be freed of constraints currently imposed on UN peacekeeping operations, for instance.[35] Although these factors, if true, may indeed be reasons to favour an international force, they are not the most ethically significant reasons. We suggest that the creation of such an international military force would have the potential to ameliorate the foundational issues we have identified, provided that it took the right sort of institutional form.

4.1. Reducing the Threat to Social Structures

An internationalized military force would not be an agent of a single political community. In favourable circumstances, therefore, such a force could substantially reduce the risk that intervention will disrupt the social structures that serve and constitute individual interests. This is for two reasons.

First, an intervening force that does not have a national culture of its own can be expected to do less violence to the social structures of the society in which it intervenes. Ideally, a genuinely internationalized military force would be continuous with and expressive of the social structures within those societies that contribute to it. This continuity would be achieved in a reciprocal fashion: the social structures of contributing societies would shape the character of international institutions; at the same time, participation in those international institutions would shape the institutions within individual societies. The existence of an international force would, in this way, 'globalize' the participating states. This is a demanding conception of internationalization because it goes well beyond the establishment of international agreements or mere accommodations among national elites. The postwar history of Europe can be seen as a partial illustration of the model we have in mind. The endurance of peace between and comparative harmony among the major European powers provides some evidence that international institutions, created originally by elites, can become continuous with the underlying social structures of those societies.

Second, any intervention carried out by a genuinely internationalized force would less readily be perceived both by those who are undertaking it and by those who are subject to it as an attempt to impose an alien social structure on the society that is the target of intervention. A foreign military force cannot aspire to this, no matter how well-intentioned it might be, because of its location within the domestic social and political structure of another country and the necessarily parochial outlook and commitments that flow from this. Perceptions of this sort are hardly determinative of social reality, but they are not irrelevant to it because they inform the human behaviours that constitute that reality.[36] If mutual perceptions of this sort lead the social actors to behave in ways that presuppose the continuation of existing social structures, then those social structures will be more likely to survive the inevitable disruptions that will result from an intervention.

This is, in part, a 'policing' model of humanitarian intervention,[37] but this characterization must be used with care. The idea of policing is closely connected to the idea of law enforcement, but law enforcement is not central to our proposal, which retains defence of others as the underlying moral foundation for humanitarian intervention. Although it is likely that establishing an international military force to undertake humanitarian intervention would also involve establishing international legal principles authorizing and regulating intervention,[38] these would be declaratory of underlying moral principles and would not constitute novel permissions for action. In contrast, police typically enjoy wider ranging powers to exercise force than do the military: force can be used to execute a search, to repossess property, to arrest for questioning, and so on. All of these occasions go beyond the privilege of self-defence or defence of others, which arises only where there is an opportunity to avert imminent harm.

Nevertheless, the internal norms of an international military force of the sort we propose might be better characterized as policing norms than military ones. Although police enjoy wide-ranging powers to exercise force, they are much more constrained in the level of force they can use and the objectives they can aim at. For instance, when a police officer forcibly enters a home to prevent an occurrence of domestic violence, the officer can certainly arrest the perpetrator, but she cannot take up residence! We suggest that these norms, which implicitly constrain the sorts of outcomes police may legitimately pursue, play a critical role in justifying the authority of the police to use force on such a wide range of occasions. If the citizenry were less confident in police adherence to such norms, then there would be much stronger grounds for disobedience of police orders. These *limiting* norms seem highly applicable to an international intervention force.[39] First, soldiers notoriously behave extremely badly when in foreign territory. Rape and looting are ubiquitous features of military conflict. It may not be feasible to eradicate these behaviours, even in an internationalized force, given the particularly chaotic environment in which military operations typically occur, but, to the extent that it is possible, establishing very strong norms of this sort will be central to building confidence that interventions are military actions of a different character from aggression.[40] Second, as we pointed out earlier, the history of intervention has shown that it almost always results in the radical change of the governmental structure of a society, often in ways that involve the ongoing exercise of power and influence by the intervening party. In anticipation of such an outcome to intervention, there is a greater case for legitimate resistance. A properly constituted international force, however, should be a force that is understood on all sides to be limited in its ambitions. Like the police officer, it will enter the territory to try to stop violence, but it will not seek any ongoing control, nor will it seek to appropriate property.

4.2. Justifying the Liability of Soldiers to Harm

Creating a multinational force of the sort we have described promises to better resolve the problems concerning the liability to harm suffered by individual soldiers, in at least three ways:

1. *Defusing the justification for defence against intervention.* The adherence of an intervention force to limiting norms will reduce the tendency of intervention to escalate in violence. Consider a soldier, conscripted for the purposes of national defence. The soldier's government, which is somewhat despotic and engaged in serious wrongdoing against its opponents, orders that the military defends the national territory against an intervening force. Even in cases where the humanitarian crimes that trigger the intervention are egregious and known to be so, the intentions of a unilateral

intervening force are of doubtful legitimacy and can often reasonably be perceived as aggression. Consequently, there is an enormous burden on a soldier to make the appropriate judgment whether or not to support the defensive effort or to refuse orders and surrender. If it is known, however, that an intervening force subscribes to the limiting norms described earlier, then the decision for our hypothetical soldier becomes a much easier one. Because, as suggested earlier, an internationalized military would ideally be one with stronger norms that constrain behaviour so as to limit the degree of control and influence the interveners will attempt to exert, it becomes far more difficult for that soldier to accept any rationale provided by a criminal government that an act of aggression is under way. And, knowing this, the intervening force can itself plan on facing lower levels of military resistance and hence itself deploy military techniques less likely to prove disruptive to fundamental social structures. That is, there is hope that a virtuous circle of de-escalation might operate, rather than the vicious circle of escalation described earlier.

2. *Improving the justification for anticipatory self-defence by intervening forces.* As argued earlier, the permissibility of harming defending soldiers in the course of undertaking humanitarian intervention depends in part on the exercise of privileges of anticipatory self-defence. There is, therefore, the risk that escalation of violence will be so great that commencing the intervention may be impermissible. As we have just seen, however, an internationalized intervention force is less likely to lead to escalating violence via intervention. The degree of permissibility of the exercise of anticipatory self-defence by the soldiers in the intervening force is, therefore, correspondingly greater.

3. *Strengthening the justification for participation in an intervening force.* An internationalized military will be one that is purpose-built for humanitarian intervention. Individual soldiers who volunteer to serve in it, therefore, have no grounds to complain that they should not be liable to face lethal risks in carrying out intervention. Indeed, a former UN peacekeeper has written that 'modern military personnel', who are primarily volunteer professionals, 'view the task of protecting people or even saving lives as an honourable one' and suggests that UN peacekeeping could be strengthened by building on this fact.[41] Would it be permissible to conscript soldiers to such a force? We do not take a side on that question, which depends on the moral weight one gives to the pursuit of non-national humanitarian purposes.

5. Prospects

What are the prospects for an international humanitarian intervention force of the sort we have described? UN peacekeepers are subject to limiting norms in respect of the military objectives they can pursue, but also are limited to the use of force in self-defence. They are generally forbidden from using force in defence of others. Articles 43–47 of the UN Charter come closer to our proposal, but to date have not been used.[42] These provide for

> a Military Staff Committee to advise and assist the Security Council on all questions relating to the Security Council's military requirements for the maintenance of international peace and security, the employment and command of forces placed at its disposal, the regulation of armaments, and possible disarmament.[43]

The mentioned forces are to be made available to the UN Security Council by member states and are to include air forces immediately available to undertake urgent action.[44] Member states are obliged to make such forces available but remain entitled to participate in decisions concerning the deployment of their armed forces.[45]

An internationalized intervention force would need to differ from these arrangements in at least two respects. First, its members would have to have as their primary identity their membership in the force, rather than their membership in a national armed force.[46] Second, the UN Charter gives particular international power to the permanent members of the Security Council, who enjoy a power of veto over its decisions relating to international peace and security and hence over its decisions pertaining to intervention.[47] The Charter also provides that the 'Military Staff Committee shall consist of the Chiefs of Staff of the permanent members of the Security Council or their representatives'.[48] This governance structure hinders the development of a fully reciprocal relationship between the international organization and the member communities.[49] However, establishing a governance structure that does not respect current international dispositions of power and thereby leads to a somewhat autonomous international organization would pose its own risks of a domineering world government disconnected from, and attempting mastery over, the societies of its members.[50] It is difficult to predict the consequences of radical change to the UN structure, even if such change could somehow be brought about.

However, the UN Charter also states that the Military Staff Committee 'may establish regional subcommittees'.[51] This provides a possible kernel for institutional developments of the sort we have suggested. In particular, beginning regionally rather than globally makes the prospects for reciprocal integration of an internationalized force with the structures of particular societies more feasible.[52] Although substantial changes in relation to the organizational structure of any international forces, and particularly the manner of their accountability to contributing states, would be necessary before these UN Charter provisions would provide a firm basis for morally permissible intervention, they provide a better starting point than unilateral intervention and allow the possibility of building on existing peacekeeping practices. Supporters of humanitarian intervention therefore have a reason to encourage their governments to try to activate these presently inactive provisions of the UN Charter.

The development of these sorts of arrangements could also contribute to solving other transnational problems where unilateral action, either domestically or by way of intervention, is inadequate. Arguably the most pressing such contemporary challenge is the threat of anthropogenic climate change resulting from the release of carbon dioxide and other greenhouse gases. The interests at stake in this issue are different across different societies, and the sorts of changes to social structures necessary to reduce greenhouse gas emissions are likewise varied. Although some initial steps have been made to reach cooperative agreements on climate change, the temptations of free-riding on these agreements remain enormous and will only become greater if more stringent agreements are negotiated. To make these sorts of agreements effective, some sort of enforcement mechanism will be required, and it is almost impossible to imagine that conventionally constituted military forces will be the appropriate means by which to achieve that enforcement.[53]

Notes

1. Michael Walzer, 'The Moral Standing of States', *Philosophy & Public Affairs* 9 (1980), 217–219.
2. John Rawls, *The Law of Peoples, with 'The Idea of Public Reason Revisited'* (Cambridge, MA: Harvard University Press, 1999).
3. See, e.g., Michael Walzer, *Arguing About War* (New Haven, CT: Yale University Press, 2004), 42.
4. Cf. Jeff McMahan, *Killing in War* (Oxford: Clarendon Press, 2009); Cécile Fabre, *Cosmopolitan War* (Oxford: Oxford University Press, 2012).
5. UN Charter, *signed* 26 June 1945 (entered into force 24 October 1945), Articles 2(4),(7), 51.
6. UN Charter Articles 41, 42; and see Mindia Vashakmadze, 'Responsibility to Protect', in *The Charter of the United Nations: A Commentary*, 3rd ed., edited by Bruno Simma et al. (Oxford: Oxford University Press, 2012).
7. Michael Walzer, *Just and Unjust Wars* (Harmondsworth: Penguin Books, 1977), 101–102.
8. Carl Schmitt, *The Concept of the Political*, translated by George Schwab (Chicago: University of Chicago Press, 2007), 54; Joseph Raz, 'Human Rights Without Foundations', in *The Philosophy of International Law*, edited by John Tasioulas and Samantha Besson (Oxford: Oxford University Press, 2010), 330–331.
9. For discussions of the issue of legality, including the tradeoff between failing to remedy immediate injustice and threatening the long-term stability of the international system, see Helen Frowe, *The Ethics of War and Peace: An Introduction* (London: Routledge, 2011), 86–87; George P. Fletcher and Jens David Ohlin, *Defending Humanity: When Force Is Justified and Why* (Oxford: Oxford University Press, 2008), 133–135.
10. Walzer, 'The Moral Standing of States', expresses support for the value of sovereignty but within a framework of nonindividualist pluralism. For criticism of Walzer's approach, see Patrick Emerton and Toby Handfield, 'Understanding the Political Defensive Privilege', in *The Morality of Defensive War*, edited by Cécile Fabre and Seth Lazar (Oxford: Oxford University Press, 2014). For a variant on Walzer's approach, focussing on political culture as expressive of collective agency, see Christopher Kutz, 'Democracy, Defence and the Threat of Intervention', in *The Morality of Defensive War*, edited by Cécile Fabre and Seth Lazar (Oxford: Oxford University Press, 2014).

11. Allen Buchanan, 'Taking the Human Out of Human Rights', in *Human Rights, Legitimacy, and the Use of Force* (Oxford: Oxford University Press, 2010), 40.
12. Cf. International Covenant on Economic, Social and Cultural Rights, adopted 16 December 1966, G.A. Res. 2200A (XXI), 21 UN GAOR, Supp. No. 16, UN Doc. A/6316 (1966), 993 UNTS. 3 (entered into force 3 January 1976) [hereinafter ICESCR], Article 12(2)(b),(c).
13. Cf. ICESCR, Article 12(2)(d).
14. Cf. ICESCR, Article 12(2)(a).
15. Cf. ICESCR, Article 13(2)(a). The right to receive a primary education has been stated to include literacy as a component: Committee on Economic, Social and Cultural Rights, General Comment 13, 'The right to education' (Twenty-first session, 1999), UN Doc. E/C.12/1999/10 (1999).
16. Cf. ICESCR, Article 6(1).
17. Cf. ICESCR, Article 8(1).
18. For an expression of concern that an unthinkingly universal human rights rhetoric and practice runs the risk of imposing institutions that are purely parochial in their capacity to fulfil human interest, see Charles R. Beitz, *The Idea of Human Rights* (Oxford: Oxford University Press, 2009), 203–205.
19. See, e.g., H. L. A. Hart, *The Concept of Law*, 2nd ed. (Oxford: Clarendon Press, 1994), 117.
20. For a more conventional account of the value of sovereignty as instrumentally valuable merely insofar as it helps the residents of a state secure basic human goods, see Frowe, *The Ethics of War and Peace*, 87.
21. There is some disagreement regarding the preferred use of the word 'incommensurate'. We simply intend it to mean that neither scenario is better than the other, nor are they equally valuable. For discussion, see Nien-he Hsieh, 'Incommensurable Values', in *Stanford Encyclopedia of Philosophy*, edited by Edward N. Zalta (Stanford University, 1997–), http://plato.stanford.edu/entries/value-incommensurable/.
22. Michael Mandler formally proves the way in which a willingness to trade incommensurate goods can lead to a dominated outcome and, further, that status quo preserving decision rules are—at least to some extent—protective against such outcomes: 'Status quo Maintenance Reconsidered: Changing or Incomplete Preferences?', *Economic Journal* 114 (2004); 'Incomplete Preferences and Rational Intransitivity of Choice', *Games and Economic Behaviour* 50 (2005). For other discussions in moral philosophy see, e.g., John Broome, 'Are Intentions Reasons? And How Should We Cope with Incommensurable Values?', in *Practical Rationality and Preference: Essays for David Gauthier*, edited by Christopher W. Morris and Arthur Ripstein (Cambridge: Cambridge University Press, 2007); Toby Handfield, 'Rational Choice and the Transitivity of Betterness', *Philosophy and Phenomenological Research* 89 (2014).
23. Nor is our hesitancy about intervention due to relativism or anti-individualist communitarianism, contra the diagnosis of in-principle objections to a liberal defence of its permissibility advanced by Fernando R. Tesón, 'The Liberal Case for Humanitarian Intervention', in *Humanitarian Intervention: Ethical, Legal and Political Dilemmas*, edited by J. L. Holzgrefe and Robert O. Keohane (Cambridge: Cambridge University Press, 2003), 100–105.
24. Fabre suggests a principle along these lines: *Cosmopolitan War*, 194.
25. Walzer agrees: Michael Walzer, 'Arguing for Humanitarian Intervention', in *The New Killing Fields: Massacre and the Politics of Intervention*, edited by Nicolaus Mills and Kira

Brunner (New York: Basic Books, 2002), 28. For an argument that such civilians sometimes are legitimate targets, see Igor Primoratz, 'Michael Walzer's Just War Theory: Some Issues of Responsibility', *Ethical Theory and Moral Practice* 5 (2002); for a reply that defends civilian immunity from attack, see Robert Sparrow, '"Hands Up Who Wants to Die?": Primoratz on Responsibility and Civilian Immunity in Wartime', *Ethical Theory and Moral Practice* 8 (2005).

26. On the value of national defence, see Emerton and Handfield, 'Understanding the Political Defensive Privilege'.
27. Once the intervention has commenced and war is therefore under way, rights of soldiers on both sides to exercise the defensive privilege against one another may arise by a mechanism that does not rely on culpability: Patrick Emerton and Toby Handfield. 'Order and Affray: Defensive Privileges in Warfare', *Philosophy & Public Affairs*, 37 (2009).
28. McMahan suggests along these lines: *Killing in War*, 148–149.
29. For further discussion on anticipatory defensive violence and the justification of preventive war, see, e.g., Walzer, *Just and Unjust Wars*, ch. 5; David Luban, 'Preventive War', *Philosophy & Public Affairs* 32 (2004).
30. See the discussions in Allen Buchanan, 'The Internal Legitimacy of Humanitarian Intervention', *Journal of Political Philosophy* 7 (1999), McMahan, *Killing in War*, 100; Walzer, *Arguing About War*, 100–101, Tesón, 'The Liberal Case for Humanitarian Intervention', 124–127.
31. For a critical discussion of the duty of soldiers to serve in the interests of national defence, see Cheyney Ryan, 'Democratic Duty and the Moral Dilemmas of Soldiers', *Ethics* 122 (2011).
32. 'The Internal Legitimacy of Humanitarian Intervention', 83.
33. McMahan, *Killing in War*, 100–101.
34. Our methodology here is similar here to Allen Buchanan's, when he writes that 'The proper choice is between adherence to the just war norm and the creation of new institutions that would allow for a more permissive norm. Not just alternative norms but also alternative combinations of norms and institutions need to be evaluated': 'Institutionalizing the Just War', *Philosophy & Public Affairs* 34 (2006), 3.
35. E.g., Henry Shue 'Let Whatever Is Smoldering Erupt? Conditional Sovereignty, Reviewable Intervention, and Rwanda 1994', in *Between Sovereignty and Global Governance: The United Nations, the State and Civil Society*, edited by Albert J. Paolini, Anthony P. Jarvis, and Christian Reus-Smit (Basingstoke: Macmillan, 1998), 66.
36. See the discussion of 'default expectations' in Emerton and Handfield, 'Order and Affray', 394–396.
37. See, e.g., Fabre, *Cosmopolitan War*, 171–176 (who does not use the word 'policing' but describes the victims of oppression as transferring their right of self-help to the interveners). For discussions of law enforcement models of defence against international aggression as alternatives to traditional just war theory, see, e.g., Janna Thompson, 'Terrorism and the Right to Wage War', in *Terrorism and Justice: Moral Argument in a Threatened World*, edited by Tony Coady and Michael O'Keefe (Carlton South: Melbourne University Press, 2002), 95–96; David Rodin, *War and Self-Defense* (Oxford: Clarendon Press, 2002), 179–188.
38. Perhaps developed out of the emerging concept of 'responsibility to protect': see Vashakmadze, 'Responsibility to Protect', 1236.
39. Cf. Shue, 'Let Whatever Is Smoldering Erupt?', 62.

40. For a discussion of the wrongdoings that have been perpetrated by existing UN peacekeepers, see Muna Ndulo, 'The United Nations Responses to the Sexual Abuse and Exploitation of Women and Girls by Peacekeepers During Peacekeeping Missions', *Berkeley Journal of International Law* 27 (2009).
41. Wiebe Arts, 'Preventing Genocide Through Military Intervention: Peacekeeping Troops in the "Responsibility to Protect" Era', in *Confronting Genocide*, edited by René Provost and Payam Akhavan (Dordrecht: Springer, 2011), 126.
42. The Military Staff Committee established under Article 47 has been formally established but 'has had no meaningful role to play in the history of the UN': Brun-Otto Bryde and August Reinisch, 'Articles 44–50', in *The Charter of the United Nations: A Commentary*, 2nd ed., edited by Bruno Simma (Oxford: Oxford University Press, 2002), 770. Caney, in calling for the establishment of a UN volunteer force that would have greater organizational coherence and would be able to respond more quickly than a multinational coalition, does not note these provisions of the Charter that go some way to making such a suggestion feasible: Simon Caney, *Justice Beyond Borders: A Global Political Theory* (Oxford: Oxford University Press, 2005). ch. 7, §6.
43. UN Charter, Article 47(1); see also Article 46.
44. UN Charter, Articles 43, 45.
45. UN Charter, Articles 43, 44.
46. Arts argues for the creation of a UN school to provide peacekeeping personnel with the necessary training: 'Preventing Genocide Through Military Intervention', 124–126, 129. This would be a first step in the direction that we are advocating.
47. Article 27(3) of the UN Charter establishes the veto of the permanent members over non-procedural decisions.
48. UN Charter, Article 47(2).
49. Proponents of intervention (e.g., Caney, *Justice Beyond Borders*, ch. 7, §6) complain that it also generates a strong status quo bias towards nonintervention.
50. Rawls, *Law of Peoples*, 36.
51. UN Charter, Article 47(4).
52. Walzer observes that 'the most successful interventions in the last thirty year have been acts of war by neighboring states': 'Arguing for Humanitarian Intervention', 23.
53. We thank Robert Simpson and the editors for numerous helpful comments on earlier drafts.

CHAPTER 12

TERRITORIAL RIGHTS AND NATIONAL DEFENCE

ANNA STILZ

1. Introduction

Both just war theory and international law recognize national defence as a just cause for war. Though some have argued for extending just war theory to other causes—such as humanitarian intervention or preventive warfare—the defence of one's own state and its territory is usually taken to be the core example of a just cause.[1] Yet just war theorists have done little to explore what might give the state a territorial right of this kind.

We can define a state's territory as that area of the Earth's surface in which it exercises supreme jurisdiction.[2] Territorial integrity is a claim to exercise political power over this area, free from interference by rival power wielders. This is a complex right, one that can be decomposed into three elements:

1. the state's right to exercise political power, by making, enforcing, and applying laws (*Legitimate Jurisdiction*);
2. the state's right to exercise that political power over a particular geographical space (*Territorial Claim*);
3. the state's right to immunity from interference with its rule over that entire area by attempts at regime change, annexation, or colonization (*Political Independence*).[3]

Offhand, it might seem that *Political Independence* is sufficient to justify national defence. But this is too simple because national defence also involves defence of the state's territory, and the state as an institution is separable from its current territory. The state might continue to exist in some other space or perhaps only in part of its previous territory (as France continued to exist after it lost Alsace-Lorraine). So national defence also depends on a claim to the area controlled by that state, a claim somewhat akin to a property right.[4]

This paper is a much-revised version of a previous essay of the same title published in *The Morality of Defensive War*, ed. Cécile Fabre and Seth Lazar (Oxford: Oxford University Press, 2014).

In what follows, I develop an approach to justifying this complex right.[5] On my view, a state has a right to its territorial integrity if and only if (1) the individuals represented by that state have a claim to occupy the area it rules (*Territorial Claim*), (2) the state imposes a legitimate legal system on the territory by enacting and enforcing personal and property law there (*Legitimate Jurisdiction*), and (3) the citizenry has established a relationship of political cooperation that is reasonably and widely affirmed (*Political Independence*). I shall develop these conditions in turn. In the final section, I take up the question of whether a state that satisfies these conditions is entitled to defend its territorial integrity with lethal force.

2. Occupancy Rights

An account of the state's territorial integrity must rest in part on a prior 'property-like' entitlement to the area it governs. But, in my view, this prior entitlement does not belong to the state itself. Although states exercise rights over particular spaces, they do so on behalf of another party (much as a trustee makes decisions concerning my property when I set up a trust). It is the state's inhabitants who are the underlying possessors of rights in their territory. The state gets its right to territory indirectly, as an agent of its members.[6]

One might think there is no need to invoke the language of property here. Michael Walzer instead argues that territorial rights are grounded purely on communal self-determination:

> Territorial integrity . . . does not derive from property; it is simply something different. . . . It is the coming together of a people that establishes the integrity of a territory. . . . It is for the sake of this common life that we assign a certain presumptive value to the boundaries that mark off a people's territory and to the state that defends it.[7]

If a state protects its citizens' common life, it is a legitimate institution, and it has a right to its territory because that common life requires some geographical space within which to unfold.

Walzer's approach is attractive because it promises to circumvent the problems deriving from the fact that few states have a 'clean' historical title to their lands. States have gained territory through arbitrary processes including conquest, dynastic unions, and the boundary-drawing efforts of colonial rulers. But despite its attractions, Walzer's approach fails. To see why, consider the following case:

> *Forced Removal:* Suppose a group of settlers gets together, overthrows the state of Chad, and drives out all the inhabitants, who then become refugees in neighbouring states. This group then sets up a perfect state on the territory. It rules justly, protects a common life, and enjoys the unanimous consent of all its inhabitants.[8]

I believe this perfect state lacks any right to its territory, at least at the moment of its founding. This is because the settlers have no claim to construct a common life there in the first place. A state's territorial integrity therefore needs to be grounded in a prior account of its members' claims to a geographical space.

In my view, the prior claim that grounds a state's territorial integrity is its inhabitants' right to *occupy* that area.[9] While less robust than a property right, occupancy does have some 'property-like' qualities. An occupancy right comprises two main elements:

> *First*, a liberty to reside permanently in a particular geographical space and to make use of that space for social, cultural, and economic practices. This extends to the liberty to travel freely through the area in order to access the places in civil society where those practices occur. (An occupancy right does not confer liberty of access to others' private property, but it does entitle one to access public spaces, e.g., parks, roads, byways, as well as businesses or buildings that offer services to the general public, whether publicly or privately owned.)
>
> *Second*, a claim-right against others not to remove one from that area and not to interfere with one's use of the space in ways that undermine the shared social practices in which one is engaged.

While occupancy does confer some 'property-like' incidents—namely, claims to secure access and use of a particular geographical area—it is distinct from an ownership right because it confers much more limited incidents of control. Occupancy rights are not exclusive: many people can share occupancy of the same area, and occupancy does not confer rights to alienate, to derive income, and so on. Still, the fact that inhabitants have occupancy rights in their territory is important: although they do not fully 'own' their country, local inhabitants have special claims to live there and to use the area for their social, cultural, and economic practices, and that is why actions like removal, ethnic cleansing, and exile are wrong.

What grounds occupancy rights and makes them important? I believe that the claim to territorial occupancy is rooted in the role that geographical space plays in individuals' most important projects and relationships. Many of our comprehensive goals require us to form expectations about the use of and secure access to a permanent place of residence. Geography and climate may affect the economic and subsistence practices we take up, thus making it difficult for us to reconstitute those in some very different place. Our religious, cultural, and recreational activities also often have territorial components. Finally, people form personal bonds and enter work, religious, and friendship relations in part because they expect to remain spatially arranged in certain ways. We structure our daily activities and associate together under the assumption that current patterns of residence will not be massively disrupted. I call these situated goals, relationships, and pursuits our *located life plans*.

We can separate out several significant categories of located life plans:

1. *Economic practices.* Many economic practices can only be carried on in a territory with certain geological, ecological, or infrastructural characteristics. The Sioux

Indians' economy was based on hunting wild buffalo, so they had an interest in living somewhere that could sustain these animals. Many modern Americans work in white-collar professional jobs, so they have an interest in living where there is office space, internet access, etc.

2. *Membership in religious, social, cultural, educational organizations.* Many located life plans require individuals to have access to spaces that are shared with other people. For a person to have the option to pursue a religious, recreational, educational, or work activity means being able to access the physical spaces and infrastructure—churches, mosques, schools, meeting houses, and so on—where these activities occur.
3. *Personal relationships.* People are engaged in networks of relationships—with colleagues, family, and friends—that are fundamental to their well-being. They have an interest in continuing these relationships with the particular people that matter to them, and that requires living near enough to do so. Since individuals are tied to differing networks, it is difficult to draw bounds around communities such that we could move all and only these people without breaking any personal ties. Sustaining people's important personal relationships requires maintaining their current spatial arrangements to a significant degree.
4. *Attachment to locality.* Some, though not all, people have fundamental projects based on a special identification with a unique locality. The Taos Pueblo's religious rituals centre on Blue Lake, the Sioux attribute spiritual significance to the Black Hills, and the Highland culture of Switzerland is focused specifically on the Alps.

Taken together, these reflections show that the people who live on a territory have important *plan-based interests* in continuing to occupy that place and in using it for the located social, cultural, and economic practices they value. Along with these plan-based interests in our territory, we also have an autonomy interest in being in charge of controlling and revising the fundamental commitments that are central to the structure of our lives. When other people interfere with or prevent us from pursuing very fundamental goals, such as working in our chosen occupation, practicing our religion, or forming intimate friendships and family relationships, this jeopardizes our sense of authorship over our own life. One form that such interference can take is expulsion from territory.

Showing that people have an interest in the area that is fundamental to their located life plans is the first step in an argument that they have a *right* to occupy that space. But we must also assess whether their interest is sufficiently weighty to justify imposing a duty on others to respect it. In most cases, I have difficulty conceiving of a significant countervailing interest in being able to remove or expel others from their territory or to interfere with their occupancy in ways that undermine their shared social practices. Nor does compliance with duties to respect others' occupancy seem especially burdensome: as long as an outsider enjoys flourishing located life plans where she now lives, depriving her of the liberty to interfere with others' use of territory isn't unduly costly to her.

There are two kinds of cases, however, where imposing duties to respect occupancy is quite burdensome. If someone does not enjoy flourishing located life plans where he now is, then he has a significant interest in acquiring some space in which to pursue those plans, even if that space is currently occupied. This suggests that we should add an *equitable distribution* constraint to our account: in occupying a territory, one must leave others with access to enough space to secure their interest in located life plans. Deciding which of many candidate distributional principles should apply to territorial occupancy is difficult. But I believe enjoyment of sufficient territory for a decent life is a plausible minimal requirement for an equitable distribution of space, so any good theory will allow for at least this. On a sufficiency approach, if outsiders lack access to space that is adequate for a decent life, then current occupants will be obliged to share their territory with them or provide those resources in some other way.[10] I do not claim special status for sufficiency here; I use it to illustrate the role that distributional constraints play in my account. If some more demanding principle—like equal per capita shares—turns out to apply, then I assume my theory of occupancy can be revised accordingly.

Another exceptional case is prior expulsion. It would be radically unfair to hold that by expelling a victim and forcing her to reorder her life, a wrongdoer could then gain rights in her territory. The formation of located life plans does not confer occupancy rights when the establishment of those plans involved dispossessing people with prior claims. Just as someone who commits an assault renders himself liable to bodily harm by his victim or the police, so, too, wrongful dispossessors make themselves liable to territorial removal.[11] This is despite the fact that they may have formed located life plans in the area, and they may have an interest in sustaining those plans. Wrongful dispossessors have no justified complaint if they are expelled by way of their victims' reclaiming their place of residence.

As long as equitable distribution and no expulsion constraints are met, however, I believe that our interest in stable located life plans is significant enough to justify imposing duties on others not to remove us from our territory and not to interfere with our use of it in ways that undermine our social, cultural, and economic practices. This is because (1) the security afforded to located life plans by recognizing such duties is of great benefit to us, and (2) our interest in not having such duties imposed is quite weak by comparison.

I should stress that I understand occupancy as a *preinstitutional* moral right: occupancy is not the product of positive law or of a society's conventional practices. Even people without a legal system—like a non-state tribe—or people in a situation of state collapse, like the population of Somalia today, can have a right to the area they occupy. It is wrong to remove them or to interfere with their use of that place.

I should also stress that the bearers of occupancy rights are individuals, not national groups. People living in close proximity may have interests in different spaces and participate in different practices yet share occupancy rights in roughly the same area. A Cuban immigrant has a claim to live in Miami because it contains his family, his workplace, his Catholic church, and his fellow Spanish-speakers, whereas a Jewish Miamian has an occupancy claim there because it contains his soccer club, his synagogue, and his school. Although there is little overlap between the social practices in which these two people participate, each has a right to live *in Miami* because it contains shared spaces that are fundamental to him. Unlike nationalist theorists, then, I do not attribute the right to occupy territory to a transgenerational, culturally unified group.[12] Instead it is the individual inhabitants of a place who are the ultimate possessors of it, and people with diverse cultural attachments may share occupancy rights in the same space.

To sum up this account, I offer a more formal statement as follows:

> *Occupancy Rights*: A person has a moral claim to occupy a particular area if (1) he resides there now or has previously done so, (2) access to spaces in that area is fundamental to his located life plans, and (3) his connection to that area was established without wrongdoing on his part, including no expulsion of prior rightful inhabitants and no infringement of others' claims to an equitable distribution of space.

3. State Legitimacy

So far, I have argued that the state's inhabitants are the ultimate possessors of the area it governs. But how does the state acquire its jurisdiction over that space? In an initial stateless condition, I believe that states can acquire jurisdiction simply by imposing a just scheme of law in an area. This is because the residents have a natural duty to support a legitimate state because they cannot live together in a condition of justice without one. Simply by making itself the salient choice, then, a state can give individuals a reason to accept its authority if there is no rival institutional scheme.[13] I note here that I do not define a 'state' as a modern, Western, bureaucratic institution. As long as an association allows for collective rule-setting and publicly controlled enforcement, we can apply the term 'state' to it in a suitably broad sense. Many non-Western or indigenous political forms can be considered 'states' in this wide view.

Why are states necessary? Justice, on my view, is a necessarily institutional value: it cannot be secured through individuals' private actions, no matter how well-disposed they may be. Our duties of justice are in part institutionally mediated: a legitimate state is required to provide a unitary interpretation of rights that binds everyone and to enforce those rights consistently with individuals' reciprocal independence. If a state exists and enforces a legitimate system of law in an area, then the inhabitants ought to comply with it because it is only through such an institution that they can do justice to others.

To explain, it is helpful to borrow elements from Kant's account of state authority. Kant argues that each person has an equal innate claim to freedom-as-independence, which requires that he not be forced to obey the will of another person. This is a right to be one's own master, to pursue one's own purposes without subjection to another's choices.[14] Each person is also under a basic moral duty to respect the freedom-as-independence of others. To realize independence, the individual must enjoy a set of guaranteed rights, including rights to person and property. Kant argues that the state is a necessary intermediary for the interpretation and enforcement of these rights, however, because only the state can overcome the problems of unilateralism that arise when individuals attempt to interpret and enforce their rights themselves.

There are three relevant problems: (1) some moral rights—especially property rights—are indeterminate in a state of nature; (2) even where moral rights are determinate, individuals may disagree about what justice requires in particular cases; and (3) when faced with disagreement, individuals lack the standing to coerce others to submit to their judgments.

Consider first indeterminacy. Even if a group shares an understanding of their moral claims, what they should do together to protect them often remains underdetermined. To illustrate, consider property rights. There are many different schemes of property rules that would protect our most basic moral interests. In order to say which particular goods a person has a right to, we must refer to some institutional background rules and the legitimate expectations they create. Surely, it is foolish to believe that the terms of these various rights can be made determinate simply through abstract moral reflection. Partly, the problem is one of coordination: even if each person has a basic interest in the goods necessary for his survival, that does not determine any answer as to how to structure many other issues, including property in the means of production, rights to transfer (subject to tax? at what level?), or rights of bequest. Due to this indeterminacy, even individuals who are in full agreement as to what their most basic interests are will not be able to translate this agreement into a consensus on which rules of justice to recognize (including rules about property, tort law, contract, exploitative agreements, fraud, and the distribution of opportunities, education, and income). It is unlikely that individuals could resolve these problems without granting authoritative institutions a role in defining many of their rights. One cannot specify what property and contractual claims a person has without reference to the system of rules that is actually in force in the society where she lives and the expectations these rules create.

State-of-nature individuals would also face a second problem: the problem of moral disagreement. Even where moral rights are determinate, often individuals will not share a common understanding of these rights in particular cases. Each person's good-faith attempt to do justice to others may not lead him to respect the claims that other persons take to be significant. In circumstances of disagreement, it is difficult for individuals to recognize one another as attempting to do justice in their personal behaviour.

Consider an example: almost everyone agrees, at an abstract level, that individuals have a right to life. Many people believe this can ground a claim to material resources essential for one's survival. And many, in turn, believe this grounds a claim to adequate medical care. But not all who agree on the importance of the right to life support these conclusions. For example, Christian Scientists think that poor health is a sign of erroneous spiritual beliefs that must be corrected through faith healing. And libertarians believe that while the right to life is important, it imposes only negative duties, not positive duties, on others. In the pre-state situation, these Christian Scientists and libertarians would not recognize any duty to secure others' interests in medical care. When people lack a common understanding of their rights in particular cases, their attempts to respect the rights that, by their lights, other individuals have will not strike these others as an effort to respect their rights. These divergent moral understandings will lead to injuries and conflict.

Because individuals disagree on what their moral interests are, how these interests should be protected by coordinated rules, and which is the best of the many schemes that could protect these interests, even individuals acting in good faith may have great trouble coordinating their behaviour so as to effectively and publicly respect each other's rights in the absence of a political authority. Because individuals will disagree in attempting to do justice to others, they must not only ask themselves substantive questions about justice—for example, what rights and duties do we all have, on my best understanding? Instead, they face an equally important procedural question of justice, namely: when we disagree about our rights and duties, how are we to do justice to one another? Kant's argument for state authority is that a group of individuals should not do justice to one another by acting unilaterally (i.e., by demanding that others conform to their beliefs about what justice requires and privately enforcing this demand). In cases of indeterminacy and disagreement, we ought to do justice by constructing a common authority that can define and enforce public rules regarding our rights.

This third problem of unilateral enforcement builds on the other two. Even when you privately enforce what you take to be the correct scheme of rules, you may still wrong other people by doing so unilaterally in accordance with a nonpublic conception of justice. In effect, you are claiming a superior political standing over others that, as an equal, you do not have. Other individuals are equally authoritative interpreters of justice, which means they will perceive your well-meaning attempts to enforce justice as an arbitrary assumption of power, not as something that places them under any obligation. A Kantian does not deny that one party to these disputes may be right, while the other one is wrong. We simply deny that his being correct is enough to give him a right to use force on the other person in order to implement his view. In cases of good-faith disagreement, these others remain entitled to submit only to an impersonal institution governed by commonly recognized laws, not to an act of private coercion.[15]

Because individuals who disagree about justice have no way (1) to publicly establish what moral interests they are all committed to respecting, (2) to decide which of many conventional rules to protect those interests they collectively wish to adopt, and (3) to enforce justice without wrongly claiming private authority over their moral equals, they are unable to establish justice through unilateral action. States are of significant moral value, then, because they allow individuals to resolve indeterminacies in their rights, to accept a common interpretation of these rights amid moral disagreement, and to enforce these rights without private subjection. States provide us an essential means of defining and enforcing our rights in a nondominating way.

There are important reasons—pertaining to the state's role in establishing clear property rights—to believe that to carry out these tasks, states will need to be territorially defined. To secure property rights, people who live in proximity and interact regularly will need to have reference to the same set of rules. If each person signed up for the jurisdictional organization of his choice, carrying around his own personal definitions of property, contract, and tort, interaction between persons in a contiguous space would continue to generate conflicts and disputes. So there is an important reason for those who are located in a contiguous space to support the same institution.

Note, too, that this Kantian argument provides support only for sufficiently legitimate states. The most basic moral reason for supporting the state is a reason of justice: we owe it to our fellows to respect their status as independent equals, and therefore we ought to define and enforce justice through an impartial institution, not through private coercion. There is some essential minimal content to what could reasonably count as a state that was aiming to impartially interpret and enforce justice on behalf of its subjects. If the system of law enacts at least this minimal justice content, then it gives subjects moral reasons for their support and outsiders reason for their respect.

How are we to tell if a state is aiming at doing justice for its subjects? We must demand that it give at least minimal consideration to each member's interests by delineating a set of basic human rights as a standard for state legitimacy. I believe such a minimal standard will include many of the core rights set down in the Universal Declaration of Human Rights, including rights to life, liberty, and security; rights against slavery, torture, and arbitrary imprisonment; rights to equal protection of the law and a fair trial; to freedom of conscience and freedom of association; and rights to some form of political participation. Violation of these basic rights voids the state's status as a legitimate authority.

To sum up the argument thus far, I have claimed that a state will have a claim to exercise political power over a particular territory if (1) it qualifies as a legitimate authority, imposing a scheme of personal and property law that protects the basic interests of the persons situated there, and (2) the area within which the state's legal system is in force corresponds to the area rightfully occupied by the state's inhabitants.[16]

4. Political Independence

My third and final condition holds that a state's right to territorial integrity depends on a further claim to political independence—a claim to noninterference with its exercise of political power in the area it rules through acts of regime change, annexation, or colonization (*political independence*).

Why is this additional condition necessary? Although my argument so far has established that states are morally necessary institutions, it hasn't shown why particular states have authority over particular territories. Something more needs to be said about how—among a range of legitimate states—we single out this particular state as the one with a right to rule over this population and this space. I believe that a state that is self-determining is specially singled out in this way. A minimally just state may have a pro tem moral permission to issue and enforce binding law and policy among some population. But a self-determining state has an additional claim-right not to be displaced by equally just rival powers. Because a self-determining state reflects its people's shared priorities, it ought not to be interfered with or removed.

Some support for self-determination's importance is provided by our intuitive judgments about colonial rule, military occupation, and annexation. Consider two cases:

> *Annexation:* In 1945, the Allies occupied Germany in a just use of force. Suppose that instead of restoring the territory to the German people, the United States had annexed its zone of occupation, turning it into an additional state of the union. After annexation, the United States ruled legitimately: it protected the Germans' human rights and granted them rights of democratic participation in the now-unified polity. Could the annexed people of Germany rightly have attempted to recover their political independence?
>
> *Benevolent Colonialism:* One historically influential defence of colonialism was the 'civilizing mission': European rule over non-Western peoples was alleged to better guarantee liberal rights and good governance when compared to indigenous regimes. Suppose that a 'civilizing' empire did a reasonably good job of protecting its subjects' rights and delivering enlightened governance. Wouldn't its colonial subjects still have a morally significant complaint, on grounds that they were denied the right to rule themselves?

The best way to characterize our intuitions about these cases is, I believe, to say that annexed, colonized, or occupied populations have a *pro tanto* claim to self-rule: to govern themselves independently and to order their institutions as they choose. This claim is defeasible and may sometimes be outweighed by competing concerns, as in a justified military occupation or humanitarian intervention. But where weighty countervailing considerations are not at stake, the claim to self-rule ought to be respected.

In accepting a claim to self-rule, we view the state's legitimate authority as having two distinct dimensions. Mainstream liberal theory (including the Kantian view I outlined earlier) has focused primarily on the state's role in benefiting its members. This 'taker' dimension of evaluation is concerned with the quality of state institutions, independent of anyone's attitudes to them. But I believe a state's institutional quality is not all that matters. Instead, individuals have an additional interest in being the 'makers' of their political institutions. It is as important that their political institutions reflect their priorities and contributions (in their role as 'makers') as that these institutions be good ones (from their perspective as 'takers'). Political institutions are important for individuals, then, in part because those individuals *created* their institutions together with others, and they see those institutions as reflecting a shared project they value.

How might ordinary people relate to their political institutions as 'makers'? To be self-determining, citizens must appropriately see themselves as joint authors of their institutions through participation in a cooperative enterprise they value and affirm. This relation matters because it is especially significant for individuals to be ruled by an authority that reflects, in some way, their own values and priorities. Of course, since individuals must share the political world with others, no individual's personal priorities can be mirrored in every law. Yet there is a second-order sense in which an individual's priorities *are* often reflected in his institutions: namely, when they are shaped through his participation in a cooperative enterprise that he affirms. Although this 'maker' interest is an interest of individuals, it can be furthered by an individual's membership in a self-determining group, to the extent that he values participation in that group.

To develop this idea, note that sustaining the state shares many features with the joint activity of everyday cooperative groups. Of course, states feature formal governance institutions, like the legislative, executive, and judicial branches; the police; and the bureaucracy. These formal institutions typically direct citizens' activities. But still, it is the everyday contributions of ordinary citizens—their intentions to 'play their parts'—that make formal institutions effective and stable. Ordinary citizens coordinate their behaviour in a number of ways that help support their government's rule. They cooperate with officials, judges, and policies, and they comply with the law. By paying taxes, the people contribute to their governing institutions. And where they have political representation, citizens offer input into the overall shape of their cooperative enterprise. They voice opinions about which priorities they wish to see coordinating their activity. Although they do not know each other personally, then, citizens still participate in a shared venture together: they uphold, reproduce, and sometimes direct a common scheme of law.

In other joint cooperative activities, members often value their participation partly for its own sake. Consider a group running a coffee shop together. As they cooperate over time, this group will likely develop some shared commitments about how their enterprise should run. This does not mean that the partners will converge in all their personal judgments. More probably, they will divide on some issues, as, say, whether or not to stay open on Sundays. Perhaps one partner, Amy, thinks it best that the coffee shop stay open for the extra business. But after hearing the views of her partners and noting the importance they place on a day of rest, she decides to go along with a Sunday closure policy. Amy can freely accept this group policy, although it differs from her first-order judgments. She does so because she values the cooperative venture and wishes to see it continue and because, as part of that shared activity, she values the process of making decisions together even when that means accepting some decisions with which she disagrees.

While there are many important differences between a modern state and a small-scale partnership, I believe that, ideally, a state's citizens ought to relate to the cooperative enterprise that undergirds its institutions in a similar fashion. This occurs, I suggest, when a member *reasonably affirms* her participation in the shared political project. A citizen *affirms* participation when she reflectively endorses her own intention to 'play her part', understanding the group's shared purposes and the role which her contributions play in their achievement. In order to appropriately see herself as a 'co-author', a member must also have the opportunity to contribute to forming the group's shared commitments. This requires a channel—in the form of basic liberties of conscience, speech, and association—by which her opinions can be expressed and taken notice of by other members. Moreover, to be *reasonably* affirmed, the shared venture must be genuinely valuable. A shared political project must be at least minimally just if it is to be reasonably affirmed.

Imagine a scenario, then, in which all citizens reasonably affirm their cooperation together in sustaining a minimally just state. I am going to call this the ideal case. In this case, I believe the group's self-determination is valuable for each individual member of that group. The basic thought is that, in this case, the purposes of the state count as the citizenry's own purposes to a significant degree. There are several individual interests that are served by self-determination in the ideal case, including interests in political stability and in well-being. But here I discuss what I consider the most important interest: an interest in political freedom.

When individuals live under a *hierarchical* and *coercive* institution like the state, I believe their relationship to its imposed demands is different when they affirm their participation in it than when they do not. Citizens who affirm their participation together experience political freedom under coercive authority.

How is affirmation related to political freedom? Consider that many joint enterprises—including the modern state—are large and complex. Tasks are often parcelled out among various roles in an overall plan. In the state, that concrete plan is specified and enforced by a hierarchical and coercive government. As an occupant of a role, the demands of the enterprise can often seem burdensome, unfulfilling, or pointless. When this happens, we can say that a participant is *alienated* from the shared enterprise. It has no meaning for her.

To some extent, alienation is to be expected in any complex institution. And often alienation may not present a problem: if the demands of one's professional role seem pointless, one has the option of abandoning this role and pursuing some other occupation. But alienation is a bigger problem when the institution is a coercive one that pervasively shapes a person's social environment, and the role she plays in it is one she has no option to abandon. In that scenario, her duties may seem not just onerous, but imposed by a threatening and hostile force that exercises near-complete control over her life. Since the state determines so many aspects of our lives—many more than other collective institutions like universities, churches, or business corporations—alienation from the state is an important concern.

In other institutional contexts, often we have a good response to alienation: a participant can reflect on the way in which her performance of a task furthers the achievement of a shared enterprise that she values. Feeling alienated and overburdened by the mundane tasks of university administration, for example, a professor might recall that these tasks are necessary to running a successful university. When we carry out this kind of reflection, we relate to the demands of our roles quite differently. Administrative tasks may still seem burdensome, of course; we do not suddenly acquire a spontaneous desire to engage in them. But we now see a *point* to the task, and so the role's demands are imbued with new significance. We see reason to hold ourselves to this task, even though we have no desire to do so.

Having available this kind of response to alienation is of great importance when an institution is pervasively controlling and coercive and our membership in it is involuntary. When one is alienated from an institution of this kind, substantial aspects of one's life can come to seem dominated by a menacing power. Yet suppose that one is able to reflect on how one's performance of burdensome duties furthers a collective enterprise whose overall goals one endorses. In the wake of that reflection, these requirements no longer seem threatening; instead, they have new significance. Seeing that connection is valuable because it furthers citizens' *political freedom*. Even though their civic duties may be onerous, citizens who affirm their cooperation together as a people can impose these duties on themselves as part of a meaningful joint project. For that reason, an individual's interest in authorship over his own life can be furthered by membership in a collectively self-determining state.

Because of this connection with political freedom, the desire not to be alienated from one's political community is more than a mere preference. Rather, it is connected to a significant human need to be at home in one's social and political world. One of the most destructive effects of colonialism was the coercive imposition onto a subject population of a political order that bore no relation to their own priorities and values. Those who lived through this experience tell of a sense of powerlessness and a radical loss of orientation and control. This alienation is distinct from the other abuses perpetrated by colonial institutions, and it persists as a legacy of bitterness and resentment. Obviously, alienation and affirmation are matters of degree: one can reject many aspects of one's social institutions without suffering meaninglessness and loss of control. Still, the coerced imposition of a social order that fails in any way to reflect the values and priorities of those governed by it often leads to serious harms to the population's well-being and sense of self-respect. It treats them as pawns to be forced into compliance, without any regard for whether they can endorse the authority's aims. For that reason, persistent alienation from one's political institutions is a very important concern.

To sum up, then, I believe a state will have a claim to political independence when it reflects a shared political project that is widely valued by its members. The ideal of self-determination holds that each citizen should relate to the political order by affirming his involvement in the cooperative political enterprise that undergirds it. Only then can he see himself as a co-author of the institutions that govern his life.[17] When a minimally just state is widely affirmed by its citizens, it gains a special right to rule its people and their territory in the absence of interference by rivals.

5. Thoughts on Lethal Force

Let me turn to my final question: does a state that satisfies these three conditions have a right to defend its territorial integrity with lethal force? Recall that the conditions are (1) its citizens have a right to occupy its territory, (2) its scheme of law is minimally just, and (3) the relationship of political cooperation that supports its institutions is reasonably and widely affirmed. National self-defence is a morally fraught question.[18] Nevertheless, our reflections provide some basis for thinking about it.

To begin, consider David Rodin's distinction between the subject of the right of national defence and the end of that right.[19] The subject of a right is its bearer, the entity that can exercise it. For national self-defence, this subject is the state as a corporate entity. But the more interesting question is about the end of this right. Although the right of national defence is exercised by the state, the ends it protects are not necessarily statist in character. Indeed, metaphors that characterize the state as a 'trust' suggest that the state wields its power on behalf of some other entity and is obliged to exercise that power in a fiduciary manner. So what ends might national defence protect? There are three: the interests of individuals, the shared priorities of a political community, and the objective value of just institutions.

The individual interests protected by national self-defence include interests in continued occupancy of the territory, in the protection of basic rights, and in the provision of public goods and a fair scheme of distributive justice. National self-defence also protects the shared priorities of the political community: as I emphasized in the last section, a group who willingly cooperates to sustain a state will share an interest in the institutions they have together created, insofar as they value their political project and wish to see it continue. We should note, too, that membership in such a self-determining group is also important for individuals because it safeguards their interest in political freedom. Finally, the defence of a just state serves important *objective values.* If my Kantian argument for the 'institutional mediation' of duties of justice is correct, then states are necessarily part of the realization of justice in the world. *Everyone* has a reason to support the effective functioning of legitimate states because these institutions play a fundamental role in establishing justice.

I don't believe these three ends are quite robust enough to support the common-sense conviction that fighting for one's state is not only justified, but even a patriotic duty. But they can establish a defensive privilege in at least a central range of cases.

Consider first a war of territorial removal. This is a fairly uncontroversial case. Individuals have extremely weighty interests in their place of residence and the preservation of their located life plans. Territorial removal generally causes the loss of an individual's home, disruption of his social ties, and the utter transformation of his life. Removals can also cause grievous harms through hunger or disease and may result in the expellees becoming refugees with no permanent residence at all.

Individuals themselves would have the right to use force in defence of their occupancy in a 'state of nature'. For this reason, their state may also exercise this right on their behalf. Many theorists of self-defence have argued that lethal force is only warranted when an attacker threatens harm to extraordinarily vital interests, such as the interest in not being killed, severely wounded, raped, or kidnapped.[20] For some—notably David Rodin—interests in property are not sufficiently vital to warrant lethal force. But the interest in territorial occupancy (a limited form of property) is indeed a vital interest. Being made a refugee from one's territory may not involve bodily injury, but it can be just as grievous as a loss of limb.

Next, consider a case in which a community faces an aggressive invader that does not threaten their lives or occupancy but wishes to impose an unjust political order on them. Say that these imposed institutions would not go so far as to threaten their most vital interests (perhaps they would not allow for fair trials, the right to vote, or freedom of speech). These institutions would be unjust, but not so unjust as to threaten personal security or survival. Can they engage in national self-defence?

Yes. There are two types of considerations that support defensive action here. First, individuals have justice-related interests as beneficiaries of legitimate institutions. Taken one by one, each person's interest in free speech or a fair trial may not be sufficiently valuable to warrant using lethal force against possibly innocent enemy soldiers, but surely they warrant some forceful action. And when we consider the fact that we are protecting the nonvital rights of a great many people, the use of lethal force may become proportionate even though it would not be warranted in just one person's case.[21]

Second, recall that legitimate institutions are objectively valuable as a means to establish justice. If, simply by making an aggressive threat, an invader could make it incumbent on us to give up our legitimate institutions, then he would have the power to prevent the achievement of justice in the world. But this seems absurd. If people have fundamental interests in living under legitimate institutions, then there are important reasons for adopting a rule that will allow us to act in their defence. Otherwise, we would be unable to deter the aggressive destruction of such institutions. This is an important difference between national defence and individual self-defence within an existing legal system, where the state takes care of background deterrence. When deterrence is not a factor, the privilege to use force is correspondingly constrained. But without the right to impose deterrence, the fate of just institutions would be highly insecure. So even if individuals' nonvital interests as beneficiaries of just institutions do not suffice to make their defence of these institutions proportionate, when considerations of deterrence are added in, I believe the argument justifies national defence, all things considered.

The most difficult case for national self-defence, in my view, is an invasion by an aggressor who does not threaten citizens' lives, nor their territorial occupancy, nor does he wish to impose on them unjust institutions. Instead, the aggressor wishes to destroy their current institutions and substitute in their place a different but also reasonably just state. Call this a case of *mere political aggression*: the aggressor aims at regime change or territorial acquisition, not at oppression or injustice to individuals. In this case, we are precluded from appealing to a number of the important ends we outlined earlier: individuals' occupancy interests, their interests in the receipt of justice-related benefits, and also the objective interest in the institutional establishment of justice.

Can national defence be justified here? I am unsure. In a provocative recent paper, David Rodin draws an analogy between a hostile corporate takeover and a war of political aggression.[22] According to Rodin, much like the state, the Cadbury Corporation—recently merged with Kraft in a hostile takeover—was a distinctive community with shared values and a common way of life. Yet no one argued that the defence of Cadbury's independence warranted the use of lethal force. So what is the transcendent value that might justify killing to protect the independence of the state? This question takes on particular force in a war of mere political aggression, one in which it is *only* the independence of the state—not the rights of individuals—that is at stake.

Yet there are significant differences between a modern state and a private corporation, and Rodin places insufficient weight on these differences. Consider:

1. a modern state is *coercive*—it can punish people who refuse to 'play their parts';
2. a modern state is *involuntary*—whereas Cadbury employees freely joined their association, most citizens are born into theirs, and they may have no reasonable option to leave it.

These distinctive features make self-determination a weightier interest in the case of the state than in the corporate case. This greater weight is grounded in self-determination's special connection with the political freedom of individuals who must live under coercive institutions. If the Cadbury employees don't like their new corporate culture, they can always look for another job, and, with time, they are likely to find one. If they find repugnant Kraft's emphasis on the bottom line, they cannot be threatened with violent penalties for their refusal to comply. Finally, the workplace is only one—albeit significant—association in their lives. It does not exercise comprehensive power over all aspects of their social world. These differences mean that the hostile imposition of a political order that does not reflect its subjects' priorities is much more debilitating than the equivalent takeover of a corporation. The kinds of remedies that might safeguard individual autonomy in the face of a corporate takeover simply aren't available in the case of the state. After a political takeover, individuals may not be able to leave their state, they will be threatened with coercion for their refusal to comply with the new rules, and they cannot escape the regime's power by taking refuge in other social associations.

If there is a justification for national self-defence in the face of mere political aggression, I believe it rests on the importance to individuals' political freedom of being governed by coercive institutions that partly reflect their values and priorities. The fact that many colonized populations have experienced such severe disaffection and resentment in the face of alien rule suggests that political freedom is significant. Still, one must ask: how significant? Even if political freedom is quite important, its value must truly be of vital weight to justify the killing of human beings in its defence. Is co-authorship of our coercive institutions sufficiently fundamental to justify the use of lethal force? I am unsure. In certain cases, it seems so. Prolonged colonial rule has led to massive social despair on the part of some conquered subjects (e.g., among indigenous peoples). But alien rule may not always have such horrific consequences. In cases where the imposed institutions are not wholly incompatible with the subject population's values, a hostile takeover may only lead to milder forms of political apathy. In that scenario, I doubt that the good of political freedom would be of sufficient weight to justify the destructiveness of war. It is therefore difficult, in my view, to give an account of the values behind national self-defence that fully justify our pretheoretic intuition that defending one's state from aggression is always permitted or even required. But if we can offer a justification that accounts for the most central and compelling cases, then perhaps that is convincing enough.

Notes

1. T. Hurka, 'Proportionality in the Morality of War', *Philosophy and Public Affairs*, 33:1 (2005), 34–66; J. McMahan, 'Just Cause for War', *Ethics and International Affairs*, 19:3 (2005), 1–21.
2. See T. Baldwin, 'The Territorial State', in *Jurisprudence: Cambridge Essays*, edited by Hyman Gross and Ross Harrison (Oxford: Clarendon Press, 1992); D. Copp, 'The Idea of a Legitimate State', *Philosophy and Public Affairs*, 28:1 (1999), 3–45. I take as my central case here the state's control over land, and I do not address issues of control over airspace or territorial waters.
3. In formulating these conditions, I have been influenced by Buchanan and Yong. See A. Buchanan, *Justice, Legitimacy, and Self-Determination* (Oxford: Oxford University Press, 2004); and C. Yong 'Towards a Theory of Territory', January 2012, unpublished paper on file with author.
4. D. Miller, 'Territorial Rights: Concept and Justification', *Political Studies* 60:2 (2012), 3.
5. This account is part of my ongoing project on state rights to territory, parts of which have been published in A. Stilz, 'Why Do States Have Territorial Rights', *International Theory* 1:2 (2009), 185–213; 'Nations, States, and Territory', *Ethics* 121:3 (2011), 572–601; and 'Occupancy Rights and the Wrong of Removal', *Philosophy and Public Affairs* 41:4 (2013), 324–356.
6. Miller, 'Territorial Rights', 2.
7. Walzer, *Just and Unjust Wars* (New York: Basic Books, 1977), 56–57.
8. See my 'Nations, States and Territory', 583.
9. This section adapts and extends some remarks in my 'Occupancy Rights and the Wrong of Removal'.
10. The question of what makes a territory adequate for a decent life is also complex. But I would highlight that people must enjoy adequate natural resources, including food, shelter, and a liveable environment. And people must also enjoy adequate social institutions, institutions that guarantee their basic security and protect their essential interests in forming and pursuing life plans by allowing them to practice their religion and culture and associate together with others, including being free to form family relationships.
11. Jeremy Waldron argues that entitlements based on life plans can fade after dispossession, perhaps even within the victim's own lifetime. See Waldron, 'Superseding Historic Injustice', 19. An account of rights forfeiture avoids this implication. For other discussions of forfeiture, see Jeff McMahan, *Killing in War* (Oxford: Oxford University Press, 2009), 1–37; and Christopher Wellman, 'The Rights Forfeiture Theory of Punishment', *Ethics* 122:2 (2012), 371–393. On my view, only wrongdoers forfeit their occupancy rights; their descendants—who are innocent of any injustice—do not.
12. For contrasting nationalist views, see Tamar Meisels, *Territorial Rights* (Dordrecht: Springer, 2005), and David Miller, 'Territorial Rights', 259.
13. See J. Waldron, 'Special Ties and Natural Duties', *Philosophy and Public Affairs* 22:1 (1993), 3–30.
14. A. Ripstein, *Force and Freedom* (Cambridge, MA: Harvard University Press, 2009), 35–37. My remarks here draw on my 'Why Does the State Matter Morally', in *Varieties of Sovereignty and Citizenship*, edited by Sigal Ben-Porath and Rogers Smith (Philadelphia: University of Pennsylvania Press, 2012), 244–264.

15. For a useful discussion of these issues, see L. P. Hodgson, 'Kant on Property Rights and the State', *Kantian Review* 15:1 (2010), 57–87. Kant's argument does not entail that in a situation where there *are* no authoritative institutions, individuals may not defend themselves through private force. But by resorting to self-help in this way, individuals fall short of the fullest ideal of justice, and, where a legitimate institution exists or can be set up, they have a duty to accept its jurisdiction.
16. Can states claim additional rights beyond territorial jurisdiction, such as rights to own the natural resources present on, in, and under their territories? States do have a right to manage these resources in the name of their citizens, to ensure their survival and decent livelihood. But I doubt that states have a full property right in, for example, the mineral and oil resources of their territories. If states decide to exploit these resources, they may be legitimately subject to an international taxation scheme.
17. In sketching this account, I do not claim that the existing configuration of state boundaries adequately realizes self-determination. No existing state is an ideal case. My view therefore implies that persistently alienated subgroups sometimes have claims to redraw political boundaries. While an account of internal autonomy or secession is beyond the scope of this chapter, I should note that not every alienated group's claim can be addressed. In concrete cases, we will need to weigh the claims of persistently alienated groups against the countervailing risks to just institutions, including the potential for civil unrest, instability, ethnic conflict, or rights violations. Sometimes the risks of reconfiguring our institutions will be so great as to outweigh persistent alienation. And some kinds of alienation should be discounted entirely, as with groups that are persistently alienated because they hold unjust aims.
18. I should note that the Kantian argument I outlined in Section 3 implies that states, like individuals, are obliged to construct an international legal institution that can decide their disputes without recourse to war. Any state that uses force to defend its rights will always fall short of the ideal of justice. Still, states may be provisionally justified in defending their territorial integrity with lethal force because that kind of international institution is not yet realized in the world. And, even under an international enforcement system, states may retain certain defensive privileges in the case of direct territorial incursions, analogous to the individual privilege of self-defence in existing legal systems.
19. D. Rodin, *War and Self-Defence* (Oxford: Oxford University Press, 2002), 123–127.
20. Idem, 43–44.
21. For this point, see T. Hurka, 'Proportionality in the Morality of War'.
22. David Rodin, 'The Myth of National Self-Defence', in *The Morality of Defensive War*, edited by Cécile Fabre and Seth Lazar (Oxford: Oxford University Press, 2014), 69–89.

CHAPTER 13

LAST RESORT AND PROPORTIONALITY

HENRY SHUE

THE best war possible now is a bloody nightmare. Wars rarely fulfil hopes, moral or empirical. For these two reasons—the horror of war itself and the deep propensity for wishful thinking to obscure the reality—any resort to war can be justified only by genuinely satisfying multiple necessary conditions. The one certain fact about every war is that its results will include deaths, wounds, and destruction and that many of these will be inflicted wrongfully in violation of basic rights. Most clearly, people who are not participating in the conflict will die, be injured, or lose their property, and almost all wrongfully so. And, as I will explain a little more fully herein, many combatants on both sides of most conflicts are not morally liable to incur the terrible deaths and the disabling wounds that they suffer—such grievous calamities far exceed what is appropriate to any degree of moral liability that such young people, even on the less well-justified side, are likely to bear.[1] Wars result in evil on all sides—this is abundantly clear from reflection on history. In the following, consequently, I shall be suggesting that a decision to go to war can be justified only if it satisfies at least four interrelated necessary conditions: just cause, reasonable prospect of success, last resort, and proportionality of resort, with most extensive analysis of the last.

1. Just Cause

Steven Lee, who has written the best recent analysis of the requirements for justified resort to war,[2] suggests helpful labels—'the resisted evil' and 'the created evil': 'The evil that arises out of a war may be called the *created evil*, while the evil a war is meant to avert may be called the *resisted evil*. Proportionality is tied to just cause because the main resisted evil is the wrong that provides a just cause.'[3] In the just war tradition 'just cause' is the terminology, drawing on Aristotle's 'final cause' or purpose, for the end that grounds the justification for the use of military means. The evils that wars themselves create are sufficiently serious that the only possible 'just cause' is the prevention of evils that are still greater. By 'evil', I mean specifically violations or infringements of fundamental individual rights (like arbitrary wounding or killing) or seriously wrongful harms (like wanton destruction of the environment), not simply impersonally bad outcomes. So, the first necessary condition for a justified resort to war is the clear identification of great evil that might be preventable by military means.

The moral impermissibility of putative just causes other than the prevention of significant evil is reflected in the evolution of international law over recent centuries, in which war has ceased to be accepted as a normal instrument of statecraft to be used, for instance, to redress an unfavourable balance of power by taking an adversary down a few notches, as was common on the part of eighteenth- and nineteenth-century European powers, arguably up through World War I, which had little other point.[4] The prohibition on the initiation of war by the United Nations Charter in 1945 can be construed as expressing the position that the clearest—and possibly the only—case of an evil significant enough to provide adequate cause for permitting military action is an aggression in violation of this very prohibition on all nondefensive war. But defensive war's being permitted by international law does not, of course, mean that it is a good solution.

2. Reasonable Prospect of Success

Specifying the evil to be resisted is only the merest beginning of an adequate justification for resorting to war. The second necessary condition for justifying war is empirical: a demonstration that, wishful thinking aside, military means have what in the just war tradition was called 'a reasonable prospect of success'.[5] Most great evils cannot be eliminated by military means. It must be shown that the specific evil in question can be prevented through war, and specifically through the kind of war that is likely to result if a war is launched there and then to attain that purpose. Empirical questions tend to make philosophers nervous because they are not our strong suit. But anyone who wishes to engage in practical reasoning about a particular war must investigate such empirical questions as which actions are likely to lead to which results[6]; specifically, whether the military struggle advocated is likely in fact to achieve the cessation of the evil promised as its justifying ground. Otherwise, one simply adopts unquestioningly whatever empirical assumptions war advocates make. The next step, then, ought to include a showing of empirical possibility. Many proposed military campaigns ought to be rejected at the bar of possibility, although sadly their infeasibility often is recognized only too late through the bitter, futile experience of fighting the war.

And the mere practical possibility of actually securing the just cause is not good enough—'success' must have a 'reasonable prospect'. Success certainly need not mean full military victory, much less unconditional surrender by the adversary, demands for which tend to lengthen wars greatly. And reasonable prospect may vary inversely with the importance of the just cause, at least at the extreme. For example, if the very survival of some community, one's own[7] or others', is at stake, as in an attempted genocide, perhaps it is enough that prevailing is not entirely impossible.

This second necessary condition amounts to a required showing that a military means of preventing the evil that is claimed to constitute the 'just cause' for war in fact exists.

3. Last Resort

That clearly leads to the next question: since military actions always create their own evils, is military force the least evil alternative? The just war tradition approached this question in two stages, employing terminology that may have done as much to obscure the issue as to elucidate it. One can analyze the issue of whether war is the least evil alternative in two steps by asking, first, is military force the least evil means by which to accomplish the end of stopping the evil that might be resisted? And then, second, if so, is the evil that will be created by attempting to resist less than the unresisted evil? First, what is the least evil means of resisting? Second, is resisting by the least evil means available less evil than not resisting and thereby avoiding the evil likely to be created by the resistance? The less than ideal traditional terminology for raising these two questions sequentially was to ask, first, is war the last resort? And, second, would war be proportional?

'Last resort', like 'just cause', is to modern ears somewhat oddly named. General Guthrie and Secretary Quinlan note that: 'the criterion of "last resort" does not mean that war is not to be embarked upon until every other option has been tried out'.[8] Common sense, like the just war tradition, suggests that one ought actually to try only alternatives that appear to have some reasonable prospect of success. Running through every alternative to war, however unpromising, is pointless at best and likely to waste time. 'Time is often by no means neutral. . . . The early application of force may do more good and less harm than delaying until the situation has grown worse and harder to put right. . . . [But] it is possible to resort to military force too soon as well as too late, and no formula can displace the need for honest practical judgment in the particular circumstances'.[9] Lee observes that 'in the case of a humanitarian crisis, the cost of delay is likely to be great'.[10]

Consideration of whether a resort to war can be justified has already moved on to questions of means, specifically the effectiveness of military means, when it turns to reasonable prospect of success. The issue about 'last resort' is whether warfare is the effective means that accomplishes the end with the least evil. Such minimizing tests, like maximizing tests, are exceptionally strong requirements. But if a less evil means to the same goal has reasonable prospects of success, it is not necessary to resort to war. In this respect, the requirement of last resort is a necessity requirement, as David Rodin observes.[11] One may fight a war only if war is necessary to prevent great evil. The requirement of 'last resort', then, can be expressed far more straightforwardly by simply saying: if war is to be an acceptable means when alternative means ordinarily create less evil, it will ordinarily be because the other means do not in this case lead to the end. That they do not is a largely empirical judgment.

But it is important to appreciate that the hypothesis that other means will cause less evil than war is also a largely empirical generalization and must be investigated in each case. For instance, the sanctions regime against Iraq between 1991 and 2003, approved by the United Nations Security Council on the urging of the United States and dominantly managed in meticulously cruel detail by the United States, caused extensive wrongful harm to Iraqi civilians, including highly vulnerable children, over more than a decade.[12] Even if one had granted the existence in this case of some evil, such as the proliferation of weapons of mass destruction, that could rightly be resisted, it is far from clear that these sanctions produced less evil than some highly limited military actions might have. One has no basis for simply assuming that sanctions, no matter how extreme, unrelenting, and long-lasting they are, will cause fewer deaths and less suffering than limited military action. However, apart from what are now, thanks to the distressing Iraq case, known as 'dumb sanctions' (as distinguished from 'smart sanctions'; i.e., far more selective and carefully targeted ones), alternatives to war ordinarily cause less evil.

A war, then, must be necessary in the sense that there is no effective means to the prevention of the evil that might be resisted that will create less evil than war will. Only then does the question of the proportionality of the resort to war arise.

4. Proportionality of Resort: Whose Evils?

Even the least created evil possible from warfare may still be too much for the sake of the end in question—the prevention of the evil to be resisted may not be worth the evil that a war would create. However, in the face of great enough evils (e.g., the 1994 Rwandan genocide and its spillover into several million deaths in the chaotic and vicious fighting in the eastern Democratic Republic of Congo that is still under way twenty years later[13]), one ought to have acted to prevent those evils while doing as little evil in the process as one could. Questions about how far forward 'reverberating effects' ought to be foreseen and counted are increasingly discussed within military circles, although primarily in the context of proportionality of conduct.[14] This and many other facets of how evils—serious wrongful harms—are to be calibrated involve deep issues that cannot be tackled here. 'As little evil as possible' would not, for example, necessarily entail as few casualties as possible or even, in an extreme case like a genocidal adversary, fewer casualties than would otherwise be perpetrated. In order to prevent the genocide of a certain number of people, it might be a lesser evil to inflict an even larger number of casualties—this would depend on how evil genocide is. And many further complexities remain about what is, after all, only a soothingly simple metaphor: 'balancing' evils.

Nevertheless, it is useful to keep reminding oneself of what one is fundamentally doing in resorting to war. Even on the best case for war, one will be doing evil—killing and wounding people in violation of their rights—in order to prevent others from doing greater evil. The most one can hope is that the created evil is very significantly less than the resisted evil—which is the basis of the just cause—and that one can therefore be justified in the evil one creates. Many people give much higher priority to responsibility for not doing evil than to any responsibility for not allowing evil—this is sometimes put as negative responsibility taking priority over positive responsibility.

These general issues about agency and about negative and positive responsibility cannot be settled here. But I want to acknowledge that it is perfectly coherent instead to refuse to take the least evil alternative if it involves the commission of evil oneself and some other alternative does not. On the one hand, if one gives full (lexical) priority to not doing evil, one must be a pacifist, because it is never in fact possible to fight a war without contributing to the killing of people who are not morally liable to be killed, some of whom will be civilians and some of whom, as we see later, will be opposing combatants whose responsibility for any moral errors is not great enough to make them liable to death and the other worst calamities of war, like wounds that never heal. If, on the other hand, in spite of acknowledging a strong responsibility not to do evil, one believes that a duty to protect others against wrongful harm perpetrated by third parties can sometimes outweigh the duty not to inflict wrongful harm oneself, one can engage in war at least in those rare instances in which the evil resisted is indeed much greater than the evil created by the resistance.

5. Proportionality of Resort: Which Evils?

But we cannot avoid confronting this question: exactly which wrongs ought to be counted among the created evils? This section and the following two sections each examine one particular challenge faced when one tries concretely to specify the central created evils of war. A first especially difficult component question that concerns responsibility is: does one count only the wrongs that one's own side can be expected to cause, for instance, the civilians who can be expected to be killed unintentionally by one's own forces, or all the civilians who will be wrongfully killed by all sides if one chooses to resort to war, including the civilians who can be expected to be killed by the side one is resisting when it fights back against one's opposition? Lee argues as follows:

> When a state M launches a defensive war, its opponent N will respond with (further) military force, and this will involve its committing wrongs against individuals that would not have occurred without M's having gone to war. The question is whether these wrongs must be taken into account when M calculates proportionality. The

> answer seems to be no. In the domestic case, if some action of A results in B's committing a wrong, B's wrong is not, in general, also A's wrong, unless B is acting under A's authority. Otherwise A and B are responsible for their own wrongs. So wartime wrongs suffered by individuals in M committed by N do not count in M's proportionality calculations.[15]

I am not fully persuaded but am inclined to think instead that the proportionality assessment should consist of overall judgments about all the evil that can be reasonably expected if war is chosen. All the harms that were wrongfully inflicted, it seems to me, have to count in any ex post facto judgment about whether a war was worth the evil it created. And, insofar as they were reasonable to expect in advance, all these evils should have been included in the ex ante assessments of the proportionality of the resort to war. Various evils would be the primary responsibility of various different agents, but a certain total collection of evils will all descend if war is taken up by the agent making the proportionality assessment. One ought, then, to count in the calculation of evil created by the war all the evil that can be expected to result from the war that would not have been expected to occur if there had been no war. All the evil consists of at least three noteworthy categories: (1) evil one could expect to inflict oneself—unintentional but foreseeable, (2) evil one could expect others whom one ought to protect to suffer at the hands of third parties, and (3) evil one could expect yet others whom one has no duty to protect to suffer at the hands of third parties. No one denies that one must count (1), the evil one can expect to do oneself, so I discuss (2) and (3).

One reason why it is not the case that 'wartime wrongs suffered by individuals in M committed by N do not count in M's proportionality calculations' is M's special duty to protect particular people. This means that one must count (2), the evil one could expect others whom one ought to protect to suffer at the hands of others. If M chooses to go to war against N's aggression, this is presumably in large part to protect as many as possible of the people (potential combatants as well as civilians) it is bound to protect. Part of the source of my disagreement with Lee here may, then, turn on different criteria for different types of responsibility. One way in which a government can be responsible for a wrongful harm to a society is that the government inflicted the harm on the society; in this case, the government is guilty of directly harming the society. But another, more indirect way in which a government can be responsible for a wrongful harm to a society is the following. The government has a duty to protect the society, but a second government inflicts a harm on the society because the first government's protection is inadequate. In this case, the first government is not guilty of harming the society—the second government is. But the first government is at least partly responsible for the society's being harmed by the second because the first failed to protect the society against the second's attack, as it was obligated to do. Perhaps in this second case Lee would be impressed by the fact that the first government is not guilty of wrongfully harming the society and so, in that respect, is not directly responsible. But I am impressed by the fact that the first government is responsible for having failed to protect the society. If the attack on the society would not have occurred if the first government had not done something it chose to do (e.g., confront the second government in an attempt to prevent it from taking yet some other action), then it seems to me that the first government is all the more responsible for the first society's being wrongfully harmed. The first government's decision to confront the second might be a causally necessary condition of the second government's wrongfully harming the first society.

One must, of course, think hard about whether the people for whom one is responsible will in fact suffer less evil if one resists militarily than if one does not. In war, it is folly to ignore either the risk of losing or the risk of reiterated escalations, win or lose. War usually does not go according to plan. A nation as militarily powerful as the United States has failed to achieve some of its main objectives in several recent wars (intervention in Vietnam in the 1960s, invasion of Afghanistan in 2001, and invasion of Iraq in 2003), but it suffered astronomical economic costs and substantial human losses and inflicted great death and destruction on civilians and opposing forces through these military involvements.[16] David Rodin emphasizes especially strongly that one of the risks one bears only if one chooses to go to war is the risk of losing the war and that 'to fight and to lose is often worse than not fighting at all'.[17] It is helpful to distinguish the costs of fighting, regardless of whether one wins, from the costs of losing. Ordinarily, unless one's adversary is especially murderous or genocidal, one suffers more casualties from resisting than from not resisting, even if the fight is militarily successful—this depends in part on what one's adversary is committed to doing if not resisted. As mentioned earlier, it is conceivable that these losses can be justified, as in the interest of those intended to be protected in light of other values served by resisting, but the costs of fighting cannot be ignored. The costs of losing are rarely mentioned by politicians promoting war, who tend to talk as if one is going to win. Again, much depends on the nature of the adversary and its basic goals. At the extreme, if it is genocidal from the start, losing is unlikely to be materially worse than not resisting and may be more honourable.

But, in more ordinary cases, losing itself can bring severe additional penalties, including imposed surrender conditions (possibly including unjust reparations), military occupation, and whatever additional destruction of military forces and civilian infrastructure results not simply from being at war but being at war and being on the losing side—often considerable destruction is suffered before defeat is conceded. Rodin cites Clausewitz's famous observation that war normally tends to escalate: the side that believes itself to be losing redoubles its attacks, which tends to provoke the adversary to redouble its attacks, and so on. Some of the costs of escalation are simply the costs of fighting, win or lose, but if one is on the receiving end of a final decisive escalation by one's adversary that one cannot resist, the harms inflicted can be considerable, especially if one resists to the bitter end.

The most difficult case is (3), evil one could expect yet others whom one has no duty to protect to suffer at the hands of third parties. If one is not in any respect responsible for these people, it might seem that one need not count the evils they will suffer if one chooses war. And yet the basic argument for any war must be that war is the lesser evil overall in the case at hand. But if the war produces less evil only because one decided that some of the resulting evil should not count, the proportionality assessment seems fundamentally dishonest. If one chooses war, these people will suffer evil that they would evidently not have suffered if you had chosen against war—merely not at your hands and not in the face of any special responsibility of yours to protect them. Your choice of war will nevertheless foreseeably bring evil upon them. I do not see how that evil could not count in what is supposed to be not an assessment of one's own guilt or responsibility, but instead an overall assessment of whether less evil occurs if there is a war than if there is none.[18] If this is correct, it is obligatory to include consideration of all the wrongful harms to be expected, including those wrongful harms for which one's adversary in the war would be directly to blame legally and morally.

The need to be inclusive for this purpose becomes especially clear when one considers that in assessing the resisted evil (the evil that will occur if one does not go to war), one is counting only evils for which one is not responsible oneself. If one is sometimes justified in engaging in humanitarian military intervention, those resisted evils would include ones suffered by individuals for whom one has no special responsibility. One could not honestly count evils for which one is not responsible suffered by people to whom one is not responsible on one side of the balance and ignore them on the other.

So it appears that the fundamental question that one ought to be asking before launching a war is basically this: would a war be worth it morally?[19] Is what is at stake in this conflict—the evil that war might prevent in this case—worth all the evil that this war can be expected to create? Therefore, looking beyond the negative duty not to harm and special duties to protect, one ought to count all the evil the war can reasonably be expected to inflict because one will be tipping the scales in favour of war by omitting some of its worst evils if one does not count on both sides of the balance the evils for which one is not responsible. The central question here is not for which evils will one be responsible, but, instead which evils will one in fact unleash if one goes to war? So when I use Lee's phrase 'created evil', I shall not mean, as he seems to, the evil that the side carrying out the calculation of proportionality could rightly be held directly and primarily responsible for, but all the evil that it is reasonable to foresee being created if they choose to go to war. It takes only one side to have a massacre or an invasion, but two sides to have a war. If one chooses war, one decides that all that war's evils—whatever they turn out to be—will be committed. In choosing for or against war, one should count all the evils that will predictably occur, not only the evils one will do oneself.

5.1. Proportionality of Resort: Which Harms Are Evils?

We turn now to a third component of the general challenge of specifying the most relevant kinds of created evils: whether, in addition to losses inflicted on civilians, only losses to one's own forces or also losses to at least some of the opposing forces ought to be counted among the created evils.

When one goes to war, one would like to believe that the casualties on the opposing side either deserve or are morally liable to their fates. And philosophers endlessly assume the most simple of all possible cases: 'the just side and the unjust side'. Reality, however, is far messier than these wishes and assumptions. A full explanation would require detailed examinations of numerous historical cases, for which sufficient space is not available here, but we cannot proceed on the basis of a black-and-white caricature of military conflict. First, obviously, one may be mistaken in one's belief that the side on which one is fighting is justified. I will largely leave this aside because some cases, like resistance to the Nazis and resistance to the Rwandan genocide, were or would have been as fully justified as it is reasonable to expect complex human affairs to be. Nevertheless, the mere possibility that one is oneself an unjustified killer and that there is no excuse for harming anyone in the opposition is a reason not to inflict any casualties that are not entirely necessary for victory, however certain one feels that one is justified in pursuing victory. I will, however, ground my position instead on the other three complications that follow.

Second, one's own side may be, all things considered, justified, but only barely or only partly. In almost all wars, wrongs have been committed on both sides prior to the resort to war. Some of one's adversaries may be fully justified in resisting some of the wrongs done by one's own side even if most of the opponents are fighting on different grounds that do not justify their fighting. Any given adversary combatant may be one of those who is justified in fighting you or one who is not justified in fighting you. And even in a case in which one's own side is not justified, like the misguided American and British invasion of Iraq in 2003, consider the enormous variety of types of Iraqis who resisted, including some engaged in justified defence against groundless invasion and others who were murderous fanatics bent on ethnic or religious slaughter of their own compatriots.

Third, many wars—I am inclined to believe most wars—have two unjust sides: no party to the war adequately satisfies the necessary conditions for resort to war that this chapter is discussing. These are wars that should never have occurred. But, as the war progresses, many on each side become motivated primarily to defend their own country and comrades against the attacks from the other side, which are indeed without adequate justification. To some degree, no one was justified in the beginning and everyone is justified in the end—which individuals are morally liable to be wounded or killed? Perhaps the majority of wars are almost pure tragedy.

Fourth, and most important, even if one takes the neatest possible (and rarest) case in which one side is justified in resorting to war and its adversary is not justified, two crucial multiplicities that compound each other yield arbitrary outcomes. On the one hand, the individuals who fight in wars—on both sides—suffer an exceptionally wide spectrum of harms, ranging from returning home largely unscathed to suffering minor wounds or serious wounds that heal; to suffering irreparable wounds like blindness, paralysis, and life-long mental trauma and psychological dysfunction; to not returning home at all. On the other hand, individual fighters bear equally great varieties of types and degrees of responsibility for fighting. Some are well-informed, well-educated, and thoughtful people who have voluntarily consented to fight. Others participate not only voluntarily but also ruthlessly and hatefully. Others are conscripted by law or by poverty or otherwise coerced into participation in a conflict they know almost nothing about. Some are poorly educated, badly informed, and not capable of meaningful consent. Others come out of a perhaps in-itself-admirable loyalty to their immediate comrades with only the dimmest understanding of what is at stake in the war as a whole—they know only that 'we are under threat'. And so on—by any normal standard of moral responsibility for one's actions, some combatants are highly responsible, some are not responsible at all, and most are scattered somewhere on the very wide spectrum in between.

Much of the horror of war consists in the intersection of the cruel diversity of fates with the wide variation in responsibility: the randomness with which the radically different fates are distributed across the radically different degrees of responsibility. If only the enthusiastically hateful died and all the reluctantly coerced and the uneducated and ill-informed were wounded and then healed, war might seem an almost tolerable extreme method of dispute resolution. But we have no reason whatsoever to believe that among those fighting on the unjust side either the distribution among dead, wounded, and unscathed (or the distribution across wounds among life-shattering, serious, and minor ones) matches in any way individuals' varying degrees of moral responsibility. The least morally responsible may return home quadriplegic and emotionally shattered, while the most responsible survive unscathed and covered in medals. Just as markets do not reward the industrious with wealth and the lazy with poverty, wars do not assign death to those responsible for injustice and scratches to the nonresponsible and the excused.[20] It is a consolation to believe that those on the wrong side of a war suffer only harms to which they are morally liable. Unfortunately, this consolation is baseless—it is, as Kant, probably alluding to a central insight in the Book of Job, understood, 'only sorry comfort'.[21] Wars are far more deeply tragic in their random, if not perverse, dispersal of pain, injury, and death.

Until this changes, we must count at least some—I would say, many—of the losses on the opposing side among the evils created by the war irrespective of whether the opposing side is justified or unjustified in having resorted to war.[22] Thousands and sometimes millions suffer harms to which they are not morally liable. Exactly why are they not liable? Outside of war, we think that people can sometimes do things that make them liable to be harmed, either punitively or in defence, so that the harms inflicted on them do not wrong them. But we also think that there should be some fit between the harms they suffer and what they have done to make themselves liable. This is obviously true for punitive harm, but it is also true for defensive harm. Any justifiable harm must meet a standard of appropriateness. To become liable to be permanently maimed, for example, a person must have done something that warrants that liability. But in war, the harms that unjust combatants suffer are routinely far out of proportion to their degree of responsibility and are wrongful for that reason. Harms suffered by justified combatants are, unless those particular combatants are also contributing to an unjustified goal, even more likely to be wrongful. So we need to consider, when assessing the proportionality of the war as a whole, both the harms inflicted on combatants engaged in justified combat and many of the harms inflicted on those who are contributing to unjustified combat but whose terrible fate in war is utterly inappropriate to their meagre degree of responsibility.[23]

Although this is an issue we cannot pursue adequately here, a further question remains: which harms inflicted on those who are not liable to those harms are inflicted wrongfully? One intermediate position would be, for example, that many killings and woundings are wrongly suffered because not appropriately distributed according to individual liability but can nevertheless be inflicted excusably if they are necessary in the course of fighting an all-things-considered justified war. But what is crucial here is that as long as the harms are suffered wrongly, they still count among the created evils from the war, and they are no less evil in themselves for the agents of their creation being excused, when they are. My conclusion, then, is that combatants on both sides in any war are likely to suffer wrongly considerable harm to which they are not liable in addition to the harm suffered wrongly by civilians. Therefore, a responsible calculation of proportionality must include reasonable expectations about the full extent of all these categories of war-created evil.

6. Proportionality of Resort: Further Evils

David Rodin has made a valuable suggestion about a fourth kind of created evil that ought to be included in assessments of the proportionality of a resort to war.[24] In this section, we note this additional category and then mention a final evil. I have mentioned several times the unpredictability of war, which experienced military leaders regularly invoke as a caution against the easy resort to war. Rodin observes that when financial accountants are doing a cost–benefit analysis for a large, long-term project, they add on top of the predictable costs a category called 'the contingency'. The contingency is for further costs, the particulars of which are entirely unknown but the general likelihood of which is almost guaranteed by the nature of things to be high—one can be fairly sure that there will be other costs beyond those one can think of. Allowing for nasty surprises is only prudent, and, even with the contingency, ambitious projects are notorious for cost overruns. Rodin suggests that every proportionality calculation should include what he calls a *moral contingency*, an additional quantum of probable evil beyond the specific evils that one reasonably expects. This category is for the moral equivalent of nasty surprises: the unexpected massacres, the soldiers run amok, the fatal 'cock-ups' (British) and lethal 'SNAFUs' (American) that any veteran can tell you are endemic to the chaos of war.[25]

Adding a moral contingency to the assessment of proportionality obviously means putting a finger on the side of the scale with the created evil, thereby making any given war a little harder to justify. One could object that, in theory, there could be positive contingencies—pleasant rather than nasty surprises—and the two might cancel out. However, first, a look at history reveals far more nasty than pleasant surprises from wars. Second, given the incorrigible tendency of politicians to get into unnecessary or unwinnable wars, as well as current excessive technological optimism, making the justification a bit harder is in general an excellent idea. Third, some unforeseen evil is fairly well guaranteed to turn up, and making provision for it can be seen as simply implementing a standard of care. Naturally, the contingency ought not to be exaggerated, or it would amount to smuggling in pacifism by the back door through making the proportionality requirement impossible to satisfy in practice. But a bit of extra caution seems in order before any decision is made to 'let slip the dogs of war'.

Finally, I would briefly add one obvious further kind of evil created by almost all wars: predictable environmental destruction. Even if extreme atrocities (e.g., the long-lasting human genetic effects of the herbicide Agent Orange employed in gigantic quantities against Vietnam by the United States in the 1960s) are avoided,[26] wars still routinely tend to wreak havoc in the natural world.

7. Proportionality of Resort: Summing Up the Evils Created by War

It may be useful now to draw together the various created evils discussed in the four preceding sections. Altogether, wars create at least four known, readily predictable evils: wrongful harm to civilians (on both sides: a civilian is a civilian, and the evil of wrongful harm to them is not variably weighted into 'theirs' and 'ours'); wrongful harm to combatants on both sides in excess of any individual moral liability to be harmed; possible defeat of the better justified side and the consequent suffering of additional wrongful harm; and the inevitable pollution and environmental destruction. Then, fifth, there are the unpredictable evils that a standard of care would recommend providing for with Rodin's suggestion of a category for moral contingency. A judgment about proportionality should consider at least these five types of evil created by virtually every war.

8. Proportionality of Resort Versus Proportionality of Conduct

A final source of confusion remains. The wrongful harms that ought to be weighed in the balance against the resisted evil in the assessment of proportionality that must precede any decision to resort to war (proportionality *jus ad bellum*, if one likes Latin labels coined in the nineteenth century) are far wider than the harms that are ordinarily considered in the calculus of proportionality during the conduct of the war (proportionality *jus in bello*). The criteria of proportionality are so divergent between the two cases that 'proportionality' is fundamentally equivocal between the circumstances of resort and the circumstances of conduct, for reasons briefly sketched here. It is important to appreciate this divergence lest one unthinkingly assume that the relation between the proportionality of the resort to war and the proportionality of the constituent operations in the conduct of the war is the relation of whole to parts. In particular, one might think that if the individual operations in the war satisfy proportionality of conduct, then the war as a whole will satisfy proportionality of resort. But this is a fallacious inference because it ignores the equivocation over 'proportionality' resulting primarily from the differences in which harms the two kinds of proportionality respectively consider and other differences as well.

The generally accepted definition of proportionality of conduct is the one embodied in the 1977 Geneva Protocol I and acknowledged in principle by the vast majority of the world's militaries, as shown by their governments' ratification of Protocol I. The laws of war take a common-sense approach: when parties have committed themselves to going to war, one ought then to do everything possible to restrain their conduct of the war irrespective of whether they are justified in going to war—indeed, especially if they are not. The circumstances for the assessment of proportionality of conduct are vastly different from the circumstances for the assessment of proportionality of resort. In the case of resort, no decision has yet been made on the question of whether one would be justified in going to war, so one clearly ought to take into account everything important that is relevant, especially all the evils that will result only if one chooses war; I have argued that these include at least the five categories of evil listed earlier. Judgments about the proportionality of the conduct of a war, by contrast, arise only after one has made the decision to go to war and presuppose that, having committed oneself to battle, one is attempting to be successful on behalf of the just cause for which one takes oneself, rightly or wrongly, to be fighting. One can—and should—reassess during the course of the war whether the decision to resort to war was correct, which means repeatedly returning to all the necessary conditions for justified resort (including the proportionality of resort) and considering whether they still seem to be fulfilled. One might, for instance, discover that what one had thought was the just cause was merely a pretext and that the real purpose of the war is quite different from what one believed in advance.

But insofar as one is committed to continuing to fight the war, one ought, according to the international law that governs warfare, to judge the proportionality of every attack that one is contemplating launching. While proportionality of resort weighs all the resisted evils expected from the entire war against all the created evils expected from the whole war, proportionality of conduct asks about a particular attack in the war 'whether the civilian losses an attack would be expected to produce are excessive, compared to the military advantage it is also expected to yield'.[27] Only a specific operation in the war is assessed, not the whole war, and the test for each operation is extremely narrow on both sides of the scale: proportionality of conduct narrowly weighs only the military advantage expected from the attack against only the civilian losses expected from the attack. None of the evils of war is included except civilian losses. Proportionality of conduct is sharply focussed on its sole purpose: protecting civilians during each military action. Wrongful infliction of losses on combatants, for example, is ignored. And the only 'good' considered on the other side of the balance from civilian losses is the military advantage of one's own side, which a party committed to war will assume is good for as long as it is committed to fight. To question whether its own military advantage is a good would be to question whether it ought to be fighting. Many parties to war ought to be questioning precisely that, but the purpose of proportionality of conduct is to protect civilians against *all* sides, including the sides that ought to be questioning their own justification for fighting but are not.

Why? Why should the focus in the midst of the war be so much narrower than before a war has begun? I may appear here to be abandoning morality—or at least the best morality—and settling for law or some second-best morality. But the best moral rules demand the best that is humanly possible in the circumstances of the decision facing the agent. The best that one can do in the midst of a contest in inflicting harm, which is what war is, is obviously not going to be very good. But it may be the best within those circumstances, and one can do better only by refusing to be in those circumstances, for which there is much to be said.[28] This is not the place to present the full case, but here briefly are some leading considerations.[29] First, it makes sense to focus on the protection of civilians because, for as long as battle continues to be joined, combatants on each side are committed to attempting to kill or wound each other insofar as necessary in order to succeed militarily. Wars are competitions in death and destruction. Being committed to a war is being committed to significant destruction of one's adversary's military capabilities. The only restraint that fighters committed to military success are at all likely to observe is to concentrate on killing each other and on avoiding killing civilians.

Second, judgments about proportionality of conduct must be able to be made by the lowest level combatants, those actually doing the fighting. Accordingly, decisions must demand only the amounts and types of information that fighters are likely to be able to acquire and responsibly process quickly while in mortal danger themselves. All combatants ought frequently to reconsider whether the war they are fighting is on the whole justified, but, during the preparation for an attack and the attack itself, they cannot reflect on all the complex necessary conditions for justified resort to war. As the US Army's latest *Training Circular* begins, 'Modern combat is chaotic, intense, and shockingly destructive. In your first battle, you will experience the confusing and often terrifying sights, sounds, smells, and dangers of the battlefield. . . . You might hear the screams of a wounded comrade'.[30] What combatants can, and therefore ought to, do is focus vigilantly on taking care not to inflict on any civilians the death and wounds they have been trained to inflict on adversaries. In the 'fog' and mortal danger of battle, this discrimination is already a demanding task that is frequently not achieved.

Third, in order to provide maximum protection for civilians, it is critical that both sides in battle—more justified and less justified—abide by the same standard of proportionality; this has nothing to do with any mythical 'moral symmetry' of combatants, which is a misguided and irrelevant notion.[31] Each side tends to cut itself slack on the assumption that they are the 'good guys'—this is one common route to the brutality of 'holy wars'. So there needs to be one well-known standard for what constitutes excessive civilian losses, the standard needs to be the minimum losses compatible with the success necessary for a specific military advantage, and those who believe they are fighting on the right side should not be allowed to cut themselves any slack whatsoever.[32] The tight standard for excessive civilian losses should, to the maximum extent possible, be enforced on all fighters by their own sense of honour, their own commanders, their own *courts martial*, and international criminal courts.

It is, of course, true that abiding by the standard of proportionality in conduct does nothing to change the fact that a party that is not justified in being at war in the first place may not be justified in anything that it is doing. When the standard permits a party committed to war to pursue its own military advantage, it is in no way granting that military success for that side is in fact morally good. The standard applies to the expectations of all combatants in advance of a decision to attack. The standard says: whatever advantage you could reasonably expect to be accomplished by your military operation, you may not launch an attack that can reasonably be expected to harm a number of civilians that would be excessive for that much of an advantage as judged by standard military practices. This is a very low standard, but it can serve the elementary moral purpose of saving civilian lives by imposing some restraint even on forces who entirely falsely believe that they are justified in being at war. A number of contemporary philosophers think, on the contrary, that some higher and more objective standard should be workable, but they have so far completely failed to specify one that could be adopted by all parties committed to fighting.[33] A workable higher standard would obviously be welcome.

Because, for the sake of effectiveness, the focus of proportionality of conduct is so narrow, it would be entirely possible for every single attack throughout a war to satisfy proportionality of conduct, but the war as a whole grossly to fail to satisfy the standard of proportionality of resort because the evils created, including the proportionate civilian losses satisfying the standard of proportionality of conduct in each attack, combined with all the other evils created by the war exceeded the resisted evil. Proportionality of conduct considers only one of the five kinds of evil relevant to the resort to war. The two kinds of proportionality, then, play radically different but vital roles. Proportionality of resort restrains people from getting into wars. Proportionality of conduct restrains how they fight the wars they get into, irrespective of whether they ought to be in them.

9. Conclusion

Last resort and proportionality of resort are, then, each one ineliminable further necessary conditions for the justification of any war, even a war that would have reasonable prospects of success in serving a just cause by resisting a great evil. Unfortunately, proportionality is at best quite vague, and governments that want to promote wars find it easy to manipulate it by playing down the evils the war will create and playing up the evils to be resisted. Citizens of major military powers are constantly told that their security and possibly their very existence is threatened by some unprecedented evil like communism or terrorism against which the only solution is military victory. If practical reasoning is to counter such false claims, it must take on their empirical elements as well as make conceptual arguments. A purely conceptual argument cannot be practical. Whether a war would be proportional depends on what it is in fact likely to achieve and to harm, as well as the moral significance of both any reasonably expected accomplishments and all reasonably expected evils.

Notes

1. Janina Dill and Henry Shue, 'Limiting the Killing in War', *Ethics & International Affairs*, 26 (2012), 312–319. Here, we challenge the views of Jeff McMahan, Cécile Fabre, and Helen Frowe.
2. Steven P. Lee, *Ethics and War: An Introduction* (Cambridge: Cambridge University Press, 2012), 68–108 and 136–149.
3. Lee, *Ethics and War*, 86.
4. Niall Ferguson, *The Pity of War* (London: Allen Lane, 1998), 462; Richard Norton-Taylor, 'First World War Abridged', *The Guardian*, 13 August 2013.
5. See, for example, Francisco Suárez, *Metaphysical Disputations*, XIII, Section IV, 10; rpt. in Gregory M. Reichberg, Henrik Syse, and Endre Begby (eds.), *The Ethics of War: Classic and Contemporary Readings* (Oxford/Malden, MA: Blackwell, 2006), 352.
6. Henry Shue, 'Making Exceptions', *Journal of Applied Philosophy* 26 (2009), 307–322.
7. Danny Statman, 'On the Success Condition for Legitimate Self-Defense', *Ethics* 118 (2008), 659–686.
8. Charles Guthrie and Michael Quinlan, *Just War—The Just War Tradition: Ethics in Modern Warfare* (London: Bloomsbury, 2007), 33.
9. Idem, 33–34.
10. Lee, *Ethics and War*, 136.
11. David Rodin, 'The War Trap: Dilemmas of *jus termination*', *Ethics* 125 (2015), note 6.
12. Joy Gordon, *Invisible War: The United States and the Iraq Sanctions* (Cambridge, MA: Harvard University Press, 2010); Henry Shue, 'Force Protection, Military Advantage, and 'Constant Care' for Civilians: The 1991 Bombing of Iraq', in *The American Way of Bombing: Changing Ethical and Legal Norms, from Flying Fortresses to Drones*, edited by Matthew Evangelista and Henry Shue (Ithaca, NY: Cornell University Press, 2014), 146–147.
13. Gérard Prunier. *Africa's World War: Congo, The Rwandan Genocide, and the Making of a Continental Catastrophe* (Oxford: Oxford University Press, 2009).
14. Henry Shue, 'Force Protection, Military Advantage, and "Constant Care" for Civilians', 154–156.
15. Lee, *Ethics and War*, 89.
16. Neta Crawford et al., *Costs of War Project* (Providence, RI: Watson Institute of Brown University, 2013), http://costsofwar.org.
17. Rodin, 'The War Trap', 677.
18. William V. O'Brien, *The Conduct of Just and Limited War* (New York: Praeger, 1981), 28.
19. Cheyney Ryan, 'Pacifism', this volume, *s.v.*
20. This is overwhelmingly obvious from almost any memoir or novel by someone who has fought in or observed war, but see, e.g., Martha Gellhorn, *The Face of War* (New York: Atlantic Monthly Press, 1988); Michael Herr, *Dispatches* (New York: Avon

Books, 1978); John Keegan, *The Face of Battle* (London: Penguin Books, 1976); or Bao Ninh, *The Sorrow of War*, translated by Frank Palmos (London and New York: Vintage, 2005).

21. Immanuel Kant, 'Toward Perpetual Peace', in *Practical Philosophy*, translated and edited by Mary Gregor, Cambridge Edition of the Works of Immanuel Kant (Cambridge: Cambridge University Press, 1996 [1795]), 326 [8:355]; and Howard Williams, *Kant and the End of War: A Critique of Just War Theory* (Basingstoke, Hampshire: Palgrave Macmillan, 2012), 60–65.
22. For a concrete ethical argument along these lines, see Richard W. Miller, 'Civilian Deaths and American Power: Three Lessons from Iraq and Afghanistan', in *The American Way of Bombing*, 158–171.
23. I am grateful to Seth Lazar for the formulation in this paragraph and for his dogged rejection of several less adequate ones. A conflicting view of moral liability in war has been extensively articulated by Jeff McMahan.
24. Rodin, 'The War Trap', 685.
25. Phil Klay, *Redeployment* (Edinburgh and London: Canongate, 2015).
26. Stockholm International Peace Research Institute, *Ecological Consequences of the Second Indochina War* (Stockholm: Almqvist & Wiksell, 1976).
27. Henry Shue, 'Proportionality in War', in *Encyclopedia of War*, edited by Gordon Martel (Oxford: Blackwell Publishing, 2012), *s.v.*
28. See Ryan, 'Pacifism'.
29. Henry Shue, 'Laws of War, Morality, and International Politics: Compliance, Stringency, and Limits', *Leiden Journal of International Law* 26 (2013), 271–292. Also see Pablo Kalmanovitz, 'Modern Sources of the Regular War Tradition,' this volume, *s.v.*
30. US Department of the Army, Headquarters, *The Warrior Ethos and Soldier Combat Skills*, TC 3-21.75 (Washington, DC: Headquarters, Department of the Army, 2013), xiii.
31. Adam Roberts, 'The Principle of Equal Application of the Laws of War', in *Just and Unjust Warriors: The Moral and Legal Status of Soldiers*, edited by David Rodin and Henry Shue (Oxford: Oxford University Press, 2008), 226–254; Dill and Shue, 'Limiting the Killing in War'.
32. Janina Dill, 'The American Way of Bombing and International Law: Two Logics of Warfare in Tension', in *The American Way of Bombing*, 131–144.
33. Thomas Hurka, 'Proportionality in the Morality of War', *Philosophy & Public Policy*, 33 (2005), 34–66; McMahan, *Killing in War*, 107–110; Rodin, 'The War Trap'.

CHAPTER 14

PACIFISM

CHEYNEY RYAN

The term 'pacifism' comes from the Latin for 'peacemaking'. It was coined a century ago during a heyday of war glorification, when many political leaders saw war as an intrinsically good thing, a theater of masculine virtue and a source of political regeneration. Theodore Roosevelt, America's first modern president, praised war as 'bully fun' and once urged invading Canada if no other war could be found. Initially, a 'pacifist' was simply someone who rejected such nonsense, who saw war as an intrinsically bad thing and sought alternatives to it, like international arbitration. Self-proclaimed pacifists included prominent politicians like William Jennings Bryan in the United States and Jean Jaurez in France and thinkers like William James and Bertrand Russell. During World War I, pacifism became associated with feminist figures like Jane Addams who linked militarism with sexism and argued that women have a special interest in peace making.[1]

After World War I, the term was increasingly associated with what was previously termed '*nonresistance*'. This is what nineteenth-century Christians like the Quakers, and figures like Tolstoy called the personal rejection of all killing. Finally, in the twentieth century, pacifism became associated with '*nonviolence*', the political practice of figures like Gandhi, Dr. Martin Luther King, Jr., and Cesar Chavez that rejects violent strategies.[2]

Pacifism, then, is a complex tradition.[3] Any account of it is as much a proposal as a description. I distinguish two types here. Both fundamentally oppose war and pursue peace but from different perspectives.

Political pacifism opposes war as a social practice. This pacifism attacks the 'war system', by which it means the practices of killing and destruction that characterise war *making* and the practices of mobilising human and material resources to those ends that characterise war *building*. Political pacifists have differed on how expansive the war system is (i.e., how much other practices like racism or sexism are included in it). I shall focus on its core elements. Political pacifism's solutions are institutional: they involve both peace-making (movements to prevent or stop war) and peace-building (mechanisms to resolve conflicts peacefully). Its sources are secular, originating in the

Enlightenment, specifically eighteenth-century republicanism. It coalesced in the nineteenth century, in response to the Napoleonic Wars.

Personal pacifism opposes killing as an act, hence opposes war as involving instances of that action. Its peace-making focus is more individual: it promotes acts of personal refusal to participation in war and personal transformation in developing more peaceful relations. Its sources are religious, originating in the West with the first Christians.

A key issue for the philosophy of pacifism is the relation between these pacifisms. They can overlap, but they differ in their logic.

Most importantly, they differ in *why* they oppose war. The political pacifist is like the death penalty opponent who objects to the *kind* of killing the practice involves. Death penalty opponents object to 'legal' killing (death by government), political pacifists object to 'political' killing (death by states). But just as those who oppose the death penalty may permit killing in other circumstances, political pacifists may permit it as well (personal self-defence, say). The personal pacifist is like the death penalty opponent who objects to it because she is opposed to killing per se, whatever the context. So this type of pacifism finds personal self-defence problematic. (Their differences around personal self-defence do not translate into differences about war because both think that war has about as much to do with personal self-defence as rape has to do with procreation.)

Both types of pacifism *unconditionally* oppose war, but in different ways. Political pacifism opposes the practice of war in the same way that many people unconditionally oppose the practice of torture. Its focus is the *illegitimacy* of the practice: individual wars, like acts of torture, are condemned as instances of the practice, whatever justification they might have in isolation. The thinking here is from the top down. By contrast, personal pacifism's is from the bottom up. It unconditionally opposes the act of killing in the same way that people oppose the act of infanticide; hence, it opposes *any* endeavour involving that act.

The issues raised by pacifism are of interest whatever one thinks of its response to them. Personal pacifism, as its name suggests, approaches war as a matter of personal responsibility, not just public policy. It compels us to ask: how am I implicated in the warlike proclivities of my society, how should my opposition to it translate into my own words and deeds? If this personalises war, political pacifism historicises it. It compels us to step back from judging war one more time and address what Clausewitz called 'the question of war itself': the legitimacy (or illegitimacy) of war as a distinct human practice. My account of pacifism will consider how it addresses both issues. At the start, though, several challenges are worth noting.

Pacifism has been primarily a *practical* tradition whose principal audience has been the marginalised. Its main voices have been political activists, inordinately people of color and women. It has never had a presence in academia (for much of the twentieth century, pacifists were barred from teaching in American public universities). So theoretical work on it is minimal and undeveloped; hence, the problem of parochialism.[4] Another challenge comes from the opposite direction. Anyone comparing a century ago to now might say that yesterday's pacifism has become today's common sense. No one thinks that war is 'bully fun'. A candidate who urged invading Canada would not be elected president; they would be judged insane. John Mueller writes, 'War is no longer regarded like eating or sex, as something inevitable to the human condition. It is seen as something grafted onto human existence, like duelling, which human beings can well do without'.[5] Alongside what might be termed this 'grand disillusion' is what might be termed the 'great defection': the refusal of ordinary people to participate in the war enterprise. (A recent study of this is James J. Sheehan's *Where Have All the Soldiers Gone?*[6]) It used to be that the mark of a pacifist was refusing to fight in one's country's wars. Now, hardly anyone wants to fight in them. The upshot is that it's increasingly difficult to say what is *distinctive* about the pacifist position, as opposed just war views that doubt if their standards are ever met.

Let's call this the 'demarcation problem'. For some versions of pacifism, there *is* no sharp distinction: pacifism is what you get from taking just war principles seriously. This has been called 'just war pacifism'. But my discussion will stress the differences between the two approaches by construing pacifism as an 'absolutist' position, considering what this means, and how it can be defended.

I begin with what it means.

1. Pacifism as Fundamental Opposition to War

Pacifism (as I'll construe it) is fundamentally opposed to war. I take this to mean two things. Pacifism is *unconditionally* opposed to war. The pertains to the extent of its opposition. And, it is *absolutely* opposed to war. This pertains to the depth of its opposition.

It is its unconditional and absolute opposition that most distinguishes pacifism from more fastidious forms of just war theory. It is also what makes people uncomfortable with it. Its unconditional opposition reeks of *dogmatism*, a refusal to look at things case by case, and its absolute opposition reeks of *fanaticism*, a refusal to countenance countervailing moral claims. Something must be said about both.

1.1. Unconditional Opposition

To be unconditionally opposed to war means being opposed to every *instance* of war, regardless of what kind of war it is. Nineteenth-century political pacifism arose contemporaneously with abolitionism, so it might be termed 'war abolitionism'. It does not distinguish good/just wars from bad/unjust wars any more than abolitionism distinguished good/just instances of slavery from bad/unjust ones. Some of the objections to it are objections to *any* position of this kind. Jeremy Waldron writes of unconditional opposition to torture, 'In these troubled times, it is not hard to make the idea of an absolute prohibition on torture, or any absolute prohibition, look silly, as a matter of moral philosophy'.[7] Much criticism of pacifism's unconditional opposition to war has aimed to do just this. But note that pacifism's 'absolutism' does not distinguish it from just war theory insofar as many just war theorists are equally uncompromising in their opposition to violations of *jus in bello* or extreme instances of them (like poison gas). The difference between them and pacifists is not 'absolutism' per se but what they are absolutists *about*: pacifists are opposed to war in *all* its aspects—they are *totally* opposed to war, we might say.

Complications arise because people can be unconditionally opposed to war yet disagree about what *counts* as 'war'. The same was true of slavery: nineteenth-century abolitionists unconditionally opposed slavery yet disagreed about what counted as 'slavery' (specifically, whether prisons were a form of slavery).

Two such disagreements stand out. Nineteenth-century political pacifists disagreed whether *self-defence* counted as war. Given self-defence's prominence in today's justifications of war, this may seem like fudging. But the preoccupation with self-defence is a relatively recent phenomenon. Indeed, prior to the twentieth century, self-defence was often distinguished from war proper. (The U.S. Constitution distinguishes them, for example.) More recently, pacifists have disagreed whether collective security actions count as war. Ultimately, what counted as 'slavery' was determined by a larger account of slavery's historical and institutional character and why it bore condemning. The same holds true for what counts as 'war'. I return to this in Section 3.

To say that pacifism is unconditionally opposed to war is to say that it is opposed to every actual instance, past and present. I also construe it as opposed to every possible war. But this a strong claim: does it mean opposing every *imaginable* instance of war?

The question arises because hypotheticals play such a big role in today's philosophical discussions of war. I think this reflects the total lack of agreement about *real* cases—specifically, about which, if any, actual wars are justified. This is striking: 14,600 wars in recorded history, 3,200 major ones—and people cannot agree on a *single* case of 'just war'![8] Imagine if philosophers of punishment could not agree on a single case of justified punishment. (Has any other practice has been so discredited by history, yet philosophers still labor to justify it?) At most, people agree on *one* war, World War II, although they typically mean one aspect of that war, the resistance to Hitler, and not others, like the 1943 Bengali Famine, in which 2–4 million perished as food was sent elsewhere for military reasons.[9]

Preferring fantasy, then, pacifism's opponents chastise it for opposing wars where no one is hurt, or the only ones harmed are legions of criminal psychopaths, or the fate of the universe depends on it.[10] (Then they berate pacifism for not being 'realistic'!) Pacifism cannot withstand appeals to science fiction for the simple reason that no position can. Pacifism is the critique of *actually existing war*, meaning that it concerns itself with what is practically possible, not 'theoretically' possible in some unconstrained sense. Judgments of what is possible or not in this sense cannot be made a priori; again, they require a serious study of war in its historical and institutional reality.

The 'possibility' of just wars seems to distinguish the pacifism here described from 'contingent' pacifism (CP), now much discussed.[11] The term was first used by Rawls as holding that 'the possibility of a just war is conceded but not under present circumstances'.[12] There were, or could have been, just wars in the past, but current conditions, like nuclear weapons, render them a practical impossibility. Turn-of-the-century pacifists like William James and Jane Addams saw war as outdated. The moral and political obsolescence of war is explored in Martin Shaw's important writings on 'historical pacifism'.[13]

A stronger version is advanced in Larry May's championing of CP against 'absolute' pacifism (AP). The former holds that war 'as we have known it' has not been, and seemingly cannot be, waged in a way that is morally acceptable. He specifically cites the difficulties of abiding by principles of *jus in bello*.[14] But because a justly fought war is 'hypothetically' possible, the contingent pacifist, like the just war theorist, must evaluate each war as it comes along. The contrast between CP and AP has several meanings here: (1) CP attends to 'war as we have known it', AP does not. Remark: this may distinguish CP from personal pacifism, insofar as the latter is only interested in killing, but political pacifists *ground* their unconditional opposition in what is known of war, just as abolitionists grounded their opposition in what was known of slavery. (2) CP grants that a just war is possible, at least hypothetically, AP does not. Remark: this depends on what we mean by 'possible'—political pacifists maintain that what we know of war shows that just war is a *practical* impossibility. Theoretical possibilities rest on ignoring what we know of war! (3) CP appraises each war as it comes along, AP does not. Remark: this speaks to the dogmatism some place at the heart of 'noncontingent' pacifisms. In the words of Martin Ceadel, 'absolute pacifism' (the 'real' pacifist, for him) refuses to look at each war 'on its merits' but 'sticks resolutely instead to [its] guess about what it will be like'.

This kind of charge could be leveled equally at an uncompromising just war theorist who does not judge each violation of *jus in bello* 'on its merits', but sticks 'resolutely' to her 'guess' about 'what it will be like'. Judging each case as it comes along seems like open-mindedness. But is it *rational*? If 14,600 wars in history have produced at most one 'just' war, is it rational to assess each new war as it comes along on the chance that another one might come along sometime in the next seven thousand years? Is such open mindedness really a virtue? In the United States, there were 6,000 lynchings from Colonial times to the 1970s. A 'justified' lynching is certainly 'possible'—but insisting that we inspect each new lynching as it comes along is an insult to the victims of lynching.

The great virtue of CP is its insisting that we attend to 'war as we have known it'. The study of war is an ongoing project. Political pacifism claims that the more seriously we study war, the more we will oppose it in all its instances.

1.2. Absolute Opposition

Pacifism is primarily a first-person view: what should *I* do—specifically, should I kill (in war)? This was the question for the first Christians. By contrast, just war theory's focal concern has been policy: when may the state wage war, and when should it refrain?

The first pacifists did not concern themselves with such questions because their marginalised status meant they were excluded from any role in policy.

The pacifist is absolutely opposed to war. I take this to mean that, for the pacifist, there is always a compelling reason to reject war. But this can be taken in two ways: that the reasons for rejecting war are always *as* strong as any reasons to do otherwise, hence we are never irrational in rejecting war; or, that our reasons for rejecting war are always *stronger* than any reasons to act otherwise, hence we are irrational in not always rejecting war. The first view says that the rejection of war is always a moral option. If the pacifist regards it a moral necessity for him, a matter of personal integrity in Bernard Williams's sense, it is not a moral necessity for everyone.[15] This is why many pacifists reject war but do not condemn those who act otherwise. The moral option view is less absolutist, but it is still incompatible with the war as practiced in the modern state, which until recently demanded full allegiance of a type that left no room for the claims of conscience.

But the pacifist is not just someone who opts for peace over war when the occasion arises, anymore than the abolitionist was someone who opted for freedom over slavery when the occasion arose. Pacifism is a moral *conviction*: the pacifist *cares* about peace in ways that make it not just a political position but a personal vocation. Following Harry Frankfurt, we might say pacifists choose peace 'wholeheartedly': their reasons are ones they identify with in ways that inform other choices they make and compel them to make sacrifices that the less committed avoid.[16] Pacifism, then, is an uncompromising position insofar as it does not make exceptions, and it is an unwavering position insofar as it does this despite the personal costs. Commitments of this sort—to ending war, to ending slavery, and the like—always seem fanatical to the mild-mannered.

Kant's quasi-pacifism is an interesting variation. In some writings, he condemned war as illegitimate. He likened it to duelling in that both were approaches to resolving disputes but without the larger juridical framework to legitimate them. There was always a good reason to resist war, then, but sometimes there were equally good reasons to engage in it, like self-defence. But the right to do so was a 'provisional' one insofar as it presumed taking seriously our duty to work for peace; that is, to create a global legal/political framework that would render collective force legitimate. (He granted a provisional right to engage in duelling on similar grounds.) We might distinguish between regarding the practice as illegitimate and regarding the practice as *fundamentally* illegitimate, with the latter being one that we never have a reason for engaging in.

2. Personal Pacifism

Personal pacifism originated with the first Christians. Just war thinking began with Augustine's merging of the Gospel ethic with Roman stoicism. So the personal pacifist tradition can be understood as rejecting that merging and the compromise with Roman imperialism it signified.

Personal pacifism opposes killing as an individual act, hence opposes every instance of war as involving instances of that act. It doesn't concern itself with what counts as war as long as there is killing. Many, if not most, people today equate 'pacifism' with personal pacifism, or they say that this is what it means to be a 'real' pacifist or a 'true' pacifist. But this is like saying that one 'really' or 'truly' opposes the death penalty only if one opposes all killing. If anything, the term 'pacifism' was coined a century ago as a *contrast* to the rejection of all killing (termed 'nonresistance').

One reason for equating the two is the belief that one can only unconditionally oppose all war if one unconditionally opposes all killing; hence, the only meaningful pacifism is personal pacifism. For example, it might be argued that some wars are just agglomerations of individual acts of self-defence, hence one can only oppose such wars if one opposes the individual act. But no actual war fits this description. Wars have certainly involved individual acts of self-defence—any form of mob violence does. But they've involved a great deal more, the moral costs of which outweigh any claims of individual self-defence. So, the claim must be that war *could* be just this, and, if so, could only be opposed by opposing individual self-defence. But this will depend, for starters, on what we mean by 'war'. We distinguish spontaneous acts of group violence like 'riots' from 'war' proper by the *institutionalised* dimensions of the latter—for example, states and their militaries. The question is whether these institutions are intelligible as agglomerations of individuals acting in self-defence. David Rodin has challenged this picture of state self-defence in his *War and Self-Defence*. The idea that soldiers are just individual self-defenders has been contested since Hobbes and Locke.[17] The laws of war have limited the right of *non*combatants to defend themselves. A better question might be what collective force would look like if it were only concerned with the defence of individuals. Thinkers like Mary Kaldor have argued that it would bear no resemblance to war as we've known it throughout history.[18]

2.1. The Rationality of Personal Pacifism

How should personal pacifism's opposition to all killing be understood? We can identify two main traditions here. One is that of the first Christians and their followers today. It is a type of virtue ethics, which holds that killing is incompatible with living a righteous life, the model for which is the life of Jesus. The most sophisticated proponents of this view, like John Howard Yoder, do much to explain the nature of the righteousness that Jesus exemplified—especially in contrast to the corrupt Roman practices of Jesus' time—and how those persist today. The righteous life eschews all killing. Essential to this vision is that such a life cannot be achieved alone; it can only be achieved in the kind of community that Jesus and his followers sought to establish. So, this is a theologically laden view, plus it is a 'perfectionist' one in acknowledging that its ethic is difficult if not impossible to achieve fully.

The other tradition is a type of deontological ethic, or what Yoder calls a 'pacifism of principle'.[19] The principle is that one must never take human life because of the sanctity of human life. This is not a requirement to minimise the taking of human life, nor is it a requirement to prevent the taking of human life any more than the Kantian requirement to treat people as ends implies such things. The appeal to the sanctity of life is often given theological underpinnings, but this is not the only approach to grounding it. One approach has appealed to the experience of killing, or attempting to kill, and what is revealed about the ethical status of fellow creatures in the resistance to doing so. I have sketched a view of this sort in my own writings; other variants can be found in the writings of Tolstoy and Emmanuel Levinas.[20]

Proponents of this view recognise that, especially in today's culture, it will seem radically unreasonable—although it's worth noting that proponents of it, like Martin Luther King, Jr., have been among the most influential political figures of our time. (Andre Trocme argues in *Jesus and the Non-Violent Revolution* that it motivates people because it is unreasonable![21]) The renunciation of all killing is not just a call to act differently but to be a different type of person and construct a different type of community than the kind most people take for granted. But a separate question is whether it is *irrational*. I think a philosophical defence must address this, which is why it must address Jan Narveson's well-known critique of pacifism.[22]

Narveson claims that pacifism—by which he means personal pacifism—is guilty of a logical contradiction. The charge that pacifism is 'incoherent' and its proponents 'deeply confused' is a familiar one. Narveson aims to fill it out with reference to self-defence.

His argument proceeds thus:

The pacifist's condemnation of killing rests on the right not to be killed. But inherent in the logic of rights is that 'the right not to be subjected to X' implies 'the right to defend oneself against X'. Hence, the right not to be killed implies the right to defend oneself against killing, which Narveson construes as the right to do whatever is necessary to defend oneself—including killing the aggressor. So the pacifist's denial of the right to kill in self-defence conflicts with its grounds for condemning killing in the first place; hence, its incoherence. Now a first problem with this argument is that personal pacifism as a tradition has never grounded itself in individual rights (Narveson cites no actually existing pacifists in his characterisation of the view), nor has it ever denied the 'right' to self-defence. (Martin Luther King, Jr., termed his a "realistic pacifism" that was mindful of the moral dilemmas involving killing that neither pacifist or the non-pacifist could escape.[23]) I have said it finds self-defence 'problematic', but this does not mean denying we have the 'right' to do so. When Jesus said 'Turn the other cheek', he was not claiming we have no right to do otherwise. Indeed, the moral force of 'turning the other cheek' may rest on its being permissible, in a juridical sense.

But let us consider Narveson's argument as it stands. The weakest part of his argument is the claim that the right not to be killed implies the right to do *whatever* you need to do to resist the aggressor, including killing him.[24] The right not to be killed implies the right to do some things to resist an aggressor. No pacifist has denied this. Narveson construes the pacifist as opposing all 'force'. But pacifists have always regarded nonviolence as a *type* of force (Gandhi called it 'truth force') and have permitted physical force short of killing.[25] The question, then, is whether the right to kill implies a right to defend oneself that includes killing. It may or may not, but it's hard to see that this follows from the 'logic of rights' alone. There are many cases where the right to resist X does not imply the right to do that same X in defence against it. I cannot torture someone if that is the only way to prevent being tortured by them. Indeed, some maintain that what it *means* to have a deontological prohibition against doing X is that one is prohibited from doing X oneself, even to prevent X. (Narveson's argument gains force from beginning with rights rather than prohibitions.)

Still, the great virtue of Narveson's argument is challenging personal pacifists to unpack their view in ways that speak to a nonreligious audience and clarify its relation to things like self-defence.

2.2. The Politics of Personal Persuasion

The first Christian pacifists did not construe their position as a political position aimed at influencing the state because they were excluded from any role in it. Later Christian pacifists generally ignored the political realm as one of sinfulness. Insofar as they had a social ethic, it could be described as a politics of counterculture: the creation of communities of nonviolence by bearing witness to an ethic of nonviolence in word and deed. This politics of persuasion has remained central to personal pacifism. It was embodied in Leo Tolstoy, the leading personal pacifist of the late nineteenth century.

Personal pacifism's political turn came with the Society of Friends (the Quakers), whose influence on reform politics in eighteenth- and nineteenth-century England and the United States cannot be exaggerated. For them, pacifism meant commitment to a larger reform agenda that especially included ending slavery. Hence, nineteenth-century America's leading abolitionist, William Lloyd Garrison, was also its leading pacifist. One of the most influential writings of American politics, Henry David Thoreau's 'Essay on Civil Disobedience', exemplifies this orientation. It was written in protest of both war and slavery, articulating a politics of personal refusal: conscience, abiding by what Thoreau called the 'higher law', obliges us to refuse all connection with practices of war and slavery. Gandhi cited this essay as a major influence on his thinking.[26]

The irony of personal pacifism is that, although sceptical of political projects, it has had at times significant if less obvious political impact. A case in point is Dorothy Day, founder of the Catholic Worker Movement. Hers was a spiritually based pacifism, pure if not purist in its convictions. Her opposition to any involvement with the war system extended to refusing to pay all taxes. But, over the years, her personal example and that of her circle had a profound impact on the American Catholic Church, a powerful political force in American life. She is credited with playing a major role in transforming it from a bellicose institution into a leading advocate for peace and justice.[27] Similar stories can be told of other countries.

I have suggested that a contribution of personal pacifism is that it provokes us to regard war as a matter of our own personal responsibility, not just impersonal public policy. The fact that war *is* a structured institution, not just people fighting one at a time, means that our personal connections to it are easily ignored; indeed, the institutions of war aim to obscure these connections. Recent just war thinking is increasingly concerned with the personal responsibility of soldiers in war. Personal pacifism begins with the question of the personal responsibility each of us has for war.

3. Political Pacifism

Political pacifism opposes war as a social practice.[28] Let's consider first what it means by 'war', then why its opposition to it is unconditional.

3.1. The War System

War is a protean phenomenon with no fixed essence any more than the family has a fixed essence. Like the family or any other social institution, it must be approached historically and institutionally.

Political pacifism's characterisation of war has been strongly tied to the state or the state system generally. (This reflects its emphasis on war-building because states are instruments of war-building.) But war preceded the state as a political form; indeed, the state is largely a product of war. Does reference to the state render it parochial? When nineteenth-century abolitionists condemned slavery, their picture of it was strongly tied to the slavery of their day. They didn't concern themselves with archaic forms of it in which, say, slaves might be quite privileged. But no one thought this detracted from their basic point. Political pacifists will say the same of their analysis. If we are now moving beyond the state, our understanding of this must start with the state.

War is the collective organisation of killing and being killed. It is more than this, of course, but it is always at least this. War is a 'political' phenomena insofar as that organisation aims to transform killing into power. It is the organised nature of both war-making and war-building that distinguishes war from spontaneous acts like rioting. It is the priority of killing that distinguishes war from other violent practices, like rugby. My emphasis on *being* killed marks the fact that dying, too, assumes ritualised forms in war (think of modern war memorials). Types of war are distinguished by *how* the killing and dying are organised.

In the modern state system, that organisation has an 'internal' dimension—how states mobilise their own human and material resources for conflict. Throughout history, domestic law has always been shaped by this purpose. But states are also part of a larger state *system*, itself organised; hence there is an 'external' dimension of state–state relations, how they deal with each other. International law regulates these relations. A final complexity is that, especially since the 'discovery' of the Americas, Europe's state system has closely interacted with a world of *non*-states. Indeed, the first international law addressed how states related to each other in their combined dealing with the Americas. This gave war a twofold character. War between European states was a finite act in which parties recognised each other as reasonable adversaries, and victory involved reconciliation. Wars between ('civilised') European states and ('savage'/'barbarian') non-European non-states were ongoing states of hostility, where foes were regarded as irrational enemies and victory meant annihilation.

Just war thinking can be understood in this context. It prescribed rules for conflict between 'civilised' states, whereas conflicts between the 'civilised' and 'savages'/'barbarians' were held to few if any rules at all. The aim of regulating conflicts between states was to prevent 'civilised' war from *becoming* 'savage' war; that is, unconstrained endless slaughter. When this failed, European wars become 'hyper-wars', where Europeans treated each other the way they'd treated non-Europeans. The first such conflict, the Thirty Years War, led to the Treaty of Westphalia; the second, the Napoleonic Wars, led to the Concert of Europe; and the third, World Wars I and II, led to the United Nations—all attempts to constrain war more effectively.

Political pacifists hold that attempts at constraining war will ultimately fail, that the only solution lies in ending war itself. One reason lies in the 'internal' organisation of war. (Political pacifism arose after the Napoleonic Wars, and here its account of the 'war system' parallels that of its contemporary, Clausewitz.) War as a system has two dimensions: war-making (battle) and war-building (the mobilisation of human and material resources for battle). The great shortcoming of received thinking is to focus on the first to the exclusion of the second. Thus, just war thinking has focused on the rules of conflict while ignoring the organisational conditions of that conflict. But war-building is crucial for two reasons.

First, it explains why we have states at all. The state prevailed over competing political forms by its success at war-building, and the forms of the state have succeeded each other by their success at this. Second, it explains the instability of the system as a whole. If success at war-making ultimately depends on success at war-building, the latter will increasingly dominate every aspect of society. This is the extremist logic that Clausewitz perceived in modern war, leading to the 'contradiction': if the purpose of war-making is to serve political ends, the nature of war-building is to serve only itself. Political pacifists saw this confirmed in the arms races of the late nineteenth century and in the twentieth-century's two world wars. Where they disagreed with Clausewitz was whether society was condemned to this logic, whether it could escape the war system. This disagreement has involved the very nature of power: whether the power achieved by organised killing/being killed is the only (or ultimate) political power or whether nonviolent power is a true possibility. This puts things crudely, of course. A central issue is whether the end of the Cold War brought an end to this extremist logic and, if so, how this impacts our account of the 'war system'. The writings of Jonathon Schell and Mary Kaldor on 'new wars' address this.[29]

3.2. The Critique of the War System

Political pacifists have leveled two quite different charges against the war system, both implicit in the foregoing. The first involves what I'll term the *inhumanity* of the system. Basically, this is the claim that war takes on a life of its own in ways that escape all human agency and ignore, and usually negate, legitimate human ends. This is most evident in eras of hyper-war, like World War I, when many came to see the war as a 'Frankenstein monster' transcending all human control and purpose. This was a prominent theme for political pacifists like Randolph Bourne and for soldiers-turned-pacifists whose experience of combat led them to see war an uncontrollable 'machine', rendering all moral appraisal problematic.[30] Political pacifists see this as an inherent tendency of war per se, meaning that the step from war to hyper-war itself escapes human control. Hence, their unconditional opposition to war is in part 'pragmatic': any tolerance of war can trigger its extremist logic.

This helps illuminate the aforementioned disagreement among political pacifists about what counts as 'war'. The claim that war escapes human control is inherited from the civic republican tradition and its critique of standing armies. Kant voiced this concern, but he held that this extremist logic need not apply to collective self-defence if properly conducted—by a citizens' militia, not a standing army. Such thinking led nineteenth-century political pacifists to hold that self-defence, thus conducted, did not count as 'war' because it escaped war's main vice. And it led some twentieth-century political pacifists to hold that collective security arrangements not only escaped war's principal vice but served to constrain it and hence fell under a different category. In the end, of course, what matters is not the terminological issues but whether the problems identified are real ones and how address them.

A second charge pertains to the *injustices* of the war system. One pacifist argument holds that war is incapable of abiding by the just war principles of *jus ad bellum* and *jus in bello*. This concern has become more prominent as just war theorists have formulated these principles more precisely. Attention has focused on the proportionality requirement (the harms imposed on innocents must not exceed the evils averted by war's aims): contingent pacifists have argued that, whatever the good achieved, the number of noncombatants killed can never be justified by their role in war. Furthermore, they have argued that the killing of many unjust soldiers cannot be justified either, given the circumstances in which they came to fight or continue to fight. These pertain to the illicit harming others. But political pacifism stresses war as an enterprise of both killing and *dying*; hence, it asks if a soldier's 'sacrifice' of his own life violates an obligation to himself. The problem is not just whether the reasons given soldiers for sacrificing their lives are false or trivial. The logic of militaries actively discourages reflection on such matters of the sort required for soldiers to make meaningful choices.

These pertain to the injustices of war-making. But the more important issue for political pacifism is war-*building*. How do the practices of states in mobilising the human and material resources for war themselves violate fundamental human rights? Here are some examples:

The state prevailed over other political forms by its superior ability at war mobilisation, especially in mobilising populations within its borders. This was achieved by the homogenisation of its populations, involving, in the nineteenth century, their transformation into 'nations'. War-building was both a mechanism of this (conscription was key to nation building) and a beneficiary of it; it always involved great violence and coercion. Conflict over war mobilisation was a persistent feature of nineteenth- and twentieth-century nation states. The 1863 New York City draft was the largest civil disturbance in American history; the so-called Easter riots of 1918 in Canada, provoked by conscription, were among its most violent disturbances (similar events occurred in Ireland's conscription crisis); the mass violence engendered by Russia's World War I mobilisation led directly to the Bolshevik revolution; and so on. War mobilisation has always meant massive violations of civil liberties. The mass internment of Japanese Americans in World War II was, after segregation, the most significant violation of American civil liberties in the twentieth century. Liberals are not indifferent to the latter, of course. But political pacifists regard all these problems as crucial features of the war system.

Martin Shaw's 'historical pacifism' argues that the exigencies of war mobilisation are the key to understanding modern genocide.[31] The mobilisation of populations has meant the extermination of groups identified as not 'belonging', as hostile to state purposes. Both the Turkish genocide of Armenians and the German genocide of Jews and others were war measures, construed as acts of national security. Indeed, the genocide of native peoples in the United States and other settler states were justified on security grounds. Shaw extends this analysis to the late twentieth century. Again, the claim is not that nonpacifists ignore or minimise these problems but that they do not regard them as a feature of war, much less intrinsic features. Arguments about social practices are often of this sort. Supporters of slavery did not always ignore its many repugnant features; they did not regard them as an intrinsic of slavery, as abolitionists did.

3.3. Opposing the War System

> Defining effective international government in this way is of course setting an idealistic goal; but it less idealistic than the idea that military action could be truly an instrument of justice.
>
> —John Howard Yoder[32]

John Dewey wrote, 'How long have we been taking steps to do away with war, and why have they accomplished nothing? Because the steps have all been taken under the war system. It is not a step we need, it is an about-face; a facing in another direction'.[33] Political pacifists agree, although they differ among themselves on what such an 'about face' means.

Political pacifism's privileging of war-building dictated its practice in the past. Strategies were from the bottom up. If conscription was the principal means for generating soldiers, political pacifism meant opposition to and disruption of conscription.

If taxes were the principal means for generating resources, political pacifism meant opposing war taxes. But strategies have also been top down. Political pacifists have sought to influence governments not just on particular acts of war-making but on the mechanisms of war-making generally. A notable example in the United States was the proposal that the country should only go to war after a national referendum approving it. This was first proposed by William Jennings Bryan in 1914, revived during the debate about America's entry into World War I, and then advanced as a proposed constitutional amendment by Rep. Lewis Ludlow in the 1930s (polls consistently showed a majority of Americans supporting it).

As the twentieth century concluded, political pacifists continued to oppose particular acts of war-making. But the problem of war-building changed in two ways. The end of conscription and the rise of deficit financing to pay for war meant that traditional methods of draft resistance and tax refusal were no longer relevant. At the same time, the widespread disillusionment with war generally meant that the question was less 'War, pro or con'? and more 'What are viable means for addressing conflict, if *not* war'? From the bottom up, political pacifists have participated in discussions of global civil society as an alternative to the state system and its warlike proclivities. From the top down, they have concerned themselves with mechanisms of global governance of the type that constrain the state system but in ways that look beyond. These are places where the difference between being a political pacifist or someone deeply critical of war, although not so unconditionally, blurs in importance.

4. What Is To Be Done?

> The analysis of war is too important to be left to the intuitionists.
>
> —Quincy Wright

The problems posed by political pacifism are as much empirical as normative. Its opposition to war generally compels us to consider what we mean by 'war'—generally. This requires attention to the history of war as a practice, just as any judgment of, say, slavery, requires attention to its history. Compounding the problem is a further fact. We live in a time of profound rethinking of violence. This animates the renewed interest in both just war thinking and pacifism. But both just war thinking and political pacifism emerged as responses to the state system and to war as a feature of that system. Put simply, just war theory has assumed the legitimacy of the state system and sought to regulate it; political pacifism has asserted the legitimacy of war and hence sought to replace the state system with some kind of global community. Both perspectives remain tied to the statist framework, though.

The quarrel between pacifism and just war theory cannot be addressed, much less resolved, without expanding our perspective. The problem is that, whereas war has been with us for thousands of years, the study of war is in its infancy. We need what I call a *critical war theory*. Such a theory is historical, it is attentive to how war has developed and changed over time, and how the normative frameworks for assessing war, including those of international law, have developed and changed over time. It is institutional, insofar as war is a matter of war-building as well as war-making. It is as much a matter of how societies mobilise the resources for war as how they employ them in war. Finally, the approach is critical insofar as it does not prejudge the question of whether war is justified; it is open to the pacifist alternative in the same way that a critical theory of state is open to the anarchist alternative. In these respects, it is truly interdisciplinary, as any valid social theory must be.

Notes

1. Jane Addams, *Essays and Speeches on Peace* (New York: Continuum, 2005).
2. Leo Tolstoy, *The Kingdom of God Is Within You* (New York: Cassell Publishing, 1894); Martin Luther King, Jr., 'My Pilgrimage to Nonviolence' in *Stride to Freedom* (Boston: Beacon Press, 1988); Mohandas K. Gandhi, *Gandhi on Nonviolence*, edited by Thomas Merton (New York: New Directions 1965/2007).
3. On pacifism as tradition of argument, see David Cortright, *Peace: A History of Movements and Ideas* (New York: Cambridge University Press, 2008) 30. In general, see Martin Ceadel, *Thinking About Peace and War* (Oxford: Oxford University Press, 1987); Peter Brock, *Pacifism in Europe to 1914* (Princeton, NJ: Princeton University Press, 1972); Brock, *Freedom from Violence: Sectarian Nonresistance from the Middle Ages to the Great War* (Toronto: University of Toronto Press, 1991); Brock and Nigel Young, *Pacifism in the 20th Century* (Syracuse, NY: Syracuse University Press, 1999); John Howard Yoder, *Christian Attitudes to War, Peace, and Revolution* (Ada, MI: Brazos Press, 2009).
4. Excellent philosophical works on pacifism include Richard Norman, *Ethics, Killing and War* (Cambridge University Press, 1995); Jenny Teichman, *Pacifism and the Just War* (Oxford: Basil Blackwell, 1986); Robert Holmes, *On War and Morality* (Princeton, NJ: Princeton University Press, 1989); and Andrew Fiala, *Practical Pacifism* (Algora Publishing, 2004).
5. John Mueller, *Retreat from Doomsday* (New York: Basic Books, 1989), 38.
6. James J. Sheehan, *Where Have All the Soldiers Gone?: The Transformation of Modern Europe* (New York: Mariner Books, 2009).
7. Jeremy Waldron, 'Torture and Positive Law: Jurisprudence for the White House', *Columbia Law Review* 106:6 (October 2005), 1712–1713.
8. Jeff McMahan notes, 'Even the acknowledged experts—the theorists of the just war—disagree among themselves about the justice of virtually every war'. *Killing in War* (Oxford: Oxford University Press, 2009), 120.
9. See Max Hastings, *All Hell Loose: The World at War 1939–1945* (New York: Harper, 2011), 422–426; Gerhard Weinberg, *A World at Arms—A Global History of World War II* (Cambridge: Cambridge University Press, 1994), 493–496.
10. For example, Caedel writes (op. cit, 145–146), 'The pacifist holds that, even if a state fought an extraordinarily successful and costless war, it would nevertheless have committed an impermissible act and would have done better to have submitted stoically to assured butchery and enslavement'.

11. Andrew Fiala, 'Contingent Pacifism and Contingently Pacifist Conclusions', *Journal of Social Philosophy* 45:4 (2014), 463–477; Saba Bazargan, 'Varieties of Contingent Pacifism', in *How We Fight*, edited by Helen Frowe and Gerald Lang (Oxford: Oxford University Press, forthcoming).
12. John Rawls, *A Theory of Justice* (Cambridge: Harvard University Press, 1971), 382.
13. See, among his other writings, Martin Shaw, *Post-Military Society: Militarism, Demilitarization and War at the End of the Twentieth Century* (Philadelphia: Temple University Press, 1991).
14. Larry May, 'Contingent Pacifism and the Moral Risks of Participating in War', *Public Affairs Quarterly*, 25:2 (April 2011), 95–111.
15. See his 'Critique of Utilitarianism' in Williams and J. J. C. Smart, *Utilitarianism: For and Against* (Cambridge: Cambridge University Press, 1973).
16. Harry Frankfurt, 'Identification and Wholeheartedness', in *The Importance of What We Care About* (Cambridge: Cambridge University Press, 1988), 159–176.
17. David Rodin, *War and Self-Defense* (Oxford: Oxford University Press, 2004).

    See my discussion of Hobbes and Locke in 'War and the State', in *For and Against the State: New Philosophical Readings*, edited by Jan Narveson and Jack Sanders (Lanham: Rowman and Littlefield, 1996).
18. Mary Kaldor, *Human Security* (London: Polity, 2007), chapter six, 'Just War and Just Peace'.
19. John Howard Yoder, *Nevertheless, Varieties of Religious Pacifism* (Scottdale, PA: Herald Press, 1971), 32–38. Yoder's work is the starting point for understanding personal pacifism today. See his *The Politics of Jesus*, 2nd ed. (Philadelphia: William B Eerdmans, 1996) and subsequent writings.
20. See Cheyney Ryan, 'Pacifism, Self-Defense, and the Possibility of Killing', *Ethics* 93 (1983), 508–524; Tolstoy, 'Certain Things Christians Cannot Do', in John Yoder, *What Would You Do: If a Violent Person Threatened to Harm a Loved One?* (Harrisonberg, VA: Herald Press, 1983), 45–49; Emmanuel Levinas, *Totality and Infinity* (Pittsburgh, PA: Duquesne University Press, 1961).
21. Henry David Thoreau, *Walden* (New York: Plough Publishing, 2014).
22. Jan Narveson, 'Pacifism: A Philosophical Analysis', *Ethics* 75: 4 (1965), 259–271.
23. Martin Luther King, Jr., at Note 2.
24. See my discussion of this in 'Pacifism, Self-Defense, and the Possibility of Killing'.
25. See Gandhi, at Note 2.
26. See George Hendrick, 'The Influence of Thoreau's "Civil Disobedience" on Gandhi's Satyagraha', *New England Quarterly* 29:4 (December 1956), 462–471.
27. Mel Piehl, *Breaking Bread: The Catholic Worker and the Origin of Catholic Radicalism in America* (Philadelphia: Temple University Press, 1982). See also my 'The One Who Burns Herself for Peace', *Hypatia* 9:2 (Spring 1994), 21–39.
28. Andrew Alexandra, 'Political Pacifism', *Social Theory and Practice*, 29:4 (2003), 589–606; David Carroll Cochran, 'War-Pacifism', *Social Theory and Practice*, 22:2 (1996), 161–180. Also my articles, 'Pacifism(s)', *The Philosophical Forum* (Spring 2014), and 'Pacifism, Just War, and Self-Defense', *Philosophia, Philosophical Quarterly of Israel* 41:4 (2013).
29. Jonathan Schell, *The Unconquerable World: Power, Nonviolence, and the Will of the People* (New York: Owl Books, 2004); Mary Kaldor, *New & Old Wars: Organized Violence in a Global Era* (Stanford, CA: Stanford University Press, 2013).

30. Randolph Bourne, *War and the Intellectuals: Collected Essays, 1915–1919* (Indianapolis: Hackett, 1999); also Lewis Mumford, *The Myth of the Machine: Technics and Human Development* (New York, Harcourt, 1967) and *The Myth of the Machine: The Pentagon of Power* (New York: Harcourt, 1970).
31. Martin Shaw, *War and Genocide: Organized Killing in Modern Society* (London: Polity Press, 2003).
32. John Howard Yoder, *The Christian Witness to the State* (Harrisonburg, PA: Herald Press, 2002), 47.
33. Cited in Joseph Ratner, ed. *Intelligence in the Modern World: John Dewey's Philosophy* (New York: Modern Library, 1939), 515.

CHAPTER 15

LEGITIMATE AUTHORITY IN WAR

YITZHAK BENBAJI

TRADITIONAL just war theory is divided into two independent codes. *Jus ad bellum* defines the conditions that wars must meet in order to be justified. *Jus in bello* concerns the question of what conduct within wars is permissible. The *jus ad bellum* code comprises six individually necessary and jointly sufficient conditions. Just wars have a *just cause* (mostly national defence). They are fought by a *legitimate authority*: usually a state that represents its citizens and is recognized as such by the international community. Just wars are *necessary*: there is no way to attain their purpose except by using force. They are fought with the *right intention*: to achieve that just cause. Just wars might incidentally (and unintentionally) harm innocents, but the good effects of just wars outweigh the evil they cause; that is to say, just wars are *proportionate*. Finally, just wars have a *reasonable chance of success*.

The requirement of legitimate authority (hereafter 'the Requirement')[1] was originally introduced in the writings of Augustine, Aquinas, and Pufendorf. Their assertion that 'the right of initiating war in a state lies with the sovereign'[2] implies that the right to resort to war is enjoyed by states (entities that effectively rule by law in a certain territory). As it is now understood, however, the Requirement can also be satisfied by non-state actors. It acknowledges the possibility of just independence and civil wars and, therefore, grants normative power to non-state actors to fight such wars: political movements that represent stateless or oppressed political communities are entitled to fight in the name of such communities and on their behalf for national liberation, decolonization, and basic civil rights.

This extension of the Requirement follows from the standard reading of the current post-World War II legal system. According to this reading, the international community justifiably treats national defence and defence of territorial integrity as just causes for war. The right of stateless peoples to use force in order to attain political independence in a territory to which they are entitled is the other side of same coin. Wars fought by political societies (which claim to be wrongfully denied the attributes of state sovereignty) meet the Requirement if the subgroup that actually conducts the war represents the community in whose name and on whose behalf it fights. In one obvious respect, this extension reasserts the general statist tendency of the traditional just war theory: it is precisely in virtue of their aspirations for statehood that non-state actors can claim just cause.[3]

The entities that can, in principle, meet the Requirement are, then, legitimate states (and their political elites) and members of the elite of a stateless political society who demand political independence in its name. The Requirement distinguishes well-functioning states from rogue or failed states. It further distinguishes movements like the Taliban (in Afghanistan) or al Qaida (in the Arab world) from movements like the Palestinian Liberation Organization or the African National Congress. The former two are based on the charisma and brute force of local leaders, whereas the latter two are authentic representatives of the stateless political societies they lead.

The Requirement seems to convey certain moral convictions. Rare cases aside, wars declared and fought by persons in their capacity as private individuals are unjust even if they satisfy the other *ad bellum* conditions. Usually, such wars are (or ought to be) fought in the name of a larger group and on its behalf and, as such, need its authorization.[4] Another normative conviction underlying the Requirement is that certain entities—criminal gangs, mafias, terror organizations, landlords—cannot represent any larger group and therefore lack normative power to fight in its name.[5]

Even at this preliminary stage of their formulation, these moral convictions raise questions. If the use of force is justified—it has a just cause, it is necessary, it is directed against culpable aggressors by those who have righteous intentions, the incidental damage it causes to innocent civilians is proportionate—why does it matter who wields it? Why are only states or well-organized state-like political movements (and their agents) entitled to fight wars? A related worry might be put thus: if a war meets all the other conditions, it ought to be fought by those who can carry it out. If so, shouldn't the relevant group bestow its authorization on the agent who can fight it?

The second conviction seems as problematic. Gangs lack permission to do violence—whether on their own behalf or on behalf of a larger group—when their purposes are nefarious. These are not examples of groups that lack legitimate authority, but rather of people who tend to engage in wrongful harming. They can be representatives of larger groups—there's nothing to stop a landlord becoming a trade union leader or a church elder. What they cannot do is use force to achieve their ends, whether they represent a larger group or not. Or so the objector argues.

In this chapter, I present what seems to me to be the best reading of the traditional requirement of legitimate authority and articulate a cogent moral conviction that supports it. The argument is shaped in light of the difficulties just put forward. Section 1 offers a detailed account of the Requirement as I think it should be understood. Section 2 presents cases that exemplify the presumption that wars are just in virtue of their intrinsic features, such that, normatively, it does not matter who fights them. It further points out that this argument follows from a more general scepticism about the very possibility of legitimate authority. Sections 3 and 4 accordingly examine two widely accepted arguments for that possibility. Section 3 shows that Joseph Raz's 'normal justification thesis' supports conferring authority to veto war on two (usually overlapping) collectives: those on whose behalf the war is fought and those who will bear its costs. This implies that wars that meet the Requirement are more likely to satisfy the other central *ad bellum* conditions. Section 4 advances a proceduralist justification of the Requirement: violating it compromises the ideal of fair political participation. Section 5 notes that, according to the analysis of Sections 2–4, the Requirement has important scope restrictions. Section 6 concludes.

1. The Legitimate Authority Requirement: The Common Understanding

This section presents what I take as a charitable interpretation of the legitimate authority requirement. On this interpretation, the Requirement is linked to three distinct but importantly related moral conjectures. The first is that an entity must have the right sort of status in order for its wars to be just.[6] Usually, only courts are entitled to decide legal cases, only a police officer is entitled to arrest a suspect,[7] only certain officials can distribute drivers' licenses, and so forth. Likewise, only a legitimate state, or something that shares some of its important features, can perform the act of justified war.[8]

A second conjecture connects the Requirement to the just cause condition. Only certain kinds of statist/communal aims can justify war, hence—mind the obvious logical gap here—only states/communities may possess a justification for achieving these aims by means of war.

A third conjecture links the Requirement to the morality of the *in bello* code: when individuals fight in the name of a legitimate state or a stateless political community they are subject to different rules and regulations than if they fought in the name of other entities. Most explicitly, according to the teaching of early jurists and natural law theorists, the authority of the sovereign explains why soldiers acting under orders from the prince do not violate God's proscription against killing.[9]

Recently, I offered a secularized articulation of this idea.[10] Since modern wars involve mass participation, they cannot be effectively conducted without the obedience of those who actually fight the war. But only legitimate political authorities are entitled to command the obedience of their combatants; only such authorities possess the normative power to divide the labour between decision-makers and enactors in a way that allows the enactors to blindly follow the orders of the political leadership. Individuals, in their private capacity, and, *a fortiori*, evil terror organizations and mafias, have no such power. The third conjecture does not support the Requirement, but instead appeals to the authority of political persons who satisfy it in order to explain the morality of the *in bello* code. This aspect of the Requirement is, therefore, beyond my scope here.

The following account of the Requirement will develop the first two moral conjectures; in later sections, I will argue that, properly modified and weakened, these conjectures are defensible.[11]

1.1. Contextualizing the Legitimate Authority Requirement

My interpretation of the Requirement assumes that most wars meet what I call the '*factual condition*', at least in part:

1. There is a group whose members actually fight the war: call this collective Actor. It is composed of two overlapping subgroups: decision-makers and enactors (generally, the decision-makers form a government and the enactors are members of an army).
2. Actor represents a larger group of individuals—Political Society—in whose name the war is fought. A war fought by the American army is fought in the name of the American people. By declaring war, the president takes America into war.
3. The war is fought in order to secure a public good for a third group of individuals, Beneficiary.
4. The resources with which the war is fought belong to individuals who constitute a fourth collective, Bearer. Those individuals also bear the internal risks of the war.

Routinely, Political Society is identical to Beneficiary, and Beneficiary to Bearer. In wars of national defence, Actor wages a war in order to advance the interest of Political Society in territorial integrity, national security, economic prosperity, or political clout. In such circumstances, the government and its army fight on behalf of *and* in the name of the citizens of a state by employing means that belong to them and by exposing them to substantial risk.

The distinctions between the various groups identified within the factual condition are nevertheless important. In wars of humanitarian intervention, for example, a state fights in the name of one political community (Political Society) on behalf of another (Beneficiary); the aim of the intervention is protecting the human rights of non-citizens. According to some politicians, the intervention in Iraq in the second Gulf War was made in the name of the American people but on behalf of the Iraqis. Here, the Bearer might be a third group, which includes the Iraqis and citizens of other states required to cover some of the internal costs of the war. In principle, Americans might bear no risk (because of the huge power inequalities) and invest no material resources in such a war.

Another illustration of the disparities among Political Society, Beneficiary, and Bearer comes from the Security Council-authorized first Gulf War. Although the Allies fought in the name of the United Nations, those who bore the costs of this war constituted a radically smaller group. The Beneficiary was the citizens (or, perhaps, the ruling elite) of Kuwait, who had to bear almost no internal cost.

On the interpretation I advance and defend here, wars that partly or fully meet the factual condition (and wars that ought to meet it) are subject to the Requirement. That is, wars fought by Actor in the name of Political Society, on behalf of Beneficiary, by employing means that belong to Bearer and by exposing members of Bearer to internal risks ought to be fought by a legitimate authority. More specifically, I suggest that, according to the Requirement, Political Society, Beneficiary, and Bearer are entitled to veto these wars.[12]

I said that the Requirement applies not only to wars that meet the factual condition, but also to wars that ought to meet it. To illuminate this distinction, consider the Israel–Hezbollah conflict. Although it is an officially recognized political party in Lebanon, Hezbollah's use of force against Israel is not undertaken in the name of the Lebanese people. But it is widely believed that, because Hezbollah's war takes advantage of Lebanon's sovereignty and territory, it *ought* to be fought in the name of Lebanon or not fought at all. If my interpretation of the Requirement is sound, it follows that Hezbollah's war can be just only if the Lebanese authorize Hezbollah to fight it in their name; Hezbollah might not meet this condition even if its war against Israel fulfils all the other *ad bellum* conditions.

1.2. The Authority of Whom?

So understood, the legitimate authority requirement is constituted by three subrequirements: Political Society Authority, Beneficiary Authority, and Bearer Authority. Let us look at each of them.

Political Society Authority says that if a war is fought *in the name* of a group of individuals (or ought to be fought in its name), then this group is entitled to veto the war. The moral conviction on which this rule is based is straightforward. Typically, acting in the name of a person is permissible only if the actor has the authority to do so. Typically, the authority to act in the name of another person is gained by authorization—a process characterized as authority-conferring in virtue of being a fair procedure. Thus, there can be circumstances in which Actor fights in the name of Political Society but has no authority to do so; Political Society Authority prohibits such wars. This subrequirement, I suggest, underlies the American Constitution, which empowers Congress to veto a war the president is determined to carry out; an American president who takes the country to war without the approval of Congress violates this duty.[13]

To understand the role of Political Society Authority in current political discourse, another assumption should be explored: that it is necessary for the Actor to pass basic moral tests in order to have the normative power to act in the name of Political Society. If a political organization is sufficiently evil, it cannot represent a political community; its members can act only in their private capacity. Thus, a sufficiently bad terror organization cannot gain authority to act in the name of a people, even if it fights for a just cause and enjoys popular support (expressed in a procedurally fair election). As we shall see, states implicitly appeal to this assumption in condemning the non-state actors they fight against. Properly interpreted, their view is that the Requirement functions as an independent constraint thanks to the further assumption that political representativeness is a moralized relation.[14] (Admittedly, the view that evil is a disqualification from authority is questionable. One might plausibly believe that a group can be totally heinous, yet still representative and democratic; what matters to representativeness is whether the political organization is actually conceived by the community to be acting in its name. For example, one might believe that a murderous Jewish mafia could have had the authority to fight the Nazis in the name of the Jews.)

Another implication of Political Society Authority is noteworthy. Consider armed individuals who patrol the borders of the United States in order to prevent illegal immigration from Mexico. Suppose the patrollers ought to act in the name of the political society to which they belong.[15] Suppose further that, in the American legal context, representation is not gained by informal popular support; one may use force in the name of the community only if formally authorized to do so by the state. Since they hold no public position, the patrollers act in their private capacity, even if ordinary Americans support them and are willing to authorize them to act on their behalf.[16] Their violent activity is in violation of Political Society Authority, whether or not its cause is just.

The account offered here identifies questions to which we need answers if we are to apply the Requirement, but it leaves these questions open. It does not specify when Actor fights in the name of Political Society or when it ought to do so. It does not tell us what it is for a Political Society to veto a war fought in its name. Nor does it specify what moral features are demanded of an Actor who has the normative power to act in the name of Political Society.

Humanitarian interventions highlight the complexity of these questions. A common argument implies that the intervener ought to act in the name of the international community. The intervention in Kosovo, David Luban argues, was justified because 'as human beings, we should be ashamed to remain bystanders in the face of evil when evil rises to the level of barbarism'.[17] Conjoined to the Requirement, this justification suggests that intervention is permissible only if the intervener has the authority to fight in the name of the international community. Luban, and others, believe that the United States had this authority because its military hegemony created expectations for leadership and because others were unlikely to act without its active support.[18]

Interestingly, critics also appeal to Political Society Authority in order to repudiate US interventionism. Humanitarian intervention is needed in many places—Bosnia, Kosovo, Somalia, Rwanda, Burundi, Sierra Leone, Congo, Sudan, Syria, and elsewhere—but the United States selectively intervenes only to promote its national interests. Past US campaigns provide no reason to believe in American commitment to humanity and human rights. Hence, so the argument runs, US interventions fail the Requirement: the United States has no normative power to act in the name of the international community because of its features as a self-interested or even a hypocritical state. Note that the objection to US interventionism is based on the idea of authority/representation and not on the idea of (lack of) right intention: the fact that the Kosovo intervention, say, was a humanitarian effort makes no difference.[19] Some take this line of thought further, claiming that whatever the nature of interventionism, ideally it 'ought not to be left to individual states acting on their own initiative. Rather, it must become the responsibility of international institutions with their own standing, professional military force created and maintained specifically for this purpose'.[20]

The other two requirements—Beneficiary and Bearer Authority—are that those groups on whose behalf the war is fought and who provide the necessary resources are entitled to veto the war. Beneficiary Authority is evident in the conviction that humanitarian intervention 'must either be requested, or there must be at least compelling evidence that the intended beneficiaries would welcome rather than oppose it'.[21] To see the bite of Beneficiary Authority, consider the Russia–Finland war in 1941.[22] Finland's military defeat was obvious from the beginning. The war was fought for one purpose only: in order not to surrender without a fight. The war had the symbolic value of fighting for political freedom. Beneficiary Authority says that Finland's government (Actor) was justified in getting the Finns to fight this war only if the public good that the war was to secure was sufficiently important to them—only, that is, if the community on whose behalf the war was fought valued the cause of the war.

The intervention in Kosovo exemplifies the distinction between Bearer Authority and Beneficiary Authority. If bearers are unprepared to tolerate loss of human life, Bearer Authority would allow only an intervention in which force protection is maximal. This aspect of the Requirement might be the moral consideration to which President Bill Clinton implicitly appealed in deciding against an intervention in Kosovo if boots on the ground rather than an air campaign were required.[23] If Bearer Authority is a cogent requirement, proportionate collateral damage externalized on beneficiaries and enemy civilians is acceptable even if soldiers could lessen it by assuming greater risk.[24]

1.3. The Statist Tendency of the Requirement

The interpretation of the Requirement that I offered in the preceding section implies that states, just like any other entity, can violate it. Yet it is common understanding that outsiders are entitled to assume that the Requirement is satisfied by any war waged by a recognized state in defence of its own interests. In contrast, outsiders who witness an independence or civil war should support it only after ensuring that the Requirement has been satisfied.

The privileged standing of states vis-à-vis the Requirement is rooted in a morally problematic presumption: the government of a state recognized as an equal member in the UN represents its citizens, knows their interests, and cares for them. As most interpreters of international law and most observers of international life would confirm, the presumptive legitimacy of such states is an essential element of the common morality of the society of states. Hence, whereas the Requirement applies to all wars, the question of whether it has been satisfied really arises in nontraditional wars between states and non-state actors.[25]

This asymmetry between states and non-state actors enables states that fight guerrillas to deny them the moral power of representing the larger group in whose name they fight, without being subject to a similar critique. Thus, Israel insists that Hamas's attacks on military targets are illegitimate, as Hamas's war against it fails Political Society Authority. Moreover, Israel insists that even if Hamas was fairly elected by the majority of the Palestinian community in Gaza, it cannot fight in its name because of its moral failures. In the eyes of the international community, Israel's own moral failures seem irrelevant to the justice of its war against Hamas.[26]

The United States' treatment of al Qaida is similar. First, its normative power to act in the name of a larger group is challenged on the basis of its moral failures. Second, al Qaida's leaders usually present its war as anti-imperialistic: they fight in the name of the Ummah of Islam (the supernational community that follows Islam) against 'Western imperialism'. Suppose (for the sake of argument) that the cause of al Qaida's war is just: the United States supports friendly dictators in a way that justifies military resistance. Even if this were true, al Qaida ought to fight in the name of the larger group that it claims to represent. The common view within the international community is that the war fails to satisfy the Requirement because al Qaida has no authority to wage war in the name of this group. Hence, its war is unjust, whether or not its cause is just and whether or not its warriors target only combatants and military objects.[27]

As I shall argue later, these statist tendencies of the Requirement are only partly justified: the presumption that an internationally recognized state represents its citizens and that it is sufficiently just to have the normative power to do so might be defeated in clear cases like Stalin's USSR or Hitler's Germany.

2. The Legitimate Authority Requirement Challenged

A general realizes that his country is under imminent unjust threat from a military rival. A prevalent misconception blinds the political leadership; the politicians are unaware of the danger. Waiting for the command to initiate a pre-emptive attack would cause the wasteful death of thousands of innocent people on both sides. The general violates the chain of command and pre-emptively attacks the aggressor. He manages to conceal the provocative nature of his action; the politicians are under the impression that the other side was the first to use force. The war is fought in the name of the relevant community and on its behalf: the general occupies a public role and acts in his capacity as a high-ranked officer. The war meets the factual condition and yet, the objector asserts, the fact that it fails the Requirement does not render it unjust.[28]

A similar counterexample is offered in Cécile Fabre's cosmopolitan critique of the Requirement. She argues that it is unreasonable to insist that America's World War II would have been unjust had Roosevelt dispensed with the approval of Congress or even with the approval of the American people. She concludes that 'it is not necessary that a state be able to secure the consent of its people in order for its war to be just'. Hence, 'it is not necessary that an individual acting alone . . . be able to secure the consent of those on whose behalf she goes to war, in order for their war to be just'.[29]

Our objector might concede that there are considerations that speak against embarking on a war that does not meet the Requirement. The general has a prima facie reason not to violate the chain of command: he is duty-bound to support just institutions, and he is under a further, contractual duty to respect the institutions within which his role is defined. Violating the directives on which this regime is based is a violation of these duties. The objector argues that meeting the Requirement is morally prima facie desirable but denies that it is necessary for a war's being justified. The same is true of the president in Fabre's example: an unauthorized war defies the law and the democratic values on which the presidential office is based. Still, the objection goes, the reasons *for* going to the just wars imagined in these examples outweigh the cogent, yet less weighty reasons against.

Such cases might invoke general scepticism regarding the very idea of legitimate authority or less radical (but no less general) doubts as to the scope of the normative power of authorities. To understand these doubts, I introduce here the notion of a content-independent and pre-emptive reason for action.[30] A command to ψ issued by an entity that claims legitimate authority is a *content-independent* reason to ψ if it gives its addressee a reason to obey the command (i.e., a reason to ψ) irrespective of whether or not he had a reason to ψ, absent the command. The command is a *pre-emptive* reason to ψ if it is a second-order reason not to consider (some of) the other merits and demerits of ψ-ing: the command replaces these reasons. According to Joseph Raz, the notion of content-independent and pre-emptive reasons figures in the very definition of legitimate authority.[31]

Traditional just war theory treats legitimate authority as one of the six conditions necessary for just wars. This strongly suggests that the veto conveyed by Political, Beneficiary, or Bearer Authority has a pre-emptive force. To see more clearly why, observe that even if a failure to meet the Requirement is a prima facie first-order reason against fighting an unauthorized war, the gravity of this reason is limited, and hence it is hard to understand why a war that does not meet the Requirement is unjust. But suppose the violation of the Requirement is not merely a first-order reason against the war, to be weighed alongside the reasons for fighting it. Suppose, that is, the veto of the relevant collective pre-empts almost any other consideration that tells in favour of the war. Then the idea that the traditional treatment of legitimate authority is another necessary *jus ad bellum* condition is understandable.

One way to construe the objection under discussion derives from a general argument against the Razian approach to legitimate authority.[32] Rationality demands that agents aim to act on the undefeated reasons that apply to them. Hence they never have reasons to ignore the desirable and undesirable properties of an action they consider.

A requirement to treat someone as a legitimate authority—and to treat his instruction as a pre-emptive reason—must therefore be flawed. Our story about the general illustrates this truth: the Requirement implies that considerations in favour of the general's war, whatever they are, ought to be pre-empted. But these considerations might prevail, and, unless they are taken into account, a just defensive war that will prevent a much more bloody future war won't be fought.

A less radical critique accepts the possibility of Razian authorities while levelling less anarchical objections to the Requirement. According to one objection, the general is permitted to go to war without authorization because, in this domain of action, he (and perhaps other high-ranked officers) is not subject to the authority of the political leadership. It might be further argued that, in rare circumstances, the general is entitled to act in the name of the government and in the name of the people it represents without explicit authorization of his military actions. It is, so this thought goes, an essential element of his role that in exceptional cases he will follow his judgment about what has to be done here and now.[33]

The following sections defend the Requirement from the more principled objection. I will concede that it should be further contextualized in light of the nonanarchical objections to it.

3. An Instrumentalist Defence of the Requirement

Raz's powerful argument for the possibility of pre-emptive reasons and, consequently, for the possibility of legitimate authority is based on what he calls 'the normal justification thesis'. I will appeal to this thesis to show that, conjoined to certain empirical facts, those on whose behalf the war is fought (i.e., members of the collective named 'Beneficiary') and those who bear the internal costs of the war (i.e., members of Bearer) have the authority to veto it.

Normally, argues Raz, an authority is justified if the directives the authority issues serve its addressees.[34] Such directives help their recipient to conform to reasons that independently apply to him. A subject needs the guidance the authority provides if and only if it is more likely that he will conform to the reasons that apply to him by obeying the authority, and it is less likely that he will do so if he directly attempts to respond to these underlying reasons. Suppose, for example, that state institutions are able to identify individuals who possess medical expertise, whereas ordinary citizens have no such ability. By deferring to the directives of the relevant institutions, subjects are likely to do better than if they tried to figure out for themselves on which individuals they should count for medical advice.[35]

Here is another (more controversial) example.[36] Two siblings hire an arbitrator to resolve a dispute over the just distribution of the inheritance of their late mother. Both acknowledge that they are biased towards themselves in a way that distorts their judgment of a fair resolution of their conflicting interests. If the arbitrator is more impartial than they are, his verdict is legitimately authoritative. This is because, by following his instructions, they are more likely to agree on the right distribution of the resources than if they try to resolve the conflict by themselves.

Raz observes that, for an arbitration to be serviceable, the parties must be able to rationally precommit themselves to accept its resolution, regardless of its content. Moreover, the arbitrator's verdict must pre-empt their own deliberation on the merits of the case; should the parties consider the first-order reasons for and against the arbitrator's resolution, they would have no reason to hire him in the first place. Their deliberation would obviate the need of the authoritative directive. Moreover, the parties *cannot* be subject to the arbitrator's verdict *and* to the reasons that justify its authority simultaneously, because his verdict is meant to reflect the first-order reasons that independently apply to them. Since the considerations that support the arbitrator's verdict legitimize his authority, treating the verdict as a further first-order reason would be to count those considerations twice. To avoid double-counting, the verdict must function at a different level: it must pre-empt the underlying reasons it is supposed to reflect.[37]

Conjoined to three plausible factual assumptions, Raz's normal justification thesis grounds the authority conferred on Beneficiary and Bearer to veto a war. The first assumption is that political leaders and high-ranked military officers tend to pursue fame, legacy, and political power, which might be achieved by successful (although unjust) wars. The personal risk imposed on initiators of wars is relatively low. Hence, in too many circumstances, they might have a distorted incentive to fight an unjust war despite having an undefeated reason against doing so.

To understand the second assumption, recall that wars that meet the factual condition are claimed by their initiators (the government, members of Actor) to be intended to secure a public good for a larger group (Beneficiary) on whose behalf the war is fought. The second assumption is that the alleged beneficiaries are in a better position to assess the value of this public good than are the politicians that represent them. The more important the public good for which the war is fought to alleged beneficiaries, the more likely the cause of the war to be just; a veto by Beneficiary suggests that the cause of the war is unjust.

The third assumption is that those who bear the costs of the war are likely to object to unnecessary wars. The costs inflicted on them are so high that they are likely to prefer any morally feasible peaceful alternative to going to war.[38] Of course, Bearer Authority might be satisfied by externalizing risks and costs to third parties rather than by avoiding unnecessary wars. Accordingly, the empirical assumption is weak: Bearer Authority creates a *tendency* in the political leadership to avoid unnecessary wars.

An interesting further implication of these empirical generalizations is that conferring authority on Beneficiary and Bearer to veto the war makes it more likely that the *ad bellum* proportionality constraint will be satisfied. Very roughly, a war is proportionate if its relevant good effects outweigh its relevant bad effects. Bearers are sensitive to considerations of internal costs and risks, which constitute some of the bad effects of the war. Beneficiaries are sensitive to considerations about the public goods the war is supposed to secure—the good effects. These are two crucial factors in the proportionality calculation.

Are these factual assumptions reasonable? One might worry that the populace is a poor judge of the rights and wrongs of war, especially because the self-sacrifice of ordinary people is so easy to secure. I should like to emphasize, in response, that the empirical presumption is not that those on whose behalf a war is fought and those who bear its costs are well-positioned to veto unjust wars. Rather, the assumption is that their aggregate judgments about their own interests indirectly track justice better than the politicians or military leaders who directly assess the justice of the war. The biases from which such decision-makers suffer are well-documented.

To summarize, the instrumentalist justification of the Requirement has four noteworthy advantages. First, it illuminates and extends the Requirement/just cause conviction formulated at the beginning of this section: if the Requirement is satisfied, and other things are equal, the war is more likely to have a just cause. Second, the authority of the Beneficiary and Bearer veto serves the initiators of the war: politicians are more likely to conform to the moral reasons that apply to them if they respect it. The war they would initiate and conduct is more likely to have a just cause, more likely to be necessary, and more likely to be proportionate if beneficiaries and bearers do not veto it. Third, under the normal justification-based analysis advanced here, the Requirement constitutes a second-order reason: a veto by Beneficiary and Bearer is not another reason to be added to the balance of reasons for or against the war. In and of itself, a veto cannot render a war that is content-dependently just content-dependently unjust; an authoritative veto does not directly affect a war's justice, but rather makes it unjustified for the addressees of the veto to fight it.

Fourth, the instrumentalist justification adequately contextualizes Beneficiary and Bearer Authority. A veto by Beneficiary and Bearer does not entail that going to any war (that meets the relevant clauses of the Factual Condition) would be unjustified. In cases in which public opinion is clearly mistaken, the veto would not provide pre-emptive instrumentalist reasons to avoid it (see Section 5).

The analysis has another (already anticipated) revisionist implication. Section 2's account of the way the Requirement is commonly understood suggests that wars fought by states in defence of their national interests are presumed to meet the Requirement. Is the bias of the common understanding of the Requirement towards states justifiable? The instrumentalist justification of Beneficiary and Bearer Authority suggests not. States might violate the Requirement, just like any non-state actor. For example, a war to protect the territorial integrity of a state is unlikely to have a just cause if the territory is unimportant to the citizen or the costs of defending this territory seem to them to be too high.

Having said that, let me offer a rough consideration that supports the Requirement's statism. Compared to non-state actors—liberation movements included—a state is usually in a better position to determine whether the public good for which it fights is sufficiently important to its citizens and whether its citizens are ready to bear the internal costs of fighting for this good. This is due to one of the essential features of states: they are composed of institutions that rule and are ruled by a legal system. As Hart's positivistic account of the concept of law teaches, the set of rules by which a polity is governed attains the status of a legal system only if it is accepted by the relevant officials and by the institutions within which the role of these officials is defined.[39] If all other things are equal, these relations among the state, the institutions that constitute the state, and the officials that run and maintain these institutions makes it more likely that the state will adequately respond to the preferences of the community. The relation between national liberation movements and the community it represents is much less structured. Hence, other things being equal, wars fought by states are more likely to satisfy Beneficiary and Bearer Authority than are wars fought by non-state actors.

This consideration does not imply that wars fought by states in defence of their rights or interests automatically meet the Requirement, but rather that, compared to wars fought by non-state actors, states' wars are more likely to meet the Requirement. The presumptive legitimacy of states is defeasible; states exaggerate the moral asymmetry between them and non-state actors vis-à-vis the Requirement.

4. A Proceduralist Justification of Political Society Authority

A war that meets the factual condition is fought by one group of individuals, Actor, in the name of a larger group of individuals, Political Society. The justification of Political Society Authority, which I develop in some detail in this section, is distinct from the normal justification of the authority of Beneficiary and Bearer offered in the previous section. To see why, return to the case of humanitarian intervention, which illustrates the distinction between the group in whose name the war is fought and the group on whose behalf the war is fought. A government (Actor) is involved in a military campaign, the aim of which is to protect the rights of an oppressed group of citizens of another country (Beneficiary). Political Society—the citizens of the intervening country, the individuals in whose name the war is fought—gain no material benefit from the intervention. Hence, the war is not fought on their behalf. Furthermore, the military campaign might entail almost *no* internal risk to citizens and combatants of the intervening country (because of the power differential between the intervening state and its enemy) and no internal costs (the investment in the war will be repaid from the resources of the defeated country). There is no overlap between Political Society and Bearer/Beneficiary and, therefore, the normal justification of the authority of Beneficiary and Bearer does not legitimize the authority of Political Society. Indeed, I will assume that the mere fact that a war is fought in the name of Political Society does not put its members in any special epistemic position with respect to the justice of the war.

However, the normal justification thesis does not tell the whole story about political authority. One role of political organizations is to reach decisions when there are serious disagreements over the common good and the right thing to do.[40] Let us take a case in which there is a conflict between two political parties—Greens and Capitalists—over how to use a certain amount of resources to the benefit of future generations. The resources can be used to significantly advance future industry at the price of causing slight harm to the environment. Alternatively, they can be used to significantly benefit the environment, at the cost of causing slight harm to future industrial life. If the disagreement remains unresolved, the resources will vanish.

The disagreement can be structured as follows. The current conditions of the parties vis-à-vis these resources can be represented by the ordered pair <0, 0>. If one of the parties prevails, the 'benefit' to its worldview is quite large (10) while the loser's worldview is slightly harmed (−2). The possible *ex post* states of affairs are, then, <0, 0>, <−2, 10> and <10, −2>. Accepting a fair conflict resolution procedure under which each party gets a 50 per cent chance of winning 'betters' the *ex ante* condition of both parties. The expected benefit of this move to both parties is $0.5\cdot(-2) + 0.5\cdot 10 = 4$; and <4, 4> is Pareto superior to <0, 0>. There is, then, a clear sense in which the conflict should be resolved one way or another; inaction (<0, 0>) would be wasteful.

In such a case, rational parties need the service of political authorities because, *ex ante*, they would consider it valuable to take the risk of political defeat in order to gain the chance of political victory. But should the loser respect the result of the procedure? After all, the fair procedures that both parties reasonably accept—elections, referendums, and the like—allow a political action that the loser disfavours compared to the status quo. Therefore, the authority of the procedure is not covered by the normal justification thesis. Notwithstanding, it seems that the three aspects of the procedure—(*ex ante*) mutual benefit, fairness, and its acceptance by the conflicting parties—bestow authority on it. It seems that the parties are under a prima facie duty to abide by the outcome of the procedure even if they know it to be unjust. Rather than the merits of the outcome, it is the qualities of the procedure by which the political decision is reached that obligate the participants to respect it.[41]

I suggest that Political Society Authority is such a proceduralist requirement. The authority of the individuals in whose name the war is fought to veto the war derives, I suggest, from the fairness requirement to which political decision-making is subject. The individuals in whose name the war is fought ought to be included in the process by which the decision to go to this war is taken. Indeed, the political decision ought to be sensitive to the value judgments of those individuals—even if the war would have no impact on their quality of life and would not require any substantial sacrifice from them.

Consider, in light of this requirement, the counterexamples discussed in Section 2 from the perspective of Political Society Authority. The war initiated by the general is fought in the name of the citizens of a country, but these citizens had no say in the decision-making process that led to the war. The Requirement was violated because—in the imagined society—the chain of command is the accepted procedure that resolves the disagreement between the general and the politicians as to whether to go to war at this early stage. Similarly, suppose that the president takes Americans into a paradigmatically just war without the permission of Congress, which authentically represents the American people. They have been excluded from the decision-making process. The process is defective in that it was unresponsive to the value judgments of those in whose name the war is fought.

Like wars that fail Beneficiary and Bearer Authority, a war that fails Political Society Authority might meet all other *jus ad bellum* conditions; contrary to a violation of the just cause requirement or the necessity and proportionality conditions, a violation of Political Society Authority does not imply that the war is unjust (even if it is wrong for Actor to fight it, for reasons unrelated to the justice of the war). There is, however, a crucial difference between Political Society Authority and Beneficiary and Bearer Authority. Under the normal justification, a veto on a war conveyed by bearers and beneficiaries indicates that the war in question most probably fails other *ad bellum* conditions. The veto of these collectives reflects independent reasons against going to war. In contrast, under the proceduralist justification, a veto by Political Society merely makes it the case that—whatever the merits of the war—the decision to fight it would be morally defective. The veto of Political Society does not reflect the other first-order reasons that speak against the war. Therefore, the proceduralist argument cannot appeal to the Razian argument from double-counting in order to show that reasons that speak in favour of fighting are excluded by the veto of Political Society.

It might be concluded that politicians and high-ranking military officers are entitled to weigh the moral reasons in favour of the war against the fact that the decision to fight it must be morally defective (given popular opposition to the war). If these procedural reasons are outweighed, it could be permissible to initiate a war that does not meet Political Society Authority.[42]

I believe, however, that the disanalogy between the normally justified authority of Beneficiary and Bearer and the procedurally justified authority of Political Society should not be overstated: pre-emption is essential to the possibility of conflict of values resolution by a fair procedure. The parties' acceptance of the procedure would be pointless unless they give each other a sincere assurance to respect its outcome, whatever it is. Otherwise, it would be irrational for them to respect a verdict of a fair conflict-resolving procedure in case it goes against their best judgment of the right way to go: however weighty the first-order reasons provided by the fact that assurance has been given, as a first-order reason of limited weight, it can be easily overridden by the reasons that speak against honouring it. Therefore, for the procedure to resolve the disagreement between the parties, the commitment to respect its outcome must somehow pre-empt most countervailing reasons against conformity. Notwithstanding Political Society's lack of normally justified authority, the requirement to secure fair political participation in the decision-making process is pre-emptive; it involves a requirement not to attend to the first-order reasons that speak against the veto Political Society conveys.[43]

Is Political Society Authority statist, like its sisters Beneficiary and Bearer Authority? The presumption that every war fought by a state in defence of its interests meets Political Society Authority is groundless; states might violate the Requirement, just like non-state actors. Still, other things being equal, wars fought by states in defence of their interests are more likely to meet Political Society Authority than independence or civil wars fought by non-state actors. State institutions have a history; they have been founded and maintained thanks to the cooperation of many individuals over generations; the collective agency of these individuals generates a concrete shared interpretation of the ideal of fair political participation. In contrast, the institutional history of stateless political societies is usually shorter and poorer, and hence the procedures by which political participation is secured are underdeveloped.

5. The Scope Restrictions of the Requirement

The defence of the legitimate authority requirement offered in the previous sections presents it as a highly circumscribed *jus ad bellum* condition. Its scope restrictions have two main sources. First, and most importantly, the Requirement applies only to wars that partly or fully meet the factual condition and to wars that ought to meet it. The second source follows from the philosophical defence of it that I have offered. Beneficiary/Bearer Authority functions as a second-order test; wars that satisfy these conditions are more likely to meet the other *jus ad bellum* conditions. Political Society Authority is a secondary condition: waging a just war that violates it offends the ideal of political participation. The Requirement functions as if it were a pre-emptive second-order reason. Therefore, in at least some cases, following it could bring about bad results (in terms of conformity to the underlying reasons for or against the war it forbids).

In order to explore the first source of scope restriction, I should make a preliminary remark: the *Oxford English Dictionary* definition of war seems to imply that wars meet the factual condition as a matter of conceptual necessity: 'hostile contention by means of armed forces, carried on between nations, states, or rulers, or between parties in the same nation or state; the employment of armed forces against a foreign power, or against an opposing party in the state'.[44] An individual who explodes bombs in a series of attacks against a government that violates her basic rights commits a justified or unjustified criminal act. On this conceptual view, the importance of states to the Requirement derives from their having the capacity to wage war.

I side with Fabre, who argues that wars that do not meet some of the clauses of the factual condition are easily imaginable. There is no point in denying that the individual bomber just described goes to war against the government.[45] Moreover, as far as I can see, the semantic disagreement has no normative implication. Imagine a case whose description as a private war is much more natural. A small group of citizens fights an oppressive regime. Realizing that they cannot defeat and replace it, they do not intend to fight on behalf of or in the name of other citizens. They use force to protect the unrecognized borders of the oppression-free zone in which they (rather than any larger group) live; they maintain their limited political liberty by making it harder for the oppressive regime to get into the small territory in which they live. Actor—the group that actually fights the war—does not need authorization to fight the war from any larger group for a simple reason: it is identical to Political Society, to Beneficiary, and to Bearer. The Requirement is therefore irrelevant.

It should come as no surprise that early proponents of the Requirement applied it only to public wars. Grotius argued that when a war endangers the state itself, the sovereign authority alone has the right to fight it, but that, alongside such public wars, wars might be justly fought by individuals in their private capacity.[46] Similarly, Vitoria claimed that only a commonwealth may punish by war, but 'any person, even a private citizen, may declare and wage a defensive war'.[47]

Consider a more problematic case of private war, in which an intrinsically evil mafia (or terror organization) is the Actor, and the enemy is a dehumanizing genocide-seeking state. Following the common understanding of the Requirement, let us suppose that, unlike legitimate governments and legitimate non-state actors, the mafia cannot act in the name of members of the relevant Political Society. Does it follow that the mafia's war in defence of the rights of the innocents fails Political Society Authority? Not necessarily. We might deny that a war against the genocide-seeking state ought to be fought in the name of Political Society. After all, the morality of other-defence implies that, like all other private individuals, members of the mafia are allowed to defend potential victims by using force. (Other approaches to the morality of other-defence argue that self-appointed saviours are allowed to kill a culpable aggressor in the victim's defence only if the potential victim allows them to act on his behalf.) The rule of Political Society Authority does not apply to such a war because those who fight it do not act in the name of any larger group, nor ought they to do so. The use of force by the mafia is justified, even if it cannot act in the name of those on whose behalf they fight.

Turning to the second source of the Requirement's scope restriction, the Requirement's moral standing leaves room for authoritative, yet mistaken, vetoes by the relevant collectives. Actor has a pre-emptive reason not to fight the vetoed war in virtue of Actor's undefeated reason not to attend to considerations that make the war all things considered justified. Yet, as Raz notes, a normally justified authority ought not to be obeyed if it is clearly mistaken. He insists that this proviso is consistent with the pre-emptive nature of legitimate authority: 'establishing that something is clearly wrong does not require going through the underlying reasoning'.[48] You are not rationally required to obey clearly mistaken commands issued by a legitimate authority.

A different limitation of the Requirement is related to the empirical generalizations on which it is based, according to which the Beneficiary/Bearer opposition to the war symptomizes its injustice. There might be exceptional circumstances in which beneficiaries and bearers are radically uninformed. Then their veto has no authority over Actor.

These various limitations and restrictions of the Requirement raise an understandable worry. The Requirement cannot effectively constrain politicians who are determined to violate it; they have too many ways to excuse a decision to ignore or bypass it. My analysis of the Requirement treats it as a moral constraint rather than as a legal rule. Moral constraints are *not* designed in light of facts about the predicted level of compliance or enforceability. They have no built-in tendency towards generality and robustness. It is the role of the laws of war to accommodate the Requirement as an element of a system of enforceable rules whose application and violation can be easily identified as such.

6. Conclusion

Most wars are fought by a relatively small group in the name and on behalf of a larger group by imposing risks on members of this larger group and by employing means that belong to them. This chapter argues that traditional just war theory is best interpreted as conferring authority to veto a war on some of these groups. Let me highlight four propositions on which the legitimate authority requirement is based, according to the argument I offered. First, if a war is opposed by Beneficiary or Bearer, it is less likely to meet the substantive *jus ad bellum* conditions of just cause, necessity, and proportionality. Second, approval of the war by those in whose name it is fought furthers the fulfilment of the ideal of fair political participation. Third, the reason to respect the vetoes invoked by Political Society, Beneficiary, and Bearer are pre-emptive. Finally, like non-state actors, states can easily violate the Requirement. Yet, other things being equal, states are in a better position than non-state actors to know and to adequately respond to the values and preferences of the individuals they represent. They are also in a better position to fulfil the ideal of fair political participation by imposing and respecting a fair political decision-making process.

Acknowledgements

Thanks to Hagit Benbaji, Hanoch Dagan, Avihai Dorfman, Cécile Fabre, Jeff McMahan, Michael Walzaer and especially to Jonathan Parry and to the Editors of this volume, Helen Frow and Seth Lazar for helpful conversations and comments.

Notes

1. The Requirement receives little attention in contemporary literature. Michael Walzer's classic *Just and Unjust Wars: A Moral Argument with Historical Illustrations*, 4th ed. (Basic Books, 1996) devotes to it no substantive discussion. For Walzer, the legitimate authority issue arises in civil and guerrilla wars (96, 179–183). For interesting attempts to illuminate the Requirement and define its scope, see Anthony Coates, *The Ethics of War* (Manchester: Manchester University Press, 1997), 123–145. For discussion of the Requirement in the US Constitution, see Paul Christopher, *The Ethics of War and Peace: An Introduction to Legal and Moral Issues*, 3rd ed. (Upper Saddle River, NJ: Prentice Hall, 2004), 87–88.

2. Augustine, *Contra Faustum* XXII, 74–75; Aquinas, *Summa Theologiae* II, Q. 40: Pufendorf, *On the Duty of Man and Citizen*, para. 16–18: quoted in Cécile Fabre, 'Cosmopolitanism, Legitimate Authority and the Just War', *International Affairs* 84 (2008), 963–976, at 967, 968.
3. Fabre makes this point in her 'Cosmopolitanism, Legitimate Authority', 968; Helen Frowe makes it in her *The Ethics of War and Peace* (Routledge, 2011), 59–60.
4. This preliminary account is influenced by David Luban, 'Intervention and Civilization: Some Unhappy Lessons of the Kosovo War', in *Global Justice and Transnational Politics*, edited by Pablo de Greiff and Ciaran Cronin (Cambridge, MA: MIT Press, 2002), 79–115, who states that 'It takes an army to fight an army and it will be states, not heroic little bands . . . that carry out . . . humanitarian interventions . . . no reasonable law of peoples can tolerate vigilante interventions . . . [because] it gets hard in principle to distinguish self-appointed saviours . . . from mafias' (84–85).
5. This formulation follows Lionel K. McPherson, 'Is Terrorism Distinctively Wrong?', *Ethics* 117 (2007), 524–546, taking into account Coates's warning that, under one reading of the Requirement, any 'revolutionary' political movements might be regarded as 'terrorist' organizations due to their failure to achieve adequate legitimacy (*The Ethics of War*, ch. 5). Indeed, the suspicion that non-state actors are not legitimate authorities explains 'the hesitancy of just war theory to engage with the issue of non-traditional wars' (Jonathan Parry, 'Legitimate Authority, Irregular Belligerency and Orthodox Just War Theory' [unpublished manuscript], on files with the author). The sharpest contrast to the reading of the Requirement offered here can be found in Nicholas Fotion, 'Two Theories of Just War', *Philosophia* 34 (2006), 53–64.
6. There might be another explanation why only certain entities can fight a just war. If I blow up the houses of Parliament, it is not an act of war (even if I act on behalf of my animal rights group). But if the US Army drops a bomb, that's an act of war (even if the United States is motivated by concerns about the UK's treatment of animals, and, like my animal rights bomb, it fails all the other *ad bellum* conditions). It's an act of war because of who does it. I reject this view later (see Note 13 and Section 5).
7. Citizen's arrest is an exception.
8. A powerful argument in Malcolm Thorburn, 'Justifications, Powers and Authority', *Yale Law Journal* 117 (2008), 1070–1130, suggests that, in criminal law, 'conduct is legally justified only if the appropriate person validly decides that it is justified. The mere fact that there are good reasons to engage in certain conduct is not enough to justify it. . . . The appropriate decision maker must consider those reasons and make an authoritative decision on the matter' (1083).
9. As Fabre remarks: 'Cosmopolitanism, Legitimate Authority', 968.
10. See Yitzhak Benbaji, 'The Moral Power of Soldiers to Undertake the Duty of Obedience', *Ethics* 122 (2011), 43–72.
11. I owe the distinctions offered in the preceding two paragraphs to Jonathan Parry, who suggests that 'the authority requirement serves not only to identify the parties who are capable of declaring and waging *just* wars, it identifies the kinds of parties who are capable of waging war *simpliciter*, whether just or unjust' ('Legitimate Authority'). See also Christopher Finlay 'Legitimacy and Non-State Political Violence', *Journal of Political Philosophy* 18 (2010), 287–312, at 288. Cf. Note 6.
12. For simplicity, I will focus on wars that actually and fully meet the factual condition.

13. There's some nuance here. The president can deploy troops for a period of time, after which he must have the approval of Congress to keep them stationed.
14. It might be further argued that, even if the mafia pursues unjust ends, this doesn't mean it is unrepresentative. It means merely that it lacks the authority to act on behalf of those it represents for the Lockean reason that representative agents only have the authority to perform actions that their principals themselves have the right to perform. I owe these formulations to Helen Frowe (private communication).
15. The patrollers reject this claim: they say that they are entitled to act in their own name.
16. Cf. Avihai Dorfman and Alon Harel, 'The Case Against Privatization', *Philosophy & Public Affairs* 41 (2013), 67–102.
17. Luban, 'Intervention and Civilization', 105.
18. Idem, 88.
19. Luban, ibid., presents, but does not endorse this argument it. It seems to him sufficient that the intervention in Kosovo was a humanitarian effort. The same is true of Walzer: 'Kosovo', in his *Arguing About War* (New Haven, CT: Yale University Press, 2004).
20. Jeff McMahan, 'The Ethics of Killing in War', *Ethics* 114 (2004), 693–733, at 707.
21. Jeff McMahan, 'Just Cause for War', *Ethics and International Affairs* 18 (2005), 1–21, at 13. He follows Walzer, *Just and Unjust* Wars, 101–103. Cf. Fernando Tesón, *Humanitarian Intervention*, 3rd ed (Ardsley, NY: Transnational, 2005), who excepts 'those extreme situations [in which individuals] have lost their autonomy' (160). The Requirement is denied in Andrew Altman and Christopher Heath Wellman, 'From Humanitarian Intervention to Assassination: Human Rights and Political Violence', *Ethics* 118 (2008), 228–257.
22. Discussed in Walzer, *Just and Unjust Wars*, 70–73.
23. Walzer criticises Clinton's policy. The ability 'to fight a war without using armies' allows leaders to go to war 'without convincing the country the war is necessary' (*Arguing About War*, 101).
24. Suppose, though, that the bombing campaign in Kosovo would cost each US citizen $1 000, but would save 10 000 lives. You might think citizens are under a natural duty to support the political decision to go to war. A veto would be morally invalid. This view treats Bearer Authority as based on the role of consent in a permissible use of some people to benefit others. But the defence of Bearer Authority that I advance in the following sections is very different.
25. The factual observation regarding the role of presumptive legitimacy of states in the international community is expressed in both Michael Walzer, 'The Moral Standing of States: A Response to Four Critics', *Philosophy & Public Affairs* 9 (1980), 209–229, and David Luban, 'Just War and Human Rights', *Philosophy & Public Affairs* 9 (1980), 160–181.
26. As Jonathan Parry points out (private communication), the failure to meet Political Society Authority may have a further implication, one rooted in the connection between the morality of the *jus in bello* and the Requirement. One could argue that Hamas's agents are not combatants, even if they attack only Israeli combatants, because they lack belligerent status and therefore their actions fall outside the jurisdiction of orthodox just war theory.
27. Al Qaida can satisfy the authority requirement simply by modifying its claim to representativeness: 'we claim to represent only fundamentalists'. But bootstrapping the authority in this way is possible only at the cost of losing the just cause of the war: al Qaida militants have no right to fight for fundamentalists' liberation and moderates' oppression.

Compare Frowe's objection (*The Ethics of War and Peace*, 59–60) to McPherson's thesis in 'Is Terrorism Distinctively Wrong?'.

28. I used this example in Yitzhak Benbaji, 'The War Convention and the Moral Division of Labour', *Philosophical Quarterly* 59 (2009), 593–618, at 609–610.
29. Fabre, 'Cosmopolitanism, Legitimate Authority', 973.
30. Joseph Raz, *The Morality of Freedom* (Oxford University Press, 1986), 39–45. For an illuminating discussion of Raz's views, on which I rely heavily here, see Scott Shapiro, 'Authority', in *The Oxford Handbook of Jurisprudence and Philosophy of Law*, edited by Scott Shapiro and Julius Coleman (Oxford University Press, 2004).
31. See especially Raz, *The Morality of Freedom*, 56–75.
32. See Scott Shapiro, 'Authority', 391–393.
33. Thanks to Jonathan Parry for pressing this point.
34. See Shapiro, 'Authority', 402–406, based on Raz, *The Morality of Freedom*, 56–75.
35. Shapiro, 'Authority', 403.
36. Raz, *The Morality of Freedom*, 41–42; Shapiro, 'Authority', 404–405.
37. Thus, according to Raz (*The Morality of Freedom*, 58), pre-emption is related to two distinct features of legitimate authorities: that they exist to serve their subjects and that their directives reflect the underlying reasons that apply to their citizens. Cf. Shapiro, 'Authority', 404.
38. Recall Walzer's critique of Clinton's policy of not putting US soldiers at risk (see Note 26). In the terms used here, if there are no internal risks, Bearer Authority is met automatically; therefore, a powerful tool to make sure that the war is a necessity is lost.
39. H. L. A. Hart, *The Concept of Law*, 2nd ed. (Oxford: Oxford University Press, 1994), especially chapters 5–6.
40. I rely on Shapiro's 'Arbitration Model' of the service conception of authority, lucidly developed in his 'Authority', 431–434.
41. Cf. Shapiro's explanation of the moral standing of the outcome of a fair decision-making process; it is, he says, 'deference to a power-sharing arrangement that is socially necessary, empowering and fair' ('Authority', 435).
42. This is Jonathan Parry's view (private communication).
43. Consider a case in which a purely self-interested person is asked to give a sincere assurance to pay $10 in the future in return for a 50 per cent chance of gaining $100 now and a promise that dishonouring the assurance would involve no costs. David Gauthier famously argues that the gambler can give the assurance despite having no interest in honouring it: 'Assure and Threaten', *Ethics* 104 (1994), 690–721. Scott Shapiro shows that even if Gauthier is wrong, as many think, precommitments might function *as if* they were pre-emptive reasons. By subjecting themselves to the authority of the procedure, the parties might be capable of affecting the feasibility of nonconformity: 'Authority', 418–419.
44. Quoted in Fabre, 'Cosmopolitanism, Legitimate Authority', 969. Cf. Brian Orend: 'War is a phenomenon which occurs *only* between political communities, defined as those which either are states or intend to become states' ('War', *Stanford Encyclopaedia of Philosophy*, http://plato.stanford.edu/entries/war/).
45. Fabre, 'Cosmopolitanism, Legitimate Authority', 970.
46. Hugo Grotius, *The Rights of War and Peace*, I–3, I–4, I–5, quoted in Fabre, 'Cosmopolitanism, Legitimate Authority', 970.
47. Vitoria, *On War*, Q. 1, 2–3, quoted in Fabre, 'Cosmopolitanism, Legitimate Authority', 970.
48. Raz, *The Morality of Freedom*, 62.

CHAPTER 16

CIVIL WAR AND REVOLUTION

JONATHAN PARRY

1. Introduction

It is often claimed that war just isn't like it used to be.[1] Most strikingly, the majority of armed conflicts now occur within, rather than across, state borders (or combine the two). According to one study, of the 118 armed conflicts that have occurred between 1989 and 2004, only seven were interstate wars.[2] At the time of writing, a horrific civil war has raged in Syria for more than four years, Ukraine teeters on the brink of descending into internecine conflict, and the fledgling Iraqi state is facing violent opposition from powerful substate actors. In short, intrastate conflict is now the norm rather than the exception.

Interestingly, however, there have been few sustained treatments of civil war within the recent resurgence of interest in the ethics of war.[3] Most discussions remain focused on traditional conflicts between states.[4] In this chapter, I aim to show that this is an oversight worth rectifying. My strategy will be largely comparative, assessing whether certain claims often defended in discussions of interstate wars stand up in the context of civil conflicts and whether there are principled moral differences between the two types of case. In Section 2, I argue that thinking about intrastate wars may help us make progress on an important theoretical debate in recent just war theory. In Section 3, I consider whether certain kinds of civil wars are subject to a more demanding standard of just cause, compared to interstate wars of national defence. Finally, in Section 4, I assess the extent to which having popular support is an independent requirement of permissible war, and whether this renders insurgencies harder to justify than wars fought by functioning states.

To provide a frame for our inquiry, I will, following Cécile Fabre, understand civil wars to be armed conflicts that (1) are fought between substate groups and their own government or amongst non-state factions within a community, (2) are fought over political goals, (3) involve a level of violence that passes a threshold of severity, (4) in which each belligerent party has the ability to impose significant casualties on the other.[5]

2. The Theoretical Significance of Nontraditional Conflicts

While the majority of my discussion will concern the substantive permissibility of resorting to civil war, I begin by discussing how the issue of intrastate war bears on a central debate in contemporary just war theory at a more theoretical level.[6]

2.1. Two Approaches to the Morality of War

A key fault line within current discussions concerns how we should understand the relationship between the moral principles that govern warfare and those that apply to 'ordinary' acts of violence carried out in nonmilitary contexts. Positions on this question can be divided into two broad camps.

A *reductivist* approach treats warfare as morally continuous with all other activities, with its permissibility determined solely by familiar justifications for killing and injuring that we accept in all other circumstances.[7] On this view, for any act of justified killing in war, there are justified killings outside of war that are justified on precisely the same grounds. In terms of identifying these grounds, reductivists standardly hold that intentional killing in war is primarily justified in terms of individuals' rights of self- and other-defence, with collateral killing justified by considerations of lesser evil. Justified war is simply an aggregation of violent acts, each of which is justified in one of these two ways.

In opposition, *exceptionalist* approaches deny that the morality of war is exhausted by ordinary interpersonal morality. In conditions of war, the standard moral principles governing harming are either replaced or (more plausibly) supplemented by additional moral considerations. On this view, for at least some acts of justified killing in war, there are no justified killings outside of war that are justified on the same grounds. An exceptionalist view is often motivated by arguing that there are classes of killing in war that are intuitively permissible or impermissible, but that cannot be justified or prohibited solely by appealing to individuals' defensive rights or to standard lesser evil justifications.[8] If these judgments are to be vindicated, we must identify additional moral properties in war capable of generating additional permissions to kill (or restrictions on killing) beyond those identified by reductivists. What differentiates exceptionalists is the particular properties that they identify as playing this role. Here, I outline four prominent versions, which need not be exclusive.[9]

2.2. Varieties of Exceptionalism

One important strand of exceptionalism locates the relevant properties in features of the belligerent groups participating in an armed conflict. On a *collectivist* version of this view, reductivism is incomplete because it ignores the fact that war is something that individuals do *together* as co-members in morally important forms of association. More specifically, the claim is that the relationships between co-members in certain kinds of group are capable of altering the moral status of acts of violence carried out by members.[10] On one interpretation of this view, these relationships generate additional moral reasons for or against killing in war that defeat whatever reasons would otherwise determine their permissibility. On another, the relevant deontic alterations follow from the different ways in which participants in collective actions bear responsibility for their actions, compared to private actors.

A different version of group-based exceptionalism focuses on the idea that the leaders or governing institutions of certain organizations possess legitimate authority over their members. This authority consists in the moral power to issue commands and, by doing so, place the subjects of those commands under obligations to act as directed.[11] *Authority-based* exceptionalism holds that, under certain conditions, individuals may be all-things-considered required to obey commands to cause (or refrain from causing) harm in war. Importantly, this may include cases in which harming would be impermissible (or permissible) on the basis of the command-independent reasons.[12] Authoritative commands may thus provide an independent source of permissions and constraints.

An alternative strand of exceptionalism emphasizes the fact that warfare is a highly structured and convention-bound practice. The central claim is that the existence of conventional norms makes an important difference to the moral permissibility of killing in war, compared to killing in the absence of these conventions. This view is most at home within a broader contractualist moral theory, according to which the moral status of (at least some) actions are (at least partly) the product of agreement, either actual or idealized, among a relevant class of contractors. For *contractualist* exceptionalists, the moral permissibility of certain actions in war is determined by whether a norm permitting or prohibiting those actions would be accepted as binding by belligerents. For example, on Yitzhak Benbaji's development of this view, a class of killing in war is morally permissible if it is sanctioned by a convention that is (1) mutually advantageous to opposing parties, (2) fair, and (3) accepted (at least tacitly) by participants.[13] This may include killings that would be prohibited by precontractual moral principles.

A different convention-based view does not ground exceptional norms in the transformative power of agreement, but instead in the moral importance of the outcomes promoted by conventions containing those norms, such as reducing suffering in war. This view—which I term *pragmatic humanitarian* exceptionalism—is typically motivated by the thought that norms for war must be implementable and action-guiding in real-world scenarios. Since (by hypothesis) combatants will be unable or unwilling to act in accordance with the moral principles identified by reductivists and institutionalizing these principles in law would be counterproductive, they are practically irrelevant. Instead, war ethicists should be concerned with identifying rules for war whose implementation would do as much good as realistically possible, taking the abilities and motivations of actual participants in war into account.[14]

2.3. The Relevance of Nontraditional Conflicts

We can begin to appreciate how intrastate conflicts bear on the reductivist/exceptionalist debate by noting a key difference between these two approaches. Whereas reductivism is universal in scope, evaluating all acts of killing and injuring in terms of two invariant principles, exceptionalist approaches are necessarily scope-restricted. On these views, the moral status of (at least some) acts of killing depends on whether those acts take place within a conflict that has the particular properties that exceptionalists identify as generating additional moral permissions and/or restrictions. [15] For example, it may depend on whether the conflict is fought by certain kinds of collective or political authority, or whether it falls within the scope of a binding agreement or pragmatically justified convention.

With this in mind, the key feature of modern conflict that I want to emphasize is its sheer diversity. In particular, compared to the traditional Westphalian paradigm of warfare between sovereign states, today's conflicts are fought by a wide range of 'irregular' belligerents. This diversity poses three related challenges for exceptionalist views, although the extent to which each bites will depend on the particular form of exceptionalism under consideration. By contrast, none of these challenges arises for reductivism, given its universality.

The first holds that exceptionalism, even if correct in principle, fails to have much practical significance because the relevant exceptionalist properties are far less likely to obtain in irregular conflicts than in traditional interstate wars. Given the infrequency of interstate wars, exceptionalist approaches will not offer much guidance in the majority of real-life conflicts. This objection is perhaps most clear in the case of contractualist exceptionalism, which almost always takes states (or perhaps only 'decent' states[16]) to be the relevant parties to the agreement. Hence, in conflicts in which at least one party is not a (decent) state, exceptional norms will not arise. But a similar point can be made, *mutatis mutandis*, against group-based versions of exceptionalism. Since it is no easy task to show that even functioning states possess the kind of collective agency or political authority required to bring exceptionalist norms into play, we may be sceptical that more loosely structured substate groups will do so.

A second challenge begins by noting an important adequacy requirement for exceptionalist approaches: if one holds that the permissibility of harming depends on whether it takes place within a conflict that has specific properties, then one must be able to draw a clear boundary between the conflicts that exhibit those properties and those that do not. Call this the *demarcation requirement*.[17] Without demarcation, exceptionalism will assign an indeterminate moral status to many acts of harming—as neither permissible nor impermissible—which is a serious defect in any normative theory. Given this, a potential challenge for exceptionalism (and group-based exceptionalism in particular) is that modern wars hugely complicate the task of demarcation. In a world in which the de facto ability to employ large-scale organized violence is restricted to clearly identifiable state actors, demarcation may appear relatively straightforward. But this is not our world. Instead, the empirical messiness of contemporary conflicts presents a spectrum of cases—ranging from regular interstate wars down to mere large-scale banditry—that exhibit exceptionalist properties to greater and lesser degrees. To satisfy the demarcation requirement, exceptionalists must venture into the untidy range of cases between these two poles and provide nonarbitrary criteria that both clearly identify the relevant thresholds at which exceptionalist norms are activated and do so without generating unintuitive results in particular cases (more on this later). This is a pretty demanding task.

A third challenge questions whether exceptionalism can make good on its promise to vindicate certain intuitive judgments about the permissibility of killing in war, when applied to nontraditional conflicts. These cases may reveal a lack of alignment between these judgments and the properties that exceptionalists invoke to explain them. More specifically, irregular conflicts may provide cases in which (1) the intuitive judgments persist though the putative explanatory properties are absent, or (2) the properties remain but our judgments of permissibility shift dramatically. Such counterexamples would suggest that the exceptionalist has either failed to identify the relevant properties that explain the judgments or that the original judgments ought to be jettisoned, in which case the appeal to exceptionalism lacks motivation.

For example, contractualist exceptionalism is often invoked to support the intuition that combatants are permitted to kill their armed opponents in war, independently of whether their wars are just or unjust. However, if this permission is grounded in a contract between states then, presumably, it will not apply to soldiers who fight in unjust wars against non-state belligerents. These individuals therefore commit serious moral wrongs by fighting. But I doubt that defenders of the equal permission think that its scope is restricted in this way. If so, we will have cases in which the target judgment persists in the absence of the putative explanatory properties. A similar problem emerges if one takes the prohibition on targeting noncombatants to be grounded in contractual considerations, even if the class of contractors is somehow broadened to include non-state parties. This is because it is unlikely that a contract prohibiting these tactics would satisfy the mutual advantage, fairness, and actual acceptance conditions in conflicts involving militarily weak substate actors, who may be significantly disadvantaged by the ban.[18] If we think that the prohibition still holds strong in these cases, it is not clear that contractualism can account for our judgments.

Collectivist versions of exceptionalism may also be susceptible to counterexamples. Again, one application of this view is that it helps support common views about killing in war that are difficult to subsume within ordinary morality, such as the permission to fight in wars that lack a just cause. But, as David Rodin has pointed out, appealing to the moral significance of collective action risks extending the scope of these permissions to conflicts in which they intuitively do not apply, since 'Football violence, warring criminal gangs, mafia vendettas, family feuds, and most forms of ethnic and racially motivated violence are also mediated through group relations'.[19] To avoid this implication, the relevant collectivist properties need to be refined. One plausible response restricts exceptional permissions to *political* belligerent collectives, as groups 'engaged in violence in support of political goals, in the sense of aiming at creating (or restoring) a new collective ordering'.[20] This certainly excludes many groups, but it still seems controversially inclusive. For example, the group calling itself Islamic State (IS) surely counts as a political collective on this conception, but I think most just war theorists would be reluctant to attribute any special permissions to IS combatants, even if, counterfactually, they restricted their attacks to military targets.[21] However, once we start tightening up the collectivist conditions even further, it is hard to see how we can avoid excluding many states from the scope of exceptionalist permissions. For example, one obvious way of excluding organizations like IS is to appeal to the moral undesirability of the group's aim. However, once we employ such a moralized conception of what counts as a political collective, then it looks like states fighting unjust wars will also be excluded.[22] Nontraditional conflicts thus provide a rich source of tricky cases in which to test our intuitions, which in turn impose additional constraints on the task of demarcation outlined earlier.

Pragmatic humanitarianism may also have rather revisionary implications when extended beyond core cases of interstate conflict. This is surprising because the view is typically deployed in support of certain legal orthodoxies, such as the equal impunity granted to all combatants in war provided they attack only military targets. The claimed justification for this neutrality is that it incentivizes restraint, thereby reducing the suffering that war causes. However, consistency would seem to demand that the same pragmatic rationale for determining the *content* of rules for conduct in war should also determine their *scope*. If a set of rules is justified in virtue of the valuable outcomes their implementation promotes, then we should recommend their application to any conflict in which doing so has a sufficiently good chance of achieving this result. To demonstrate, consider a nontraditional conflict such as the Mexican drug 'war', which causes huge amounts of suffering, especially to civilians. Furthermore, imagine that it were possible to impose a neutral system of rules on this conflict, one that granted equal impunity to state soldiers and to armed cartel members, and that doing so would significantly reduce harm to civilians. Under these conditions, practical humanitarianism should recommend doing so.[23] If we find this intuitively unacceptable, or at least troubling, this casts doubt on whether practical humanitarianism successfully justifies these practices in the standard interstate cases.[24]

The challenges sketched here clearly do not suffice to settle the reductivism/exceptionalism debate. As mentioned, much will depend on the particular brand of exceptionalism and the specific substantive judgments that it is invoked to support. But I hope to have shown that thinking about cases of nontraditional conflict provides a useful standpoint from which to make progress on this issue.

3. Insurgencies, Interstate Wars, and Just Cause

I now turn to the moral justification of resorting to civil wars, focussing on an important subset of these cases in which members of a substate group resort to war against their own state. Term these *insurgencies*. These include cases of *revolution* (in which insurgents aim to replace the government of their state), *secession* (in which insurgents aim to annex and govern a portion of their state's territory, leaving the state's sovereignty over the remainder of its territory unchallenged), and *rebellion* (in which insurgents aim to force specific policy changes or concessions without challenging the regime's general claim to govern).

Despite several prominent figures in the history of political philosophy denying that violently opposing the state is ever permitted—Kant most notoriously—few, if any, contemporary theorists accept this extreme view. While it is uncontroversial that insurgencies *could* be justified under certain circumstances, the specific question I will consider is whether insurgencies are subject to a different justificatory burden at the bar of *jus ad bellum* compared to traditional interstate wars of national defence.

There are several fairly obvious respects in which insurgents may be morally disadvantaged. First, substate actors typically lack the military and material resources that states possess and so may find it more difficult to satisfy the requirement that war have a reasonable chance of success. However, the mere fact that insurgents cannot achieve their aims by conventional military means does not license the conclusion that they fail the success condition because nonconventional warfare could still be effective.

This reveals a second possible justificatory asymmetry, since nonconventional methods may be additionally morally objectionable even if effective. For example, in certain cases, effectively waging an insurgency may require intentionally targeting noncombatants, either to weaken the enemy or to coerce support for the insurgents.[25] Assuming that attacking noncombatants is particularly difficult to justify, wars that require such methods inherit this additional justificatory burden.

Third, insurgencies may be more difficult to justify in terms of the requirement that war be the last resort, because substate groups may be able to press their claims by legal means or by nonviolent resistance.[26] This is particularly likely to be true within broadly liberal-democratic societies.[27] By contrast, these options may not be available for states facing outside aggression. However, this cuts both ways because substate groups often lack access to international arbitration procedures that are available to states.[28]

Fourth, the fact that substate groups generally have fewer members than states is not only relevant to their ability to satisfy the success condition, but also to whether insurgencies fought on their behalf are proportionate. This is because the amount of collateral harm that it is permissible to cause in pursuit of a war aim is sensitive to the number of individuals who will benefit from its achievement. Holding the amount of collateral harm constant, the smaller the group contemplating resorting to insurgency, the harder it will be to satisfy the proportionality criterion.[29]

However, although practically important, the foregoing asymmetries are of limited philosophical interest. They can be viewed as merely tracking contingent differences in the non-normative facts, rather than any deep moral distinction between the two types of conflict. By contrast, as Cécile Fabre has emphasized, two factors are genuinely distinctive about insurgencies: they involve the use of organized violence (1) by *non-state* actors (2) against *their own* state and its officials.[30] Our topic, then, is whether the *political status* of the insurgents and the *special relationship* between them and their *state* can ground a deeper justificatory asymmetry between insurgencies and interstate conflicts. I return to political status in the next section. Here, I discuss the moral significance of insurgents' relationship to their state.

One natural way of appealing to the special relationship between insurgents and their states concerns the requirement of just cause. More precisely, it may be argued that this relationship affects the threshold of severity at which rights violations become candidates for remedy by military means. Perhaps the relationship places an additional constraint on resorting to war against one's own state, thereby raising the threshold of injustice required to generate a just cause for insurgency, compared to a war against outside aggressors.[31] On this view, there is a *restrictive asymmetry* between insurgencies and interstate wars.

This line of argument has recently been forcefully opposed. For Fabre, the fact that belligerents in civil wars stand in a state–subject relationship is irrelevant to whether or not the insurgents possess a just cause for war, and so 'what counts as a just cause for an interstate war also counts as a just cause for a civil war, and *vice versa*'.[32] Term this the *equivalence thesis*. An important part of assessing the comparative permissibility of insurgencies will thus depend on the truth of the equivalence thesis. In what follows, I set out three possible challenges.

3.1. National Partiality

The first, which forms Fabre's main target in defending the equivalence thesis, appeals to our having special obligations towards co-nationals in order to justify a restrictive asymmetry. On this view, considerations of partiality impose a higher threshold of injustice in order to justify resorting to war against one's own state, compared to external aggressors, because doing so requires killing and injuring one's co-nationals.

However, the normative claim underpinning this view is more controversial than one might think. First, one cannot simply appeal to the widely shared anti-cosmopolitan intuition that partiality to co-nationals is *permissible* in order to show that co-nationality makes insurgencies harder to justify. For this is compatible with the permissibility of weighing the interests of co-nationals and outsiders equally. Instead, it must be claimed, more strongly, that partiality towards co-nationals is *obligatory*. Second, it is questionable whether these obligations are able to do the moral work required. For example, the view seems to imply that if a gang of thugs threaten to inflict a certain level of harm on me, the amount of harm it is permissible for me to cause in self-defence (either to the attackers or to bystanders) depends on whether I am attacked by co-nationals within my home territory or by foreigners while aboard. This seems highly counterintuitive.

Furthermore, even if defensible, the normative claim may not in fact support the desired conclusion. For when a community has fissured to the point where civil war is a genuine possibility, often along ethnic or cultural lines, it seems doubtful that there exist particularly strong bonds of co-nationality between members of the belligerent groups capable of grounding special obligations. Hence, it is unclear that the distinction between those to whom we have special obligations and those to whom we do not will reliably track the distinction between those we must kill in order to wage an insurgency and those we must kill in order to resist external aggression.

3.2. The Obligation to Obey

A different argument in defence of a restrictive asymmetry focuses on the fact that states claim a right to rule, correlated with an obligation to obey on the part of their subjects. The central idea is that these political obligations impose an additional constraint on waging war against one's own state. Given this, a greater injustice is required to generate a just cause for insurgencies because these obligations must be overridden.

However, the defender of the equivalence thesis is unlikely to be moved by this. Modern consensus holds that states have legitimate authority in virtue of serving or benefitting their subjects in some relevant respect. When a state fails to carry out its legitimating functions, it forfeits its right to rule, thus relieving its subjects of any obligation to obey. If we understand a just cause for war as consisting, roughly, in threatened rights violations of sufficient gravity to warrant remedy by large-scale lethal force, then it seems uncontroversial that if a state is committing wrongs of this magnitude against its own citizens, it must thereby have forfeited its authority. In other words, if a rights violation is serious enough to warrant remedy by means of war when imposed by an external aggressor, then it is also serious enough to void a state's right to rule.[33] Hence, political obligations cannot constrain just causes for insurgency.

Interestingly, however, the conjunction of two common views regarding, respectively, the limits of political authority and the permissibility of national defence casts some doubt on the obviousness of this claim. First, it is generally accepted that states do not have to be maximally just or infallible in order to successfully perform their legitimating functions. States may retain a right to rule while still committing 'tolerable' injustices.[34] Second, common intuitions about permissible national defence suggest that the threshold at which injustices generate a just cause for war is considerably lower than that of serious violations of basic human rights, such as genocide and severe oppression. For example, many believe that it is permissible to wage war against 'bloodless aggressors', who aim to violate only 'lesser' rights, such as those to political self-determination, territory, property, or certain social and political goods.[35]

The equivalence view is most plausible if we set a high threshold for just causes for war in terms of grievous breaches of human rights. It is very doubtful that a state could commit such wrongs against its citizens while retaining its legitimacy.[36] However, the lower we set the just cause threshold—in line with common views about bloodless aggression—the weaker the equivalence thesis becomes. For if wars are permissible in defence of comparatively minor interests, then it is not obviously implausible that states could retain their authority while committing injustices comparable to bloodless aggression. If so, political obligations could potentially constrain just causes, thus supporting a restrictive asymmetry between insurgencies and interstate wars.

Of course, this brief argument does not suffice to show that the equivalence thesis is mistaken. It remains open to a defender of the thesis to argue that we reject one of the two views with which it is in tension. Most plausibly, they may argue that we should jettison intuitions about permissible national defence and instead adopt a higher just cause threshold. In fact, one may invoke intuitions about the permissibility of insurgency directly in support of doing so. A quick glance around the world reveals a fairly large number of non-state groups suffering what may be called 'bloodless injustice' at the hands of their state, such as a frustration of rights to political self-determination. But I doubt that many of us think that such groups have a straightforward just cause for lethal resistance, in the same way that we are inclined to believe in the case of states *facing* bloodless aggression.[37] Unless there is some principled explanation (as I have suggested there may be) for the intuitive asymmetry between killing in *defence* of rights to self-determination that are currently enjoyed and killing in order to *realize* those rights when they are wrongly denied, consistency requires taking either a considerably more permissive view of insurgency or a more restrictive view of national defence. To me, the latter seems the more palatable.[38]

3.3. Fiduciary Obligations

It is also possible to challenge the equivalence thesis on the ground that the threshold of injustice required to generate a just cause for insurgencies may be *lower* than that for interstate wars. In other words, there is a *permissive* justificatory asymmetry between insurgencies and interstate wars. To my knowledge, no one in the contemporary literature has explicitly advanced this view.[39] However, an argument for it can be constructed by combining two arguments that have been advanced in other contexts and that are at least *prima facie* plausible.

The first argument begins with the idea that states and their officials stand in a fiduciary relationship to their subjects, having a special obligation to protect them and to act in their interests.[40] These obligations obtain regardless of how well or poorly the state in fact serves its citizens; it is not a condition of having certain responsibilities that one does a good job of discharging them. In virtue of these obligations, states and their officials can wrong their subjects in a distinctive and particularly egregious manner.[41] For example, John Gardner has argued that a victim is more gravely wronged if he is unjustly harmed by a police officer rather than by an ordinary citizen, for the same reasons that one would be if harmed by one's parent rather than a stranger.[42] This thought may gain further support from the idea that the distinctive wrongness of crimes against humanity lies in the fact that, in these cases, the institutions of the state are turned on those they are meant to protect.[43] This argument, if successful, establishes a moral asymmetry between unjust harms inflicted by one's own state and equivalent harms imposed by external aggressors.

It does not, however, show that there is a permissive asymmetry between just causes for insurgencies and interstate wars. To do so, a second argument must be invoked from the self-defence literature, one concerning the factors that determine whether defensive harm is proportionate. While there is general agreement that the amount of defensive harm it is permissible to inflict on aggressors is sensitive to the amount of physical harm their victims would otherwise suffer, several theorists argue that the degree of *wrongfulness* of the harm is also relevant.[44] The basic thought is that individuals have an interest not simply in avoiding harm, but also in avoiding being wronged or disrespected by others, an interest that ought to be reflected in the content and limits of our defensive rights. Other things being equal, the graver the violation threatened, the greater the amount of harm it is permissible to cause to prevent it. For example, victims may inflict more harm in defending themselves against intentional rather than merely negligent harm, or against being harmed as a means rather than as a side effect.[45]

Taken together, these two arguments support the conclusion that the threshold of unjust harm required to generate a just cause for insurgencies may be lower than the threshold for defence against external aggression, other things being equal.[46] The existence of fiduciary obligations magnifies the wrong individuals suffer when they are harmed by their own state, thereby justifying defensive actions that would not be permissible in their absence. This is in contrast to the equivalence view, which gives the impression that victims of states that grossly fail to perform their legitimating functions should regard their assailants as morally on a par with strangers.

4. Authority, Consent, and Popular Support

As we saw in the previous section, insurgents may, as a contingent matter, be at a disadvantage in terms of their ability to satisfy the requirements of last resort, reasonable prospect of success, and proportionality. In addition, the special relationship between insurgents and their state opponents may affect whether a given injustice generates a just cause for war. But these do not exhaust the standard requirements of *jus ad bellum*. Mainstream just war theory also includes the criterion of 'legitimate authority'. In the broadest terms, the criterion holds that, to be justified, wars must be initiated and fought by a certain kind of belligerent entity. This is standardly interpreted to mean a state, a coalition of states, or, more permissively, certain non-state entities that aspire to statehood. Although comparatively undertheorized in contemporary debates, the authority criterion is clearly crucial to answering our next question: to what extent does the political status of insurgent groups ground a justificatory asymmetry between insurgencies and traditional interstate wars? If the standard interpretation of the criterion is correct, at least the majority of insurgencies will be automatically unjustified.

However, for precisely this reason, many find the authority criterion extremely implausible. Most obviously, it seems open to clear counterexamples. For one, it implies that the members of a substate group facing genocide or enslavement could not permissibly wage war against their oppressors, *even if* they satisfied all other requirements for just war. This is very hard to believe. More theoretically, the criterion is also deeply at odds with a broadly reductivist approach, according to which the initiation and waging of wars can be justified as a composition of acts of permissible defensive harming between individuals. Since it is not a necessary condition of permissible self- or other-defence that one have a certain political status or be authorized by someone who does, the authority criterion seems morally redundant.

Two conclusions may be drawn from these objections. An *abolitionist* view holds that the authority requirement should be entirely jettisoned.[47] If a war satisfies the remaining *ad bellum* criteria, this is sufficient for its permissibility. On this view, the political status of belligerents cannot ground any deep moral asymmetry between insurgencies and interstate wars. A *reformist* view denies the sufficiency claim. Instead, it aims to retain the criterion in a more plausible form, one that both avoids absurd implications and is compatible with justifying war in terms of the rights and interests of individuals.

One promising way of rehabilitating the criterion, suggested by several writers, is to replace the formal property of statehood with the normative notion of consent.[48] The underlying claim is that it is an independent and necessary condition of permissible defensive force that the beneficiaries consent to it or, at very least, do not overtly refuse it. Term this the *consent principle*.[49] On this view, an entity's having the authority to wage war consists in its being authorized to do so by those on whose behalf the war is fought. Without this authorization, waging war is impermissible, even if all other conditions are met.

Although consent is intended to impose an independent constraint on all forms of armed conflict, it is particularly salient in the case of wars fought by substate belligerents because these groups typically lack the institutional mechanisms to demonstrate that they have popular support, and are often criticized for claiming to fight in the name of others without a sufficient mandate. So, although this reformist view does not automatically disqualify these groups from having the authority to wage war (thus avoiding the counterexamples just mentioned), it may still provide support for the claim that insurgencies are harder to justify than wars fought by functioning states (if we grant the empirical assumption that subgroups are less likely to be representative of those they fight on behalf of). The question, then, is whether and to what extent the consent principle does impose a genuine constraint on war.

4.1. Against the Consent Requirement

The consent principle gains considerable support from our judgments about simple cases of other-defence. Consider the following example:

> *Elevator*: Victor is taking a ride in an elevator. Agatha hates Victor and begins to saw through the elevator cable in order to kill him. Richie is walking by and is able to shoot Agatha with his sniper rifle before she succeeds in killing Victor. However, Victor is committed to nonviolence and refuses Richie's defensive assistance.

In this case, it does seem wrong for Richie to kill Agatha in defence of Victor (assuming that Victor is mentally competent, aware of the facts, etc.). Victims occupy a morally privileged position within the morality of defence—it is *their* interests that are at stake after all—and this gives them the exclusive right to decide if and how those interests are defended.[50] The role of consent thus tracks an important distinction between there merely *being* a potential justification for defensive harm and a particular agent's actually *having* that justification. For the latter, the will of the victim must be engaged. Rescuers thus wrong the victim by defending him against his express wishes, even if they do not wrong the attacker. More specifically, they commit the distinctive wrong of paternalism.[51]

Despite its appeal in these cases, an obvious difficulty with invoking the consent principle as a constraint on war is that groups are not simply individuals writ large. There is no straightforward sense in which a victim group can consent to or refuse the use of force on its behalf in the same way that an individual victim can. However, an obvious solution in these cases, often proposed in discussions of humanitarian intervention, is to appeal to majority consent. Although the proportion of consent required is unlikely to be precise, it seems plausible that if a clear majority of the members of a victim group refuse war on their behalf, then defending them would violate the consent principle and so be impermissible.

The problem, however, is that intuitive judgements militate against the straightforward move to a majoritarian version of the consent principle. Consider the following case:[52]

> *Multiple Elevator*: Victor and four others are taking a ride in an elevator. Agatha begins to saw through the elevator cable in order to kill its occupants because she hates them. Richie is walking by and is able to shoot Agatha with his sniper rifle before she succeeds in killing the five. Victor consents to Richie's defensive assistance, but the remaining four victims refuse due to their commitment to nonviolence.

In this case, a clear majority of victims explicitly refuse defence, yet it seems permissible for Richie to use defensive force nevertheless. The explanation of why defence is impermissible in the original Elevator case does not apply here. While individuals may have the right to decide whether or not *their own* lives are defended, this does not extend to the lives of others. This seems true even if the victim group is not a pure aggregate of individuals, but is instead composed of individuals linked by morally significant 'unifying relations' such as shared ethnicity, culture, or conception of the good.[53] As Andrew Altman and Christopher Heath Wellman put it, when lives are at stake, 'It seems dubious to hold that a group has this type of normative dominion over its members'.[54]

Given this result, some conclude that it cannot be a necessary condition of permissible war that the majority of the victim group consent to its prosecution or even that many consent.[55] In cases where (1) consent is mixed among the members of a victim group, and (2) defending those who do not consent is a condition of defending those that do, a lack of consent does not render defence impermissible. In other words, provided that some members of a victim group consent to defence (or are not competent to refuse), the consent principle is satisfied.[56]

Of course, this is not to deny that consent may play an important indirect role in justifying war. For example, widespread refusal may provide good evidence that a proposed war would not be justified or render it unlikely to succeed.[57] The claim is that the consent of the victims does not place an *independent* constraint on defensive war, at least in any minimally realistic case. If this sceptical view is correct, then the fact that insurgents are typically less representative of those they fight on behalf of, compared to state belligerents, would not provide any independent support for the claim that insurgencies are harder to justify.

4.2. A Qualified Defence of Consent

In my opinion, both the simple majoritarian view and the strong sceptical view are mistaken. The correct account of the role of consent in justifying war lies somewhere between these two views. Though the sceptics are correct that majority or widespread consent is not always required for permissible defence, this does not license the stronger conclusion that it is never (or rarely) required. In order to defend a more robust consent requirement, one must identify a relevant moral difference between defensive wars and mixed-consent cases like Multiple Elevator, which explains why broad consent may be required in the former but not the latter. Here, I sketch two possible responses of this type.

4.2.1. *Individual Versus Collective Rights*

One strategy identifies a distinction in the kinds of rights that are at stake in the two types of case. It points out that just causes for war not only include preventing rights violations such as death, enslavement, and other atrocities, but also defending rights to political and social goods such as territory, independence, and self-determination.[58] The argument concedes that majority consent is not a requirement for defending the former class of rights (as in the Multiple Elevator case), but holds that it is required for defending the latter. Since wars and insurgencies are often, perhaps typically, justified by appeal to political goods (national liberation struggles spring to mind most obviously), majority consent is therefore usually required.

But why should this difference in rights ground a difference in the consent requirement? One answer points to a difference in the *strength* of the interests that the rights protect. While the value of majority rule may trump the importance of protecting less weighty political rights, when it comes to our most stringent rights (such as those to life and limb), this value pales in comparison.[59] However, this doesn't seem to be the right answer. Consider a variation on the Multiple Elevator case, in which Agatha threatens to inflict a much less severe harm on her five victims, a vicious pinch say, which Richie can avert by defensively pinching Agatha. If the severity-based explanation were correct, we would expect to judge that defending the victims in the face of majority refusal would be wrong. Yet defence still seems permissible. As in the original case, though each victim has the right to decide whether his interest is defended, this does not extend to the interests of others.

A more promising explanation appeals to a distinction in the *type* of rights at stake, rather than the weight of the interests they protect. On this view, majority consent among the members of a victim group is required when the rights violations threatened are *collective* rights, such as those to territory or self-determination, but not when the relevant rights are *individual* rights, such as those to life and limb. A full account of collective rights is far beyond the scope of this chapter. But, for our purposes, we need only highlight one important feature of collective rights, which that is that while such rights can be *grounded* in the interests of individuals—namely, individuals' interests in enjoying certain collective or communal goods—they can only be *exercised* collectively.[60] No one member can unilaterally exercise a collective right on his or her own, including authorizing third parties to act on that right.[61] Rather, some collective procedure is required in order to successfully do so, majority decision-making being a paradigmatic example.

This feature of collective rights, it may be argued, explains why, in certain cases, the consent of the majority of the members of a victim group is a necessary condition for justifying defensive war. When a just cause for war is based purely on individual rights (such as a war of defence against mass murder or enslavement), each individual right-holder has the moral power to authorize a third party to defend his or her rights, which is unaffected by the refusal of other victims. By contrast, if the just cause is grounded in the defence of interests that are protected by collective rights, that right can only be permissibly acted upon by those who have been collectively authorized to do so. So, while it is false that majority consent is a necessary condition for *all* wars, it may be true for a (possibly large) subset.

It should be noted, however, that one could resist this conclusion by adopting a high threshold view of just cause, as discussed in the previous section. If the interests protected by collective rights are not important enough to justify large-scale killing, then having the consent of the victims of collective rights violations is irrelevant to justifying war in their defence.

4.2.2. *Consent and Proportionality*

A different strategy aims to show that widespread consent among the victim group may be required even when the rights threatened are purely individual. It locates the relevant difference between defensive wars and cases like Multiple Elevator in the fact that the former typically involves collaterally killing innocents, which must be justified as a matter of proportionality. On the view under consideration, the consent of the victims plays two distinct roles in establishing whether defending them is proportionate, by determining (1) whether certain good effects are *admissible* in the proportionality calculation and (2) whether certain bad effects are *discounted.*

The argument for the first claim rests on a particular view of the normative effect that follows from a victim refusing defensive assistance. The basic thought, familiar from discussions of paternalism, is that, by refusing, the victim removes his interests from the 'pot' of values that may be appealed to in justifying defensive harm. One way of capturing this idea is by thinking of an individual's refusal as morally equivalent to their nonexistence, for the purposes of justifying harm. Hence, in justifying defence, rescuers may only invoke the interests of victims who have not refused defensive assistance.

This view accounts for why majority consent is intuitively not required in the Multiple Elevator case. Although each of the four nonconsenters successfully withdraws their interests from the pot of admissible values, this does not render defence impermissible because the interests of the single consenter are sufficient to justify the total amount of defensive harm. Were the nonconsenters not to exist, it would still be permissible to kill Agatha in defence of Victor. It is this particular feature of the case that explains why the number of refusing victims seems morally irrelevant. But, crucially, this feature is absent in cases where defending members of a victim group also requires collaterally killing innocent persons, such as in defensive wars. To demonstrate, consider a variation on the Multiple Elevator case:

> *Collateral Elevator*: Victor and four others are taking a ride in an elevator. Agatha begins to saw through the elevator cable in order to kill its occupants because she hates them. Richie is walking by and is able to blow up Agatha with his grenade before she succeeds in killing the five. However, doing so will also kill an innocent bystander as a side effect. Victor consents to Richie's defensive assistance, but the remaining four victims refuse due to their commitment to nonviolence.

In this case, the interests of the single consenter are *not* sufficient to justify defence. Were the four nonconsenters not to exist, Richie would not be permitted to defend Victor because collaterally killing one innocent person would be disproportionate. In fact, the absence of just *one* of the victims could be enough to render defence disproportionate, depending on where one sets the relevant threshold.

If we accept the idea that individuals have this kind of normative control over their good, the refusal of members of the victim group may be much more relevant to the permissibility of defensive force than the sceptic alleges. By refusing, victims diminish the amount of value that may be invoked in order to justify collateral harm. Since wars usually involve considerable amounts of collateral harm, widespread refusal by the intended beneficiaries of that war may significantly count against it being proportionate.

Whereas the first argument for the dependence of proportionality on consent focusses on victims *qua* beneficiaries, the second focusses on victims *qua* objects of collateral harm. It will often be the case that defending a group of victims by means of war will risk significant collateral harm to members of that group (perhaps especially so in the case of insurgencies, which are often fought in close proximity to their putative beneficiaries). The argument rests on the plausible idea that the amount of harm it is permissible to impose in order bring about a good effect is sensitive to whether those *who will be harmed* (as opposed to benefitted) consent to its imposition. For example, consider the standard Trolley Case, in which one person is collaterally killed in order to save five. Let's stipulate that five lives is the precise threshold at which killing one is permissible. Now imagine a variation in which there are only four victims on the main track, but the single person on the side-track freely consents to being killed for the greater good. In this case, the victim's consent intuitively makes all the difference, rendering permissible an otherwise disproportionate act of collateral killing.

Generalizing somewhat (and ignoring some important complications), this result suggests that defensive actions that would otherwise be disproportionate in virtue of the risk of harm imposed on members of the victim group can be rendered permissible in virtue of the consent of a sufficient number of those victims. This is because consent can permit discounting certain bad effects in the proportionality calculus.

As with the argument from collective rights, these two proportionality-based arguments do not show that widespread consent within a victim group is necessary in order to justify *all* defensive wars. But, taken together, they provide firm support for the idea that insurgents may be at a moral disadvantage compared to state actors (on the empirical assumption that insurgent groups are generally less likely to be representative of those on whose behalf they claim to fight).[62]

5. Conclusion

According to perhaps the most popular method for doing moral and political philosophy, one systematically compares one's judgments about particular cases and about general principles and then goes through a process of revising these judgments where necessary in order to bring them into a state of coherence and mutual support. If there is a general lesson to be learnt from issues I have sketched in this chapter, it is that when it comes to the task of uncovering the morality of war, we will need to include our judgments about a much wider range of cases as inputs into this reflective process. These may require some interesting revisions in order to be accommodated.

Acknowledgements

Thanks to Cécile Fabre, Henry Shue, Cheyney Ryan, Janina Dill, Michael Gibb, and Bernard Koch for stimulating discussion of a very early draft at the Oxford War Workshop, and to Seth Lazar and Helen Frowe for detailed and extremely helpful comments.

Notes

1. For an influential example, see Mary Kaldor, *New and Old Wars: Organised Violence in a Global Era*, 2nd ed. (Cambridge: Polity Press, 2007).
2. Lotta Harbom and Peter Wallensteen, 'Armed Conflict and Its International Dimensions', *Journal of Peace Research* 42:5 (2005), 623–635.
3. As William V. O'Brien observed more than thirty years ago, 'Logically, there should be an elaborate *jus ad bellum* and *jus in bello* for revolutionary war, but development of such a doctrine has never been seriously attempted'. William V. O'Brien, *The Conduct of Just and Limited War* (New York: Praeger, 1981), 23.
4. Although the tide does seem to be turning. See, Ned Dobos, *Insurrection and Intervention: The Two Faces of Sovereignty* (Cambridge: Cambridge University Press, 2012); Cécile Fabre, *Cosmopolitan War* (Oxford: Oxford University Press, 2012), ch. 4; Christopher Finlay, 'Legitimacy and Non-State Political Violence', *Journal of Political Philosophy* 18:3 (2010), 287–312; Allen Buchanan, 'The Ethics of Revolution and Its Implications for the Ethics of Intervention', *Philosophy and Public Affairs* 41:4 (2013), 292–323; Allen Buchanan, 'Self-Determination, Revolution, and Intervention', *Ethics* 126:2 (2016), 447–473; Mattias Iser, 'Beyond the Paradigm of Self-Defense? On Revolutionary Violence', in *The Ethics of War*, edited by Saba Bazargan and Sam Rickless (Oxford: Oxford University Press, forthcoming). In addition, two monographs have recently been published: Christopher Finlay, *Terrorism and the Right to Resist: A Theory of Just Revolutionary War* (Cambridge: Cambridge University Press, 2015); Michael Gross, *The Ethics of Insurgency: A Critical Guide to Just Guerrilla Warfare* (Cambridge: Cambridge University Press, 2015).
5. Fabre, *Cosmopolitan War*, 135.
6. The following section draws on Jonathan Parry, 'Just War Theory, Legitimate Authority, and Irregular Belligerency', *Philosophia* 43 (2015), 175–196.
7. For book-length reductivist treatments of war, see Jeff McMahan, *Killing in War* (Oxford: Oxford University Press, 2009); Fabre, *Cosmopolitan War*; Helen Frowe, *Defensive Killing* (Oxford: Oxford University Press, 2014).
8. For both sides of the objection, see Seth Lazar, 'The Responsibility Dilemma for Killing in War: A Review Essay', *Philosophy and Public Affairs* 38:2 (2010), 180–213.
9. For a more detailed discussion, see Seth Lazar's chapter in this handbook.
10. See, for example, Christopher Kutz, 'The Difference Uniforms Make: Collective Violence in Criminal Law and War', *Philosophy and Public Affairs* 33:2 (2005), 148–180; George Fletcher, *Romantics at War: Glory and Guilt in the Age of Terrorism* (Princeton, NJ: Princeton University Press, 2002).
11. For useful introductions, see Joseph Raz, 'Introduction' in *Authority*, edited by Joseph Raz (Oxford: Oxford University Press, 1990), 1–19; Scott Shapiro, 'Authority' in *The Oxford Handbook of Jurisprudence and Philosophy of Law*, edited by Jules Coleman and Scott Shapiro (Oxford: Oxford University Press, 2002), 382–439.
12. For discussion, see David Estlund 'On Following Orders in an Unjust War', *Journal of Political Philosophy* 15:2 (2007), 213–234; Jonathan Parry 'Authority and Harm', *Oxford Studies in Political Philosophy*, Vol.3 (forthcoming); Massimo Renzo, 'Democratic Authority and the Duty to Fight in Unjust Wars', *Analysis* 73:4 (2013), 668–676; Massimo Renzo, 'Duties of Citizenship and Just War' (unpublished manuscript); Cheyney Ryan, 'Democratic Duty and the Moral Dilemmas of Soldiers', *Ethics* 122:1 (2011), 10–42.

13. Yitzhak Benbaji, 'The Moral Power of Soldiers to Undertake the Duty of Obedience', *Ethics* 122:1 (2011), 43–73; 'The War Convention and the Moral Division of Labour', *The Philosophical Quarterly* 59:237 (2009), 593–617.
14. See, for example, Henry Shue, 'Do We Need a 'Morality of War'?' in *Just and Unjust Warriors: The Moral and Legal Status of Soldiers*, edited by David Rodin and Henry Shue (Oxford: Oxford University Press, 2008), 87–111.
15. Thanks to Seth Lazar for helping me formulate this thought more clearly.
16. Benbaji, 'The Moral Power of Soldiers to Undertake the Duty of Obedience', 45.
17. For a discussion of demarcation in the context of the laws of war, see David Luban, 'War Crimes: The Laws of Hell' in *War: Essays in Political Philosophy*, edited by Larry May (Cambridge: Cambridge University Press, 2008), 266–288.
18. Benbaji comes close to conceding this, but attempts to show, on empirical grounds, that weak parties would consent to a revised version of the prohibition. Yitzhak Benbaji, 'Justice in Asymmetric Wars: A Contractarian Analysis', *Law and Ethics of Human Rights* 6:2 (2012), 172–200. For further discussion of the moral force of agreements in the context of asymmetric wars, see Fabre, *Cosmopolitan War*, ch. 7.
19. David Rodin, 'The Moral Inequality of Combatants: Why *jus in bello Asymmetry is Half-Right*', in *Just and Unjust Warriors*, 44–68, at 65.
20. Kutz, 'The Difference Uniforms Make', 176.
21. On this point, see Robert E. Goodin, *What's Wrong With Terrorism?* (Malden, MA: Polity Press, 2006), ch.1.
22. Rodin, 'The Moral Inequality of Combatants'.
23. For an argument that elements of the laws of war should be extended to this conflict, see Carina Bergal, 'The Mexican Drug War: The Case for a Non-international Armed Conflict Classification', *Fordham International Law Journal* 34 (2011), 1042–1088.
24. For a more detailed version of this objection, see Kutz, 'The Difference Uniforms Make'. For further discussion, see Finlay, 'Legitimacy and Non-State Political Violence'. David Rodin pursues a structurally similar line of objection regarding the content of pragmatic humanitarian norms, as opposed to their scope. David Rodin, 'The Morality and Law of War', in *The Changing Character of War*, edited by Huw Strachan and Sibylle Scheipers (Oxford: Oxford University Press, 2011), 446–463.
25. For detailed discussion of the latter, see Buchanan, 'The Ethics of Revolution and its Implications for the Ethics of Intervention'.
26. Fabre, *Cosmopolitan War*, 150.
27. Jeff McMahan criticizes Palestinian terrorist attacks for this reason (among others). Jeff McMahan, 'Just Cause for War', *Ethics and International Affairs* 19:3 (2005), 1–21, at 12.
28. On this point, see Anna Moltchanova, 'Stateless National Groups, International Justice and Asymmetric Warfare', *Journal of Political Philosophy* 13:2 (2005), 194–215.
29. Some have found it unintuitive that whether a political community may resort to war depends on the size of its population; for example, Seth Lazar, 'National Defence, Self-Defence, and the Problem of Political Aggression', in *The Morality of Defensive War*, edited by Cécile Fabre and Seth Lazar (Oxford: Oxford University Press, 2014), 11–39, at 33. However, it seems to me far more implausible to claim that the numbers don't matter.
30. Fabre, *Cosmopolitan War*, ch. 4.
31. It is worth pointing out that potential just causes for insurgency need not involve the target state violating the rights of *its own* citizens. Injustices committed by a state against non-members could also generate a just cause for insurgency, even if it is internally benevolent.

32. Fabre, *Cosmopolitan War*, 165.
33. Idem, 137.
34. For a defence of the claim that unjust states may still be legitimate, see David Copp, 'The Idea of a Legitimate State', *Philosophy and Public Affairs* 28:1 (1999), 3–45.
35. For extensive discussion of bloodless aggression, see the collection of essays in Fabre and Lazar (Eds.), *The Morality of Defensive War.*
36. In defending the equivalence thesis, Fabre invokes precisely this type of violation. Similarly, Buchanan's discussion of permissible revolution is explicitly limited to those waged against 'Resolute Severe Tyrannies': 'The Ethics of Revolution and Its Implications for Intervention'.
37. As Seth Lazar has pointed out to me, it may be objected that this intuition is not tracking the fact that these groups lack a just cause, but the fact that are likely to fail to meet some other *ad bellum* requirement. Admittedly, it is hard to tell. But, in support of my claim, we might imagine that these groups have a magic button, which if pressed will result in their instantly having a fully functioning state of their own but will cause the deaths of, say, 5000 soldiers and police officers of the (bloodlessly) oppressive regime, as well as 1000 civilians. Given the certainty of success and the favourable numbers, if we think (as I am inclined to) that pushing the button would be impermissible, this suggests that the intuition is in fact tracking the just cause requirement.
38. For a more detailed version of this argument from consistency, see Jeff McMahan, 'What Rights May We Defend by Means of War?' in *The Morality of Defensive War*, 114–155, at 133–135.
39. Though Mattias Iser defends several of the elements of such an argument. Iser, 'Beyond the Paradigm of Self-Defense? On Revolutionary Violence'.
40. See, e.g., Evan Fox-Descent, 'The Fiduciary Nature of State Authority', *Queens Law Journal* 31 (2005), 259–310.
41. See, Iser, 'Beyond the Paradigm of Self-Defense? On Revolutionary Violence'.
42. John Gardner, 'Criminals in Uniform', in *The Constitution of Criminal Law*, edited by Anthony Duff, Lindsey Farmer, Sandra Marshall, Massimo Renzo, and Victor Tadros (Oxford, Oxford University Press, 2012), 97–118.
43. See, e.g., Richard Vernon, 'What is a Crime Against Humanity?', *Journal of Political Philosophy* 10:3 (2002), 231–249; David Luban, 'A Theory of Crimes Against Humanity', *Yale Journal of International Law* 29 (2004), 85–163.
44. Jonathan Quong offers the most detailed argument for this position of which I am aware. 'Proportionality, Liability, and Defensive Harm', *Philosophy and Public Affairs* 43:2 (2015), 144–173. For other endorsements, see Iser, 'Beyond the Paradigm of Self-Defense? On Revolutionary Violence'; Yitzhak Benbaji, 'Culpable Bystanders, Innocent Threats and the Ethics of Self-Defense', *Canadian Journal of Philosophy* 35:4 (2005), 585–622; Frances Kamm, 'Self-Defense, Resistance, and Suicide: The Taleban Women', in *How We Fight*, edited by Helen Frowe and Gerald Lang (Oxford: Oxford University Press, 2014), 75–86; Frowe, *Defensive Killing*, ch. 5.
45. Quong, 'Proportionality, Liability, and Defensive Harm'.
46. One possible exception being cases in which the just cause for insurgency is grounded solely in the target state's treatment of outsiders. See Note 31.
47. See, e.g., Fabre, *Cosmopolitan War*, chs. 3–4; Uwe Steinhoff, *The Ethics of War and Terrorism* (Oxford: Oxford University Press, 2007), ch. 1.

48. Finlay, 'Legitimacy and Non-State Political Violence'; Anne Schwenkenbecher, 'Rethinking Legitimate Authority', in *Routledge Handbook of Ethics and War*, edited by Fritz Allhoff, Nicholas G. Evans, and Adam Henschke (Abingdon, UK: Routledge 2013), 161–170; Lionel McPherson, 'Is Terrorism Distinctively Wrong?', *Ethics* 117:3 (2007), 524–546; Seth Lazar, 'Authorisation and the Morality of War', *Australasian Journal of Philosophy* 94:2 (2016), 211–236.
49. Here I borrow Allen Buchanan's terminology. 'The Ethics of Revolution and its Implications for the Ethics of Intervention'.
50. For endorsement and more detailed discussion, see Cécile Fabre, 'Permissible Rescue Killings', *Proceedings of the Aristotelian Society*, 109 (2009), 149–164; Finlay, 'Legitimacy and Non-State Political Violence'.
51. On a fairly standard characterization, an action is paternalist if it involves (1) interference with an individual, (2) against their will, (3) for the sake of their good.
52. Based on a case in Andrew Altman and Christopher Heath Wellman, 'From Humanitarian Intervention to Assassination: Human Rights and Political Violence', *Ethics* 118:2 (2008), 228–257, at 244.
53. I borrow this phrase from McMahan, 'Intervention and Collective Self-Determination'.
54. Altman and Wellman, 'From Humanitarian Intervention to Assassination', 243.
55. For different arguments against the consent principle, see Buchanan, 'The Ethics of Revolution and Its Implications for the Ethics of Intervention'.
56. McMahan, 'Humanitarian Intervention, Consent, and Proportionality'.
57. Altman and Wellman, 'From Humanitarian Intervention to Assassination'. Interestingly, however, there is empirical evidence that civilian support for insurgencies often depends on military success, rather than vice versa. Kalyvas, *The Logic of Violence in Civil War*, chs. 4–5.
58. Although this will depend on one's views about the bloodless aggression/injustice question raised in the previous section.
59. Schwenkenbecher, 'Rethinking Legitimate Authority'. For a different take on the link between severity and consent, Fabre, *Cosmopolitan War*, 155.
60. On this point, see Allan Buchanan, *Secession: The Morality of Political Divorce from Fort Sumter to Lithuania and Quebec* (Boulder, CO: Westview Press, 1991), 74–75. See also, Joseph Raz, *The Morality of Freedom* (Oxford: Oxford University Press, 1986), 208.
61. For a related discussion of authorization in the context of defending jointly held rights, see Fabre, *Cosmopolitan War* (esp. ch. 2) and Seth Lazar's review of the same in *Ethics* 124:2 (2014), 496–412.
62. For different arguments in support of a similar conclusion, see Lazar, 'Authorisation and the Morality of War'.

PART IV

CONDUCT

CHAPTER 17

THE MORAL EQUALITY OF COMBATANTS

CHRISTIAN BARRY AND LARS CHRISTIE

THE doctrine of the moral equality of combatants—we'll refer to it throughout this chapter as Equality—holds that combatants on either side of a war have equal moral status so long as they abide by certain norms governing how wars must be fought. Proponents of Equality distinguish sharply between the issue of whether the resort to war is justified (*jus ad bellum*) and moral norms guiding justified conduct in war (*jus in bello*). Proponents of Equality agree that there are constraints on what soldiers may do in war—they can become guilty of criminal offenses when they use unjust means in pursuing their war aims. However, that they are involved in an unjust war and even that they are fighting for an unjust cause is, as Walzer puts it 'the king's business—a matter of state policy, not of individual volition'.[1] Their participation in the war is not something for which they can be held to account morally. The debates about Equality are closely related to other hotly contested issues, such as whether combatants on either side should have the same legal protections and whether and how the moral distinction between combatants and noncombatants is justified.[2] In this chapter, we will set aside those debates to focus squarely on the moral justifications that can be offered for Equality, as well as the critiques of those justifications.

1. A Puzzle About Killing

Common morality affirms stringent constraints against intentional killing. Since killing occurs routinely during war—which we stipulatively define as armed conflict involving political communities—justifying war is notoriously difficult. At the same time, however, the killing that does occur in wars tends to be assessed differently from that which occurs in non-war contexts. People who fight and kill in wars that (seem) manifestly (to) lack a just cause, or which are either disproportionate or unnecessary (we will refer to such people as unjust combatants), are not commonly regarded in the same manner as those who kill in non-war contexts without justification. Indeed, so long as unjust combatants abide by the constraints of *jus in bello*—justice in the fighting of war—they are not held legally accountable for the killing that they do and are not typically singled out for moral censure. At the same time, a just combatant fighting for a manifestly just cause (say national self-defence or humanitarian intervention) is provided no legal protection for her right to life, even if the war and means employed are proportionate. The value of just combatants' lives in war seems radically discounted compared to the lives of noncombatants—and, indeed, the universal value that we ordinarily attribute to human life.

In non-war contexts, there are extremely strict legal and moral constraints on killing. The notion of a moral equality of parties to a violent conflict in peace time—between, say, an armed assailant and her victim or between a police officer and an armed criminal— is morally absurd and would have no place in any sane legal system. What, then, can explain the differential treatment of lethal conflicts in war and non-war contexts? Can such differential treatment be justified?

2. Collectivist Approaches to the Moral Equality of Combatants

To defend the claim that there is moral discontinuity between killing in war and killing in non-war contexts, one needs to explain why there is such a discontinuity and what it consists in. One way of doing so argues that what makes killing in war special is that it is essentially collective. According to this collectivist line of argument, the difference between the use of violence in relatively peaceful domestic settings and in war lies not in the plain facts that stakes are higher in war or that a greater number of people are involved. Rather, the difference is that war involves violence employed on behalf of a collective and not on behalf of individuals. On this view, a person's moral status, especially his rights and liabilities, can be affected by his membership in a collective, irrespective of his behaviour. The idea is that individuals possess moral rights and privileges qua members of a collective that exceed those they possess considered as individuals. As we shall see, the collectivist position can be used to argue both for and against Equality. We'll begin by exploring collectivist arguments that seek to vindicate this doctrine.

2.1. Collectivist Defences of the Moral Equality Doctrine

The most influential modern collectivist defence of Equality can be found in Michael Walzer's work, and especially his *Just and Unjust Wars*.[3] Walzer's premise is that all people begin with immunity against being deliberately attacked—a right against others that these others not attack them.[4] Soldiers have lost their immunity to attack because they have allowed themselves to be conscripted and thereby 'made dangerous'.

The doctrine of the moral equality of combatants, as presented by Walzer, is based on a conception of combatants as both responsible moral agents and innocent victims. They are innocent in that they have *been made* dangerous by their king or state. Consequently, they cannot be blamed morally or held legally accountable for the harm they inflict in war, as long as they fight according to the rules of war.

If combatants were entirely innocent, however, it would be hard to see how they could lose their immunity to lethal harm. Even in cases of conscription, combatants have in some sense consented to become combatants and thereby traded in their immunity for a license to harm and kill enemy combatants. So, by Walzer's lights, they are also responsible because they have *allowed* themselves to become dangerous: '[A combatant] has been made into a dangerous man, and though his options may have been few, it is nevertheless accurate to say that he has allowed himself to be made into a dangerous man'.[5] Yet, although responsible for becoming 'a dangerous man', a combatant is not held responsible for the justness of the cause for which he fights. This, according to Walzer, is because he is fighting on behalf of a morally significant political collective. Since the combatant is not fighting in his capacity as a private individual but as a representative of a collective, moral responsibility for the cause he fights for should not be attached to him. According to Walzer: 'We draw a line between the war itself, for which soldiers are not responsible, and the conduct of the war, for which they are responsible, at least within their own sphere of activity'.[6] Quoting a soldier from Shakespeare's play *Henry V*, Walzer grants all combatants, including those pursuing a unjust cause, the following line of defence: 'We know enough if we know we are the king's men. Our obedience to the king wipes the crime of it out of us.'[7]

On Walzer's view, there is no difference between soldiers fighting for a just cause in a justified war and those fighting for an unjust cause in an unjustified one since each imposes the risk of severe harm on the other. Just and unjust combatants are morally symmetrical: each has a 'license to kill' one another, which, according to Walzer, is 'the first and most important of their war rights'.[8] A combatant gains this privilege by trading in her immunity to lethal harm. As Walzer puts it: 'You can't kill unless you are prepared to die'.[9]

Combatants are morally liable to attack, according to Walzer, in the sense that their moral rights to life are not violated if they are attacked by other combatants who fight in accordance with the rules of *jus in bello*. It is worth noting that Walzer's account, as with most defences of Equality, employs the concepts of immunity and liability to defensive harm somewhat differently from the critics of Equality. On the most general level, both sides of the debate take liability to attack to entail a loss of immunity against attack. However, Walzer holds that liability to be attacked does not entail the loss of a right to self-defense against attack. Critics of Equality, whose views we discuss at length later, disagree. They insist that one cannot have the right to defend oneself against harm to which one is liable. Immunity against being attacked and rights of self-defence are granted or lost together. For Walzer, a combatants right to inflict harm is a privilege and not a claim right. Privileges, unlike claim rights, are not morally protected from outside interference. Hence, possession of such a privilege does not morally prevent a combatant from trying to thwart her opponent's exercise of his (symmetrical) privilege.

One of the distinctive aspects of Walzer's version of Equality, then, is that it makes it possible to fulfil the requirements of *jus in bello* even if one is fighting an unjust war with an unjust cause.

Christopher Kutz has developed a somewhat different collectivist defence of Equality: 'When individuals' wills are linked together in politics, this affects the normative valence of what they do individually as part of that politics, even to the point of rendering impunible what would otherwise be criminal'.[10] Kutz argues that a collective can grant permissions to kill to its members. He argues: 'the logic of collective action can make appropriate a limited scope for an essentially political permission to do violence, because when I do violence, I do it as a member of one group towards another. The privilege to kill as part of a collective is not a moral permission attaching to the individual soldier'.[11] The privilege is derived from combatants' 'individual commitments to the collective: their mutual orientation around each other as fellow agents in a collective project'.[12]

Kutz limits the privilege to groups who pursue political goals, which he defines as 'aiming at creating (or restoring) a new collective ordering'.[13] According to him, these groups must possess a certain degree of internal ordering, as well as a certain degree of success in achieving their aims.

In sum, collectivists aim to absolve agents of individual moral responsibility for participation in war on the ground that they are fighting on behalf of a political community rather than in their private capacity. They also typically stress that individual soldiers are subject to duress and epistemic limitations. Only the first argument is distinctly collectivist; the second appeals to circumstances that mitigate the individual moral responsibility of combatants and can—as we will see—also be invoked by those who defend Equality on individualist grounds.

2.2. Collectivist Critics of the Moral Equality Doctrine

The challenge for collectivist critics of Equality, such as Saba Bazargan and Noam Zohar, is to explain why it is permissible for just combatants to target unjust combatants even when they are failing to contribute to their side's war effort or when they are morally innocent for their contributions. Bazargan and Zohar use collectivist premises to justify the conviction that most or all unjust combatants are liable to attack—an intuitive conclusion that individualist critics of Equality may be unable to support (more on this later).

Zohar shares Walzer's starting point. Nonpacifists, according to him, must explain how a person can come to lose his immunity to be attacked. On his view, it cannot be permissible to kill morally innocent threatening people in individual self-defence as a matter of individual morality. For Zohar, then, the main challenge becomes this: 'But if even the [unjust] enemy *soldiers* are mostly innocent, can there be any justification for killing them?'[14] Zohar attempts to provide a positive answer to this question by adopting a collective perspective. He writes: 'The reality of international confrontation is not adequately described by reduction to individualistic terms. We are not only individuals facing other individuals but also a nation confronting another nation'.[15] Zohar thus drives a wedge between individual self-defence and collective self-defence. 'For defensive war, as for private self-defense, the moral sanction relies on a crucial tipping of the scales. But whereas in self-defense this requires a minimal measure of individual guilt, in warfare the issue is and must be weighed on the great collective scale'.[16] Zohar argues on this basis that unjust soldiers who are morally innocent can be killed because they are part of a collective which is pursuing an unjust cause: 'Only viewing it as a collective aggressor can sanction the very killing of combatants, despite the impossibility of determining their individual guilt or innocence, for in fact we cannot act against the enemy as a collective without killing particular persons'.[17] The fact that combatants use violence in the pursuit of a collective cause does not, on his view, provide combatants with any moral protection. Rather, it strips them of protection they would have possessed were they acting on their own behalf.

Saba Bazargan also employs a collectivist perspective to attribute liability to most unjust combatants while exempting just combatants from liability. He rejects Equality but argues that individualist accounts of killing in war cannot support the claim that most unjust combatants are liable. Bazargan's concern is not that many of the unjust combatants are morally innocent, but that many of the unjust combatants do not pose threats. For him, the challenge is to explain how it can be permissible to kill combatants who are neither direct threats nor contribute to threats posed by their fellow soldiers. Bazargan's solution is to emphasize the cooperative nature of warfare. On his view, war is a cooperative project that 'consists of individuals who share participatory intentions'.[18] A participatory intention, according to Bazargan is an intention to act according to a role, the function of which is to contribute to a cooperative act: 'When individuals have participatory intentions with roles that have one and the same cooperative act as their objects, these individuals *share* participatory intentions'.[19] On Bazargan's view, 'an ineffective participant in a cooperative project can' in virtue of her participatory intentions 'be complicitously liable to be killed, provided that doing so averts substantially wrongful threats posed by her effective co-members in furtherance of the project's unjust aims'.[20] Bazargan's account aims to explain how one can become complicitously liable to be harmed to prevent a threat to which one does not actually causally contribute. As with accomplice liability in criminal law, he suggests that complicitous liability to attack attaches to fellow participants in a wrongful cooperative enterprise. Like Zohar, then, Bazargan employs the collectivist perspective to argue why a combatant who would not be liable considered individually becomes liable once he takes part in a collective pursuit of an unjust cause.

3. Individualist Approaches to the Moral Equality Doctrine

Just as Equality can be both defended and challenged from a collectivist perspective, so too can it be rejected and defended on individualist grounds. We will begin by looking at individualist critiques of Equality that have played a generative role in recent just war theorizing.

3.1. Individualist Critics of the Moral Equality Doctrine

Jeff McMahan has been the most influential individualist critic of the moral equality doctrine. McMahan challenges the idea that posing a threat of severe harm is sufficient to make a person liable to attack. In particular, McMahan argues that combatants who fight fairly in a just war of self-defence against an aggressing army have done nothing to make themselves liable to deliberate attack. After all, in all other interpersonal contexts, a person does not become liable to lethal attack unless he has done something wrong. Conversely, since unjust ends in principle cannot be pursued by just means, McMahan considers it impossible for combatants fighting for an unjust cause to meet the requirements of *jus in bello*. His denial of Equality is categorical.

McMahan employs the following analogy: if a murderer is in the process of killing a number of innocent people and the only way to stop the murderer is to kill him, then the police officer who opens fire does not thereby make himself morally liable to defensive action, and if the murderer in self-defence kills the officer, he will become responsible for one more wrongful death.[21] Both in war and outside of it, it is morally wrong to kill unless the cause for which one kills is just.[22] The just combatant certainly poses the threat of severe harm to the unjust combatant, but she does not thereby make herself liable to attack. The unjust combatant who kills the just combatant does so in the service of an unjust cause. 'Not all combatants are legitimate targets of attack in war. Unless they fight by wrongful means, just combatants do nothing to make themselves morally liable to attack. They neither waive nor forfeit their right not to be attacked. They are not, therefore, legitimate targets'.[23] Hence, the differential treatment of killing in war and non-war contexts cannot be justified and neither can Equality.[24]

Individualists differ about what, precisely, makes someone liable to deliberate attack. For McMahan, a person can become liable to attack only if she is morally responsible for a threat of unjust harm.[25] The view that liability can only be derived from responsibility for a threat of unjust harm distinguishes this account from Equality: unlike unjust combatants, just combatants who fight by just means do not pose a threat of unjust harm. The requirement that those liable to attack be morally responsible for the threat of unjust harm means that only wholly nonresponsible threats—such as a person who against his will is fired from a cannon at others, is controlled like an automaton, is invincibly ignorant that he poses any threat at all—escape liability to attack.[26] Responsible agency is necessary for liability.

McMahan and other individualist critics also argue that Equality, understood as a public doctrine governing killing in war, has nefarious consequences. The supposition that unjust combatants do no wrong when they fight in an unjust war helps facilitate the recruitment of combatants to fight in unjust wars. If combatants were to reject Equality and instead to hold the view that they can fight justly only when they fight for a just cause, they would be less likely to fight in wars whose causes were apparently unjust or whose causes were of questionable moral status. As a result, the incidence of unjust wars would be lower.[27] He writes, 'Wars are now and have always been initiated in the context of the general and largely unquestioned belief that the moral equality of combatants is true. If that background assumption were to change—if people generally believed that participation in unjust or morally unjustified war is wrong—that could make a significant practical difference to the practice of war.'[28]

Individualist critics of Equality provide a kind of 'error theory' for this doctrine, explaining how people have falsely taken it to be the same as or entailed by other, much more plausible claims about unjust combatants.[29] For example, people may support Equality because they have confused the morality of war with the law of war.[30] There may be good reasons, these critics point out, to uphold the legal equality of combatants as international law does, not least because it is difficult to provide combatants with authoritative guidance about whether the specific wars in which they fight are just or unjust. However, these considerations do not justify Equality as a moral doctrine.[31]

3.2. Individualist Defences of Equality

The preceding section indicated some forceful objections to Equality when defended on collectivist grounds. Several philosophers have defended Equality, however, without committing to a collectivist position. In this section, we examine their arguments.

Some have argued that combatants *consent* to be attacked by taking up arms. Thomas Hurka, for instance, adopts this position:, arguing that 'by voluntarily entering military service, soldiers on both sides freely took on the status of soldiers and thereby freely accepted that they may permissibly be killed in the course of war'.[32] Hurka leaves open the possibility that the degrees of voluntariness be taken into account. That is, combatants who are coerced into joining the army might be awarded a different status from that of volunteer soldiers. This possibility, however, does not alter the claim about equal status of just and unjust combatants since it applies equally to both. Hurka concludes that, insofar as a just and an unjust combatant target each other, 'both act permissibly and neither's acts are wrong. In that important respect they are moral equals'.[33]

Alternatively, one might follow David Estlund and claim that when an 'institutional process producing the commands is duly looking after the question whether the war is just, the soldier would be wrong to substitute his own private verdict and thwart the state's will. . . . [W]hen the state and its procedures are of the right kind the soldier's participation in an unjust war is sanitized precisely because he was following orders'.[34] Note that these defences of Equality are not categorical. They explain how moral equality could obtain between *some* unjust and just combatants.

Yitzhak Benbaji has offered a contractualist defence of Equality.[35] Observing that members of domestic societies have a right not to be attacked by others he also notes that we possess a power to waive such a right, either explicitly or through tacit acceptance. He writes: 'By entering the ring, a boxer waives this right and in return gains a privilege to attack his rival . . . [T]he convention which covers boxing is considered by both sides to be fair and mutually beneficial. This is why we can safely presume that the boxers accept it. The redistribution of rights within the ring is not produced by explicit agreement. Rather, it is generated by tacit acceptance of the rules, which is indicated by the combatants entering the ring'.[36]

Benbaji's main idea is that the tacit acceptance of rules of practices which are deemed to be fair and mutually beneficial (by participants in that practice) is sufficient to justify those rules, even if the practice seems to involve conduct that would otherwise be considered unjustified.

3.3. Discussion

A major weakness of the collectivist defence of Equality, especially as Walzer formulates it, is its categorical nature. It is simply implausible to claim that combatants can never be held responsible for the cause they are fighting for. In fact, the implausible implication of this view seems to be recognized by Walzer himself when he discusses General Eisenhower's refusal to accept a visit from a captured German general before he was sent to captivity. Walzer quotes Eisenhower at length to illustrate that Eisenhower blames the general not for violating the laws of war, but for participating in the war in the first place.[37] Walzer is unable to bring himself to reject Eisenhower's reaction, expressing sympathy with it, despite its evident tension with Equality. It seems clear, although Walzer does not admit this, that one cannot easily support both Eisenhower's very plausible attribution of blame to the German general and defend Equality by denying that combatants can be held responsible the ends for which they fight (and not only for the means by which they pursue them). Moreover, on Walzer's position, it seems impossible to explain why deserting from an army that is waging an unjust war can ever be required or morally justified except when the army violates *in bello* requirements. This categorical form of Equality seems to imply that the only aspects a citizen ought to consider when deliberating whether to join the war effort would be whether the personal costs would exceed what she has a duty to bear for her fellow compatriots. This way of conceptualizing an individual's choice of whether or not to participate in a given war seems highly problematic.

Kutz's defense of Equality is less categorical since he argues that it does not hold in wars which are outright criminal or unjust.[38] He maintains that there are restrictions on a combatant's privileges to engage in political violence as opposed to mere criminal violence. It is hard, however, to see how this supports Kutz's conclusion. Political and criminal goals are not mutually exclusive categories. Even on Kutz's own definitions of political goals—'creating or restoring a new collective ordering'— this should be clear. Collective orderings, too, can be outright criminal, as the examples of many political regimes past and present can attest.

Collectivists who reject Equality may also seem to defend an overdrawn conclusion. According to Zohar, *all* combatants on the unjust side are legitimate targets simply in virtue of being an agent of the unjustly aggressing collective. Bazargan's view is slightly less categorical since it holds that ineffective unjust combatants who are conscripted under severe duress are exempted from liability.[39]

One important challenge for a collectivist approach is whether it can restrict the collective whose members should be considered liable in a plausible way. Does it only include combatants or also noncombatant members of the army? Should government officials and politicians be excluded from the collective that is liable to attack? And what about taxpayers and citizens? Zohar argues that only combatants should be regarded as legitimate targets since 'combatants are those marked as participating in the collective war effort, whereas the rest of the enemy society retain their exclusive status as individuals'.[40] Bazargan recognizes that a typical tax-paying civilian may turn out to contribute as much to an unjust war as an ineffective combatant does, yet insists that only the ineffective combatants and not the taxpayers are liable to attack. The essential difference, according to Bazargan, is the combatant's intention to fill a formal role 'designed to contribute to a degree far greater than the typical civilian's'.[41] On these views, then, a person's liability may depend in some measure on the choices of the political leaders or generals who decide who should be 'marked' as participating in the war effort and who 'designs' the function of a combatant's formal role. One implausible implication of both accounts is that they do not treat irregular fighters who pursue an unjust cause as liable to attack. On Zohar's account, irregular fighters escape liablity simply because they are not members of the armed forces and not therefore not 'marked' as participants in the collective war effort. On Bazargan's account, too, an irregular and ineffective unjust combatant presumably would not be liable, as opposed to an ineffective unjust combatant who is member of the army since only the latter fills a formal role designed to contribute towards the war's end. Both views seem to assume that a society can engage in unjust aggression and then unilaterally decide which of its members are legitimate targets and which are not. But, as Helen Frowe points out, 'It would be very odd if those posing an unjust threat got to decide amongst themselves who was liable to be killed to avert that threat, making it impermissible for their victim to aim defensive force at some group members rather than others. Liability to defensive harm doesn't seem like something we get to allocate by agreement'.[42]

In addition, these approaches fail to recognize the non-liablity of certain members of the army. Consider infiltrators or army members who deliberately sabotage their own side's war effort. During World War II Werner Heisenberg was one of the scientists central to the German nuclear project. Heisenberg's real motivations have been a matter of debate, but some observers claim that Heisenberg and his team deliberately slowed down the work to prevent Hitler from getting the nuclear bomb. Let us assume that this was true. One natural way of exempting Heisenberg and his team from liability in this scenario would be by reference to facts which distinguish them (their motivations and contribution to slowing the advance of German weaponized nuclear science) from other combatants in the army. Yet, on the accounts we have been considering, they would still be liable to attack since they are still members of the unjust army, 'marked as participating in the collective war effort' and filling a formal role which is 'designed to contribute' towards the war effort. If, on the other hand, we exempt these people from liability, it is not clear why we shouldn't also assess the liability of the other members within the army (and outside it) according to their individual contributions and intentions.

There are forceful objections to individualist defences of Equality too. Consider Hurka's claim that combatants consent to be attacked by taking up arms. Even if successful, this defence significantly limits the scope of Equality, since it would apply only to wars involving volunteer armies. It is unclear how it would apply when soldiers act under duress. In addition, it is not clear that just combatants do indeed consent even when they are not conscripted. As McMahan has stressed, the fact that combatants assume risks does not mean that they agree to be attacked, any more than anyone choosing to walk through a dangerous neighbourhood agrees to be attacked.[43] The appeal to the role-based duties of unjust combatants, which require them to follow orders and attack on command, is also vulnerable since it is hard to see how any such obligation could override very stringent negative obligations not to kill people when they have done nothing wrong.[44]

Would a soldier's participation in an unjust war be sanitized because he was following orders, as David Estlund claims, so long as the state for which he fights and its procedures are of the right kind? It is very hard to see that the institutional processes leading to decisions to go to war have the epistemic value that Estlund's account would require. And Estlund's claim seems highly questionable: if an agent knows that following an order will involve committing a grave wrong, nothing in the institutional process producing the command will sanitize his conduct, even if the costs of disobeying it will at least partially excuse it.[45] Nor does the fact that unjust combatants may be coerced into fighting sanitize their conduct—as advocates of Equality recognize with respect to obeying the requirements of *jus in bello*, where the coercion imposed on soldiers to carry out commands that violate them is likely to be extreme.

Benbaji's appeal to tacit acceptance of rules of practices of the war convention that are deemed to be fair and mutually beneficial (by participants in that practice) is also open to challenge. Critics of Equality care not only about what combatants in fact, tacitly or otherwise, consent to, but also what they *ought* to consent to. Even if we take combatants' tacit acceptance as a starting point, this consent is clearly compromised by the duress under which it is typically given since refusing these rules would not mean peace but total and indiscriminate war. Assuming that the traditional war convention can indeed be considered fair and mutually beneficial, it is far from clear that the analogy employed by Benbaji is successful in supporting Equality. Boxers, after all, must typically give explicit consent before entering the ring—they sign waivers and contracts and so on—and would not be permitted by trainers or promoters to fight without having done so for the simple reason that these people, along with their opponents, would otherwise become liable for injuries suffered in the ring. Even in informal sparring between boxers who have signed the relevant waivers, boxers must touch gloves and explicitly acknowledge to each other that they are ready to fight. And there is very good reason to insist on explicit consent in boxing. Given the potential harms of engaging in this activity, the fact that they give their consent is at least an imperfect indicator that the participants in the practice believe that they are not exposing themselves to *undue* risk of severe harm. Furthermore, while the boxing model might seem plausible for wars involving two parties that both fight for unjust causes, McMahan points out that it seems much less plausible for wars in which just combatants fight against unjust combatants.[46] Insofar as the unjust combatants are guilty of aggression, then a more apt boxing analogy would be one in which the just combatant was having a picnic in the ring with his family and is attacked by the unjust combatant or came upon the unjust combatant beating a custodial worker senseless in the middle of the ring but was able to run to the custodial worker's assistance.[47] In these cases, the just combatant does not seem to have waived his right not to be attacked when he defends himself and others from the assaults of the unjust combatants—certainly his merely entering of the ring does not signify any such waiver.

McMahan's individualist faces challenges of its own. His notion of nonculpable moral responsibility from which liability is derived is so minimal that no unjust combatant can ever plausibly escape liability.[48] Although he sometimes seems reluctant to endorse this categorical conclusion, allowing that there might be some nonresponsible unjust combatants, it is hard to see how his theory justifies that reluctance.[49] On McMahan's account, the only way an agent can be nonresponsible for posing unjust threats is if she is acting in a manner that does not foreseeably cause a risk of harm.

As an example of a nonresponsible threat, McMahan provides a case where a villain has tampered with a man's cell phone in such a way that if its owner presses the 'send' button, he will detonate a bomb that will kill an innocent person. Even if the cell phone operator constitutes a threat of unjust harm to a nonliable person, he escapes liability since it is not foreseeable that his action will cause unjust harm. But could unjust combatants ever be in an analogous position to the cell phone operator? Surely, combatants are not unaware that they are engaged in activities that can cause harm. And, according to McMahan, any agent engaged in what she knows is a harmful activity must know that there is a chance she is mistaken about the facts and might end up causing unjust harm. So all unjust combatants, to varying degrees, would seem to be liable by virtue of the fact of their moral responsibility and the unjustness of their cause. McMahan places the threshold of moral responsibility low enough that even child soldiers fighting under duress are caught in the liability net if they fight for the unjust side.[50] It might be thought that McMahan's notion of nonculpable moral responsibility for an objectively unjustified threat is too narrow a basis for a moral asymmetry between an innocent aggressor who poses a wrongful threat and innocent people whom they risk harming. At least some amount of culpability, as opposed to McMahan's narrow notion of non-culpable responsibility, might be thought necessary to make the agent who is responsible for the threat liable to lethal or even very significant force.[51] Recall that when one is liable to attack, one cannot claim that one has been wronged when one is attacked, and one lacks a claim to compensation for damages thereby suffered. Yet it doesn't seem far-fetched to suppose that if John (who is innocent) must cut off the leg of Jocelyn (a nonculpable aggressor) in order to save his hand, then John should try to compensate Jocelyn for her loss in some way, even if we believe that John's defensive conduct was fully justified, all things considered. As McMahan himself notes, in criminal law, full excuses typically negate legal liability, and, insofar as an agent lacks culpability altogether, it is not obvious why she should nevertheless remain morally liable.[52]

Consider an episode that occurred in New York in 1962 that gave rise to a legal case.[53]

> *People v. Young*. Young came upon two middle-aged men beating and struggling with a youth. Reasonably believing the youth was being unlawfully assaulted, Young went to his rescue, pulling on or punching at the seeming assailants. They turned out to be plain-clothes detectives trying to make an arrest for disorderly conduct. One of them suffered a broken leg in the struggle.

The legal philosopher Kent Greenawalt claims, plausibly, that the behaviour displayed by Young does not warrant criminal liability. It is not obvious that he should be considered morally liable to defensive harm either. If a third party, knowing all the facts of the situation, were to intervene, it is not clear why he should take there to be a moral asymmetry between the plain-clothes detectives and Young. It seems permissible to harm Young to some degree to prevent him from harming the detectives. But it is not clear that the third party could inflict more harm on Young than could be permissibly inflicted on either detective. One reason for exempting agents from liability when their actions inflict unjust harm is that such agents sometimes act in a manner that is either strongly justified, required, or supererogatory given the evidence available to them. As Greenawalt writes, 'Young is to be praised, not blamed, for what he did, and members of society would wish that others faced with similar situations requiring instant judgment would act as Young did'.[54] It seems odd that an agent who acts on what is, given her epistemic position, a moral requirement (or positively exceeds it) should become liable if his action turns out to cause wrongful harm. It is a further question, of course, how many unjust combatants should be exempted from liability due to their epistemic position. Perhaps a young Taliban soldier whose innocent family members were collaterally killed in a drone strike when he was a child and who has been 'educated' in a school run by fanatics would qualify as being justified in believing that he is morally required to defend his village from further attacks. Or consider an indoctrinated North Korean soldier who, in the event of a North Korean attack, might be justified in believing that the North Korean side is actually acting in obligatory self-defence rather than aggression. Wherever one wants to draw the line, it seems clear that if one accepts that Young should be exempt from liability, then *some* unjust soldiers may also be exempt from liability.

Kutz raises this issue when he points out that the unjust side may be innocently mistaken about the justness of its cause (e.g., innocently but mistakenly thinking that a genocide is under way or that a hostile country is amassing weapons of mass destruction).[55] David Rodin considers Kutz's objection but thinks it can be brushed aside. He writes 'The problem of ambiguous or emerging evidence . . . can be unproblematically dealt with using standard moral and legal concepts, in particular the standard of reasonable belief and the concepts of objective and subjective justification. . . . War leaders are held responsible for the decisions they make in light of the facts as they honestly and reasonably believed them to be. It is at the very least unclear why we should not hold soldiers responsible in the same way'.[56]

This doesn't really undermine Kutz's argument, however.[57] If unjust combatants and their leaders escape liability whenever they act on a reasonable belief that their cause is just, then a significant number of unjust combatants will presumably be nonliable. Accepting the analogy between moral liability to defensive harm and criminal liability is an important concession and severely undermines the categorical rejection of Equality since people have to be at fault (must act culpably) in order to be criminally liable.

The manner in which some individualists have rejected, categorically, the moral equality doctrine depends on the assumption that (in sharp contrast to criminal liability) liability and blame can come apart. This view seems counterintuitive when agents are acting in a positively praiseworthy manner, as Young did in the case previously considered. If we agree that agents such as Young ought to be exempt from liability, new questions arise as to how we might make an exception for praiseworthy agents or whether this ought to motivate a wholesale move to accounts on which an agents' liability is determined by the evidence available to them.

Jonathan Quong has argued that we should not exempt from liability agents who act with subjective justification so long as they are mistaken about the liability of the person they threaten. He argues that even in circumstances where the soldiers don't bear responsibility for their mistaken belief that their enemy is unjust, they can be liable.[58] He uses the following example to illustrate his point:

> *Duped Soldiers*: A group of young soldiers are successfully fooled by a totalitarian regime into believing that the regime is good and just and is under repeated attacks from their evil neighbours, the Gloops. The regime's misinformation campaign is subtle and absolutely convincing: the soldiers are justified in believing what they are told by the regime. Once the misinformation campaign is complete, these Duped Soldiers are given orders to attack and destroy a Gloop village on the border which, they are told, is really a Gloop terrorist camp plotting a major attack. In fact, everything the regime has said is a lie, and the Gloop village contains only innocent civilians. The Duped Soldiers prepare to shell the village and are about to (unknowingly) kill all the innocent civilians in it. A peacekeeping force from a neutral third country patrols the border and could avert the attack but only by killing the Duped Soldiers.

Quong argues that it is implausible that the excused Duped Soldiers are exempt from liability simply because they are blameless for believing that they fight for the just side.

He rejects the idea that the Duped Soldiers and the Gloops are equally nonliable to attack. If this were the case, he claims, then the peacekeepers have no grounds to attack the Duped Soldiers to prevent the attack. At first blush, this might seem like the right conclusion. Note, however, that mistaken nonliable parties need not be thought to be protected from third-party intervention. Rather, the mistaken threats could be treated as on a par with the innocent victims. If the peacekeepers stop the attack by harming fewer Duped Soldiers than the number of Gloop civilians who would otherwise be killed in the wrongful attack, such an account would permit or even require peacekeepers to intervene. Nevertheless, it might seem intuitive that the peacekeepers should intervene even if they had to harm significantly more Duped Soldiers than Gloop civilians who would otherwise be harmed. But destroying an entire village in order to take out a terrorist cell is something any soldier, regardless of her mistaken belief in her own just cause, should surely realize is wrong since it would clearly violate reasonable principles of proportionality.[59] More importantly, constructing the example so that the peacekeepers have the choice between saving innocent civilians or duped soldiers trades on a further commonly held view that it is worse to harm defenceless and vulnerable civilians than soldiers—even if the soldiers are on the just side and are just as innocent as the civilians. This is, however, a separate discussion that does not relate to the debate over whether a complete excuse can exempt you from liability. If we alter Quong's case so that there are two groups of combatants who oppose each other, and where the unjust combatants are convincingly described as innocent (or even praiseworthy because they take on individual risk to reduce enemy casualties), the claim that unjust combatants are liable is considerably less intuitive.

Conclusion

The recent debate concerning the moral equality doctrine has taken Walzer's collectivist and McMahan's individualist positions as points of departure. This chapter has suggested, however, that the most forceful defence of at least a more limited form of the moral equality doctrine may be mounted from an individualist perspective.

The main challenge for collectivist defences of Equality is to show how a group of individuals can somehow acquire the normative power to authorize a subset of its numbers to inflict unjust harm on individuals outside the group. The main challenge for the collectivist critics of Equality is why individuals who either do not contribute to the war effort or who even deliberately subvert it may lose their protection against harm simply because they are part of the army on the unjust side.

Individualist defenders of Equality, on the other hand, struggle to point out why defending oneself and others from a combatant on the unjust side can make one liable. Individualist critics of Equality typically argue that agents can be liable without being culpable. A challenge for this view, presented in the previous section, is that it fails to explain the intuitive verdict that agents who act in a way that, given their epistemic situation, is either required or praiseworthy ought not to be liable to attack if they turn out to be mistaken through no fault of their own. Insisting, as McMahan does, that excuses *never* exempt morally responsible agents in such situations from liability may seem too harsh.

In our view, the strongest direct challenge to individualist views such as McMahan's comes from considering agents (like Young) who pose an objectively unjust threat while acting in a way that is justified or indeed supererogatory relative to their epistemic position. This objection does not take issue with McMahan's claim that excuses that arise from duress are insufficient to exempt an agent from liability to defensive harm. It does however point to a plausible and morally relevant distinction between excuses that arise from epistemically justified mistaken beliefs and excuses that arise from duress. There are different ways to express this distinction. One is to say that excuses arising both from duress and from mistaken beliefs are fully exculpating but should be considered separately. In the case of duress, the agent knows that he is acting wrongly but cannot be blamed for his conduct because acting rightly would require more than could be expected from a 'reasonable person'. In cases where agents act on a justified mistaken belief, the agent cannot even know, given his epistemic situation, that what he does is wrong. Another way is to say that excuses arising from duress, unlike those which arise from justified mistaken beliefs, are never fully exculpating since the agents involved knowingly do wrong. The fact that we might be reluctant to blame someone who is coerced does not mean that they are not blameworthy or culpable.[60]

In addition to the class of agents who act on the justified belief that they are acting in a supererogatory manner, it seems equally implausible that agents who act on what they reasonably take to be moral requirements should be considered liable if they cause harm to innocents through no fault of their own. Yet conceding this may not necessarily commit one to the view that culpability is necessary for liability. Critics of Equality may attempt to draw a line between different types of agents who act in an objectively unjust but blameless way. They may distinguish between those who are epistemically justified in believing their actions are either morally required or supererogatory and those epistemically justified in believing that their act is morally permissible.

To us, this indicates a fruitful way forward for debates concerning Equality. The debate might then focus on the conditions under which combatants who are epistemically justified in their mistaken belief that their enemy lacks a just cause should be seen as acting on subjective justifications or requirements (like Young) or merely on a subjective permission.[61]

In this chapter, we have argued that views that categorically reject *or* support Equality are problematic whether mounted from an individualist or collectivist position. In our view, the most plausible position is the individualist one that accepts that nonculpable combatants may be exempt from liability. At most, this would result in a limited defence of Equality since this clearly would not hold for all unjust combatants. Moreover, it differs from the view that the defenders of Equality reviewed here have argued for since it does not claim that unjust and just combatants may be equally liable or that both parties would have a licence to kill each other. To the contrary, our limited defence of Equality merely claims that, in some instances, combatants on either side may be equally nonliable.[62] In such circumstances, waging a just war may be considerably harder to justify since the intentional targeting of nonliable unjust combatants would constitute a grievous wrong.[63]

Notes

1. Michael Walzer, *Just And Unjust Wars: A Moral Argument with Historical Illustrations*, 2nd ed. (New York: Basic Books, 2000), 39.
2. For an illuminating discussion of these connections, see Seth Lazar, 'The Responsibility Dilemma for Killing in War: A Review Essay', *Philosophy & Public Affairs* 38 (2010): 180–213.
3. Walzer, *Just And Unjust Wars*. See also Walzer, 'Terrorism and Just War', *Philosophia* 34 (2006), 3–12, and 'Response to McMahan's Paper', *Philosophia* 34 (2006), 43–45.
4. They also have a right against being attacked nondeliberately (as a side effect), but this right can be overridden more easily.
5. Walzer, *Just and Unjust Wars*, 145.
6. Idem, 38.
7. Idem, 39. Walzer makes clear that this defence does not extend to violations of jus in bello: 'Not that his obedience can never be criminal; for when he violates the rules of war, superior orders are no defence. The atrocities that he commits are his own, the war is not', 39.
8. Idem., 36.
9. Michael Walzer, *Arguing About War* (New Haven & London: Yale University Press, 2004), 101. See also Walzer, *Just and Unjust Wars*, 136: 'Simply by fighting, whatever their private hopes and intentions, they [soldiers] have lost their title to life and liberty, and they have lost it even though, unlike aggressor states, they have committed no crime'.
10. Christopher Kutz, 'The Difference Uniforms Make: Collective Violence in Criminal Law and War', *Philosophy & Public Affairs* 33 (2005), 148–180 at 156.
11. Idem., 173.
12. Idem., 176.
13. Ibid.
14. Noam J. Zohar, 'Collective War and Individualistic Ethics: Against the Conscription of "Self-Defense"', *Political Theory* 21 (1993), 606–622 at 607.
15. Idem., 616.
16. Idem., 617.
17. Idem., 616–617.
18. Saba Bazargan, 'Complicitous Liability in War', *Philosophical Studies* 165 (2013), 177–195 at 184.
19. Idem., 185.
20. Idem., 182.
21. Idem., 14.
22. Idem., 6.
23. Idem., 205.
24. McMahan also rejects the view that posing a threat of harm (being the agent of the threat) is necessary for creating liability to attack, and thus he does not endorse the blanket moral immunity (with the exceptions just noted) that Walzer grants to civilians. Idem., 206–208.

25. Fabre, by contrast, requires that their responsibility for and contribution to the threat be more substantial. Cécile Fabre, 'Guns, Food, and Liability to Attack in War', *Ethics* 120 (2009), 36–63 at 62.
26. Idem., 162–163, 165. This view seems shared by many prominent individualists.
27. Idem., 3.
28. Idem., 6–7.
29. McMahan, *Killing in War*, 105–122.
30. Idem., 108. See also Jeff McMahan, 'The Morality of War and the Law of War', in *Just and Unjust Warriors: The Moral and Legal Status of Soldiers*, edited by David Rodin and Henry Shue (New York: Oxford University Press, 2008), 19–43.
31. McMahan, *Killing in War*, 110. It is worth noting, however, that some critics have suggested that we might reform substantially the legal and institutional practices surrounding war in light of concerns about their moral basis. See David Rodin, 'The Moral Inequality of Soldiers: Why *Jus in Bello* Asymmetry Is Half Right', in *Just and Unjust Warriors: The Moral and Legal Status of Soldiers*, edited by David Rodin and Henry Shue (New York: Oxford University Press, 2008).
32. Thomas Hurka, 'Liability and Just Cause', *Ethics & International Affairs* 21 (2007), 199–218 at 210.
33. Idem., 216.
34. David Estlund, 'On Following Orders in an Unjust War', *Journal of Political Philosophy* 15 (2007), 213–234 at 213.
35. See especially Yitzhak Benbaji, 'The War Convention and the Moral Division of Labour', *Philosophical Quarterly* 59 (2009), 593–617, and Yitzhak Benbaji, 'A Defense of the Traditional War Convention', *Ethics* 118 (2008), 464–495.
36. Benbaji, 'The War Convention and the Moral Division of Labour', 598–599.
37. Walzer, *Just and Unjust Wars*, 36.
38. McMahan, *Killing in War*, 175, 178.
39. Bazargan, 'Complicitous Liability in War', 192.
40. Zohar, 'Collective War and Individualistic Ethics', 618.
41. Bazargan, 'Complicitous Liability in War', 189.
42. Helen Frowe, 'Non-Combatant Liability in War', in *How We Fight: Ethics in War*, edited by Helen Frowe and Gerald Lang (New York: Oxford University Press, 2014), 179.
43. McMahan, *Killing in War*, 52.
44. Idem., 70.
45. For an extended discussion of Estlund on this point, see Gerhard Øverland and Christian Barry, 'Do Democratic Societies Have a Right to Do Wrong?' *Journal of Social Philosophy* 42 (2011), 111–131.
46. McMahan, *Killing in War*, 57.
47. This objection is developed in Uwe Steinhoff in 'Benbaji on Killing in War and "The War Convention"', *Philosophical Quarterly* 60 (240), 656–663.
48. Seth Lazar has raised an important criticism of McMahan's account by pointing out that it is unable to distinguish between combatants and noncombatants since the many noncombatants will be equally or more morally responsible for the threat their country poses. See 'The Responsibility Dilemma for Killing in War'. Since the focus of this chapter is exclusively on the moral equality of combatants, we will not pursue this influential criticism of McMahan's defence of Equality here.
49. 'Although the vast majority of unjust combatants are Partially Excused Threats, some are Culpable Threats, others are Excused or Innocent Threats, and a few may be

Nonresponsible Threats. Apart from those who are Nonresponsible Threats, unjust combatants in all these categories are liable to defensive attack to one degree or another'. McMahan, *Killing in War*, 189.

50. Idem., 202. Fabre criticizes him for this; see Fabre, 'Guns, Food, and Liability to Attack in War'.
51. Although the view that culpability is relevant to liability (e.g., affecting the proportionality constraint) is old, few contemporary authors defend the view that culpability is necessary for liability. Rodin, for example, thinks culpability is relevant for liability (especially to proportionality) but does not claim that it is necessary for it. He distinguishes between agency-diminishing excuses, which are 'fully exculpating for the purposes of punishment' and agency-defeating excuses that also exempt agents from liability to defensive harm. According to Rodin, reasonable mistakes of fact are only agency-diminishing and do not exempt an agent from liability. See David Rodin, 'Justifying Harm', *Ethics* 122 (2011), 74–100 at 84. Jeff McMahan once defended the view that culpable responsibility is necessary for liability but later abandoned it. See Jeff McMahan, 'Self-Defense and the Problem of the Innocent Attacker', *Ethics* 104 (1994), 252–290. For a defence of the view that culpability is necessary for liability to defensive harm in the context of individual self-defence, see Kim Ferzan, 'Justifying Self-Defense', *Law and Philosophy* 24 (2005), 711–749. Ferzan does not herself discuss Equality; but her view implies that unjust combatants will not be liable as long as they are not culpable (Zohar, who shares Ferzan's view that culpability is necessary for liability, argues that nonculpable unjust combatants can nevertheless permissibly be attacked due to the collective nature of war). John Gardner and François Tanguay-Renaud argue for the relevance of desert to punitive and defensive harming alike. John Gardner and François Tanguay-Renaud 'Desert and Avoidability in Self-Defense', *Ethics* 122 (2011), 111–134. To claim that desert is relevant to defensive harming is different from claiming that culpability is relevant to defensive harming since desert, but not culpability, entails that there is reason to inflict harm on the aggressor beyond the instrumental one of averting the threat. Seth Lazar endorses a disjunctive view according to which an agent can become liable to defensive harm either through nonculpable responsibility for a 'causally substantial' contribution to an unjustified threat or culpable responsibility for a 'relatively slight causal contribution' to an unjustified threat. Seth Lazar, *Sparing Civilians* (Oxford: Oxford University Press, 2015), 94.
52. McMahan, *Killing in War*, 157.
53. *People v. Young* 183 NE 2d 319 (1962).
54. Kent Greenawalt, 'The Perplexing Borders of Justification and Excuse', *Columbia Law Review* 84 (1984), 1897–1927 at 1919.
55. Christopher Kutz, 'The Difference Uniforms Make', 175.
56. David Rodin, 'The Moral Inequality of Soldiers: Why *Jus in Bello* Asymmetry Is Half Right', 67–68.
57. Rodin's response is also puzzling given that, on his view, reasonable mistakes can exempt a person from criminal liability but cannot exempt him from moral liability to harm. See David Rodin, 'Justifying Harm', 84.
58. Jonathan Quong, 'Rights Against Harm', *Proceedings of the Aristotelian Society Supplementary Volume*, 89 (2015), 249–266.
59. Except perhaps if a terrorist cell was about to launch a nuclear attack on a different city. The case as described provides no indication that the duped soldiers believed this (reasonably or otherwise).

60. A person can be blameworthy yet it might be impermissible for another to blame her if he would not have acted differently in the same situation. Whether it is appropriate for others to blame a blameworthy person may therefore depend on whether these others have moral standing to do so. It is not implausible to think that this is the best way of understanding cases of duress: although the coerced agent who does wrong is blameworthy (i.e., culpable), others are not in a position to blame him since they probably would have done the same were they similarly situated.
61. For a defense of the view that other defense can only be forbidden or required, but never merely permissible, see Helen Frowe 'Claims Rights, Duties and Lesser Evil Obligations', *Proceedings of the Aristotelian Society Supplementary Volume*, 89 (2015), 267–285.
62. Although our view suggests that some degree of culpability is necessary for liability (with the exception of coerced agents), we have not addressed the further question of whether causal responsibility for an unjust threat should be seen as necessary for liability. If causal responsibility is not necessary for liability, then a *just* combatant who is ignorant of the just cause of his side and who fights for reasons that are blameworthy could in principle become liable to preventive harm. We cannot explore this issue here but, for discussion, see Richard J. Arneson, 'Just Warfare Theory and Noncombatant Immunity', *Cornell International Law Journal* 39 (2006), 663–668 and Lars Christie, *Harming One to Save Another: Liability and Lethal Luck* (Oslo: Universitetet i Oslo, 2016).
63. For discussion of how wars under these conditions can nonetheless be permissible, see Lazar, *Sparing Civilians*.

CHAPTER 18

NONCOMBATANT IMMUNITY AND WAR-PROFITEERING

SABA BAZARGAN

1. Background

1.1. Noncombatant Immunity and the Combatant's Privilege in International Law

In Article 155 of what came to be known as the 'Lieber Code', written in 1866, Francis Lieber wrote '[a]ll enemies in regular war are divided into two general classes—that is to say, into combatants and noncombatants'.[1] As a legal matter, this distinction does not map perfectly onto the distinction between members and nonmembers of an armed force. For example, armed forces typically include medics and religious personnel, yet they do not qualify as combatants. Likewise, the distinction between combatants and noncombatants does not map perfectly onto the distinction between those who take up arms in a war and those who do not. For example, unlawful combatants are sometimes characterized as 'civilians who take up arms without being authorized to do so by international law'.[2] On this view, 'just as guerrillas and militias are a subset of "combatant", unlawful combatants are a subset of "civilian"'.[3]

In international law, bearing the status of 'lawful combatant' (from here on, I refer to them simply as 'combatants') comes with considerable privileges. According to Article 43.2 of Additional Protocol I to the Geneva Convention, combatants 'have the right to participate directly in hostilities'. This means that it is legally permissible for them to engage in hostilities, and it is legally permissible to target them, provided that they have not surrendered, been captured, been injured, or shipwrecked.[4] This has come to be known as the '*combatant's privilege*'. International and common law prohibits warring parties from intentionally targeting noncombatants.[5] Civilians will almost always qualify as noncombatants. (Exceptions include cases in which a military leader is also the head of state.) But what is a civilian? Article 50.1 of Additional Protocol I defines civilians negatively. It states that any person who is not a member of (1) the armed forces of a party to the conflict; (2) other volunteer corps, including organized resistance movements; (3) regular armed forces who profess allegiance to a government not recognized by the detaining power; or (4) a *levée en mass*, is a civilian. Under Additional Protocol I, 'making the civilian population or individual civilians the object of attack' constitutes a grave breach—a war crime of such seriousness as to entitle any state to exercise jurisdiction over any perpetrator.[6] This legal doctrine forbidding the targeting of civilians is the *principle noncombatant immunity*. Killing civilians *collaterally* (i.e., as an unintended but foreseen side effect of targeting a military (or dual-use) installation) is acceptable if the civilian casualties are not disproportionate to the anticipated military advantage that the attack affords.

In international law, the legal permission to target combatants is based on their status, rather than on their conduct, in that it is not whether she poses a threat that makes a combatant a permissible target but rather the very fact that she qualifies as a combatant (although if a civilian participates directly in hostilities she *eo ipso* qualifies as a combatant). Many combatants—such as cooks, administrative personnel, grave-registration teams, musicians, lawyers, and the like—contribute to the war effort in ways that do not pose threats to anyone. Yet since they qualify as combatants, they 'may be attacked at any time until they surrender or are otherwise hors de combat, and not only when actually threatening the enemy'.[7] This means that a combatant remains a combatant even when she is not actually fighting. A soldier bivouacked and sleeping retains her status as a combatant, which means she is a legitimate target.

As with the combatant's privilege, the basis of the principle of the noncombatant immunity lies not in the individual's conduct. What makes noncombatants illegitimate targets of attack is not the fact that they generally do not contribute substantially to the war being fought; influential journalists, lobbyists, and politicians advocating for the war, as well as scientists and engineers working on technologies likely to be used in weapons substantially furthering the war effort, are (for example) not legally targetable in spite of their contributory conduct.

1.2. The Orthodox and the Revisionist Views

So far, I have described, if only roughly, the legal versions of the combatant's privilege and the principle of noncombatant immunity. Many assume that the morality of war parallels international law, at least with respect to laws articulating the legal permission to target combatants and the legal prohibition against targeting not noncombatants. I call this assumption the '*orthodox view*'.

Among those who defend the orthodox view, the most influential is Michael Walzer. In his book *Just and Unjust Wars*, he argued that civilians cannot be permissibly targeted since they are *materially* innocent—which is to say that they are harmless. The presumption is that it is morally wrong to target materially innocent people but permissible to target those who are *not* materially innocent. Walzer argues that no active-duty combatants during wartime are materially non-innocent, since they are all 'currently engaged in the business of war'.[8] Even those whose actual contribution to the war is small or non-existent are not materially innocent; by virtue of their status as combatants, they have made themselves dangerous. Accordingly, all combatants are morally permissible targets of attack by other combatants. Although civilian journalists, lobbyists, politicians, scientists, and engineers might individually contribute substantially to a war, they are not themselves dangerous men or women; moreover, their contributions to the war do not fall under the aegis of a state's (or substate actor's) attempt to project violent force.

This argument in favour of the orthodox view has been subjected to withering criticism. Jeff McMahan is the most prolific of these critics. He has argued that material non-innocence is neither a necessary nor a sufficient condition for losing one's right not to be killed. Those who pose morally justified threats do not thereby lose their right not to be killed, no more than the victim of a culpable aggressor attempting murder loses her right not to be attacked once she engages in necessary and proportionate self-defence against the culpable aggressor. Correspondingly, combatants fighting in accordance with the rules of war in furtherance of morally just aims cannot be permissibly targeted, as a matter of morality. Although such combatants are not *materially* innocent, they are nonetheless *morally* innocent: they have done nothing to lose their right not to be killed. And it is an individual's moral innocence, rather than her material innocence that (partly) determines whether she is liable to be killed.

Combatants acting in furtherance of a war's unjust aims are, on the other hand, *morally liable to be killed*: they have forfeited their right not to be killed, so killing does not wrong them, provided that doing so is necessary to achieve a good of sufficient importance. Combatants participating in furtherance of an unjust aim are morally liable to be killed because such a combatant (provided she is a full-fledged agent—e.g., she is not a child soldier) is responsible for her contribution to an end which (by hypothesis) violates the rights of others. Even if such a combatant limits her targets to military installations and personnel, she acts impermissibly because those who are only defending against an unjust aim retain their right not to be harmed. So the orthodox view is mistaken in its claim that all combatants are morally entitled to kill enemy combatants. On McMahan's '*revisionist view*', only combatants fighting against an unjust cause (or against a just cause pursed by unjust means) are entitled to target enemy combatants.[9]

There have been attempts, aside from Walzer's, to defend some version of the orthodox view.[10] For instance, Thomas Hurka has argued that enlistees waive the right not to be killed. He writes: 'by voluntarily entering military service, soldiers on both sides freely took on the status of soldiers and thereby freely accepted that they may permissibly be killed in the course of war'.[11] This is because, he claims, 'the common conception of military status' includes the combatant's privilege—that is, an entitlement to target enemy combatants. One problem with this view, however, is that although it might accurately describe the intentions and expectations of *some* who voluntarily join the military, there is little reason to believe that this is true of *all* enlistees.[12] In any case, even if all combatants by virtue of enlisting waive their rights not to be killed, this would only mean that they do not wrong one another by attempting to kill one another. But they still contribute to the achievement of that unjust aim, which makes what they do morally impermissible, again suggesting that the combatant's privilege is mistaken at the level of morality.[13]

On the revisionist view, the moral basis of the prohibition against targeting *noncombatants*—that is, the principle of noncombatant immunity—is that everyone has by default a right not to be killed and an even more stringent right not to be killed intentionally. According to the revisionist view, noncombatants typically do nothing to forfeit that right. Whether an individual has done something to forfeit such a right depends on her degree of responsibility for the wrong which harming her helps avert. As Robert Holmes suggests, the degree of responsibility an individual bears for a war varies with the degree and kind of contribution that individual makes to the war, with 'initiators of wrongdoing (government leaders)' and 'agents of wrongdoing (military commanders and combat soldiers)' bearing the most responsibility and the paradigmatically innocent bearing the least.[14] Because the typical civilian bears very little to no responsibility for the wrongs committed by her government, she is not morally liable to be targeted in order to avert those wrongs.

But the claim that civilians are not liable to be killed (whereas noncombatants are) is a statistical claim in that only typically will noncombatants be less responsible than combatants. Although the aforementioned influential journalist, lobbyist, politician, scientist, or engineer, are civilians, they make (by hypothesis) substantial contributions to the unjust war their government is fighting; on the revisionist view, they would be morally liable to be targeted if doing so is necessary to save any number of innocent lives. So noncombatants do *not* enjoy blanket immunity from intentional attack on the revisionist view. Rather, only those who are not responsible for substantial contributions to the war are immune (in the sense that they are not morally liable to be killed).

This does not mean that influential pro-war lobbyists, politicians and the like can be targeted at whim in war—rather, on the revisionist view, they can be targeted only if doing so is the least harmful way of saving (any number of) innocent lives. So targeting influential pro-war pundits on the opposing side is likely to be unjust, if only because their violent deaths are more likely to aid their cause than avert further harm. But those scientists and engineers contributing to an unjust war (and who are in a position to recognize that what they are doing is wrong) would indeed be morally liable to be killed *if* their contributions wrongfully endanger innocents and *if* killing the contributors is necessary to avert that threat.[15] McMahan has defended this sort of view.[16] Cécile Fabre similarly suggests that that although contributing civilians are morally immune from intentional attack, this is only for highly contingent reasons—namely, that most wars include both just and unjust aims and that civilians typically cannot know which aims their contributions are promoting.[17]

1.3. Challenges to the Revisionist View

The revisionist view faces a number of challenges. According to the revisionist, culpability is not a necessary condition for liability to a lethal harm. This view might strike some as draconian; if an individual contributes to a wrongful threat nonculpably, then she cannot be liable to lethal harms. If this criticism is correct, then many combatants fighting in furtherance of an unjust cause will qualify as morally innocent. This is because the indoctrination, manipulation, and coercion of these young and consequently cognitively underdeveloped combatants by their culture, state, and military might serve as partially excusing conditions combining to substantially diminish their culpability for what they do.[18] Some have pointed out that a significant portion of combatants—such as those who occupy highly subsidiary support roles, as well those involved in actual combat but who are ineffective as fighters—might contribute no more to the war effort than the typical civilian does.[19] If those combatants are nonetheless liable to be attacked, then the threshold of contributory responsibility is so low that the typical civilian will be liable as well. If we raise the threshold of contributory responsibility so that the typical civilian is *non*liable, then the highly subsidiary and the ineffective combatants will be nonliable as well. The former option has the absurd consequence of rendering the typical civilian liable to be targeted. The latter option invites a version of pacifism, insofar as it is pragmatically impossible to conduct a war requiring us to discriminate between liable and nonliable combatants, if their liability is grounded in their individual conduct.[20] This problem has been dubbed the '*responsibility dilemma*'.[21]

In an attempt to diffuse the dilemma, McMahan argues that the constraint against killing intentionally is not violated when we reasonably although mistakenly believe that the target is liable to be killed.[22] If this is correct, the weight assigned to the deaths of nonliable combatants is discounted substantially, thereby averting the pacifism horn of the responsibility dilemma. To diffuse the 'total war' horn of the dilemma, McMahan argues that when civilians causally contribute to unjust wars fought by their governments, they typically do so through tax payments serving a plurality of worthy aims that justify these payments, thereby precluding liability to defensive action.[23] Bradley Strawser, in defence of the revisionist view, suggests an emendation: abandoning the binary 'combatant or noncombatant' distinction, in favour of a conflict-sensitive rubric that tracks differing levels of liability based on what he calls their 'reasonable perceived liability'. He writes that '[t]he distinctions could range from 1st, 2nd and 3rd-degree combatants and the like (or more, as needed) and similar degrees for non-combatants'.[24] I have argued that supplementing the revisionist view with an account of complicitous liability provides a basis for thinking that nearly all combatants—including ineffective and highly subsidiary ones—bear complicitous liability.[25]

Others have maintained that we cannot justify intentional killing in war by appealing to the liability of combatants. For example, Janina Dill and Henry Shue argue that even if combatants are liable to some harms due to their individual contributions to an unjust cause, most of them do not contribute enough to make *lethal* attack necessary and proportionate.[26] Since a liability-based justification is unavailable, a war is morally justified only if it is the lesser evil relative to refraining from waging the war. And since the enemy combatants are not liable to be killed, the calculation determining whether the war is a lesser evil must weigh the deaths of enemy combatants as heavily or nearly as heavily as the deaths of enemy civilians.[27] Dill denies, however, that this restrictive view of war should be enshrined in international law since, on her view, it is not to the role of international law to vouchsafe the moral acceptability of war.[28] Nonetheless, if wars are only morally justified as the lesser evil, then a version of contingent pacifism is likely correct: given how wars are actually fought, it is practically impossible for any wars to be just. Larry May is the most prominent supporter of this view.[29]

Although I think the revisionist view is largely correct, it is critically incomplete. Implicit in this picture of the morality of war is the presumption that causation is a necessary basis for liability to lethal harms. Accordingly, the discussion of liability in war has focused on *what sort* of causal contributions serve as a basis for liability to be killed and *how great* that contribution must be to entail such liability. In these discussions, the possibility that civilians can be liable to be killed without having causally contributed to the war fought by their government has been met with scepticism, partly because it has been assumed that such arguments would have to rely on accounts of vicarious or collective responsibility. Some have defended this sort of expansive view of responsibility. In particular, Virginia Held[30] and Igor Primoratz[31] have argued that civilians in a democracy who support their government's unjust war can, at least in principle, be liable to be attacked, even if their causal contributions to the war are minimal or nil.

But I will argue for a noncausal basis of liability to lethal harms, one that does not rely on any notions of vicarious or collective responsibility. Specifically, I will argue that certain kinds of *war-profiteers*—those who buy or sell in substantial quantities resources wrongfully misappropriated from a civilian population through armed force—will sometimes be morally liable to be killed even if they have done nothing to contribute to that war. Such a war-profiteer can be liable on the grounds that she has failed in her duty of restitution toward the relevant civilians insofar as she is under a duty to return to the civilians the wrongfully misappropriated resources (or its equivalent value). A failure to discharge a duty of restitution does not usually render an unjust beneficiary liable to lethal corrective force because (1) there are usually alternative corrective mechanisms available, (2) harming her will not prevent the wrong that made the unjust beneficiary's enrichment possible, and (3) her failure does not result in or contribute to lethal harms. But I will argue that when these conditions do not obtain, a culpable failure to discharge a restitutionary duty can indeed render a person liable to lethal harm. And these conditions often fail to obtain in war.

So, in one sense, the revisionist view is not revisionist enough: we ought to abandon the notion that causally contributing to war is a necessary condition for moral liability to lethal harm. Victor Tadros has argued in favour of a position like this. On his view, noncombatants are made liable if they benefit from the unjust activity of combatants—activity for which the noncombatants are intended beneficiaries.[32] Restricting our defensive violence solely to unjust combatants increases the chances that such combatants will be harmed, in comparison to a case in which we achieve our defensive goal by dispersing the defensive violence so that it is not concentrated solely on combatants. In deciding how to disperse a fixed amount of necessary defensive violence, it is unfair to 'rule out' the intended beneficiaries of those whose unjust acts necessitated the resort to violence. In such a case, 'Fairness determines the distribution of liability, and fairness militates against a strict causation requirement on liability'.[33] Still, Tadros explicitly denies that noncombatants are liable to be killed—only that they are liable to sublethal harms.

I argue, on the other hand, that certain noncontributing civilians are indeed morally liable to be lethally targeted in war. Thus, the principle of noncombatant immunity is mistaken at the level of morality, not just because some civilians contribute substantially, and not just because civilians are in the intended beneficiaries of their military's unjust acts, but also because some unjustly enriched civilians culpably fail to discharge their restitutionary duties to those whose victimization made the unjust enrichment possible—or so I will argue.

2. On War-Profiteering in General

The term 'war-profiteer' is a vague pejorative. The American government tends to regard war-profiteers as subcontractors who defraud the government in the course of providing goods or services supporting a war. But my use of the term is broader than this; it is inspired by Brigadier General Smedly D. Butler's famed tract 'War Is a Racket'.[34] On my usage, a war-profiteer is someone who derives substantial monetary benefits from an unjust war by either (1) selling goods and services supporting the war (this includes defence contractors, private security contractors, and risk-management companies), (2) trading in resources misappropriated in the course of that war, or (3) selling services or goods aimed at postwar reconstruction. I will call (1) 'support-related' war-profiteers, (2) 'resource-related' war-profiteers, and (3) 'reconstruction-related' war-profiteers. These are not clean divisions; some services fall under more than one category. For example, London-based Erinys and Nour USA was granted $80 million and $136 million, respectively, to secure Iraq's oil pipelines during the US-led war in Iraq—a service that can be categorized under both support-related and resource-related profiteering.

Note that it is possible to seek and gain substantial monetary benefits from an unjust war without doing so wrongly and thereby without qualifying as a war-profiteer. For example, the unpopularity of the Vietnam War led many potential conscripts to enrol in universities in an effort to avoid the draft; even if this served as a financial boon to certain private universities, those who benefited did not qualify as war-profiteers because they did not derive these benefits wrongly. Of course, this requires an account of what qualifies as a wrongful benefit. (I provide part of such an account in subsequent sections.)

I have distinguished war-profiteers along one dimension: the sort of goods or services they provide (support-based, resource-based, or reconstruction-based). I will also distinguish war-profiteers along another dimension: whether they contribute to the war. One can contribute to a war by aiding materially in the war effort (e.g., by manufacturing armaments) or providing an incentive to wage the war (e.g., by lobbying the government in favour of the war). Consequently, all three types of war-profiteers can be contributory, even if they provide goods or services only *after* hostilities have ended (as is often the case with resource-based and reconstruction-based war-profiteers), provided that, prior to the war, they incentivize the decision to wage the war.

But not all war-profiteers contribute to the war. Although support-based war-profiteers will almost always be contributory, resource-based and reconstruction-based war-profiteers might not be if they were simply unwilling or unable to effectively lobby the government in favour of the war. This is most obvious in cases where the corporation did not exist at the outset of the war (as was the case with Nour USA, which was formed only after the US-led war in Iraq was under way). I will call war-profiteers who derive substantial benefits from a war without actually contributing to the war 'opportunistic' (rather than 'contributory') war-profiteers.

If the revisionist view is correct, and hence the principle of noncombatant immunity is mistaken, contributory war-profiteers can be morally liable to be killed when doing so is necessary to save the lives of any number of innocents. In what follows, though, I will motivate the even more controversial view that certain *opportunistic* war-profiteers—specifically, resource-based war-profiteers—can be liable to be killed, even though, by definition, they are not contributing to an unjust war (or at least not contributing to a degree any greater than the average civilian does).

3. Examples of Resource-Based War-Profiteers

Resource-based war-profiteers derive monetary benefits from an unjust war by gaining access to resources misappropriated in the course of that war. There are several ways to categorize resource-based war-profiteers. We can distinguish resource-based war-profiteers who benefit by wrongly *selling* resources from those who benefit by wrongly *buying* resources.

Recall that a resource-based war-profiteer is someone who trades in resources misappropriated in the course of an unjust war. A resource-based war-profiteering exporter sells misappropriated resources, thereby earning a profit. The resources are misappropriated in the sense that some or all of their value belongs to civilians who were wrongly dispossessed of the resources or the land from which it was extracted. Suppose, for example, an unjustly aggressing country gains a foothold in the country it is aggressing against; the former now has effective control over resource-rich land properly belonging to the latter. The aggressing country then grants a corporation access to that resource-rich land for development. If a fair portion of the profits derived from the corporation's activities are not transferred to the people of the country to whom the land and resources properly belong, then they are deprived of that to which they a have a proper claim. The corporation thereby misappropriates the country's resources and sells them at a profit, which qualifies the corporation as a resource-based war-profiteering exporter.

Of course, what counts as a 'fair share' is debatable. I will pass the buck by simply stating that failing to pay a fair share—*whatever it is*—constitutes a misappropriation of the relevant resources. I am assuming, though, that the relevant territory and the resources in it rightfully belong to at least some of the people of the country in which the territory is located; consequently, even the most ardent libertarian would admit that the 'fair share' is something greater than zero.

But suppose that the people to whom the resource-rich territory properly belongs lacked the means or inclination to develop it in the way necessary to extract its resources. It might seem, then, that they are deprived of nothing if the territory is developed without their consent. Or, more precisely, it might seem that what they are deprived of is limited to whatever value the use of the territory had for the people using it. Suppose they were using it as a park; the corporation, without the people's consent, destroys the park by converting it into a mine, thereby depriving the people of the park. The corporation consequently owes the people a park or its equivalent value in compensation. What it does not owe, one might argue, is a percentage of the value of the resources extracted from the mine; this is because those resources were effectively out of the people's reach in any case. I will respond to this argument in the next section. Until then, I will assume that those who own the territory in which natural resources are located thereby also own the natural resources; consequently, they must be compensated for the extraction or use of those resources.

Historical examples of resource-based war-profiteering exporters abound. For instance, the CIA in 1964 led an invasion of Guatemala, subsequently deposing its democratically elected leader by recruiting, training, and arming 480 mercenary soldiers commanded by an exiled right-wing Guatemalan Army officer. The resulting military junta annulled former President Jacobo Arbenz Guzmán's agrarian reform legislation and new Labour Code, which had threatened American corporate interests—specifically that of the United Fruit Company. Following the coup, the United Fruit Company could cultivate and export its products without properly compensating its workers or the country's people. It thereby qualified as resource-based war-profiteering exporter.

A resource-based war-profiteering *importer* purchases rather than sells misappropriated resources in a war. Suppose an armed group (such as a substate insurgency) unjustly gains effective control over territory with natural resources. It then develops those resources and sells them on the international market in order to finance arms purchases. In doing so, the group is able to sell the resources at below-market cost by failing to properly compensate the workers extracting the resources or the people living on the acquired territory to whom the resources properly belong. Now suppose that a foreign state or corporation agrees to purchase the resources at below-market cost even though it is common knowledge that the reason why the resources are available at such low cost is that they were procured without adequate compensation. The buyer consequently qualifies as a resource-based war-profiteering *importer* insofar as it is knowingly purchased wrongfully acquired goods and benefitted from doing so.

For example, the Forces Démocratiques de Libération du Rwanda (FDLR)—a Rwandan Hutu rebel group in the east of the Democratic Republic of the Congo opposed to Tutsi influence in the region—has been engaged in armed conflicts since its formation in 2000. The group, through its control of mining fields such as those in the North Kivu province, has been able to smuggle out and sell minerals (such as coltan and cassiterite) to international buyers. In 2008, a United Nations expert panel argued that 'targeting companies complicit in systematically trading materials with FDLR and promoting due diligence within the international minerals supply chain represent effective ways of cutting off the financial support of FDLR'. These international buyers qualify as resource-based war-profiteering importers.

Sometimes the government of a country colludes with foreign states or corporations in the misappropriation of the country's resources during an internal armed conflict in order to procure funds in furtherance of defeating the insurgency. If the government is illegitimate, and if it defrauds its people by entering into a deal that denies them their fair share of the resource's value, and if the foreign state or corporation agrees to the deal without subsequently transferring a fair share of the resource's value to the people, then it qualifies as a resource-based war-profiteer. The group in question has, after all, obtained access to goods without the consent of the persons to whom the goods belong and without compensating them for the conversion of the goods' value. For example, in 2000, during the Second Liberian Civil War, Charles Taylor's regime officially collected only $6.6 million in taxes from the $186 million in sales of timber. China and French logging interests were the main importers (46 per cent and 18 per cent, respectively). Much of the untaxed funds were used to finance Charles Taylor's side of the war against rebel groups. The Chinese and French logging interests qualify as resource-based war-profiteering importers.

We might be inclined to think that unscrupulous private parties who want to benefit from an unjust war will *always* lobby in favour of the war, thereby contributing positively to the decision to wage that war. But this overstates both the influence and instrumental rationality of war-profiteers. Sometimes they are simply not in a position to lobby the government. At other times, attempts to influence decision-making in favour of the war are ineffective. And, in still other cases, they simply fail to recognize that the candidate war will in fact benefit them. Suppose an unjustly aggressing warlord gains control of a lawful government's alluvial diamond mines, which he intends to mine using forced labour. But flight from local violence has deprived him of enough manpower to run the mines. The warlord failed to foresee this eventuality. Unexpectedly, though, a third-party conglomerate (hitherto unknown by the warlord) expresses interest in leasing access to the mine. The warlord consents. In this case, the third party derives financial benefit from the wrong of wresting control of the diamond mine from the proper authorities, without (ex hypothesi) causing or contributing to that wrong. After all, by the time the third party leases the mine, it is already handily in the warlord's control. In this case, the third-party conglomerate qualifies as a purely opportunistic rather than a contributory resource-based war-profiteering exporter.

In what follows, I argue that opportunistic resource-based war-profiteers (whether importers or exporters) can bear substantial liability even though they do not contribute to the unjust war from which they benefit.

4. Duties of Redress

Wrongful appropriation of goods can generate duties of redress. If someone wrongfully commits theft and subsequently transfers the property (or converts it to an equivalent value which is transferred) to a third party who knows the property was stolen, the third party thereby acquires a (defeasible) duty to return to the victim the property (or its equivalent value if it has been irretrievably converted, damaged, or lost). The third party has such a duty even if she did not contribute to or cause the theft in the first place. In this case, the wrong for which the third party is responsible is not the theft; as I stipulated, she did not cause or contribute to that wrong. Rather, the wrong for which the third party is responsible is the wrong of failing to return to the victim the goods (or its value) that she currently has in her possession.

Now consider a case not of theft, but of *unjust enrichment*. Suppose that Thief steals Victim's car, just to see if she could get away with it. Now in possession of an unwanted car, Thief, on a whim, gives it to Beneficiary as a gift. Beneficiary knows that the car was stolen; she in no way encouraged or otherwise contributed to the theft. Beneficiary then rents the car to others (who are nonculpably ignorant that the car was stolen) as part of a car-rental business, thereby deriving profit from its use. In such a case, Beneficiary is *unjustly enriched* by her wrongful use of the car. She has a duty to return not only the car but the profits that she derived from its wrongful use.

There are several reasons for thinking that the unjustly enriched beneficiary is morally required to disgorge the wrongfully obtained benefits, provided that she knew how it was obtained. The relevant cardinal principle in tort and criminal law in general, and in the law of restitution specifically, is that the defendant should not benefit from her wrongdoing.[35] There are, of course, pragmatic reasons for this: we have an interest in ensuring that the expected utility for wrongdoing remains negative. But there are, in addition, moral reasons of interpersonal fairness for requiring the unjust beneficiary to transfer the enriched benefits: deriving gains from flouting moral norms makes those who abide by them comparatively worse off, which is unfair. Suppose that I commit a murder, and I benefit from it by subsequently publishing a book about my heinous deeds. This makes nonmurderers comparatively worse off, which is unfair.

But one might point out that this shows, at best, that Beneficiary should disgorge the profits she made by wrongly using Victim's car—and not that it should be transferred to Victim specifically. After all, Beneficiary has not deprived Victim of anything other than the car (given that Victim was not going to rent out the car herself). It seems, then, that Beneficiary owes Victim only the car, or its value, and not the profit derived from it. But, interestingly, this is not borne out in tort law. According to the so-called '*user principle*',[36] the plaintiff is owed the amount that the defendant *would* have been willing to pay for the use of the plaintiff's property. So, for example, where a trespasser has taken a shortcut across a plaintiff's land, she will be required to pay damages assessed by reference to the fee that she should have had to pay to obtain the plaintiff's permission to use the land. Indeed, where a defendant has wrongfully interfered with the plaintiff's property, damages should go to the plaintiff even if it is clear that the plaintiff would not have bargained with the defendant for use of the property.[37] In such a case, instead of saying that the unjust beneficiary is liable to restore a benefit to the victim, she is instead liable to transfer the value of a benefit to the victim. That is, the unjust beneficiary has a *restitutionary* (rather than restorative) duty.

If the user principle is correct as a matter of morality, then this suggests that resource-based war-profiteers have a restitutionary duty to those whose resources were misappropriated by developing and exporting the resources without properly compensating those to whom the resources belong or by acquiring such resources through their purchase. This duty is discharged by transferring to the victims a share of the wrongfully derived profits—specifically, the amount that they should have paid *ex ante*.

This restitutionary duty can serve as grounds for liability. Specifically, the opportunistic resource-based war-profiteer is liable to certain harms necessary to force her to transfer the unjustly derived benefits to the victims if she culpably fails to discharge that duty. But what harms are these? In the context of domestic tort law, the harms to which such an individual is liable are highly circumscribed. She might be liable to fines, but she will not be liable to physical harms, such as maiming and killing, even if imposing such harms is necessary to force her to disgorge her wrongly derived benefits. And whatever harms she is indeed liable to suffer in the context of civil society are subject to the constraint of due process, in that the victim cannot take it upon herself to force her wrongdoer to discharge her restorative duty. Rather, the victim must proceed by way of the courts. But outside the context of civil society, the harms to which an individual becomes liable are more substantial and are free of due-process constraints. Consider this example:

Food. In a failed state stricken with famine, and without a functioning criminal justice system or police force, Thief steals Victim's supply of food, which rightfully belongs to Victim (in virtue of having produced it). Without it, Victim will likely die. Thief mistakenly drops the parcels of food while driving away. A third party, Beneficiary, witnesses these events unfold from afar. He takes the food, despite knowing that it belongs it to Victim.

Clearly, Beneficiary is obligated to return the food to Victim, even if Beneficiary needs the food to survive. By culpably ignoring this obligation he makes herself liable to proportionate harm necessary to force him to return the food. Now suppose that the only way to force Beneficiary to do so is to kill him. It seems to me that killing Beneficiary would *not* violate his right. That is, Beneficiary is liable to be killed if necessary to force him to return the food to Victim. This is because Beneficiary's culpable failure to return the food is particularly egregious, considering that Victim not only has a right to the food, but also needs it to live.

It is important to recognize that although Beneficiary had no control (we can assume) over Thief's actions, he does indeed have control over whether he returns the food he has wrongfully procured. In this sense, Beneficiary can avert his own culpable wrongdoing, which is a condition that any plausible moral principle must satisfy. Now consider an analogous case of unjust enrichment:

Well. In a failed state stricken with famine and without a functioning criminal justice system or police force, Thief culpably invades Victim's farmland and takes over her well, which properly belongs to Victim. In doing so, Thief badly injures Victim. Thief had planned on using the well himself, but finds he has no use for it. So he instead leases the well to Beneficiary, who knows how the well was obtained. Beneficiary uses the well to water her crops; she consequently derives a substantial profit. Victim, who is penniless, needs resources equivalent to a substantial proportion of those profits to survive the injuries she sustained in the initial attack.

In this case, it seems that Beneficiary has a restitutionary duty to Victim in that Beneficiary is obligated to transfer to Victim (in accordance with the moral version of the user principle) the earnings derived from the well's use equivalent to the market value of renting out the well for that period of time. (Any additional gains made from the well's illicit use would be transferred to Victim or disgorged.)

In general, a restitutionary duty can be overridden or outweighed when the party owing the funds needs it for something much more important than what the party to whom the funds are owed will use it for. But in Well, not only is Victim's life at stake, but it is at stake *as a result of* the well's appropriation, which was used as a means to enrich Beneficiary. So the user principle, in combination with (1) the fact that Beneficiary does not need the profits much more than Victim does and (2) the fact that Beneficiary knows that the well was wrongfully appropriated, gives us reason to think that Beneficiary has a restitutionary duty to Victim, even though she did not cause or contribute to Victim's harm.

The upshot is that culpable unjust enrichment can, in certain circumstances, ground duties of restitution. What counts as unjust enrichment, though, depends on how the beneficiary was enriched. Suppose Thief uses the car she stole from Victim by renting it out to unwitting third parties, thereby deriving $500 in profits. As I have noted, she is unjustly enriched and thereby owes Victim at least $500. But suppose Thief invests $500 in a stock the value of which subsequently increases. Does Thief now owe Victim, in addition to the $500, the increased value of the stock? As a legal matter, in most Anglo-American jurisdictions the answer would be 'no', since those dividends did not arise 'directly' from the wrongful use of the victim's car (this describes the so-called '*direct use*' standard). Instead, Thief would owe only the $500 in benefits she obtains from the car's use. Virgo Graham contends that such a limiting principle is necessary to prevent 'over-protection of the claimant'.[38] But there is another oft-noted consideration in favour of the 'direct use' standard: as the 'dirty' profits derived from renting the car are alloyed with 'clean' money and together used in economic activity yielding returns, which is itself used in further investments, it becomes hard to determine in a principled way how much should be disgorged. And as the economic benefits ramify through the economy (including the benefits derived by those who innocently rented the car), it becomes difficult to force disgorgement without harming third-party innocents.

The problem with the direct use standard, though, is that it is unclear what counts as 'direct use'. Fortunately, I need not address this issue here, since on any existing interpretation of the standard, the profits derived from wrongfully and culpably developing and selling what rightfully belongs to others—such as the resources extracted from one's land—falls within the scope of 'direct use'.

5. Failures of the Duty to Redress

What happens if the unjust beneficiary fails to discharge her restitutionary duty? Suppose she is in a position to recognize that she has such a duty, and she is able to discharge this duty but culpably fails to recognize the moral importance of doing so.

In certain cases, a culpable failure to discharge a restitutionary duty can make an individual liable to harms exceeding the amount that she owes, if such harms are necessary to force restitution. To motivate this view, return to *Well* example. Recall that Thief badly injures Victim in the course of wrongly appropriating Victim's well, which Thief leases to Beneficiary, who knows that it properly belongs to Victim. I claimed that, under the user principle, Beneficiary owes Victim the unjustly derived proceeds she gains by her wrongful use of the well.

Suppose, though, that Beneficiary refuses to discharge her duty of restitution; she refuses to hand over the proceeds, even though she can easily do so. Suppose further that the only way to force her to disgorge the wrongfully derived benefits is by imposing a cost on her substantially greater than the value of those benefits. Specifically, as a result of her refusal to comply, the only way to gain access to the wrongfully derived benefits from the use of the well is to kill Beneficiary.

It seems to me that, under these circumstances, she is morally liable to be killed if necessary to force her to disgorge the wrongfully derived proceeds. At first, this might seem draconian; Beneficiary is neither the one who forced the well from Victim, nor was she a cause of Victim's injury. More generally, a fiscal duty of redress is typically not so strong as to invite lethal liability in the event that the duty is culpably ignored. But when discharging the duty is necessary to save a life endangered by the very act enabling the beneficiary's unjust enrichment, it seems that the duty to redress is made substantially stronger. The victim already has claim to what the beneficiary unjustly appropriated—the issue here is whether the victim's need *enhances* that claim. We might say that, in general, the greater the legitimate need that the victim has for what the beneficiary unjustly appropriated, the stronger the beneficiary's duty to transfer the benefits. But for those who find this claim too expansive, we can attenuate it by adding the caveat that the victim's legitimate need enhances the strength of the duty to discharge the benefit *only if* the victim's need is a result of wrongful acts enabling the beneficiary's unjust enrichment.

If this is right, Beneficiary's duty can be characterized as a stringent duty to engage in *life-saving* restitution to Victim. *This* is why culpably failing to discharge the duty can make Beneficiary liable to be killed if necessary to force her to do what she culpably chooses not to do. To be clear, the duty to save Victim's life is *not* a duty of beneficence; arguably, a duty of beneficence to save another's life is typically not strong enough to make culpable violators liable to be killed. There might be a 'ceiling' on the harms to which one is liable resulting from violations of the duty of beneficence owed to another individual in need. But there is no analogous ceiling for restitutionary duties.

The duty of beneficence is usually cast as an agent-neutral utilitarian duty to make things go better or best. Critics of consequentialist theories of normative ethics fear that an unrestricted version of this duty might take over our lives by requiring us to forego all unnecessary benefits that, when transferred to others, will do more good impersonally measured. In order to limit the scope of this duty, some have argued that there is a protected sphere of conduct in which we are permitted to act in ways that do not promote what is impersonally best. Put in the jargon of normative theory, we have an agent-centred prerogative to pursue our own projects even if doing so precludes doing what makes things go best. Samuel Scheffler called this the '*liberation strategy*' for limiting the demands of consequentialism.[39] Now, if this strategy circumscribes the scope of impersonal utilitarian demands, then it stands to reason that it circumscribes their stringency as well—which means that there are limits to the harms we are liable to suffer for violating the duties of beneficence that survive the liberation strategy. Tadros argues that at least some of our impersonal utilitarian duties are enforceable, in that a failure to abide by them makes it permissible for others to force us to act accordingly. That is to say, we have no right not to be forced to comply with some duties of beneficence, which means we are liable to be so used.[40] But if the stringency of the impersonal utilitarian duty is circumscribed, then the degree of harm to which we are liable in furtherance of enforcing that duty is limited as well.

But the liberation strategy cannot similarly circumscribe the stringency of *restitutionary* duties. This is because incurring such duties is relevantly within our control. The purpose of the liberation strategy is to prevent the moral demands of the impersonal standpoint from enjoining us to do what would make things go best overall. But there is already a mechanism in place to prevent restitutionary duties from similarly 'taking over' our lives: we can simply refrain from unjustly enriching ourselves. (If we are unable to do so—if it is prohibitively difficult to rejected or disgorge such benefits—then there is no restitutionary duty.) So there is no basis for thinking that the liberation strategy imposes a ceiling on the stringency of our duties of redress, whereas there *is* a reason for thinking that it imposes a ceiling on the stringency of our duties of restitution.

Absent a principled reason for imposing a ceiling on the stringency of restitutionary duties, there is no reason to think that a culpable failure to discharge such a duty cannot ground lethal liability in certain circumstances. It is important to stress, though, that the claim is *not* that unjustly enriched person are, in general, morally liable to be killed as a means of forcing them to discharge their restitutionary duties; this would typically violate the constraint of proportionality. But, in the case at hand, killing Beneficiary as a necessary means of forcing her to discharge her duty does not violate the constraint of proportionality because Victim is not only owed the funds, but also needs them to survive because of the harms imposed on her in the course of enabling Beneficiary's unjust enrichment.

What I have claimed, then, is this: if (1) an unjustly enriched individual has restitutionary duties, (2) fulfilling these duties will save the life of the individual to whom it is owed, (3) discharging the duty will not cost the unjust beneficiary significantly more than what refraining from discharging the duty will cost the individual to whom it is owed, (4) the beneficiary culpably refrains from discharging her duties herself, (5) there are no effective judicial institutions to defer to as a means of enforcing the claim against the unjust beneficiary, and (6) there is no way to force the unjust beneficiary to discharge her restitutionary duties other than by killing her, *then* the unjust beneficiary is morally liable to be killed.

One of the conditions that I've claimed must be satisfied in order for an unjust beneficiary to be liable to be killed as a necessary means of enforcing a life-saving restitutionary duty is that the beneficiary must be *culpable*. To be culpable in the relevant sense, she must not only fail to discharge her restitutionary duty, but she must also be in a position to recognize that (1) there is a significant chance that she has appropriated resources rightfully belonging to someone else, (2) appropriating resources rightfully belonging to someone else is wrongful, (3) she owes the wronged persons restitution for having misappropriated their resources, (4) there are means by which to discharge this duty, and (5) in the course of dispossessing the wronged persons of their resources, they were harmed in such a way as to put them in dire need of life-saving assistance.

Of course, in tort law, defendants of civil suits found liable to substantial monetary restitution, and who culpably refuse to pay, cannot be permissibly killed even if this is necessary to force them to pay what they owe. But this is because it has probably never been the case that killing a defendant is necessary to save the plaintiff's life. There are several reasons why this is so. In a well-functioning civil society, there will almost always typically be other means by which the plaintiff can obtain life-saving medical treatment. And, second, even if there aren't such alternative means, it is hard to envision a case in which killing the unjustly enriched defendant would be useful in saving the plaintiff's life. It is no surprise, then, that civil law does not countenance killing as a means of enforcing culpable violations of civil suits—the circumstances in which doing so would be morally permissible are so unlikely to obtain that permitting lethal enforcement is more likely to be abused than it is to prevent injustice. But we shouldn't make the mistake of concluding from the fact that there is no lethal enfacement in civil law that there is, *in principle*, a low ceiling on the harms to which an unjust beneficiary is liable to suffer when she culpably refuses to discharge life-saving benefits to the individual harmed in the course of enabling the beneficiary's unjust enrichment. Outside a well-functioning civil society, as in the cases described in our examples—and in the context of war—circumstances arise in which killing an unjust beneficiary is the only way to save the life of the victim.

6. The Liability of War-Profiteers

If what I've argued is correct, resource-based war-profiteers can owe redress to those civilians whose resources were misappropriated, even if the profiteer did not contribute to the act that dispossessed the civilians of their resources. That is, *opportunistic* resource-based war-profiteers can owe redress to those civilians whose resources were misappropriated. If, in the course of dispossessing them of their land or resources, the civilians' lives are endangered (by way of injury, starvation, disease, dehydration, etc.), and if discharging the restitutionary duty will avert that loss of life, then the restitutionary duty owed to them is especially stringent. This is, again, because the stringency of a restitutionary duty is determined in part by the severity of the harms that discharging that duty will avert; or, more conservatively, it is determined in part by the severity of the harms imposed on the victims in the course of enabling the beneficiary's unjust enrichment.

One way for a resource-based war-profiteer to avoid such duties is to simply cease any profitable association with the corporations or groups through which the profiteer derives her benefits. To the extent that the profiteer has already wrongly derived such benefits, she can discharge her duty of redress through individual financial donations to charities and humanitarian organizations focussed on alleviating the suffering of the victims in the wronged country. If no such charity operates in the relevant region, there might still be other ways to discharge a duty of redress, perhaps by contributing the unjustly derived profits to politically oriented efforts aimed at stopping the war (or unjust operations in the war).

It is important to note that it is not enough for the profiteer to benefit just *any* civilian unjustly victimized by their government; the profiteers have duties of redress to those civilians specifically who were harmed in the course of wrongly appropriating their resources—resources by which the profiteers were enriched. Alleviating the suffering of *other* civilians in the country (or, for that matter, the famine-stricken elsewhere in the world) does nothing to satisfy the duty of redress that a profiteer owes to those whose suffering enabled the profiteer's enrichment, any more than donating to Oxfam would satisfy a duty of redress I have to an individual whose car I illicitly used as part of a rental business.

If there is nothing a resource-based war-profiteer (who has since ceased the activity by which was unjustly enriched) can do to discharge her duties to the relevant victimized civilians, the profiteer is still morally required to disgorge her earnings. This is because there are *two* injustices associated with unjust enrichment. First (in accordance with the cardinal principle that wrongdoers should not benefit from their wrongdoing), it is wrong for the unjustly enriched party to keep and thereby benefit from what she has wrongly derived. Second (in accordance with the user principle), the victim is owed at least part of what the unjustly enriched party wrongly derived from the misappropriation of the victim's resources. So, even if it is prohibitively difficult to address the second wrong, the profiteer can still address the first by disgorging her wrongly obtained benefits.

Resource-based war-profiteers are typically culpable for their wrongful misappropriation of resources and their failure to engage in restitution. Any worldly adult of reasonable intelligence is at least in a position to recognize (even if she fails to do so) that resources appropriated from a zone of armed conflict are unlikely to have been rightfully appropriated. If the territory is under dispute, then any putative claim of ownership by those in control of the territory (including the government) ought to be treated sceptically. Consequently, the profiteer is in a position to recognize that there is a significant chance that she is not entitled to the benefits of selling or purchasing those resources. If it is at all clear who was dispossessed of the resources, and there are means (such as charities) by which to transfer some of those benefits to the rightful party, and the profiteer fails to avail herself of these means, then she is a *culpable* opportunistic resource-based war-profiteer—that is, she culpably fails to discharge her life-saving restitutionary duty. Indeed, even if it is not at all clear who was dispossessed of the resources that the profiteer has appropriated, it is still clear that they do not belong to the profiteer—a failure to disgorge the resources (or its converted value) is itself a culpable failure.

If the resource-based war-profiteer has an opportunity to fulfil her duties of redress to the innocents who were harmed in the course of dispossessing them of their land and yet fails to do so, then the profiteer can be forced to discharge her life-saving duty by killing her, if that is the least harmful means by which to save those lives.

At first, this might seem implausible. Culpably failing to discharge a duty of redress is typically not worth a human life. And even if killing the profiteer will save the lives of innocents who were harmed in the course of dispossessing them of resources that enriched the profiteer, it seems as if this benefit cannot be included in the 'benefits column' of the proportionality calculation determining the degree of harm to which the profiteer is liable because she is not responsible for the harms that those civilians face. After all, by hypothesis, the *opportunistic* resource-based war-profiteer has contributed neither to the harms nor to the actual theft of the resources. So it seems that the amount of harm that can be permissibly imposed upon such a profiteer to force her to discharge her restitutionary duties is small.

But this is an illusion. Suppose the resource-based war-profiteer can discharge her restitutionary duty by writing a cheque to the relevant aid agencies; doing so will save the lives of some of the innocents who were harmed in the course of dispossessing them of the resources that the profiteer has since sold or purchased. If the resource-based war-profiteer has a moral obligation to write that cheque, thereby saving those lives, then the consequences of a failure to do so can indeed be included in the proportionality calculation determining the degree of harm that can be permissibly imposed on the profiteer. This is because the profiteer is obligated to save those lives by donating the funds. She is so obligated because the benefits she has garnered were unjustly derived from the victimization of those innocents; she consequently owes them restitution that, it so happens, will save lives. If this is right, the profiteer can indeed be preventively killed if doing so is necessary to achieve the good that she was obligated to do and had culpably failed to do. Of course, killing the profiteer won't result in her giving to charity. But if killing her is an effective means to saving the relevant lives of civilians, then killing the profiteer is a means of forcing her to discharge a duty she culpably failed to fulfil on her own—a duty to engage in life-saving restitution. This is, again, consonant with Tadros's account of the relation between duties and liability; he argues that a person's failure to act in accordance with an enforceable duty makes her liable to harms necessary to force her to do what she was obligated to do or to avert the harm that she was obligated to avert.[41]

It might be pointed out that once civilians have been killed in the course of dispossessing them of resource-rich territory used to enrich war-profiteers, there is nothing such a profiteer can do to help such civilians; they are, after all, already dead. The profiteer would have, at best, a restitutionary duty to the families of the victims. But since this is not a life-saving restitutionary duty, it cannot be enforced through lethal means. However, the majority of civilian deaths due to warfare come from postcombat conditions, rather than from the use of armaments. Neta Crawford has concluded that 'although it is difficult to estimate the number of those killed indirectly by war with confidence, it is safe to say that indirect deaths outnumber direct deaths'.[42] And, based on data on armed conflicts between 2004 and 2007, the Geneva Declaration Secretariat suggests that, 'a reasonable average estimate would be a ratio of four indirect deaths to one direct death in contemporary conflicts'.[43] Regardless of what the exact figures are, it is clear that the excess morbidity and mortality among civilians resulting from armed conflicts are often, if not usually, the indirect rather than the direct result of combat. This means that even *after* civilians have been dispossessed, through armed conflict, of land and resources, many of them will die preventable deaths from disease, starvation, injuries, and dehydration. Insofar as these deaths are caused in part by the armed conflict dispossessing the civilians of their land and resources, and if aid agencies can prevent at least some of these deaths, then the resource-based war-profiteers unjustly enriched by those resources have a restitutionary duty to transfer the wrongly derived benefits to those aid agencies, thereby saving the lives of those innocents. Consequently, the restitutionary duties of resource-based war-profiteers will not be limited to redressing the families of those wrongly killed in the course of the armed conflict that forcibly dispossessed the victims of their land and resources; in addition, and more importantly, their restitutionary duty will be to *save the lives* of those who will die from the effects of the armed conflict that forcibly dispossessed them of their land and resources.

So far, I have argued that if killing an opportunistic resource-based war-profiteer who has culpably failed to discharge life-saving restitutionary duties to the relevant victims is the only available way of saving the lives of any number of those victims, then the opportunistic resource-based war-profiteer is morally liable to be killed as a way of enforcing her restitutionary duty. But in what circumstances would killing an opportunistic resource-based war-profiteer save the lives the innocents who were harmed in the course of armed conflicts that dispossessed them of their land and resources? Recall that an opportunistic resource-based war-profiteer contributes neither to that specific military operation nor to the war in general (or, more carefully, she does not contribute to a degree greater than the typical civilian does). It is indeed difficult to envision how targeting opportunistic resource-based war-profiteering importers would help save the lives of the relevant victims. These profiteers will typical reside in foreign countries—often countries that are not party to the conflict in question. Targeting nationals of a foreign country on their own soil is likely to antagonize the foreign government, possibly expanding the conflict. So, although opportunistic resource-based war-profiteering importers who have culpably failed to discharge their life-saving restitutionary duties would be liable to be killed if killing them were effective in saving the lives of the relevant innocents, it is (fortunately for the profiteers) unlikely that this condition will obtain in any given conflict.

But the situation is crucially different for opportunistic resource-based war-profiteering *exporters*. These profiteers often reside or do business in the very country where civilians were or are in the process of being forcibly dispossessed of their land and resources. (Indeed, as the various instanced outlined earlier illustrate, these profiteers often share the same nationality or allegiance as the group that victimized the civilians.) This means that targeting opportunistic resource-based war-profiteering exporters is not pragmatically problematic in the same way that targeting opportunistic resource-based war-profiteering importers tends to be because it typically will not require violating the sovereignty of a third-party country. If the lives of opportunistic resource-based war-profiteering exporters are threatened, this might very well coerce them into pressuring the unjustly warring party to cease or at least diminish the scope or intensity of its campaign. This is not an unreasonable presumption given that resource-based war-profiteering exporters tend to be among the social and economic elite, with more political influence than the average civilian. (Recall from Section 2 that the profiteers in question are those who are in leadership positions in the corporation in question. What counts as a leadership position, of course, need to be examined; for purposes here, I leave the category vague.) Targeting these profiteers in a context where it is made clear *why* they are being targeted can motivate them to use this influence to yoke the military conduct of the unjustly warring party. This, in turn, is likely to save lives, thereby enforcing the restitutionary life-saving duty of the resource-based war-profiteering exporter.

But recall that the resource-based war-profiteer has a life-saving restitutionary duty not towards just anyone, or even just towards the victims of the war, but rather towards the specific civilians whose land or resources were wrested from them and who as a result are in need of life-saving assistance. The resource-based war-profiteer is *not* liable to be killed to save just anyone, but instead to save *them* specifically. But, generally, the longer a war lasts, the greater the rate of morbidity and mortality of those who were not killed during the war—which will likely include at least some of those civilians displaced, injured, diseased, or starving as a result of the military operations that dispossessed them of the resources from which the resource-based war-profiteers are unjustly enriched. So if killing a resource-based war-profiteer helps bring an end to the conflict, then that killing is likely to enforce the restitutionary life-saving duty of the resource-based war-profiteering exporter, even though that duty is towards specific civilians.

There are two empirical presumptions that I am making here: (1) that killing the opportunistic resource-based war-profiteering exporter will help save lives and (2) that it will help save the lives of the civilians to whom the profiteer has a life-saving restitutionary duty. It is hard to know how certain we must be of these empirical facts in order to be justified in thinking that a profiteer is indeed liable to be killed. But this is a problem that plagues every aspect of war that involves killing; indeed, the epistemic challenges are even more pronounced in cases where we must decide whether collaterally killing innocent civilians is justified by the predicted benefits of destroying a military target. And despite the epistemic challenges, we accept, at least in principle, that collateral innocent deaths can be morally permissible. Likewise, despite the epistemic challenges, I think we should accept, at least in principle, that opportunistic resource-based war-profiteers are sometimes liable to be killed in war.

The upshot is that there have been and will be circumstances in which not only contributory but also opportunistic resource-based war-profiteering importers will be morally liable to be killed by combatants fighting in furtherance of a just cause, even if the profiteers have not contributed to any unjust aims. Of course, when resource-based war-profiteers—such as the controlling interests in a corporation buying or selling misappropriated resources—are unjustly enriched, the benefits derived will likely 'trickle down' to subordinates as well as to other groups and individuals with whom the profiteer does business. This might seem to suggest that they, too, owe restitutionary duties. But as I noted in Section 4, the wronged victims' claim to the unjust benefits diminishes as these benefits are dispersed throughout the economy. There are three reasons for this. First (which I noted earlier), as these benefits becomes increasingly mixed with legitimate economic activity, disgorging the former will also thereby unjustly threaten the latter, which provides a prima facie reason to forgo forced restitution in those cases. Second, like ripples in a pond, the benefits from a profiteer's unjust enrichment tend to diminish as they pass from one individual to the next. So, even if downstream beneficiaries owe restitution, the amount that they will be require to transfer will accordingly shrink. And third, downstream beneficiaries of the profiteer's unjust enrichment are less likely to be in a position to identify the causal history of these benefits—specifically, that they were derived from an unjust armed conflict in which innocents were dispossessed of their land and resources. Consequently, these downstream beneficiaries will not bear the culpability necessary to enforce their restitutionary duties through violent means.

7. The Law of War and the Morality of War

As mentioned in Section 1, advocates of the revisionist view deny that the principle of noncombatant immunity is correct, at least at the level of morality. Civilians who contribute substantially to an unjust war, who are in a position to recognize that they are making such a contribution, and who can refrain from doing so at no great cost to themselves are morally liable to be targeted if doing so is necessary to save any number of morally innocent lives. Contributory war-profiteers can, then, be morally liable to be killed, on this view. Their status as civilians does not insulate them against liability, given their conduct. I have pushed this argument further by arguing that culpably contributing to an unjust war is not a necessary condition for liability to be lethally targeted. An unjust beneficiary, by culpably failing to discharge a life-saving restitutionary duty, can be liable to be lethally targeted if doing so is necessary to save the lives of those whose victimization enabled the beneficiary's wrongful enrichment. This is further reason to think that the principle of noncombatant immunity is mistaken—at least at the level of morality.

But this does not mean that there should be no *legal* prohibition against targeting noncombatants. The fact that it can be, in principle, morally permissible to target civilians does not mean that such conduct should be made legal. Normally, the fact that a type of conduct is morally permissible suggests that it ought to be legally permissible as well. But this is not always the case (and not merely due to the existence of *malum prohibitum* laws and statutes). Sometimes legally permitting morally permissible behaviour has bad consequences. There are several reasons for thinking that this is likely to be true if we legally permit targeting certain types of civilians, such as opportunistic resource-based war-profiteers.[44]

As mentioned earlier, there is an epistemic challenge in determining, on any given occasion, whether the candidate resource-based war-profiteer is morally liable to be killed. The epistemic difficulty of making a reliable determination combined with the natural inclination to err on the side of self-interest by killing likely means that legally permitting such targeting will result in the intentional killing of many civilians who should not be intentionally killed. (Indeed, for similar sorts of reasons, it seems to me that collaterally killing civilians should be illegal as well, despite that it is sometimes morally permissible. But such a law would be tantamount to outlawing warfare, which is presumably unenforceable.)

In addition, there are widespread cross-cultural social mores against targeting civilians. Although as a moral doctrine this blanket prohibition is too crude (precisely because there are some civilians who are indeed morally liable), the widespread agreement has been hard-won and has almost certainly done more good than ill. A legal permission to target certain civilians might have a corrosive effect on this valuable social more by weakening it beyond what would be morally prescribed. It is not hard to imagine events unfolding in this way: a legal permission to target resource-based war-profiteers results not only in such profiteers being targeted, but their subordinates as well, and eventually *anyone* who is or is perceived to benefit from a war. Such an outcome would be morally catastrophic; it is better, then, to be risk-averse. We should keep intact the mores against intentionally killing civilians by legally prohibiting all such killings, even though, in principle, certain civilians are morally liable to be killed. In the meantime, resource-based war-profiteers can count themselves fortunate that they cannot be legally targeted even though they are morally liable.

But, of course, these are just armchair predictions. It might turn out that legally permitting combatants to target resource-based war-profiteers will *prevent* bloodshed. Wars are often funded on profits from trading in resources and commodities dispossessed from others. An 'open season' on such profiteers might cause them to think twice before buying or selling such resources, thereby starving a group of funds otherwise needed to wage war.

Ultimately, the point here is not to argue for or against weakening the legal prohibition on intentionally targeting noncombatants, but rather to point out that whether the principle of noncombatant immunity is correct at the level of morality *under-determines* whether an exceptionless version of the principle should be enshrined in law. That question cannot be settled without the help of historians and social-psychologists.

Notes

1. Lieber, Francis, 'Avalon Project—General Orders No. 100: The Lieber Code', Avalon Project—General Orders No. 100: The Lieber Code, http://avalon.law.yale.edu/19th_century/lieber.asp.
2. Expert opinion, 'On Whether Israel's Targeted Killings of Palestinian Terrorists Is Consonant with International Humanitarian Law' (2006), www.hamoked.org/Document.aspx?dID=7901.
3. Gary D. Solis, *The Law of Armed Conflict: International Humanitarian Law in War* (New York: Cambridge University Press, 2010), 208.
4. Yoram Dinstein, *The Conduct of Hostilities Under the Law of International Armed Conflict*, 2nd ed. (Cambridge: Cambridge University Press, 2010), 34.
5. See 'Rule 1' of the ICRC's volume on Customary International Humanitarian Law.
6. Protocol Additional to the Geneva Conventions of 12 August 1949 and relating to the Protection of Victims of International Armed Conflicts (Protocol I), Article 51.3, 8 June 1977.
7. Marco Sassòli and Olson M. Laura, 'The Relationship Between International Humanitarian and Human Rights Law Where It Matters: Admissible Killing and Internment of Fighters in Non-international Armed Conflicts', *International Review of the Red Cross* 90 (2008), 605.
8. Michael Walzer, *Just and Unjust Wars: A Moral Argument with Historical Illustrations*, 3rd ed. (New York City: Basic Books, 2000), 43.
9. For a comprehensive treatment of McMahan's revisionist view, see Jeff McMahan, *Killing in War* (New York: Oxford University Press, 2009).
10. For an attempt to provide a collectivist defence of the view that combatants on all sides in a war have an equal permission to kill, see, e.g., Christopher Kutz, 'The Difference Uniforms Make: Collective Violence in Criminal Law and War', *Philosophy & Public Affairs* 33 (2005), 148–180. Also see Jeff McMahan, 'Collectivist Defenses of the Moral Equality of Combatants', *Journal of Military Ethics* 2007, 50–59.
11. Thomas Hurka, 'Liability and Just Cause', *Ethics & International Affairs* 21 (2007), 210.
12. McMahan makes this point in Jeff McMahan, 'The Morality of War and the Law of War', in *Just and Unjust Warriors: The Moral and Legal Status of Soldiers*, edited by David Rodin and Henry Shue (Oxford: Oxford University Press, 2008), 25.
13. McMahan, 'The Morality of War and the Law of War', 26.
14. Robert L. Holmes, *On War and Morality* (Princeton, NJ: Princeton University Press, 1989), 187.

15. For an actual examination of these empirical assertions, see Seth Lazar, 'Necessity and Non-Combatant Immunity', *Review of International Studies* 40 (2013), 53–76.
16. Jeff McMahan, 'Pacifism and Moral Theory', *Diametros* 23 (2010), 44–68.
17. Cécile Fabre, 'Guns, Food, and Liability to Attack in War', *Ethics* 120 (2010).
18. This was McMahan's early view. See Jeff McMahan, 'Innocence, Self-Defense and Killing in War', *Journal of Political Philosophy* 2 (1994), 193–221. See also Robert L. Holmes, 'Pacifism & Wartime Innocence—A Response', *Social Theory and Practice* 20 (1994), 200.
19. See Holmes, *On War and Morality*, 187. Also see Mark Vorobej, 'Pacifism & Wartime Innocence', *Social Theory & Practice* 20 (1994), 181–182.
20. Larry May presses this point. See Larry May, 'Contingent Pacifism and the Moral Risks of Participating in War', *Public Affairs Quarterly* 25 (2011), 104. Noam Zohar does as well, although by arguing that the basis of liability is the collective rather than individual conduct of combatants. See Noam Zohar, 'Collective War and Individualistic Ethics', *Political Theory* 21 (1993), 631–633. See also Henry Shue, 'Laws of War, Morality, and International Politics: Compliance, Stringency, and Limits', *Leiden Journal of International Law* 26 (2013), 277.
21. Seth Lazar, 'The Responsibility Dilemma For Killing in War—A Review Essay', *Philosophy & Public Affairs* 38 (2010), 180–213.
22. Jeff McMahan, 'Who Is Morally Liable to be Killed in War?', *Analysis* 71 (2011), 557–558.
23. Idem, 550.
24. Bradley J. Strawser, 'Walking the Tightrope of Just War', *Analysis* 71 (2011), 541.
25. Saba Bazargan, 'Complicitous Liability in War', *Philosophical Studies* 165 (2012), 177–195.
26. Janina Dill and Henry Shue, 'Limiting the Killing in War: Military Necessity and the St. Petersburg Assumption', *Ethics & International Affairs* 26 (2012), 311–333.
27. Lazar explores this possibility in detail, in Lazar, 'The Responsibility Dilemma For Killing in War—A Review Essay'.
28. Janina Dill, 'Should International Law Ensure the Moral Acceptability of War?', *Leiden Journal of International Law* 26 (2013), 253–270.
29. Larry May, *Aggression & Crimes Against Peace* (New York City: Cambridge University Press, 2008), 25–45. Larry May, 'Contingent Pacifism and the Moral Risks of Participating in War', 95–112.
30. Virginia Held, *How Terrorism Is Wrong* (New York: Oxford University Press, 2008), 20.
31. Igor Primoratz, 'Michael Walzer's Just War Theory: Some Issues of Responsibility', *Ethical Theory and Moral Practice* 5 (2002), 221–243.
32. Victor Tadros, 'Orwell's Battle with Brittain: Vicarious Liability for Unjust Aggression', *Philosophy & Public Affairs* 42 (2014), 42–77.
33. Idem, 45.
34. Smedley D. Butler, *War Is a Racket: The Antiwar Classic by America's Most Decorated Soldier* (Port Townsend, WA: Feral House, 2003).
35. See Graham Virgo, *The Principles of the Law of Restitution*, 2nd ed. (Oxford: Oxford University Press, 2006), 431, 460, 538, 551.
36. Idem, 459.
37. See, in particular, *Strand Electric and Engineering Co Ltd* v. *Brisfored Entertainment Ltd* [1952] 2 QB 246; *Penarth Dock Engineering Co Ltd* v. *Pounds* [1963] 1 Lloyd S Rep 259 and *Gondal* v. *Dillon Newspapers Ltd* [2001] RLR 221. [430].
38. Virgo, *The Principles of the Law of Restitution*, 534–535.
39. Samuel Scheffler, *The Rejection of Consequentialism* (Oxford: Oxford University Press, 1982).

40. Victor Tadros, 'Duty and Liability', *Utilitas* (2012), 259–277.
41. Ibid.
42. Neta Crawford, *Accountability for Killing: Moral Responsibility for Collateral Damage in America's Post-9/11 Wars* (New York: Oxford University Press, 2013), 151.
43. Geneva Declaration Secretariat 2011, 32.
44. For a more in-depth discussion of the relation between the morality and the law of war, see, e.g., McMahan, 'The Morality of War and the Law of War', in *Just and Unjust Warriors: The Moral and Legal Status of Soldiers*, edited by David Rodin and Henry Shue (Oxford: Oxford University Press, 2008), 19–43. See also Henry Shue, 'Do We Need a "Morality of War"'? (2008), 87–111.

CHAPTER 19

HUMAN SHIELDS

ADIL AHMAD HAQUE

In contemporary armed conflict, combatants fight where civilians live. Often, it is both morally and legally permissible to conduct military operations in civilian areas. As in all things, the risks combatants impose on civilians must be proportionate to the military advantage they seek. However, it is unlawful (indeed, it is criminal) to use civilians as human shields, either by moving civilians near military targets (active shielding) or by moving military targets near civilians (passive shielding) for the purpose of preventing or dissuading attacks on those targets.[1]

The moral bases of this legal prohibition are not hard to find. Combatants who use human shields opportunistically take advantage of the presence of civilians, place those civilians at grave risk, and often occasion foreseeable harm to those civilians. In addition, the use of human shields often involves coercing civilians into involuntary service. Strikingly, Cécile Fabre argues that forcing civilians to serve as human shields is not as morally problematic as it seems.[2] I take up her arguments shortly.

Importantly, the use of civilians as involuntary shields by one party does not release the opposing party from its legal obligations not to target these civilians, to avoid harming these civilians, and not to inflict excessive incidental harm on these civilians.[3] Nevertheless, some scholars argue that death or injury to civilians used as involuntary shields should be disregarded or at least discounted in determining proportionality.[4] On their view, an attack that would be disproportionate if some number of civilians is near the target by chance may be proportionate if the same number (or an even greater number) of civilians is near the target due to the wrongful actions of the opposing party. I hope that, for many readers, to state this view is to refute it. However, since this view is increasingly prevalent in both public and academic discourse, it is worth examining in some detail.

Finally, the moral status of voluntary shields remains controversial. Some scholars insist that all voluntary shields forfeit the moral protections ordinarily enjoyed by civilians. Others insist that voluntary shields who physically obstruct military operations forfeit these protections while other voluntary shields retain these protections in full.

In contrast, I will argue that most voluntary shields compromise but do not lose their moral rights.

Before proceeding further, let me introduce some terminology and normative assumptions. Combatants are members of the armed forces of a party to an armed conflict, except for medical, religious, and civil defence personnel. Civilians are neither combatants nor participants in a *levée en masse*. Voluntary shields are civilians who freely choose to remain near military targets for the purpose of preventing or dissuading attacks on those targets. Involuntary shields include civilians who are forced by the defending party to remain near military targets, as well as civilians who have military targets moved near them but do not remain near those targets for the purpose of averting an attack.

Civilians are, first and foremost, human beings with basic rights not to be killed, injured, coerced, or endangered. Civilians can forfeit their basic rights through their voluntary conduct, thereby making themselves morally liable to be harmed. Paradigmatically, civilians can forfeit their basic rights by directly participating in hostilities on behalf of an unjust cause. In contrast, innocent civilians bear insufficient moral responsibility for an unjust war effort to lose their basic rights. As we shall see, the moral status of supportive civilians—those who indirectly contribute to an unjust war effort, for example, by paying taxes to a state engaged in an unjust war—remains hotly disputed.

In addition, the basic rights of innocent civilians can be overridden. Importantly, intentionally harming innocent civilians is morally worse (i.e., harder to justify) than unintentionally harming innocent civilians. In general, it is morally permissible to collaterally harm an innocent person as an unintended side effect of preventing substantially greater harm to others. In rare cases, it is morally permissible to intentionally harm an innocent person as a necessary means of preventing far greater harm to others.

In what follows, I will describe tactical encounters between an attacking force that might kill human shields if it attacks and a defending force that uses human shields for the purpose of averting an attack.[5] I will assume that it is morally impermissible for combatants pursuing an unjust cause to use civilians as involuntary shields or to kill civilians serving, voluntarily or involuntarily, as human shields. Objectively speaking, it is morally impermissible to threaten or harm anyone in pursuit of an unjust cause. I will instead ask whether it is ever morally permissible for an attacking force pursuing a just cause to use civilians as human shields or to kill civilians serving, voluntarily or involuntarily, as human shields for a defending force pursuing an unjust cause.

1. Using Involuntary Shields

Most people believe that it is morally reprehensible to use civilians as involuntary shields. Remarkably, Cécile Fabre argues that many supportive civilians who indirectly contribute to an unjust war effort are morally liable to be used as involuntary shields by combatants fighting for a just cause. On this view, if combatants fighting for a just cause enter their adversary's territory, then these combatants may use civilians supportive of their adversary as human shields. In addition, Fabre argues that the right of innocent civilians not to be used as involuntary shields may be overridden as easily as their right not to be collaterally harmed.

Fabre starts from the premise that, although few supportive civilians contribute enough to an unjust war effort to render themselves morally liable to intentional killing, many supportive civilians contribute enough to render themselves morally liable to unintentional killing.[6] Fabre also observes that it is morally permissible to unintentionally kill innocent civilians as a necessary and proportionate side effect of pursuing a just cause.[7] Fabre then argues that using civilians as involuntary shields is easier to justify than intentionally killing them and no harder to justify than unintentionally killing them. Fabre concludes that supportive civilians who are morally liable to intentional or unintentional killing are also morally liable to be used as involuntary shields and that combatants may use innocent civilians as involuntary shields as a necessary and proportionate means of pursuing a just cause.

Importantly, Fabre argues that using civilians as human shields is in one way easier to justify than unintentionally killing civilians because it is the opposing party that will directly kill the civilians. On this view, 'killing is generally worse than contributing to causing someone to die at the hands of third parties'.[8] Fabre admits that using civilians as involuntary shields is in another way harder to justify than unintentionally harming civilians. The former opportunistically uses civilians as a means, taking advantage of their presence to obtain tactical advantages that would not be possible in their absence. Fabre suggests that these competing considerations—intervening agency and opportunistic use—offset one another, leaving the harmful use of human shields morally comparable to collaterally harming civilians.

I reject every step of Fabre's argument. First, Fabre is wrong to think that someone can be morally liable to unintentional killing but not to intentional killing.[9] Human beings do not have one right not to be intentionally killed and a separate, lesser right not to be unintentionally killed such that it is possible to forfeit one but not the other. On the contrary, human beings have one basic right not to be killed that protects our basic interests and reflects our basic humanity. One cannot retain this basic right with respect to intentional killing but lose this right with respect to unintentional killing. Moral liability to intentional harm and moral liability to unintentional harm stand or fall together. If supportive civilians are not morally liable to intentional killing then they are not morally liable to unintentional killing either.

No doubt, it is harder to justify infringing (i.e., overriding) this basic right intentionally than to justify infringing this basic right unintentionally. On some views, the intent to kill adds a morally objectionable feature, such as special disrespect, to the foreseeable infliction of death that requires additional justification. On my own view, the causal consequences of infringing this right and the side effects of the infringing act do not count equally in favour of its infringement. In particular, the prevention of substantially greater harm to others may justify the infringement of this basic right if it occurs as a side effect of the infringing act but not if it occurs as a consequence of the infringement itself.

On my view, our basic right not to be killed generates both a first-order reason not to kill us as well as a second-order reason that excludes or silences the first-order reasons others ordinarily have to bring about good consequences when those good consequences would result from killing us.[10] If we intentionally kill the innocent as a means of preventing substantially greater harm to other innocent people, then our motivating reason is not a justifying reason. In contrast, if we unintentionally kill the innocent as a side effect of preventing substantially greater harm to other innocent people then our motivating reason is also a justifying reason.

On my view, it is disrespectful to kill an innocent person as an intentional means of producing good consequences because killing an innocent person is not a morally acceptable causal means of producing good consequences, not independently and not the other way around. In other words, the moral significance of intention and foresight tracks the moral significance of the causal relations between the good and bad consequences of our actions. The moral significance of these causal relations, in turn, expresses (or perhaps constitutes) one dimension of our moral status. To the extent that the good consequences of killing us count in favour of killing us, morality itself regards us as mere means. To the extent that the good consequences of killing us are excluded or silenced, morality regards us as inviolable ends in ourselves.[11]

Because human beings have one basic right not to be killed, supportive civilians are morally liable to unintentional killing if and only if they are morally liable to intentional killing. Supportive civilians who are not morally liable to intentional killing are not morally liable to unintentional killing either.

Suppose that Fabre is right that supportive civilians, in principle, could be morally liable to unintentional killing but not to intentional killing. Fabre's argument would still fail because supportive civilians, in fact, are not morally liable to unintentional killing (let alone intentional killing).

Ordinarily, it is morally impermissible to unintentionally kill innocent civilians except as a necessary side effect of preventing substantially greater harm to other innocent people. In contrast, if supportive civilians are morally liable to unintentional killing, then it is permissible to unintentionally kill supportive civilians as a side effect of preventing substantially less harm to other innocent people. On this view, the small, indirect, and overdetermined causal contributions of supportive civilians to an unjust war effort invert the substantial moral asymmetry between doing harm and allowing harm. Yet, intuitively, only substantial moral responsibility for an unjust threat can invert such a substantial moral asymmetry. Similarly, intuitively, only great moral responsibility for an unjust threat can invert the great moral asymmetry between intentionally doing harm and unintentionally allowing harm.

For Jeff McMahan, civilians who support an unjust war effort are morally liable to both intentional and unintentional killing because they bear *comparatively* greater responsibility for the conflict than either combatants or civilians on the just side.[12] On his view, defensive force is a matter of justly distributing indivisible harms: if harm must befall either civilians supporting the unjust side or combatants fighting for the just side (or civilians supporting the just side), then it is morally preferable that the harm befall the former rather than the latter. This view rests on a mistake. Killing in war is not a matter of distributing some fixed amount of inevitable harm falling from the sky. Nor is killing in war a matter of redirecting a pre-existing threat away from some and toward others. Killing in war is a matter of intentionally or unintentionally doing harm to some people rather than allowing harm to other people.

Put another way, because the possession of moral rights rests on the noncomparative properties of human beings, the loss of moral rights should turn on noncomparative responsibility of a degree commensurate with the importance of the rights lost. We can lose our basic rights by posing unjust threats individually, jointly with others, or indirectly through others under our control. Perhaps we can also lose our rights by making large, direct, or necessary contributions to unjust threats posed by others. But it is hard to believe that we can derive liability to be killed or maimed from small, indirect, and overdetermined contributions to unjust threats posed by others.

Finally, even if Fabre could show that supportive civilians are morally liable to unintentional killing, it would not follow that supportive civilians are morally liable to use as involuntary shields. Fabre is wrong to think that using civilians as involuntary shields is morally comparable to unintentionally killing civilians. On the contrary, using civilians as involuntary shields is morally comparable to intentionally killing civilians.

First, there is hardly any moral difference between opportunistic use that occasions unintended harm and opportunistic use that inflicts unintended harm. Suppose that a defending force positions civilian shields between it and an attacking force, and the civilians are unintentionally killed in the crossfire. It makes little moral difference, if any, whether the lethal bullets are fired by the attacking force or by the defending force. Put another way, it is hard to imagine that the moral permissibility of forcing civilians into the line of fire turns on the relative likelihood that they will be killed by the attacking force or by the defending force.

Second, opportunistic use that inflicts unintended harm is morally comparable to intentional harming. Indeed, the very category of opportunistic harming was developed to capture cases of strictly unintentional harming that are morally comparable to intentional harming.[13]

It follows that opportunistic use that occasions unintended harm is morally comparable to intentional harming. In particular, it follows that using civilians as human shields and thereby occasioning their deaths is morally comparable to intentionally killing those civilians. So, if it is morally impermissible to intentionally kill supportive civilians, then it is morally impermissible to use supportive civilians as involuntary shields. Finally, if it is morally impermissible to intentionally kill innocent civilians, then it is morally impermissible to use innocent civilians as involuntary shields.[14]

2. Killing Involuntary Shields

Under what circumstances is it morally permissible for an attacking force pursuing a just cause to kill civilians forced to serve as involuntary shields by a defending force fighting for an unjust cause? Although it is generally accepted that involuntary shields are not morally liable to be killed, this consensus requires some explanation. In particular, we must explain why conscripts who involuntarily fight for an unjust cause are morally liable to harm whereas civilians who involuntarily serve as human shields on behalf of an unjust cause are not.

Importantly, several leading commentators insist that attacking forces may fully or partly discount collateral harm to involuntary shields, proceeding as if no civilians or fewer civilians are in harm's way. Put another way, a military advantage insufficient to justify collateral harm to some number of civilian passersby may be sufficient to justify comparable collateral harm to the same (or an even greater) number of involuntary shields. These commentators argue that their position reflects the responsibility of the defending force for any harm that befalls involuntary shields as well as the need to deter defending forces from using involuntary shields in the future. I take up these arguments shortly.

2.1. Shields and Conscripts

Commentators almost universally agree that civilians forced to serve as involuntary shields retain their basic rights. Some involuntary shields are physically incapable of avoiding military targets, whereas others are not morally responsible for their actions. At the same time, many involuntary shields consciously choose to go or remain in or near military targets, albeit under duress. This point is significant because most commentators agree that conscripts who will be killed if they refuse to fight for an unjust cause are morally liable to defensive force if they choose to fight.[15] Why, then, are civilians who will be killed if they refuse to serve as involuntary shields not morally liable if they choose to serve rather than die?

The answer must turn on the different kinds of contributions that conscripts and shields make to the unjust threats posed by the defending force. Many conscripts who fight on behalf of an unjust cause kill innocent people, either individually, jointly with other combatants, or through other combatants under their effective control.[16] It is wrong for them to do so, even to save their own lives. Other things equal, it is permissible for me to save my own life rather than save someone else's life. In contrast, it is wrong for me to kill an innocent person to avoid my own death because doing harm is worse than allowing harm.

Unlike conscripts, shields do not kill or otherwise harm innocent people. At the same time, shields do not simply allow innocent people to be killed. Shields make it harder for attacking forces to prevent defending forces from killing innocent people. Ordinarily, when we fail to save another person, we leave that other person no worse off than she would have been in our absence. In contrast, shields make innocent people worse off than they would have been in the shields' absence.[17] However, it does not follow that shields are morally liable.

Imagine that A, an innocent person, is drowning. B could toss A a life preserver were it not for the fact that C is in the way. However, the only way for C to get out of the way will result in C's death. In this case, C's presence makes A worse off than A would be in C's absence. Nevertheless, it seems permissible for C to remain in the way rather than die. Moreover, it seems impermissible for B to kill C in order to save A.[18]

Similarly, shielding an unjust threat to an innocent person is morally close enough to allowing harm to that innocent person that both are permissible to avoid one's own death, and neither render one morally liable to be killed to save that innocent person. On my view, involuntary shields threatened with death are not morally liable to be killed because they do not pose unjust threats and are morally justified in shielding unjust threats.

2.2. Responsibility

Some who advocate partly or wholly discounting harm to involuntary shields claim that if a defending force uses civilians as involuntary shields and an attacking force kills those civilians in subsequent attacks, then the defending force is partly or wholly morally responsible for these deaths.[19] On this view, the attacking force need only justify civilian deaths to the extent that it is responsible for them. To the extent that the defending force is responsible for the deaths of involuntary shields, the attacking force has less or nothing to justify. On this view, it is as if some or all of the civilians are killed by the defending force while some or none of the civilians are killed by the attacking force.

As we have seen, a defending force that uses involuntary shields is morally responsible if doing so occasions their deaths. It does not follow, however, that the attacking force is not also morally responsible for their deaths. After all, it is the attacking force that kills these civilians; that is, that directly causes their deaths without further intervening agency. Moreover, the attacking force generally chooses to attack knowing that civilians are in or near the targets. Importantly, the bases of the attacking force's responsibility (ultimate control and direct causation) are exactly the same whether the civilians are being used as human shields or are simply in the wrong place at the wrong time. Ultimately, it is up to the attacking force to either kill the civilians or spare them.

To see the moral significance of direct causation and ultimate control more clearly, compare the following cases. In one case, if you attack a legitimate military target, then you will kill some number of nearby civilians. In a second case, the defending force threatens that, if you attack a legitimate military target, killing no civilians, then the defending force will kill the same number of civilians as you would kill in the first case.[20] There may very well be some number of civilians such that it would be permissible to attack in the second case but not in the first case. Although the same number of civilians would die, in the first case you would ultimately choose to directly kill them whereas in the second case the defending force would ultimately choose to directly kill them. Importantly, cases like these do not support discounting the lives of involuntary shields because it is the attacking force and not the defending force that ultimately chooses to directly kill involuntary shields.

The moral responsibility of the defending force for the deaths of involuntary shields does not affect the moral permissibility of the attacking force choosing to kill them. To see this, consider the following scenario.

> *Involuntary Shields*: You can strike a legitimate military target from the North or from the South. If you strike from the South, you will kill nineteen civilians who are merely passing by. If you strike from the North, you will kill twenty civilians forced to serve as involuntary human shields.

It is worse to kill the twenty shields than to kill the nineteen passersby. If either strike would be proportionate, then you ought to strike from the South. It is almost always worse to kill more than to kill fewer, and the previous scenario does not seem like an exception. The involuntary shields have done nothing to lose or weaken their moral rights. It does not matter that the defending force is responsible for the presence of the shields but not for the presence of the passersby. What matters is that the shields are not responsible for their presence near the target.

Indeed, the responsibility of the defending force would give you no reason to kill twenty involuntary shields rather than *twenty* passersby. The responsibility of the defending force is not even a moral "tie-breaker." If anything, it might be slightly worse to kill twenty involuntary shields than to kill twenty passersby. For one thing, as hard as it is for passersby to avoid military targets, particularly in dense urban environments, it is even harder for involuntary shields to avoid military targets. As we shall see, the moral wrongfulness of harming an individual can vary somewhat in degree depending on how easily the individual could have avoided being in harm's way.

Killing involuntary shields might also be slightly worse than killing passersby on roughly prioritarian grounds.[21] In general, it is better to confer a benefit on the potential recipient who is comparatively worse off; similarly, it is worse to impose a cost on the potential victim who is comparatively worse off. Because involuntary shields have been threatened and coerced by the defending force, they are in some respects worse off than passersby. It might therefore be worse to kill involuntary shields than passersby.

It follows that harm to involuntary shields should not be discounted in determining the proportionality of an attack. If it is disproportionate to strike from the South, then it is also disproportionate to strike from the North. If the harm an attack will inflict on involuntary shields is not justified by the military advantage anticipated from the attack, then that harm cannot be justified by adverting to the responsibility of the defending force.

To conclude, if an attacking force inflicts proportionate harm on involuntary shields, then the defending force has violated the rights of those civilians but the attacking force has not. In one sense, then, the defending force is morally responsible (i.e., morally *blameworthy*) and the attacking force is not. However, if an attacking force inflicts disproportionate harm on involuntary shields, then both the defending force and the attacking force violate the rights of those civilians. In this sense, proportionality determines moral responsibility, not the other way around.

2.3. Deterrence

Some scholars argue that if attacking forces ignore or discount the presence of involuntary shields, reducing the tactical benefits of using involuntary shields, then defending forces will use involuntary shields less often. By killing civilians currently used as human shields, attacking forces will reduce the number of civilians used as human shields in the future. On this view, in determining the proportionality of an attack that kills involuntary shields, we should consider not only the immediate benefit of, say, destroying a legitimate target but also the deterrence of future use of involuntary shields.[22]

Presumably, consequentialist arguments for killing civilians should rest on strong evidence that the desired consequences will follow. Yet there is no reason to expect that killing involuntary shields will reduce their use by defending forces. Neither ignoring nor discounting the presence of involuntary shields makes the defending force worse off than it would be if it did not use human shields. It follows that defending forces will continue to use human shields if they expect any substantial benefit from doing so. Because many observers will in fact (correctly or incorrectly) believe that attacking forces act wrongfully by killing these civilians, defending forces may expect to gain new recruits and additional support or to politically isolate their adversaries. It follows that ignoring or discounting the presence of involuntary shields is unlikely to deter their use.

More fundamentally, the causal consequences of civilian deaths ordinarily do not count in favour of killing civilians. Certainly, we cannot justify targeting involuntary shields on the grounds that their deaths will reduce the future use of involuntary shields. Nor can we justify unnecessarily killing involuntary shields as a side effect of targeting a military objective (killing more when we could kill fewer, killing some when we could kill none) on such grounds. I submit that we also cannot justify otherwise disproportionately killing involuntary shields on such grounds.

On my view, the proportionality of an attack that kills innocent civilians generally excludes good consequences of the attack that are causally downstream from the civilian deaths. By denying justificatory weight to the consequences of civilian deaths, morality gives substance to the inviolability of every human being. It follows that, if an attack that kills civilians would be disproportionate but for the good consequences of the civilian deaths, then that attack *is* disproportionate and therefore impermissible.

It might be objected that, although it is wrong to launch an attack *in order to* deter the use of involuntary shields, it is not wrong to launch an attack in order to destroy a legitimate military target *on the condition* that doing so will deter the use of involuntary shields.[23] However, on my view, what matters is that the attack is proportionate only if killing involuntary shields is a morally acceptable causal means of producing good outcomes. If these good outcomes do not objectively count in favour of killing involuntary shields, then the attacker necessarily acts on the basis of insufficient reasons.

Alternatively, it might be objected that it is not the deaths of the involuntary shields that deters but rather the demonstrated willingness of the attacking force to attack despite their presence. If, by luck, the involuntary shields survive the attack, then the deterrent effect of the attack will still be sufficient to render the attack proportionate.[24] On these facts, the attacking force nevertheless makes opportunistic use of the involuntary shields because the attack would be disproportionate in their absence. After all, the attack can only deter the future use of involuntary shields if some involuntary shields are present. Moreover, as we have seen, opportunistic use that foreseeably results in harm is morally comparable to intentional harming. Because it is wrong to intentionally kill involuntary shields, it is also wrong to opportunistically use the presence of involuntary shields, foreseeably killing them, for the sake of deterrence. We should deter the use of involuntary shields by criminally punishing those who so use them, thus imposing costs on wrongdoers rather than on their victims.

Before moving on, it is worth noting that many advocates of discounting harm to involuntary shields observe that it is unfair that defending forces may gain tactical advantages over attacking forces through wrongful conduct. Some argue that attacking forces should wholly or partly deprive defending forces of such unfair advantages by ignoring or discounting the presence of involuntary shields.[25]

War, like the rest of life, is often unfair. Killing civilians who have done nothing to forfeit their basic rights cannot correct but can only compound the unfairness of war, shifting the unfair burdens imposed on the attacking force not onto the defending force but onto their civilian victims. We should annul the unfair advantages gained through the use of involuntary shields by prosecuting those responsible for war crimes. We should not, in effect, punish involuntary shields for war crimes committed against them.

3. Killing Voluntary Shields

Under what circumstances may attacking forces fighting for a just cause intentionally or unintentionally harm civilians who voluntarily serve as human shields on behalf of defending forces fighting for an unjust cause?

Before considering the objective permissibility of harming voluntary shields, let me say a word about the epistemic permissibility of harming voluntary shields. In general, we should presume that individuals retain their basic rights absent decisive reason to believe that they have made themselves morally liable to defensive force. It follows that it is epistemically impermissible to target civilians, or to discount collateral harm to civilians, absent decisive reason to believe that they are neither involuntary shields nor passersby. Because decisive evidence of voluntary presence and intent to shield is hard to come by in armed conflict, it is seldom epistemically permissible to target or discount collateral harm to voluntary shields.[26] Nevertheless, the objective permissibility of harming voluntary shields is worth exploring in its own right.

3.1. Physical Shields and Moral Shields

Many commentators distinguish between voluntary shields who create physical obstacles to attacking legitimate targets (physical shields) and voluntary shields who create moral or legal obstacles to attacking legitimate targets (moral shields).[27] Imagine a civilian who voluntarily moves in front of a combatant who is firing on opposing soldiers, using his or her own body to physically protect the combatant from return fire. This civilian creates a physical obstacle to attacking the combatant. In contrast, imagine that the civilian instead stands beside or behind the combatant. Depending on the stakes, the proximity of the civilian might render an attack on the combatant disproportionate, thereby creating a moral obstacle to attacking the combatant. Some commentators maintain that physical shields are liable to intentional and collateral harm but that moral shields retain their basic rights in full.[28] Others maintain that, because both physical shields and moral shields may avert the destruction of legitimate targets, both forfeit their basic rights.[29] Both positions strike me as too extreme.

First, we may be misled by cases of civilians who actively serve as physical shields to combatants currently engaged in combat operations. In many such cases, the combatants and the civilians exercise joint agency, each intending to perform their respective roles within a coordinated attack. In such cases, the civilians do not merely shield a threat posed by others but jointly pose a threat with others. In contrast, imagine a group of civilians conversing among themselves when an unarmed combatant runs between them and convinces them to stand still and thereby physically shield his escape from opposing forces. These civilians passively serve as physical shields to a combatant who poses no immediate threat. It is hard to believe that these civilians are morally liable to intentional killing or to nearly unlimited collateral harm.

More broadly, if voluntary shields (either physical or moral) forfeit their basic rights, then they count for little or nothing in determining the proportionality of an attack. On this view, so long as the target is legitimate, voluntary shields may be collaterally harmed virtually without limit. Yet it seems wrong to kill twenty, fifty, or one-hundred civilians as a foreseeable side effect of killing one ordinary combatant simply because the civilians are near the combatant voluntarily with the intent to dissuade an attack. This is true even if the combatant may pose unjust threats in the future. The conduct of these civilians does not seem sufficiently morally comparable to the conduct of the combatant to render them all morally liable to be killed.

On one hand, an attack that kills some number of voluntary shields may be proportionate even though an attack that kills the same number of involuntary shields or civilian passersby would be disproportionate. Consider the following scenario:

Voluntary Shields: You can strike a legitimate military target from the North or from the South. If you strike from the North, you will kill twenty civilians voluntarily serving as human shields. If you strike from the South, you will kill twenty civilians who are merely passing by.

In this case, it seems worse to kill the twenty passersby than to kill the twenty voluntary shields. If either strike would be proportionate, then you ought to strike from the North. Moreover, depending on the importance of the target, it might be proportionate to strike from the North but not from the South.

On the other hand, it seems that harm to voluntary human shields can render an attack disproportionate. Consider the following scenario:

Voluntary Shields 2: You can strike a legitimate military target from the North or from the South. If you strike from the North, you will kill twenty civilians voluntarily serving as human shields. If you strike from the South, you will kill two civilians who are merely passing by.

In this case, it seems worse to kill the twenty voluntary shields than to kill the two passersby. If either strike would be proportionate, then you ought to strike from the South. Moreover, depending on the importance of the target, it might be proportionate to strike from the South but not from the North.

Cases like these suggest that voluntary shields compromise but do not lose their basic rights. Put another way, it seems easier to justify harming voluntary shields than to justify harming ordinary civilians, yet harming voluntary shields still requires substantial justification. In the following sections, I explore a possible moral basis for this intermediate position.

3.2. Avoidability and Liability

In most cases, voluntary shields can avoid being harmed in attacks on military targets more easily than can civilian passersby. To be sure, at the moment of attack, voluntary shields are just as vulnerable as passersby. However, before an attack, voluntary shields can more easily reduce their future vulnerability. The voluntary shields know they are near a military target, know that an attack may be imminent, and presumably have no other compelling reason to be there. The passersby presumably lack this knowledge or have other compelling reasons for being where they are.

Now, the fact that you can easily avoid some harm does not entail that you are morally liable to suffer that harm, let alone that you deserve to suffer that harm—only that inflicting that harm upon you is less wrongful (i.e., easier to justify) than it would be if you could not easily avoid that harm. Ordinarily, if some action will prevent some harm to one person but inflict a comparable harm on another person then that action is impermissible. However, if the person whom the action will harm can easily avoid being harmed, or could have easily avoided a situation in which one of the two people will be harmed, then the action may be permissible.

Similarly, on my view, voluntary shields do not forfeit their rights not to be killed, nor do they deserve to die. Nevertheless, it is less wrongful to kill voluntary shields than to kill passersby because the former could more easily avoid being killed than the latter. Put the other way around, it is more wrongful to kill passersby because they have less control than voluntary shields over whether or not they will be killed.[30] Because the moral gravity of losses to voluntary shields is reduced by their ability to avoid these losses, military advantages that would not justify given losses to civilian passersby may justify similar losses to voluntary shields. It is for this reason that collateral harm that would be disproportionate if inflicted on civilian passersby may be proportionate if inflicted on voluntary shields.

As we have seen, the comparative avoidability of harm is morally relevant but is not morally dispositive. Although it is worse to kill one passerby than to kill one voluntary shield, it is not ten times worse to kill one passerby than to kill one voluntary shield. Of course, it is hard to say precisely how much worse it is to kill passersby than to kill voluntary shields. A conservative view is that avoidability offsets the general moral asymmetry between doing harm and allowing harm. On this view, an attack that collaterally kills some number of voluntary shields is proportionate if it is necessary to save a comparable number of innocent civilians. A more permissive view is that avoidability inverts this asymmetry. On this view, an attack that collaterally kills some number of voluntary shields is proportionate if it is necessary to save a substantially smaller number of innocent civilians. It is hard to determine which view is correct. But the view that avoidability obliterates this asymmetry, rendering it proportionate to collaterally kill a very large number of voluntary shields to save a very small number of innocent civilians, seems far too strong.

Some readers may feel that many voluntary moral shields choose to create a situation in which either the attacking force will kill them or (at some point) the defending force will kill either innocent civilians or combatants fighting for a just cause. On this view, voluntary moral shields are morally liable to be killed in order to resolve a moral dilemma of their own making. However, if the innocent civilians or combatants fighting for a just cause could easily avoid being killed by the defending force, then it seems wrong to kill the voluntary shields. So, on this view, it is permissible to kill the voluntary shields to the extent that they could have avoided the situation comparatively more easily than the innocent civilians and combatants.

This view resembles McMahan's view that it is permissible to kill A to save B if A is comparatively more responsible than B for the fact that B will be killed unless A is killed. However, as we have seen, just as the possession of basic rights depends on noncomparative properties of our status, the loss of basic rights depends on our noncomparative degree of moral responsibility. No doubt, voluntary shields generally bear greater moral responsibility than innocent civilians for the fact that either they will be killed or innocent civilians will be killed. Similarly, generally, it is easier for voluntary shields than for innocent civilians to avoid situations in which either voluntary shields will be killed or innocent civilians will be killed. As we have seen, it does not follow that the voluntary shields are morally liable to be killed. Instead, comparative responsibility and comparative avoidability entail only that it is comparatively easier to justify killing voluntary shields than to justify killing innocent civilians.[31]

3.3. Shielding and Wrongdoing

Some readers may feel that civilians have moral duties not to aid combatants fighting for an unjust cause and not to interfere with combatants fighting for a just cause. These readers may feel that voluntary moral shields violate these moral duties and thereby forfeit their basic rights.

In general, the stringency of a moral duty should determine the moral consequences of its violation. If morality requires you to suffer some harm rather than violate some duty then, if you violate that duty, it may be fair to inflict the same degree of harm on you to correct or prevent the unjust result of your violation. You cannot complain about suffering such harm because you had a moral duty to suffer similar harm to avoid producing such unjust results in the first place.[32] However, it would be disproportionate to inflict a greater harm on you than you had a duty to suffer. Put another way, moral constraints protect moral prerogatives: I am under a moral constraint not to harm you for some end because you have a moral prerogative not to accept that harm for that end.[33]

For example, the duty not to kill the innocent is very stringent. In general, we are morally required to die rather than breach this duty. It is therefore fair to kill someone who tries to kill an innocent person; in doing so, we only inflict a harm on them that they have a duty to accept. Conversely, the duty to save the innocent is less stringent. In general, we are not morally required to die or suffer serious injury to save an innocent person from comparable harm. It is therefore unfair to kill one innocent person to save another; in doing so, we impose a harm that person has no duty to accept.

Importantly, if civilians have a moral duty not to shield military targets from combatants fighting for a just cause, then this duty is not very stringent. After all, civilians are not morally required to die or suffer serious injury rather than serve as involuntary shields. Because civilians need not risk death or serious injury to avoid shielding military objectives, it is presumptively wrong to kill or seriously injure civilians who do so.

It may be objected that, although civilians are not required to die rather than shield military targets, voluntary shields do not, in fact, shield military targets under threat of death. True enough. My point is not about the motivations of voluntary shields but about the stringency of the moral duty they violate. On my view, stringency rather than motivation should determine moral liability to be killed. For example, on my view, an adult who fails to save a drowning child for a trivial or wicked reason is not morally liable to be killed to save that child. True, the adult does not fail to save the child in order to avoid being killed. However, the moral duty that the adult violates is insufficiently stringent to result, when violated, in moral liability to be killed.

In most cases, voluntary shields, involuntary shields, and civilian passersby perform similar actions: they go or remain near military targets. They differ primarily in their motivation. On my view, the duty not to shield military targets is insufficiently stringent to result, when violated, in moral liability to be killed. The fact that voluntary shields breach that duty for reasons other than fear of death does not make them morally liable to be killed.

It may be further objected that voluntary shields *culpably* breach their duty not to shield military targets—they intend to shield military targets and are free from duress—and that the moral blameworthiness of the breach combines with the stringency of the duty to yield moral liability. Indeed, because involuntary shields retain their basic rights, some form of moral fault must be necessary for shielding to result in moral liability. Of course, it does not follow that culpability is sufficient for shielding to result in liability to be killed. But I will pursue a different point.

Presumably, almost all civilians willing to serve as voluntary shields subjectively believe that the defending force they aid fights for a just cause. Often, their belief is reasonable; that is, epistemically justified by the evidence available to them. Civilians who serve as voluntary shields in support of what they reasonably believe is a just cause are not morally blameworthy even if they intend to shield and are not coerced. Indeed, it is remarkable that defenceless civilians would make themselves vulnerable to death and dismemberment for the sake of what they believe to be a just cause. Certainly, such civilians are not so morally blameworthy that by shielding military targets they forfeit their basic rights.

4. Conclusion

In this chapter, I have defended three claims. First, it is morally impermissible for combatants fighting for a just cause to use civilians supporting an unjust war effort as involuntary human shields. Second, civilians who are forced to serve as involuntary shields by combatants fighting for an unjust cause retain their basic rights. These civilians are not morally liable to intentional harm, and the proportionality of collaterally harming them is not affected by the wrongful conduct of the unjust combatants. Finally, civilians who voluntarily serve as human shields for unjust combatants compromise but do not lose their basic rights. Such voluntary shields are not morally liable to collateral harm, although it may be proportionate to inflict collateral harm on voluntary shields in pursuit of a given military advantage that it would not be proportionate to inflict on involuntary shields or passersby in pursuit of a comparable military advantage.

Acknowledgments

Special thanks to Helen Frowe, Lisa Hecht, Seth Lazar, and Victor Tadros for their comments and suggestions. Many thanks also to participants in the Lethal Agency

Workshop at the Stockholm Centre for the Ethics of War and Peace, the International Law Workshop at William & Mary Law School, and the faculty workshop at Cardozo Law School.

Notes

1. Protocol Additional to the Geneva Conventions of 12 August 1949, and Relating to the Protection of Victims of International Armed Conflicts, art. 51(7), 8 June 1977, 1125 U.N.T.S. 3 (entered into force 7 December 1978); Jean-Marie Henckaerts and Louise Doswald-Beck, *Customary International Humanitarian Law* (Cambridge University Press, 2005), 339–340; Rome Statute of the International Criminal Court, art. 8(2)(b)(xxiii), 17 July 1998, U.N. Doc. A/CONF.183/9.
2. Cécile Fabre, *Cosmopolitan War* (Oxford University Press, 2012), 256–267.
3. Most dramatically, Protocol I prohibits the use of human shields in Article 51(7) and then, in the very next provision, states that '[a]ny violation of these prohibitions shall not release the Parties to the conflict from their legal obligations with respect to the civilian population'. Protocol I, art. 51(8). Strikingly, the U.S. Department of Defense recently took the position that harm to human shields 'would be understood not to prohibit attacks under the proportionality rule'. U.S. Department of Defense, *Law of War Manual* (2015), 5.12.3. For a response, see Adil Ahmad Haque, 'Off Target: Selection, Precaution, and Proportionality in the DoD Manual', *International Law Studies* 92 (2016), 31.
4. See, e.g., Thomas Hurka, 'Proportionality in the Morality of War', *Philosophy & Public Affairs* 33 (2005), 47–50; Yoram Dinstein, *The Conduct of Hostilities under the Law of International Conflict* (Cambridge University Press, 2nd ed. 2010), 131.
5. Note that the defending force in a given tactical encounter may have initiated the broader conflict, launched recent attacks, or planned future attacks.
6. Fabre, 77. In her discussion of human shields, Fabre writes that many supportive civilians are morally liable to nonlethal harm or to *the risk* of being unintentionally killed (Fabre, 265). This might seem like a weaker claim. However, Fabre supports the latter claim solely by reference to her earlier, stronger claim. Indeed, supportive civilians cannot be liable to the risk of unintentional killing unless they are liable to unintentional killing. Risks of *unjust harm* (harm to which we are not liable) are, necessarily, *unjust risks* (risks to which we are not liable) the imposition of which can only be justified as a lesser evil. Note finally that liability to nonlethal harm does not entail liability to a risk of lethal harm, just as liability to the loss of one arm does not entail liability to a 50 per cent chance of losing both arms. I will therefore address Fabre's stronger, foundational claim.
7. Fabre, 266.
8. Fabre, 267.
9. It appears that Jeff McMahan introduced the notion that someone could be liable to unintentional killing but not to intentional killing. Jeff McMahan, *Killing in War* (Oxford University Press, 2009), 219–221. McMahan's arguments at most show that it is comparatively easier to justify collaterally harming supportive civilians than to justify collaterally harming innocent civilians.
10. See Adil Ahmad Haque, 'Torture, Terror, and the Inversion of Moral Principle', *New Criminal Law Review* 10 (2007), 636–639. The scope of the second-order reason is not

unlimited. The good consequences of harming innocent people can justify harming them if those good consequences exceed some high threshold. Our moral inviolability is not absolute.

11. My view is a 'downstream theory' or is at least 'downstreamish'. See F. M. Kamm, *Intricate Ethics* (Oxford University Press, 2006), 138.
12. McMahan, 228–229. See also Helen Frowe, *Defensive Killing* (Oxford University Press, 2014).
13. See Warren Quinn, 'Actions, Intentions, and Consequences: The Doctrine of Double Effect', *Philosophy & Public Affairs* 18 (1989), 334. For example, Quinn considers a terror bomber who narrowly intends to create a large explosion over a civilian area that will convince the adversary's political leaders that the civilians below have been killed. This terror bomber does not strictly intend the deaths of the civilians but instead 'strictly intends to involve them in something (to make his bombs explode over them) in order to further his purpose precisely by way of their being involved' (Idem at 343 n. 16). Quinn concludes that this terror bomber commits a moral wrong much closer to intentionally killing civilians than to unintentionally killing civilians.
14. Fabre also argues that combatants pursuing a just cause can fairly conscript their own civilians to serve as human shields, just as they can fairly conscript civilians to serve as combatants (Fabre, 260–265). Because civilians forced to serve as human shields are never, in fact, selected through a fair procedure, I will not discuss this argument further.
15. See, e.g., McMahan, 183.
16. Of course, many conscripts do not harm innocent people in any of these ways or even enable other combatants to do so. The permissibility of killing such conscripts rests on other considerations.
17. For similar reasons, Helen Frowe argues that involuntary shields should be considered innocent threats rather than innocent bystanders. See Frowe, *Defensive Killing*.
18. For more on the costs we must bear to avoid contributing in different ways to unjust threats, see Frowe, *Defensive Killing*. On Frowe's view, individuals need not bear lethal costs in order to avoid obstructing the defensive options of others.
19. See, e.g., Hurka, 47–50; Michael Walzer, 'Responsibility and Proportionality in State and Nonstate Wars', *Parameters* (Spring 2009), 40–52.
20. I adapt these cases from Seth Lazar, 'On Human Shields', *Boston Review* (Aug. 5, 2014), http://www.bostonreview.net/world/seth-lazar-human-shields.
21. For more on prioritarianism, see Derek Parfit, 'Equality and Priority', *Ratio* 10 (1997), 202–221.
22. See, e.g., Michael Walzer, 'Can the Good Guys Win?', *European Journal of International Law* 24 (2013), 438; Noam Zohar, 'Risking and Protecting Lives: Soldiers and Opposing Civilians', in *How We Fight: Ethics in War* edited by Helen Frowe and Gerald Lang (Oxford University Press, 2014), 168.
23. On the distinction between acting in order to bring about an outcome and acting on the condition that an outcome will occur, see Kamm, 101–102.
24. This objection resembles the 'closeness' objection to the traditional doctrine of double effect.
25. Cf Michael N. Schmitt, 'Human Shields in International Humanitarian Law', *Israel Yearbook on Human Rights* 38 (2008), 17, 49 ('An extreme view urges that involuntary shields should be ignored . . . because an enemy violating the law should not be allowed to benefit from its malfeasance').

26. For more on epistemic permissibility in war, see Adil Ahmad Haque, 'Killing in the Fog of War', *Southern California Law Review* 86 (2012), 63; and Seth Lazar, 'In Dubious Battle' (forthcoming).
27. See, e.g., David Rodin, *War and Self-Defense* (Oxford University Press, 2002), 82. Fabre draws a similar distinction, between 'shields-as-targets' and 'shields-as-deterrents' (Fabre, 258). Cf. International Committee of the Red Cross, *Interpretive Guidance on the Notion of Direct Participation in Hostilities under International Humanitarian Law* (ICRC, 2009) (prepared by Nils Melzer), 56–57; Ian Henderson, *The Contemporary Law of Targeting* (Brill, 2009), 217–218.
28. Idem.
29. See, e.g., Helen Frowe, 'Threats, Bystanders and Obstructors', *Proceedings of the Aristotelian Society* 108 (2008), 365. Cf. Schmitt, 41–43.
30. Interestingly, it is also worse for combatants pursuing an unjust cause to kill civilian passersby than to kill voluntary shields. To the extent that combatants kill in furtherance of an unjust cause, it is impermissible for them to kill anyone. But some impermissible killings are worse than others. See Seth Lazar, *Sparing Civilians* (Oxford University Press, 2015).
31. Compare Hurka, 47 ('[B]y placing themselves near [military targets, voluntary] shields arguably take upon themselves some responsibility for their deaths and remove it from us, so their deaths count less against our attack's proportionality'). Obviously, counting less is better than not counting at all.
32. I started thinking along these lines after reading Victor Tadros, *The Ends of Harm* (Oxford University Press, 2011). Although I disagree with Tadros on many points, I share his general position that liability to suffer harm is related to the duty to accept harm in important ways.
33. Of course, moral rights and moral constraints can be overridden, such that it may be permissible to harm one person to prevent greater harm to others even if the one person has no moral duty to accept that harm (i.e., a moral prerogative not to accept that harm).

CHAPTER 20

DIMENSIONS OF INTENTIONS

Ways of Killing in War

VICTOR TADROS

THE idea that there is an important difference between intentional killing and killing as a side effect has played a significant role in just war theory. Few rule out intentional killing altogether. Killing a culpable attacker who poses a lethal threat in self-defence is clearly permissible even if the killing is intentional.[1] Why this is so is a matter of controversy. Perhaps killing an attacker in self-defence is justified because such a person is liable to be killed to avert the threat she is responsible for posing,[2] or because doing so prevents her from violating one's rights,[3] or even perhaps because she deserves to be killed.[4]

More controversially, it might be argued that some noncombatants are liable to be killed and hence may be targeted. A now familiar, but contested, question concerns whether noncombatants are liable to be killed in virtue of their causal and moral responsibility for the threats that combatants unjustly pose. They may be causally and morally responsible in virtue of providing moral support, munitions, food, health care, and finances to combatants.[5] Even more controversially, it might be argued that noncombatants are liable to be harmed to avert the threats that unjust combatants pose, even if they are not causally or morally responsible for the posing of these threats—they may be vicariously liable to be killed, for example.[6] Even if there are circumstances in which intentionally killing noncombatants is permitted, though, it is normally wrong to target noncombatants lethally.

Of course, one reason why intentionally killing noncombatants is typically wrong is that killing them is typically useless. Killing a combatant may be useful in averting the threat that she poses. Killing noncombatants does not normally serve any legitimate purpose.[7] But many people regard intentional killing of noncombatants as wrong even if doing so is useful in securing victory in a war. Consider:

Terror Bomber: A pilot on the just side of a war bombs a school killing 500 children. The only way in which this will contribute to the war is by terrorising those on the

> unjust side. The war effort on the unjust side will be undermined, and 10000 innocent lives will be saved.

Saving 10,000 lives is a legitimate aim for the pilot. Nevertheless, many think it wrong for the pilot to kill the 500 in virtue of the pilot's intentions.

This is not to say that it is always wrong to kill noncombatants. Killing noncombatants is typically regarded as permissible if (1) they are killed as a side effect of an action done in service of a just cause, and (2) killing them is proportionate given the importance of the goal pursued. Consider:

> *Tactical Bomber*: A pilot on the just side of a war bombs a munitions factory. Doing so is necessary to deprive the unjust side of weapons, which will save 10000 innocent lives. However, the munitions factory is next to a school, and the blast will kill 500 children as a side effect.

Most people believe that bombing the plant is permissible if it is done in order to save the 10,000. Killing 500 is proportionate to the saving of 10,000, and the 500 are not intentionally killed.

This familiar approach to the significance of intentions is highly contested. No single essay can do justice to the complex range of issues involved in evaluating the significance of intentions. A wide range of arguments for and against intentions having any significance to permissibility is to be found in the literature, but here I will be concerned with only a smaller group of arguments. And if intentions are relevant to permissibility, then there is a great deal more to be said about why they are relevant and the implications of their relevance. I aim to defend the significance of intentions to permissibility against critics and to explore some different views about their relevance. I do so by exploring a range of contexts in just war theory, in which views about the significance of intentions make a difference to our judgments about the permissibility of military action.

The structure of this chapter is as follows. The next section situates the discussion by introducing the doctrine of double effect (DDE). I clarify two components of the DDE and distinguish different versions of it by exploring two disputes. I indicate my preferred views without defending them here. The next three sections compare the DDE with some competitor explanations of the intuitive difference between terror bombing and tactical bombing. Section 2 shows that neither the combatant/noncombatant, nor the importance of military advantage, can adequately explain the difference. Section 3 explores a version of the principle prohibiting treating a person as a means that does not rely on intentions. It shows that the DDE is superior to this version and addresses some arguments that have been mounted against the DDE. Section 4 is concerned with the question of whether the prohibition on opportunistic harming can do all of the work that the DDE does without relying on the significance of intentions. It shows that, even if opportunism is important, there is plenty of remaining work for the DDE to do. Overall, I offer a partial defence of the DDE.

1. Introduction to the Doctrine of Double Effect

There is no single agreed-upon formulation of the DDE. On all formulations, it has two components: a more stringent prohibition on intentional harming and a less stringent prohibition on harming as a side effect. There is disagreement about both components. I briefly focus on the second component first, because it is not my main focus, before considering different versions of the first component.

1.1. Harming as a Side Effect

The prohibition on killing as a side effect is often thought more stringent than the prohibition on letting die. It may be wrong, for this reason, to kill ten as a side effect of an action that saves eleven. The better outcome—the net saving of a life—is insufficient to justify killing ten. The view that there is a more stringent prohibition on harming than failing to prevent harm is known as the doctrine of doing and allowing (DDA).

The DDA is commonly defended on roughly the following basis: if one kills, then one is more deeply responsible for the deaths that one causes than the deaths one lets occur; the more deeply we are responsible for a death that we could have averted, the more powerful our justification for this death needs to be; hence, the prohibition on killing is more stringent than the prohibition on letting die.

Those who endorse the DDA may also think that there are considerations other than the relationship between the magnitude of the good done and the harm done that are important in determining whether it is permissible to harm others. For example, some believe that there is a difference between (1) diverting a threat away from some people towards others and (2) saving some people from a threat by creating a new threat to others. To illustrate this idea, those who think it permissible to divert a trolley away from five towards one may think that it is wrong to create a medicine that will save five from being killed by a disease that they have contracted if doing so releases toxins into the atmosphere that will kill one as a side effect.[8]

Like the DDA itself, responsibility may explain this view: a person who has created a threat is responsible for the existence of the threat; the person who diverts a threat is not responsible for its existence: responsibility for a threat transfers to responsibility for the deaths that will be caused if it is realized; therefore there is a more stringent prohibition on creating than on diverting threats.

The right view about the DDA is important for just war theory. If we are more deeply responsible for threats that we have created than for threats that we have diverted, some familiar actions during war are easier to justify than others. For example, it may be easier to justify diverting an enemy attack from a more populated city to a less populated city than it is to kill noncombatants as a side effect of one's own fighting.

I think that the difference between creating and diverting threats is not terribly important. The person diverting the threat has created the threat in the important sense: she has caused the circumstances in which a person who was safe is now threatened. It is difficult to see why it matters very much whether the object that gives rise to a threat that a person brings about was already threatening others. If we have intuitions about a moral difference between creating and diverting, we should reject those intuitions.

Nevertheless, there may be other differences between different kinds of side-effect harms; the DDA, as stated, may be too simple to capture the moral reality. For ease of exposition, I will work on the basis of a simplified version of the DDA whilst acknowledging that this may be some distance from the truth.

1.2. Variations on the Significance of Intentions

A very ambitious version of the DDE holds that intentionally harming the innocent is always wrong.[9] A more modest view is more plausible: certain intentions render harming others more difficult to justify. We can see that this view is more plausible in virtue of the fact that small-scale intentional harming is surely permitted to secure very large-scale goals. Intentionally targeting some noncombatants is permitted to prevent Nazi world domination, for example. Those who endorse this more modest view are called 'threshold deontologists'.[10] Almost all deontologists endorse thresholds, though they disagree about how thresholds are explained.[11]

Here are two further disagreements. First, some believe that the significance of intentions is limited to using. Others believe that a person's intentions can render her act wrong even if the person who is affected by her intentions is not used. This disagreement reflects a deeper disagreement about the source of the significance of intentions.

A standard argument for the first view is that the significance of intentions is derived from the status of those who will intentionally be harmed. Roughly, because individuals have rights to pursue their own ends, intentionally harming them for the sake of another person's ends, even her good ends, is prohibited. But this idea, it might be argued, only implicates using and not other intentional harming, or it implicates using much more powerfully than other forms of intentional harming.[12]

The second view extends claims about responsibility to intentions. Suppose, as I suggested earlier, that the stringency on the prohibition on harming another person depends on the extent of the person's responsibility for the harm that will be caused. The extent of a person's responsibility for harm caused may depend on whether it is caused intentionally. This has at least some plausibility in virtue of the fact that intentional action is at the heart of responsible agency.[13]

We need not decide between these views here. Intentions may be significant for more than one reason. The prohibition on using is, I think, more stringent than the prohibition on other forms of intentional harming. Yet intentions may be relevant to permissibility even when the person is not used.[14]

A second dispute: some believe that the relevant intentions are intentions to harm people or to do things that are close to harm; others believe that what matters is not whether harm itself, or something close to harm, is intended but rather whether the person intends to affect others in a way that causes them to be harmed.[15]

To illustrate this disagreement, consider:

> *Simulated Terror*: In the course of a just war, a pilot launches a gas attack that renders 500 noncombatants unconscious to induce the belief in combatants on the unjust side that the civilians are dead. Rendering them unconscious will not cause them significant harm in itself. The belief that these noncombatants are dead will impair the motivation of the unjust combatants to fight and hence advance the just cause, saving 10000 lives. However, as the noncombatants have been rendered unconscious they will not be able to defend themselves against marauding wolves, resulting in the deaths of all 500.

Because the execution of the pilot's plan does not depend on the deaths of the noncombatants, he can harm them without intending them to be harmed. He need not even intend to do something that is close to harm. He need only intend to render the civilians unconscious. Rendering them unconscious causes them to be harmed. But whether they are harmed is neither here nor there for the pilot's plan.

The view that only intentions to harm or to do something close to harm are relevant to permissibility implies that the pilot acts permissibly. The view that it is wrong to use others, in contrast, might be coupled with the view that it does not matter whether the using is harmful or merely causes harm. I think that the latter view is preferable to the former. I doubt that it is very significant whether harm or something close to harm is intended if there is an intention to affect a person in a way that will cause him to be harmed.[16]

2. Military Advantage and the Combatant/Noncombatant Distinction

Many philosophers reject the DDE on the grounds that bad intentions are relevant only to whether a person or her acts are blameworthy and not to permissibility.[17] A person's intentions may derivatively affect permissibility—for example, by altering the predictable consequences of one's acts. But intentions do not nonderivatively render acts wrong. If an action causes harm, but the harm is outweighed by some benefit, the action is permissible. If the person performs the action for bad reasons—such as to cause the harm—the person may be blamed, and perhaps her action is also blameworthy, but she has not acted wrongly.

One challenge for such views is to explain cases which, intuitively, come apart with respect to permissibility and that might be explained by referring to intentions—such as in the *Terror Bomber* and *Tactical Bomber* scenarios. Of course, if we cannot find a morally powerful explanation for our intuitions, we should reject them. We should at least be inclined, though, to explain these intuitions. Few who reject the significance of intentions are willing to endorse the counterintuitive conclusion that these cases are morally on a par (either that both are permissible or both are wrong).

This section is concerned with two explanations offered by T. M. Scanlon. Here is the first:

> Those who believe that there is an important difference between tactical bombing and terror bombing need to defend some version of the combatant/noncombatant distinction. But they need not be saddled with the additional burden of defending the relevance of intent, or the doctrine of double effect.[18]

This explanation is opaque. Its problems emerge when it is clarified. There is more than one way to understand the combatant/noncombatant distinction. On one view, this is a distinction about who may be harmed during war. However, understood in this way, it will not, on its own, explain the contrast between *Terror Bomber* and *Tactical Bomber*. Noncombatants are harmed to the same degree in both cases.

Another way of understanding the combatant/noncombatant distinction is that it is a distinction about who may be targeted during a war: it is permissible to target combatants but not noncombatants. This version does not prohibit harming noncombatants as a side effect, as in tactical bombing. But this way of understanding the distinction relies on the significance of intentions to permissibility because it prohibits targeting noncombatants whilst permitting harming them as a side effect. Targeting a person cannot be explained without referring to the intentions of the person doing the targeting.

Scanlon's alternative explanation is that killing in war is justified only if secures a military advantage.[19] This fares no better. It faces two problems. First, terror bombing is often done to secure a military advantage. Demoralizing unjust combatants, for example, is a military advantage—it reduces the military capacities of the unjust side—and is a standard military goal. After all, killing combatants, destroying their weapons capabilities, and so on, are often done in part to demoralize those on the unjust side. Yet killing noncombatants to terrorize combatants seems wrong. The aim of demoralizing the enemy, then, is a legitimate military goal; yet we reject some ways of pursuing that goal.

Second, the idea that military advantage has fundamental moral significance is much more difficult to believe than the idea that intentions have fundamental moral significance. The reason why securing a military advantage is the main aim of warfare is that securing a military advantage is typically the best way to avert unjust threats. But terror bombing also averts unjust threats—the whole point of the pair of examples is that, in both cases, unjust threats are averted. How could it be fundamentally significant whether securing a military advantage averts unjust threats or if it is done in some other way? Scanlon avoids the difficult burden of justifying the DDE at the cost of saddling himself with the need to defend something much more difficult to defend—the moral significance of military advantage itself.[20]

Overall, Scanlon's explanations are too far from the DDE to plausibly explain the intuitive contrast between the cases.

3. Means Without Intentions

Others who reject the DDE endorse one of its closer relatives. For example, whilst she denies that intentions are relevant to permissibility, Frances Kamm believes (roughly) that there is an important distinction between cases where some good is brought about only in virtue of something inherently evil being its cause and cases where the good is or could have been brought about without the inherently evil thing being its cause. An inherently evil thing might be harm itself or might be causal involvement that leads to harm—hence, Kamm rejects the significance of closeness considered earlier. She calls this the doctrine of productive purity (DPP). A good is productively pure if it is not caused, or at least need not be caused, by evil.[21]

The DPP, like some versions of the DDE, might be understood as a version of the *means principle*: the principle that a greater good is normally insufficient to justify harming a person if that person is the means by which the greater good is produced. One version of the DDE holds that harming a person in this way is wrong because the person harmed is harmfully used as a means to the greater good. The DPP holds that it is wrong because of the causal relationship between the harmful act and the good. Thus, the DPP, like the DDE, prohibits the bombing of the school in the terror bomber example; in contrast with the *Tactical Bomber* example, the event that affects the children in a way that harms them is the means by which the good comes about. But the DPP explains this verdict without appealing to the pilot's intentions.

I consider two arguments that might support the DPP over the DDE. The first claims that the DDE cannot explain cases in which, intuitively, a person does the right thing for the wrong reasons. If the person acts for the wrong reason, the right thing becomes the wrong thing on the DDE. Second, the version of the DDE that gives primacy to the significance of using people as a means cannot explain the wrongness of killing that is useful but which is not done in virtue of it being useful. I find both arguments wanting.

3.1. The Exclusionary DDE

The DDE, at least as it is most commonly defended, implies that it is wrong to harm a person intentionally even if harming that person in the same way would have been permissible as a side effect of an action which brings about the greater good. The DPP does not have this implication. To illustrate, consider:

> *Bad Bomber*: A pilot in a just war bombs a munitions factory next to a school. Bombing the factory saves 10000 lives and is the only way to save these lives. 500 children in a school near the munitions factory will be killed as a result of the bombing. However, the pilot does not care about the 10000. He bombs the factory because he hates the children and wants to see them die.

Kamm believes that the pilot's bad intentions cannot render his act wrong. If it is permissible to bomb the factory with the intention only to save the 10,000 and not to kill the children, then it is also permissible to bomb the factory with the same result but without the intention to save the 10,000 and with the intention to kill the children.

Many people who reject the significance of intentions to permissibility are moved by cases like *Bad Bomber*—they think that when other things are equal, merely altering a person's intentions makes no intuitive difference to permissibility. Different responses are available to friends of the DDE. Some aim to show that the DDE does not imply that the pilot acts wrongly in *Bad Bomber*;[22] others agree that the DDE implies this, but they accept the verdict.[23] Both strategies are forceful. I offer a new argument in favour of the view that the relevance of intentions to permissibility in cases like *Terror Bomber* does not imply that the pilot acts wrongly in *Bad Bomber*. Yet, I suggest, we have independent reasons to believe that the pilot acts wrongly in *Bad Bomber*.

In *Bad Bomber*, the 500 children are harmed as a means. Furthermore, they are harmed as a means to achieve something bad—the satisfaction of the pilot at the suffering of the children. If it is wrong to harm the children as a means to a greater good, as in *Terror Bomber*, it is even more gravely wrong to harm them as a means to the bad. Some might conclude that if the DDE prohibits killing in *Terror Bomber*, it necessarily prohibits killing in *Bad Bomber*.

Friends of the DDE need not accept this argument. It is consistent to claim both: (1) the saving of the 10,000 cannot justify the killing of the children in *Terror Bomber* in virtue of the fact that the children will be used as a means to save the 10,000, and (2) the fact that 10,000 will be saved in *Bad Bomber* renders it permissible for the pilot to kill the 500 even though the 500 will be used as a means to a bad end. These verdicts are consistent because the children will not be used as a means to save the 10,000 in *Bad Bomber*. What matters, it might be argued, is not whether a person is used as a means to a bad end, but rather whether they are used as a means to a good end.

This view might seem puzzling: surely, as I have just noted, it is worse to be used as a means to a bad end than a good end. However, this objection misunderstands the central way that intentions can be relevant to permissibility: it excludes certain considerations that would otherwise be sufficient to justify an action. Some good that would normally be morally salient in justifying an act is not morally salient if the person performing the act intends something evil—such as the harmful using of a person—as a means to produce the good. For example, in *Terror Bomber*, the good of the 10,000 being saved is excluded as a consideration in favour of the pilot's act in virtue of the fact that something evil is intended as a means of bringing the good about. Call this *the exclusionary DDE*.

A powerful rationale can be offered for the exclusionary DDE. The reason that certain goods cannot play the justificatory role that they usually play in cases where the person is used as a means is that doing so amounts to imposing the good on the person as an end. If a good is insufficiently weighty to ground a duty on a person to pursue an end at a certain cost, it is also normally insufficiently weighty to permit others to force that person to promote that good at the relevant cost. And if it is wrong to force a person to promote a good, it is also normally wrong to use a person to promote that good.

Terror Bomber illustrates this argument. The 500 are not required to sacrifice their lives to save the 10,000. They are free to pursue other ends. It is therefore wrong for others to force the 500 to sacrifice their lives for the 10,000. Because it is wrong to force the 500 to do this, it is also wrong to use them in service of this end. Doing so is tantamount to imposing the end of the saving of the 10,000 on the 500 at the cost of their lives. Therefore, the saving of the 10,000 cannot be used to justify the killing of the 500.

The exclusionary DDE does not imply that the pilot's bad intentions render his act wrong in *Bad Bomber*. This is because the saving of 10,000 is sufficiently important to justify the killing of 500, and the bomber does not intend harmfully to use the children as a means to save the 10,000. Whilst the pilot in *Bad Bomber* has bad intentions, these intentions may not exclude the moral significance of the saving of the 10,000. The pilot does not intend the killing of the 500 as a means to save the 10,000, so the end of saving the 10,000 is not imposed on the 500. Hence, it might be argued, the moral significance of their being saved remains. Those who find it implausible that the pilot acts wrongly in *Bad Bomber* thus need not reject the DDE: they can accept the exclusionary DDE.

The exclusionary DDE is superior to the DPP. This is because it is generally easier to motivate the idea that there is an especially strong constraint on using a person as a means than it is to motivate the idea that the causal relationship between the evil and the good is inherently morally significant.[24] Although the exclusionary DDE and the DPP have similar implications, we should prefer the former in virtue of its explanatory power.

Now consider an objection to the exclusionary DDE. It involves evaluating:

> *Psycho Bomber*: As in *Terror Bomber*, except the pilot does not care about saving the lives of the 10000. He bombs the school only in order to kill the children.

The pilot does not kill the children as a means to the greater good. Clearly, if the pilot acts wrongly in *Terror Bomber*, he also acts wrongly in *Psycho Bomber*. But in *Psycho Bomber*, as in *Bad Bomber*, (1) the pilot acts only in order to kill the children, (2) he does not intend to kill the children as a means to save the 10,000, and (3) the 10,000 are in fact saved by his action. Does the exclusionary DDE implausibly imply that the pilot acts permissibly in *Psycho Bomber*? If it does, we should reject the exclusionary DDE.

However, it is not difficult to see how to respond to this objection. I suggested that the reason that the saving of the 10,000 could not justify the killing of the 500 in *Terror Bomber* is that the moral significance of the fact that 10,000 will be saved is ruled out in virtue of the fact that the 500 will be used as a means to save the 10,000. We should now notice not only that the 10,000 are saved in *Terror Bomber* only by using the 500 as a means, but also that a person *can* execute an intention to save the 10,000 only by executing an intention to use the 500 as a means. Defenders of the DDE might claim that the moral salience of a good to permissibility depends on the possibility that this good could be used to justify the action. And it could be used to justify an action only if a well-motivated person might be motivated by it. A well-motivated person would only kill 500 in order to save an even greater number. A person who executes an intention to save the 10,000 necessarily executes an intention to use the 500 as a means and hence executes an impermissible intention. Hence, the saving of the 10,000 cannot motivate a well-motivated person. Hence, the pilot acts wrongly both in *Terror Bomber* and in *Psycho Bomber*.

The proper conclusion to draw about *Terror Bomber*, then, is that the best that can be said for the permissibility of killing the children is that it will lead to the greater good. If the means principle disallows this, other bad reasons that might be given for harming the children cannot render the action permissible.

This also deflates another attack that has been mounted against the DDE. It is sometimes claimed that the DDE is false either because (1) people cannot act for the right reasons or (2) because they cannot be expected to act for the right reasons. Return to *Bad Bomber*. One argument that Scanlon offers against the significance of intentions to permissibility is that the pilot cannot choose to form the intention to save the 10,000. He can choose whether or not to bomb the munitions factory. If he chooses to do this, he cannot choose the reasons for which he does it. If this is so, he must be permitted to intentionally kill the children: the only alternative is that the 10,000 are not saved, and this is not the desired result.[25]

There are a number of ways to meet this concern. One way attacks the importance of the pilot having a choice about whether to act in order to save the 10,000.[26] It might be doubted that having such a choice is required to render acting in order to kill the children wrong. A second attacks the idea that there is a morally salient sense of choice in which the pilot lacks a choice to kill the children only in order to save the 10,000.[27] In the morally salient sense in which a person can choose how to act, a person can choose the reasons for which she acts.

A third way to meet the concern evades Scanlon's challenge by accepting that it is permissible for the pilot to kill the children without intending to save the 10,000. The aim is then to show that the DDE does not imply that the pilot in *Bad Bomber* acts wrongly. This verdict is open to defenders of the version of the DDE that I have been considering so far. Overall, the exclusionary DDE is capable of responding to many attacks that have been mounted against the DDE.

3.2. The Salience of Bad Intentions

The exclusionary DDE leaves it open whether two acts that harm some and benefit others—and that are identical with respect to their causal structure—can differ with respect to permissibility in virtue of the intentions of the person performing the act. The exclusionary DDE holds that the pilot in *Terror Bomber* acts wrongly *even if* he acts in order to save the 10,000 because the moral salience of the fact that 10,000 are saved is vitiated or diminished in virtue of the fact that 500 must be used as a means to execute an intention of saving the 10,000. It does not imply that the pilot in *Bad Bomber* acts wrongly if he acts in order to kill the children.

How should friends of the exclusionary DDE respond to *Bad Bomber*, though, where the moral salience of the saving of the 10,000 is not excluded? Could the pilot's bad intentions and lack of good intentions nevertheless render his act wrong? If the pilot's action in *Bad Bomber* is wrong, then it is most plausibly wrong in virtue of the fact that the children are wronged. When a person is wronged, we can usually mount objections on their behalf. It might be argued, though, that the 500 have no objection to being killed with bad intentions rather than good intentions; they have no strong reason to care about the intentions of the person killing them. Their deaths matter to them, not the intentions with which their deaths are brought about. Hence, killing them with bad intentions rather than good intentions does not wrong them.

The children in *Bad Bomber* are no worse off than they would be were the bomber to have good intentions. But the wrongness or otherwise of an act does not depend only on whether that act renders the person worse off than he would be were some permissible act to be performed. There are many actions that violate people's rights even though they render the person no worse off than he would have been had the action not been performed: paternalistic interference is an obvious example.

Furthermore, a person's rights may be violated even if that person is rendered no worse off than he would have been had some alternative permissible action been performed. For example, suppose that the pilot had two options: either he could kill the children and save the 10,000 or just kill the children. If the pilot chooses the latter option, he clearly violates the rights of the children. But this action renders them no worse off than a permissible action (the action of killing the children to save the 10,000).

Furthermore, intentions clearly sometimes make a difference to permissibility, other things equal. It is difficult to see the difference between such cases and cases like *Bad Bomber*. Hence, we have some reason to believe that the pilot acts wrongly in *Bad Bomber*.

Consider:

> *Pre-emptive Killer*. Killer 1 kills Victim. Had he not succeeded, Killer 2 would have killed Victim. Killer 2 employs an especially cruel method of killing and would have been certain to succeed.

Killer 1 clearly acts wrongly if he does not act in order to preempt Killer 2, but only for the fun of killing. If Killer 1 kills for fun, Killer 1 acts wrongly. Someone has wrongly murdered Victim. That person is not Killer 2, so it is Killer 1. But Victim has a powerful interest in being killed by Killer 1, given that this is the only way to prevent him being killed more cruelly by Killer 2. For this reason, if Killer 1 acts in order to preempt the cruel killing by Killer 2, Killer 1 acts permissibly.

Why might Victim object to being killed by Killer 1 if Killer 1 acts with bad intentions, given that he is benefited overall by his actions? After all, he surely prefers this to being killed by Killer 2, even if Killer 1 acts with bad intentions. One answer is that although Victim prefers to be killed by Killer 1 with bad intentions to being killed by Killer 2, he also prefers to be killed by Killer 1 with good intentions than to be killed by Killer 1 with bad intentions.

Another way to see this: why should Killer 1 be able to exploit the fact that Victim is doomed to die to fulfil his own murderous desires? Why should Victim not have a right to demand that Killer 1 not do this? Perhaps it might be argued that Victim has an interest in this demand not being made of Killer 1 because then he would be less likely to save Victim from an even crueller death. In response, the scope of moral permissions does not depend on how they will affect the badly motivated. Whilst we have good reason to alter laws to respond to the existence of the corrupt, moral principles are immune from such alterations. They respond to what the person can do, not what he or she will do.[28]

It is not obvious why our analysis of *Bad Bomber* should be any different from our analysis of *Preemptive Killer*. Hence, we have good reason to think that bad intentions render the pilot's action wrong in *Bad Bomber*. The fact that we would prefer the pilot to act on bad intentions than not to act does not render it permissible for him to act on bad intentions. He could act on good intentions. If he decides to kill the 500, he ought to do so to save the 10,000 and not to fulfil his sadistic desires.

The role of intentions, then, is not restricted to the role that the exclusionary DDE gives them. A person who lacks good intentions and acts for bad intentions can act wrongly where a person with good intentions and lacking bad intentions acts permissibly.[29]

4. Opportunism

Here is another way of explaining the contrast between *Terror Bomber* and *Tactical Bomber* that some have found superior to the DDE. Consider two different explanations for why it is especially wrong to kill nonliable people as a means to terrorize others to end a war. One explanation draws on the idea that there is a stringent prohibition on incorporating a person into one's plan to secure a goal if that person does not consent to being used in that way. This explanation implies that intentions are relevant to permissibility, and hence a version of the DDE.

A second explanation draws on the idea that it is especially wrong to harm a person if that person is harmed in the course of exploiting an opportunity that exists only because of this person's presence. The second explanation does not depend on intentions. Some claim that the second explanation is superior to the first, and hence that the first has either a less important role, or no role, in determining what it is permissible to do.[30]

Warren Quinn, whose work has been heavily influential in the philosophy of self-defence and just war theory, referred to both ideas in his account of the DDE. But he also tended to run them together.[31] This tendency has been exacerbated by the use of the label 'opportunistic agency' to refer to the use of a person as a means. It is better to restrict the term 'opportunistic agency' to refer to cases in which a person is harmed in the course of exploiting an opportunity that exists in virtue of that person's presence. This is to be contrasted with using a person, or her body, as part of one's plan to secure an end, which we can label 'manipulative agency'.[32]

Standard cases of self-defence involve intentional harming, but they are neither opportunistic nor manipulative. This helps to explain why harming a person who poses a lethal threat in self-defence is typically permitted, even if the person who is killed has little or no culpability for the threat he poses. Harming the person is not opportunistic, for were this person not to be present, the person defending herself would be better off. Hence, in harming this person, a new opportunity to avert a threat is not exploited. Nor is harming the person manipulative—neither the attacker herself nor her body is used as a means to avert a threat. Harming her is the means by which the threat is averted, but she is not used as a means.

Terror bombing is both opportunistic and manipulative. However, killing noncombatants in war is sometimes manipulative even though it is not opportunistic and vice versa. To consider whether opportunism, manipulation, or both is morally significant, we should consider cases which have one feature but not the other. I will not be able fully to examine the issues here, but I believe that both manipulation and opportunism are morally significant, but that manipulation is more morally significant than opportunism.

To begin, consider:

> *Kill the Supporters*: A engages in an unjust war on B. Some noncombatants support the war. Others are opposed to it. Were it not for the presence of the supporters, the war would not have gone ahead. If B kills sufficient supporters, other supporters will be terrorised and the war will end.

If B kills supporters, terrorizing others, B is no better off than she would have been had these supporters not existed. Thus, B has not benefited from the existence of these supporters. These supporters do not provide B with an opportunity that she would have lacked were these supporters not to have existed because the existence of these supporters causes the threat. However, these facts are insufficient to warrant terror bombing. This provides some support to the view that manipulation is morally significant independently of opportunism. The view that opportunism but not manipulation is morally significant renders terrorism too easy to justify.

Perhaps the idea of opportunistic agency can be adjusted to meet this concern. If B is permitted to terrorize these civilians, B is no better off than she would have been had these civilians not *ever* existed. But B is better off than she would have been had these civilians not existed *now*. But although this revised view yields the right judgment, it is ad hoc. Let me explain. Quinn's idea of opportunistic agency might be understood as drawing on the following idea, which is intuitively important. If opportunistic agency is permitted, then a person who uses another benefits from the existence of that other person. There is a sense in which this other person is then treated as a resource. But a person is not a resource. Her fundamental importance is 'for herself', not 'for others'. In contrast, if a person is harmed eliminatively, she is not treated as a resource. Rather the harming action prevents her existence from disadvantaging others. Because she must take steps to prevent herself from disadvantaging others, eliminative harming is not as stringently prohibited.

In other words, the distinction between eliminative and opportunistic agency depends on the distinction between a person's responsibility not to cause harm and a person's responsibility for preventing harm. If a person's responsibility not to cause harm is more stringent than a person's responsibility to prevent harm, we can also explain why eliminative harming is permissible but opportunistic harming is not.

This explanation of the contrast between opportunistic and eliminative agency does not apply to *Kill the Supporters*, however. If the supporters are killed, then they are prevented from disadvantaging others. They will thus not be treated as though they are simply a resource available for the benefit of others. Thus, we need other principles to explain why it is wrong to kill in *Kill the Supporters*. The fact that the supporters will be killed manipulatively provides the obvious explanation.

A further way to support the idea that manipulation is independently morally significant is to consider cases in which a new opportunity arises in virtue of a person's presence, but the person is not used as a means. Consider:

> *Kill the Builders*: Destroying a munitions factory will make a very significant difference to the advancement of country B's just war. The munitions factory is on the other side of a river. Fortunately, some of A's noncombatants, on the other side of the river, have built a bridge prior to the war. B's tanks can get to the munitions factory only by crossing the bridge. If the munitions factory is bombed, the noncombatants who built the bridge will be killed.

The existence of the civilians provides the bombers with an opportunity to bomb the munitions factory that they would otherwise have lacked. Hence, if they are killed, they are killed opportunistically. Yet even if it is more difficult to justify killing the noncombatants in *Kill the Builders* than it would be were they not to have built the bridge, the prohibition on killing these people is nowhere near as stringent as the prohibition on terror bombing. The plausible explanation is that, although the civilians provide an opportunity to bomb the factory that the bombers would otherwise have lacked, they are only harmed as a side effect and not as a means to destroy the factory.

Relying on the difference between eliminative and opportunistic agency thus seems insufficient to explain our reaction either to *Kill the Supporters* or *Kill the Builders*. Even if the distinction could be gerrymandered to meet these concerns, it is difficult to see how the basic idea of the distinction between eliminative and opportunistic agency can explain the judgments that we make about these cases. I conclude that although the distinction between opportunistic and eliminative agency is important, the DDE is also important, and more so.

5. Conclusion

The DDE has been very important in the history of just war theory. However, recently, a more complex range of moral ideas has emerged that have significance for just war theory. The simple claim that intending harm is worse than harming as a side effect is insufficient to capture the moral significance of intentions. Whilst there is a great deal of dispute between defenders and attackers of the DDE and between different defenders of the DDE, I think that the idea that intentions make a difference to the permissibility of acts of war has considerable force and in more than one way.

Acknowledgements

I am grateful to Helen Frowe and Seth Lazar for excellent comments on a previous draft.

Notes

1. There are those who argue that killing in self-defence is not intentional killing—the intention is to avert the threat posed to the person. Killing may not be the means by which this is done. See John Finnis 'Intentions in Tort Law', in *Philosophical Foundations of Tort Law*, edited by David G. Owen (Oxford: Oxford University Press, 1995), 246–247. This may typically be true, but it is not very plausible that it is always wrong to execute an intention to kill.
2. See Jeff McMahan, *Killing in War* (Oxford: Oxford University Press, 2009).
3. See Judith Jarvis Thomson, 'Self-Defense', *Philosophy and Public Affairs* 20 (1991), 283.
4. See John Gardner and François Tanguay-Renaud, 'Desert and Avoidability in Self-Defence', *Ethics* 122 (2011), 111.
5. For some of the extensive debate that has arisen, see McMahan, *Killing in War*; Cécile Fabre, 'Guns, Food, and Liability to Attack in War', *Ethics* 36 (2009), 120; Seth Lazar, 'The Responsibility Dilemma for Killing in War: A Review Essay', *Philosophy and Public Affairs* 38 (2010), 180; Helen Frowe 'Noncombatant Liability in War', in *How We Fight: Ethics in War*, edited by H. Frowe and G. Lang (Oxford: Oxford University Press, 2014).

6. See Victor Tadros, 'Orwell's Battle with Brittain: Vicarious Liability for Unjust Aggression', *Philosophy and Public Affairs* 42 (2014), 42–77, though there I defend only the liability of noncombatants to be harmed, not to be killed.
7. The importance of this fact in a pragmatic defence of a principle of noncombatant immunity should not be underestimated. See Frowe, 'Noncombatant Liability in War', but see S. Lazar. 'Necessity and Noncombatant Immunity', *Review of International Studies* 14 (2014), 53, for a survey of the empirical literature claiming that harming noncombatants is sometimes effective.
8. See, e.g., James A. Montmarquet, 'On Doing Good: The Right and the Wrong Way', *Journal of Philosophy* 79 (1982), 439; Phillipa Foot 'Killing and Letting Die', in *Moral Dilemmas* (Oxford: Oxford University Press, 2002); Judith Jarvis Thomson, 'The Trolley Problem', in *Rights, Restitution, and Risk: Essays in Moral Theory*, edited by (Cambridge, MA: Harvard University Press, 1986). For doubts, see Warren Quinn (1993) 'Actions, Intentions, and Consequences: The Doctrine of Doing and Allowing', in *Morality and Action*, edited by (Cambridge: Cambridge University Press, 1993), 159–160; Frances M. Kamm, *Morality, Mortality vol. II: Rights, Duties and Status* (Oxford: Oxford University Press, 1996), 162–166.
9. See, e.g., Thomas Scanlon's formulation in *Moral Dimensions: Permissibility, Meaning, Permissibility, Blame* (Cambridge, MA: Harvard University Press, 2008), 1.
10. For a good discussion, see Shelly Kagan *Normative Ethics* (Boulder, CO: Westview, 1998), 78–84. John Rawls, 'Fifty Years After Hiroshima', in *John Rawls: Collected Papers*, edited by Samuel Freeman (Cambridge, MA: Harvard University Press, 1999), argued that intentional targeting of noncombatants would have been permissible to prevent Nazi domination.
11. See, further, Tadros, *The Ends of Harm*, ch. 6.IV.
12. See, e.g., Quinn, 'Actions, Intentions, and Consequences: The Doctrine of Doing and Allowing'; Tadros, *The Ends of Harm*, ch. 6.
13. See, e.g., Thomas Nagel, *The View from Nowhere* (Oxford: Oxford University Press, 1986) 175–180; Ralph Wedgwood, 'Defending Double Effect', *Ratio* 24 (2011), 384.
14. For further discussion, see V Tadros 'Wrongful Intentions Without Closeness' *Philosophy and Public Affairs* 43 (2015), 52.
15. For discussion, see, e.g., Phillipa Foot, 'The Problem of Abortion and the Doctrine of Double Effect', in *Virtues and Vices* (Oxford: Oxford University Press, 2002); Quinn, 'Actions, Intentions, and Consequences'; Jeff McMahan, 'Revising the Doctrine of Double Effect', *Journal of Applied Philosophy* 11 (1994), 201; Jonathan Bennett, *The Act Itself* (Oxford: Oxford University Press, 1995); John Martin Fischer, Mark Ravizza, and David Copp 'Quinn on Double Effect', *Ethics* 103 (1993), 707; FitzPatrick 'The Intend/Foresee Distinction and the Problem of "Closeness"', *Philosophical Studies* 128 (2006), 585; Frances Kamm, *Intricate Ethics: Rights, Responsibility, and Permissible Harm* (Oxford: Oxford University Press, 2007) ch. 3; Neil F. Delaney, 'Two Cheers for "Closeness": Terror, Targeting and Double Effect', *Philosophical Studies* 137 (2008), 335; Wedgwood, 'Defending Double Effect; Dana K. Nelkin and Samuel C. Rickless '"So Close, Yet So Far": Why Solutions to the Closeness Problem for the Doctrine of Double Effect Fall Short', *Noûs* (forthcoming); Tadros, 'Wrongful Intentions Without Closeness'.
16. For a defence of this view, see Tadros, 'Wrongful Intentions Without Closeness'.
17. See Judith Jarvis Thomson, 'Self-Defense'; 'Physician-Assisted Suicide: Two Moral Arguments', *Ethics* 109 (1999), 497; Kamm, *Intricate Ethics*, ch. 5, and *Ethics for*

Enemies: Terror, Torture, and War (Oxford: Oxford University Press 2011); Scanlon, *Moral Dimensions*. For different responses to this challenge, see William J. Fitzpatrick, 'Acts, Intentions, and Moral Permissibility: In Defence of the Doctrine of Double Effect', *Analysis* 63 (2003), 317; 'Intention, Permissibility, and Double Effect', in *Oxford Studies in Normative Ethics* vol. 2, edited by Mark Timmons (Oxford: Oxford University Press, 2012); Jeff McMahan, 'Intention, Permissibility, Terrorism, and War', *Philosophical Perspectives* 23 (2009), 345; Wedgwood, 'Defending Double Effect'; Tadros, *The Ends of Harm*, ch. 7; Matthew Liao, 'Intentions and Permissibility: The Case of Acting Permissibly with Bad Intentions', *Law and Philosophy* (forthcoming).

18. Scanlon, *Moral Dimensions*, 32.
19. Idem, 29.
20. For further discussion of Scanlon's view, see McMahan 'Intention, Permissibility, Terrorism, and War'.
21. Kamm, *Intricate Ethics*, ch. 5.
22. See, e.g., Fitzpatrick, 'Acts, Intentions, and Moral Permissibility' (2012); 'Intention, Permissibility, and Double Effect'.
23. See, e.g., McMahan 'Intention, Permissibility, Terrorism, and War'; Tadros, *The Ends of Harm*, ch. 7.
24. See, further, Tadros, *The Ends of Harm*, 149–155. For the claim that differences in causal paths are not morally relevant, see also Scanlon, *Moral Dimensions*, 120–121.
25. Scanlon, *Moral Dimensions*, 56–62.
26. See McMahan, *Killing in War*.
27. See Tadros, *The Ends of Harm*; Nelkin and Rickless, 'Three Cheers for Double Effect', *Philosophy and Phenomenological Research* (forthcoming).
28. For further defence of this idea, see Tadros, *The Ends of Harm*, ch. 7.
29. To be complete, we should consider cases of mixed motives. I leave such cases aside here.
30. See, e.g., Alec Walen, 'Wrongdoing Without Motives: Why Victor Tadros Is Wrong About Wrongdoing and Motivation', *Law and Philosophy* 32 (2013), 217, and 'Transcending the Means Principle', *Law and Philosophy*, 33 (2014), 427; and Gerhard Øverland, 'Moral Obstacles: An Alternative to the Doctrine of Double Effect', *Ethics* 124 (2014), 481.
31. See Quinn, 'Actions, Intentions, and Consequences', 186; McMahan, *Killing in War* (2009), 170–173; Jonathan Quong 'Killing in Self-Defense', *Ethics* 119 (2009), 507.
32. For related discussion of these different ideas, with contrasting views about their moral significance, see Walen, 'Wrongdoing Without Motives: Why Victor Tadros Is Wrong About Wrongdoing and Motivation'; 'Transcending the Means Principle'; and Victor Tadros, 'Responses', *Law and Philosophy* 32 (2013), 241, 289–291.

CHAPTER 21

PROPORTIONALITY AND NECESSITY IN *JUS IN BELLO*

JEFF MCMAHAN

1. Introduction

In the traditional theory of the just war, the requirements of proportionality and necessity appear twice, once among the principles governing the resort to war (*jus ad bellum*) and again among the principles governing the conduct of war (*jus in bello*). The theory insists, in other words, not only that a war itself be proportionate and necessary but also that each individual act of war be proportionate and necessary.

My topic in this chapter will be the *in bello* proportionality and necessity constraints. I will focus primarily on proportionality, offering a few remarks on necessity at the end. I will begin by providing a general characterisation of the difference between proportionality and necessity. I will then, in Section 2, give a brief account of *ad bellum* proportionality, which will be essential for explaining why, in my view, the traditional accounts of *in bello* proportionality and necessity are mistaken—at least as a matter of morality, if not of law.

Whether an instance of defensive action (which we may take to include both wars and acts of war) is proportionate is a matter of the relation between the bad effects it causes and those it prevents. The assessment of proportionality thus requires a comparison between the bad effects (mainly harms to individuals) that the act will cause to occur with those that the act will prevent from being caused by others. If the bad effects the act will cause are not excessive in relation to those it will prevent, the act is proportionate. Comparisons with other means of defence or with acts with other aims are irrelevant to proportionality.

It is the necessity constraint that requires comparisons between an act of defence and alternative means of achieving the same defensive aim. In what is perhaps its most familiar formulation, the necessity constraint is that an act of defence is permissible only if there is no less harmful means of defence. I will explain in the final section why this and other common formulations of the necessity constraint are inadequate.

2. Proportionality in *Jus ad Bellum*

These brief characterisations of proportionality and necessity are considerable oversimplifications. Some of the complexities in the notion of proportionality emerge when we consider proportionality in the resort to war. *Ad bellum* proportionality weighs the harms that war inflicts against those it prevents but, according to the traditional theory of the just war, not all the harms inflicted count. To my knowledge, no traditional just war theorist has ever argued that the victims of an aggressive war might be morally prohibited from engaging in defensive war on the ground that their doing so would cause disproportionate harm to the aggressing combatants. They have assumed that all combatants are morally liable to any harms that might impair their ability to contribute to their side's war—that is, any harms at all—and that harms to which people are liable do not count in the assessment of proportionality. (They would not, until quite recently, have used the term 'liability', but would instead have said that all combatants are 'noninnocent' and that harms to the noninnocent do not count in the assessment of proportionality in war.) The only harms that might make war disproportionate, on this traditional view, are those inflicted on people who are not liable to them—that is, noncombatants or civilians. Moreover, since the intentional harming of people who are not liable to be harmed is prohibited by the requirement of discrimination, proportionality is assumed to be concerned with harms inflicted on innocent civilians as a *side effect* of attacks on military targets (what is often referred to euphemistically as 'collateral damage'). A clear instance in which war could be disproportionate in this way would be if defensive war against unjust aggression had a high probability of escalation to nuclear war, which would kill millions or billions of people in countries not involved in the conflict.

The idea that harms to combatants do not count in the assessment of proportionality is, however, mistaken.[1] In most instances in which individual self-defence or defence of others is disproportionate outside the context of war, the explanation is not that the defensive action causes harm to innocent bystanders as a side effect but that it causes harm to the threatener that is excessive in relation to the threat he poses and thus exceeds the harm to which he is liable. But if defensive harm inflicted on threateners can be disproportionate outside the context of war, it can also be disproportionate in war. Although actual cases of this sort are rare, it is possible that there could be unjust wars with aims that would be so limited and comparatively trivial that none of the soldiers involved in their implementation would be liable to be killed, although they might be liable to certain lesser harms. More importantly, it can sometimes be known that certain soldiers on the unjust side are both morally innocent and almost certain not to make any significant contribution to their side's unjust war. It might be proportionate to capture such a soldier but disproportionate to kill him, unless he came to pose a significant threat in resisting capture.[2]

The foregoing remarks presuppose a distinction between two forms of proportionality—namely, what are often referred to as narrow and wide proportionality.[3]

Narrow proportionality is a constraint on a liability justification for the infliction of harm. When a threatener is morally liable to harm that is inflicted on him, the harm is proportionate in the narrow sense. When the harm inflicted exceeds that to which he is liable, it is disproportionate in the narrow sense. Wide proportionality, by contrast, governs harms to which the victims are not liable. It is a constraint on a lesser-evil justification for the infliction of harm. The infliction of harm on a nonliable person can be justified in this way when inflicting it is necessary to prevent a substantially greater amount of harm from being suffered by others who are also not liable to that harm. When the infliction of harm on a nonliable person can be justified as the lesser evil, it is proportionate in the wide sense. When it exceeds what can be justified in this way, it is disproportionate in the wide sense. It is possible that harm that exceeds that to which a person is liable, and is thus disproportionate in the narrow sense, can nevertheless be justified as the lesser evil, and therefore be proportionate in the wide sense. (Although a lesser-evil justification is concerned with consequences, impartially considered, it is nevertheless a nonconsequentialist form of justification. It recognises that there are deontological constraints on action but is acknowledged by non-absolutist deontologists as capable of overriding them.)

In war, there are liability justifications for the infliction of certain harms and lesser-evil justifications for the infliction of other harms. The standards of justification are different in these cases. Whereas a liability justification permits the infliction of harm greater than that which is prevented, a lesser-evil justification permits only the infliction of significantly less harm than that which is prevented. In other words, wide proportionality is a more stringent constraint than narrow proportionality. For this reason, among others, these two forms of proportionality must be kept distinct.

Having considered the harms that war might inflict, consider next those it might prevent. I say 'might' because one cannot, in advance of acting, have precise knowledge of what harms a war would cause or prevent. At most, one can have some information about probabilities, such as the probabilities that aggression will cause different forms and degrees of harm in the absence of defensive war, the probability that defensive war will succeed, the different probabilities that war will inflict different degrees of harm on innocent bystanders as a side effect, and so on. So, when it is said that proportionality depends on the amount of harm war would prevent, this could refer to the amount that it is *most likely* to prevent, the amount that it is *intended* to prevent, the amount that it *actually does* prevent, or the average of all the different harms it might prevent when each such harm is weighted for the probability of its occurrence.

It may be that more than one of these considerations is relevant. Suppose, for example, that the harm one reasonably expects to prevent is very great but the harm one in fact prevents is tiny, or that the harm one expects to inflict is tiny but the harm one actually inflicts is very great. When such divergences occur, it may be that different senses of proportionality are important for different reasons—for example, one depending on probabilities ('evidence-relative proportionality') and another based on what actually happens ('fact-relative proportionality').[4] I will not attempt to adjudicate among the various options here, although each has its advocates. I will instead follow custom and write as if it were known both what harms war would inflict and what harms it would prevent.

Thus far I have, for brevity of exposition, said that in the assessment of proportionality, what weighs against the harms that war inflicts are the *harms* it *prevents*. This is an oversimplification. In *ad bellum* proportionality, what mainly weighs against the harms war causes is the achievement of the just cause for war. Of course, since most just war is defensive in one way or another (national self-defence, defence of an ally, defence of foreign citizens against their own government, and so on), the just cause normally consists in the prevention of harm or of the continuation of harm, which can include the removal of obstacles to the acquisition of benefits. But there are aims that can be a just cause for war other than the prevention of wrongful harm. These include the rectification of wrongs (for example, the recovery of territories or freedoms lost when earlier defensive action failed) and the prevention of effects that are bad only impersonally (for example, preventing a state from adopting a policy that would greatly lower the quality of life in the future but, because of the Non-Identity Problem, would not be worse for anyone who ever lives).[5] I will refer to good effects that are constitutive of the achievement of a just cause for war as 'just-cause goods'.

It is universally recognised that just-cause goods count in the assessment of *ad bellum* proportionality. Assuming that aggressing combatants are liable to attack, just-cause goods weigh against harms inflicted on them in the assessment of narrow proportionality. And they also weigh against harms inflicted on innocent bystanders as a side effect in wide proportionality. Indeed, the achievement of the same just-cause good can offset both harms to which combatants are liable and harms to which noncombatants are not liable—just as, in individual self-defence, the prevention of serious harm to an innocent victim can provide both a liability justification for harming the threatener as a means of defence and a lesser-evil justification for causing much lesser harm to an innocent bystander as a side effect.

Yet it is acknowledged by virtually all just war theorists, whatever their conception of just cause may be, that not all good effects that might be produced by war are just-cause goods.[6] In my view, only the prevention or rectification of a moral *wrong* (including, of course, the wrongful infliction of harm) can be a just cause for war. And even the prevention or rectification of a wrong can be a just cause only when those whom it is causally necessary to attack are liable to attack because of their responsibility for the wrong that is to be prevented or corrected. In short, a just cause for war is a liability justification for the resort to war, although there must also be a lesser-evil justification for the inevitable infliction of harms on people who are not liable to them.[7] (This is the account of just-cause goods that I favor. Some just war theorists accept that there could be a just cause for war even when some whom it would be necessary to attack as a means of achieving it would not be liable to attack. Some of these theorists claim that there could be a just cause even when it would be impermissible to pursue it because no one was liable to be attacked as a means of pursuing it.)

On this or any other plausible account of what can be a just cause for war, there are some good effects that a war might produce that would not be elements of the achievement of a just cause—for example, the exhilaration that some soldiers experience in combat. We can call such good effects 'non–just-cause goods'.

Suppose a country has no just cause for war but nevertheless goes to war to pursue aims that are unjust. One might wonder whether, if this war produces a range of non–just-cause goods as side effects, it could in principle be proportionate. But this question presupposes that the notion of proportionality is univocal, whereas the answer may be different depending on whether the question refers to narrow or wide proportionality. As regards narrow proportionality, the answer is 'no'. This is because, in the absence of a just cause, none of those who are attacked in the war is liable to attack, at least according to the account of just cause sketched earlier. According to that account, none of the harms inflicted can be proportionate in the narrow sense because no one is liable to them.

The answer in the case of wide proportionality is more difficult. One might think the question is irrelevant since the war is already ruled out as impermissible on the ground that its aims are unjust. Suppose, however, that the non–just-cause goods produced as a side effect are so extensive that, even though the war is intended to achieve unjust aims, there could be a lesser-evil justification for fighting the war as a means of producing those good effects. In that case, one might concede that the war is proportionate in the wide sense even if one believes it is impermissible because of its intended aims.

Suppose that a country that will not fight for unjust aims has a lesser-evil justification for fighting a war to produce non–just-cause goods. Because there is no just cause, this war requires attacking people who are not liable to attack; yet the harms it inflicts on them are morally outweighed by the prevention of much greater harms to other people who are also not liable to them. Because there is a lesser-evil justification for the harms inflicted in such a war, the war is proportionate in the wide sense. Because it lacks a just cause, this war is unjust. Yet it is morally justified. Although such wars are very rare, it seems that they are possible. Suppose, for example, that there is famine in one state. An adjacent state could mitigate or relieve the famine, but only at the cost of imposing great hardship—although not starvation—on its own people. Suppose it is therefore justified in refusing to help. It might nevertheless be justifiable for the state in which people are starving to use military force to seize food from the adjacent state.

Finally, in a war that has a just cause and does not pursue any aims other than those constitutive of the just cause, non–just-cause goods do not count in narrow proportionality but may count in wide proportionality.[8] Narrow proportionality is a constraint on a liability justification, and the justification for harming people as a means of achieving a just cause is a liability justification. Those responsible for the wrong to be prevented or rectified are liable to attack; otherwise, there is no just cause. Yet these people are not liable to attack as a means of producing non–just-cause goods. If they were, those good effects would be just-cause goods. To harm these people as a means of producing non–just-cause goods in addition to just-cause goods would therefore be to harm them beyond their liability. It would be disproportionate in the narrow sense.

There might, however, be different justifications for inflicting different harms on the same person. There might, for example, be a liability justification for harming an unjust combatant as a means of pursuing the just cause and also a lesser-evil justification for harming him in another way as a side effect (or even, in extreme circumstances, as a means) of producing some non–just-cause good. (For completeness, it may be worth noting that there could be both a liability justification and a lesser-evil justification for inflicting the same harm on the same person, in which case the justification would be overdetermined.)

It is a familiar idea in just war theory that it can be permissible to harm an innocent civilian as a side effect of attacking a military target.[9] When this is permissible, the reason is most often that the harm is proportionate in the wide sense in relation to the contribution the attack makes to the achievement of the just cause. Yet it is also possible that, in a war intended to achieve a just cause, harm caused to innocent civilians as a side effect could also be offset by non–just-cause goods. Suppose that military action by the just side causes, as a side effect, some innocent civilians on the unjust side to suffer certain economic losses. Yet other military action by the just side causes civilians on the unjust side to receive certain economic benefits, again as a side effect. It seems that the economic losses can be offset in wide proportionality by the economic gains, even though the latter are non–just-cause goods.

If the victims and the beneficiaries are the same people, it may be that the harms can be offset by benefits of the same magnitude—that is, the benefits may not need to be greater than the harms for the infliction of the harms to be proportionate in the wide sense. Yet if, as is likely, the victims and the beneficiaries are different people, it seems that the lesser-evil standard applies—that is, that the harm to some may be offset only by a substantially greater benefit to others, even when the benefit consists in the prevention of harm.

3. Proportionality in *Jus in Bello*

In summary, there are three elements of traditional just war theory's view of *ad bellum* proportionality that are important for our purposes. First, the only form of proportionality in war is wide proportionality. Second, in a war with a just cause, harms to innocent civilians can be offset in wide proportionality both by just-cause goods and, in some instances, by non–just-cause goods. Third, because a war fought for aims that are unjust is highly unlikely to achieve just-cause goods as a side effect (if any are even possible in the context) and because it is also highly unlikely to produce enough non–just-cause goods as a side effect to offset the inevitable harms to innocent people, it is virtually impossible for a war fought for unjust aims to be proportionate in the wide sense. Hence it seems that, in a war in which one side has a just cause and the other fights for unjust aims, only the just side's war can be proportionate.

But if the unjust side's war is inevitably disproportionate, it seems that many or most of the acts of war that together constitute that war must also be disproportionate. For if all the acts of war that together constitute one side's war were proportionate, that would seem to guarantee that the war as a whole must be proportionate. Yet traditional just war theory denies this. It maintains instead that it is possible for every act of war by combatants on the unjust side to satisfy the *in bello* proportionality constraint, even though their war itself is disproportionate.[10]

The explanation of how traditional just war theory can consistently claim that a war that is disproportionate can consist entirely of acts that are proportionate is that the theory presupposes that the good effects that can offset the harms caused to innocent civilians by individual acts of war are neither just-cause goods nor non–just-cause goods as ordinarily understood. Indeed, there is, according to the theory, only one good effect that weighs against the harms inflicted by any act of war in determining whether that act is proportionate: namely, military advantage.[11] In this matter, the traditional theory is in agreement with the law of war, which is quite explicit. The clearest statement of *in bello* proportionality in law is in Article 51(5) of Additional Protocol I of the 1977 Geneva Conventions, which prohibits any 'attack which may be expected to cause incidental loss of civilian life, injury to civilians, damage to civilian objects, or a combination thereof, which would be excessive in relation to the concrete and direct military advantage anticipated'.[12]

The problem with this restriction on the good effects that are allowed to count in wide *in bello* proportionality is that military advantage is in itself neither impartially good nor impartially bad. Whatever value it has is instrumental and depends on the value of whatever the military advantage is advantageous *for*. Military advantage is impartially good only when it is instrumental to the achievement of a just or at least morally justified aim. When forces pursuing unjust aims gain a military advantage, that is impartially *bad*.

A military advantage for the Nazis may, of course, be good *for the Nazis*, but that kind of relative good cannot weigh against or offset the infliction of harms on people who are not liable to them. Effects that are good only in this relative way, and not impartially, are irrelevant to proportionality. No one supposes, for example, that the benefits that a man derives from inheriting a fortune weigh against the harm of death in the determination of whether his murdering his wealthy uncle is proportionate in the wide sense. It is not that the question of proportionality cannot arise in such a case, for there could in principle be a lesser-evil justification for the murder of his uncle. It is, rather, that the pure benefits he would gain from his uncle's death are irrelevant even in a lesser-evil justification. Only effects that are impartially good count in a lesser-evil justification for harming a nonliable person.

Given that there is this obvious objection to the idea that only military advantage weighs against harms inflicted on innocent civilians in *in bello* proportionality, one must wonder why both traditional just war theory and the law of war have embraced this idea. The explanation is that both are committed to the independence of *jus in bello* from *jus ad bellum*.[13] Whether a combatant acts permissibly in the conduct of war is independent of whether his war is just or unjust. An unjust combatant whose war lacks a just cause and who fights for aims that are unjust acts permissibly provided that he obeys the principles of *jus in bello*. But he can fight in obedience to those principles only if they are satisfiable in the absence of a just cause. Hence *in bello* proportionality cannot weigh unintended harms to civilians only against the contribution that an act of war makes to the achievement of a just cause because then no acts of war by unjust combatants could satisfy the *in bello* proportionality constraint. And it would be absurd to suppose that *in bello* proportionality can weigh harms inflicted on civilians against any impartially good effects *except* just-cause goods—that is, that the only good effects that *cannot* count in *in bello* proportionality are the only good effects that *can* count in justifying the resort to war.

Yet any understanding of *in bello* proportionality that allows just-cause goods to count along with other impartially good effects would give just combatants a moral advantage by making their acts of war more likely to be able to satisfy the *in bello* proportionality constraint than those by unjust combatants. Traditional just war theory and the law of war are, however, committed to the view that all combatants are moral and legal equals. Neither just nor unjust combatants are in a morally or legally advantaged position in the conduct of war.

The main reason for this is that both moral and legal theorists want to promulgate and inculcate principles that can, in practice, successfully constrain the action of combatants on both sides.[14] But because no principles, moral or legal, will prevent people from fighting unjust wars, there *will* be unjust combatants who *will* fight. When they do so, it is obviously desirable to motivate them to restrain their action in certain ways. Telling them that it is permissible for them to fight provided that they refrain from acting in certain ways may arguably be more effective in constraining their action than simply telling them that all or virtually all of their acts of war are impermissible so that the only permissible course of action for them is to stop fighting.

One reason for this might be that most unjust combatants mistakenly believe that they are *just* combatants and thus, to the extent that they seek to abide by moral principles, will apply those principles to their own conduct on the assumption that the aims for which they perceive themselves to be fighting are just. In these circumstances, it may well be that they will exercise greater restraint if they think they must weigh the harms that their action might cause to civilians against the military advantage it might provide rather than against the contribution that they think the action would make to the achievement of an imagined just cause—because people may be less morally inhibited about causing harm to innocent people (that is, people who are not liable to any harm at all) when they believe they are serving the cause of justice.

Hence just war theorists and international lawyers have settled on military advantage as the one effect of military action against which harms caused to civilians are to be measured in the assessment of *in bello* proportionality. It is, in one sense, a natural measure of proportionality because it is the immediate aim of virtually all military action that harms civilians as a side effect. It also seems a neutral measure because, in general, it is no more available to just combatants than to unjust combatants. Yet military advantage is not in fact a neutral measure because it is only impartially good when it is gained by just combatants (or by combatants fighting in a war that is unjust but nevertheless morally justified because it is the lesser evil). When it is gained by combatants fighting for unjust aims, it is impartially bad and cannot, in the assessment of *in bello* proportionality, offset harms that those combatants may cause to civilians. It is not coherent to suppose that military action could be morally permissible despite causing harm to innocent civilians on the ground that the harm is offset by the fact that the action better enables the combatants who cause it to achieve unjust aims.

As a matter of morality, wide *in bello* proportionality has to weigh the harms that an act of war inflicts on people who are not liable to them against the act's impartially good effects—mainly the contribution the act makes to the achievement of a just cause, but also, in some instances, certain non–just-cause goods as well. It must, in other words, test whether harms to innocent civilians are proportionate in the same way that traditional just war theory requires in the determination of wide *ad bellum* proportionality. This means that what traditional just war theorists have been unwilling to say to unjust combatants is in fact true—namely, that most of their acts of war are morally impermissible. That these acts are impermissible may be overdetermined by a variety of considerations. But one reason they are generally impermissible is that, even if they are intended to attack only military targets, the harms they inflict on innocent civilians as a side effect are disproportionate in the wide sense because these acts have few or no impartially good effects by which these harms could be offset. The harms cannot be justified on the ground that they are the lesser evil in the circumstances.

It may be that the consequences would be worse if combatants came to accept this understanding of wide *in bello* proportionality rather than the orthodox account that weighs harms inflicted against military advantage. But, even if that were so, it would be irrelevant to the truth of the view.

This leaves open the question of what the law of *in bello* proportionality ought to be. I can think of four options, although there may be others. One is for the law simply to restate the truth of morality.[15] The implication would be that, in general, only combatants who fight for just or justified aims can engage in acts of war that are proportionate. The exceptions would be acts of war by unjust combatants that would cause no harm to innocent civilians or that would produce sufficiently extensive non–just-cause goods as a side effect to justify the harms the acts would cause to civilians as the lesser evil.

The second option is to keep the law as it is while acknowledging, although perhaps rather quietly, that the legal measure of *in bello* proportionality has no moral significance in its application to unjust combatants. Once it is conceded that harms to innocent people cannot really be offset by a military advantage in the pursuit of unjust aims, a problem in the application of this view becomes conspicuous—namely, determining how great a military advantage would be necessary to provide legal justification for the killing of a certain number of innocent civilians. Any response to this problem must, at least in one important sense, be arbitrary in its application to combatants who fight for unjust aims.

The third option would avoid this latter problem. According to this third suggestion, *in bello* proportionality is a relation between the harm that military action would cause to innocent civilians and the harm that it would prevent the combatants who inflict it from suffering. For example, the killing of one civilian as a side effect might be proportionate if it were an unavoidable effect of saving the lives of two combatants. The attractions of this option are that the relevant effects are obviously commensurable and that it confines the relevant good and bad effects to the battlefield, making no reference to the ends for which the conflict is fought.

Finally, a fourth option is to assess what combatants might reasonably believe to be the just cause of their war and then to weigh the harms an act of war inflicts on innocent civilians against the contribution the act might make to the achievement of that aim. Suppose, for example, that combatants believe that their war's aim is to capture or destroy weapons of mass destruction that an enemy state is otherwise likely to use unjustly, when, in fact, the enemy state has no weapons of mass destruction. An act of war by these combatants might be proportionate in an evidence-relative sense if it *would* have made a sufficiently significant contribution to preventing the enemy state from using weapons of mass destruction *if it had had them*.

In my view, none of these options is really viable. I have sought elsewhere to show why the third and fourth options are hopeless.[16] At present, the least bad of the possibilities is probably to keep the law as it is, if only because the law itself fails to provide reliable and authoritative guidance to combatants in determining whether they are fighting in a just and legal war or in an unjust and illegal war. If international legal institutions could provide such guidance, that might make it possible for the law to achieve closer congruence with morality.[17] The law might then acknowledge that any military action by unjust combatants that causes harm to civilians is highly likely to be disproportionate in the wide sense, so that any such action would be presumptively illegal. That it would be illegal need not entail that it would also be criminal and therefore punishable. But the law might hold that the more harm unjust combatants cause to innocent civilians in the course of military action, the more likely it is that their action will pass a threshold for criminal disproportionality. It is also possible that the notion of military advantage could have a role here because unjust combatants' disregard for the lives and well-being of civilians would be more egregious the greater the disparity between the harm an act of war inflicts and the military benefits it provides. It is worse, at least in one way, to sacrifice the lives of innocent people for the sake of trivial relative benefits than to sacrifice them for relative benefits of greater importance.[18]

4. *In Bello* Proportionality in Its Application to Just Combatants

Although what I claim is the correct account of wide *in bello* proportionality (as a matter of morality rather than law) may seem problematic in its application to acts of war by unjust combatants, it is intuitively highly plausible in its application to acts of war by just combatants who harm innocent civilians as a side effect. It implies that even if an act of war makes a contribution to the achievement of a just cause, and even if it is intended to do so, any harms it causes to innocent civilians are disproportionate unless there is a lesser-evil justification for inflicting them—that is, unless the harms to innocent people that the act prevents are substantially greater than those it causes. This proportionality standard presupposes the rejection of both absolutism and consequentialism. Unlike absolutism, it accepts that it can be permissible to inflict harm on innocent people, even intentionally—although it is generally assumed that, to justify harming innocent people as an intended means of preventing harm to others, the harm prevented must be greater than the harm it would be necessary to prevent to justify the infliction of the same harm on innocent people as a side effect. But it also insists, contrary to traditional consequentialism, that it is insufficient to justify an act that inflicts harm on innocent people that the act would prevent more harm to innocent people than it would cause. The harm prevented must instead be substantially greater.

Skeptics about proportionality often object that although one can make such claims about comparisons between harms inflicted and harms prevented in the abstract, the necessary comparisons are almost impossibly difficult to make in the context of war, not just because of epistemic problems but also because the relevant effects of different types are only very imprecisely comparable. This is clearly true in many cases—for example, when one has to weigh the killing or wounding of a large number of innocent people as a side effect against the preservation of certain political freedoms of a much larger number of innocent people. Yet there are cases in which the harms inflicted and those averted are of the same type or types. In these cases, it is possible to make surprisingly precise judgments about wide *in bello* proportionality.[19]

The various invasions of Gaza by Israel in recent years are good examples of this. In each instance, the justification that the Israeli government offered was that the invasions were necessary to prevent Palestinian militants from killing Israeli civilians. The proportionality calculus therefore required a comparison between the number of innocent Palestinian civilians killed as a side effect and the number of innocent Israeli civilians prevented from being killed. (The Gaza wars raise a special issue of *ad bellum* necessity. Preventing the killing of innocent Israeli civilians is a just cause for war but can justify the resort to war only if there is no morally better means of addressing the terrorist threat. It is arguable that there is an alternative means that is both less harmful and, in the long term, far more effective than war—namely, responding appropriately to the Palestinians' legitimate grievances, which would require, among other things, allowing them to have a state in the territories that Israel currently occupies. This option does not, I think, require the Israelis to sacrifice anything to which they are morally entitled. I will, however, put this issue aside in the following discussion.)

The best way to think about wide *in bello* proportionality in wars in which the just cause is simply the prevention of the wrongful killing of innocent civilians is to consider our beliefs about parallel issues in the morality of individual self- and other-defence. It is generally agreed that the most common justification for self-defensive harming is a liability justification—that is, a justification that appeals to the fact that a threatener has made himself morally liable to be harmed by virtue of his responsibility for threat of wrongful harm to another.[20] Because this form of justification is agent-neutral, it seems that the amount of harm it permits a third party to cause to innocent bystanders as a side effect of defending another person is the same as the amount that that person is justified in causing as a side effect of self-defence. Yet there may be other justifications for defensive action that apply in some cases that have different implications for 'other-defence' by third parties. According to one such view, which I will discuss below, third parties may not be permitted to cause as much harm to innocent bystanders as a side effect of defending another person as that person is permitted cause in self-defence. And there is another view according to which at least certain third parties may be permitted to cause more harm to innocent bystanders as a side effect of defending another person than that person is permitted to cause in self-defence.

Suppose that Victim will be wrongly killed by Threatener unless she acts in self-defence. Assume that Threatener is morally liable to whatever Victim must do to him to eliminate the threat he poses. There are, however, innocent bystanders present, and Victim's only effective means of defence will kill some of them as a side effect. People's intuitions about how many bystanders Victim may permissibly kill as a side effect of defending herself differ. Some people, myself included, believe that it is not permissible for her to kill any, even as a side effect rather than as a means of saving her own life.[21] One reason some of us believe this is that we think the moral reason not to kill an innocent person is in general stronger than the moral reason to save an innocent person's life. The choice that Victim must make is between killing an innocent person (Bystander), thereby saving an innocent person (herself), and allowing that innocent person to be killed. If the reason not to kill is stronger than the reason to save, the presumption is that Victim ought not to kill Bystander as a side effect of saving herself. This is certainly true of defence by a third party. Suppose that Victim is unable to defend herself but that Third Party, who is not specially related to any of the others, can effectively defend her, although only by killing Bystander as a side effect. It seems clear that this would be wrong. Or, suppose again that Victim can act in self-defence but that Third Party can, without directly harming her, prevent her from doing so, thereby preventing her from killing Bystander. It is arguable that it is permissible, and perhaps even required, for Third Party to do this, even though it would result in Victim's being killed by Threatener.

Some philosophers have argued, however, that self-defence is morally different from defence by a third party in that each person has an 'agent-relative permission' to give some degree of priority to her own life over that of another equally innocent person. These philosophers have appealed to the claim that people have an agent-relative permission in an effort to explain the permissibility of killing a nonresponsible threatener in self-defence.[22] Because such a person is wholly nonresponsible for the threat he poses, it is difficult to defend the claim that he is morally liable to be killed. Yet, unless he is killed, he will kill another equally nonresponsible and nonliable person. If the potential victim has an agent-relative permission, it could explain and justify the common view that it is permissible for her to kill the nonresponsible threatener in self-defence. But if there can be an agent-relative permission to kill a nonliable person as a *means* of self-defence, it seems that there must also be an agent-relative permission to kill a nonliable person as a *side effect* of self-defence.[23]

Almost everyone accepts that there is an agent-relative permission to save oneself rather than save two other people to whom one is unrelated. It is more controversial, however, to suppose that there can be such a permission to *kill* a wholly innocent or non-liable person in the course of saving one's own life. And it is, of course, even more controversial to suppose that there might be an agent-relative permission to kill two, or three, innocent bystanders as a side effect of saving oneself. Defenders of the agent-relative permission recognise that its scope is limited. Few, I suspect, would defend the claim that each person has an agent-relative permission to kill more than two innocent bystanders as a side effect of saving her own life, whether in self-defence or self-preservation.

One question that arises here is whether, if a person does have an agent-relative permission to kill an innocent bystander as a side effect of self-preservative action, that permission can be transferred to a third party who might then act on the person's behalf. Suppose that Victim has an agent-relative permission to kill Bystander as a side effect of defending herself against Threatener but is unable to defend herself. She hires Bodyguard to protect her. In doing so, does she effectively transfer her agent-relative permission to Bodyguard, so that he, acting as her agent, is permitted to kill Bystander as a side effect of preventing Threatener from killing her? There is a case for thinking that the permission is genuinely *agent*-relative and thus cannot extend to anyone else.[24] But I will not take a position on this question here.

There is another way, though, to defend the view that at least *some* third parties may be permitted to do in defence of an innocent victim as much as the victim is agent-relatively permitted to do in her own defence. This is to appeal to the duties and permissions that people have to protect the well-being of certain people to whom they are specially related in certain ways.[25] Perhaps the morally most significant special relation is the parent–child relation. Because of the moral significance of the relation, parents have special duties to protect the well-being of their children. Suppose again that Victim has an agent-relative permission to kill Bystander as a side effect of defending herself against Threatener but is unable to defend herself. If Third Party is Victim's parent, his special duty to protect her may make it permissible for him to do as much in her defence as she is agent-relatively permitted to do. It may, for example, be permissible for him to kill Bystander as a side effect of defending Victim. Indeed, it might be that certain special relations, such as the parent–child relation, are morally *more* significant than self-identity or the difference between self and others. On that assumption, it might, in principle, be permissible for Victim's parent to cause more harm to innocent bystanders in defending Victim than she would be permitted to cause in her own defence. It might be, for example, that she has an agent-relative permission to kill at most one innocent bystander as a side effect, whereas her parent is permitted to kill two.

These views about what potential victims and third parties are permitted to do might combine in various ways. Some of the possibilities are:

1. Individuals have no agent-relative permission and no third party may cause more harm to innocent bystanders as a side effect of defending a potential victim than the victim is permitted to cause in self-defence.

2. Individuals have no agent-relative permission, but a third party who is specially related to a potential victim is permitted to cause more harm to innocent bystanders as a side effect of defending the victim than the victim is permitted to cause in self-defence.
3. Individuals have an agent-relative permission, but it cannot be transferred to a third party and no specially related third party is permitted to cause more harm to innocent bystanders as a side effect of defending a potential victim than the victim would be permitted to cause in self-defence *if she had no agent-relative permission*.
4. Individuals have an agent-relative permission that can be transferred to a third party, and a specially related third party may cause as much harm to innocent bystanders as a side effect of defending a potential victim as the potential victim is agent-relatively permitted to cause.
5. Individuals have an agent-relative permission that can be transferred, and a specially related third party may cause *even more* harm to innocent bystanders in defending a potential victim than the victim is agent-relatively permitted to cause.

These do not exhaust the possibilities, but they are sufficient for our purposes.

The application of these views to *in bello* proportionality in wars such as those in Gaza is not entirely straightforward. Our question is how much harm combatants whose just cause is to prevent innocent civilians on their own side from being killed may inflict as a side effect on innocent civilians on the unjust side. *If* people have an agent-relative permission and *if* it can be transferred to a third party defender, we can assume that civilians transfer their agent-relative permission to the soldiers whose job it is defend them. But even though soldiers are specially related through co-citizenship to the civilians they defend, and even though some special relations may make it permissible for third parties to do in 'other-defence' as much as or more than potential victims are permitted (whether agent-relatively or not) to do in self-defence, co-citizenship does not seem to be a very significant special relation. Certainly, it is substantially less significant than the parent–child relation, which I used to illustrate the point that special relations can be a factor in the permissibility of third-party defence.

One question here is whether the moral effect of a transferred agent-relative permission (assuming there are such) and the moral effect of a special relation are additive. I will assume that they are. It is not unreasonable to suppose, for example, that soldiers who are defending the inhabitants of their home town are permitted to cause more harm to innocent civilians as a side effect of defending their friends and neighbors than foreign mercenaries would be permitted to cause.

The other important question is whether mere co-citizenship is a sufficiently important special relation to make any difference to how much harm soldiers are permitted to cause to innocent civilians as a side effect of defending their civilian co-citizens. My own view is that whereas co-citizenship is highly important for certain distributional issues involving institutions (such as the provision of free health care and education for some but not others), it is largely irrelevant to the weight that unintended killings of innocent people have in *in bello* proportionality. Let *n* be the minimum number of innocent people to whom a person is related by co-citizenship that it is permissible for that person to save at the cost of killing one innocent non-citizen as a side effect. I find it implausible to suppose that it is not permissible, other things being equal, for that same person to save *n* non-citizens at the cost of killing one innocent non-citizen as a side effect—that is, that the number of non-citizens saved would have to be greater than *n* to justify killing a non-citizen as a side effect. But this is, of course, controversial.

We can now consider the issue of wide *in bello* proportionality on the basis of assumptions we have considered—both those that are most permissive and those that are most restrictive. The most permissive assumptions are (1) that individuals have an agent-relative permission to give some priority to their own life, (2) that this makes it permissible for them to kill up to two innocent bystanders as an unavoidable side effect of saving their own life, (3) that the agent-relative permission is transferrable to third parties, (4) that soldiers are recipients of their fellow citizens' agent-relative permissions, and (5) that the relation of co-citizenship is sufficiently important to make it permissible for them to kill more innocent bystanders as a side effect of defending the life of a fellow citizen than that citizen is permitted to kill as a side effect of self-defence. Assumptions 1–4 imply that it is permissible for a soldier to kill up to two innocent civilians as a side effect of preventing the killing of one civilian fellow citizen. And we can suppose that assumption 5 implies that it can be permissible for a soldier to kill as many as three innocent enemy civilians as a side effect of saving one civilian fellow citizen. On the basis of these permissive assumptions, one can conclude that an act of war by a just combatant that kills three innocent civilians must save the life of at least one of the combatant's civilian fellow citizens to be proportionate.

It is usually, of course, impossible to make such fine-grained judgments about the effects of a single act of war. In the most recent Gaza war, for example, the presumed saving of the lives of Israeli civilians came not from the elimination of specific threats to specific individuals but from the combined effects of Israeli military action in destroying missile launchers and tunnels and killing Hamas militants. In such a war fought to prevent the killing of innocent civilians, judgments of *in bello* proportionality may therefore, in general, be best derived from the most objective possible judgment of *ad bellum* proportionality made after the war has concluded. If the war has killed 3*n* civilians but can be reliably judged to have saved more than *n* innocent civilians on the just side, the war can be judged to have been proportionate according to the permissive assumptions stated earlier. And one can presume on that basis that most individual acts constitutive of the war were proportionate as well. Only if some act of war killed civilians but made little or no contribution to the overall strategy for protecting civilians could it be singled out as objectively or fact-relatively disproportionate. (Some acts of war can be disproportionate even when the war as a whole is proportionate because other acts of war often produce 'surplus' good effects beyond what is necessary to render them proportionate.)

According to the permissive assumptions, then, in a war whose just cause is the prevention of the killing of innocent civilians, an act of war, to be proportionate, must save one civilian for every three it kills as a side effect. Consider now the most restrictive and, to my mind, more plausible assumptions. These are (1) that individuals have no agent-relative permission to give priority to their own life over that of another innocent person when doing so would involve killing, (2) that it is therefore not permissible for a person to defend or save her own life when that would unavoidably involve killing one or more innocent bystanders as a side effect, and (3) the relation of co-citizenship is insufficiently significant to make it permissible for soldiers to cause more harm to enemy civilians as a side effect of defending one of their civilian fellow citizens than that person is permitted to cause as a side effect of defending herself. According to these assumptions, soldiers on the just side are not permitted to kill even one innocent enemy civilian as a side effect of saving one of their civilian fellow citizens.

There is, of course, *some* number of their civilian fellow citizens that it would be proportionate for soldiers to save at the cost of killing one innocent enemy civilian as a side effect. We might refer to a highly familiar thought experiment for guidance here—namely, the Trolley Problem. In this example, a runaway trolley is headed for five innocent people who are trapped on the track. A bystander can divert it onto a branch track where one innocent person is trapped. Most people intuitively believe that it is permissible to divert the trolley, killing one as a side effect of saving five. The many philosophers who have used this example or one of the many variants in their work have presumably retained the original number of five people on the main track because that is the lowest number that people can be expected to accept as sufficient to justify the killing of one innocent bystander as a side effect. If the number of people who could be saved were reduced to four, or to three, presumably significantly fewer people would accept that it would be permissible to kill one innocent person as a side effect of saving them. If this speculation is correct, it suggests that common sense moral thought accepts that the constraint against killing an innocent person, even as a side effect, can be overridden only when the killing is necessary to save five or more innocent people. Indeed, many people think that it is necessary to the permissibility of killing the one in the Trolley case that the killing occurs through the redirection of a preexisting threat rather than through the creation of a new threat.[26] They think that if those on the main track could be saved only by detonating a bomb that would both destroy the trolley and kill an innocent bystander, more than five would have to be saved to make it permissible to detonate the bomb. Since most 'collateral' killings of innocent civilians in war occur as a result of the creation of new threats, consideration of the Trolley Problem suggests that many people's intuitions seem to commit them to the view that it can be proportionate for a just combatant to kill an innocent civilian on the unjust side only if doing so would be a side effect of the saving of *six or more* innocent civilians on his own side. This will no doubt strike many people as excessively restrictive. But they then face the challenge of reconciling a more permissive view with common intuitions about the Trolley Problem.

These claims about wide *in bello* proportionality presuppose that the standard of proportionality in war is the same as the standard of proportionality in individual self- and other-defence. Yet many people believe, to the contrary, that wide proportionality in war is substantially less stringent than wide proportionality in private defence or even in law enforcement. Although I cannot argue for this here, I have argued elsewhere that it is a mistake to suppose that the moral principles governing killing in war are any different from those governing killing outside the context of war.[27] The moral justifications for killing are the same in war as in other contexts, and the constraints on those justifications are the same as well. No new moral principles come into effect in conditions of war, and the standard of proportionality in killing does not change.

There is obviously much more to be said about *in bello* proportionality than there is space to say here. Another dimension of wide proportionality that I have not discussed is the extent to which the prevention of harm to just combatants counts among the good effects against which the killing of innocent civilians as a side effect weighs in the determination of proportionality. I will offer only a couple of remarks on this issue.

One might think that, when just combatants fight only for a just cause and only by permissible means, they do nothing to make themselves liable to be harmed, so that the prevention of harms to them must count the same in wide proportionality as the prevention of equivalent harms to innocent civilians. But it also seems that, when they become soldiers, they accept a professional role that comes with duties to accept risks to themselves as a means of avoiding harming innocent bystanders in the course of fulfilling their other duties, such as their duty to protect their civilian fellow citizens.[28] It is thus possible that harms to just combatants have somewhat less weight in wide proportionality than equivalent harms to innocent civilians. The duty to accept risks may, however, be to some extent offset by the fact that self-defence by just combatants is instrumental to the fulfillment of their duty to protect their fellow citizens.

There is, however, another reason for doubting that the prevention of harms to just combatants can always offset harms these combatants would otherwise cause as a side effect to civilians. When civilians are threatened with being wrongly killed, there is a limit to the amount of harm that it can be proportionate to inflict on innocent bystanders as a side effect of preventing the killings. But when soldiers intervene to save the threatened civilians at some risk to themselves, they thereby increase the overall amount of harm that the unjust side will try to inflict on innocent people (as they are themselves innocent in the relevant sense). We can ask whether their decision to put themselves at risk can increase the amount of harm they may permissibly cause to innocent bystanders relative to what it would be if they could intervene in complete safety.

Suppose, for example, that just combatants can save 100 of their civilian fellow citizens but only in a way that will kill 20 innocent enemy civilians as a side effect, which we can stipulate is the maximum number it is proportionate for them to kill (that is, it is proportionate to kill an innocent bystander as a side effect of saving five other innocent people but not as a side effect of saving fewer than five). If the just combatants intervene to save the hundred, however, ten of them will be killed by unjust combatants unless they engage in self-defensive action that will kill two more innocent enemy civilians as a side effect. It may seem that, if they intervene, they will then be preventing 110 innocent people from being wrongly killed, so that their killing 22 innocent bystanders as a side effect will be proportionate (since they save five for everyone one they kill as a side effect). But this, I think, is a mistake. The only people who are initially at risk are the 100 innocent civilians. If the just combatants expose themselves to risk as a means of saving the 100 and then kill two innocent bystanders as a side effect of averting the risk to which they have exposed themselves, they will in effect have killed 22 innocent civilians as a side effect of pursuing their means of saving the 100. And killing 22 as a side effect of saving 100 is, by our earlier stipulation, disproportionate. In the circumstances, therefore, the just combatants ought not to intervene to save the 100 unless they are willing to allow ten among themselves to be killed in the course of doing so.[29]

Suppose, however, that the same just combatants are epistemically justified in believing that they can save the 100 civilians in a way that will unavoidably kill the 20 enemy civilians as a side effect but without exposing themselves to any risk of being killed. They therefore undertake what they reasonably believe will be a proportionate rescue mission. But well into the mission they are ambushed in a way that they could not have foreseen. Ten of them will be killed unless they engage in defensive action that will kill two enemy civilians as a side effect. Whether or not they engage in self-defense, they, or the survivors among them, will still be able to save the 100 at the cost of killing 20. It may seem that what I have argued implies that they must not engage in defensive action, thus allowing ten of their number to be killed. But in fact I think that in *these* circumstances, it is permissible for them to save the ten at the cost of killing the two. This is because assessments of proportionality must always be entirely prospective. The choice they must make now is not whether to save the 100 at the cost of killing 20 *and* making it the case that ten others will be killed unless they kill two more. Rather, their choice is simply whether to save ten innocent people at the cost of killing two others as a side effect, which we have stipulated is proportionate.[30]

5. *In Bello* Necessity

I will conclude with a very brief discussion of *in bello* necessity.[31] It is often thought that what this principle says is that an act of war is permissible only if there is no less harmful means of achieving the same aim (which, for purposes of discussion, we can assume is a defensive aim). There are, however, two problems with this formulation of the necessity constraint. One is that it fails to distinguish between harms inflicted on those who are liable to those harms and harms inflicted on those who are not liable to them. Suppose, for example, that there are two ways that just combatants can prevent ten innocent people from being wrongly killed. One is to kill the two unjust combatants who are culpably attempting to kill the ten. The other is to incapacitate the two unjust combatants without harming them, although that will unavoidably kill an innocent bystander as a side effect. Assume that both options are proportionate. Although the second would cause less harm, it would clearly be wrong to choose it rather than the first.

The second problem is that this formulation of the necessity constraint fails to take account of the fact that different means of defence may have different probabilities of success. Suppose that just combatants have two possible means of trying to prevent the wrongful killing of 100 civilians. These means are mutually exclusive in the sense that pursing one is certain to provoke the enemy to make the other impossible. The first of these means would be certain to save 100 innocent civilians but would also be certain to kill one innocent bystander as a side effect. The other would have an 80 per cent probability of successfully defending the 100 civilians but would not kill any innocent bystander. While the first means would cause more harm—harm, moreover, that would be inflicted on someone who would not be liable to it—its significantly greater probability of success shields it from the charge of causing unnecessary harm because the harm it would cause is an unavoidable concomitant of its greater probability of success.

A more plausible formulation of the necessity constraint, which also frequently appears in the just war literature, explicitly takes account of the probability of success. According to this view, an act of war is permissible only if there is no alternative act of war that (1) would have an equal or higher probability of achieving the same aim or another equally important aim and (2) whose bad effects would be less bad, taking into account both considerations of liability and considerations of agency (such as the distinction between harming as a means and harming as a side effect).

Yet this understanding of the necessity constraint is also unacceptable. Suppose again that just combatants have two mutually exclusive means of attempting to prevent 100 innocent civilians from being wrongly killed by unjust combatants. The first would require killing ten unjust combatants and would have a 99 per cent probability of successfully defending the lives of the 100 civilians. The second would have a 100 percent probability of saving the 100 civilians, would not involve harming or killing any unjust combatants, but would kill two innocent bystanders as a side effect. Assume that both these options are proportionate (the first in the narrow sense and the second in the wide sense). The only ground for choosing between them is necessity. According to the second interpretation of the necessity constraint, the second option is necessary because there is no other option that promises to be as effective in achieving the just defensive aim. One might say, echoing what I said earlier, that the harm to the two innocent bystanders is necessary because it is an unavoidable concomitant of the second option's greater probability of success.

It seems clear, however, that the first option is morally better than the second. Although the first option has a slightly lower probability of saving the 100 civilians, and even though it would kill more people, and even though it would kill them as an intended means rather than as a side effect, it is morally better because its slightly lower probability of success is outweighed by the fact that it would not inflict any harms to which the victims were not liable, whereas the second option would kill two people who are not liable to any harm. In cases such as this, in which neither option would involve greater cost to the agents than the other, it would be perverse for the necessity constraint to rule out the morally better option. And the morally better option is not necessarily the one that has the highest probability of successfully achieving the just aim. Rather, an act's probability of success must be weighed against the harms the act would inflict on victims who would not be liable to those harms.

I suspect that many people have been misled by the thought that the *necessity* condition must permit whatever means is *necessary* for the achievement of a just aim, where a means is understood to be necessary, even if it is not certain to achieve the aim, if it has a higher probability of achieving the aim than any other possible means. But necessity cannot plausibly be understood in this way, as the example just considered shows. It has to be sensitive to tradeoffs between the harm prevented and the harm caused, even when the harms that might be caused by alternative means would all be proportionate. Leaving aside considerations of cost to the agent, what the necessity constraint requires is that one choose, from among the proportionate defensive options, the one that is overall morally best. This is what we would naturally expect in the moral constraint on defensive harming that requires comparisons among different possible means of defence.

Like the wide principle of *in bello* proportionality, this more complex principle of necessity cannot be coherently applied to many acts of war conducted by unjust combatants. This is because one cannot coherently trade off the probability of success in achieving unjust aims against harms to which the victims are not liable. There are, however, certain rather simple cases in which a crude form of necessity constraint applies to the action of unjust combatants. If, for example, unjust combatants have two options for the achievement of a military aim and each has an equal probability of success but one would cause more harm to innocent bystanders than the other, it is a genuine moral requirement that *if* the unjust combatants are going to do wrong by pursuing one of these options, they *ought* to choose the one that would cause less harm to innocent bystanders. This is an implication of the simple requirement, which is a form of necessity requirement, never to cause harm wholly wantonly or gratuitously.

Acknowledgements

I am very grateful to Susanne Burri for written comments on an earlier draft, to Tom Dannenbaum and Victor Tadros for helpful discussion, and to Frances Kamm for her commentary when I presented an earlier draft at Harvard. I am particularly indebted to Seth Lazar for extensive and perceptive written comments.

Notes

1. Compare Gabriella Blum, 'The Dispensable Lives of Soldiers', *Journal of Legal Analysis* 2 (2010), 115–170.
2. Jeff McMahan, 'What Rights May Be Defended by Means of War?' in *The Morality of Defensive War*, edited by Cécile Fabre and Seth Lazar (Oxford: Oxford University Press, 2014).
3. See Jeff McMahan, *Killing in War* (Oxford: Clarendon Press, 2009), 20–24.
4. I briefly explore this possibility in a review of Helen Frowe's book, *Defensive Killing*, forthcoming in *Ethics*. My thinking about the relevance of probabilities to proportionality has been greatly influenced by unpublished work by Patrick Tomlin.
5. The relevance to the morality of war of effects that are comparatively bad but not worse for any particular people is the topic of work in progress by Michael Robillard. On the

Non-Identity Problem, see Derek Parfit, *Reasons and Persons* (Oxford: Oxford University Press, 1984), part 4.

6. See, for example, Jeff McMahan and Robert McKim, 'The Just War and the Gulf War', *Canadian Journal of Philosophy* 23 (1993), 501–541; Thomas Hurka, 'Proportionality in the Morality of War', *Philosophy and Public Affairs* 33 (2005), 34–66; and Kamm, *Ethics for Enemies*, chapter 3.
7. Jeff McMahan, 'Proportionality and Just Cause: A Comment on Kamm', *Journal of Moral Philosophy* 11 (2014), 428–453.
8. This implicitly repudiates the position for which I argued in 'Just Cause for War', *Ethics and International Affairs* 19 (2005), 1–21. That article was written before I came to understand the importance of distinguishing between narrow and wide proportionality.
9. Just war theory has, for many centuries, generally assumed that it makes a difference to the permissibility of harming innocent people that the harm is a side effect rather than an intended means. This assumption has recently been forcefully challenged. For one influential challenge, see Judith Jarvis Thomson, 'Self-Defense', *Philosophy and Public Affairs* 20 (1991), 283–310, esp. 289–296.
10. In an as-yet-unpublished paper ('Proportionality in War: A Surprising Finding'), Patrick Tomlin ingeniously demonstrates that in a war in which the harms necessary for victory are overdetermined, it could be that every act of war is proportionate while the war as a whole is disproportionate. This would not, however, be for the reasons given by traditional just war theory. He also shows that, granting certain widely accepted assumptions in population ethics, it is possible that there could be a war in which every act of war is disproportionate but the war as a whole is proportionate. Again, however, this would not be for reasons deriving from traditional just war theory.
11. See Shue's chapter, in this volume. The assumption that harms to civilians must be weighed against military advantage is found in discussions in moral philosophy in which issues in the morality of war are merely illustrative. See, for example, T. M. Scanlon, *Moral Dimensions: Permissibility, Meaning, Blame* (Cambridge, MA: Harvard University Press, 2008), 28–32.
12. '1977 Geneva Protocol I Additional to the Geneva Conventions of 12 August 1949, and Relating to the Protection of Victims of International Armed Conflicts', in *Documents on the Laws of War*, edited by Adam Roberts and Richard Guelff (Oxford: Oxford University Press, 1982), 416.
13. As Michael Walzer puts it, judgments about *jus ad bellum* and judgments about *jus in bello* 'are logically independent'. Walzer, *Just and Unjust Wars* (New York: Basic Books, 1977), 21. For further discussion, see the essays in *Just and Unjust Warriors: The Moral and Legal Status of Soldiers*, edited by David Rodin and Henry Shue (New York: Oxford University Press, 2008).
14. See, for example, Henry Shue, 'Do We Need a "Morality of War"?', in *Just and Unjust Warriors*, edited by Rodin and Shue; and Janina Dill and Henry Shue, 'Limiting the Killing in War: Military Necessity and the St. Petersburg Assumption', *Ethics and International Affairs* 26 (2012), 311–333.
15. See David Rodin, 'Morality and Law in War', in Hew Strachan and Sibylle Scheipers, eds., *The Changing Character of War* (Oxford: Oxford University Press, 2011).
16. Jeff McMahan, 'War Crimes and Immoral Action in War', in *The Constitution of Criminal Law* edited by Antony Duff et al. (Oxford: Oxford University Press, 2013), 181–183.

17. See Jeff McMahan, 'The Prevention of Unjust Wars', in *Reading Walzer*, edited by Yitzhak Benbaji and Naomi Sussman (London: Routledge, 2013).
18. Two theorists who have been developing suggestions along these lines are Adil Haque and Seth Lazar. See Haque, *Law and Morality at War* (Oxford: Oxford University Press, forthcoming) and Lazar, *Sparing Civilians* (Oxford: Oxford University Press, 2015).
19. In the following paragraphs, I draw on some ideas that appear in Jeff McMahan, 'Gaza: Is Israel Fighting a Just War?' *Prospect Magazine* online (5 August 2014). Available at http://www.prospectmagazine.co.uk/philosophy/gaza-is-israel-and-hamass-conflict-a-just-war
20. See, for example, Jonathan Quong, 'Liability to Defensive Harm', *Philosophy and Public Affairs* 40 (2012), 45–77; and Helen Frowe, *Defensive Killing* (Oxford: Oxford University Press, 2014).
21. Thomson, 'Self-Defense'; and Michael Otsuka, 'Killing the Innocent in Self-Defense', *Philosophy and Public Affairs* 23 (1994), 74–94.
22. Nancy Davis, 'Abortion and Self-Defense', *Philosophy and Public Affairs* 13 (1984), 175–207; and Jonathan Quong, 'Killing in Self-Defense', *Ethics* 119 (2009), 507–537.
23. For discussion, see Jeff McMahan, 'Self-Defense Against Justified Threateners', in *How We Fight: Ethics in War*, edited by Helen Frowe and Gerald Lang (Oxford: Oxford University Press, 2014), 104–137.
24. Jonathan Quong, 'Agent-Relative Prerogatives to Do Harm', *Criminal Law and Philosophy* (forthcoming); Seth Lazar, 'Associative Duties and the Ethics of Killing', *Journal of Practical Ethics* 1 (2013), 3–48; and Seth Lazar, 'Authorization and the Morality of War', *Australasian Journal of Philosophy* (forthcoming, 2015).
25. Jeff McMahan, *The Ethics of Killing: Problems at the Margins of Life* (New York: Oxford University Press, 2002), 217–228. For a discussion of the relevance of special relations to the morality of war, see Lazar, 'Associative Duties and the Ethics of Killing'.
26. Judith Jarvis Thomson, 'The Trolley Problem', *Yale Law Journal* 94 (1985), 1395–1415.
27. Jeff McMahan, 'Rethinking the 'Just War', Part 2', *New York Times Opinionator* (November 12, 2012). Available at http://opinionator.blogs.nytimes.com/2012/11/12/rethinking-the-just-war-part-2/?_r=0
28. For discussion, see Jeff McMahan, 'The Just Distribution of Harm Between Combatants and Noncombatants', *Philosophy and Public Affairs* 38 (2010), 366–369; and Gerhard Øverland, 'High Fliers: Who Should Bear the Risk of Humanitarian Intervention?', in *New Wars and New Soldiers: Military Ethics in the Contemporary World*, edited by Paolo Tripodi and Jessica Wolfendale (Farnham, Surry: Ashgate, 2011).
29. For a further dimension of the problem that I cannot discuss here, see Gerhard Øverland, 'Moral Obstacles: An Alternative to the Doctrine of Double Effect', *Ethics* 124 (2014), 481–506; and Alec Walen, 'Transcending the Means Principle', *Law and Philosophy* 33 (2014), 427–464.
30. For a defence of the claim that proportionality is entirely prospective, see Jeff McMahan, 'Proportionality and Time', *Ethics* 125 (2015), 696–719.
31. For a much more detailed and comprehensive discussion of the requirement of necessity, see Seth Lazar, 'Necessity in Self-Defense and War', *Philosophy and Public Affairs* 40 (2012), 3–44. Also see Jeff McMahan, 'The Limits of Self-Defense', in *The Ethics of Self-Defense*, edited by Christian Coons and Michael Eric Weber (New York: Oxford University Press, forthcoming).

CHAPTER 22

TERRORISM

SUZANNE UNIACKE

How is terrorism relevant to the ethics of war? My question is prompted by two considerations. First, terrorism can occur within civil society as well as in contexts of armed combat or war. In this chapter, I shall be concerned with how the moral wrongfulness of terrorism as a distinct phenomenon can shed light on an important aspect of the ethics of war.[1]

The second consideration is the claim that, as a means of fighting, terrorist tactics are answerable to principles that govern ethically acceptable conduct of war, not the other way around. The first part of this claim is sound, but it does not follow from this that the ethics of terrorism can add nothing to our critical understanding of the principles of *jus in bello*. Recent philosophical discussions of whether terrorist tactics can ever be morally justified might attest to this last point insofar as they engage with the question of whether the *jus in bello* principle of discrimination that prohibits targeting innocent people ought to represent an absolute prohibition as opposed to a very stringent constraint. In this chapter, I argue for a different, deeper point: namely, that examination of the structure of terrorism and its distinctive wrongfulness is relevant to how we should morally interpret the *jus in bello* principle of discrimination.

My argument will depend on understanding what terrorism is. Terrorism is a contested notion in the philosophical literature, across policy documents, and in public discourse. In Section 1, I provide a characterization of terrorism that highlights its central features without claiming to be definitive. Although I reject a strongly moralized conception according to which terrorism is morally wrongful by definition, a satisfactory characterization of terrorism will include normative elements that have a significant bearing on its ethical evaluation. I turn more directly to ethical issues in Section 2 and conclude the discussion in Section 3.

1. What Is Terrorism?

Conceptions of terrorism have shifted over time.[2] Our focus in this chapter is contemporary terrorism, as opposed to various historical understandings and instances of terrorism. Here, we need to elucidate 'terrorism' in its everyday sense, as opposed to how 'terrorism' might best be defined in policy or law. As commonly understood, terrorism has somewhat imprecise boundaries: its motivation may be religious or ideological as well as political; it could include actions, such as cyber-attacks, that are not strictly speaking violent; and it can extend to, for example, assassination perpetrated by groups who use terrorism as part of a broader political agenda.

In characterizing contemporary terrorism in terms of its central features I shall draw on prominent recent philosophical definitions. 'Terrorism' is not a term of art, and philosophical conceptions that are too removed from common contemporary understandings become arcane and ill-suited for the purposes of practical ethics, for making a useful contribution to public debate, and for having an input to shaping or evaluating policy or laws on terrorism.[3] Nonetheless, a satisfactory characterization will need to stipulate to an extent, since alongside related terms such as 'violence', 'terrorism' is frequently used loosely in everyday discourse. (This looseness sometimes trivializes what 'terrorism' in its more legitimate sense(s) conveys and can thus undermine the effect intended by those who inappropriately label as terrorism nonterrorist activities that they seek to vilify by association.) Whereas a satisfactory characterization will capture much of what is commonly understood by 'terrorism' and allow both for some imprecision of use and also for the inclusion of nonparadigmatic instances of terrorism (such as so-called *lone-wolf terrorism* involving someone acting on his own), at the same time, it needs to respect significant distinctions that are sometimes neglected in everyday parlance between, for example, terrorism and subversion, and terrorism and other types of political intimidation and coercion.

We can begin by identifying common features of a range of individual, coordinated, and collective activities that are widely regarded as paradigmatic instances of terrorism. Examples include a long list of aircraft hijackings across the world; the sarin gas attack on the Tokyo subway by members of Aum Shinrikyo in March 1995; the car bomb attack by the Real IRA in Omagh, Northern Ireland in August 1998; the coordinated attacks by members of al-Qaeda in New York City and Washington DC in September 2001; the bombing attacks by members of Jemaah Islamiyah in Bali in October 2002; the bombings conducted by a group of Islamists in London in July 2005; the shooting and bomb attacks by members of Lashkar-e-Taiba in Mumbai in November 2008; the sequential bombings and mass shootings by Anders Breivik in and near Oslo in July 2011; the multiple shootings and hostage-taking in a shopping centre in Nairobi, Kenya in September 2013 by members of the Somali militant group al-Shabab; and, in 2014, the abduction of more than 200 schoolgirls by the al-Qaeda-linked militia Boko Haram in Nigeria, and the mass killings of civilians, including 'demonstration' beheadings of hostages, by members of the Islamic State of Iraq and the Levant (ISIL). Instances of attempted terrorism include the actions of Richard Reid (in 2001) and those of Umar Farouk Abdulmutallab (in 2009) who tried unsuccessfully to detonate explosive devices on civilian aircraft. These and similar examples involve attempted or actual attacks, either with conventional weapons (e.g., knives, guns, bombs) or by nonconventional means (e.g., hijacked civilian aircraft used as missiles). Terrorist activity more broadly includes incitement to terrorism and intentional support for terrorism in the form of weapons supply or funding, as well as active planning and preparation for terrorist attacks.

From the preceding examples we can identify terrorism as paradigmatically a type of violence that aims to achieve political ends by coercive means, usually through instilling terror, fear, or significant insecurity through unpredictable attacks on illegitimate targets. Typically, terrorism is conducted by non-state actors who directly target a limited number of innocent people as (an attempted) means of exerting influence over decision-makers or a larger group or of fomenting social upheaval.

Each aspect of the preceding characterization can be queried as an essential element of terrorism. For instance, in characterizing terrorism as a political tactic involving the deliberate frightening of people for political advantage, Robert Goodin makes no explicit mention of violence;[4] in this respect, he differs significantly from many accounts including those of C. A. J. Coady[5] and Tamar Meisels.[6] As Claudia Card notes, terrorist acts can be motivated by revenge or intended as communicative as opposed to coercive.[7] And whereas terrorism is usually associated with non-state actors, there can be state terrorism and state-sponsored terrorism where, for instance, a government might use chemical weapons in order to coerce its own population, or a state might target another state's civilian population as a way of undermining morale or turning them against their own government.

A number of theorists, including Stephen Nathanson and Igor Primoratz, identify terrorism as having a distinctive normative structure and tactical purpose whereby it directly targets innocent people as (an attempted) means of indirectly intimidating or coercing others into a course of action they would not otherwise take.[8] This particular tactical aspect of terrorism is absent from or attenuated in the accounts of Walter Sinnott-Armstrong, David Rodin, and F. M. Kamm.[9] I think that reference to (a threat of) serious violence used against some people as a political tactic that is intended to intimidate or coerce others can be important in differentiating terrorism from, for example, political strike action involving essential services and also from other types of political violence such as genocide, assassination, sabotage, or riot. Nonetheless, the direct targets of terrorism might include (some of) those whom it is intended to intimidate (as happens when, e.g., animal rights militants target researchers), and terrorism can directly target infrastructure or property (e.g., communications systems, public transport, commercial buildings, power plants).

Some theorists develop definitions that explicitly link terrorism to what they regard as its central moral wrongfulness; namely, that it directly targets innocent people.[10] However, definitions according to which the direct targets of distinctively terrorist violence are innocent—that is, people who are not themselves threatening or otherwise legitimate targets—need not be morally motivated in this way.[11]

Terrorism is sometimes described as a tactic of the weak or politically powerless.[12] This generalization makes the point that terrorist tactics are often a means of fighting used by a party to a conflict who is manifestly the weaker in terms of conventional military capability or political power, who attempts to use its own specific relative advantages in order to exploit particular vulnerabilities of the stronger party. An imbalance in military capacity or political power has no necessary connection with terrorism, however. Clearly, not all weaker adversaries resort to terrorist tactics to compensate for a significant disadvantage in their conventional fighting capacity or political strength relative to a (perceived) much stronger adversary, and terrorist tactics are not exclusively a weaker party's weapon.[13]

The relative advantages that terrorists exploit include their own willingness to use conventional and nonconventional weapons to operate outside both domestic and international law. Terrorists target their adversaries' vulnerabilities, such as their unprotected civilian population and public facilities, their reliance on infrastructure, and their operational limits in responding to threats. Their adversaries also often have *normative* vulnerabilities, such as constraints on their responses to terrorism grounded in a concern to uphold particular values and individual rights, such as freedom of movement and privacy, and in their commitment to domestic and international law.

Terrorism represents an unconventional means of fighting, not simply as contrasted with conventional military methods of conducting warfare, but also insofar as terrorist action directly contravenes domestic law or central elements of the laws of war embodied in international humanitarian law, the most salient being the *jus in bello* principle of discrimination that prohibits directly targeting innocent people.

2. Ethical Issues

Terrorism as I have characterized it is not morally wrongful by definition. Nonetheless, as a type of coercive political violence that targets innocent people, on any defensible normative moral theory, terrorism is seriously morally objectionable. Terrorist attacks such as those listed in Section 1 violate their direct victims' most basic human rights, often to devastating effect; moreover, the fear, insecurity, and harm that (threatened) terrorist violence causes is intended, usually as a means of intimidation and coercion for political ends. Where terrorist action is intended as primarily communicative as opposed to coercive, it nonetheless aims to exert pressure or influence by means of (threatened) violence directed against innocent people or property.

The further, substantive question of whether, despite their presumptive grave wrongfulness, terrorist tactics could ever be morally justified all things considered has received extensive detailed attention in recent philosophical discussions that tend to differ from one another within a narrow but significant range, either maintaining that terrorism is never morally permissible or else providing heavily qualified defences according to which terrorist tactics could be morally justifiable in a just cause, in desperate circumstances, and under strict moral conditions.[14]

Theorists who regard terrorism as always morally impermissible do not always do so from the same basis in normative moral theory, and the same is true of those who offer heavily qualified defences of terrorist tactics. Nonetheless, for such accounts, and also for closely related discussions such as that of Cécile Fabre,[15] the question of whether characteristic terrorist tactics could ever be morally justified focuses on whether the *jus in bello* principle of discrimination represents an absolute moral prohibition that gives nonthreatening people complete moral immunity against direct attack, as opposed to its being a stringent moral constraint open to permissible infringement under strict conditions. (To my mind, the latter terminology better expresses a nonabsolutist interpretation of this principle, the contravention of which morally wrongs its direct victims by infringing their basic rights against harmful interference, as compared with Fabre's contention that the principle itself may be 'relaxed' under strict conditions.)[16] While this particular focus on the principle of discrimination addresses the central terrorist tactic in the context of an important, more general question of normative ethics that concerns the intentional harming of innocent people, it also risks obscuring the fact that some actions that arguably have the normative structure of terrorism seem to lack its distinctive moral wrongfulness. This focus also tends to downplay the relationship between the moral wrongfulness of terrorism and that of some other morally objectionable means of fighting.

Before taking up these more specific points, it is important to address the general significance of the just war norm to the ethics of terrorism. This is because scepticism is sometimes aired about the relevance of this norm both to the ethical evaluation of so-called *new wars* that can differ radically in their causes, agents, or methods from those of traditional or conventional wars, and also to the evaluation of violent conflicts and terrorist attacks that occur outside an established war or fall short of the scale and duration associated with warfare.[17]

2.1. The Significance of the Just War Norm

Many recent philosophical discussions of the ethics of terrorism invoke the prevailing just war norm as a lodestar. (Michael Walzer's discussion of guerrilla war and terrorism is a key influence.)[18] Alongside this, there are genuine and important questions to be addressed about the interpretation of elements of the just war norm as applied in circumstances of violent conflict where previously relatively clear concepts, categories, and distinctions have become less clear both in theory and also in practice. (These questions include, for example, who or what has the legitimacy to wage war; the conditions under which a threat is actual, as opposed to potential or merely possible; and who or what is a legitimate target.)[19] All the same, in my view, scepticism that is sometimes expressed about the *relevance* to the ethics of terrorism of the just war norm should be addressed in the following terms.

The *jus ad bellum* conditions of just cause, last resort, and proportionality represent broader ethical principles and constraints that have very weighty purchase in our moral thinking about whether and when the infliction of intended or foreseeable harm on others by the use of violence can be justified. The use of violence always requires significant moral justification for which the onus lies squarely with the actor. First and foremost, a resort to violence (including defensive violence) must be justified in terms of considerations that are represented by the central elements of *jus ad bellum* that address the basic conditions that could justify going to war. The use of violence against other people and their property can be justified only if it has a legitimate purpose; it is unavoidable if its legitimate purpose is to be attained; and its use, with the harm it is likely to cause, is proportionate to the purpose it aims to achieve. Other conditions of *jus ad bellum*, such as the requirements that the decision to go to war is made by a legitimate authority and that the war has a reasonable prospect of success, are more appropriate to the ethics of political violence in my view.[20]

As with the more basic conditions of *jus ad bellum*, the *jus in bello* principles of discrimination and of necessary and proportionate force that govern permissible conduct within war represent ethical principles and constraints that are applicable to the justification of the use of violence more generally. People who are innocent in the sense that they do not threaten unjust harm to others have moral rights against harmful interference, and they are morally wronged when these rights are violated or infringed.[21] Moreover, the infringement of the rights of innocent people as an incidental effect of a well-intentioned action is morally unjustified if it is avoidable or disproportionate in relation to the action's intended good purpose. These more general principles apply even to individual self-defence against unjust attack. For instance, an innocent person under attack cannot permissibly push an innocent bystander into the line of fire so that the bystander's body becomes a shield against the attacker's bullets, nor can she cause unnecessary or disproportionate collateral harm to innocent bystanders by defending herself by otherwise legitimate means.

2.2. The Wrongfulness of Terrorism

Although the conditions of *jus ad bellum* are fundamental to consideration of the ethics of terrorism as an instance of political violence, it is the characteristic features of terrorism as a distinguishable type of political violence that are most salient to its ethical evaluation. Since terrorism typically involves a strategic attack against innocent people as (an attempted) means of achieving political ends, the conditions of *jus in bello* and the principle of discrimination, in particular, understandably receive most philosophical attention in this regard.

However, a narrow focus on the *jus in bello* principle of discrimination as pivotal to the question of whether terrorist tactics could ever be morally justified can divert attention away from the complexity of terrorism's moral wrongfulness. Of course, the fact that terrorist attacks target innocent people is a morally central feature: such acts are (presumptively) gravely morally wrong because they are murderous. (Not forgetting that the deliberate destruction of property, public facilities, and so on is also wrongful in the absence of an overriding justification.) But this is a feature that terrorism shares with some nonterrorist attacks on innocent people, such as racist attacks. Terrorist attacks also (attempt to) intimidate and coerce people and this feature, too, is sufficient to make such actions (presumptively) seriously morally wrong. But again, (attempted) coercion is a morally significant feature that terrorism shares with some nonterrorist actions such as extortion or unjustified strike action, which holds a community to ransom by withdrawing essential services. Moreover, the simple combination of these two morally significant features is also something that terrorism, so characterized, could share with cases of nonterrorist violence; for instance, with the setting of land mines where this is intended both to dispatch particular people who habitually use the mined areas and also to keep other people away.

So, although the violent and the coercive aspects of terrorism are sufficient to ground its (presumptive) grave moral wrongfulness, these particular features, taken either individually or in combination, are not morally distinctive of terrorism and fail sufficiently to capture the moral wrongfulness of terrorism *qua* terrorism. For this reason, various theorists, including Card and Primoratz, have emphasized the normative structure of terrorism as fundamental to its distinctive moral wrongfulness and the need to focus on this structure in order fully to appreciate the nature of the wrong done to the direct victims of terrorism, in particular.[22] Primoratz, for instance, maintains that what is morally distinctive about terrorism is that it is 'a deliberate violence against innocent people—innocent civilians in the context of war, or common citizens, in a conflict that falls short of war—perpetrated for the sake of intimidation or coercion. No other type of action, however similar to terrorism in some respect, exhibits this type of combination of wrongs.'[23] As Primoratz puts it, this is not simply because terrorism compounds the wrong of violence directed against innocent people with the wrong of deliberate intimidation or coercion: that is to say, because terrorism uses violence against some *and* coerces others (as in the land mines example presented earlier). Rather, it is because, as Card also emphasizes, typically terrorism aims to intimidate or coerce people by means of violence directed against other, innocent people.[24] In so doing, terrorism treats its direct targets merely instrumentally by targeting violence against them as a means of coercing or manipulating others. In so doing, it violates not just particular rights (against harmful interference) of its direct targets but also their human dignity.

The *harm* inflicted on the direct victims of terrorism is loss of liberty, injury, or death, and innocent victims of such intended harms are thereby morally wronged (their rights are violated). However, the *injustice* that is done to the direct victims of terrorism essentially also involves using them as merely a means, violating their human rights as a way of coercing or manipulating others (and thereby to achieve political aims). Of course, terrorism's coercive purpose often relies on the fact that its indirect targets (those whom it aims to coerce) recognize the human dignity of terrorism's direct victims (those who are instrumentally maimed or killed). But, from the terrorists' own perspective, the direct victims of terrorism are treated as 'dispensable'.

Although Card and Primoratz rightly emphasize the significance of the structure of terrorist violence to an appreciation of the nature of its moral wrongfulness, I think that what Primoratz regards as the distinctive moral wrongfulness of terrorism is in fact something that terrorism shares with some instances of (criminal) duress or abduction where, for example, innocent members of a person's family are harmed as a means of coercing that person. Here, too, the moral wrong that is done to the direct, innocent victims involves using violence against them as a means of intimidating or coercing others into a course of action they would not otherwise take. If this is right, then terrorism is not the only type of action that has this normative structure and that, thereby, instantiates this particular kind of moral wrongdoing.

Of course, other characteristic features of terrorism can distinguish it from nonterrorist violence against some innocent people that is used as a means of coercing others. Terrorism is a political tactic that typically aims to coerce people by causing terror, fear, or significant insecurity; usually, it aims to achieve this by using unpredictable serious violence or the threat of such violence against innocent people, exploiting their vulnerability as they go about their everyday lives. Innocent people who are abducted, raped, maimed, or killed as direct targets of terrorism are not simply harmed as a means of coercing others (morally terrible as these violations might be) for any ends; they are targeted as a means of coercing other people for political aims. (Primoratz distinguishes nonpolitical, as opposed to political terrorism.[25] However, criminal gangs who terrorize communities for nonpolitical or nonideological ends are not engaged in terrorism as commonly understood. The families of witnesses in criminal trials who are harmed in order to intimidate the witnesses themselves are not victims of terrorism.)

What is distinctive about terrorism, both conceptually and morally, is due to the convergence and interaction of its characteristic features. The salient point here concerns the *nature* of the moral wrong done to the direct victims of terrorist violence, as opposed to the scale or the seriousness of the harm or the moral wrong done to them (and others). To be killed in a genocidal attack is worse for its direct victims than were they instead to be abducted and subsequently freed as direct victims of terrorism, and to kill a thousand innocent people unnecessarily while bombing a military target, out of gross indifference to the value of their lives, could be morally a much worse offence than using terrorist violence against a very few people. But to target people for genocidal reasons or to kill them recklessly during war does not morally wrong them in the same way as would deliberately killing them as a means of coercing others for political ends.

Once we appreciate the nature of the moral wrongfulness of terrorism as it is usually perpetrated, it is clear that the question of whether terrorist tactics could ever be justified all things considered should not be simplified (as it sometimes is) by asking whether it can ever be justified to use serious (including lethal) violence against some innocent people as a means of preventing far greater harm or evil being done to others. The relevant question about terrorism must include whether it could be morally justified to use serious (including lethal) violence against innocent people in an instrumental and intrinsically morally objectionable way that disregards their human dignity by using them merely as a means of coercing others for political ends.

We can note that terrorist attacks can disregard the human dignity of their direct victims in distinguishable ways. For instance, the direct victims of terrorism whose lives are treated as dispensable in the service of political ends include those who are forcibly used as terrorist weapons (e.g., young children used as suicide bombers) as well as those people who are randomly targeted (e.g., anyone who happens to be on a particular bus). Other direct victims of terrorism, such as political satirists, who are selectively targeted because of the values that their activities represent, are disposed of from revenge as well as to intimidate or coerce others.

2.3. Terrorism and Targeting the Innocent

An appreciation of the complex moral wrongfulness of terrorism is important to a satisfactory understanding of the ethics of terrorism and to the more specific question of whether terrorist or terrorist-related tactics could ever be morally justified all things considered. On this basis, I shall now maintain that some actions that both contravene the *jus in bello* principle of discrimination as conventionally understood and that also contain central elements of the normative structure of terrorism nonetheless lack the distinctive moral wrongfulness of terrorism. Reflection on why this is so can shed light on how we should morally interpret the principle of discrimination.

My argument proceeds from an example cited by Claudia Card, in which, during World War II, partisan resistance fighters bombed trains en route to the Nazi death camps in Poland.[26] Card regards these bombings as *terrorist* because, in addition to their directly disrupting a significant part of the Nazi extermination programme, they were intended as a means of drawing the attention of the international community to the significance of those trains. Moreover, Card regards these bombings as a paradigm instance of *justified* terrorism.

I think that Card's characterization and evaluation of this particular example can be open to question. The first issue is that the example is arguably although not paradigmatically an instance of terrorism. The bombings were conducted by non-state actors (armed civilians) and were aimed at a nonmilitary target. But, even if we accept Card's claim that the bombings were intended to draw international attention to the significance of the Holocaust trains, it is a further step to maintain that the people being deported on those trains were themselves directly targeted as a means to this end. Presumably, bombing the trains provided a possible—perhaps the only possible—means of escape for those who were headed for the Nazi death camps in locked and windowless cattle wagons. And, if so, arguably, those on the trains who were in fact victims of the bombings in the sense that they were killed when the trains were bombed were not themselves directly targeted in the sense of being intended, as opposed to foreseen, victims of the bombings. On the other hand, their presence on the trains was not incidental to the point of the bombings since the trains were bombed precisely because those on board were being taken to the death camps.

The second issue is that the moral justification of bombing Holocaust trains should give pause for a number of reasons, even on what I take to be the uncontroversial assumption that guerrilla warfare by the partisans against the Nazis was justified. Those people who were captive on the trains were very serious candidates for rescue, and if, say, there had been a way of trying to save the lives of people on a particular train with a realistic chance of success, then killing them by bombing that train would have been morally impermissible. A more general consideration is that while it is reasonable to presume that many of those killed when the trains were bombed would otherwise have been exterminated by the Nazis, presumably some of them might otherwise have survived the death camps.[27] A judgment on whether bombing the trains was a proportionate means to achieving the partisans' aims would need to include consideration of how many people killed by the bombings might otherwise reasonably have been expected to survive the death camps as well as whether it was realistic to expect that some people would escape when the trains were bombed.

In my view, the preceding considerations complicate the characterization and evaluation of these particular bombings as justified terrorism. But let's accept for the sake of argument that the bombings did directly target the innocent people who were captive on the trains and also that this was justified as a means of drawing international attention to the significance of the trains. Nonetheless, these particular bombings seem to lack the distinctive moral wrongfulness of terrorism. I think this is because alongside the features outlined earlier that arguably make the train bombings morally problematic, two other related considerations morally distinguish this example from paradigmatic contraventions of the *jus in bello* principle of discrimination.

The first of these considerations is that whereas those on the trains were illegitimate direct targets under the principle of discrimination as conventionally understood, they were not akin to noncombatants or civilians who are directly targeted while going about their legitimate or everyday activities. On the contrary, the people on the bombed trains were already endangered as captive victims in a grievous moral outrage from which bombing the trains spared them the final terrible outcome (the death camps). The second consideration is that, insofar as these bombings were aimed at drawing international attention to the significance of the trains, they were intended as a response to the gross disregard for human dignity being perpetrated against the trains' occupants and to expose and oppose this moral atrocity on behalf of those who were captive on the trains, as well as for the sake of similar future victims.

These two considerations point towards a significant respect in which a moral justification for the partisan bombing of Holocaust trains is distinguishable from the more familiar contemporary philosophical arguments that provide a heavily qualified defence of resort to terrorist tactics in some circumstances. The latter arguments constitute what I shall call an 'overriding' defence. This is the view that, whereas the innocent direct victims of terrorist tactics are morally wronged (unjustly targeted), this particular moral wrong might be overridden in the sense of being morally justified, all things considered, under strict conditions and in response to a dilemma that Fabre, following Rodin, expresses in the following way: Since some belligerents cannot successfully prosecute their just cause unless they resort to asymmetric tactics that are prohibited under the conditions of *jus in bello*, we must either deny such actors the right to resort to those means or else grant them such a right and thereby weaken the traditional protections afforded to noncombatants.[28]

This type of 'overriding' justification concerns the direct targeting of innocent people going about their daily lives or legitimate activities who are not otherwise directly endangered and whose human dignity has not (yet) been contravened. By contrast, the purchase that the partisan bombing of Holocaust trains has as an instance of (purportedly) justified contravention of the principle of discrimination is that it not only spared (many of) its direct victims the genocidal fate to which they were otherwise doomed, but it also directly opposed the moral outrage to which these very people were being subjected. The moral immunity from direct attack of the innocent people being deported on the trains was already being grossly violated, and, although the bombings (presumably) killed many people on the trains, at the same time, these very actions *affirmed* the human dignity of those same people in circumstances in which it was not simply being disrespected but atrociously denied.

The point I draw from the foregoing discussion is that some acts that (arguably) have the normative structure of terrorism insofar as they direct violence at illegitimate targets in order to bring political pressure to bear on others might nonetheless lack a very significant element of the distinctive moral wrongfulness of terrorism that represents a profound disregard for the human dignity of its direct targets. To be sure, the particular World War II example just discussed is very unusual in this respect, but it serves both to highlight the importance of this particular aspect of the moral revulsion that terrorism usually attracts and also the fact that those who argue that terrorist tactics might be justified in desperate circumstances and under strict conditions usually have in mind examples in which the actions involved would directly violate the human rights of some people as a means of preventing far greater violations of the human rights of other people. Although such arguments concede that resort to such tactics would be a grave moral wrong to the victims and thus very deeply morally regrettable, there is no getting around the fact that, for such 'overriding' justifications, those who are directly targeted are treated as 'dispensable'. It is a substantive question whether this kind of injustice perpetrated against some people for the sake of others could be justified as the lesser moral evil and, if so, under what conditions. However, any such (purported) justification needs to distinguish such acts from examples such as the partisan bombings of Holocaust trains, the (purported) moral justification of which does not seek to outweigh or override committing a grave moral injustice to some (otherwise morally unthreatened) people as a means of preventing a greater violation of the rights of others.

A somewhat stronger, but in my view defensible claim is that bombing the Holocaust trains did not perpetrate the type of moral wrong against its direct victims that the *jus in bello* principle of discrimination rejects and, hence, that this particular example is better seen as a moral exception to this particular principle, as opposed to a morally justified infringement of it. Here, it is useful to contrast the example of bombing the Holocaust trains with a hypothetical example that F. M. Kamm invokes in order to argue for her view that innocent people could permissibly be intentionally terror bombed when this is not further against their interests because there is an alternative course of action in which these same people could permissibly be terrified or killed as collateral harm of bombing a military target.[29] Even were we to accept Kamm's (contentious) view that innocent people might permissibly be intentionally terror bombed in the circumstances that she outlines, to target them in this way would morally wrong them in a manner in which bringing about their deaths as (unavoidable and proportionate) collateral harm would not. The fact that these same people might otherwise permissibly be terrified or killed as collateral harm does not annul the type of wrong done to them by intentionally terror bombing them, although in Kamm's view it weakens that wrong.[30] Unlike the bombing of the Holocaust trains, the intentional terror bombing of innocent people in Kamm's example disrespects, as opposed to affirms, the human dignity of its direct victims.

2.4. Wider Implications

Profound disrespect for the human dignity of its victims is something that terrorism shares with some other, distinguishable types of political violence that directly target innocent people, such as genocide.

Moreover, some means of fighting that do not directly target innocent people nonetheless disrespect the human dignity of their victims, and, to the extent that they do so, they share something of the moral wrongfulness of terrorism. Alongside the principle of discrimination, the *jus in bello* principles of necessary and proportionate force also serve to emphasize that appropriate respect is owed to the lives of all those who are endangered by fighting. C. A. J. Coady claims that while the form and effects of attacks that cause unacceptable collateral damage are very different from terrorism, they 'share something of the spirit of terrorist attacks'.[31] Significantly, such attacks fall outside what Coady and some others regard as the central morally wrongful feature of terrorism: namely, that it directly targets innocent people. So if indeed attacks that kill people unacceptably as collateral damage do share something of the 'spirit of terrorism', as I believe they do, this is because, like terrorism, such actions disrespect the human dignity of their victims by killing them unnecessarily or disproportionately out of indifference to the value of their lives. However, the type of disrespect that is due to indifference to the value of a person's life is not the same as the disrespect constituted by treating her life as disposable as a means to a political end.

Practices that bear much closer comparison with terrorism are *tactics* that use innocent people as involuntary human shields or as hostages. The laws of war prohibit these practices alongside the direct targeting of innocent civilians by, for example, firing on them or bombing them. The impermissible use of innocent people as shields and also hostage-taking can and do occur in the context of terrorism; however, philosophical discussions of terrorism in relation to the *jus in bello* principle of discrimination usually regard these other practices as distinguishable moral offences since people who are used as human shields are treated as barriers against attack by others, and people who are taken hostage are subjected to conditional or contingent threats (from the hostage takers or others), as opposed to being directly targeted. Nonetheless, to the extent that the direct victims of these tactics are morally wronged by being treated as objects (e.g., when their bodies are used as physical shields against a threat), or as moral shields against attack (e.g., when military facilities are deliberately located next to schools or hospitals), or as 'bargaining chips' (hostages), these practices share significantly in the distinctive wrongfulness of terrorism.

3. Concluding Remarks

In this chapter, I have taken the view that in addressing the ethics of terrorism it is important to attend to its distinctive features and to the nature of the moral wrongs that it perpetrates. It is important also to a moral evaluation of terrorism not simply to invoke the *jus in bello* principle of discrimination as a moral principle, even though this principle is clearly applicable and central to the wrongfulness of terrorism. We need critically to reflect on the nature of the moral wrongdoing that the principle of discrimination prohibits, alongside the different and morally distinguishable ways in which people can be directly targeted for political ends. From the example of the partisan bombing of Holocaust trains, we can recognize that some methods of fighting that both formally contravene the *jus in bello* principle of discrimination and that are also structurally akin to acts of terrorism can nonetheless affirm values that are central to that particular principle's moral rationale.

On the basis of an examination of the distinctive wrongfulness of terrorism, we can also appreciate that some other types of actions, such as unnecessary or disproportionate bombing, that do not strictly contravene the principle of discrimination nonetheless compromise it by undermining the values that it represents. In disrespecting the human dignity of their victims, such actions can be said to share something of the moral wrongfulness of terrorism. Methods of fighting that treat innocent people as objects or that hold them to ransom as means of political coercion, although structurally distinguishable from terrorism, can be seen more closely to approximate the type of moral wrong that terrorism inflicts on its direct victims.

Notes

1. The contrasting legal frameworks of terrorism-as-crime, as opposed to terrorism-as-war are arguably relevant to ethical issues of terrorism and counter-terrorism; see Seumas Miller, *Terrorism and Counter-Terrorism: Ethics and Liberal Democracy* (Oxford: Wiley-Blackwell, 2009, chapters 4 and 5). I shall not take issue with this contention here.
2. Igor Primoratz provides an outline in *Terrorism: A Philosophical Investigation* (Cambridge: Polity Press, 2013), 10, 30–35.
3. Here we might consider, for example, F. M. Kamm, *Ethics for Enemies: Terror, Torture and War* (Oxford: Oxford University Press, 2011), chapter 2.
4. Robert E. Goodin, *What's Wrong with Terrorism?* (Cambridge: Polity Press, 2006), 156.
5. C. A. J. Coady, 'Terrorism, Morality and Supreme Emergency', in *Terrorism: The Philosophical Issues*, edited by Igor Primoratz (Basingstoke: Palgrave Macmillan, 2004), 80–96.
6. Tamar Meisels, *The Trouble with Terror* (Cambridge: Cambridge University Press, 2008), chapter 1.
7. Claudia Card, *Confronting Evils: Terrorism, Torture, Genocide* (Cambridge: Cambridge University Press, 2010), 131–132.

8. Stephen Nathanson, *Terrorism and the Ethics of War* (Cambridge: Cambridge University Press, 2010), chapter 1; Igor Primoratz, *Terrorism: A Philosophical Investigation* (2013), chapter 1.
9. Walter Sinnott-Armstrong, 'On Primoratz's Definition of Terrorism', *Journal of Applied Philosophy*, 8 (1: 1991): 115–120; David Rodin, 'Terrorism Without Intention', *Ethics* 114 (4: 2004): 752–771; F. M. Kamm, *Ethics for Enemies*, chapter 2.
10. Examples include C. A. J. Coady, 'Terrorism, Morality and Supreme Emergency'. For critical discussion of terrorists' denials of the innocence of their direct targets, see Igor Primoratz, *Terrorism: A Philosophical Investigation*, 47–64.
11. Uwe Steinhoff, *On the Ethics of War and Terrorism* (Oxford: Oxford University Press, 2007), chapter 5.
12. For example, Robert Young, 'Political Terrorism as a Weapon of the Politically Powerless', in *Terrorism: The Philosophical Issues*, 55–64.
13. Uwe Steinhoff, *On the Ethics of War and Terrorism*, 137; Rod Thornton, *Asymmetric Warfare* (Cambridge: Polity Press, 2007), 4.
14. Contributions to this debate include C. A. J. Coady, 'Terrorism, Morality and Supreme Emergency'; Virginia Held, 'Terrorism, Rights and Political Goals', in *Terrorism: the Philosophical Issues*, 65–79; Stephen Nathanson, *Terrorism and the Ethics of War*; Igor Primoratz, *Terrorism: A Philosophical Investigation*; Uwe Steinhoff, *On the Ethics of War and Terrorism*.
15. Cécile Fabre, *Cosmopolitan War*, 242–256.
16. Idem., 255
17. For a discussion, see Daniel Brunstetter and Megan Braun, 'From *Jus ad Bellum* to *Jus ad Vim*: Recalibrating Our Understanding of the Moral Use of Force', *Ethics and International Affairs* 27 (1: 2013), 87–106. See also Jonathan Parry's contribution to this volume.
18. Michael Walzer, *Just and Unjust Wars* (3rd edition) (New York: Basic Books, 1977), 176–206.
19. In *Cosmopolitan War*, 141–156, Fabre addresses the question of the legitimacy of non-state actors to wage war; Paul Gilbert discusses this issue with specific reference to sub-state terrorist groups in *New Terror New Wars* (Edinburgh: Edinburgh University Press, 2003), 26–31. Issues of prevention, pre-emption, and liability to attack are canvassed in Henry Shue and David Rodin, eds., *Preemption: Military Action and Moral Justification* (Oxford: Oxford University Press, 2007).
20. Suzanne Uniacke, 'Self-Defence, Just War and a Reasonable Prospect of Success', in *How We Fight*, edited by Helen Frowe and Gerald Lang (Oxford: Oxford University Press, 2013), 62–74.
21. The conventional protections granted to military personnel who are *hors de combat*, together with the conventional wearing of combat uniforms or adoption of other means whereby fighting personnel can readily be identified as combatants and distinguished from the civilian population, can also derive an ethical rationale from the *jus in bello* principle of discrimination.
22. Claudia Card, *Confronting Evils*, chapter 6; Igor Primoratz, *Terrorism: A Philosophical Investigation*, chapter 7.
23. Igor Primoratz, *Terrorism: A Philosophical Investigation*, 125. (Contrary to what Primoratz might be taken to suggest here, terrorist violence within civil society can be directed against noncivilians, e.g., soldiers standing guard at national monuments.)
24. Claudia Card, *Confronting Evils*, 135.

25. Igor Primoratz, *Terrorism: A Philosophical Investigation*, 23.
26. Claudia Card, *Confronting Evils*, 154. The example is from R. M. Hare, 'On Terrorism', *Journal of Value Inquiry* 13 (1979), 240–249.
27. The chances of surviving the death camps were significantly worse for Jewish as compared with political deportees, for instance. A little less than half of the political deportees sent by train from France to the death camps survived, whereas only around 3 per cent of Jewish deportees survived. Of more than 10,000 Jewish children sent to the death camps on trains from France, only 300 survived; see Caroline Moorehead, *Village of Secrets: Defying the Nazis in Vichy France* (London: Chatto & Windus, 2014), 316.
28. Cécile Fabre, *Cosmopolitan War*, 240–241; David Rodin, 'The Ethics of Asymmetric War', in *The Ethics of War: Shared Problems in Different Traditions*, edited by R. Sorabji and D. Rodin (Aldershot: Ashgate, 2006), 153–168.
29. F. M. Kamm, *Ethics for Enemies*, 105.
30. Idem., 101. Kamm claims that 'the right not to be treated in the manner involved in terror bombing is weakened when the effects on one's life are no different from the effects of the act that would otherwise have permissibly been done'. Expressed more abstractly, this claim could imply that if an innocent person could permissibly be killed as an incidental effect of defending the lives of, say, six other innocent people against an unjust attack, then this weakens that person's right not to be killed by being used as an involuntary human shield to prevent a larger number of innocent people from being killed by the attacker.
31. C. A. J. Coady, *Morality and Political Violence* (Cambridge: Cambridge University Press, 2008), 161.

References

Daniel Brunstetter and Megan Braun, 'From *Jus ad Bellum* to *Jus ad Vim*: Recalibrating Our Understanding of the Moral Use of Force', *Ethics and International Affairs* 27 (1: 2013), 87–106.

Claudia Card, *Confronting Evils: Terrorism, Torture, Genocide* (Cambridge: Cambridge University Press, 2010).

C. A. J. Coady, 'Terrorism, Morality and Supreme Emergency', in *Terrorism: The Philosophical Issues*, edited by Igor Primoratz (Basingstoke: Palgrave Macmillan, 2004), 80–96.

C. A. J. Coady, *Morality and Political Violence* (Cambridge: Cambridge University Press, 2008).

Cécile Fabre, *Cosmopolitan War* (Oxford: Oxford University Press, 2012).

Paul Gilbert, *New Terror New Wars* (Edinburgh: Edinburgh University Press, 2003).

Robert E. Goodin, *What's Wrong with Terrorism?* (Cambridge: Polity Press, 2006).

Richard Hare, 'On Terrorism', *Journal of Value Inquiry* 13 (1979), 240–249.

Virginia Held, 'Terrorism, Rights and Political Goals', in *Terrorism: The Philosophical Issues*, edited by Igor Primoratz (Basingstoke: Palgrave Macmillan, 2004), 65–79.

F. M. Kamm, *Ethics for Enemies: Terror, Torture and War* (Oxford: Oxford University Press, 2011).

Tamar Meisels, *The Trouble with Terror* (Cambridge: Cambridge University Press, 2008).

Seumas Miller, *Terrorism and Counter-Terrorism: Ethics and Liberal Democracy* (Oxford: Wiley-Blackwell, 2009).

Caroline Moorehead, *Village of Secrets: Defying the Nazis in Vichy France* (London: Chatto & Windus, 2014).

Stephen Nathanson, *Terrorism and the Ethics of War* (Cambridge: Cambridge University Press, 2010).

Igor Primoratz, *Terrorism: A Philosophical Investigation* (Cambridge: Polity Press, 2013).

David Rodin, 'Terrorism Without Intention', *Ethics* 114 (4: 2004), 752–771.

David Rodin, 'The Ethics of Asymmetric War', in *The Ethics of War: Shared Problems in Different Traditions*, edited by R. Sorabji and D. Rodin (Aldershot: Ashgate, 2006), 153–168.

Henry Shue and David Rodin (eds.), *Preemption: Military Action and Moral Justification* (Oxford: Oxford University Press, 2007).

Walter Sinnott-Armstrong, 'On Primoratz's Definition of Terrorism', *Journal of Applied Philosophy* 8 (1: 1991), 115–120.

Uwe Steinhoff, *On the Ethics of War and Terrorism* (Oxford: Oxford University Press, 2007).

Rod Thornton, *Asymmetric Warfare* (Cambridge: Polity Press, 2007).

Suzanne Uniacke, 'Self-Defence, Just War and a Reasonable Prospect of Success', in *How We Fight*, edited by Helen Frowe and Gerald Lang (Oxford: Oxford University Press, 2013), 62–74.

Michael Walzer, *Just and Unjust Wars* (3rd edition) (New York: Basic Books, 1977).

Robert Young, 'Political Terrorism as a Weapon of the Politically Powerless', in *Terrorism: The Philosophical Issues*, edited by Igor Primoratz (Basingstoke: Palgrave Macmillan, 2004), 55–64.

CHAPTER 23

TORTURE

Rescue, Prevention, and Punishment

F. M. KAMM

1. Some Conceptual Issues

In this section, we will try to develop a clearer understanding of what torture is and will consider differences among various legal and philosophical conceptions of torture.

There are several different legal definitions of torture. One is from the United Nations Convention Against Torture, and Other Cruel, Inhumane or Degrading Treatment or Punishment (CAT). It says torture is:

> Any act by which severe pain or suffering, whether physical or mental, is intentionally inflicted on a person for such purposes as obtaining from him or a third person information, punishing him for an act he or a third person has committed or is suspected of having committed, or intimidating or coercing him or a third person, or for any other reason based on discrimination of any kind, when such pain or suffering is inflicted by or at the instigation or with the consent of a public official or other person acting in an official capacity. It does not include pain or suffering arising only from, inherent in, or incidental to lawful sanctions.

This definition first points to what is imposed on a person, then for what purpose, and then by whom. Here are some things to consider about this definition: (1) it does not specifically say that the person does not consent to the treatment or that it is against his interests. Both these seem important to torture. However, suppose someone who had wanted, but was unable, to divulge information requested that he be made to suffer because only that would trigger his memories. Could not what was done to him still be torture even though he requested such treatment? (2) The definition is limited to torturing persons and so it makes it impossible to torture an animal. (3) The definition excludes the real possibility that someone might be tortured by an ordinary person, not someone in an official capacity, who imposes the suffering. (4) The definition makes it impossible to be tortured if there is no additional purpose beyond inflicting mental or physical suffering as an end in itself. (5) The definition enumerates various specific purposes for inflicting suffering on someone, such as getting information. But some have argued that there is a unifying, antecedent purpose to torture that is a means to achieving other purposes: namely, 'breaking someone's will'.[1] However, someone may simply decide to change his behaviour to get suffering to stop, and this suggests that attempting to break someone's will need not be a goal of all torture. (6) It is important to see that, according to CAT, pain and suffering inherent to a sanction is not torture if the sanction is lawful. This is problematic if it implies that it would be consistent with CAT to pass a law permitting torture.

A second definition of torture is present in the US Torture Statute (USTS): 'An act committed by a person acting under the colour of law specifically intended to inflict severe physical or mental pain or suffering other than pain or suffering incidental to lawful sanction, upon another person within his custody or physical control'. The USTS further specifies 'severe mental pain or suffering' as 'the prolonged mental harm caused by or resulting from among other things, the threat of imminent death and intentional infliction of physical pain and suffering'.

A crucial addition to CAT in the USTS is that torture requires that a person be in the custody *or* physical control of the person inflicting the pain or suffering. According to this statute, it is conceptually possible to torture someone who is not in custody but over whom one nevertheless has physical control, but it is conceptually impossible to torture someone who is not in custody and also not under physical control (e.g., when he has some ability, however small, to defend himself). This is a dubious result. Note also that being in custody is consistent with someone becoming a threat, for example, by acquiring a weapon. If an official's fighting him with pain to get him to drop his weapon is not torture, then, contrary to the USTS, intentionally imposing suffering 'under the colour of law' on someone who is in custody does not suffice for an act to be torture.

By contrast to the USTS, the CAT allows that torture can occur to someone not in custody and not in the physical control of those who would impose pain and suffering. It might therefore allow that fighting a threatening person with pain could be torture, at least if its aim is to coerce or intimidate. However, it may rule this out if the pain inflicted on an unjustly threatening person is inherent to a 'lawful sanction'. The USTS also differs from the CAT in not speaking of pain 'inherent in' but only 'incidental to' an act as not undermining its status as a lawful sanction.

By contrast to the USTS's emphasis on someone being in custody *or* under physical control, Henry Shue characterizes standard torture as involving the infliction of severe distress on someone who presents no threat *and* is defenceless.[2] (Notice that person B could present a threat to person A while being defenceless to person C's attack on him to stop his threat. If fighting B with severe pain in this circumstance would not be torture, it is because he is a threat although defenceless. If, as suggested earlier, inflicting severe distress on someone who can mount only a weak defence could count as torture, then someone's defencelessness is neither necessary nor sufficient for torture to occur.) Shue thinks that sometimes the ability to reveal information that would make torture stop is a form of defence that could be had even by those who are physically under another's control: such people are not, therefore, strictly defenceless. Thus, on Shue's view, someone could satisfy a *strengthened* USTS conditions for being tortured—being in custody *and* under physical control—but not count as being tortured because he is not defenceless.

By contrast to Shue, David Sussman believes that when someone in custody refuses to reveal information that would both stop a threat he has started and stop torture of himself, he is continuing his threat, not merely refusing to defend himself against those who harm him.[3] On this view, someone in custody and under physical control might still be a threat and so, on Shue's view of torture, imposing suffering on him would not be torture.

The US Military Commission Act of 2009, War Crimes Act, and the Torture Victims Protection Act add to the USTS the requirement that specific purposes like those described in the CAT be the aim of causing pain or suffering.[4]

The views we have so far discussed do not focus only on the type of pain and suffering being imposed, but also consider their purposes and by whom and when (e.g., in custody or under physical control) they are imposed. Hence, these views narrow the application of 'torture' (e.g., one cannot torture an animal to get a confession). David Sussman's characterization (which is not a definition) further narrows the application of 'torture'. He says: 'At minimum, torture involves the deliberate infliction of great pain or some other intensely distressing affective state . . . on an unwilling person for purposes the person does not and could not reasonably be expected to share'. But he adds:

> [Torture] seems to require that its perpetrators and victims be placed in a distinctive kind of social setting and relationship to one another. Victims of torture must be, and must realize themselves to be, completely at the mercy of their tormentors . . . the victim takes her tormentor to be someone who can do anything he wants to her . . . the torturer confronts no moral or legal impediments stemming from the victim's will . . . a victim might know that her torturers operate under some significant restrictions . . . the victim's grounds for such beliefs . . . come from how these torturers choose to present themselves. . . . Typically a torture victim has no independent way of corroborating.[5]

Sussman adds that interrogational torture has a distinctive wrong-making characteristic not had, for example, by imposing pain and suffering on someone as punishment or to get someone else to reveal information. Unlike the CAT, he does not accept that such impositions are torture; he calls them 'ordeals'. The distinctive characteristic they lack is trying to control someone's agency—getting him to do something—by affecting his body (or mind, presumably). This might involve getting the person to decide to act differently to stop the suffering or his will being 'taken over' by the torturer for whom he acts. Hence, on Sussman's view, imposing distress on someone that interferes with his completing a freely chosen act (as when electric shocking someone for a long time causes him involuntarily to drop information he is holding onto) is not torture. In addition, Sussman's conception implies that governments that are known by all, through sources independent of the torturer, to abide by court-imposed limits on what they will do so that victims know they are not 'completely at the mercy of their tormentors would not be engaged in torture.[6] This, I believe, is too narrow a conception of what counts as torture and is morally problematic because it allows too many to escape the charge of torturing wrongfully.

Our discussion so far shows that there are different conceptions of torture that do not overlap and have problematic features.

Consider a Bomb Threat Case: A is not in custody or under anyone's physical control. He is deliberately setting a bomb to kill B. The only way that will either (a) stop his act, (b) get him to stop his act, (c) get him to give information needed to stop his act, or (d) stop his act from harming B (by, for example, eliciting movements from him that make a protective screen drop around B) is for police to repeatedly shock A for an hour, causing him intense pain as he is setting his bomb. Categories (b) and (c) could include getting him to decide to stop his act or to give information in order to stop the shocks or his will being 'broken' by the shocks. Category (a) by contrast would bypass his will by physically interfering with his act. In category (d), we cannot stop A's act but can use pain in A to cause movements of his or get him to decide to move so that he causes a protective screen to drop around B. In the Bomb Threat Case, A is actively threatening someone, and we would rescue the person from A's threat during A's act, so most of the preceding conceptions of torture would not count this as torture. But my own view is that in an ordinary, everyday sense of torture, we would be torturing A. Those who disagree might claim that this is only a case of fighting with pain by using a sublethal weapon.

Regardless of whether this case involves torture, it shows that, for at least some (and possibly all) cases that satisfy the preceding definitions of torture (in particular, pain inflicted on a captive after he has set a bomb to get him to stop it from shortly killing his intended victim), we can imagine a hypothetical case in which someone is in the midst of actively threatening his victim, and the same pain or suffering would be imposed on him during his act. This could be done when he is not in custody or under physical control by public officials for some of the same specific purposes (e.g., getting information, getting him to make movements) with the same general purpose of saving the life of victims he threatens. In the documents just discussed, conduct prohibited as torture in addition to imposing pain involves imposing prolonged standing or stress positions, sleep deprivation, denial of medical treatment, food deprivation, or exposure to excessive auditory stimulation.[7] Hence, we could imagine variants of the Bomb Threat Case involving each or all of these means applied to someone during his threatening act. Because inflicting severe suffering on someone during his act may not be considered torture according to those documents' conceptions of torture, let us call doing this 'torture*' by contrast to torture. Here are two important questions:

Question 1: Is torturing* A, with the purposes I have described, morally permissible to prevent his harming B?

Question 2: Suppose such torture* of A is permissible. Now imagine Bomb Threat Case 2: It is known that the bomb is already set by A and is about to kill B. In an ordinary sense of action (which does not include A's merely refraining from stopping his set bomb), it is post-A's act.[8] A is in custody, and officials (like police) impose the same suffering on him as in the previous case, with some of the same purposes (e.g., to get A to give information) and the same general purpose of rescuing B from A's bomb. Since it was permissible to torture* A, is it morally permissible to torture him in this case?

What if, given the specific content I have assigned to torture* in my discussion, the answer to Question 1 was 'no'? Then we could revise the content of torture* and ask the two questions again. The general argumentative strategy is to find the least bad type of treatment that would still be considered torture* and torture and see if it yields 'yes' answers to Questions 1 and 2. If there is such, we would know that not all torture is morally impermissible.

2. Normative Issues

Both these questions are concerned with whether, in virtue of their inherent properties and independent of considering further societal consequences or a moral obligation to obey any laws, torture* and torture in our imagined cases are morally permissible.

With respect to Question 1, it does seem permissible to engage in torture* with the content described against A. It would even be permissible to intentionally kill him if this were necessary and sufficient to save his victim. Being tortured* is better for A than being killed from a well-being point of view, and both are contrary to his will. However, perhaps it still could be wrong to torture* rather than kill if doing so was more disrespectful than killing A. To make this issue clearer, consider another case: an aggressor is threatening to kill someone. Police can stop her in only two ways. One is to kill her from a distance. The second involves getting the aggressor away from her victim and closer to where she can be captured without injuring her. The only way to do this involves using a racist or sexist to shout insulting remarks at the aggressor so that she becomes justifiably angry and moves toward attacking the insulter instead of her original victim. Arguably, the second way to save her victim is more disrespectful of the aggressor than simply killing her. It is manipulative and involves use of her weaknesses, in addition to using insulting verbal content. Yet, I suggest, it is morally permissible because not killing her takes priority over not being disrespectful, given the unalterable aim of saving the victim. I think the same would be true in the Bomb Threat Case were it true that torture* is more disrespectful than killing.

Suppose we are physically unable to kill A, so torturing* him does not improve on a fate he would otherwise have actually suffered. Torturing* A still seems proportionate to the harm he will otherwise do to B and so permissible. Torturing* A is permissible because he is responsible for the large threat to B and so is liable to being tortured* to avert that threat. Indeed, he even seems to owe it to his victim to suffer significant losses that will accomplish any of (a)–(d) rather than harm him.

To consider Question 2, recall that we know with certainty that A has activated the bomb that would kill B and need not actively do anything further to kill B. Since A is no longer engaged in harmful actions and is in custody, Question 2 is about torture and not torture*. To save B, officials must torture A either for information to stop the bomb, or to make him stop it himself, or to trigger a device that will protect B against the bomb's effects once it goes off. Does our answer to Question 1 and the way of reaching it lead us to a conclusion about Question 2?

Suppose torturing* A were permissible only because it is the morally preferred substitute for permissibly killing A, but killing A post-act to harm B is not permissible even to stop that harm to B. Then the permissibility of torturing* would not bear on the permissibility of torturing A.[9] However, torture* seemed permissible even if it were impossible to kill A and so torturing* would not substitute for killing. Indeed, I suggest that even if killing A during his harmful action were impermissible, torturing* would be permissible because it is proportionate to what A would do to B. If this is so, then even if killing A post-act were impermissible, this would not rule out torturing him in the way described in our case.

Furthermore, suppose mildly Tazering A for only a minute during his act is not torturing*and is permissible to get A to stop his threat to B. If permissible torturing* had implications for permissible torture, then should permissible Tazering of A during his act have implications for permissible Tazering of him post-act if this is the only way to save B? (This is not Question 2 but related to it.)

Assume that killing A during his act to harm B would be permissible were it necessary and sufficient to stop the harm to B. Should it not then also be permissible to kill A post-act if it is necessary and sufficient to prevent the harm to B? For example, suppose A hid instructions to defuse the bomb in a pellet lodged in his heart and removing his heart (without causing any suffering), thereby killing him, is necessary and sufficient to save B. If permissible torturing* had implications for permissible torturing, should permissible killing during A's act have implications for permissible killing of A post-act for some of the same purposes? (This is not Question 2 but related to it.)

On the one hand, it seems that if what may permissibly be done to A during his act has straightforward implications for the post-act case, the permissibility of intrusions greater than torture (death) and also less than torture (Tazering) should have implications for the permissibility of these after A has acted. On the other hand, if such acts would be impermissible post-act, even though their counterparts would be permissible during A's act, then this implies that deliberate harmful intrusion upon someone's body (or in controlling his mind) post-act is morally problematic whether or not the intrusion is torture. Post-act Tazering and killing suggest that the focus on torture per se is misleading; what really seems to matter is the relation between violability of the agent during his act and after it.

Our analysis so far suggests two new questions that may help us answer Question 2:

Question 3: Are there morally significant differences between our torture* and torture cases that make imposing this harm on perpetrators impermissible post-act although it is permissible during their action?

Question 4: Could these differences, if any, be consistent with the permissibility of some types of post-act harm but not other types?

Consider Question 3. One might try to justify an asymmetry between harm during and post act in this way: Torture* is permissible because it involves stopping or getting A to stop his act. Torture is impermissible because it cannot stop or make A stop his act, which has already occurred. A related proposal is that torture* is permissible because it does not involve using A as a mere means opportunistically to help B; instead, it involves eliminating A's threatening act.[10] The problem with these proposals is that we already saw that torture* seemed to be permissible if it did not stop or get A to stop his act and instead used pain to A as a mere means to protect B by getting a screen to drop around him. When we do this, we use A as he acts without stopping his act to get the benefit of improving B's condition relative to the expected decline in his prospects as A acts. So this seems to be a crucial case.

However, even if torture* benefits B, it only puts him in the condition he would have been in if A had not been present at the time we torture* him, since A's absence would also have eliminated the threat.[11] By contrast, in Bomb Threat Case 2, torturing A to drop a screen around B uses A to provide a benefit that puts B in a better condition than he would be in if A were not present at the time we torture him, given that we could not help B except by harming A.[12] Is this difference morally significant if torturing A only puts B in the condition he would have been in if A had not presented his threat at all? I suspect not. Furthermore, suppose that A is present at the time officials torture him to drop the screen because he was captured at the only time capture was possible. Otherwise, he would have been elsewhere and inadvertently done something that dropped the screen. Then torturing A would not put B in a better condition than he would have been in had A not been present at the time we torture him. Could this difference alone make torture of A permissible when it would not be otherwise? I don't see why it should.

Another proposed answer to Question 3 is that torture involves trying to get A to save B whereas torture* involves preventing him from harming B. Many think that one can be required to bear greater costs to avoid harming someone than one must bear to save someone. In response: it could be noted that the moral difference between preventing harm and providing aid collapses in some cases. If someone has begun a process that will harm another, then in virtue of starting the threat and not saving his victim from it, he will wind up harming someone rather than merely not aiding him. Hence, arguably, the costs he morally must bear to save are the same as those required so as not to do the harmful act. Moreover, even if saving the victim physically requires the agent to bear losses beyond those he has a duty to take upon himself, he may still be liable to others imposing the loss on him.

However, sometimes the losses to which one is liable during one's harmful act (or during a harmful event due to one's act) seem to be different from those to which one is liable to save one's victim from one's threat at another time. Consider a driver whose brakes fail through no fault or negligence on his part. His car careers toward a pedestrian. Suppose the only way to save the pedestrian is for the police to shoot the driver, which will cause a screen to drop and shield the pedestrian. Arguably, the driver may be shot, especially if the harm to him would be less than the harm that would come to his victim. But suppose the driver is thrown from the car as it continues heading toward the pedestrian. The driver is no more or less responsible for or in control of the threat than when he was in the car. Yet it seems impermissible for police to shoot him on the sidelines even if the lesser harm to him would drop the screen.[13]

This Car Case is importantly different from the Bomb Threat Cases. The driver, although responsible for starting the car, is not at fault; A was. Still, if there is a morally relevant difference between harming the driver when he is part of the threat and harming him when he is on the sideline, then something like that difference might exist in the Bomb Threat Cases despite A's being at fault in both. A's culpability might discount the force of the difference, but it could still account for some variation in what may be done to A during his act and post-act. This sort of account would provide an answer to Question 4: some imposition on A's body could be morally permissible post-act—this might include some torture—but not the full range that was permissible during his act.

Caspar Hare, for one, denies that harming a villain post-act is morally different from harming him during his act.[14] He imagines that a villain directed a trolley toward several people who will die if it hits them. The only way to save them is to topple the villain from the bridge where he stands so that he lands in front of the trolley so that his body stops it. We might even (as Hare suggests) have to hold the villain on the tracks to ensure he is hit and killed for the five to be saved.

In Hare's case, I believe, the person responsible for the threat is post-act made into a shield for those he has threatened. A similar arrangement would occur in Bomb Threat Case 2 if officials who have A in custody could move him post-act so that he blocks his bomb's effect on B and is killed (or suffers in ways comparable to torture) by it instead of B (Bomb Threat Shield Case). In both cases the villain is moved against his will (e.g., the trolley or bomb is not merely redirected away from his victim and to him), and he is the victim of his own threat. Using the villain as a shield does seem permissible in both cases. The Bomb Threat Shield Case is useful for showing that it is not duties of care to someone in our custody that stand in the way of torturing since they do not stand in the way of our using him as a shield.

However, would matters differ morally if Hare's villain had to be thrown in front of a different moving trolley from the one he started in order to save his victims (as Hare further imagines)? Would matters differ morally if the villain had to be shot to stop the trolley he started, so that in this way we create a different threat to him from the one he started? It is such cases that should be compared with Bomb Threat Case 2.

Regardless of the answers to these questions and to Questions 1–4, our discussion shows that the issues crucial to whether torture is permissible may often differ from what is commonly thought. For example, it is commonly thought that it is crucial that in torture cases (a) a type of harm is to be done to someone that should never be done to anyone without his consent; (b) this harm is distinctive relative to other types of harm that do not involve torture; and (c) many lives of potential victims are at stake. But in our cases, none of these issues is crucial. With regard to (a), torture harms the subject in the same way, without his consent, as does torture*, and yet torture* is sometimes permissible. So (a) alone cannot explain the impermissibility of torture. With regard to (b), objectors to torture would probably also object to painlessly surgically removing information pellets from someone's heart or even from his ear when this causes partial deafness. If the objections to these nontorture post-act bodily invasions were at least as strong as to torture, (b) would not be a crucial reason for the impermissibility of torture. With regard to (c), in our case, it would have been permissible to torture* the perpetrator to save only one victim. If torture were no less permissible than torture*, saving even one victim from his perpetrator could justify some torture. Then (c) would not be necessary for torture to be permissible. Rather, in our cases, what seems crucial is (1) responsibility for the threat by the agent who would be tortured* or tortured to (2) stop the harm to his victim, (3) the proportionality of the torture* or torture to the harm to be stopped, and (4) (possibly) whether harm is imposed during or after the agent's act. (Possibly some of these factors will not be crucial in other cases. We consider this later.)

How should the moral status of torture in our cases affect its legal status? Some think that torture should always be legally wrong because it is always morally wrong.[15] However, this ground could not justify outlawing all forms of torture if torture were not morally wrong in our cases. A different argument would be needed.

Some think that legalizing any torture would lead to an uncontrollable 'culture of torture' because regulation would be difficult, and there would be a slippery slope to instances of torture that are in themselves morally wrong.[16] But does this argument also apply to torture*? For example, when a perpetrator is severely harming someone else, should it be illegal for officials to continuously deprive him of food and sleep, shocking to keep him in stress positions, and the like if doing these things are the only way to stop or get him to stop his actions? If not, then we need to know why we think that torture* can be regulated so that a 'culture of torture*' does not develop while denying the same with respect to torture.

Officials commonly shoot at or physically coerce people into dropping their weapons. This has sometimes resulted, or threatened to result, in a culture of police brutality. Yet the answer to this is commonly thought to be regulation of physical harm in defence or protection of others—not its elimination. Might we apply the same logic to post-act harms? For example, if police are required to wear cameras so that their harmful behaviour during a perpetrator's act can be monitored, could post-act physical harm be similarly monitored?

Our hypothetical cases of torture* and torture so far have involved officials being certain of who the perpetrator is and what he would deliberately do. It was also certain that torturing him was necessary and sufficient (given other innocent things that will be done) to stop the imminent harm to his victim. We could vary these conditions in several ways. Here are some examples.

1. Suppose officials remain certain of who the culpable perpetrator is and what will happen if they do not intervene. They know torture is necessary to stop the harm to his victim, but they do not know that it will actually save him. For example, any information gotten may come too late. Presumably, it would be permissible to torture* or otherwise harm such a perpetrator during his act even if officials were not certain that this would help his victim but thought it was sufficiently likely to do so. It is not clear how low the probabilities of success must be for it to become impermissible to torture* or otherwise harm the active perpetrator in this way; at minimum, usually these things should not be done if it is certain no good for the victim will come of it. If torture and torture* were equally permissible, the same would hold for torture: hence, when it is certain who the culpable perpetrator is, that he will kill his victim, and his being tortured is necessary to save his victim, then that torturing the perpetrator is not very effective at stopping the harm (which is often pointed to in arguing against torture) may not rule out its permissibility if there is a chance that it will avert the perpetrator's harm.
2. What if we are not sure that torture* of a known culpable perpetrator is necessary to prevent the harm? In keeping with the idea that the least harmful and disrespectful techniques should be used, if torture* is more harmful and disrespectful than some other mechanisms, they should be used instead of torture* when the probability of saving the victim is the same (or increases). If torture* had implications for torture, the same would be true of torture. What if the fruition of a harmful act is not imminent but will come about in the further future (e.g., a year) unless we torture* or torture now in order to avert that later harm? If imminence per se is important only because it correlates with necessity of acting now, then we should sometimes deal with imminent and more remote threats similarly.[17]
3. What if officials are not certain that the person they would torture* or torture is an agent whose deliberate actions will kill someone? It might nevertheless be reasonable, relative to evidence they have and that it is reasonable to require them to have, that they believe that they are dealing with such actions. For example, they might not be certain that the agent pointing a gun at someone has a real (rather than a toy) gun or that he is able to hit his target. But if it would be farfetched to doubt the evidence of danger, it might be permissible to torture* the agent to stop or get him to stop what is reasonably believed to be his harmful act. If torture* has implications for the permissibility of torture, torture might also be permissible even if it turned out that, contrary to grounds for reasonable belief, there was no threat to a victim.[18]

In our Bomb Threat cases there is now someone who will definitely be harmed if we do not *rescue* him. Call these rescue type cases. However, many cases in which torture of a perpetrator is imagined to be necessary and useful to save his victim are cases in which harm will definitely come to someone if we do not torture, but the person who will be harmed is now among many, each of whom has only a small risk of being harmed by the perpetrator. (Call these prevention cases. These cases are said to involve 'statistical deaths'.) For example, suppose a terrorist puts a bomb somewhere in a large city. It has only a very small chance of killing any given person in the city, but, given the enormous number of people in the city, it is certain that if nothing is done someone will be killed by the perpetrator (City Case). In such a case, we need to *prevent* there being someone who will be threatened whom we will not be able to rescue once the bomb is about to kill him. *If* it were permissible to torture* or torture a perpetrator in our earlier rescue cases, would this imply that it is permissible to torture* or torture a perpetrator in prevention cases at a time when the risk to any person of being the victim is still small but we know someone will die?

Some think that rescue and prevention cases are not morally equivalent because we have a stronger duty to protect someone who is certain to die than to protect people each of whom has only a small risk of dying. This view emphasizes that what is morally important is what we owe to each person as an individual (not aggregated with others) given his or her known risk of dying, not how many people overall will die. (As such, this view might be associated with a certain sort of contractualist moral theory.) However, some think that it is compatible with this view to weigh the number who would die in deciding whom to help if many people will die in the group whose members each have only a small chance of dying.[19] There being a moral difference between rescue and prevention cases might imply that even if torture* and torture of a perpetrator were permissible if there is someone who needs to be rescued in rescue cases, it might not be permissible to do the same to prevent comparable harm certainly befalling even somewhat more people in prevention cases.

To decide if the difference between the two types of cases bears on the permissibility of torture* and torture in cases involving a deliberate wrongdoer, recall that what distinguished the types was a difference in the probability of harm to any given innocent person at the time when we would have to torture* or torture the wrongdoer. So, consider the Old Gun Case, in which a villain deliberately aims at someone a very old gun that is known to have only a small chance of killing anyone.[20] This is like a rescue case insofar as there is a known potential victim, but he has the same small risk that each person in a prevention case has (although, unlike the prevention cases that I have imagined, there is a strong possibility that no one will die). Because this case involves a known deliberate wrongdoer, I believe it might be permissible to torture* him if this were necessary and useful to eliminate any possibility of the gun killing his victim. Why should this not also be true in prevention cases like the City Case, where there is the same small risk of death to each of many people, especially if some one of the many will certainly be killed? If the permissibility of torture* bears on the permissibility of at least some types of torture, then torturing a perpetrator who has already set up a threat that will go off in order to prevent the harm to his victim in a prevention case might be morally permissible.

In sum, one should be wary of moving directly from discussing torture* and torture in rescue cases like Bomb Threat to discussing the application of these means to prevention cases like City.[21] Nevertheless, if a perpetrator's wrongdoing causes a threat in prevention cases, and someone is certain to die, then the significance of the rescue/prevention difference to the permissibility of torture* or torture may be reduced.

There are other categories of people whom it might be useful to torture in addition to a perpetrator whose being tortured will save only his own victim from the harm he would impose. Assuming (only for the sake of argument) that some torture could be permissible in the latter case, we should assess the permissibility of torturing these other people. Consider six categories:

1. *People innocent of actual or potential harmful wrongdoing who nevertheless might be useful in preventing a perpetrator's harm (e.g., because if they are harmed a perpetrator will confess or because they have information about his location)*: Prima facie, these people are not liable to being tortured to save victims whom they would not have a duty to rescue at the cost of undergoing torture. Presumably, one should place greater weight on not torturing an innocent person to get a perpetrator to confess than on rescuing other innocent victims. The inviolability of an innocent person stands in the way of his being used to save other victims even from acts disrespectful of their inviolability.[22] However, someone who is withholding information relevant to saving a victim is, arguably, doing something wrong and so is not completely innocent. His failing in the duty to aid at a low cost might make him subject to having greater costs imposed on him to save others. Nevertheless, if there is a moral distinction between killing and even wrongly letting die, this person may not be committing a serious enough wrong for him to be liable to torture to save victims.

However, suppose the number of people that could be saved grows to millions (e.g., a nuclear bomb will explode in a large city unless information to stop it is obtained by torture from someone not in that city). Such a scenario is in some ways like the ticking-time bomb cases used by some to justify torture of the perpetrator. According to what is known as 'threshold deontology', the inviolability of even an innocent (or insufficiently noninnocent) person can be overridden by the extraordinary bad consequences of not harming him, and this might justify torture of those in category 1.

2. *People who are suspected on statistical grounds of being involved in or knowing about plots to harm others (e.g., suspected because they are young, male, and unemployed), not because there is particular data relating them to a threat (e.g., some eyewitnesses saw them plant a bomb)*: Is it any more permissible to torture such people than ordinary innocents to save victims just because there is a greater probability of finding a perpetrator or someone who knows about one? A person whom statistical evidence indicates may only know more than most innocents should be treated even less badly than those in category 1 whom we know have information. Hence, it is only the chance of finding a perpetrator whose being tortured could help a victim that could be at issue. What if the statistical evidence was so good that it made

the probability of torturing a nonperpetrator minuscule? Would this case differ morally from torturing someone whom it is reasonable to believe is a perpetrator on the basis of multiple eye witnesses?

3. *People who belong to a group with a member known to be a guilty perpetrator*: Some of these are responsible for supporting the threatening goals of a group but not actually performing or providing material support for threatening acts. Is being such a group member a sufficient wrong to make one liable to be tortured to prevent the harm done by a fellow member? It is usually thought that someone has a moral (and in liberal democracies a legal) right to hold, and associate with others holding, immoral beliefs so long as he does not engage in or materially support harm against others. Hence, it does not seem that a person in category 3 engages in conduct that makes him specially liable to be tortured to stop someone else's harmful conduct.
4. *People who* unsuccessfully *attempted to harm in the same way as a current perpetrator either that perpetrator's current target or others*: These people did what they have no moral right to do—attempt to harm someone. A case in which someone attempted to harm the very person who will now be harmed by someone else unless the earlier attempter is tortured can be modelled on the following revised version of Jeff McMahan's Attempter Case: Aware that several villains independently plan to kill you, the police provide protection. On one occasion, a villain confronts you in an alley and fires all his bullets at you but fails to hit you. A second, independent villain is preparing to kill you from behind a narrow basement window but you are unable to flee. The police cannot accurately fire through the window; they can save you only by wounding the first villain, causing him to slump in front of the window so as to block the second villain's line of fire and stop him from shooting.[23] A particular theory of punishment (such as that proposed by Victor Tadros)[24] might be needed to justify using the first attempter to stop the attack for which he is not responsible. It involves reasoning as follows: (1) consider what it would be permissible to do to a perpetrator to stop or get him to stop harming his victim before we know his attempt would fail (call this amount x). (2) The permissible punishment for a mere attempt would be less than x (i.e., $x - n$). (3) Suppose the justification for punishment (which is always post-act) were the wrongdoer's liability to protect his attempted victim from future attacks by deterring others from attacking him. (4) Then a known wrongdoer might also have cost $x - n$ imposed on him post-act to stop (or prevent harm from) an actual ongoing attack by someone else on his attempted victim.[25] If torture fell within $x - n$, it could be permissible to impose it on the attempter to stop someone else's attack on his attempted victim. Surprisingly, if this argument were correct, it would justify some torture as *punishment* undertaken to rescue particular people. Call this a punishment case. However, if either the theory of punishment relied upon to reach this conclusion is not correct or torture is a type of harm that should not be imposed on someone to stop an attack for which he is not responsible, then we would not have provided a justification for torturing those in category 4.

For the sake of argument, suppose this justification succeeded. What if the person who currently needs protection from a threat is not the same person whom the mere attempter had threatened? One possibility is to make use of an 'exchange-of-debts-among-victims' mechanism also suggested by Tadros in his theory of punishment. That is, suppose attempter A owes $x - n$ assistance to save his own attempted victim B from C's attack but C is attacking D, not B. However, even an innocent person like B has a duty to rescue D at small cost to himself. Hence, following Tadros, it might be suggested that B has a duty to transfer A's protective services owed to B to D. If transfer were permissible, and torture fell within $x - n$, then torture of an attempter might be justified to rescue someone (such as D) whom he had never attempted to harm. An objection to this conclusion is that it is not generally true that strenuous services owed to B by A may permissibly be transferred by B to D merely because doing this is easy for B. (For example, offspring may not transfer their parents' unused services owed to them to a friend.)

5. *People who are now threatening or have set up a device that threatens someone but who are useful only in preventing harm to someone else*: Category 5 might involve a perpetrator whose own victim can only be saved by police torturing another perpetrator when this second perpetrator's victim can only be saved by their torturing the first perpetrator. In this case, the perpetrators are each liable to being harmed to some degree to save those they did not threaten because this is a necessary means to each indirectly saving the person he did threaten, and it is being assumed (only for the sake of argument) that he is liable to some harm post-act to save his own victim. However, what if no one is able to help the first perpetrator's victim? It might again be argued that this victim has a duty to transfer his right to be helped by the first perpetrator to the potential victim of the second perpetrator. This transfer proposal raises the same concerns voiced in regard to its use with category 4.

In discussing the permissibility of some torture in categories 1–5, we considered rescue cases. In particular, in the transfer of a protective debt from one victim to another, we considered cases in which there is a second victim who needs to be rescued from certain death. But many cases in which it would be useful to harm a wrongdoer to save people other than his victim are prevention type cases. Our previous discussion suggests that we should also consider whether torture* or torture could be justified in each of the categories on the ground that lives will certainly be saved, even though this would happen by eliminating only the small chance that each of many people has of being the ones who will be harmed.[26]

6. *People from whom we seek confessions of wrongdoing*: It is sometimes argued that confessions elicited by torture are worthless because individuals will falsely admit to a crime merely to stop the torture. This may be true, but suppose that we knew that the innocent would never falsely confess and the guilty would always tell the truth in response to torture. There would still be reason not to torture to acquire

confessions if this results in our having tortured innocents who had a right not to be tortured. In addition, suppose only saving victims from threats could justify some torture of perpetrators. Then, unless confessions helped in this way, even torture that got confessions only from actual perpetrators would not be justified.[27]

Notes

1. See Seamus Miller's *Terrorism and Counter-terrorism* (Blackwell, 2009).
2. In his 'Torture', *Philosophy & Public Affairs*, 7 (Winter 1978), 124–143. I discuss Shue's views in my *Ethics for Enemies* (Oxford University Press, 2011), ch. 1.
3. David Sussman, 'What's Wrong with Torture', *Philosophy & Public Affairs* 3 (Winter 2004), 1–33.
4. Descriptions of the CAT, the US Statute, and other Acts can be found in *The Report of the Constitution Project's Task Force on Detainee Treatment*, appendix 1.
5. Sussman, idem, 5–8. Given the inability to corroborate independently, it seems odd to say the victim 'might know'.
6. For a more complete discussion of Sussman's views, see *Ethics for Enemies*, ch. 1 (which is also the basis for Sections 3–6 of the following discussion).
7. As described in *The Report of the Constitution Project Task Force on Detainee Treatment*, appendix 1.
8. If refraining involved continuing to act, many cases that are now thought to involve torture would involve torture*.
9. Except possibly if killing A during his act was replaced with torture post-act in A's own interests.
10. These distinctions derive from those drawn by Warren Quinn between opportunistic and eliminative agency in his 'Actions, Intentions, and Consequences: The Doctrine of Double Effect,' *Philosophy & Public Affairs* 18 (4: 1989), 334–351.
11. I think this is consistent with agency being opportunistic, as the following case helps show: A villain threatens Joe only because he wants to impress innocent Jane standing nearby. If Jane were not there, the villain wouldn't threaten Joe. Jane cannot get away, and the only way to save Joe is to shoot her in the leg to cause a screen to drop around Joe. The benefit obtained from using Jane does not make the situation better than if Jane were not there. Yet shooting her, although impermissible, would involve opportunistic agency.
12. This contrast was pointed out by Kristi Olson.
13. In another case, the driver is in control, backing out of his driveway taking all precautions, but a child is blown into the car's path. Compare what may be done to the driver during and after his act in order to save the child from the car.
14. In his 'Torture—Does Timing Matter?', his commentary on *Ethics for Enemies*, in *The Journal of Moral Philosophy* (July 2014), 385–394.
15. See Charles and Gregory Fried, *Because It Is Wrong* (W. W. Norton & Company, 2010).
16. See, for example, Jeremy Waldron's 'Torture and Positive Law: Jurisprudence for the White House', *Columbia Law Review* 105 (6: October 2005), 1681–1750.
17. David Luban made this point in his 'Preventive War,' *Philosophy & Public Affairs* 32 (3: June 2004), 207–248.

18. The use of 'permissible' in this analysis depends on an evidence-relative rather than fact-relative sense of the term.
19. Johann Frick makes these points in his 'Treatment and Prevention of HIV/AIDS and the Question of Identified vs. Statistical Lives' (unpublished).
20. A similar case is presented by Charles Fried in *Right and Wrong* (Harvard University Press, 1978) for other purposes.
21. Something similar seems true when justifying punishment. For example, Victor Tadros (in his *The Ends of Harm*, Oxford University Press, 2011) often moves from considering (i) what may permissibly be done to a perpetrator when there is his victim who faces certain death unless we act, to conclusions about (ii) what may permissibly be done to a perpetrator as punishment to deter future crime and save people, each of whom had only a small risk at the time we punish of being some perpetrator's future victim.
22. My *Morality, Mortality: Vol. II* (Oxford University Press, 1996) discusses inviolability of the innocent.
23. McMahan's original case is in his 'The Basis of Moral Liability to Defensive Killing', in *Philosophical Issues* 15 (2005), 386–405.
24. In his *The Ends of Harm*; I use his approach as illustration without necessarily endorsing it or implying that Tadros would justify torture.
25. Steps 1–3 follow Tadros's analysis. Step 4—a move from deterring attacks to interfering with them—is my extension of Tadros's approach.
26. Similarly, when punishment is used for deterrence, it is not usually true that there is an individual whose would-be attacker is deterred from harming him due to a transfer from one person to another of a claim to protective services. Rather, each of a great number of people is spared a small chance that he will be someone who is criminally attacked.
27. For comments, I am grateful to Shelly Kagan, Seth Lazar, Jeff McMahan, Kristi Olson, and Larry Temkin.

CHAPTER 24

DRONES AND ROBOTS

On the Changing Practice of Warfare

DANIEL STATMAN

1. Introduction

The history of warfare has witnessed many changes following the introduction of new weaponry. However, although many inventions, such as gunpowder, had dramatic effects in their world, none of them changed the basic character of war as a direct and violent confrontation between combatants on more or less defined fields of battle. Until recently, modern wars retained this essential characteristic. The only difference was that instead of meeting the enemy in personal combat with a sword or a knife, he was met with a rifle, an armored vehicle, or a missile fired from an aircraft. But now, with the rapid development of unmanned technology—drones and robots of various types—humanity seems to be moving towards a state of affairs in which fighting is increasingly less between human beings and more between human beings, on the one hand, and machines, on the other. At present, these machines are operated by humans, but they are becoming increasingly autonomous.

Some people believe that, from a moral point of view, this development is worrisome. An important human rights organization went so far as to refer to the use of such weapons as a case of *losing humanity*.[1] The assumed moral defects of the new technologies pertain mainly to fully autonomous offensive systems ('killer robots'), in which humans are completely 'out of the loop'. But strong criticism is also mounted against automated systems that require a human operator: systems in which humans are either 'in the loop' (when the decision to fire is theirs) or 'on the loop' (when they maintain the option of intervening in the 'decisions' made by the system).

This chapter takes an opposing view. I seek to show that, in spite of some drawbacks, the new technologies overall mark significant moral progress in the history of warfare. In what follows, I focus mainly on drones because it is their use that has drawn the most attention in discussions about the changing practice of warfare. But what holds true for drones applies, *mutatis mutandis*, to other unmanned platforms, be they airplanes, submarines, or armored vehicles.

The question regarding the morality of drones is a good illustration of a wider theoretical question: namely, whether, and in what ways, technological developments that transform traditional practices necessitate changes in the norms that govern these practices. In a sense, the answer is obviously affirmative because the application of moral principles always depends on premises about the factual reality. If reality changes, the moral norms also change. What is less obvious is whether the underlying moral principles change as well.

Although drones and other automated weapons can be used in conventional warfare, their actual use has been limited to unconventional, asymmetric warfare between states and non-state groups (see Chapter 21). Hence, although there is no essential connection between the use of drones and asymmetric warfare, the two issues are, albeit contingently, strongly connected. In particular, since drones, when used for attack, are employed mainly in the targeted killing of assumed members of hostile organizations, the moral debate about drones is very much entangled with the debate about the morality and legality of targeted killing. The first sections of the chapter, then, are devoted to the debate about drones and killer robots, after which I turn to the issue of targeted killing.

2. The Advantages of Drones

Drones are just a tool of war, one among many: there are tanks, cannons, aircraft, submarines, and now there are also drones. The question of their moral legitimacy is one, therefore, of *jus in bello*. If drones raise any special difficulties beyond those raised by other tools of war, this can only be because they pose some special threat to the central goal of *jus in bello*, which is the protection of civilians. (For those who believe that *jus in bello* is also about reducing harm to combatants, see below.) Recall that *jus in bello* incorporates two main constraints on the conduct of war: (1) never attack noncombatants directly, and (2) when indirectly harming noncombatants, do not inflict disproportionate harm on them. How does the use of drones fit these constraints?

There is no reason to think that drones are more dangerous than other tools of war in terms of the intentional killing of noncombatants. To be sure, they can be used to attack noncombatants directly, but so can tanks and aircraft. Moreover, if some country decided to attack enemy civilians directly, drones would be less effective than other tools in its arsenal. Carpet bombing would cause more extensive harm to the enemy than the precise 'surgical' attacks carried out by drones.

What about collateral damage? Does the use of drones put civilians at higher risk of harm than alternative measures? The crucial point to remember here is that the alternative to the use of drones is not the avoidance of violence altogether, but employing other, more conventional, lower tech measures, such as tanks and helicopters. These, though, would almost certainly lead to more civilian casualties rather than fewer. True, there could be times when the greater collateral harm inflicted by low-tech measures would render the attack disproportionate to the particular military objective and hence rule it out. Then civilians would be made worse off by the possibility of drone use because, without it, they would not be exposed to harm at all. But this seems an unlikely scenario. If states believe that they are under a serious threat that justifies resort to military force and think that by the use of drones they could neutralize the threat, it is hard to imagine that they would refrain from doing so only because they realize that the results would be disproportionate. In the real world, the alternative to drones would be artillery or bombers, which are either less precise or more destructive (or both).

One might argue that while the use of drones in state-on-state wars would pose no special problem in terms of *jus in bello*, asymmetric wars are different. Does the use of drones in these contexts put civilians at special risk, thus giving us a reason to consider banning their use? Again, the alternative to using drones in fighting against organizations such as al Qaeda is not peaceful negotiation, but other, far less discriminate, measures. So if lethal measures (under the rubric of war rather than under that of law enforcement) are permitted in these conflicts at all, it is hard to see why drones should be seen as especially worrisome. Needless to say, drones might be abused, but so could other tools of war. At any rate, the danger of abuse should not make us lose sight of the great moral promise at hand. Other things being equal, *the more precise a weapon is, the better its use can comply with the requirements of discrimination and proportionality.*[2]

I have been assuming so far that the main point of *jus in bello* is the protection of noncombatants. Some philosophers believe that the ethics of warfare should also be concerned about the protection of combatants. As Kasher and Yadlin put it, combatants' blood is no less red and thick than that of civilians.[3] But from this perspective, too, drones should be welcomed. Their availability on the battlefield enables those using them to be more precise in their attacks—for example, by targeting officers rather than privates. Another moral advantage of drones is the reduced risk to a country's own soldiers. The availability of unmanned measures means that countries can, and hence should, expose their soldiers to the lowest possible risk in defence against their enemies. Bradley Strawser derives this duty from a wider moral principle that he terms 'the principle of unnecessary risk': if X gives Y an order to accomplish some good goal G, then X has an obligation not to expose Y to unnecessary risk in doing so.[4]

Reducing casualties among the soldiers of one's own side is not only a moral issue, but a prudential one, too. Not only do losses undermine the army's ability to withstand its enemy, but 'sensitivity to military losses has increased in democratic societies since the 1960s, playing a key role in limiting the state's freedom of operation in deploying the armed forces for military missions'.[5] This aversion to casualties is influenced by the public's assessment of the success of the military campaign.[6] Since asymmetric wars are typically long, indecisive, and without a clear end point, the aversion is expected to be especially high. As drones and other unmanned devices reduce the risk of casualties, their role might turn out to be critical in the winning of such wars.

Furthermore, lowering the risk to soldiers by using unmanned weapons may encourage states to get involved in humanitarian interventions[7] and would make such interventions less problematic in terms of the risks incurred by the soldiers of the intervening countries. It is not easy to justify forced participation in war to defend one's own country, still harder to justify war to defend *another* nation from an oppressive or genocidal regime.[8] Reducing the risk to soldiers by using drones helps alleviate this problem. (Some might regard this as an argument *against* drones; see section 5 below.)

The option of carrying out effective attacks by drones might also have the advantage of delaying full-scale war or even avoiding it altogether. Drone attacks might be sufficient to convince the enemy to desist, thus obviating the need to mobilize troops and get involved in bloody battles on the ground.[9] Finally, as Strawser points out, potentially worthwhile cost savings can be made by using drones.[10]

To conclude, drones seem to have significant moral advantages:

1. other things being equal, they comply better than other tools of war with the requirements of discrimination and proportionality;
2. they enable states to reduce the risk to their own soldiers;
3. they weaken moral arguments against involvement in wars of humanitarian intervention;
4. they make it possible to respond effectively against perceived aggression without the need to engage in a full-scale war;
5. they are cheaper in comparison to human-operated tools of war and thus leave more public money available for other causes.

Nevertheless, many critics are still quite worried by the increasing use of drones and even more so by the development of killer robots. The next sections are devoted to the evaluation of their arguments.

3. Unfair, Disrespectful Warfare: Arguments Against the Use of Drones and Killer Robots

This section examines arguments against any (lethal) use of drones even if humans are still in or on the loop; Section 4 goes on to discuss arguments that apply only to fully autonomous weapons—killer robots.

3.1. Disrespectful Death

Imagine a person walking in his neighborhood when suddenly, literally out of the blue, he is shot and killed by a drone that he can't even see. Now compare this to the death of a soldier on the battlefield. Arguably, there is something disturbing about the former kind of death, something particularly disrespectful or humiliating.[11] The intuition underlying this argument seems to be:

> that a human being deserves to be able to at least point at his or her killers (and condemn them, if they are unjust) even if his or her killers are cruising 20 000 feet above in a plane. The thought is that at least a human being in a plane high above is less of a 'faceless' death wrought upon someone than a robot being operated remotely would be.[12]

But what exactly is disrespectful in being killed by a robot—in comparison to being killed by a tank or a helicopter? Why is 'being killed by remote control' so 'powerfully disturbing and morally troubling'?[13] Maybe it is because when a human being does the killing, that human being acknowledges, albeit in a paradoxical manner, the humanity of his victim. He identifies the victim as a fellow human being, though one posing a threat to him. For a very short time, they meet on the same plane, so to say, thus mutually affirming each other's existence and humanity. In contrast, when a drone shoots and kills a person, no such meeting takes place; hence, the humanity of the victim is denied or, at any rate, does not receive the acknowledgement it merits.

There is something appealing about this argument, although on reflection I don't find it convincing. First, it is unclear in what sense a helicopter pilot 'affirms the humanity' of her victim when she targets and kills her from afar. Second, the argument works best when one thinks of a physical, close confrontation between combatants, in which they see the faces of one other and, in some sense, thereby acknowledge their humanity. But most fighting has long lost this feature. Operators of cruise missiles don't see the faces of their victims, nor do pilots or, typically, even tank operators. The victims of such weapons are no less 'faceless' than those of drones.

Arguments against drones and killer robots must be powerful enough to explain why they are morally wrong—without implying that conventional weapons, the legitimacy of which is universally accepted, are also morally wrong. The denial of such legitimacy would lead to a position close to pacifism; indeed, we shall see that most objections to drones fall very close to this position.

3.2. Unfair or 'Dirty' Killing

Maybe the sense of disrespect just mentioned grows out of a sense of unfairness. One might regard the killing of the person walking in his neighborhood as 'fighting dirty', probably because the victim stands no chance against the drone. But soldiers are often similarly defenceless against combat aircraft or long-range artillery.

There seem to be two separate arguments here, though they overlap: one against unfairness in the sense of asymmetric military force[14] and one against unfairness in the sense of visiting death upon the enemy by using 'dirty' measures and tactics. But both of them fail. To realize just how weak and unstable the argument from unfairness is, one should note its resemblance to the arguments formerly raised against submarines and military aviation,[15] or even, much earlier, against the crossbow—'a moral abomination that made warfare into a depersonalized and dishonourable "point-and-click" affair, disrupting the existing code of ethics and balance of power'.[16] Unless one wants to rule out machine guns (the modern version of crossbows), submarines, and jets, one cannot rule out drones on the basis of their being unfair or dishonourable means of warfare.

3.3. Riskless Killing Undermines the License to Kill in War

In Paul Kahn's view, the morality of law is caught in a paradox. On the one hand, countries have a moral obligation to minimize the risk to their soldiers and to create what he calls an 'asymmetrical situation' in which they can totally overpower their enemies. On the other hand, beyond a certain threshold, such asymmetry undermines the very license to kill in war. Why is that so? Kahn contends that due to their youth, indoctrination, and pressures from peers and superiors, most combatants are not morally guilty for their participation in war and, insofar as such guilt is concerned, are no worse than noncombatants. If the mutual killing of combatants in war is permissible, it must have a different ground. In Kahn's view, this is mutual self-defence: each side is defending itself from the threat posed by the other. But to say that each side poses a threat to the other is just a different way of saying that they impose a risk on each other, or that *both sides are exposed to some nontrivial risk when in combat*. What follows is that when such mutual exposure to risk does not exist because the power relation between the warring parties is manifestly asymmetrical, the paradigm of war is inapplicable, together with the mutual license it entails to kill enemy combatants. 'Without reciprocal imposition of risk', asks Kahn, 'what is the moral basis for injuring the morally innocent?'[17]

Kahn's argument for the mutual license to kill in war reflects a widespread intuition that 'it is the willingness to die that creates the license to kill'.[18] Since the drone operator 'kills but does not live with the risk of sacrifice',[19] she has no license to kill enemy soldiers. Thus, the more warfare consists of drones and killer robots, the less justified these operators are in bringing death and destruction on their enemies. This argument is unconvincing. First, drone operators are not the only combatants whose risk is close to zero. The same is true for those who fire artillery or cruise missiles far away from their targets, for those who fly aircraft that drop bombs in circumstances where the enemy has no effective anti-aircraft weapons, and so on. Second, the use of drones is unlikely to lead to a situation in which most soldiers face no, or merely nominal, risk. In the near future, drones will provide invaluable help to armies in carrying out their missions, but they will not completely replace them. It will remain true that soldiers in general (not each individual one) undertake risks.

Third, if incurring risk were a condition for engaging in warfare, then humanitarian intervention by third parties would hardly ever be justified.[20] Since the soldiers of such third parties are antecedently under no threat at all, they could not claim to be acting in self-defence. Most humanitarian interventions would be ruled out, even if Kahn's analysis applied only to the *jus in bello* level, because democracies, increasingly hesitant to risk their troops in humanitarian missions, limit military activities of this nature to attacks from the air or from a distance with very low risk to their personnel. Kahn's view would rule out such attacks—leaving the international community with no effective (and morally justified) way of preventing humanitarian crises.

3.4. Wars Without Virtue

With drone operators taking very low risk upon themselves, not much room is left for the virtue of courage, which is mainly manifested on the battlefield, or for other martial virtues, such as honour, comradeship, and loyalty. Is 'war without virtue'[21] a reason to object to drones? Hardly so. First, in the foreseeable future, wars will continue to involve operations on the ground[22] in which the martial virtues will be no less relevant than they were in the past. Second, courage in combat is arguably an 'instrumental virtue' whose value depends on its contribution to a perceived worthwhile goal—in this case, the defeat of the enemy.[23] If this goal can be achieved without courage, courage simply loses its value. To avoid a new method of war that is expected to be more effective and less destructive just because it makes the martial virtues redundant is to get things the wrong way round.[24]

4. Arguments Against Fully Autonomous Killer Robots

Among critics of drones there are some whose concern stems mainly from the fear that drones are just one step behind the 'shocking and unacceptable'[25] development and use of fully autonomous killer robots. In their view, drones put us on a slippery slope at the bottom of which we'll be giving 'machines the power to make decisions about whom to kill'.[26]

Note that nobody objects to the use of automated systems for defence, such as the 'Iron Dome' system that automatically intercepts and destroys rockets directed against populated areas. Indeed, it is hard to see on what ground one might object to systems of this kind. The problem lies, at least prima facie, with automated systems that lethally attack human beings. Critics have in mind a scenario where drones (or some kind of ground robots) with artificial intelligence make their own decisions about where and whom to attack. For the sake of the present discussion, I ignore the question of how likely it is that such automated systems will in fact be developed and employed in the near future[27] and ask merely whether there is ground for moral concern.

4.1. Robots and the Conditions for *Jus in Bello*

Critics view the ability of robots to comply with the two main requirements of *jus in bello*—discrimination and proportionality—as much poorer than that of humans.

Hence, to take humans 'out of the loop' would be a serious moral fall. While the identification of combatants is relatively easy in conventional wars, it is much more difficult in asymmetric warfare in which regular armies struggle against fighters who wear no uniforms and are not situated in clearly defined locations closed to noncombatants. In such circumstances—the majority of armed conflicts today—there are no clear criteria that could be programmed into a robot to make sure it attacks only combatants. The ability to discriminate depends on many cues that are not explicit and hence cannot be translated into orders to robots ('if X, then shoot; if Y, hold fire and check whether Z; if Z, then withdraw; etc.'). Calculating proportionality is even more problematic[28] and is inevitably left to the subjective evaluation of the military commander or the soldier on the ground. But the ability to make such subjective evaluations is precisely what robots lack.

However, I see no reason to rule out a priori the possibility of robots doing just as well—and even better—than humans in both these respects. Not that long ago, many were skeptical about the possibility of a driverless car that could bring us safely from one point to another. The amount of tacit knowledge and subjective judgment involved in driving seemed impossible to feed into a machine. But such cars now exist, and riding in them will soon be safer than driving a regular car. Similarly with killer robots. There is no reason to despair of being able to translate the cues that help us distinguish between combatants and noncombatants into computer language. Robots might make mistakes or be misled by the enemy, but the same is true of humans.[29]

If there are no objective standards to determine the right proportion between military achievements and harm to civilians, then there is no basis for saying that robots do worse than humans. If such objective standards, however imprecise, exist, there is again no reason to rule out the possibility that they could be programmed into a computer that could then be trusted to be no less sensitive than humans in issues of proportionality.

At any rate, *if* robots are ever to be programmed to carry out attacks under the *in bello* constraints, things like necessity and proportionality—currently vague at best—will need to be codified. The same for target selection: a much more precise definition of the distinction between legitimate and illegitimate targets will be required. The robot's default position vis-à-vis targets outside the definitions programmed into it will also need to be set. In other words, in case of doubt, should the robot be programmed to fire or to refrain from doing so? This need to rethink and redefine the *in bello* conditions is a good illustration of the point mentioned at the outset about technological developments calling for a change in norms or their redefinition.

4.2. Accountability

When a drone operated by a human being fires a missile at a group of civilians, there is an address for moral and legal complaint and measures: namely, the operator. What happens when a fully automated robot makes such a mistake and carries out what would regularly be termed a war crime? Who can/could be held accountable? In Robert Sparrow's view, no one.[30] Surely not the robot itself, to which no moral responsibility could be assigned. Nor the programmer who, in essence, cannot fully predict and control the behaviour of a fully autonomous robot. The last option is the officer who ordered the use of a killer robot, but this seems unsatisfactory, too. Let's assume that the officer has good reason to believe that killer robots would lead to better results, both tactically and morally, than other measures. Given the autonomy of such devices, there is no way she could predict that something will go wrong. Hence, it seems unfair to hold her accountable for the 'crimes' committed by robots.

What exactly is so bothersome in having nobody accountable for (unpredictable) violations of the war convention by killer robots? One answer is that it contradicts the requirement of respect for people: 'the least we owe our enemies is allowing that their lives are of sufficient worth that someone should accept responsibility for their deaths'.[31] Another answer is consequentialist: with nobody held responsible for unjust deaths, the incentive to avoid them diminishes. This, though a common objection to fully automated robots,[32] is not very compelling. What is meant by the idea of respect owed to other people is always ambiguous. What is morally important in warfare is that only legitimate targets are attacked and that the collateral harm caused to illegitimate targets is proportionate. If these conditions are met, then, from a Kantian perspective, the enemy has been treated with respect, even if the people killed, or their relatives, never know the identity of those directly or indirectly involved in their deaths. By contrast, if the conditions for permissible killing are not met—for instance, if civilians are harmed disproportionately—then it is the impermissible killing that expresses disrespect towards them, not the fact that there is no person to whom responsibility for their deaths can be assigned.

Furthermore, there is only something disrespectful about not accepting responsibility for the harm imposed upon X when some perpetrator exists who *is* responsible for this harm and nonetheless refuses to acknowledge her responsibility, thereby adding insult to injury. In circumstances in which there is no such perpetrator—which, according to the present argument, is precisely the case with killer robots—it is unclear where the disrespect lies. In any case, I don't see why the *state* can't accept responsibility for the deaths it unjustifiably brings about. When people *accept* responsibility, it is usually because they are not responsible in the usual sense of the word: they are not blameworthy for whatever the relevant wrong is. If the robots of the state bring about unjustified harm, there is no reason why the state shouldn't accept responsibility and even apologize to the victims, thus expressing proper respect for them.

Harm caused by such robots is not unique in this sense. Given human limitations, there is no way to avoid fault altogether. Military and political leaders might make completely reasonable decisions that then lead to a disaster. They are not to blame for such decisions, but they are nevertheless expected to take responsibility for the results, apologize, and seek ways to compensate the victims.[33] The assumed relation between accountability and compliance with the laws of war is based on the thought that post hoc punishment is essential to achieving such compliance, the fear of which will assumingly deter politicians and soldiers from immoral behaviour. However, Anderson and Waxman argue that this focus is a mistake.[34]

Finally, the difficulty of allocating accountability in the cases at hand should be balanced against the unprecedented improvement in monitoring the military activity carried out by drones and robots in comparison to that carried out by traditional, low-tech military measures. When a platoon of infantrymen engages the enemy and civilians are killed, it is often very hard to find out who exactly did the killing, who gave the order, what the circumstances were, and so on. These questions are much easier to answer in the case of drones and robots because all the data fed into them are recorded, as are their 'decisions', the circumstances in which they act, and the results of their attacks, thus producing 'unprecedented accountability for military operations'.[35]

4.3. Robots and Emotions

Killer robots act in the way they are programmed, making their own 'judgments' about when and whom to attack. They feel nothing when they blow up human beings on the other side; no compassion, no reluctance, no regret. Some critics believe that removes some of the central constraints on killing in war. For Armin Krishman, this makes war 'inhumanely efficient' and 'no longer constrained by the natural urge of soldiers not to kill'.[36] Since lack of emotion is essential to robots, this is not a problem that could be fixed as technology progresses. Killer robots should thus simply be banned.

The high toll paid by civilians in the wars of the twentieth century sheds some doubt on the restraining power of human compassion. One might say, of course, that without compassion the toll would have been even higher, but the truth of this counterfactual is hard to establish. At any rate, compassion is not the only emotion active in war. There are also negative emotions such as national pride, rage, the longing for revenge, and so on, and these seem much more effective on the battlefield than compassion. Therefore, lack of emotion seems a moral advantage and not a downside.

5. Harmful Results of the Use of Drones

I leave the world of killer robots and return to drones to deal with objections based on the assumed excessive harm they cause. The main worry is that the distance between the drone operators and their victims will lead to a more callous attitude towards killing. This is a version of the argument from emotions just discussed. The idea is that sympathy with our fellow humans is intensified when we come into close contact with them—when we see them (and more so when we make eye contact), hear them, are in actual physical contact with them—and weakened the farther we get from such contact. At some extreme point of distance, human beings lose their reality, so to say, and, consequently, become (psychologically) much easier to kill.

Again, this argument leads to something like pacifism, because most killing in war today takes place from afar without the killers seeing, hearing, or smelling their victims. The psychological distance is even greater in these cases: whereas drone operators can at least see and track their victims on their monitors, this is not the case with soldiers firing artillery. And since nobody regards the use of artillery as worrisome because of the psychological distance between their operators and their targets, drones should not be regarded as worrisome either.

Peter Singer concedes that 'each new technology, from the bow and arrow to the bomber plane, has moved soldiers farther and farther from their foes' but nonetheless believes that 'unmanned systems have a more profound effect on "the impersonalization of battle" '.[37] Maybe this profound effect has to do with the fact that killing with drones resembles 'killing' in video games. The operators sit in front of computer screens and chase the bad guys just like they do when they play video games.[38] The danger is that drone operators will lose sight of the fact that, in this case, clicking the mouse doesn't gain the player extra points but instead visits death and destruction upon real human beings. I'm not sure how significant this danger is, but there are ways to deal with it—for example, by tight supervision and by requiring high-rank approval for every attack carried out.

A different objection to the use of drones is that the decreased risk they pose to soldiers may encourage countries to go to war in circumstances where doing so would be morally wrong.[39] Again, it is hard to estimate how likely this would be. Long-range missiles, especially GPS-guided ones, can cause massive destruction with zero risk to their operators; nonetheless, countries don't resort more easily to (full-scale) war as a result. Moreover, as suggested earlier, drones might allow states to *avoid* full-scale war, or at least delay it.[40] Finally, the fear of casualties is not the only disincentive to war. There is also the likely harm to civilians and to civilian infrastructure (which might increase precisely because the enemy has no military targets to attack), the economic price, and more. Nor is it the case that even combatants would be completely spared the risks and horrors of war. Hence, although drones might reduce the risk to some soldiers, the risk in going to war would still be high enough to deter countries from doing so unless they believe they have no other choice—and if this is how they see things, then, as history has taught, they will often be willing to undertake significant risk.

6. Targeted Killing

The most widespread objection to the use of drones is based on their having become the main tool for the targeted killing of assumed members of terror organizations, which is an important aspect of the changing practice of warfare. In conventional warfare, one's enemies are met on the battlefield. In most contemporary wars, one side is a non-state organization whose members instead hide in the mountains or among civilians. In these circumstances targeted killing becomes the most logical way of conducting war.[41] The alternative would be to engage in a ground attack causing many more deaths and much more harm—to both sides—with no guarantee of better results in neutralizing the relevant threats.

The morality (and the legality) of targeted killing is only contingently connected to the development and deployment of drones. One can carry out targeted killing using other measures, and one can use drones for other missions. In practice, denying the legitimacy of targeted killing in asymmetric warfare would amount to a rejection of the war model as a means of dealing with such conflicts. But this denial is not very convincing. Suppose that some aggressive organization (or, for this matter, a regular state), Aggressor, has a proper army and conducts unjust attacks against country Victim (e.g., fires rockets at its military bases). Assuming that the standard conditions for *jus ad bellum* are met, everybody would agree that Victim is permitted to defend itself by force, meaning that it has moral (and legal) permission to kill each of Aggressor's soldiers. Victim is under no obligation to satisfy the strict conditions for the use of force that are demanded by criminal law. It may carry out 'extra-judicial' killing of any member of the armed forces that fights against it (except, of course, for the wounded, POWs, and so on) with nothing like due process and with no need to establish the moral responsibility of the target or the necessity of killing him.

Now suppose that Aggressor is losing, so it orders its soldiers to remove their uniforms and avoid direct confrontation with Victim's soldiers but to continue the same kind of attacks, this time while hiding among the civilian population. The only thing that has changed is the structure and the organization of Aggressor's armed body and the strategy of its attacks against Victim. If anything, the threat to Victim has increased, because those attacking are much harder to locate and, as they find shelter among civilians, there are stronger moral constraints in fighting against them. It seems implausible that this mere change in strategy and organization could make such a normative difference; namely, render Aggressor's soldiers morally immune to the kind of regular military attacks to which they would be vulnerable in a standard war.

A helpful way to see the moral legitimacy of targeted killing is to see how it fits different versions of just war theory. In *individualism*, the license to kill human beings in war is ultimately the same license we have to kill in individual self-defence: 'justified warfare just *is* the collective of individual rights of self- and other-defence in a coordinated manner against a common threat'.[42] Since, in McMahan's theory of self-defence, the aggressor's moral responsibility is crucial in making him liable to defensive attack, it plays such a role in war, too. So formal affiliation with some organization, or even with some state, plays no intrinsic role in making a person liable to attack. The fact that al Qaeda militants are not soldiers in the usual sense of the word makes no difference to their moral status vis-à-vis the potential victims of the threats that they (individually or collectively) pose. Hence, if the only way to block such threats is to kill these activists, according to individualism, there is no reason why doing so should be impermissible. Moreover, given the voluntary nature of enlisting in these organizations and acting within them, their members seem typically *more* liable to defensive attack than conscripted soldiers in regular armies, whose responsibility for participation in unjust wars is rather weak. If the latter are legitimate targets for attack—as all nonpacifists agree—the former are certainly so as well.[43]

Individualism, then, views targeted killing not just as one permissible tactic among others, but the preferred one. It does a much better job of distributing the self-defensive harm in accordance with moral responsibility. Bear in mind still that the alternative to targeted killing is not no-killing (some form of pacifism), but *nontargeted* killing; namely, ordinary military operations which are far less sensitive to differences in moral liability. Whereas individualism is most clearly compatible with targeted killing, I show elsewhere that the same holds true for other prominent versions of just war theory, *collectivism* and *contractualism*.[44]

Pure moral considerations aside, how effective is targeted killing in deciding asymmetric conflicts? Since the main use of drones for attack is targeted killing, one could just as well ask how effective drones are as a tool of warfare. The questions are hotly debated.[45] Since they turn on empirical evaluations of social and political reality, I shall limit myself here to one comment. The level of evidence required to establish the effectiveness of attacks in conventional warfare is pretty low. Soldiers are permitted to kill enemy soldiers with no need to demonstrate that the killing of some specific individual or group of individuals is necessary for victory. If asymmetric warfare is perceived under the war model, it is unclear why the burden of establishing the effectiveness of the measures used should be any higher.[46]

7. Conclusion

The practice of war at the beginning of the twenty-first century is undergoing two major changes. First, today, there are hardly any old-style wars with proper armies confronting each other on the battlefield. Instead, wars are fought by states against non-state organizations with no clear battlefield, no clear distinction between combatants and noncombatants, and no clear idea of what victory might mean.[47] Second, weaponry is becoming increasingly automated and technologically sophisticated. These two changes are connected as we watch drones and other automated devices become the main tools of warfare against non-state organizations.

In the first sections of this chapter, I criticized arguments aimed at showing that the use of drones and killer robots is morally problematic. These arguments are so weak that one suspects that, for the most part, they are motivated not by worries about the intrinsic nature of these devices, but by a concern about the way they are actually used. In other words, drones and killer robots are assumed to be problematic because they are believed to enable and encourage a specific practice that is deemed wrongful: targeted killing. In Section 6, therefore, I aimed to show that this practice is far less problematic than critics would have us believe. If so, then the (albeit contingent) connection between drones and targeted killing does not constitute a persuasive argument against the use of drones either.

One must always be cautious in predicting the future. Nevertheless, compared with the grand battles of the past, with their shockingly high toll of casualties, drone-centered campaigns seem much more humane. They also enable a better fit between moral responsibility and vulnerability to defensive action. Judged against bombers, cruise missiles—and, obviously, against various kinds of weapons of mass destruction—the drone may well be remembered in the annals of warfare as offering real promise for moral progress.

Notes

1. Human Rights Watch, *Losing Humanity: The Case Against Killer Robots* ('Printed in the United States of America', 2012). See also Marcel Dickow and Hilmer Linnenkamp, 'Combat Drones—Killing Drones', *SWP Comments* 4 (2013), 1–8.
2. For the view that drones are effective in reducing civilian casualties, see Daniel Brunstetter and Megan Braun, 'The Implications of Drones on the Just War Tradition', *Ethics and International Affairs* 25 (2011), 348; Bradley Jay Strawser, 'Moral Predators: The Duty to Employ Uninhabited Aerial Vehicles', *Journal of Military Ethics* 9 (2010), 352; and Avery Plaw, 'Counting the Dead: The Proportionality of Predation in Pakistan', in *Killing by Remote Control: The Ethics of an Unmanned Military*, edited by Bradley Jay Strawser (New York: Oxford University Press, 2013), 126–153. For the opposite perspective, see Joint and Coalition Operational Analysis (JCOA), 'Drone Strikes: Civilian Casualty Considerations', https://info.publicintelligence.net/JCOA-DroneStrikesSummary.pdf.
3. Asa Kasher and Amos Yadlin, 'Military Ethics of Fighting Terror: An Israeli Perspective', *Journal of Military Ethics* 4 (2005), 3–32.
4. Strawser, 'Moral Predators', 342.
5. Yagil Levy, *Israel's Death Hierarchy: Casualty Aversion in a Militarized Democracy* (New York: New York University Press), 2.
6. Christopher Gelpi, Peter Feaver, and Jason Reifler, *Paying the Human Costs of War: American Public Opinion and Casualties in Military Conflicts* (Princeton, NJ: Princeton University Press, 2009), 21.
7. See Zack Beauchamp and Julian Savulescu 'Robot Guardians: Tele-operated Combat Vehicles in Humanitarian Intervention', in *Killing by Remote Control*, 106.
8. For a helpful discussion of this dilemma regarding humanitarian intervention, see Michael Gross, *Moral Dilemmas of Modern War: Torture, Assassination and Blackmail in an Age of Asymmetric Conflict* (New York: Cambridge University Press, 2010), ch. 9.
9. Brunstetter and Braun, 'The Implications of Drones', 339.
10. Strawser, 'Moral Predators', 344.
11. See Yitzhak Benbaji, 'Culpable Bystanders, Innocent Threats and the Ethics of Self-Defence', *Canadian Journal of Philosophy* 35 (2005), 623–640.
12. Strawser, 'Moral Predators', 357.
13. Jai Galliott, 'Closing with Completeness: The Asymmetric Drone Warfare Debate', *Journal of Military Ethics* 11 (2012), 355.
14. Idem, 353–354.
15. Kenneth Anderson and Matthew C. Waxman, 'Law and Ethics for Autonomous Weapon Systems: Why a Ban Won't Work and How the Laws of War Can' (American University

Washington College of Law Research Paper No. 2013-11, 2013), 8, http://papers.ssrn.com/sol3/papers.cfm?abstract_id=2250126).

16. Patrick Linn, 'Drone Ethics Briefing—What a Leading Robot Expert Told the CIA', *The Atlantic,* December 2011, 321.
17. Paul Kahn, 'The Paradox of Riskless Warfare', *Philosophy & Public Policy Quarterly* 22 (2002), 2. Kahn first developed this line of thought in his critical discussion of the US intervention in Kosovo: Paul Kahn, 'War and Sacrifice in Kosovo', *Report from the Institute for Philosophy and Public Policy*, 19:2 (1999).
18. Paul Kahn, 'Imagining Warfare', *European Journal of International Law* 24 (2013), 218.
19. Idem, 224.
20. Jeff McMahan, 'Foreword', in *Killing by Remote Control*, xii–xiii.
21. Robert Sparrow, 'War Without Virtue?' in *Killing by Remote Control*, edited by Bradley Jay Strawser (New York: Oxford University Press, 2013), 84–105.
22. Idem, 103.
23. Edmund L. Pincoffs, *Quandaries and Virtues Against Reductivism in Ethics* (Lawrence: University Press of Kansas, 1986).
24. For a similar argument, see Saul Smilansky, *Ten Moral Paradoxes* (Oxford: Blackwell, 2007), ch. 7.
25. Human Rights Watch, *Losing Humanity*, 26.
26. Noel Sharkey, 'Saying "No!" to Lethal Autonomous Targeting', *Journal of Military Ethics* 9 (2010), 381.
27. See Peter Singer, *Wired for War: The Robotics Revolution and Conflict in the Twenty-first Century* (New York: Penguin, 2009), and the criticism by Werner Dahm, 'Killer Drones Are Science Fiction', *Wall Street Journal*, 12 February 2012. See also Anderson and Waxman, 'Law and Ethics for Autonomous Weapon Systems', 2.
28. Sharkey, 'Saying "No!"', 380. See also his 'Death Strikes from the Sky: The Calculus of Proportionality', *Technology and Society Magazine* 28 (2009), 16–19.
29. See Wendell Wallach and Colin Allen, *Moral Machines: Teaching Robots Right from Wrong* (New York: Oxford University Press, 2008), who predicted that 'within the next few years, there will be a catastrophic incident brought about by a computer system making a decision independent of human oversight' (4).
30. Robert Sparrow, 'Killer Robots', *Journal of Applied Philosophy* 24 (2007), 62–77.
31. Idem, 67.
32. See also Sharkey, 'Saying "No!"', 381; Ryan Vogel, 'Drone Warfare and the Law of Armed Conflict', *Denver Journal of International Law and Policy* 39 (2010–11), 136; Ugo Pagallo, 'Robots of Just War: A Legal Perspective', *Philosophy and Technology* 24 (2011), 307–323.
33. The obligation to take responsibility for results beyond our control is a case of moral luck. See Margaret Walker, 'The Virtues of Impure Agency', in *Moral Luck*, edited by Daniel Statman (Albany, NY: SUNY Press), 235–250.
34. Anderson and Waxman, 'Law and Ethics for Autonomous Weapon Systems', 17.
35. Rebecca J. Johnson, 'The Wizard of Oz Goes to War: Unmanned Systems in Counterinsurgency', in *Killing by Remote Control*, edited by Bradley Jay Strawser (New York: Oxford University Press, 2013), 172. See also Strawser, 'Moral Predators', 353.
36. Armin Krishnan, *Killer Robots: Legality and Ethicality of Autonomous Weapons* (London: Ashgate, 2009), 130. See also Human Rights Watch, *Losing Humanity*, 28–22.
37. Singer, *Wired for War*, 396.
38. See Sharkey, 'Saying "No!"', 372, for some anecdotal evidence for this attitude.

39. Idem, 376.
40. Recently, it has been suggested that the set of questions dealing with the limited use of force (by drones or other measures) short of—or instead of—full-scale war constitutes a subfield of its own, *jus ad vim*. See Daniel R. Brunstetter and Megan Braun, 'From *Jus ad bellum* to *Jus ad vim*: Recalibrating Our Understanding of the Moral Use of Force', *Ethics and International Affairs* 26 (2013), 87–106.
41. It 'is already on the way to becoming a norm'; see David Whetham, 'Drones and Targeted Killing: Angels or Assassins?', in *Killing by Remote Control*, edited by Bradley Jay Strawser (New York: Oxford University Press, 2013), 83.
42. Jeff McMahan, 'The Ethics of Killing in War', *Ethics* 114 (2004), 717.
43. See Daniel Statman, 'Targeted Killing', *Theoretical Inquiries in Law* 5 (2003), 63–82.
44. Daniel Statman, 'Can Just War Theory Justify Targeted Killing? An Investigation into Three Models', in *Targeted Killings: Law and Morality in an Asymmetrical World*, edited by Claire Finkelstein, Jens David Ohlin, and Andrew Altman (New York: Oxford University Press, 2012), 90–111.
45. On targeted killing, see Michael Gross, *Moral Dilemmas of Modern War: Torture, Assassination and Blackmail in an Age of Asymmetric Conflict* (New York: Cambridge University Press, 2010), 114–121. On drones, see Michael Boyle, 'The Costs and Consequences of Drone Warfare', *Journal of International Affairs* 89 (2013), 1–29.
46. For the recent debate about the morality and legality of targeted killing and for helpful references, see Finkelstein et al. (eds.), *Targeted Killings*.
47. See Daniel Statman, 'Ending Wars: A Contractarian View of Jus ex Bello', *Ethics* 125 (2015), 1–31.

CHAPTER 25

ENDING WARS

DARREL MOELLENDORF

FAR more often than not, wars are abominations from the moral point view. Massive endeavours, they consume vast amounts of resources and spew out human carnage and devastation usually for no reasons other than conquest and domination. From its inception, the just war tradition has acknowledged that even the few wars that have been just are miserable human practices contrary to the better aspects of human nature. St. Augustine observes the dehumanizing character of war as follows:

> For it is the wrongdoing of the opposing party which compels the wise man to wage just wars; and this wrong-doing, even though it gave rise to no war, would still be matter of grief to man because it is man's wrong-doing. Let everyone, then, who thinks with pain on all these great evils, so horrible, so ruthless, acknowledge that this is misery. And if any one either endures or thinks of them without mental pain, this is a more miserable plight still, for he thinks himself happy because he has lost human feeling.[1]

ONE might expect, then, that in considering the morality of ending wars little more needs to be said than that the party pursuing a just war and employing just means should end the war only when the objective has been fulfilled and that the party pursuing an unjust war should cease hostilities immediately. On reflection, however, matters turn out to be more complicated.

In discussing the morality of ending wars, I use the term '*jus ex bello*'. David Rodin who independently, and more or less simultaneously, developed similar ideas about the underappreciated moral importance of ending wars suggests the terms '*terminatio* law'[2] or sometimes '*jus terminatio*'.[3] No settled convention in favour of one or the other usage has yet emerged. I trust that readers partial to Rodin's terminology will excuse my usage in this chapter.

With the inclusion of an account of *jus ex bello*, just war theory contains at least four different sets of concerns about the morality of war, *jus ad bellum, jus in bello, jus ex bello*, and *just post bellum*. It is tempting to think of the fundamental distinction between these as temporal: before, during, ending, and after the war. But David Rodin makes the plausible suggestion that 'a better way of conceiving them is as articulating moral reasons appropriate to distinctive forms of moral problem generated by different aspects of conflict'.[4] The form of the moral problem that *jus ad bellum* addresses is whether it is permissible to initiate a war. *Jus ad bellum* maintains that it is permissible to begin a war if and only if each member of a set of conditions is satisfied. Conceptions of *jus ad bellum* vary, of course, depending on the conditions included, their interpretation, and the understanding of the parties addressed by the doctrine.

What is the moral problem addressed by *jus ex bello*? One obvious answer would seem to be whether to end a war. It has in fact long been recognized that sometimes war in pursuit of just causes either should not be initiated or should be ended short of victory. Francisco de Vitoria argued that even just wars sometimes must not be pursued:

> But it is clear that one may have a right to reclaim a city or province, and yet find that right nullified by a danger of provoking greater conflict. As I have said, wars should only be waged for the common good; if the recovery of one city is bound to involve the commonwealth in greater damage, for instance the devastation of several cities, heavy casualties, or rivalry between princes and the occasion of further wars, there can be no doubt that the prince should cede his right and abstain from war.[5]

And if the excessive damage, devastation, and casualties can be reckoned only after the war has started, then the *ante bellum* determination of the justness of the war would require revision. But the distinction between the question addressed by *jus ex bello* and that addressed by *jus ad bellum* also entails that wars that should not have been started might be justly continued.

Two stylized examples support these two claims. In the first example, a powerful democratic country suffers a series of devastating terrorist attacks. Several thousand civilians are killed in closely timed incidents. The leadership of the country has credible evidence that the group perpetrating the attacks is being hosted in a country that, as the result of bloody internecine conflict, fell into the hands of a religiously fundamentalist political group that is hostile to the country attacked and that instituted a series of draconian laws against the freedom of women, the education of girls, and religious minorities. There is credible evidence that the terrorist group intends additional attacks imminently. The country attacked demands that the host country immediately close the terrorist training camps, arrest the terrorist leadership, and hand them over for trial in order to pre-empt additional imminent attacks. These demands are ignored. As a response, the country attacked and its allies initiate an aerial bombing campaign and a subsequent ground invasion, with the aim of capturing the terrorist leadership, closing the terrorist camps, and overthrowing the host government. Let's suppose this war satisfies the criteria of *jus ad bellum*.

Ten years later, a new government hostile to the previous one is in power in the invaded country. The camps have been closed, the religiously fundamentalist group has been deposed, and legal progress has been made in recognizing the rights of women and religious minorities. But the remnants of the fundamentalist group are prosecuting an effective insurgency. They are in de facto control of large swathes of the country where they have implemented their draconian system of control. And in other areas they are mounting a destabilizing terror campaign. Thousands of lives have been lost, and the attacked country and its allies have no credible strategy for victory. Now it would not seem unreasonable to question the justice of continuing the war on grounds of either proportionality or likelihood of success.

The second example is suggested in Moellendorf.[6] The initial circumstances are as in the first example, but the attempts by the powerful democracy to achieve a diplomatic solution instead of invading were not sufficiently thoroughgoing. Although the other conditions of *jus ad bellum* were satisfied, the war failed to satisfy the condition of necessity. Once the war began, diplomatic solutions were no longer available, and a victory by the fundamentalist regime would have both secured a staging ground for future terrorist activity and strengthened the fundamentalist regime vis-à-vis internal liberation efforts. Given the lack of diplomatic alternatives and the raised stakes, it seems reasonable to conclude that continued prosecution of the war is permissible. The two stylized examples give intuitive credibility to the view that it is possible that the initial determination of the justice or injustice of a war is not determinative of the morality of a subsequent prosecution of the war.

The distinction between the *jus ad bellum* judgment of the morality of the war and the *jus ex bello* judgment of its continuation is discussed more fully in the next section. In Section 3, I turn to the issue that has been the focus of most discussion in current debates about *jus ex bello*, namely, whether the discrepancy between the *ante bellum* reasonable projection of the expected moral costs of the war and the actual moral costs should change our judgment of the war's morally permissible costs. In Section 4, I discuss an area of *jus ex bello* that remains underexplored in current debates, but about which there was some discussion in the modern period: namely, how to end a war that ought to be ended.

The claim that *jus ex bello* is distinct from *jus ad bellum, jus in bello*, and *jus post bellum* is sometimes referred to as '*the independence thesis*'.[7] In Moellendorf[8] and Fabre,[9] systematic arguments are presented for the independence thesis. In this section, I discuss the independence of *jus ex bello* from *jus ad bellum*. The latter comprises several individually necessary and jointly sufficient conditions for the permissibility of resorting to war. Certain of these conditions could be taken as either belief- or fact-sensitive. In other words, the requirement stated could depend on either objective states of affairs or reasonable beliefs about those states of affairs. Although that distinction is important for assessing whether a war is justified and attributing responsibility, it makes no difference for assessing the independence thesis.

An argument for the independence of *jus ex bello* from *jus ad bellum* goes as follows:

1. Whether resorting to war is justified depends on conditions each individually necessary and jointly sufficient.

2. Each of the aforementioned conditions also applies to the justification of continuing a war.
3. After a war begins, either the states of affairs relevant to the satisfaction of one of the aforementioned conditions, or reasonable beliefs about the states of affairs, may change, such that the truth value of one or more of the individually necessary and jointly sufficient conditions changes.
4. Therefore, the morality of continuing a war is distinct from the morality of resorting to war.

Premise 3 seems true of a set of core principles, including at least just cause, proportionality, likelihood of success, and necessity.

Suppose that, *ante bellum*, a war of regime change fails to satisfy the condition of just cause but that the continued prosecution of the war is necessary, or reasonably believed to be so, in order to protect from the imminent threat of mass atrocities a large civilian population sympathetic to the cause of regime change. The cause of the war has changed, and the new one is arguably just. Parenthetically, arguably, the identity of the war is tied to its cause, in which case this is a new war.[10] Regardless, however, of whether one takes it to be a new war, each of the other conditions must be re-evaluated because the primacy of just cause among the conditions of *jus ad bellum* entails that, as the cause changes proportionality, likelihood of success and necessity must be re-evaluated.[11] It is possible that continuing to fight is justified even though resorting to war was not.

Alternatively, proportionality and likelihood of success could change once a war begins since the unexpected is the rule in warfare. Finally, either a war that was necessary may become unnecessary as diplomatic avenues open up, or a war that was unnecessary may become necessary as the avenues close. These considerations lend credence to the third premise and hence to the conclusion that *jus ex bello* is distinct from *jus ad bellum*.

There are several possible challenges to the independence of *jus ex bello* from *jus ad bellum*. Consider first Seth Lazar's claim that 'Contra Moellendorf and Rodin, there is no principled difference between the two questions: "am I justified in taking arms?" And "am I justified in not laying my arms down?" Each reduces to the same question: is fighting justified? And this question must be asked constantly'.[12] This might be interpreted as denying the independence thesis. (But, to be fair, Lazar does not deny the importance of *jus ex bello* in that paper.) For if the question of *jus ex bello* is identical to the question of *jus ad bellum*, then perhaps these are not (in Rodin's words) 'distinctive forms of moral problem'. It is true that both *jus ad bellum* and *jus ex bello* are about whether fighting is justified, but it is false that they apply to the same kind of circumstances. *Jus ad bellum* concerns the following question: should this war be started? Meanwhile *jus ex bello* concerns a different question: should this war be continued? There is good reason to believe that the truth conditions of the answers can be different even with respect to the same war. And that is the point of the independence thesis.

An objection to the independence of *jus ex bello* from *jus ad bellum* based on Michael Walzer's views is discussed in Moellendorf.[13] Walzer claims that resistance to aggression is 'always justified' and is usually 'the morally preferred response'.[14] According to his view, if the war is justified to begin, it remains justified as long as the threat of aggression persists because if the other conditions of the justice of a war do not require independent satisfaction, then no changed conditions—other than a changed cause—would change the morality of the war. It is, however, implausible that the other conditions of the justice of the war do not require independent satisfaction. Such a view would permit wars when a satisfactory diplomatic solution existed or when the costs in terms of civilian lives far exceed the benefits and the prospects for victory are hopeless. The view is far too permissive of war to be morally acceptable.

Moellendorf[15] claims that one conclusion entailed by the independence thesis is that a war that was unjust to initiate is not necessarily unjust to continue. This is disputed in Rodin.[16] His objection is based on an analogy involving wrongfully dangling a person (the dangled) out of a window. Imagine that a person engaged in such wrongful dangling (the dangler) were to have a moral conversion and appreciate the wrongness of dangling but without being strong enough to pull in the dangled. It would be wrong for the dangler to stop dangling by letting go, even though, according to Rodin, dangling is nonetheless wrong to the dangled. This is offered, by analogy, to support the following claim: 'Prosecuting a war that fails to satisfy the requirements of *jus ad bellum* is necessarily immoral. However, it may sometimes be morally obligatory to continue to prosecute an immoral war in order to avoid the commission of even worse forms of aggravated immorality'.[17] If a war fails on grounds of *jus ad bellum*—in particular due to an unjust cause—but satisfies conditions of *jus ex bello*, Rodin claims that there is a dilemma 'in which one will do wrong no matter how one acts'.[18] The view is that a war that is unjust to initiate is necessarily unjust, even though it might also be unjust to end it.

Although Rodin claims that there is a moral dilemma in these kinds of cases owing to our inability not to do wrong, he nonetheless (and perhaps inconsistently) claims that there is a unique course of action that we morally must not take. In considering the dangling case, he asserts that, 'although dangling you from my window is wrong (and the longer I dangle the worse it is), the one thing I morally must not do is to let go'.[19] If both dangling and letting go are wrong, it is unclear how one arrives at the conclusion that one must not let go. Obviously, it is correct that the dangler morally must not let go of the dangled, but that seems to refute the claim that dangling is wrong.

One way to account for the correct judgment that the dangler must not let go is to challenge the necessary wrongness of dangling the person. Once the dangler has had the moral conversion, appreciates the wrongness of the initial dangling, and seeks to save the person dangled, the continued dangling is not necessarily wrong. Presumably, the dangler's cause of dangling before the conversion was to terrify or persecute the dangled. After the conversion, the cause of dangling is to rescue the dangled. Surely, the act of rescuing, including the continued dangling as a means of rescuing, is not wrong even though it was wrong to engage in terror-dangling. This is made clear by a change in the example. A third person (the rescuer) witnessing the dangling, prior to the conversion of the dangler, rushes to the window in an effort to save the dangled. The rescuer rips the dangled out of the hands of the dangler. But the rescuer is incapable of hauling in the dangled and must let him dangle while yelling for help. This rescuer's action of rescue-dangling is not wrong. If that is the case, then it seems that the original dangler's post-conversion action of rescue-dangling is also not wrong. The cause of the dangling has changed and is now just. As the action changes from a case of terror-dangling to rescue-dangling, its moral value changes. Of course, it might be correct to describe these as different acts—namely, persecution and rescue—but that only serves to make clearer the point that they have different moral values. Hence, there is no real dilemma. So also with a war that was unjust to initiate. Suppose the cause is now just (and it is arguably a new war), or that it is now likely to succeed, or that circumstances have changed to make one of the other conditions previously not satisfied now satisfied. In that case, the wrong making condition no longer exists.

The response to Rodin defeats a principled rejection of the possibility that a war that was unjust to begin could become just. The changed appraisal of the war with respect to several conditions common to the *jus ad bellum* and *jus ex bello* is discussed in more detail in both Moellendorf[20] and Fabre.[21]

One of the most controversial issues in the emerging debates concerning *jus ex bello* is whether the actual moral costs incurred in fighting a war provide a reason to change the moral judgment made before the war began about its budget of permissible moral costs.[22] In principle, the moral costs in war are manifold, but problems of commensurability among manifold costs are vexing.[23] So, I simplify the issue by considering only killing. The debate thus far has focused mainly on the conception of proportionality appropriate to a war that has proved to be more costly than originally expected. The concept of proportionality requires that the pursuit of a just cause not exceed some budget for the moral costs. Conceptions of proportionality can vary according to how these costs are counted.[24] One important way in which conceptions vary is in how they weigh past moral costs, in particular whether past moral costs count in a proportionality assessment or not.

Suppose that, *ante bellum*, the realization of the just cause was correctly judged to be worth no more than 10 000 killings. Moreover, a reasonable intelligence assessment projected that the just cause could be realized by killing fewer than 10 000 people. Hence, *ante bellum*, the war was correctly judged proportional. However, the war went worse than expected, and this was not due to culpable strategic or tactical failures. Perhaps freak weather conditions made prosecution of the war less accurate than it otherwise would have been. The war is 90 per cent complete, but 10 000 people have already been killed. Now a reasonable intelligence assessment projects that the war can be won at the cost of 1000 additional killings. This is a case of what Rodin[25] calls 'a sunk cost dilemma', which he characterizes as follows: '[A] situation in which it is morally permissible (or obligatory) to continue with a course of action that is *in toto* and all things considered wrong, because the sufficient wrong-making features of the course of action lie in the past and the action is morally permissible (or obligatory) on a forward looking basis'.[26] According to Rodin, these dilemmas come in two versions. In cases such as the one under discussion, continuing to fight the war mitigates, but does not eliminate, the wrong-making features of the action. In other cases, in which the war did not begin with a just cause, continuing to fight the war aggravates the sufficient wrong-making feature of the war.[27]

There is considerable controversy about whether sunk costs in warfare actually create a dilemma. One view is that continuing the war in cases like the one just described would be unjust because disproportionate[28]; hence, there is no dilemma. The original correct moral judgment about the value of fully realizing the just cause is not revised because the pursuit of the cause has proved harder than could have been expected. In contrast, another view has it that the war in pursuit of the just cause would be proportional if the remaining 10 per cent of the goal is worth killing 1000 people.[29] According to this view, the past killings should be fully discounted, and the question salient to proportionality is simply about the comparison between the value of realizing the remainder of the just cause and the killings required to achieve that remainder. Rodin draws an analogy to prudential reasoning, in which overall losses can sometimes be minimized by exceeding an initial limit on costs. He concludes that moral reasoning may sometimes allow a party to war to kill more than the correctly judged *ante bellum* budget in order to improve the ratio of costs to benefits.

As a matter of prudential reasoning, taking past costs as sunk costs and thus exceeding the original reasonable cost limits is surely sometimes rational.[30] Consider the following. Let t be some time after the beginning of the project at which the deliberation about continuing it is occurring. Let C_t be the sum of the costs from the beginning until time t, and let C_c be the sum of the projected costs incurred from t to the completion of the project. Since the *C*s are costs we take them to be negative numbers. Also let B be the sum of all the benefits that accrue upon completion of the project, which we take to be a positive number. As long as $B + C_t + C_c > Ct$, then it is rational to pursue the project. In other words, as long as the net benefits of completion (the benefit minus all the costs) are greater than the costs of stopping short of completion, then it is rational to pursue the project. It can be rational to complete a project even if the net benefits are negative (even if the sum on the left side of the formula is negative) as long it would be more costly to stop (as long as the right-side number in the formula is less than the sum on the left). Rodin[31] argues that continued pursuit of a war that exceeds the *ante bellum* correctly judged budget for securing the just cause is morally permissible if the expected net moral benefits of doing so are greater than the costs of stopping in order not to exceed the *ante bellum* limit.

McMahan[32] illustrates the forward-looking approach by means of a trolley argument. Imagine a trolley rolling down a track in the direction of five people whom it will surely kill unless diverted. Using a switch, a bystander could divert the trolley to another track, where it would kill only one person. The bystander's choice then is to kill one person or allow five to die. Let's suppose that the bystander morally should kill the one to save the five. But the example need not presuppose a moral symmetry between killing and letting die. Let's assume that there is some limit on permissible killing less than five people. For the sake of the example, we stipulate that the limit is three people. In other words, it would be proportional to kill up to (but no more than) three people in order to save five. Imagine that when the bystander first attempts to flip the switch, there is an unexpected malfunction; the trolley is not diverted, and a small explosion caused by flipping the switch kills three innocent people in the area. As luck would have it, the bystander has sufficient time to repair the malfunction and flip the switch a second time, thereby diverting the trolley, killing one more person, but saving the five.

After the accidental explosion, the choice of the bystander can be described in forward-looking terms as either to kill one person in order to save five or not to kill one and to let five die. Since by assumption it would be proportionate to kill one person in order to save five others, the correct choice is clear. But if we take account of the three people already killed, the choice is between either killing three people and letting five die or killing four to save five. Since killing four to save five is, by assumption, disproportionate, it would be wrong to flip the switch a second time. The example does not offer a compelling reason not to take account of the three already killed. It's not a compelling defence of counting only future costs.

Looking only forward when making proportionality judgments looks very congenial to the present trend in warfare, in which long wars bleed into long military occupations. Perhaps too congenial. If we consider the case of the long war in Afghanistan, fully discounting sunk costs would require proportionality judgments only in light of future killings. That would suggest that critics of the war who invoked its cumulative costs were confused about which costs proportionality counts. It would leave us with a very significant restriction of the grounds on which a war might be criticized. Perhaps it's false that the Afghan war was disproportionate; perhaps the cumulative costs were worth the value of realizing the cause. But that's to accept the critics' charge on its own terms, not to claim that they failed to make an intelligible claim because they misused the concept of proportionality.[33]

Regardless of whether one believes that fully discounting sunk costs is too permissive of current wars, there is a fundamental problem with it. The forward-looking approach is consistent with there being, in principle, no stopping point to killing.[34] As long as the expected disvalue of the next round of killing does not outweigh the value of completing the remaining portion of the just cause, another round of killing can be justified. Building on McMahan's trolley example, it is possible for there to be infinite iterations of switch-flipping, with the effect that the number of people killed in order to save five people becomes infinite. The concept of proportionality assumes that the good of realizing the just cause of a war is, in principle, limited. But fully discounting the sunk costs allows that, in principle, one may pursue a war whose cumulative costs have no limit. This suggests that the approach is not a conception of the proportionality of a war at all. Perhaps the advocates of fully discounting sunk costs would reply that the concept of proportionality has always only been related to future costs, but since proportionality discussions have typically focused only on whether to start a war, the forward-looking character of proportionality has not been appreciated. But, as we have seen, accepting such a conception of proportionality (if it is that) would come at the cost of significantly revising the terms according to which ongoing wars may be criticized.

There is another issue about the costs of a war in progress that has received little critical attention, although it is recognized in Rodin.[35] Rather than imagining a war that it is pushing up against its *ante bellum* proportionality budget, imagine instead the remarkable case of a war whose moral costs are thus far coming in well under budget. Suppose the war is approximately half over, with no good reason to suppose the second half to be more difficult than the first, but only 20 per cent of the killings permitted by the correct *ante bellum* budget have been committed. What does the fact that the war is under the proportionality budget entail for the permissible moral costs for the second half? One view would require revising the total permissible costs downwards to approximately 40 per cent of the original limit on grounds that killing in excess of that is presumptively unnecessary. Another view would permit 80 per cent of the total costs to be incurred in the second half of the war on grounds that the actual costs of the war should not affect the budget of morally permissible costs.

There may be reasons to criticize the moral costs of a war, even if it does not exceed its *ante bellum* correctly judged budget for moral costs. Samuel Pufendorf understood these to be reasons of humanity: '[h]umanity however requires that so far as the momentum of warfare permits, we should inflict no more suffering on an enemy than defence or vindication of our right and its future assurance requires'.[36] This seems generally correct. But Pufendorf's point can be made more precisely. The wrong involved in the prosecution of a war that is proportionate but that could have been fought at lower moral costs is that it involves unnecessary killings.[37]

Invoking the more precise version of Pufendorf's point, a belligerent party that pursues a strategy permissive of 80 per cent of its permitted costs accruing in the second half of the war is pursuing a strategy for ending the war that is unnecessary, even if the costs are proportional to the good of realizing the just cause. A criticism on grounds of lack of necessity in this context does not entail that the war in pursuit of the just cause is per se unnecessary. Rather, if the war could be prosecuted with substantially fewer moral costs, then the war is fought in an unnecessary manner, even if the war generally is necessary. The condition of necessity, then, can be directed at the military strategy used in pursuit of the end, rather than belligerence per se. This is a familiar concern from *jus in bello*.

There are at least two distinct questions to which *jus ex bello* responds.[38] One is whether to continue to fight or to end the war. The other is how to end a war that should be ended. Because the latter is an account of means, it might be thought to be covered by either *jus in bello* or *jus post bellum*. Conceptually, the distinction between the second doctrine of *jus ex bello* and these other two doctrines is straightforward. The question of how to end a war is a different from the question of how a war should be fought. The former concerns the morally appropriate strategies for the cessation of conflict. The latter concerns constraints on those who prosecute a war across all its phases. The question of how to end a war is also different from the question about the constraints that a morally justified peace places on the prosecution of the war. That question is not specific to strategies for ending a war.

The distinctiveness of the question of how a war should be ended can best be appreciated by surveying the kinds of constraints on ending a war that seem reasonable.

Moellendorf[39] defends five moral principles that govern the ending of a war. The first three are closely related to one another. The first of these is the principle of all due haste, which requires ending an unjust war as quickly as is reasonably possible. The idea is simple. If a war is unjust, then, prima facie, the injustice should not be prolonged. But what is reasonable to do in ending a war depends on at least two additional principles. The second principle is the principle of injustice mitigation. This principle applies insofar as the cause of the war, which should be ended, is just. Injustice mitigation requires pursuit of the just cause while the war is being wound down. An instance of this general principle is defended in Fabre[40] ; sometimes, a party pursuing a just cause that cannot be won is justified in not surrendering, but instead in suing for peace in an effort to achieve more of the objective that provides the just cause for war.[41] Even in the case of a war that cannot be won and morally must be brought to a close, the closing should advance justice to the extent possible consistent with the constraints of morality. The third principle is moral cost minimization, which requires that a war should be ended in a manner that minimizes the moral costs that arise in the process of ending. This includes the moral costs to civilians, to the institutions of a just and peaceful social and political life, and to the country's natural resources and vital infrastructure. Preventing certain kinds of wrongs, especially gross violations of human rights, requires priority. Such prevention may require some delays in ending a war that should be ended. The requirement to minimize costs to civilians is similar to the *jus in bello* constraints that also seek to protect civilians. But the *jus ex bello* principle governs specifically the tactics of the military drawdown and withdrawal.

Two additional principles governing the ending of wars are drawn from Lazar.[42] One is the requirement to negotiate for peace in good faith. Thomas Hobbes is well-known for arguing that fraud is a virtue in the conduct of war.[43] But there is a tradition of just war theorizing that holds that there are constraints on the use of fraud even during warfare. Keeping faith with one's enemies is an important theme in Book 3 of Hugo Grotius's *The Rights of War and Peace*. Samuel Pufendorf echoes a distinction drawn by Grotius between acceptable forms of wartime deceit and unacceptable breaking of faith: 'one has equal right to use fraud and deceit against an enemy, provided one does not violate one's pledged faith. Hence one may deceive an enemy by false or fictitious stories, but never by promises or agreements'.[44]

Grotius makes two arguments to support the claim that promises made to enemies, especially during peace negotiations, must be kept. One argument appeals to the right, based in natural law, which a promise creates in a promisee:

> From this Society founded on Reason and Speech, arises that Obligation from a Promise, which we now treat of. And we are not to imagine that, because it is permitted to tell a Falsehood to an Enemy, or because, according to the Opinion of several, there is no Harm in it . . . we may extend such Permission to the very Words we use in treating with the Enemy. For the Obligation to Truth arises from a Cause, prior to War, and perhaps may be in some Measure annihilated by War, but a Promise of itself confers a new Right.[45]

The right of the promisee derives, according to Grotius, from the nature of speech and reason, which he takes as constitutively aiming towards the truth. What is more, a promise that takes the form of an oath is understood by Grotius to be owed not only to the promisee but to God:

> [F]or Oaths have a Power to exclude all Exceptions which may arise from the Party we deal with, because therein we treat not only with Men, but with GOD, to whom we stand obliged by our Oaths, tho' there should arise no right at all to Man. . . . In things sworn it is necessary that our Words be true in that Sense, in which we sincerely believed those to whom we swear, understand them, so that we perfectly abhor their Impiety, who scruple not to affirm, that it is as lawful to deceive Men with Oaths, as Children with Toys.[46]

Grotius's second argument for keeping faith with wartime enemies rests on the good of peace made possible by the preservation of the norm to honour promises with enemies. He claims that, 'We ought to preserve our Faith for several Reasons, and amongst others, because without that we should have no Hopes of Peace'.[47] The discovery that a party has been fraudulent in the negotiating process would undermine the efforts to build trust, which are necessary to achieve a negotiated settlement short of decisive victory and defeat. The argument for negotiation in good faith extends beyond the pursuit of peace in the particular conflict to the value of a strong war convention incorporating the principle of good faith. Such a convention encourages the expectation that peace might be possible by means of negotiation. That expectation can spare civilians the hell of prolonged war.

Grotius anticipates the following objection: promises made under the duress, such as credible threats of death and destruction, cannot be binding, and because negotiations for peace are made in the context in which a failure to negotiate might bring destruction, no promises during war can be binding. The objection seems strongest when the threats are of consequences that are unjust. This would be analogous to a promise made by an individual under threat. In reply, Grotius invokes the great utility of the convention to honour wartime promises:

> [W]hatever promises are made in that War, or for bringing it to a Conclusion, are so valid, that tho' they were occasioned by a fear unjustly caused, yet they cannot be made void without the Consent of him to whom the Promise was made. Because as many other Things, tho' in themselves not wholly innocent, are yet by the Law of Nations reputed just, so is Fear, which in such a War is occasioned on either Side; for it were not allowed, such Wars, that are but too frequent, could be neither moderated, nor concluded, which yet are very necessary to be done for the good of Mankind.[48]

Allowing that promises made in war in response to the unjust threat of force are non-binding would be devastating to the maintenance of a wartime norm to keep faith in negotiations because such promises are a typical feature of wartime negotiations. But because that convention is immensely valuable to peace efforts, even promises in war that respond to unjust threats to use force should be taken as binding.

Although there are good moral reasons for the principle of keeping faith, it might seem unreasonable to take it as an absolute requirement. A lesser evil argument suggests that the principle is defeasible.[49] Suppose the following: a party seeking negotiation has been pursuing a war to prevent genocide; by means of fraudulent negotiating a victory would be nearly certain, and the continued fighting in pursuit of the victory would be proportional. Under such extreme conditions, negotiating in bad faith seems justified. Presumably, conditions in which a compelling lesser evil argument can be made will be very rare. And if there is to be a strong war convention that incorporates the principle of good faith in peace negotiations, the instances of bad faith would have to be few.

The other relevant principle defended in Lazar[50] is that no party to a peace negotiation is morally entitled to make demands merely on the basis of advantages acquired in war. A party ending a war has no entitlements based only on success in war. If the party was not entitled to, say, the territory prior to the war, it is not entitled to it simply because it was acquired in the war. The claim rests on the familiar distinction between the just entitlement to a good and the de facto enjoyment of the good, and its general acceptance and enforcement would discourage wars in pursuit of conquest. Rodin[51] rejects the principle of no war-based entitlements on the grounds that it makes negotiations impossible: 'it would also seem to imply that meaningful negotiation to end war is impermissible, since all negotiation grounds post war entitlement at least partly in war gains'.[52] One way to press this point is to notice that, in all wars, at least one side is unjust, and often both are. When parties fighting unjustly negotiate, they are likely to make claims that are also unjust. But we want parties to pursue peace by means of negotiation so we should not criticize negotiating claims that are unjust. That view, however, is implausible because it would reduce the primary category of criticism of the negotiating stance of parties to the strategic and tactical. The charge that a party is acting ineptly in negotiations might sometimes be appropriate, but it appeals only at its own interests. Parties may also make demands that they are unjustified in making. And it is important to evaluating the claims of other parties, observers, and historians that such criticism is recognized as possible. Of course, we often want warring parties to negotiate, but we need not abandon moral criticism of their negotiating claims in order to facilitate negotiation. Parties will often have plenty of self-interested reasons to negotiate, even if they come under moral criticism for the stances they assume in negotiations.

Negotiations do not necessarily cause states to relinquish that to which they have no rights. Fabre distinguishes between a just peace and an all-things-considered-justified peace: '[a] just peace is one in which the wronged party obtains redress for the rights-violations and (justified) rights-infringements to which it was subject'.[53] Whereas in an all-things-considered justified peace 'the wronged party receives less than what it is owed for the sake of peace and can be reasonably expected to consent to such terms'.[54] There can be a lesser evil justification for a party to concede matters to which it is morally entitled in order to shorten a costly war that it cannot win. Insofar as that is the case, then there is reason for negotiations even when a party is being unreasonable.

The moral status of a war at its commencement does not determine its moral status once the fighting begins. War changes things; it can even change the moral status of the war itself. Exactly how and under what conditions this occurs requires philosophical clarity. Although there is a discussion of the morality of ending wars that goes back at least as far as early modern political philosophy, in recent debates in just war theory, the questions of whether and how to an end a war have received comparatively little attention. In so far as these are morally important questions, and distinct ones from those that have been the focus of most just war theorizing, there is reason to consider them more carefully and thoroughly. There are encouraging signs from recent debates that this is starting to occur.

Acknowledgements

I would like to thank Helen Frowe and Seth Lazar for very helpful comments on an earlier version of this chapter.

Notes

1. St. Augustine, *The City of God*, bk. 19, ch. 7. In *Nicene and Post-Nicene Fathers*, First Series, vol. 2, edited by Marcus Dods, Philip Schaff, and Kevin Knight (Buffalo, NY: Christian Literature Publishing, 1887), http://www.newadvent.org/fathers/120119.htm.
2. David Rodin, 'Two Emerging Issues of Jus Post Bellum: War Termination and the Liability of Soldiers for Crimes of Aggression', in *Jus Post Bellum Towards a Law of Transition From Conflict to Peace*, edited by Carsten Jahn and Jann K. Kleffner (The Hague: TMC Asser Press, 2008).
3. David Rodin, 'The War Trap: Dilemmas of *Jus Terminatio*'. *Ethics* 125 (2015).
4. Idem, 2.
5. Francisco de Vitoria, 'On the Law of War', in Vitoria, *Political Writings*, edited by Anthony Pagden and Jeremy Lawrence (Cambridge: Cambridge University Press, 1991), 314, para. 33.
6. Darrel Moellendorf, 'Is the War in Afghanistan Just?' *Imprints: A Journal of Analytic Socialism* 6 (2002) http://eis.bris.ac.uk/~plcdib/imprints/moellendorf.html.
7. Bradley J. Strawser, 'Reply to Moellendorf', paper presented to Oxford Institute for Ethics of Law and Armed Conflict Conference 'Ending Wars', 30–31 August 2012.
8. Darrel Moellendorf, '*Jus ex Bello*', *Journal of Political Philosophy* 16 (2008), 123–136.
9. Cécile Fabre, 'War Exit', *Ethics* 125 (2015).
10. For a discussion of the relationship between just cause and the identity of a war, see Darrel Moellendorf, 'Two Doctrines of *Jus ex Bello*', *Ethics* 125 (2015), 19–20.
11. Jeff McMahan defends the priority of just cause in his 'Just Cause for War', *Ethics & International Affairs* 19 (2005), 1–21.
12. Seth Lazar, 'Endings and Aftermath in the Ethics of War'. CSSJ Working Papers Series, No. SJ016, November 2010, http://socialjustice.politics.ox.ac.uk/materials/SJ016_Lazar_Endings&Aftermath_War.pdf, 3–4
13. D. Moellendorf, 'Two Doctrines of *Jus ex Bello*'.

14. Michael Walzer, *Just and Unjust Wars*, 4th ed. (New York: Basic Books, 2006), 51.
15. D. Moellendorf, '*Jus ex Bello*'.
16. D. Rodin, 'The War Trap'.
17. Idem., 20.
18. Idem, 2.
19. Idem., 13.
20. D. Moellendorf, '*Jus ex Bello*'.
21. C. Fabre, 'War Exit Ethics'.
22. D. Rodin, 'Two Emerging Issues of *Jus Post Bellum*'.
23. Walzer suggests that these render proportionality judgments fatuous. *Arguing About War* (New Haven/London: Yale University Press, 2004), 89–90.
24. The concept/conception distinction derives from John Rawls, *A Theory of Justice*, rev. ed. (Cambridge, MA: Harvard University Press, 1999), 9.
25. D. Rodin, 'The War Trap'.
26. Idem, 12–13.
27. Idem, 13.
28. C. Fabre, 'War Exit' *Ethics*'; D. Moellendorf, 'Two Doctrines of *Jus ex Bello*'.
29. Jeff McMahan, 'Proportionality and Time', *Ethics* 125 (2015); D. Rodin, 'Two Emerging Issues of *Jus Post Bellum*' and 'The War Trap'.
30. D. Moellendorf, 'Two Doctrines of *Jus ex Bello*'.
31. D. Rodin, 'The War Trap'.
32. J. McMahan, 'Proportionality and Time'.
33. For a discussion of the proportionality of the Afghan war see Richard W. Miller, 'The Ethics of America's Afghan War', *Ethics and International Affairs* 25 (2011), 103–132, and the responses, including Jeff McMahan, 'Proportionality in the Afghan War', *Ethics and International Affairs* 25 (2011), 143–154, and Darrel Moellendorf, '*Jus ex Bello* in Afghanistan', *Ethics and International Affairs* 25 (2011), 155–164.
34. D. Moellendorf, 'Two Doctrines of *Jus ex Bello*'.
35. D. Rodin, 'Two Emerging Issues of *Jus Post Bellum*'.
36. Samuel Pufendorf, *On the Duty of Man and Citizen According to Natural Law*, edited by James Tully, translated by Michael Silverthorne (Cambridge: Cambridge University Press, 1991), 169.
37. See also Seth Lazar, 'Necessity in Self-Defense and War', *Philosophy and Public Affairs* 40 (2012), 6. And see page 18: 'There might be several proportionate options, only one of which satisfies necessity'. The precise relationship between judgments of proportionality and necessity requires careful philosophical analysis. An intuitively plausible view is that they make different comparisons. Necessity compares the moral costs of various means, whereas proportionality compares the costs of a particular means to the value of the just cause. But Lazar takes proportionality judgments to involve comparing the harm imposed by each available option against the harm suffered by doing nothing, and he takes necessity judgments to involve pairwise comparisons of all available options to find the least harm-imposing (19). If doing nothing is an available option, then satisfying necessity will require satisfying proportionality (18). And Thomas Hurka offers a reading of the necessity requirement as a kind of proportionality requirement compared to other means of achieving the end of the war in his 'Proportionality in the Morality of War', *Philosophy and Public Affairs* 33 (2005), 37.
38. D. Moellendorf, '*Jus ex Bello*' and 'Two Doctrines of *Jus ex Bello*'.

39. D. Moellendorf, 'Two Doctrines of *Jus ex Bello*'.
40. C. Fabre, 'War Exit' *Ethics* 125 (2015).
41. Idem, 6.
42. S. Lazar, 'Endings and Aftermath in the Ethics of War'.
43. Thomas Hobbes, *The Leviathan, in The English Works of Thomas Hobbes* vol. III, edited by Sir William Molesworth (London: Bohn, 1839–45), ch. 13, 73. http://files.libertyfund.org/files/585/Hobbes_0051-03_EBk_v6.0.pdf.
44. S. Pufendorf, *On the Duty of Man and Citizen*, 169.
45. Hugo Grotius, *The Rights of War and Peace* Bk. III, edited by Richard Tuck (Indianapolis, IN: Liberty Fund, 2005), 1535.
46. Idem, 1226.
47. Idem, 1638.
48. Idem, 1543–1544.
49. D. Moellendorf, 'Two Doctrines of *Jus ex Bello*'.
50. S. Lazar, 'Endings and Aftermath in the Ethics of War'.
51. D. Rodin 'The War Trap'.
52. Idem, 18, fn. 28.
53. Fabre, 'War Exit' *Ethics*, 11.
54. Ibid.

PART V

AFTERMATH

CHAPTER 26

WAR'S AFTERMATH AND THE ETHICS OF WAR

CÉCILE FABRE

1. Introduction

Both natural law as articulated by, inter alia, Vitoria, Suárez, and Grotius, and positivist international law as defended in the eighteenth century by Vattel and Wolff, place great emphasis on what belligerents may do to one another once the war is over. Kant himself, of course, writing a century after Grotius and at the same time as Vattel, puts the *jus post bellum* firmly on the table with his sketch of a *Perpetual Peace*.[1] And yet, until the 2003 invasion of Iraq by the US-lead coalition, and notwithstanding Walzer's brief remarks about *jus post bellum* in his seminal 1977 *Just and Unjust Wars*,[2] war ethicists have devoted far more energy to discussing the moral grounds upon which resorting to war is just (*jus ad bellum*) and the ways in which war ought to be fought (*jus in bello*) than they have to the normative issues that arise once the guns have fallen silent. Since 2003, however, there has been a steady trickle of works on *jus post bellum*—although by no means as many as one might have expected.

Although disagreements abound as to what constitutes a just postwar state of affairs, there is a relatively high degree of consensus on the following requirements: victorious belligerents should aim to restore the political sovereignty and territorial integrity of their defeated enemy; some form of compensation for wartime wrongdoings should be paid to victims; assistance should be given to the defeated enemy and its civilian population towards the reconstruction of their country; wrongdoers should be put on trial; and, crucially, a stable and durable peace should be, as far as possible, the overarching aim of erstwhile belligerents when dealing with one another.[3]

An earlier draft of this paper was presented at the Oxford War Workshop in October 2012. I am grateful to the participants, as well as to Helen Frowe and Seth Lazar, for their penetrating comments.

In this chapter, I do not review the history of *jus post bellum*, good accounts of which can be found elsewhere.[4] Nor do I attend to the various principles that, by consensus, make for a just postwar peace (see Ohlin's and Lu's contributions in this volume). Rather, taking my cue from recent work in just war theory, much of which consists in scrutinizing the relationship between *jus ad bellum* and *jus in bello*, I focus on the relationship between *jus post bellum* and those two *jura*. In so doing, I aim to offer an account of the role and place of *jus post bellum* within just war theory and to highlight avenues of inquiry on the aftermath of war that have been largely ignored so far.

I proceed as follows. In Section 2, I discuss recent arguments to the effect that *jus ad bellum* and *jus in bello* exhaust just war theory and that *jus post bellum*, far from being a key member of the family (as it were), in fact does much better as an outsider. I claim, on the contrary, that there is ample space for *jus post bellum* within just war theory; in partial agreement with those arguments, however, I agree that a full account of the ethics of war's aftermath must also draw on other fields of normative inquiry. In Section 3, I flesh out in greater details connections and disconnections between *jus post bellum* on the one hand and the other two *jura* on the other hand.

Two preliminary remarks are in order. First, the categories of *jus ad bellum, jus in bello,* and *jus post bellum* are meant to identify different phases of the war and are standardly thought to comprise normative principles that are specific to those phases. I do not think that those labels are more than a convenient expository device, but, for the sake of exposition, I shall use them to denote norms governing, respectively, the resort to war, belligerents' conduct in war, and postwar states of affairs—bearing in mind that those norms might sometimes be the same. I shall also assume, for the sake of argument, that a war is just if and only if it meets the following conditions: it has a just cause, where one has a just cause if one's fundamental human rights are violated through the use of lethal force; it is a proportionate means to avert such violations; it is not fought and won through the deliberate and indiscriminate targeting of innocent noncombatants; it stands a reasonable chance of succeeding by military means that do not breach the requirements of proportionality and discrimination; it is the only way to pursue the just cause whilst minimizing casualties; and neither its occurrence nor the way it is fought unnecessarily threaten, once it is over, the establishment of a durable and all-things-considered justified peace. Some of those requirements are recognisably *ad bellum* requirements, whilst others are standardly thought to belong to *jus in bello*.

Second, *jus post bellum* is sometimes thought to encompass two distinct phases. The first, norms for which have been dubbed *jus ex bello* by Darrel Moellendorf and *jus terminatio* by David Rodin, is the process by which belligerents stop fighting and sue for peace.[5] Once the fighting has stopped, however, attention must be given to what constitutes a just postwar state of affairs: this, in fact, is what I take *jus post bellum* to mean. My aim is to offer an analytical and normative framework for thinking about this emerging field.

2. *Jus post Bellum* and Just War Theory: In or Out?

At first sight, merely asking whether *jus post bellum* properly belongs to just war theory might seem odd, so broad is the consensus amongst war ethicists that a complete theory of the just war must, *qua* such theory, incorporate norms for regulating the aftermath of war. And yet, 'incorporatist' arguments are either remarkably cursory, deeply problematic, or both. Thus, Gary Bass argues that in so far as postwar considerations shape our ex post verdicts on the justness or lack thereof of the war, 'it is important to better theorize postwar justice—*jus post bellum*—for the sake of a more complete theory of the just war'.[6] In a similar vein, Larry May claims that 'if the object of war is a just and lasting peace, then all of Just War considerations should be aimed at this goal, and the branch of the Just War tradition that specifically governs the end of war, *jus post bellum*, should be given more attention, if not pride of place, as opposed to being neglected as is often the case'.[7] Brian Orend, one of the most prolific and earliest contemporary writers on *jus post bellum*, gives the following reasons in support of the incorporation of *jus post bellum* into just war theory: contemporary conflicts show us, if it were needed, that peace settlements are deeply controversial, and it is urgent therefore to offer a normative account thereof. Moreover, constructing an account of the *jus post bellum* helps block the pacifist objection to just war theory that the latter fails to offer comprehensive principles for a better world. Finally, 'failure to construct principles of *jus post bellum* is to allow unconstrained war termination' and 'probably prolongs fighting on the grounds'—thus raising the ire of pacifists.[8]

Pace Bass and May, however, it does not follow from the plausible claim that the end of a just war is a just peace that theorizing about the just peace is itself a part of just war theory. To illustrate, we might think, for example, that a world in which, following a war, millions of people are left without the necessities of life or millions of people are left with fewer resources at their disposal than a lucky dozen thousands is not a world where a just peace obtains. But (it might be argued), an inquiry into the correct principles of postwar distributive justice (e.g., distributing resources according to basic needs v. distributing according to some egalitarian metric) is not a branch of just war theory: rather, it is a part of a wider theory of distributive justice. *Pace* Orend, moreover, it does not follow from the claim that we should think about the justness of postwar settlements that this inquiry is, again, part of just war theory. Nor does it follow from the claim that thinking about peace after war would pacify the pacifist. Furthermore, Orend's last move rests on unsubstantiated assertions about the connection between moral inquiry and political practice: in particular, it is not clear at all that there would have been less bloodshed had it not been for the just war tradition.

The foregoing comments raise the obvious question of what it means to be 'part of just war theory'. In Section 3, I shall develop the point that, in so far as principles for a just *postwar* world are significantly shaped by belligerents' wartime relationship *qua* belligerents, it is entirely appropriate to think of *jus post bellum* as a member of the family. In the remainder of this section, I respond to some recent arguments to the effect that a theory of justice after war need not rely on a prior account of the just war—indeed, to put it more strongly—ought to be kept separate from such an account. Seth Lazar puts the point as follows.[9] *Jus post bellum*, when incorporated into a theory of the just war by its advocates, is 'relentlessly backward-looking' since its constitutive principles—as defended by *post bellum* theorists in the extant literature—are read off belligerents' breach of or compliance with *jus ad bellum* and *jus in bello*. But there are good reasons, Lazar tells us, for resisting this move. In particular, given that all sides in war are guilty of grievous wrongdoings, we simply cannot hope to achieve just rectification and compensation. Moreover, compensation and punishment are invitations to 'revisit the wrongs of war', and they do little to alleviate the enormous suffering and minimize the deep resentments which war occasions: the burdens of compensation programmes inevitably fall on the most vulnerable, and victors' justice is a recipe for the resumption of violence.[10]

What, then, should an account of justice after war look like? It should confer priority to building peace over compensation and punishment, and it should extend its reach beyond belligerents to include outsiders. As Alex Bellamy also puts it, focusing on belligerents, as most theorists of the *jus post bellum* do, is an antiquated way to think not just about war but also about peace because peace settlements are increasingly overseen by international institutions and enforced by multinational peacekeeping forces which were not themselves parties in the conflict.[11] In a similar vein, James Pattison argues that the burdens of reconstruction after war should fall on whomever is best able to rebuild effectively and not necessarily on belligerents.

As a critique of much of extant theories of the *jus post bellum*, Lazar's points strike me as overstated. For a start, as Larry May suggests in *After War Ends*, given that a great many individuals have been, or at some point will be, somehow connected to war wrongdoings through fault or unjust benefitting, it makes sense to impose on all of them, via whichever coercive institutions under whose jurisdiction they live, a duty to contribute to an international compensation fund out of which the reconstruction of war-torn communities could be rebuilt.[12] This proposal takes into account the fact (which Lazar rightly stresses) that more or less all belligerents commit grievous wrongdoings, whilst at the same time it preserves the deeply rooted intuition that being at fault or wrongfully benefitting does confer on agents obligations which they would not have otherwise.

More generally, Lazar's targets are not inattentive to the fact that punishing aggressors might jeopardize chances for peace and to the risks of victors' justice; nor do they overlook the fact that extracting compensations from the vanquished belligerent risks jeopardizing the livelihood of the most vulnerable members of that community.[13] There is also a particularly rich philosophical literature on punishment for war crimes which defends international criminal tribunals in terms that Lazar would not disavow. Whilst those authors do not always portray themselves as theorists of the *jus post bellum*, any account of contemporary works on the aftermath of war should take their views seriously.[14]

That said, I agree that a comprehensive theory of justice after war must draw on other strands of political and moral philosophy such as the philosophical foundations of the criminal law or theories of distributive justice. As Bellamy and Pattison suggest, this does imply that principles for postwar justice should not exclusively focus on belligerents. However—and this is crucial—so to conceive of such a theory does not yield the overly strong thesis that *jus post bellum* has no place within just war theory. For although it is true that articulating and defending an account of what constitutes a just postwar state of affairs requires attending to those other branches of philosophy, one cannot and should not occlude the fact that at least some of the parties in that state of affairs were locked into a lethally adversarial relationship. To put the point differently, and as in fact Lazar himself acknowledges, what is at issue here is not just peace *simpliciter*, but just peace after war—peace between Britain and Germany in the first few years following World War II rather than peace between those two countries here and now, in 2015. To be sure, there are difficulties in discerning when two erstwhile belligerents move from living in mutual postwar peace to mutual peace *simpliciter*. However, and to rehearse a familiar point, even if we cannot sharply identify when dusk is over and night begins or when dawn gives way to daytime, we can certainly distinguish nighttime from daytime. Likewise in this context. In the light of that fact, then, just war theory *qua* just war theory need not—indeed, must not—confine itself to thinking about belligerents' decision to go to war and their conduct therein and thereby overlook peace after war. If it becomes the richer for drawing on areas of moral and political philosophy with which it is not overly familiar, so much the better for it.

3. *Jus ad Bellum*, *Jus in Bello* and *Jus post Bellum*: Mapping the Relationship

If, as I have just suggested, our concern is with peace between recent belligerents (by which I mean here both communities at war and their individual members), it pays to inquire into the extent to which belligerents' *post bellum* rights and duties are partly determined and, in different ways, by the moral status of their resort to and conduct in war. In this section, I argue that they are. In so doing, I map out some of those normative connections between the three *jura*. To reiterate and to be absolutely clear: the question of what constitutes a just postwar state of affairs is not settled merely by studying the implications of belligerents' resort to and conduct in war. I focus on this particular inquiry here because my concern in this chapter is to look at *jus post bellum* in relation to *jus ad bellum* and *jus in bello*.[15]

As a starting point, let us turn to contemporary debates about the relationship between *jus ad bellum* and *jus in bello* and see whether, and if so how, different conceptions of that relationship can help us understand the ways in which belligerents' resort to and conduct in war have a bearing on their rights and duties after war. On the so-called orthodox account of the morality of war, the moral status of the war *ad bellum* has no bearing whatsoever on combatants' rights, duties, and permissions once the war has started: combatants on either side of the *ad bellum* divide (e.g., the divide between unjustified aggression and justified self-defence) have exactly the same rights and permissions (notably, the permission to kill enemy combatants); they are also similarly legitimate targets for one another.[16] As applied to the relationship between *jus post bellum* and the other two *jura*, the orthodox account so construed would hold that belligerents' rights, permissions, and obligations vis-à-vis another once the war has stopped are entirely independent of the moral status of their war *at bellum* and/or *in bello*. On the so-called revisionist account of war, by contrast, acts of killing which are carried out pursuant to an *ad bellum* unjust war are wrongful, unlike acts of killing carried out pursuant to a just war.[17] As applied to the relationship between *jus post bellum* and its counterparts, the revisionist account would hold that failing to meet the requirements of *jus ad bellum* and/or *jus in bello* entails a failure to meet the requirements of *jus post bellum*.

To assess those positions, we must draw a crucial and generally overlooked distinction between procedural and substantive justice. Generally put, substantive justice delineates agents' rights to goods and freedoms, whereas procedural justice identifies which agent is entitled to decide whether substantive justice should obtain. For example, suppose that all agents have a right to food. Suppose further that one such agent refuses the food to which he is entitled—for example, because he is a prisoner on hunger strike. The right to food is a matter of substantive justice; the claim that the prisoner has decisional authority on getting the food or (on the contrary) that prison officials are entitled to force-feed him against his wishes are claims of procedural justice. In the present context, substantive justice pertains to the content of a peace settlement, whereas procedural justice pertains to the conditions under which belligerents are deemed competent to negotiate and endorse that peace settlement. This is a deeply important issue because a just postwar world is one which (most would agree) is characterized by a peace process issuing in a peace settlement involving all parties, as opposed the unilateral and coercive imposition by the victor on the vanquished of a given state of affairs. A theory of the *jus post bellum* must therefore account for both just substance and just process. Thus, when delineating the relationship between *jus post bellum* on the one hand and *jus ad bellum* and *jus in bello* on the other hand, in the light of the orthodox and revisionist accounts of war, we must distinguish between the following views:

Independence with respect to substance: Considerations other than as derived from our moral assessment of resort to and conduct in war wholly determine the terms of the peace settlement.

Dependence with respect to substance: Whether the terms of a peace settlement are just or unjust to its parties entirely depends on the moral status of those parties' war *ad bellum* and/or *in bello*.

Independence with respect to process: Belligerents are competent to negotiate and endorse peace agreements irrespective of the moral status of their resort to war, conduct in war, or both.

Dependence with respect to process: Whether a belligerent is competent to negotiate and endorse a peace settlement is entirely dependent on the moral status of those parties' war *ad bellum* and/or *in bello.*

I should say at the outset that not all of those views are in fact held by just war theorists. In that sense, the discussion that follows is in part speculative: its payoff is a more precise understanding of belligerents' postwar *prima facie* rights and duties, *qua* belligerents. Consider first the question of substantive justice. The view that whatever wrongdoings belligerents committed *in bello* have no bearing on their rights, duties, and liabilities *post bellum* is obviously implausible because it implies that perpetrators and victims of those wrongdoings are morally on a par—such that, for example, the former do not have moral obligations to compensate the latter or are not liable to being put on trial for war crimes. It would be equally implausible, I think, to hold that *ad bellum* wrongful decisions, such as a decision to mount an unjust invasion, should have no bearing on the content of the peace settlement because such a view implies that a just peace settlement cannot compel the aggressor to withdraw its troops and that the leaders of an unjust aggressor cannot be prosecuted for the crime of aggression.

By contrast, some might be tempted by the view that the content of a peace settlement as pertains to ordinary soldiers on the unjust side should not be dictated by that side's unjust decision to resort to war *ad bellum* and by those soldiers' participation in that war *in bello*. In fact, it is on this particular point that the orthodox account of the relationship between *jus ad bellum* and *jus in bello* might be thought to provide ammunition in support of its application to *jus post bellum*. For consider. It is standardly said that combatants, particularly ordinary soldiers, act under duress when ordered by their leaders to go into battle or that they do not have access to the information they would need in order to assess whether the cause for which they are fighting is just. On both counts—duress and epistemic handicap—it would be unfair to deprive soldiers who happen to fight on the unjust side of the permission to defend their lives; by that token, of course, in so far as it would be unfair to deprive those who fight on the just side of that exact same permission, all soldiers, whatever the moral status of their cause, are permitted to kill enemy soldiers. As applied to the relationship between *jus ad bellum-jus in bello* on the one hand and *just post bellum* on the other hand, then, the orthodox account would hold that peace agreements which adversely affect unjust soldiers—particularly ordinary soldiers—are unfair precisely because the latter acted under duress, without access to proper information, or both. This, in fact, is a plausible way to read Larry May's long argument to the effect that ordinary soldiers are not morally liable to being put on trial for their participation in an unjust war.[18]

Admittedly, *to the extent* that ordinary soldiers from the defeated and unjust belligerent have acted under duress and in ignorance of the moral status of their war, it would be unfair to punish them and to demand from them payment of compensation. *If*, thus, soldiers on the unjust side are morally innocent of the wrongdoing of waging an unjust war, then there is nothing to distinguish them, morally speaking, from the victorious and just belligerent soldiers. However, the antecedent clause 'if' is crucial to the success of that argument. For if it turns out that ordinary soldiers do not act under duress and do have appropriate access to the information that is needed in order to assess their war from a moral point of view, then those who fight on the unjust side are not morally on a par with those who fight on the just side: unlike the latter, they are (*prima facie*) liable to being killed. Moreover, as the revisionist account of the ethics of war notes, far greater numbers of civilians can be deemed causally and morally responsible for the war, whether just or unjust, than is usually thought to be the case. Those civilians who are responsible for an unjust war are (*prima facie*) liable at the very least to being harmed, whereas those who are not responsible, or who somehow take part in a just war, are not. Accordingly, if soldiers and (some) civilians are responsible for an unjust war, it is plausible to deem them morally liable to being punished and to paying some compensation to their enemy.[19] My point, note, is that those agents would not be wronged by the imposition of punitive and/or compensatory harm. This is entirely compatible with the view (urged by both *post bellum* theorists and Lazar) that, when deciding whether to extract compensation or to punish, we must take into account the extent to which we would in fact threaten prospects for a durable and all-things-considered justified peace.

One should not infer from the foregoing considerations that proponents of the revisionist account of war are necessarily committed to the view that whether the terms of a peace settlement are just or unjust to its parties entirely depends on the moral status of those parties' war *ad bellum* and/or *in bello*. Orend seems to endorse that view (though he does not address separately the connection between *jus ad bellum* and *jus post bellum* on the one hand and the connection between *jus in bello* and *jus post bellum* on the other hand). As he puts it, 'failure to meet *jus ad bellum* results in the automatic failure to meet *jus in bello* and *jus post bellum*. Once you're an aggressor in war, everything is lost to you morally'.[20]

I do not think that this is right, and working out why yields a nuanced account of the relationships among the three *jura*. In particular, it matters to an unjust belligerent's postwar moral rights, liabilities, and duties how unjust its war was. Other things equal, violations of the just cause requirement are morally worse than violations of other *ad bellum* requirements because a war so started has no justification in the first instance. Suppose, for example, that *A* invades *B* at time t_1 without just cause. *B* successfully repels the invasion by force at t_2 even though measures short of war, which would have led *A* to withdraw its troops, were available. *A* decides to sue for peace at t_3 even though it still has troops on *B*'s territory. For *B* to insist that *A* should vacate its territory is entirely appropriate, even though *B* should not have used force to recover it in the first instance. Contrastingly, if *A*, who *ex hypothesi* lacks a just cause for war is victorious, it cannot rightfully insist on annexing *B*'s territory as part of the peace settlement. Although both belligerents have acted unjustly *ad bellum*, the fact that *A* lacked a just cause for war when *B* did have one makes a difference to what they can rightfully demand of one another at the negotiating table.

The point applies not just to the relationship between *jus ad bellum* and *jus post bellum* but also to the relationship between *jus in bello* and *jus post bellum*. Suppose that *A* has a just cause for war against *B* for which it cannot obtain redress other than by going to war. Suppose, moreover, that *A* could win its war without breaching the requirements of proportionality but that its forces nevertheless indiscriminately and deliberately kill 50 000 innocent civilians$_B$ and unnecessarily cause \$20 billions worth of damage within *B*. *B*, for its part, goes to war against *A* for an unjust cause in the pursuit of which its forces kill 5000 civilians$_A$ and destroy \$2 billions of infrastructure within *A*. Combatants$_A$ and citizens$_A$ are not liable to punishment and compensatory damages simply for killing members of *B* who gave them a just cause for war and for the proportionate, rightful destruction of property owned by members of *B* who are liable to incurring such a loss. By contrast, their counterparts in *B* are (*prima facie*) liable to incurring those burdens for killing without just cause. However, combatants$_A$ and combatants$_B$ who have committed those war crimes are all liable to punishment, and *A*'s and *B*'s citizenries are both liable to paying compensatory damages for the wrongful destruction of their enemy's infrastructure—although (and this is crucial) the relative magnitude of their respective wrongdoings issues in differential compensatory and punitive burdens. On that count, then, *A* and *B*, though both wrongdoers *in bello*, are not morally on a par *post bellum*.

To recapitulate, the postwar rights and duties of belligerents are partly determined both by those belligerents' decisions *ad bellum* and by their conduct *in bello*. To some extent, this is obvious. However, the foregoing discussion teaches us two lessons. First, generally, just war theorists should articulate more carefully than they tend to do what follows from the claim that a war is unjust because it has a just cause, or that it is unjust because it is not the option of last resort, or that it is unjust because it is fought indiscriminately. Second, and relatedly, bringing verdicts on the justice, or lack thereof, of a war *ad bellum* and/or *in bello* to bear on *post bellum* normative assessments is at least as complex, if not more so, than bringing *ad bellum* verdicts to bear on *in bello* conclusions.

So much for postwar substantive justice. What about postwar procedural justice? Earlier, I distinguished between two views that proponents of the orthodox and revisionist accounts of the morality of war might be tempted to endorse:

> *Independence with respect to process*: Belligerents have the standing to negotiate and endorse a peace settlement irrespective of the moral status of their resort to war, conduct in war, or both.
>
> *Dependence with respect to process:* Whether a belligerent has the standing to negotiate and endorse a peace settlement is entirely dependent on the moral status of those parties' war *ad bellum* and/or *in bello*.

To say that a belligerent has the standing to reach a peace agreement is to say that it has the (Hohfeldian) power to change its jural bundles of claims, privileges, immunities, and powers with respect to the content of the agreement's clause *and* that it is recognized as having that power by the other party. Suppose, for example, that *A* invaded *B* as a result of a long-standing dispute over some territory which had been in *B*'s possession but which *A* claimed it in fact owned. Suppose further that *B*'s leadership carpet-bombs some of *A*'s cities and that *A*'s leadership, sensing both that they will not win the war and that they nevertheless are in a position to inflict considerable losses on *B*, sue for peace. It is in the interest of both *A* and *B* to end the war. *A* and *B* agree that *A* will withdraw its troops from the disputed territory and formally renounce its claim to it; they also agree that *B* will pay part of *A*'s reconstruction costs. Setting aside the question of whether those terms are just, to say that *A* and *B* have the standing to reach a settlement with one another on those terms is to say that they both have the power to change one another's jural bundles over, respectively, the disputed territory (such that citizens$_A$ no longer have claims over it, while citizens$_B$ acquire such claims) and the resources needed for reconstructing A. In addition, the power to change jural bundles must be protected by rights as held by the relevant officials not to be interfered with when negotiating (e.g., rights not to be kidnapped, assassinated, etc.[21]) and, more foundationally, by claims against those subject to those agreements that the latter comply. Furthermore, this protected power is a fiduciary power which belligerent leaders have and exercise on behalf of their citizens. Finally—and this is crucial—neither has the standing to reach this particular settlement if the other party has a justification for refusing to grant it the power to negotiate and endorse it. By analogy, Andrew may well have the power to give his car to Bernard; but if Bernard justifiably refuses to accept Andrew's gift, for example, on the justified grounds that Andrew is a morally repugnant individual, Andrew does not, in the end, have the standing to change his jural bundles over his car vis-à-vis Bernard. Thus, standing refers both to a belligerent's authority vis-à-vis its own members and to its authority vis-à-vis its enemy.

Our task, then, is to provide an account of the conditions under which belligerents have the standing to reach a peace settlement. According to the independence view, whether belligerents have waged a just war is not a necessary condition for standing. On what I take to be the most plausible account of the power to govern in general, this seems right. For on that account, which I set out elsewhere, state officials have that power only if their directives better enable those who are subject to them to enjoy their pre-institutional moral rights and to fulfil their pre-institutional moral duties than they would have in the absence of any state or if they were included in any other feasible state.[22] It could very well be, thus, that an unjust belligerent (whether *ad bellum, in bello*, or both) would, through the peace settlement which it negotiates, provide its members as well as outsiders with better conditions overall for the protection of their moral rights and the fulfilment of their moral duties than they would have otherwise. To claim that a peace agreement is invalid simply in virtue of the fact that one or more of its parties ended up at the negotiating table thanks to conducting an unjust war risks adversely affecting individuals—typically, those who are already the weakest—for whom the alternative, in the form of a long, destructive war, might be far worse.[23] *If* the moral status of the war does not affect belligerents' de facto ability to provide such protection for its citizens and outsiders, then it seems that they have the standing to negotiate and endorse the peace settlement. By implication, under those conditions, proponents of the revisionist account of the morality of war, who hold that the moral status of acts-of-war killing is dependent on the moral status of the cause which they serve, ought to resist the view that the moral status of a belligerent as a peace negotiator and endorser is dependent on the moral status of that belligerent's war.

In some cases, however, the acts carried out by an unjust belligerent are such as to vitiate the latter's standing in either—or indeed both—of the two senses described above vis-à-vis one's members and vis-à-vis one's enemy. Thus, the Allies famously refused to negotiate with the Nazi regime in the closing stages of World War II precisely because the war the latter conducted was morally so abhorrent that its officials simply could not be granted any moral authority to act on behalf of the German people and to enter into a contractual relationship with the Allies. Likewise, in the Spring of 1994, the Tutsi Rwandan Patriotic Front refused to negotiate peace terms with Rwanda's extremist Hutu-dominated government whose officials had orchestrated the genocide of approximately 800 000 moderate Hutus and Tutsis. The question, though, is why. One possibility is that committing certain acts is in itself disqualifying. It is hard not to have sympathy for that view: the thought that Hitler, had he not killed himself, might have sat with Franklin D. Roosevelt and Winston Churchill and hammered out a peace agreement, as if on a footing of equality, is repellent. (Then again, so is the thought that Stalin, whose crimes both in war and peace plausibly equalled or at least came very close to Hitler's, *did* sit with Roosevelt and Churchill at the 1945 Yalta Conference.) That said, even with those kinds of leaders at the helm, there might not be any alternative, so that, for all that they did, they nevertheless are the best institutional actors available to represent the interests of their citizens. This does not impugn the Allies' decision not to confer negotiating standing on the Nazis, but it should alert us to the dangers of depriving some actors of standing without considering what their absence from the negotiating table might mean for those whom they would represent and who, however grievous their leaders' wrongdoings and their possible complicity in it, have not forfeited their right to be treated humanely.

Another argument for the view that unjust belligerents lack the standing to reach a peace settlement is that their wartime deeds are such that they simply cannot be trusted to do better than any other feasible alternative at the bar of the rights and duties of those who are liable to the terms of the peace settlement. A peace settlement binds two categories of agents whose trust in its justice is crucial for the realization of a durable peace: those on whose behalf the war was waged, and those against whom it was waged. Amongst the former, some may well have supported the war whilst others opposed it (notwithstanding their leaders' claim to act on their behalf and in their interest) but had little control over it. Those agents cannot reasonably be presumed to trust in a leadership which authorized the commission of crimes as grievous as the mass killings of innocent noncombatants or an unwarranted wholesale aggression against another community. In fact, they can justifiably assume that, on the balance of probabilities, those wrongdoers will negotiate and endorse peace terms which will either consist in or lead to their rights being violated or render them less able to fulfil their obligations to one another than feasible alternatives would do. On this view, it is not the commission of the wrongdoings itself which deprives wrongdoers of standing; rather, the nature of the wrongdoings is such as to suggest that trust would not be given. If those points are correct, both *ad bellum* and *in bello* wrongdoings can deprive their perpetrators of standing so long as they are sufficiently grievous.

4. Conclusion

In this chapter, I provided support, contra some recent critics, for the often-made point that just war theory, *qua* such theory, should attend to justice after war, although I agree with those critics that the content of principles for a just peace should be determined by broader considerations of (*inter alia*) distributive justice and not just by the extent to which leaders, soldiers, and civilians acted in breach of or in compliance with *jus ad bellum* and *jus in bello*. At the same time, I argued that understanding the relationship between *just post bellum* and the other *jura* of war provides some insight into the tasks which an account of justice after war must set itself. Three points in particular are worth extracting from the foregoing discussion. First, the relationship of the *just post bellum* to its *ad bellum* and *in bello* counterparts is one of partial dependence—such that the moral status of a postwar state of affairs from a belligerent's point of view sometimes, but not always, depends on the moral status, from that same point of view, of the war which led to it. Second, and relatedly, that relationship is rather complex, whether one endorses the orthodox account of the latter or is sympathetic to the revisionist account. In particular, from the point of view of belligerents' postwar rights and duties, it matters deeply which just war requirement(s) they breached. Finally, a theory of the *jus post bellum* must provide an account not just of the substantive justice of a peace settlement but also of its procedural justice. *Post-bellum* substantive justice has generated growing attention of late: procedural justice, hardly any. If this chapter succeeds in convincing at least some of its readers of the importance of that question, it will have gone some way towards achieving its aims.

Notes

1. Francisco de Vitoria, 'On the Law of War', in *Political Writings*, edited by Anthony Pagden and Jeremy Lawrance, Cambridge Texts in the History of Political Thought (Cambridge: Cambridge University Press, 1991); Francisco Suárez, '*De Bello*', in *Selections from Three Works of Francisco Suárez, S. J.: De Triplici Virtute Theologica, Fide, Spe, Et Charitate (1621)*, edited by James Brown Scott (Oxford: Clarendon Press, 1944); Hugo Grotius, 'The Rights of War and Peace', edited by Richard Tuck (Indianapolis, IN: Liberty Fund, 2005); Christian Wolff, *Jus Gentium Methodo Scientifica Pertractatum* (Oxford: Clarendon Press, 1934); Emmerich de Vattel, *Le Droit Des Gens, Ou, Principes De La Loi Naturelle Appliques Á La Conduite Et Aux Affaires Des Nations Et Des Souverains* (Washington, DC: Carnegie Institute, 1916); Immanuel Kant, 'Perpetual Peace: A Philosophical Sketch', in *Kant—Political Writings*, edited by Hans Reiss, 2 (Cambridge: Cambridge University Press, 1991).
2. Michael Walzer, *Just and Unjust Wars* (New York: Basic Books, 1977).
3. Gary Bass, 'Jus Post Bellum', *Philosophy & Public Affairs* 32 (2004); C. A. J. Coady, *Morality and Political Violence* (Cambridge: Cambridge University Press, 2008); Mark Evans, 'Moral Responsibilities and the Conflicting Demands of Jus Post Bellum', *Ethics & International*

Affairs 23 (2009); 'Balancing Peace, Justice and Sovereignty in Jus Post Bellum: The Case of "Just Occupation"', *Millenium—Journal of International Studies* 36 (2008); Larry May, *After War Ends—A Philosophical Perspective* (Cambridge: Cambridge University Press, 2012); Brian Orend, *The Morality of War* (Peterborough, ON: Broadview Press, 2006); 'Justice After War', *Ethics & International Affairs* 16 (2002); 'Jus Post Bellum', *Journal of Social Philosophy* 31 (2000); Robert E. Williams and Dan Caldwell, '*Jus Post Bellum*: Just War Theory and the Principles of Just Peace', *International Studies Perspectives* 7 (2006); David Rodin, 'Two Emerging Issues of *Jus Post Bellum*: War Termination and the Liability of Soldiers for Crimes of Aggression', in *Jus Post Bellum—Towards a Law of Transition from Conflict to Peace*, edited by Carsten Stahn and Jann K. Kleffner (The Hague: T. M. C. Asser Press, 2008).

4. See, e.g., Alexis Keller, 'Justice, Peace and History: A Reappraisal', in *What Is a Just Peace?*, edited by Pierre Allan and Alexis Keller (Oxford: Oxford University Press, 2008); Stephen C. Neff, 'Conflict Termination and Peace-Making in the Law of Nations: A Historical Perspective', in *Jus Post Bellum—Towards a Law of Transition from Conflict to Peace*, edited by Carsten Stahn and Jann K. Kleffner (The Hague: T. M. C. Asser Press, 2008).
5. Darrel Moellendorf, 'Jus Ex Bello', *Journal of Political Philosophy* 16 (2008); Rodin, 'Two Emerging Issues of *Jus Post Bellum*'.
6. Bass, 'Jus Post Bellum', 384.
7. May, *After War Ends*, 13.
8. Orend, *The Morality of War*, 160–161.
9. Seth Lazar, 'Scepticism About Jus Post Bellum', in *Morality, Jus Post Bellum, and International Law*, edited by Larry May and Andrew T. Forcehimes (Cambridge: Cambridge University Press, 2012).
10. Lazar also makes the conceptual point that a theory of the just war can be complete without tending to the aftermath of war because such a theory, *qua* theory of *war*, only means to justify and constrain fighting in war. Likewise, a theory of legitimate use of force, *qua* such theory, can be complete without attending to what should or may happen once force has been used (ibid., 218–219). I disagree: to stipulate that a theory of war is only about the justification and regulation of *fighting* is to settle the issue by definitional fiat—a move that should be resisted. As for the parallel with a theory of legitimate force, it will not convince Lazar's opponents, who may well reply, plausibly I think, that a complete theory of the legitimate use of *force* should attend to, for example, punishment for unjustified use (in so far as punishment involves the use of force) and compensatory obligations arising from unjustified use (to the extent that compensatory obligations, too, are enforced).
11. Alex Bellamy, 'The Responsibilities of Victory: Jus Post Bellum and the Just War', *Review of International Studies* 34 (2008); (James Pattison, 'Jus Post Bellum and the Responsibility to Rebuild', *British Journal of Political Science* 45 (2013).
12. May, *After War Ends*, 194–195.
13. See, *pêle-mêle*, Bass, 'Jus Post Bellum'; Evans, 'Balancing Peace, Justice and Sovereignty in Jus Post Bellum: The Case of "Just Occupation"'; Orend, 'Justice after War'; 'Jus Post Bellum'; Rodin, 'Two Emerging Issues of *Jus Post Bellum*'; Michael Walzer, 'The Aftermath of War', in *Ethics Beyond War's End*, edited by Eric Patterson (Cambridge: Cambridge University Press, 2012); Doug McCready, 'Ending the War Right: Jus Post Bellum and the Just War Tradition', *Journal of Military Ethics* 8 (2009); May, *After War Ends*.
14. See, e.g., Larry May, *War Crimes and Just War* (Cambridge: Cambridge University Press, 2007); *Crimes Against Humanity: A Normative Account*, Cambridge Studies in Philosophy

and Law (Cambridge: Cambridge University Press, 2005); *Aggression and Crimes Against Peace* (Cambridge: Cambridge University Press, 2008); David Luban, 'Fairness to Rightness: Jurisdiction, Legality, and the Legitimacy of International Criminal Law', in *The Philosoph of International Law*, edited by John Tasioulas and Samantha Besson (Oxford: Oxford University Press, 2010); R. A. Duff, 'Authority and Responsibility in International Criminal Law', in *The Philosophy of International Law*, edited by John Tasioulas and Samantha Besson (Oxford: Oxford University Press, 2010).

15. I develop a comprehensive account of justice after war in Cécile Fabre, *Cosmopolitan Peace* (Oxford University Press, forthcoming).
16. Walzer, *Just and Unjust Wars.*
17. David Rodin, *War and Self-Defence* (Oxford: Oxford University Press, 2002); C. A. J. Coady, *Morality and Political Violence,* (Cambridge: Cambridge University Press, 2008); Jeff McMahan, *Killing in War* (Oxford: Oxford University Press, 2009); Cécile Fabre, *Cosmopolitan War* (Oxford: Oxford University Press, 2012).
18. May, *Aggression and Crimes Against Peace.*
19. Interestingly, Walzer defends the imposition of punitive reparations on citizenries whose (democratic) community has waged an unjust war. See Walzer, *Just and Unjust Wars*, ch. 18.
20. Orend regards an act of aggression as morally wrong by definition—although he also endorses the view that armed humanitarian intervention is sometimes permissible. Since such intervention presumably takes the form of an *attack* on the target country, a morally neutral definition of aggression is more appropriate. See Orend, *The Morality of War*, 162.
21. In fact, in the law of treaties, just procedural conditions also include prohibitions on fraud, deception, and unjustified coercion. See the 1969 Vienna Convention on the Law of Treaties.
22. Fabre, *Cosmopolitan War*, 46–47.
23. For a similar point, see Daniel Schwartz, 'The Justice of Peace Treaties', *Journal of Political Philosophy* 20 (2012).

CHAPTER 27

JUSTICE AFTER WAR

JENS DAVID OHLIN

1. Introduction

After the conclusion of hostilities, whether formal armed conflict or not, parties must be held to account for their behaviour. This sentiment is almost universally shared, regardless of one's moral or ethical framework, although the specifics of this accounting are deeply controversial and contested. In Section 2, I offer a normative foundation for justice after war that appeals to the anti-impunity norm. I conclude that criminal trials, as opposed to nonpenal mechanisms, best vindicate this norm. In light of this conclusion, Section 3 asks how we should achieve justice after war: who should be put on trial (leaders or ordinary soldiers), who should prosecute them (national or international courts), which crimes they should be charged with (domestic or international crimes), which procedures should govern the trials, and how they should be punished.

2. Why Should We Care About Justice After War?

The moral foundation for postconflict justice is the anti-impunity norm, which posits that impunity is morally disastrous and that institutional mechanisms should be designed, along with other desiderata, to restrict impunity as much as possible. Although the norm is often defended on instrumental (i.e., consequentialist) grounds, I argue that a deontological framework provides a more convincing ground for the norm, although it needs to be carefully calibrated for the international context.[1]

The instrumental argument asserts that impunity for misconduct during war breeds further misconduct: those who engage in atrocities and escape misconduct will be prone to repeat their behaviour, and third parties who witness the impunity will be emboldened when they, too, deliberate about whether to comply with the laws of war. In contrast, robust investigation and punishment for wartime misconduct will deter violators from repeat behaviour and potential violators from engaging in the misconduct in the first instance.

The a priori argument is deeply intuitive but somewhat more difficult to articulate: punishment for wartime misconduct is an a priori good, regardless of the consequences, simply because impunity for misconduct offends the moral fabric of the universe.

The tension between instrumental and deontological justifications for international punishment is just as difficult to resolve as that between their domestic analogues in peacetime criminal law, although the international context displays some particularities not found in the domestic context. Whereas there is at least a plausible empirical claim that potential violators of domestic criminal law will be deterred in some limited circumstances by the prospect of future punishment, the same is much less likely in the war context, where decision-making is often immune from the rational deliberative process that deterrence requires as its foundation. Simply put, criminals engaged in genocide or crimes against humanity may be acting for irrational reasons that the law may have difficulty influencing with a system of rewards and punishments.[2] Although this may occasionally be true in the domestic context, the lack of systematic enforcement during war, combined with the special nature of genocidal intent, makes the problem of deterrence especially urgent in the international context. This makes a deontological justification for punishment comparatively more attractive in war as compared to domestic crime. This also produces a potential asymmetry: one can support a utilitarian justification in one context but a deontological justification in the other.

The real question is how to *ground* the anti-impunity norm. I defend a two-tiered approach to the philosophical foundation for justice after war. At the level of individual accountability for wartime conduct, a broadly retributive framework holds that individual wrongdoers should be punished simply because they deserve it and because vindicating the rule of law, in war's aftermath, has a priori value. However, there is temptation to focus on consequentialist calculations at the global level: a penal response at the individual level may incentivize victim groups to forgo reprisal attacks and submit their grievances to the rule of law. These global consequentialist considerations are important for positive law because many international institutions are empowered to act when their actions help repair international peace and security. But consequentialist aspirations should be tempered: the international community should avoid placing lofty burdens on the shoulders of international tribunals, which should concentrate their efforts on implementing retributivism at the individual level.[3] Dangers lurk when courts and prosecutors stray from individual retributivism and make decisions based on considerations of collective security—a temptation they should resist.

There are two major avenues of judicial redress for illegal conduct during armed conflict: penal and nonpenal. These different approaches offer different outcomes and also flow from different philosophical foundations regarding the nature and purpose of postconflict justice. Although there are substantive costs associated with penal mechanisms, I argue here that a criminal law approach best vindicates the anti-impunity norm and achieves justice after war.

Some states grappling with postconflict atrocities have selected nonpenal mechanisms (e.g., truth and reconciliation commissions) to achieve the demands of transitional justice. Although a full discussion of these alternative mechanisms is impractical here, the following observations are warranted. First, although alternative mechanisms of transitional justice may not necessarily result in punishment for the perpetrators, these mechanisms may do a better job of establishing a historical record of the conduct. For example, the South African government created its Truth and Reconciliation Commission with the goal of giving perpetrators an incentive to volunteer information. When channelled to the criminal process, defendants have little incentive to disclose information about their activities that will incriminate them. Seen in this light, the criminal process may actively harm the construction of the historical record, and an alternative nonpenal mechanism focussed more on information disclosure rather than punitive outcomes will produce more comprehensive information.

Second, advocates of nonpenal mechanisms occasionally argue that insisting on criminal punishment may undermine attempts to restore peace and security. In particular, local amnesties, whether for leaders or for ordinary troops, may incentivize belligerents to drop weapons and sign a peace accord. Because such amnesties are disfavoured in criminal law (and international tribunals refuse to recognize them), a criminal approach might prevent the peaceful resolution of a sticky conflict.[4]

Third, nonpenal mechanisms may better promote peace and reconciliation going forward. Under this view, *forgiveness* is central to transitional justice but unattainable within a retributivist criminal process. In contrast, a truth and reconciliation commission may encourage victims to forgive perpetrators who confess their crimes. Perpetrators might even explicitly ask for forgiveness (which is not mandated by the process) but only if their expressions of guilt and regret will not trigger convictions and punishment.

Advocates of nonpenal mechanisms frequently cite South Africa as evidence for their case. But that experience cannot be generalized; the Truth and Reconciliation Commission was truly a product of local context. Although South African apartheid was unambiguously evil, it would be wrong to equate it with international crimes like the Rwandan genocide. The South African Truth and Reconciliation Commission received support from the population because of its underlying bargain: encourage offenders to freely disclose information regarding their participation in the apartheid regime in exchange for immunity from criminal prosecution. Exchange of information facilitated expressions of remorse and, with it, reconciliation between relevant groups. This calculation worked, to the extent that it did, because of the nature of South African society and the particular crimes of the apartheid regime. The fact that the truth and reconciliation process worked so well in South Africa is not conclusive evidence that it would work in other societies.

In contrast with these nonpenal approaches, the criminal law alternative rests on arrest, public trial, and punishment. The advantages of this approach dovetail with those of criminal prosecution in peacetime: offenders are tried and punished for their crimes, future criminals are deterred from committing future offences, and the trial itself allows victims to participate in the criminal process, either as bona fide parties to the proceedings (i.e., as *partie civile*) or simply as witnesses who describe under oath the mistreatment that they have suffered. For victims, participating in the criminal process is immensely important. Finally, public trials also establish and preserve evidence regarding the crime, thus serving an important historical and pedagogical function. In many mass atrocity crimes, creating a robust historical record requires a court (with prosecutors and defence attorneys) with the incentive to assemble the relevant evidence in a coherent way and make it publicly accessible.

To be sure, the criminal law approach has drawbacks. First, mass atrocity often involves thousands of perpetrators, and the criminal justice system may be incapable of handling this many trials: prosecutors must triage which offenders are prosecuted. Second, a criminal trial may not be an appropriate—or successful—opportunity for historiography. In domestic law, criminal trials have one goal: determine guilt or innocence through procedures that protect the interests of both prosecution and defendant. Criminal trials lose focus when they try to accomplish larger global initiatives, like giving wronged groups redress or establishing a historical record. The number of witnesses and factual allegations spiral out of control, leading to lengthy trials.[5] Trial Chamber judgments at the International Criminal Tribunal for the former Yugoslavia (ICTY) commonly exceed 1000 pages, in part because judgments include not only factors relevant to guilt or innocence, but also a representative sampling of factual evidence to place the culpability of the defendant in the larger context.

Criminal courts should focus on subjecting the defendant's behaviour to the scrutiny of the legal system simply because committing international offences with *impunity* constitutes an independent and additional moral wrong, over and above the wrong associated with the underlying criminality. In this sense, the anti-impunity norm is deontically justified regardless of any consequentialist benefits achieved from criminal prosecutions; some crimes are so horrific that they demand punishment for the perpetrators. The warrant for this conclusion is largely Kantian: if perpetrators escape all meaningful consequences for violating the moral duty of humane treatment in war, then the norm itself—and the system of law designed to vindicate it—becomes an empty shell. By punishing the offender, the community at large reaffirms its commitment to the underlying norm. In this sense, the criminal process is morally justified regardless of whether one can empirically trace positive social results from it.

3. How Should We Achieve Justice After War?

3.1. Who Should Be Put on Trial?

In contemporary practice, typically, architects and planners are prosecuted in international courts whereas physical perpetrators are not. Criminal prosecutions for war crimes typically focus on leadership-level defendants who were far from the scene of the crime and must be connected to the perpetrators via complex legal doctrines that attribute legal responsibility for those who ordered, instigated, conspired, or controlled the crime from afar.[6]

There are two arguments for this approach. First, the leaders control whether the crime occurs; in most cases, if the perpetrators refuse to carry out the crime, they will be immediately replaced with more willing participants. Some international courts adopt this control-based argument to explain why high-level leaders should be viewed as principal perpetrators (or co-perpetrators), whereas the physical perpetrators should be viewed as mere accomplices. The second argument appeals to joint intentions and planning in Michael Bratman's sense of the term. The most serious offenders have a joint intention to carry out the crime—a process that inevitably requires overall coordination and the meshing of subplans. Individual soldiers rarely satisfy those criteria. Although they are clearly responsible for their own conduct, they rarely engage in high-level planning that would make them morally responsible for the entire criminal enterprise. Regardless of the moral theory used to explain the relationship between planners and perpetrators, it is clear that the former are more culpable than the latter.

For the crime of aggression, only those individuals 'in a position to exercise control over or to direct the political or military action of a State' are liable for prosecution if they engaged in the planning, preparation, initiation, or execution of the aggression.[7] The 'control' or 'direct' requirement ensures that ordinary soldiers will not be prosecuted. If they could be prosecuted for participating in a war of aggression, the dividing line between *jus ad bellum* and *jus in bello* would be compromised—this would please revisionist just war theorists but would radically reorient the law of war and its neutral conception of belligerency.

Is this reorientation necessary? Should soldiers face criminal liability for participating in an unjust war? Even if we agree with revisionists that just and unjust combatants are not truly morally equal, we should still grant the latter immunity from prosecution because mass postwar prosecutions are impractical and would hinder societal reconciliation. To the extent that something like de-Nazification is necessary, it could be achieved through nonpenal avenues.

However, we should reject the revisionist view of combatant inequality. First, the morally relevant agents in war are collective political entities for which the soldiers fight. When the state or nation launches an unjust attack, the collective is responsible for violating the moral rules regarding the use of force because the political leaders make the relevant decisions; a professional army, whether conscripted or voluntary, is an instrument—a human machine—through which policy is implemented. Individual combatants are not responsible for the injustice of their cause.

Second, combatant moral equality also preserves the professional nature of warfare—which is essential to limiting its scope. All nations and peoples benefit from a military framework in which soldiers enjoy the combatant's privilege in exchange for a moral prohibition against directly attacking civilians. Tinkering with this bargain—freedom from criminal liability unless civilians are intentionally targeted—will pull at the threads of limited warfare, ultimately pushing conflicts back into total warfare. If soldiers worry that they will be prosecuted as 'unjust combatants' at the end of an armed conflict, they will be motivated to win the war at all costs, including killing civilians in the process. The combatant's privilege gives the professional soldier a reason to comply with the moral constraints of warfare.

This bargain does not immunize civilians from all responsibility in war. Although immune from attack, they are responsible for their participation in the social and political process leading to the state's unjust war. It is therefore entirely appropriate to saddle a civilian population with the burdens of war reparations if they supported the government's unjust war. Also, in an abstract way, the civilian population rightly shares in the collective shame associated with the state's behaviour. The power of these inchoate methods of ensuring moral responsibility should not be underestimated. The German population continues to wrestle with its collective responsibility for the Holocaust—one reason why Germany today so robustly defends international law. The phrase 'never again' is more than a trite aphorism—it also structures the self-conception of a people in enduring and transformative ways.

3.2. What Should They Be Tried For?

Although the anti-impunity norm demands accountability for all wartime atrocities, only some specific offences are prosecuted before international tribunals. Although domestic courts could certainly prosecute individuals for murder, the machinery of international justice is only triggered when a defendant commits one of these international offences: aggression, crimes against humanity, genocide, and war crimes.[8] Some scholars bristle at the technicality of this typology and would prefer to replace it with a more common-sense notion of 'atrocity crimes'.[9] This would be less ad hoc and would reduce the potential for crimes to fall between the definitional cracks. For example, genocide requires an attack against a national, ethnic, racial, or religious group, but an attack on political groups does not legally constitute genocide. Similarly, a crime against humanity requires a widespread or systematic attack, which might exclude isolated or unplanned atrocities. Finally, war crimes require a nexus with armed conflict, thereby excluding atrocities committed in peacetime. Consequently, some atrocities might be excluded from these technical categories, which allegedly have no deeper normative significance or moral hierarchy. If this view is correct, then it makes no moral difference whether a defendant is convicted of crimes against humanity or genocide or even an international crime (as opposed to a domestic one) at all.

This view is mistaken. As the following brief discussion will illuminate, the core international crimes each stem from different normative commitments, and each presents unique definitional problems that require resolution. What unites them is a collective context that is uniquely different from domestic crimes. Conflating them into a single notion of 'atrocity crime' concedes too much to our folk conception of undifferentiated wartime killing. Although the technical legal definitions are not beyond criticism and reform is sometimes required, the general division is both philosophically coherent and morally justified. As David Luban and others have argued, crimes against humanity involve widespread killings, perpetrating which negates the humanity of the world community. They typically, though not always, involve a sovereign committing crimes against its subjects, thus violating a fiduciary duty and triggering a right of international judicial intervention.[10] Genocide is true collective criminality: one group attempts the existential destruction of another.[11] War crimes violate a basic prohibition against total war in favour of limited warfare that exempts civilians, as much as possible, from war's horror. I now discuss each international offence in greater detail.

3.2.1. *Crimes Against Humanity*

Crimes against humanity generally involve multiple acts of killing, rape, or torture. Many have tried to provide a normative foundation for crimes against humanity, in particular to take seriously the eponymous principle—that the offence violates humanity itself, rather than only the immediate victims.[12] This account, if convincing, helps explain the jurisdiction of international tribunals to prosecute the crime: for crimes against humanity, the world community as representative of humanity should prosecute the offence.

Positive international law supports this view with the concept of *ergo omnes*—an obligation that is owed not to specific partners but to everyone in the world. The whole point of *ergo omnes* is to limit sovereignty—a concept that traditionally places a silo around a state's internal affairs, thus rendering it immune from outside interference. When states breach bilateral or multilateral legal or moral obligations, that triggers the relevant partners' concern, but noninterested third parties lack grounds for *action* or a right of response. Classifying some legal obligations as *ergo omnes* avoids this problem.

Which crimes are sufficiently grave that they are crimes against humanity itself? Under the current doctrine, the most salient requirement is that the crimes are widespread or systematic and committed pursuant to an organizational plan or policy. These requirements make clear that crimes against humanity require true collective action. Crimes by individuals could be widespread, but not systematic, and only crimes by the relevant collectives follow an organizational plan.

But what are the relevant collectives? States, obviously. And the Nuremberg paradigm allowed organizational policies of sub-state entities like the Gestapo to count as crimes against humanity. But what of organizations outside of the law that are not subunits of *de jure* government? Recent prosecutions at the International Criminal Court (ICC) have argued that local criminal organizations (e.g., the Mungiki) could commit crimes against humanity.[13] And, in the most extreme example, prosecutors at the ICC argued that an unnamed 'Network' of perpetrators constituted the relevant organization.[14] But this dissolves the requirement entirely because we can always identify a large number of perpetrators and define them as the relevant 'organization' for the plan or policy requirement. This is a *reductio ad absurdum*. Crimes against humanity are supposed to outlaw the use of political or social structures—the corruption or cancer of politics as Luban calls it—in service of mass murder. We must lay the charge against an organization that exists independently of this criminal activity. The crime is to hijack an organized machine—whether a de jure state structure or de facto source of organizational power—to implement a machinery of death. Consequently, the *organizational* element of crimes against humanity is not only morally justified but also must be zealously guarded; attempts to water down or eliminate the requirement violate the underlying raison d'etre of the crime: to outlaw transforming sociopolitical structures into mass killing machines. That structure must exist independently of the acts that make up the crime against humanity, otherwise the organizational requirement washes away. This distinguishes crimes against humanity from the more common-sense notion of atrocity.[15]

3.2.2. *Genocide*

Genocide is an offence performed with the intent to destroy, in whole or in part, a protected group.[16] But what qualifies as a protected group? The Genocide Convention and all subsequent codifications identify only national, ethnic, racial, or religious groups—a listing that normative theory might find substantially underinclusive.[17] Many have tried to enlarge the categories to include political groups, thereby capturing atrocities such as Stalin's purges.[18] Alternatively, instead of protecting more groups, we can more loosely interpret the existing classifications, as the International Criminal Tribunal for Rwanda (ICTR) did when it ruled that the coordinated attack by Hutus on the Tutsi minority in Rwanda was genocidal.[19]

Does classifying a particular attack as genocide (as opposed to a 'mere' crime against humanity) have any special moral or legal significance? Modern international tribunals have steadfastly refused to construct or endorse a hierarchy of international crimes. In other words, international judges deny that genocide is *worse* than a crime against humanity. Without this hierarchy, what normative payoff do we gain by labelling an attack genocidal? Despite this persistent refusal from international judges, genocide represents a particular form of international criminality, one that targets groups as such: the *genos* in genocide.[20] Moreover, the law of genocide presupposes—correctly—that these groups have independent moral status. One can view them as instrumentally beneficial, as one necessary element in an account of human flourishing. Human beings are political animals, situated in groups providing meaningful connections with other human beings mediated through the raw materials of culture, language, tradition, religion, and other social artefacts. When denied these connections, human beings face substantial obstacles on the road to human flourishing.

Applying this metric, the list of groups protected by genocide law is underinclusive. Membership in some groups may be important for human flourishing even though the group is not national, ethnic, racial, or religious. In time, the list of protected groups ought to be carefully expanded. The unifying principle behind the list is the immutability of the group characteristics in question. Ethnic and racial characteristics are the most immutable and cannot easily be revised. National identity is subject to revision based on voluntary changes of citizenship, and religious identity is subject to conversion. That being said, one's birth nationality or religion can never be revised and may be a salient characteristic in genocidal campaigns. The law prioritizes the most immutable group characteristics for protection, but it seems likely that tribal or even political group membership may be immutable enough to deserve protection under an expanded conception of genocide. Members of a political group targeted for extermination—say in Stalin's purges or by the Khmer Rouge—are victims of group-based conflict best described by the word genocide.

Genocide represents a grievous moral wrong because groups have independent moral significance not exhausted by their instrumental value. Consequently, the acts that trigger genocide liability do not necessarily require *killing*, but instead might involve forced sterilization or forcibly transferring children of one group to another.[21] These acts could destroy a group without killing its members. This can only be construed as genocide once one concludes that genocide is an irreducibly collective crime designed to protect the '*genos*' as such, not just the individuals who constitute the group.

3.2.3. *War Crimes*

War crimes continue to be the one international crime that still requires a nexus with armed conflict. No war—no war *crime* (by definition). This requirement triggers tension between human rights lawyers and international criminal lawyers, two camps that usually have sympathetic or even overlapping outlooks. Prosecutors and judges at international tribunals support expansive definitions of armed conflict because only the existence of an armed conflict gives the tribunal jurisdiction over violations of *jus in bello*. In contrast, human rights activists have the opposite impulse. They wish to limit the privilege of belligerency triggered by armed conflict and so favour geographically constrained definitions of armed conflict.

Terrorist attacks are not classified as a war crime unless the attack is committed during an armed conflict. This is ironic because the 9/11 attacks *triggered* an armed conflict between the United States and al Qaeda, although there was no pre-existing armed conflict at the time (unless one backdates it to the *USS Cole* bombing in 2000). Instead of considering terrorist attacks war crimes, we might try them as crimes against humanity. However, these attacks are often isolated and do not meet the organizational plan or policy requirement described earlier. In response, the Special Tribunal for Lebanon (STL) controversially concluded that terrorism was a *distinct* international crime under customary international law, although it remains to be seen whether this precedent will have jurisprudential impact.[22]

3.2.4. *Aggression*

States that violate the international prohibition against aggressive force should be held to account for their behaviour, although there are few institutional fora where this might happen. The Security Council may issue a binding resolution condemning the aggression, but it will not do so if the aggressor is a permanent member (or even a close ally) of the Council that might exercise a veto. Wronged states may file suits before the International Court of Justice (ICJ), although the relative jurisdiction between the ICJ and the Security Council on matters of peace and security is deeply contested and unresolved. Furthermore, jurisdiction before the ICJ is largely based on consent, and the prospect of future chastisement before the court may lead a state to withdraw from the court's plenary jurisdiction, as the United States did in 1986.

If the *jus ad bellum* violation is sufficiently severe, it may constitute the crime of aggression, which figured prominently at Nuremberg under the now quaint label 'crimes against peace'. Indeed, the judges at the International Military Tribunal at Nuremberg famously referred to it as the supreme international crime because it contained within it the evil of the whole (i.e., aggressive war was the root cause of all other international crimes). Although this assumption underpinned prosecution of the Nazis for the Holocaust, it was not factually correct. The Holocaust was driven just as much by genocidal hatred as it was by aggressive expansionism, and, even if the Nazis had murdered only Jews within Germany's borders, this would have been an unspeakable crime. In the ensuing decades, serious atrocities have arisen in noninternational conflicts and civil wars where cross-border aggression was irrelevant. The break-up of Yugoslavia and the Rwandan genocide are two obvious examples (though both also had international components to their respective conflicts). However, in 1945, the international community did not yet recognize that an internal crime committed by a state against its own subjects could be a matter for international concern and prosecution. So the Nuremberg prosecutors limited their charge of crimes against humanity to the killing of European Jewry in occupied territories outside of Germany—territories that were vanquished by illegal conquest and therefore fell under the banner of aggression.

Unfortunately, Nuremberg was the last major prosecution for aggression. When the Security Council created the Yugoslav and Rwandan tribunals in 1993 and 1994, respectively, it excluded jurisdiction for aggression from their governing statutes. The ICC was denied jurisdiction over aggression when the Rome Statute was initially drafted in 1998, until the Assembly of State Parties could adopt a definition of the crime. That day came at the Kampala review conference in 2010, when state parties adopted a definition that largely matched one passed by the General Assembly in 1974.[23] The agreement was only possible because the parties also adopted a byzantine triggering mechanism that carefully circumscribed when aggression could be brought before the court.[24] The ICC prosecutor may proceed with an investigation if the Security Council determines that an act of aggression has occurred. Without this determination, the prosecutor must be preauthorized by an ICC Pre-Trial Chamber, and the Security Council can block the investigation by invoking its deferral power.[25] Furthermore, state parties to the Rome Statute can exempt themselves from jurisdiction over the crime by lodging a declaration with the Registrar. As a result of these amendments, it seems aggression will continue to go unprosecuted in the near future.

These jurisdictional obstacles undermine the anti-impunity norm. Nobody is held accountable for aggression and other less severe violations of *jus ad bellum*. That being said, informal international norms, including outcasting and noncooperation among future treaty partners, may produce social 'punishment' for states that engage in wrongful acts. Aggressive states are sometimes branded as rogue nations.[26] Nonetheless, some states are militarily strong enough to fight aggressive wars without risking geopolitical isolation. These informal measures are too toothless to ensure that crimes of aggression are properly punished.

3.3. By Whom Should They Be Tried?

Either national or international courts might conduct criminal law trials; each has its own advantages. International courts carry the legitimacy conferred by the international community as well as the expertise of international judges, prosecutors, and defence attorneys—all of whom should have substantial experience litigating accusations of mass atrocity—whereas their domestic counterparts may have no experience with criminal adjudication of wartime misconduct. Furthermore, since the crimes touch the world community, an international forum for criminal adjudication seems warranted. Finally, an international court might be more immune to charges of partiality or victor's justice levelled against domestic criminal courts convened by the winning side of an armed conflict. Precisely for this reason the Security Council granted the ICTY and ICTR primary jurisdiction that, as a matter of international law, prevailed over subordinate claims of jurisdiction from competing local courts. Under this scheme, international courts get first bite at the apple, determining which defendants are most significant, proceeding against them, and then leaving the remaining offenders to the local courts.

Although domestic prosecutions cannot represent—or stand in for—the international community as a whole, the domestic court may be more carefully attuned and sensitive to the victims' needs. The procedures of the local court will be familiar to both defendants and victims alike, and the court will be in the country or continent where the crimes occurred and where witnesses, defendant, and local lawyers are based, rather than far removed in The Hague. And a community torn apart by atrocity has a legitimate moral claim to influence or control the criminal process designed to restore justice to that community.[27]

Are local systems able to conduct such trials? Some states may be so damaged by armed conflict that their domestic criminal enforcement system cannot handle a major prosecution for genocide or crimes against humanity. Or, as with Libya, the state may have never developed independent judicial and civil institutions in the first place. So, there are reasons to doubt whether local courts can engage in prosecutions. On the other hand, prosecutions may help *develop* these judicial institutions and the respect for the rule of law that postconflict states lack. On this argument, the international community should provide financial and intellectual support for the local community to engage in its own judicial redress, which not only will prosecute offenders, but will also rehabilitate the rule of law and promote respect for judicial institutions in the aftermath of a conflict where the rule of law was completely flouted. Furthermore, a local process will be sensitive to the needs and customs of everyone involved, rather than imposing an international version of justice out of sync with local traditions.[28]

But there are also serious problems with local trials for international offences. Sometimes the local judicial system is not worth replicating or preserving because doing so would entrench existing inequities or infirmities. International trials more robustly protect due process, collect and preserve evidence using the latest forensic techniques, and feature highly qualified attorneys. Local justice, such as the regional Gacaca system in Rwanda, is sometimes procedurally deficient and meets neither the needs of defendants (who do not receive fair trials) nor, in the long run, the needs of the community (which ought to have access to a robust trial record). It would therefore seem that international justice better accomplishes the retributive goals of the criminal process. However, this must be considered alongside the opposite concern that Hague-centred justice will have inadequate buy-in from the local population—buy-in that is essential for postconflict reconstruction. For this reason, primary jurisdiction for international tribunals is waning. The Rome Statute restricts the ICC to complementary jurisdiction, so that the court can only prosecute defendants if there is no local court able and willing to prosecute them. This makes the ICC a court of last resort, designed to fill the gap when no other jurisdiction is available.[29]

Relegating international justice to a secondary role, as the complementarity principle does, is best justified on retributive grounds. The ICC's complementary jurisdiction is the clearest expression of the anti-impunity principle, whereby international institutions are justified by the need to prosecute individuals who would otherwise escape punishment for their conduct. If a local court is available to provide legal redress, the international forum is unnecessary. Instead of appealing to the priority of the local legal framework, the better justification is that international crimes *deserve* punishment and that international institutions are designed to provide that punishment when no other institution is available.

The principle of complementarity is controversial in practice. The ICC has traditionally looked at whether the forum state is both willing and able to start an investigation and prosecution of relevant individuals.[30] A pretextual investigation that exonerates an individual and never places him or her in jeopardy would signal that the state is unwilling to commence a genuine prosecution. Similarly, a state may be unable to prosecute perpetrators of individual crimes if its local judicial institutions are incapable of holding a large-scale trial, or if, as in the case of Libya, the government prosecutors do not have custody of the defendant.[31] Even if a trial is held, it is unclear whether complementarity demands particular outcomes. If the perpetrators are convicted but sentenced to ten days in jail for committing genocide, does the light punishment suggest that complementarity should be invoked? Presumably, local systems will have different standards of punishment; what counts as a harsh sentence in Rwanda will not be the same as a harsh sentence in Norway. Complementarity must allow for pluralism regarding punishment (since complementarity is animated by a respect for plural approaches). On the other hand, once a sentence falls below some extreme threshold, it becomes clear that the defendant has achieved *virtual* impunity in violation of the anti-impunity principle.

Does it matter whether a state prosecutes a defendant for an international crime or a domestic crime? Consider a state that prosecutes a war criminal for murder. Would the domestic prosecution divest an international court of jurisdiction under complementarity? The issue is labels and their significance. Under one well-known view, what matters is the length of punishment received by the perpetrator in the local court and whether it is comparable to the sentence that the perpetrator would have received if he had been convicted of an international crime before the ICC.[32] This standard is normatively convincing (because it avoids a formalistic commitment to labels), although it is difficult to apply in today's world: as of 2014, the ICC has handed down only two convictions and one acquittal. It is difficult to know what sentence a defendant would have received if he had been convicted of an international crime at the ICC.[33]

3.4. How Should They Be Tried?

Setting aside who should prosecute war criminals, we can ask next how these trials should be run, focusing on victim participation, *in absentia* trials, and plea-bargaining (negotiated justice).[34]

3.4.1. *Victim Participation*

Although the ICTY and ICTR Statutes did not include formal victim participation, the Rome Statute was drafted with victims at the centre of the process. As such, victims are formal parties to the proceedings, represented *as a group* by counsel, with authority to submit oral and written submissions on questions of fact and law. Upon conviction of a defendant, victims are entitled to compensation from a Victim Trust Fund. Although this system is all-but-unheard of in the common law, it is well known in civil law jurisdictions where the dividing line between a criminal and civil proceeding is not as clear-cut as in the common law. In some civil law systems, victims can initiate a criminal case by filing an accusatory instrument with the court and thus can be formal parties before a court with jurisdiction to decide the defendant's punishment (if any) *and* whether the victims should receive civil compensation. In contrast, the ICC does not permit victims to initiate cases themselves. The court is far more adversarial, with prosecution and defence attorneys arguing before a judge and without an investigative judge (*juge d'instruction*) as in the French system, for example. It is therefore most accurate to describe the ICC's system as adversarial with isolated civil law elements, including victim participation, grafted onto it.

But what justifies victim participation? To the extent that victims should feel like stakeholders in the process, full *partie civile* status increases their sense of ownership of the process. On the other hand, if international trials are designed simply as criminal trials (i.e., to determine the guilt or innocence of individual defendants and to protect their due process rights), then victim participation may distract the court from that narrow enterprise. Indeed, the slow pace of justice at the ICC could be ameliorated if the pre-trial and trial process was accelerated; removing victims from the process might achieve that goal.

3.4.2. *In Absentia Trials*

Must international tribunals have custody of the defendant prior to commencing the trial? Since Nuremberg, the trend has been to disfavour *in absentia* trials (consistent with the general common law approach). The assumption is that a fair trial is impossible if the defendant does not take part. However, the recent Special Tribunal for Lebanon has jurisdiction to conduct trials *in absentia*, a rule conferred on the court because the United Nations anticipated that the tribunal would have difficulty receiving custody of the accused. The issue has also been debated, in a different context, at the ICC, which does not have jurisdiction to proceed *in absentia*. However, several high-ranking politicians in Kenya, on trial for crimes against humanity, requested permission to remain in Kenya (conducting affairs of state) and appear via video-link, while defence lawyers represent them in The Hague. Although the Pre-Trial Chamber initially rebuffed these overtures, the Assembly of State Parties subsequently amended the Rules of Procedure and Evidence in order to permit, on a limited basis, such absences.[35]

Do the underlying principles of international justice countenance *in absentia* trials? If the goal of the trial is purely didactic or historical (i.e., the court is speaking to a larger audience), then why not? The *legal* justification (as opposed to the philosophical justification) for creating the ICTY, ICTR, and STL was that they would help restore international peace and security, and *in absentia* trials are better (in this respect) than no trials at all.[36] On the other hand, a more modest conception of the international trial as purely criminal, designed only to protect the due process rights of the defendant, counsels caution before permitting *in absentia* proceedings. It is hard to protect the rights of defendants when they are not even present (even if their absence is self-imposed).

3.4.3. *Plea Bargains and Negotiated Justice*

Finally, should international trials allow (or encourage) plea-bargaining? Plea bargains have obvious benefits: they reduce caseload, increase resources for trials that run to verdict, and allow parties to reduce risk (a benefit to prosecutors and defendants alike). With plea-bargaining, a tribunal can dispense with uncontested cases and encourage defendants to plead guilty in exchange for cooperating against senior-level defendants whose cases will be tried to verdict. On the other hand, plea-bargaining may frustrate the broader goals of the enterprise, such as preserving the anti-impunity norm, constructing a historical record, and giving victims a chance to participate in the process. None of these goals will be advanced if defendants short-circuit the process and skip the fact-finding stage tethered to the court's coercive investigative powers. This shows the intimate connection between the specifics of the procedural regime and the overarching normative foundation for the enterprise. If the goal is to protect defendants from unjust punishment, then one set of procedures is justified; if the goal is to serve the broader interests of collective groups writ large, then the set of relevant procedures will be different.

In this vein, it is important to contrast two arguments about international criminal procedure. We earlier discussed the tension between instrumental and deontological justifications for international criminal law generally; the same tension reappears in international procedure. So, the first view is explicitly instrumental: will the procedure advance the broader goals of international criminal justice? If it promotes the efficient administration of penal justice or advances the cause of history, then the procedure might be justified. This consequentialist account of criminal procedure requires a pre-existing account of the relevant values to be maximized. But, even with disagreement over the appropriate goods to maximize, the different positions share a common consequentialist framework. Many see procedure this way: it matters only instrumentally.

That being said, international criminal procedure's deontological foundations cannot be ignored. Criminal procedure has an inherent moral value that is not entirely reducible to its consequences.[37] In that sense, the criminal trial and its procedural mechanism represent an a priori good insofar as it constitutes criminal adjudication according to the rule of law. Vindicating the rule of law is a priori good because mass atrocity is committed during periods of legal absence. In these moments, the law is absent both substantively and procedurally, as victims are subjected to the whims of perpetrators and unspeakable violence. Subjecting this conduct to the demands of the law, through a criminal process, has obvious benefits for society. But the vindication of the rule of law represented by post-atrocity criminal trials has an inherent moral worth that is not reducible to the positive consequences that would flow from it. Lawlessness represents a transgression against human dignity and the notion that human beings are subject to normative constraints on their behaviour. Post-atrocity trials represent a return to law and order because they impose legal and moral scrutiny on conduct that came in the lawless past. In this way, post-atrocity trials transform periods of lawlessness into periods that are law-governed and, in so doing, vindicate our collective human dignity.

3.5. How Should the Guilty Be Punished?

Finally, justice after war requires both collective and individual punishment. States that engage in international wrongful acts should be punished for their conduct, although 'culpability' and 'punishment' are largely unknown terms in our modern system of public international law applied to states.[38] Punishment options include postwar reparations, loss of privileges and positions within international organizations, and a more general loss of standing within the international community.[39] And justice demands punishment for individuals who commit crimes, although circumstances will typically demand that only the most culpable individuals (at the planning level) will be punished (whether at a domestic or international tribunal), whereas those who engaged in isolated offences escape punishment.

In terms of philosophical justification, individual punishment for international crimes raises the same tensions between retributive and consequentialist frameworks as one finds in the literature on punishment in the regular criminal context. However, there are a few distinct features to punishing atrocities that are specific to the international context.[40] In the domestic literature, there is already an active empirical debate regarding the efficacy of deterrence, whether for the death penalty or incarceration. In the international context, it seems clear that deterrence (whether specific or general) is especially inapt as a particular justification for punishment. Individuals inclined to commit crimes against humanity or genocide are often motivated by intense hatred or bigotry that defies rational calculation; the possibility of future punishment in The Hague may not serve as a reliable mechanism to alter decisions. Furthermore, the nastiness of war may make the civilized Hague (with its comfortable detention facilities) seem like a benefit rather than a burden. This being said, judges at international tribunals occasionally come from domestic jurisdictions where criminal punishments are light compared to those in the United States or Africa, and the goal is simply to incapacitate a dangerous offender until he or she can be rehabilitated with educational programs and reintegrated into society—a process supported by robust state resources. But it is unclear if this paradigm of incapacitation and rehabilitation is suitable for demagogic ideologues prosecuted in the *jus post bellum* context.

This leaves retribution and expressivism as the most appropriate justifications for postwar punishment.[41] Retribution seems particularly apt in the postwar context; if anyone *deserves* punishment it is the *genocidaire*. However, retribution for wartime atrocity suffers from the very same conceptual infirmities as domestic retribution: locating the exact theoretical connection between moral desert and deprivation/suffering. Does suffering force the criminal to disgorge ill-gotten gains? Does it repair the moral fabric of society? Does it preserve the dignity of the criminal by treating him or her as a responsible (and rational) agent? There is a fine line between retributivism and expressivism; in the latter, punishment is designed to express the moral opprobrium of the world community—an element that could, in theory, be internalized as one component of a retributive theory. In this vein, punishment serves both a practical and a symbolic feature, one designed to communicate the world's determination that the acts in questions were truly reprehensible. This dovetails with the underlying principle of the substantive offences, especially crimes against humanity, whereby the real party in interest is the world community. In keeping with this principle, the community reclaims its commitment to humanity by correctly labelling the conduct as a crime against humanity and attaching the appropriate penalty.

Most punishment theories demand proportionality between the punishment and the conduct. Similarly situated defendants ought to receive similar sentences, whereas more culpable defendants ought to receive longer sentences. This framework poses problems, however, given the magnitude of international crimes and the need to reserve space at the top of the punishment scale for the worst offenders. If we reserve the top of the scale for the proverbial Hitler or Milošević or Karadžić, then the punishment of less culpable (but still tremendously guilty) offenders must be scaled down in order to maintain proportionality. At some point, offenders at the lower end of the scale are receiving trivial sentences for truly serious crimes—a counterintuitive result that demands a remedy. The correct response is to demand that the punishment accurately reflect the inherent gravity of the offence as much as possible and to give up the notion that punishments *always* express relative differences in culpability. Some crimes are so severe that we must give the same punishment (perhaps life in prison) to those at the top of the culpability scale *and* to those in positions lower down the scale.

4. Conclusion

This chapter's portrait of justice after war has focused on criminal law. Although other legal and moral mechanisms are available, criminal trials offer the best hope of vindicating the anti-impunity norm. Because of how they have acted, perpetrators of international crimes deserve punishment implemented according to the rule of law. This chapter has highlighted the manner in which these prosecutions should be conducted: the nature and location of the courts, their procedures, their substantive offences, and their sentencing. The vigorous expansion and institutionalization of postconflict criminal adjudication in the past twenty years should be heralded and accelerated.

Notes

1. For a discussion of the anti-impunity norm, see Max Pensky, 'Amnesty on Trial: Impunity, Accountability, and the Norms of International Law', *Ethics & Global Politics* 1 (2008), 40.
2. See David Wippman, 'Atrocities, Deterrence, and the Limits of International Justice', *Fordham International Law Journal* 23 (1999), 473; Julian Ku and Jide Nzelibe, 'Do International Criminal Tribunals Deter or Exacerbate Humanitarian Atrocities?', *Washington University Law Quarterly* 84 (2007).
3. See Shahram Dana, 'The Limits of Judicial Idealism: Should the International Criminal Court Engage with Consequentialist Aspirations?' *Penn State Journal of Law & International Affairs* 3 (2014), 30.
4. See Rome Statute, Article 27.
5. See Timothy William Waters, *The Milošević Trial: An Autopsy* (Oxford: Oxford University Press, 2013).
6. For a good analysis of these doctrines, see Elies van Sliedregt, *Individual Criminal Responsibility in International Law* (Oxford: Oxford University Press, 2012).
7. Rome Statute, Article 8*bis*.
8. As an example, John Demjanjuk was prosecuted for complicity in 28 060 counts of murder so as to completely avoid difficult questions regarding the state of international criminal law at the time the offences were committed.
9. See David Scheffer, 'The Merits of Unifying Terms: "Atrocity Crimes" and "Atrocity Law"', *Genocide Studies and Prevention* 2 (2007), 91.
10. See also Larry May, *Crimes Against Humanity: A Normative Account* (Cambridge: Cambridge University Press, 2004), 75.
11. Here is one area where the law's detail is clearly erroneous. Genocide involves a group conflict between enemy collectives, but the crime's definition by the International Criminal Tribunal for Rwanda erroneously suggests that a single individual acting alone (without co-perpetrators) could commit genocide. This departs significantly from the paradigm of group-against-group conflict.

12. David Luban, for example, concentrates on the 'humanness' that is the 'party in interest' in crimes against humanity. The crime touches not just the specific victims but the world community at large. Luban distinguishes this from the fact that the crime negates the 'humanness' that we all share because the crimes are so savage they call into question the distinction between humans (as political animals) and savages. See David Luban, 'A Theory of Crimes Against Humanity', *Yale Journal of International Law* 29 (2004), 85.
13. See *Prosecutor* v. *Francis Kirimi Muthaura and Uhuru Muigai Kenyatta*, Decision on Confirmation of Charges, ICC-01/09-02/11, Pre-Trial Chamber II, 23 January 2012.
14. See *Prosecutor* v. *William Samoei Ruto and Joshua Arap Sang*, Decision on Confirmation of Charges, Case No. ICC-01/09-01/11, Pre-Trial Chamber II, 23 January 2012.
15. The inquiry here is not whether the behaviour is criminal or not but what *kind* of crime has been committed: is the violation domestic or international, and, if so, should it be described as a crime against humanity or some other offence?
16. See Rome Statute, Article 6; Genocide Convention, Article II.
17. Genocide Convention, Article II.
18. See, e.g., David Nersessian, *Genocide and Political Groups* (Oxford: Oxford University Press, 2010).
19. See *Prosecutor* v. *Akayesu*, Case No. ICTR-96-4-T, Trial Chamber I, 2 September 1998, para. 702.
20. See Larry May, *Genocide: A Normative Account* (Cambridge: Cambridge University Press, 2010).
21. See Genocide Convention, Articles II(d) and II(e).
22. See Interlocutory Decision on the Applicable Law: Terrorism, Conspiracy, Homicide, Perpetration, Cumulative Charging (STL-11-01/I/AC/R176bis), Appeals Chamber, 16 February 2011.
23. See General Assembly Resolution 3314 (XXIX), 14 December 1974.
24. The triggering mechanism is codified in Article 15*bis* and 15*ter* of the Rome Statute. For a description of the US role during the negotiations, see Beth van Schaack, 'Negotiating at the Interface of Power & Law: The Crime of Aggression', *Columbia Journal of Transnational Law* 49 (2011), 505.
25. The deferral power, codified in Article 16 of the Rome Statute, allows the Security Council to block ICC investigations for one year, renewable infinitely.
26. See Scott J. Shapiro and Oona A. Hathaway, 'Outcasting: Enforcement in Domestic and International Law', *Yale Law Journal* 121 (2011), 252.
27. Some of these arguments appear in Jose E. Alvarez, 'Crimes of State/Crimes of Hate: Lessons from Rwanda', *Yale Journal of International Law* 24 (1999), 365.
28. It should be noted that one way of mediating between the competing demands of local and international justice is to split the difference with the creation of a hybrid tribunal composed of international and domestic elements. Both the Extraordinary Chambers of the Courts of Cambodia (ECCC) and the Special Tribunal for Lebanon (STL) are examples of hybrid courts. The ECCC has a dual-prosecution team spearheaded by one international co-prosecutor and one Cambodian co-prosecutor—an innovative though somewhat problematic structure when disagreements between the two prosecutors reach an impasse. The STL was created to investigate and prosecute the perpetrators responsible for the assassination of former Lebanese Prime Minister Hariri and has jurisdiction to prosecute violations of domestic Lebanese law (such as murder).

29. See Carsten Stahn and Mohamed M. El Zeidy (eds.), *The International Criminal Court and Complementarity: From Theory to Practice* (Cambridge: Cambridge University Press, 2011).
30. See Rome Statute, Article 17.
31. This is the case with Saif Gaddafi, who remains in the custody of the Zintan Rebels—a fact that figured heavily in the ICC Pre-Trial Chamber's decision that the Libyan central government was unable to prosecute Gaddafi. The Pre-Trial Chamber concluded that the ICC was permitted to exercise jurisdiction under the principle of complementarity. See *Prosecutor* v. *Gaddafi*, Decision on the admissibility of the case against Saif Al-Islam Gaddafi, Pre-Trial Chamber I, Case No. ICC-01/11-01/11 (31 May 2013).
32. For a subtle description and defence of this view, see Kevin Jon Heller, 'A Sentence-Based Theory of Complementarity', *Harvard International Law Journal* 53 (2012), 202.
33. The ICC operates a detention facility inside a Dutch prison in Scheveningen.
34. See, e.g., Sluiter et al. (eds.), *International Criminal Procedure: Principles and Rules* (Oxford: Oxford University Press, 2013).
35. See ICC Rules of Procedure and Evidence 134*bis*. It is unclear if this procedural rule is consistent with the language of the Rome Statute, which requires the presence of the accused.
36. These tribunals were created by the UN Security Council pursuant to its Chapter VII authority under the UN Charter to restore international peace and security. If this legal provision is taken seriously as a philosophical idea, it suggests a consequentialist justification based on the promise or anticipation that the creation of the tribunal will produce net social benefits for global society.
37. See Jens David Ohlin, 'A Meta-Theory of International Criminal Procedure: Vindicating the Rule of Law', *UCLA Journal of International Law and Foreign Affairs* 14 (2009), 77.
38. See Gabriella Blum, 'The Crime and Punishment of States', *Yale Journal of International Law* 38 (2013), 58 ('Since World War I, however, the moral rhetoric of state "crime and punishment" has been excised from the lexicon of international law').
39. See Shapiro and Hathaway, 'Outcasting', 258.
40. For a general discussion, see Mark Drumbl, *Atrocity, Punishment, and International Law* (Cambridge: Cambridge University Press, 2007).
41. There is an especially strong discussion of expressivism in Drumbl. See also Robert D. Sloane, 'The Expressive Capacity of International Punishment: The Limits of the National Law Analogy and the Potential of International Criminal Law', *Stanford Journal of International Law* 43 (2007), 39.

CHAPTER 28

RECONCILIATION AND REPARATIONS

CATHERINE LU

1. Introduction

After fifty-one months of war that killed 10 million people, the architects of the 1919 Versailles treaty process that concluded World War I sought to provide 'the basis upon which the peoples of Europe can live together in friendship and equality'.[1] Confronted with war's domestic, international, and transnational devastation, some hail reconciliation as having great, perhaps even the greatest, moral and political value.[2] At the same time, some find the concept of reconciliation so elusive, confusing, or objectionable that they urge abandoning it entirely.[3]

In this chapter, I aim to clarify the moral/political project of reconciliation and how it generates and conditions reparative tasks after civil, international, and transnational war. First, I distinguish between two concepts of reconciliation that address two kinds of alienation wrought by war: *relational reconciliation*, which responds to alienation arising between agents through their interactions, and *structural reconciliation*, which responds to the alienation that arises from the social and political practices and structures that mediate agents' activities and relations. After intrastate violence, relational reconciliation covers relations between individuals or between warring social groups, whereas structural reconciliation covers the reconciliation of individuals or groups to the social and political structures that mediate their relations. Internationally, relational reconciliation addresses the alienation arising from interactions between states or between states and other group or individual agents. International structural reconciliation refers to the reconciliation of individual states with the social and political structures that mediate relations between states, as well as to the reconciliation of individuals or social groups with the international order.

Second, I consider how these two concepts of reconciliation generate different accounts of the purposes of reparations, the agents responsible for reparations, and the forms that reparative measures should take. Although popular discourse and much of the theoretical literature on reconciliation focus on relational reconciliation between agents, I argue that the project of structural reconciliation is analytically prior and normatively fundamental. Reparations schemes in postwar peace settlements should aim not only to reconcile belligerents relationally to each other but also, more fundamentally, to help create a mutually affirmable and affirmed social/political order. Reparative responsibilities may extend beyond direct perpetrators of wrongs to all those who bear responsibilities for achieving structural reconciliation. With normative accounts of both relational and structural reconciliation, we can better diagnose the shortcomings and assess the normative development of historical and contemporary practices of reparation in contexts of civil, interstate, and transnational wars. The contemporary development of postwar reparative responsibilities in international law points to the unfinished project of reconciliation in international and transnational relations, especially as it relates to the legacies of empire, slavery, and colonialism.

2. The Case Against Reconciliation

Is reconciliation desirable and feasible after war? Critics worry, sometimes simultaneously, that reconciliation is too demanding, psychologically, sociologically, or morally, or not morally demanding enough.

The 'excessively demanding' charge may derive in part from Christian interpretations of reconciliation. Dostoyevsky depicts Christian reconciliation in his short story, 'The Dream of a Ridiculous Man', which contains a 'fantastic' account of 'an earth as yet undefiled by the Fall', in which human beings enjoy complete communion with themselves, each other, nature, the celestial realm, and even death.[4] Although this account is religious, the yearning for deep social unity has secular counterparts and is evident when reconciliation signals aspirations for a conflict-transcendent form of social unity. The Institute for Democracy and Electoral Assistance (IDEA)'s *Handbook on Reconciliation after Violent Conflict*, for example, presents reconciliation as 'a process through which a society moves from a divided past to a shared future', which depends on 'an over-arching process which includes the search for truth, justice, forgiveness, healing and so on'.[5] Conflict and disagreement are endemic after war, but they are also endemic to political life in peacetime. The dream of reconciliation is problematic if it aims at a kind of social unity that leaves no space for disagreement and dissent.[6] If relational reconciliation requires such fantastical social unity, some may naturally conclude that it comprises 'myths and illusions'.[7]

This 'social unity' conception of reconciliation also makes psychologically and socially infeasible demands on the victims of violent conflict. As a survivor of the

Rwandan genocide put it, 'I don't understand this word "reconciliation". I can't reconcile with people, even if they are in prison. . . . If a person comes to ask my forgiveness, I will pardon him after he has resuscitated the members of my family that he killed'.[8] Psychologically, not even retribution may guarantee sentimental social unity, especially between victims and perpetrators. More generally, individuals respond differently to similar experiences of conflict-driven loss or injury, and there may be many plausible and acceptable answers to how individuals may reconcile or not with those who have caused them grief.

Moreover, such relational reconciliation is also overdemanding because conflating social and political reconciliation with individual therapeutic models of healing and forgiveness risks sacrificing individual rights, needs, and interests for communal goals. Ultimately, focusing on agents' sentimental transformations is inappropriate for conceptualizing relational reconciliation as a political project. Suppose that some 'superior' beings suffer a serious social/political injustice or conflict, yet all are extraordinarily resilient, so do not suffer lasting damage or hold negative attitudes towards those responsible. Is the task of reconciliation fulfilled, since such beings hold no resentment against the responsible parties? Should we consider reconciliation achieved if all victims overcome their traumas through counselling? Our negative responses to both cases reveal that personal psychological healing from the traumas of war may be worthwhile but cannot account for the moral/political value of reconciliation.

When conceptions of reconciliation aim at a deep social unity that depends on sentimental transformations, they risk depoliticizing the concept and project of reconciliation, thus undermining its moral and political value.

Those who argue that reconciliation is not demanding enough typically view it as a compromise or abdication of justice. Just as reconciliation demands too much from victims (to forgive), it demands too little of the social/political order, letting off punishing perpetrators, compensating victims, and committing to structural transformations. If reconciliation entails affirming evil, it may be better to remain unreconciled. According to progressivists, when governments promote reconciliation as 'closure' after civil war, they delegitimate and demotivate continued struggle for moral and political change. In this vein, Robert Meister has criticized the liberal construct of 'transitional justice' for focusing only on victims and perpetrators of violence and basic human rights violations. Such practices obscure the structural grievances that initially led to violent political struggle, which may not be changed or settled by focusing on retribution or reparations solely for transgressions that arose in the war itself. Meister is also concerned that the beneficiaries of injustice tend to get let off the moral hook in this accounting because reconciliation is deemed to require only punishing and compensating those directly involved in or affected by violent political struggle.[9]

It would be difficult to understand how reconciliation could be a worthy moral or political value if it requires imposing undue moral and psychological burdens on individual agents, striving for a conflict-denying form of social unity, accommodating evil, and/or forestalling further progressive social and political change.

3. Two Concepts of Reconciliation

3.1. Relational and Structural Reconciliation

Reconciliation presupposes alienation.[10] Alienation may be of two kinds. First, alienation may arise from an interaction between individual or group agents. For example, individual victims of torture are alienated from their torturers, and members of a targeted group may be alienated from the police or the military if these government agents were involved in targeting them. Second, alienation may arise from the social and political institutions—both formal structures and informal practices—that mediate agents' interactions. In civil war, the most relevant structures may be domestic; in interstate and transnational wars, the pertinent structures may be international and transnational.[11] Whereas the first kind of alienation refers to agents' relational estrangement from each other, the second form refers to their structural estrangement from the social/political order. For example, faced with the devastation wrought by World War I, cynicism about societal values as well as political and social institutions—domestic and international—was pervasive:

> All of the Victorian verities came under attack . . . : progress was a myth, rationality a veneer, industry a mistake. No one in authority was to be trusted; politicians and generals had turned lying into an art form; mothers and fathers would patriotically send their sons off to die. Nothing in the newspapers was true; it was all propaganda, all the facts were invented.[12]

The experience of world war produced alienation not only between warring parties, but also structural alienation from the previous domestic and international social/political orders, from the family to the society of states.

These two distinct kinds of alienation produce two different ways of thinking about reconciliation, what it may aim to achieve, and what methods may be appropriate for realizing its aims. As already noted, I call these two concepts of reconciliation *relational reconciliation* and *structural reconciliation*.

Relational reconciliation responds to alienation between agents. Herodotus' *History*, for example, recounts the enmity between the Persians and Greeks which, according to one version, began when trading Phoenicians kidnapped a number of Greek women, including the daughter of the king of Argos, and sailed to Egypt with them. This violent interaction begins a 'series of unjust acts', with each injured party calling for satisfaction in the form of reparation or restitution, and each perpetrating party refusing to provide any because of the previous generations' failure to make reparations, when the victim and perpetrator roles were reversed.[13] Relational reconciliation between the Greeks and the Persians focuses on what the parties would have to do to transform their relationship.

The second concept of reconciliation is structural. After war and other conflicts, people are alienated not only from each other, but also from their social and political institutions. If these institutions allow some agents to treat others as if they were nothing, then they constitute an objective source of alienation for the victims, independently of the specific harms that they suffer at the perpetrators' hands. Andromache was not only alienated from Achilles, who killed her husband, Hector, or the Greeks who, out of fear of future revenge, killed her infant son, but she and the other captive Trojan women were objectively alienated from a social/political order in which conquered women became the spoils of war, to be made into concubines and slaves according to the whim of the victors.[14] Structural reconciliation aims to remedy this alienation from social institutions by creating a mutually affirmable and affirmed social/political order.[15]

The construction of a mutually affirming social/political order has objective and subjective components. Objectively, structural reconciliation involves constructing a social/political order that establishes rights and duties that allow agents to exercise their moral and political agency against a set of background conditions that ensure moral reciprocity in their institutional relations and structural conditions. Structural reconciliation also has a subjective component: agents' affirmation—acceptance or endorsement—of the validity of the rules, relations, and conditions of the domestic and/or international social/political order.[16]

In the current structure of international relations, for example, the objective component of structural reconciliation is based on declarations of human rights and humanitarian law, state sovereign equality and independence, and prohibitions on the use of force by states. The subjective component requires that all states deny the legitimacy of committing mass violations of human rights or humanitarian laws of war in the pursuit of political objectives, as well as political ambitions for world conquest or world revolution. Cultivating agents' commitment to the international order, however, may depend on whether the international order is objectively worthy of reconciliation; that is, whether the objective components successfully acknowledge the fundamental needs, rights, and interests of the relevant agents.

3.2. Reconciliation and Reparative Tasks

These two concepts of reconciliation give rise to two different, albeit related, kinds of reparative tasks after war. Relational reconciliation leads us to ask what agents involved in a damaging or harmful interaction may require of each other to make good their relationship. Typically, it focuses on the rights and needs of victims and the obligations of perpetrators to provide remedies to restore their damaged relationship. On this view, reparations repair the damaged relationship between agents; the responsible agents are those who were involved in the damaging interaction, and the forms of reparation should respond to agent-specific sources and effects of damage or injustice. After civil war, reparations programs that involve individual perpetrators repairing victims' losses aim at relational reconciliation.[17] In international relations, the agents may be states, and relational reconciliation focuses on what warring states can morally require of each other to settle damages or rectify grievances arising from their interactions.

Structural reconciliation leads us to ask what background social institutions contributed to the production of the conflict. Reparations by wrongdoers may be part of, but may not adequately fulfil, the reparative tasks generated by a concern for structural reconciliation, which is to transform alienating social structures. The responsible agents may include those involved in the conflict, but also other agents who were not involved directly but who produce the alienating background social institutions. And the forms of reparation should respond to the structure-specific sources and effects of alienating relations.[18]

International structural reconciliation focuses on the rules and practices that regulate and shape the agency of states in their interactions with each other and with non-state parties. Insofar as war is a social practice of a sovereign states system, structural reconciliation must reform alienating aspects of the international legal and political practice of war. Structural reconciliation thus involves addressing not only the grievances generated directly by the war itself, but also resolving sources of alienation from the pre-existing order that may have constituted underlying causes of the conflict or its particular brutalities. In this way, the project of structural reconciliation leaves open the need for further political struggle to overcome long-standing structural failings of the international political order. Postwar relational reconciliation is thus deeply connected to a more fundamental account of structural reconciliation that goes beyond the specific wrongs or damages done during the war itself.

Although both structural and relational accounts of reconciliation are important, structural reconciliation is normatively fundamental because its objective components establish the background conditions necessary for legitimating any negotiated settlement on relational reconciliation between agents. Neither relational nor structural reconciliation, as *political* projects, requires changing people's sentimental attitudes towards those who wronged them or contributed to their suffering and losses, although relational reconciliation may aim to recalibrate agents' senses of shame and guilt, as well as repudiate hostile, dehumanizing, and disrespectful attitudes or beliefs about other social groups.[19] Both relational and structural reconciliation may have an effect on individual psychological healing or sentiments, but changes in these features of agents do not define or fulfil reconciliation understood as a political project.[20]

At the same time, political reconciliation does not need to presuppose a fixed account of a morally ideal social/political order. Rather, reconciliation enables the relevant agents to engage in an open-ended, meaningful, and respectful struggle for a mutually affirmed social/political order. As James Tully has argued with respect to reconciliation between indigenous peoples and the settler societies into which they were forcibly incorporated, 'reconciliation is neither a form of recognition handed down to Indigenous peoples from the state nor a final settlement of some kind. It is an on-going partnership negotiated by free peoples based on principles they can both endorse and open to modification *en passant*'.[21] Given that reconciliation, so understood, does not foreclose continued political struggle over both structural and relational reconciliation, such a project allows the continuation of moral and political disagreement and does not assume a homogenizing ideal or a conflict-transcendent form of social unity.

4. Postwar Reconciliation and International Order

4.1. War and the Development of International Order

Historically, since no authoritative or binding judgement about just cause to use force was available in international relations, states enjoyed an unrestricted right to wage war for any reason, including self-aggrandizement and conquest.[22] Reparations, understood as the amends made by a state to its victims for wrongful conduct or harm, did not exist in such an international system. Rather, payment for damages caused by war, as well as any other transfers of wealth, people, territory, or other resources, were exacted by victors against vanquished in accordance with the outcome of the military contest, with the loser incurring the obligation to pay the victor no matter the moral merits of the victor's case for engaging in war.

In the 1871 Treaty of Frankfurt that concluded the Franco-Prussian War, for example, a defeated France was forced to pay huge 'indemnities' to a victorious Germany, despite the fact that Germany, led by the Prussian Chancellor Otto von Bismarck, was the main aggressor that pushed the French into declaring war.[23] Paying indemnities was the cost of making war and losing but did not signify any moral judgment. In such a self-help international order, material transfers are not guided by considerations of justice but by considerations of relative power advantage, so that 'the strong do what they have the power to do and the weak accept what they have to accept'.[24]

Similarly, the 1842 Treaty of Nanjing that concluded the First Opium War between Britain and China (1839–42), followed by similar treaties between imperial China and other Western states such as France and the United States, included payments of compensation and indemnities by the Qing to the British for destroyed opium, war costs, and outstanding debts. In addition, the Qing lost the jurisdictional authority to detain or punish prisoners who were British subjects or Chinese subjects who had collaborated with the British, Hong Kong was ceded to Queen Victoria, and five port cities were forcibly opened to European mercantile pursuits.[25] As these examples illustrate, although the practice of paying indemnities may have served the prudential function of deterring potential aggressors from initiating wars that they were uncertain of winning, it also provided a material incentive to aggressors who were confident of their military superiority.

Insofar as indemnities were guided by more than the victor's self-aggrandizement, their fundamental concern was prudential.[26] French reparations after the Napoleonic wars, for example, were determined by the prudential judgment that a 'stable, moderately strong France' was necessary for an enduring balance of power in Europe after

French hegemony. Initially, in the 1814 Treaty of Paris, the victorious Allies—Britain, Austria, Russia, and Prussia—agreed to waive all Allied claims to war damages. After Napoleon's escape from imprisonment, military remobilization, his 'Hundred Days', and subsequent recapture, however, prudence dictated a less generous Second Treaty of Paris. They exiled Napoleon far from France, left an army of occupation of 1.2 million on French soil, took more territory away from France, and imposed war reparations for the Hundred Days, as well as for the cost of the occupation and wartime damages to allied nationals. According to Eugene White, 'Reparations now became part of a tougher peace package, assessing a penalty for threatening the new European order and a deterrent against future ventures. Payment of reparations was also an incentive, whose fulfilment would allow France to resume its role as a Great Power in the management of European affairs'.[27] After the Napoleonic wars, reparations aimed to prevent future aggressions through deterrence and to provide a basis for reconciliation that involved the reintegration of France into the European balance of power.

4.2. The Failure of Political Reconciliation in 1919 Versailles

Not surprisingly, the legitimacy of states' unrestricted right to wage war was severely tested in the early twentieth century after European nationalist rivalries culminated in a devastating world war. In many historical accounts of World War I, the 1919 Versailles treaty process stands as an example of the foolish pursuit of justice at the expense of reconciliation. According to this view, the Allied powers recklessly tried to punish Germany for the war by exacting excessive reparations, thus entrenching resentment and division rather than reconciliation in European postwar politics.[28]

Although this account of the failure of Versailles is still common, contemporary historical scholarship reveals that reconciliation was a fundamental concern of the architects of the 1919 Versailles treaty process. Although strict justice might have dictated that Germany should pay to rebuild the areas it had devastated, French leaders understood that this 'would completely crush [Germany] and reduce her to a state of economic bondage which would strip away from humanity all hope of a lasting peace'. Although reparations must aim at corrective and reparative justice, they could not be designed with the aim or outcome of destroying Germany. French leaders also posited that French security would best be achieved through 'economic collaboration' with Germany and that 'the surest way of re-establishing between the two countries a peace worthy of the name is by working to join together their material interests'.[29] No matter how devastating the consequences of war, then, reparative claims against Germany had to be limited, not only practically but also morally, by considerations of a future international order that included both Germany and France. Allied powers thus recognized that the demands of structural reconciliation in international relations ought to condition the postwar reparative demands made on Germany.

With an unrepentant Germany stalling on reparation payments, however, distributive justice between the victorious powers for reconstructing the devastated areas and resolving the payment of general war costs became an issue of postwar structural reconciliation. Since structural reconciliation is a collective enterprise, Germany was not the only state that had obligations to help the victims of the war. This is indeed how the French hoped to recover economically from the war: 'French leaders looked not to Germany but to their allies for a solution'. The French Minister of Commerce in 1918, Etienne Clémentel, envisaged a global fund to restore the ravaged areas, the creation of an Allied economic bloc strong enough to restrain German ambitions, and the eventual development of an 'economic union of free peoples' into which Germans could ultimately be integrated.[30] Unfortunately, American abandonment of the wartime system of economic cooperation meant a denial of the French view of distributive justice during the period of economic reconstruction, which involved pooling war costs and reapportioning inter-Allied debt, with 'each nation paying according to its ability'.[31] The conflicts among the Allies about how to distribute the financial burdens of the war revealed their thin commitment to structural reconciliation. Jon Jacobson has argued that the economic regeneration of France and Belgium and a strong Allied economic union could have protected Europe even from an unrepentant Germany and, in time, may have provided the material basis for cultivating Germany's subjective affirmation of the international order.[32] Instead, 'the net effect of World War I and the peace settlement was the effective enhancement of Germany's relative strength in Europe, particularly in regard to her immediate neighbours'.[33]

4.3. Reparative Responsibility in International Law

The international order that emerged after World War II included greater institutionalized prohibitions against the use of force by states. As a corollary, the cost of engaging in war would include reparations for wrongful conduct. Under the Articles on the Responsibility of States for Internationally Wrongful Acts (Articles on State Responsibility), adopted by the International Law Commission in 2001, an offending state has a duty to cease a wrongful act and to make 'full reparation' for any 'material or moral' injury or damage caused by the wrongful act (Article 31).[34] As James Crawford and Jeremy Watkins have noted, 'By attaching an obligation of repair to acts which it prohibits, international law marks out a certain class of losses—namely those that follow directly from unlawful conduct—as ones which should not lie where they fall'.[35]

Under contemporary international law, reparations are the amends made by an offending state to the victims of wrongdoing to rectify the harms caused by their wrongs. Some consider this to be the only necessary and sufficient justification for a duty to make reparations, whether or not they will advance reconciliation. According to Howard McGary, 'Reparations are simply intended to rectify wrongdoing. . . . In certain cases, providing reparations to the victims of wrongdoing may allow the parties to reconcile their differences, but such reconciliation is the consequence of reparations, not the meaning of reparations or justification for them'.[36] Viewed in this way, reparations are a requirement of justice, independent of and not directly related to any concept of reconciliation. According to my account, however, justice and reconciliation are not easily separable political projects. Whereas McGary is right that reparations may or may not produce sentimental interpersonal reconciliation, I think reparative demands made against wrongdoers are justified as a component of relational reconciliation and conditioned by a more fundamental account of structural reconciliation that lays out the principles and terms of a mutually affirming social and political order.[37]

For example, an offending state cannot be required to satisfy a reparative demand in a way that is 'out of proportion to the injury' or that takes 'a form humiliating to the responsible State' (Article 37.3). There is also some acknowledgement in the practice of reparations that the populations bearing the reparative burden typically are largely 'morally blameless'.[38] Postwar peace settlements that constitute practices of reconciliation must accommodate the claims of basic justice of the citizens of defeated powers, thus necessitating limits on the reparative obligations that liable states may have. The extent of a perpetrator state's reparative obligations to victim parties, whether they are individuals, corporations, or states, must be balanced with the obligations of culpable states to provide for their own populations.[39] Indeed, nothing may justify reparations that would prevent a state from fulfilling its domestic obligations of ensuring domestic security, the administration of justice, the provision of basic health care and education, and viable economic structures that can support a basic standard of economic welfare to its population. Thus, Dinah Shelton observes that reparative obligations of wrongful parties are to be determined not only by the claims of injured parties but also by wider community interests.[40]

These wider moral considerations came to be acknowledged in the design of the United Nations Compensation Commission (UNCC) and Compensation Fund, created through Resolution 692 by the UN Security Council in 1992, following the First Gulf War that was ignited by Iraq's invasion of Kuwait.[41] Unlike the Inter-Allied Reparation Commission formed under Versailles, which was not connected to the League of Nations system, the UNCC is a creature of the UN system, with the implication that it 'does not represent the interests of a single state, for example Kuwait, nor of the coalition of states which fought for the liberation of Kuwait, but rather of the whole international community'. Andrea Gattini also observes that, as a reparative regime, the UNCC not only efficiently processed the entitlements of victims of Iraqi aggression, but also considered 'the needs of Iraq's people'.[42]

The UNCC limited the reparative obligations of Iraq in various ways: the Allied coalition forces were not eligible for compensation for the cost of the forces or their military operations against Iraq, and, with some exceptions, members of the Allied coalition force were ineligible for compensation for loss or injury sustained in military operations against Iraq. The UNCC's decisions also ranked the urgency of different types of claims, creating a hierarchy of victims that privileged individual over corporate and governmental claims.[43] Gattini observes that, in its efficient and feasible processing of reparative claims, the UNCC will 'have the chance to be remembered in the history of international law . . . as the first successful model of a collective relief system organized by the international community in response to an aggression'.[44]

Although the concept of relational reconciliation focuses on the reparative obligations of perpetrator states, a responsible state may sometimes also become an incapacitated state, especially after a major and devastating war. In such cases, the obligation to repair some categories of harms and losses that is required to support structural reconciliation may spread beyond the directly responsible state, 'through a system of international loss-spreading which extends across the community of nations'.[45] Such loss-spreading beyond the agents directly involved points to normative concerns that go beyond relational reconciliation and move towards structural reconciliation.

5. Reparations and Reconciliation in the Aftermath of Empire and Colonialism

Only recently, then, have reparations for wrongful international conduct become part of the international legal and political order's response to war. Strikingly, reparation has been, until recently, largely absent following violent political conflict between (mostly European) colonizer states and colonized peoples, including indigenous peoples. At the 1884–85 Congress of Berlin, European states, as well as the United States, agreed on the terms of recognizing colonial claims among themselves, thus allowing for a more coordinated 'scramble for Africa' as part of a competition among them for resources and national prestige. The colonial wars that ensued, characterized at the time as 'small wars', were different from interstate European wars in several ways.[46] The aims of the parties involved were quite expansive compared to those of wars between European states, which were typically more limited in their objectives. Colonizing states engaged in wars of conquest aimed to achieve 'total subjection of the population' in a territory to which they had a colonial claim; for those populations resisting colonization, their aim was thus self-determination and sometimes sheer physical survival.[47] David Olusoga and Casper W. Erichsen have observed that, 'While colonial wars were undoubtedly small by European standards, they were almost always cataclysmic for the tribal peoples concerned'. Colonial wars did not involve the clash of uniformed armies on a battlefield; rather, those who resisted European colonizers were typically killed in 'massacres, ambushes and punitive raids'. Because wars of conquest were directed by a professional army against an entire population, the conventional rules of warfare that pertained to interstate wars among European states, including distinctions between civilians and combatants, were not typically applied.[48] In Germany's campaign to colonize South West Africa (today's Namibia) in the early 1900s, for example, it is estimated that more than three-quarters of the entire Herero population (60 000 out of a population of 80 000), as well as half of the Nama people, were killed, either in battle following the

1904 'uprising' or due to harsh conditions subsequently imposed by German troops.[49] Although other experiences of colonial rule were not explicitly genocidal in intent, they entailed brutalities against indigenous groups, such as in Kenya during the Mau Mau war in the 1950s, in which Britain's colonial detention system subjected thousands of prisoners to torture, maiming, and other abuses.[50]

One challenge to thinking about reconciliation after colonial wars derives from the lack of meaningful distinction between war and peace. As Henk Wesseling points out, the treaties that ended colonial wars of conquest typically signified the start of the 'real military conquest' or 'pacification' of the population.[51] Colonial and imperial wars of conquest were not so much discrete events marking absolute and qualitative changes between war and peace as they were permanent states of war. Thus, Manjari Chatterjee Miller has observed, 'The phenomenon of colonialism was not encapsulated by a single instantaneous event but rather by many such events that would eventually become the focus of anti-colonial nationalism and mass uprisings'.[52] It is difficult, therefore, and morally less meaningful to distinguish between colonial wars as discrete, wrongful acts or events and colonialism as a normalized ongoing set of political practices of domination that were predicated on a deep structural injustice of the international social and political order.[53] Colonizer states' actions were typically not aberrant violations of international norms, and colonial injustices involved not simply wrongful acts by individual or state perpetrators. In an international order that legalized or at least did not prohibit any uses of force to achieve the subordination of colonial subject populations, the defeated were not so much reconciled as resigned to the new structures and relations of domination.

In contemporary world politics, the Articles on State Responsibility have fortified recent demands for reparations for historical international and transnational wrongful conduct, including colonialism and slavery. At the 2001 UN World Conference against Racism, Racial Discrimination, Xenophobia, and Related Intolerance, held in Durban, South Africa, state representatives discussed responses to historical injustices, including the 'provision for effective remedies, recourses, redress, [compensatory] and other measures at the national, regional and international levels'.[54] In March 2014, fourteen Caribbean countries agreed on a comprehensive plan that calls upon 'the former slave-owning nations of Europe—principally Britain, France, Spain, Portugal, the Netherlands, Norway, Sweden and Denmark—to engage Caribbean governments in *reparatory dialogue* to address the living legacies of these crimes'.[55]

Although international legal experts do not expect such a case to be legally viable, the British government did recently (in June 2013) conclude a 'full and final settlement' of a high court action brought by five victims of the Mau Mau war who suffered under the British colonial administration in the 1950s. The settlement will see 5228 Kenyans receiving compensation payments of £2600 each.[56] Although the British foreign secretary, William Hague, claimed that this settlement would not establish a precedent, historian Caroline Elkins has argued that, 'Britain's acknowledgement of colonial era torture has opened as many doors as it has closed. . . . The Mau Mau detention camps were but one site in a broader policy of end-of-empire incarceration, torture and cover-up'.[57]

In the case of the undisputed 1904 genocide of the Herero people, in 1998, the former German president Roman Herzog cited the absence of international legal reparative provisions for colonialism in the early twentieth century to support his government's decision not to pay reparations to Herero descendants.[58] Germany did eventually apologize for the Herero genocide on 14 August 2004, but it has consistently refused to accept liability or reparative obligations to Herero descendants, 'since the international rules on the protection of combatants and civilians were not in existence at the time that war crimes were being committed in Namibia'.[59]

Does the commitment of contemporary European states to development assistance for their ex-colonies make reparative demands redundant? One concern raised by Robert Meister about such forms of 'reparations' that are not directly connected to an acknowledgement of responsibility for wrongdoing is that they fail to repudiate evil adequately: 'There must also be . . . an element of moral victory for victims—a *judgment* in their favor—without which redress would merely make "forced transactions" in the past a little more *acceptable* going forward.'[60] Meister also raises the challenge of going beyond conventional 'loss-based' reparative strategies that require the identification of surviving victims whose documented harms or losses are directly traceable to past wrongs by identifiable perpetrators. Such strategies can severely limit the efficacy and scope of contemporary reparative claims and obligations and typically do not account for the continued structural disadvantages and advantages resulting from past social/political injustices. These structural consequences, however, are significant for the project of reconciliation because their persistence constitutes an objective source of alienation of contemporary agents from the social/political order. In other words, whereas reparation to individuals who suffered directly may be one component for relational reconciliation, contemporary agents also bear a political responsibility to redress the structural legacies of international or transnational historical injustices such as slavery and colonialism.

Meister thus advocates a 'gain-based approach to reparative justice' that includes the 'disgorgement of ill-gotten gains' by 'beneficiaries' of past injustice 'whether or not victims of the wrong survive and even if successors to their claims could not directly prove individual losses in an equal or greater amount'.[61] To the extent that the Articles on State Responsibility limit reparations only to states that are directly responsible for wrongful conduct and exclude disgorgement as an obligation of structural reparation, they remain too focused on the relational versus structural aspects of political reconciliation. In contrast, the Caribbean Community's idea of a 'reparatory dialogue' with former slave-owning states aims not only to repair damaged political relationships, but also to effect far more fundamental structural transformations of the international order.

6. Conclusion

According to the normative account of political reconciliation in the relational and structural forms offered in this chapter, practices of reconciliation after war are problematic if they depoliticize the project of reconciliation by focusing on individual psychological healing or by appealing to an unrealistic and undesirable form of conflict-denying social unity that, in reality, serves to pressure the politically weak to accommodate evil and injustice and forecloses progressive political struggle to redress deeper structural sources of alienation. Although we typically think about reconciliation only in relational terms, as a feature of agents' interpersonal relationships and interactions with each other, I have argued that the project of structural reconciliation of agents with the social/political order that mediates their relations is more normatively fundamental and ought to be a primary concern of postwar reconciliation efforts. While relational reconciliation focuses the investigation of responsibility for reparations on the agents who committed wrongful acts or produced harmful consequences, the project of structural reconciliation after civil, international, and transnational wars points to a distinct and more comprehensive responsibility of all those agents who participate in the relevant institutions to redress the sources of structural alienation. Emerging demands for reparations for historical wrongs associated with the practices of slavery, colonialism, and empire reveal the unfinished project of both relational and structural reconciliation in international relations.

Acknowledgements

Earlier versions of this chapter were presented and benefited from the responses of participants at various workshops and conferences, including the Moral, Political, and Social Theory workshop at the Australian National University, in Canberra (August 2013); the Research Group on Constitutional Studies workshop at McGill University in Montreal (January 2014); the Global Justice After Colonialism conference at McGill University (May 2014); and the Institute for Advanced Study colloquium in Bad Homburg, Germany (July 2014). The author wishes to thank the volume editors, Helen Frowe and Seth Lazar, as well as the organizers and all the participants of these workshops, especially Lea Ypi, Yves Winter, Natalie Stoljar, Daniel Butt, Amandine Catala, David Estlund, Katrin Flikschuh, Rainer Forst, Bob Goodin, Pablo Kalmanovitz, Jacob Levy, Murray Sinclair, and Anna Stilz for their critical comments.

Notes

1. 'Reply of the Allied and Associated Power to the Observations of the German Delegation on the Conditions of Peace, and Ultimatum [May 1919]', *The Treaty of Versailles and After: Annotations of the Text and the Treaty* (Washington, DC: US Department of State, 1947), 54.
2. This is particularly true after civil wars. Since the mid-1970s, of the thirty 'truth commissions' established in twenty-eight countries in response to civil war, intrastate violence, or oppression, at least twelve contain the word, 'Reconciliation' in their titles (Chile, Democratic Republic of Congo, Ghana, Grenada, Indonesia, Liberia, Morocco, Peru, Sierra Leone, South Africa, Timor-Leste, and the Federal Republic of Yugoslavia). See http://www.amnesty.org/en/international-justice/issues/truth-commissions.

3. For a lamentation, see Harvey M. Weinstein, 'Editorial Note: The Myth of Closure, the Illusion of Reconciliation: Final Thoughts on Five Years as Co-Editor-in-Chief', *International Journal of Transitional Justice* 5 (2011), 1–10.
4. Fyodor Dostoyevsky, 'The Dream of a Ridiculous Man: A Fantastic Story', in *A Gentle Creature and Other Stories*, translated by Alan Myers (Oxford: Oxford World's Classics, 1995), 117–122.
5. International Institute for Democracy and Electoral Assistance (IDEA), *Handbook on Reconciliation after Violent Conflict* (2003), 12. http://www.idea.int/publications/reconciliation/
6. On problematic conceptions of unity that view difference and dissent as threats to a unmediated social harmony, see Jonathan Allen, 'Balancing Justice and Social Unity: Political Theory and the Idea of a Truth and Reconciliation Commission', *University of Toronto Law Journal* 49:3 (1999): 315–353.
7. Weinstein, 'Editorial Note', 9.
8. Quoted in Weinstein, 'Editorial Note', 8.
9. Robert Meister, *After Evil: A Politics of Human Rights* (New York: Columbia University Press, 2012).
10. Although my account of 'structural reconciliation' shares many affinities with Darrel Moellendorf's normative account of reconciliation as a 'political value' and Colleen Murphy's understanding of 'political reconciliation' as 'the process of rebuilding damaged political relationships', neither employs the concept of alienation to explore what reconciliation aims to resolve. Both also confine their arguments to intrastate cases of violent political conflict or oppression such as South Africa, Argentina, Chile and Uganda. See Colleen Murphy, *A Moral Theory of Political Reconciliation* (Cambridge: Cambridge University Press, 2010), 1; and Darrel Moellendorf, 'Reconciliation as a Political Value', *Journal of Social Philosophy* 38:2 (2007), 205–221.
11. To the extent that various aspects of civil armed conflicts, including duration, supply of arms, and humanitarian and refugee assistance, may involve external or international agents and structures, alienation from various international structures and practices may also be relevant to many civil wars.
12. Gordon Martel, 'A Comment', in *The Treaty of Versailles: A Reassessment after 75 Years*, edited by Manfred F. Boemeke, Gerald D. Feldman, and Elisabeth Glaser (Cambridge: Cambridge University Press, 1998), 635.
13. Herodotus, *The Histories*, translated by Aubrey de Sélincourt, edited by John Marincola (Toronto: Penguin, 1996), I.2.
14. Euripides, *The Trojan Women*, translated by Nicholas Rudall (Chicago: Ivan R. Dee, 1999). The play was performed in 415 BC, one year after Athens invaded the island of Melos.
15. I am taking my inspiration for this concept of reconciliation from Michael Hardimon's interpretation of Hegel's philosophical project of reconciliation. See Michael O. Hardimon, 'The Project of Reconciliation: Hegel's Social Philosophy', *Philosophy and Public Affairs* 21:2 (1992), 165–195.
16. As Moellendorf rightly points out, the general acceptance of the institutional order indicative of reconciliation can be distinguished from a fuller, more complete endorsement. See Moellendorf, 'Reconciliation as a Political Value', 207.
17. Reconciliation 'still happens one encounter at a time', according to a photo-essay on a government-sponsored program in Rwanda that involves perpetrators performing reparative tasks for victims twenty years after the genocide. Pieter Hugo and Susan Dominus, 'Portraits of Reconciliation', *The New York Times Magazine*, 6 April 2014.

18. On social structures, see Iris Marion Young, *Responsibility for Justice* (Oxford: Oxford University Press, 2011).
19. See Lu, 'Shame, Guilt and Reconciliation After War', *European Journal of Social Theory* 11:3 (2008), 367–383.
20. This is not to deny the existence and desirability of reconciliation understood as an interpersonal moral project. For example, the memoirs of Eric Lomax provide a powerful story of how a British prisoner of war came to be reconciled with one of the Japanese soldiers who participated in his imprisonment and torture during World War II. See Eric Lomax, *The Railway Man* (London: Vintage, 1996).
21. James Tully, *Public Philosophy in a New Key: Volume 1, Democracy and Civic Freedom* (Cambridge: Cambridge University Press, 2008), 223–256.
22. Some of this section is drawn from my 'Justice and Reparations in World Politics', in *Reparations: Interdisciplinary Inquiries*, edited by Rahul Kumar and Jon Miller (Oxford: Oxford University Press, 2007), 193–212.
23. Michael Howard, *The Franco-Prussian War: The German Invasion of France, 1870–1871* (New York: Macmillan, 1962).
24. Thucydides, *The Peloponnesian War*, translated by Thomas Hobbes (Chicago: University of Chicago Press, 1989), book V, paragraph 89.
25. Jonathan D. Spence, *The Search for Modern China* (New York: W.W. Norton, 1990), 159–160.
26. Thucydides explained the prudential value of a strategy of restraint with respect to the demand for reparations after war, in *The Peloponnesian War*, Book 4, paragraph 19, 239.
27. Eugene N. White, 'Making the French Pay: The Costs and Consequences of the Napoleonic Reparations', *European Review of Economic History*, 5 (2001), 337–365, at 339.
28. For a scathing critique of the terms of peace, see John Maynard Keynes, 'Proposals for the Reconstruction of Europe (1919)', in *his Essays in Persuasion* (New York: W.W. Norton, 1963), 17–18.
29. Marc Trachtenberg, *Reparation in World Politics: France and European Economic Diplomacy, 1916–1923* (New York: Columbia University Press, 1980) 18, 100, 158.
30. Trachtenberg, *Reparation in World Politics*, 1, 17.
31. Idem, 21, 54.
32. Jon Jacobson, 'Is There a New International History of the 1920s?' *American Historical Review* 88:3 (1983), 617–645, at 633.
33. Sally Marks, 'The Myths of Reparations', *Central European History* 11 (1978), 255.
34. Andrea Gattini, 'The UN Compensation Commission: Old Rules, New Procedures on War Reparations', *European Journal of International Law* 13:1 (2002), 162. See Dinah Shelton, 'Righting Wrongs: Reparations in the Articles on State Responsibility', *American Journal of International Law* 96: 4 (October 2002), 833–856, 845. For the text of the Articles on 'Responsibility of States for Internationally Wrongful Acts', see http://legal.un.org/ilc/texts/instruments/english/draft%20articles/9_6_2001.pdf
35. James Crawford and Jeremy Watkins, 'International Responsibility', in *The Philosophy of International Law*, edited by Samantha Besson and John Tasioulas (Oxford: Oxford University Press, 2010), 283–298, 285.
36. Howard McGary, 'Reconciliation and Reparations', *Metaphilosophy* 41 (2010), 546–562.
37. In this respect, government-sponsored reparations programs that link interpersonal reconciliation between individual victims and perpetrators to a state reparative program to assist victims or survivors may be considered problematic if the receipt of such assistance is dependent on a victim's willingness to reconcile sentimentally with individual

perpetrators. According to my accounts of both relational and structural reconciliation, the postconflict political order has a reparative duty to victims, whether or not they can emotionally reconcile with those who wronged them.

38. Crawford and Watkins, 'International Responsibility', 290. At the same time, a growing body of theoretical literature has focused on how citizens may incur collective responsibility for the wrongful actions of their state. See Anna Stilz, 'Collective Responsibility and the State', *Journal of Political Philosophy* 19:2 (2011), 190–208; Pablo Kalmanovitz, 'Sharing Burdens After War: A Lockean Approach', *Journal of Political Philosophy* 19:2 (2011), 209–228; and John M. Parrish, 'Collective Responsibility and the State', *International Theory* 1:1 (2009), 119–154.
39. See John Rawls, *The Law of Peoples* (Cambridge, MA: Harvard University Press, 1999), 95–96, for an argument about accountability for war that precisely aims to leave open conditions of possibility for relational and structural reconciliation after interstate war. This entails understanding responsibility for war in a way that avoids demonizing and criminalizing entire peoples.
40. Shelton, 'Righting Wrongs', 838.
41. Paragraph 16 of UN Security Council Resolution 687 stated, 'Iraq is liable under international law for any direct loss, damage, including environmental damage and the depletion of natural resources, or injuries to foreign Governments, nationals and corporations, as a result of Iraq's unlawful invasion and occupation of Kuwait'. See Gattini, 'The UN Compensation Commission', 167, footnote 27.
42. Gattini, 'The UN Compensation Commission', 164, 167.
43. The UNCC concluded its work in 2007, awarding approximately US$52.4 billion for approximately 1.54 million claims, representing nearly 15 per cent of the total amount claimed. See http://www.uncc.ch/ataglance.htm
44. Gattini, 'The UN Compensation Commission', 166, 181.
45. Crawford and Watkins, 'International Responsibility', 298.
46. Charles E. Callwell, *Small Wars: Their Principles and Practice* (Book Jungle, 2009 [1896]).
47. H. L. Wesseling, 'Colonial Wars: An Introduction', in *Imperialism and War: Essays on Colonial Wars in Asia and Africa*, edited by J. A. de Moor and H. L. Wesseling (Leiden, The Netherlands: E. J. Brill, 1989), 3.
48. David Olusoga and Casper W. Erichsen, *The Kaiser's Holocaust: Germany's Forgotten Genocide* (London: Faber and Faber, 2011), 70–71.
49. Jeremy Sarkin and Carly Fowler, 'Reparations for Historical Human Rights Violations: The International and Historical Dimensions of the Alien Torts Claims Act Genocide Case of the Herero in Namibia', *Human Rights Review*, 9 (2008), 331–360, at 333. See also Olusoga and Erichsen, *The Kaiser's Holocaust*.
50. Caroline Elkins, *Imperial Reckoning: The Untold Story of Britain's Gulag in Kenya* (New York: Henry Holt and Company, 2005), 97.
51. Wesseling asks, 'Was there peace in (Belgium King) Leopold's Congo when there were no more wars, but hands and feet chopped off in the hundreds?' 'Colonial Wars', 10. For a thorough account of Belgium's brutal plunder of the Congo, see Adam Hochschild, *King Leopold's Ghost: A Story of Greed, Terror, and Heroism in Colonial Africa* (New York: Houghton Mifflin, 1998).
52. Manjari Chatterjee Miller, *Wronged by Empire: Post-Imperial Ideology and Foreign Policy in India and China* (Stanford, CA: Stanford University Press, 2013), 21.

53. See Lu, 'Colonialism as Structural Injustice: Historical Responsibility and Contemporary Redress', *Journal of Political Philosophy* 19:3 (2011), 261–281.
54. For the Declaration: http://www.un.org/WCAR/durban.pdf. Consensus could not be reached about the term 'compensatory'. See http://www.un.org/WCAR/e-kit/backgrounder1.htm
55. The Caribbean Community (CARICOM) Reparations Commission Press Statement, December 2013 (emphasis added): http://caricom.org/jsp/pressreleases/press_releases_2013/pres285_13.jsp. See also *The Guardian*, 9 March 2014: http://www.theguardian.com/world/2014/mar/09/caribbean-nations-demand-slavery-reparations
56. *The Guardian*, 3 June 2013: http://www.theguardian.com/world/2013/jun/06/uk-compensate-kenya-mau-mau-torture?guni=Article:in%20body%20link
57. Caroline Elkins, *The Guardian*, 7 June 2013. http://www.theguardian.com/commentisfree/2013/jun/06/britain-maumau-empire-waiting
58. Sarkin and Fowler, 'Reparations for Historical Human Rights Violations', 355.
59. Allan D. Cooper, 'Reparations for the Herero Genocide: Defining the Limits of International Litigation', *African Affairs* 106 (2006), 113–126, at 117. See also http://www.theglobeandmail.com/news/world/memories-of-genocide-at-the-hands-of-germany-fuels-radicalism-in-namibia/article4627436/
60. Meister, *After Evil*, 243.
61. Ibid. See also Robert E. Goodin, 'Disgorging the Fruits of Historical Wrongdoing', *American Political Science Review* 107:3 (2013), 478–491.

Index